Salesforce Advanced Administrator Certification Guide

Become a Certified Advanced Salesforce Administrator with this exam guide

Enrico Murru

BIRMINGHAM - MUMBAI

Salesforce Advanced Administrator Certification Guide

Commissioning Editor: Richa Tripathi
Acquisition Editor: Alok Dhuri
Content Development Editor: Pathikrit Roy
Senior Editor: Rohit Singh
Technical Editor: Ketan Kamble
Copy Editor: Safis Editing
Project Coordinator: Francy Puthiry
Proofreader: Safis Editing
Indexer: Pratik Shirodkar
Production Designer: Deepika Naik

First published: November 2019

Production reference: 1071119

Published by Packt Publishing Ltd.
Livery Place
35 Livery Street
Birmingham
B3 2PB, UK.

ISBN 978-1-83864-389-8

www.packt.com

To my lovely Alessandra, who supports but also stands by me when I'm deeply focused on my personal projects: life wouldn't be easy without her.

To my parents for making me the man that I am, to my family-in-law for the constant love and support, to all my friends for their genuine affection and trust, and to my online Ohana, which strongly believes in what I do and is always there to cheer my accomplishments.

To the Packt team for their valuable suggestions and help in writing my first book, which has been a dream since I was a child. And to those of you who have chosen this book.

– Enrico Murru

Contributors

About the author

Enrico Murru is a solution and technical architect at WebResults (an engineering company), an Italian platinum Salesforce partner, and ISV. He completed his MSc in Electronic Engineering at the University of Cagliari in 2007. In 2009, he joined WebResults as a junior Salesforce developer. In 2013, he launched his first blog named Nerd @ Work. In 2016, he was nominated as the first Italian Salesforce MVP due to his commitment to the Salesforce community. In the same year, he started collecting Salesforce certifications, gaining 20 of them over the next 3 years, as part of his own path to the Salesforce Technical Architect certification. In 2016, he started one of his most popular projects, the ORGanizer for Salesforce Chrome and Firefox extension.

About the reviewers

Chamil Madusanka was the first Sri Lankan Salesforce MVP and is the director of Sri Lanka's Dazeworks Technologies Pvt. Ltd. office. He has four Salesforce certifications. He is the founder of the Sri Lankan chapter of Salesforce Saturday and a program called TCICThursday.

He has authored *Visualforce Developer's Guide* and *Learning Force.com Application Development*. He has also reviewed *Salesforce Reporting and Dashboards* and *Salesforce Lightning Reporting and Dashboards*.

He completed his first degree, a BSc in computer science, at the University of Colombo's School of Computing. He achieved his MBA in management of technology at the University of Moratuwa. Chamil hails from Polonnaruwa, and can be reached via Twitter at `@chamilmadusanka`.

Himanshu Atal is a chief information officer at India's Dazeworks Technologies Pvt. Ltd. office, and a very well-known partner of Salesforce with 11 MVPs in the organization. He has more than 8 years' experience in Salesforce and has successfully delivered more than 150 projects using the Salesforce platform.

He has worked with organizations such as IBM India Pvt. Ltd. and Persistent Systems.

> *I would like to thank Chamil for nominating me for this book review.*

Packt is searching for authors like you

If you're interested in becoming an author for Packt, please visit `authors.packtpub.com` and apply today. We have worked with thousands of developers and tech professionals, just like you, to help them share their insight with the global tech community. You can make a general application, apply for a specific hot topic that we are recruiting an author for, or submit your own idea.

Table of Contents

Preface 1

Section 1: Security, Access, and Organization Management

Chapter 1: Secure Data Access 13
- **Controlling who sees what** 13
  - Licensing 14
  - The sharing model 16
- **Profiles, permission sets, and object security** 19
  - Permission sets 24
  - Object-Level Security (OLS) 27
  - Field-Level Security (FLS) 28
- **The Salesforce sharing model** 30
  - OWD sharing 30
  - Role hierarchies 33
  - Sharing rules 35
    - Public and personal groups 35
    - Working with sharing rules 36
    - Manual sharing 39
    - Apex managed sharing 42
    - Team sharing 42
      - Account teams 42
    - Opportunity teams 44
    - Case teams 45
    - Some considerations about sharing 46
- **Enterprise territory management** 47
- **Sharing within Salesforce communities** 56
  - High-volume community users 61
- **Summary** 63
- **Questions** 64

Chapter 2: Auditing and Monitoring 69
- **Delegated administration** 70
- **Monitoring your organization** 74
  - Monitoring object-specific limits 77
  - Monitoring storage 78
  - Monitoring the login history 81
  - Monitoring the identity verification history 83
  - Monitoring changes: View Setup Audit Trail 83
  - Field history tracking 86

Background job monitoring 89
Debug log monitoring 90
Monitoring email logs 95
Health check monitor 98
Event monitoring 100
Summary 109
Questions 109
Chapter 3: Change Management 113
Testing using sandboxes 113
Developer sandbox 115
Developer Pro sandbox 115
Partial Copy sandbox 115
Full sandbox 117
About sandbox flow architectures 117
Deploying changes with change sets 120
Deploying changes with packages 133
Deploying changes with other tools 135
Handling data changes 138
Importing data with the Data Import Wizard 139
Importing data with Data Loader 143
Exporting data 144
Summary 147
Questions 147

Section 2: Data Model Management

Chapter 4: Extending Custom Objects 155
Advanced aspects of object relationships 155
Master–detail relationships 158
Roll-up fields 167
Many-to-many relationships 170
Lookup relationships 171
Hierarchical relationships 173
Formula fields and relations 174
External relationships 175
Validation rules 176
VLOOKUP 180
REGEX 181
PRIORVALUE 182
Picklist management 183
Dependent picklists 189
Summary 192
Questions 192

Section 3: Sales and Service Cloud Applications

Chapter 5: Support Sales Strategies with Sales Cloud Features 199
Managing products, product schedules, and pricebooks 200
Product schedules 208
Managing quotes and quote templates 213
Quote templates creation 217
Quote versus opportunity synchronization 219
Predicting deals with forecasts 220
Setting up collaborative forecasting 223
Summary 233
Questions 233

Chapter 6: Service Cloud Applications 237
Salesforce Knowledge 237
Setting up Salesforce Lightning Knowledge 240
Handling articles 242
Managing data categories 246
Importing external knowledge 249
Configuring Omni-Channel 251
Skill-based routing 255
External routing 257
Omni-Channel Supervisor app 257
Live Agent chat and communities 258
Salesforce Community setup 259
Chat (Live Agent) Setup flow 261
Einstein Bots 268
Entitlements for SLA management (and more) 269
Summary 283
Questions 283

Section 4: Data and Content Management

Chapter 7: Improving Data Quality with Duplicate Management 289
Understanding duplicate management 289
Local duplicate management 290
Global duplicate management 299
Exploring and customizing rules 306
Customizing duplicate rules 306
Customizing matching rules 309
Considerations regarding duplicate management 313
Summary 314
Questions 315

Chapter 8: Salesforce CRM Content Management 317
Setting up Salesforce CRM Content 317

Further Salesforce CRM Content options 319
Handling content libraries 320
Adding files to libraries 328
Enabling Google Docs 331
Content packs 333
Content delivery 334
Content search 337
Summary 339
Questions 339

Section 5: Reports and Dashboards

Chapter 9: Mastering Reports 343
Building reports 343
Report types 345
Report formats 350
Filtering reports 356
Charting report data 358
Advanced highlighting for report data 360
Bucket fields 361
Formulas in reports 364
Joined reports 373
Tracking history on reports 376
Historical Tracking Reports 376
Reporting Snapshots 378
Subscribing to reports 384
Further considerations 386
Summary 386
Questions 387

Chapter 10: Visualizing Key Metrics with Dashboards 389
Building dashboards 389
Reports and dashboards folders 390
Setting up a dashboard 393
Selecting the right charting option 399
Filtering dashboards 406
Subscribing to a dashboard 413
Limitations with dashboards 414
Summary 414
Questions 415

Section 6: Process Automation

Chapter 11: Automation with Workflows 419
What is process automation? 419

Which tool should you choose? 420
Building workflow rules 422
Automated actions 428
Field updates 428
Cross-object field updates 433
Task actions 434
Email alert actions 436
Outbound message actions 439
Time-dependent actions 443
Further considerations on workflows 446
Summary 448
Questions 448

Chapter 12: Automating Record Approval with Approval Processes 451
Understanding approvals 452
Creating an approval process 453
Creating approval steps 466
Adding actions to approvals 472
Using approvals 476
Limits and considerations 483
Summary 484
Questions 485

Chapter 13: Lightning Process Builder 487
Setting up a Lightning Process Builder 488
Shaping a Process Builder 490
Trigger selection 492
Criteria definition 495
Defining action groups 500
Creating records 502
Updating records 503
Processes 505
Posting to Chatter 506
Email alerts 508
Submitting for approval 508
Flows 510
Quick Actions 511
Custom notifications 512
Apex 514
Managing the Process Builder 515
Final considerations for building with a Process Builder 516
Summary 517
Questions 518

Chapter 14: Lightning Flows 521
Flow concepts 521

Building a flow 524
Connecting flows and subflows 548
Autolaunched flows 550
Managing a flow 558
Testing a flow 559
Transactions and governor limits 560
Limits and considerations 561
Summary 562
Questions 562

Chapter 15: The Coding Approach 565
Exploring Apex triggers 565
Order of execution 566
Trigger features and rules 569
Apex trigger anatomy 571
The before event 572
The after event 583
User interface development 586
Summary 590
Questions 591

Section 7: Taking Your Certification Exam

Chapter 16: Tips and Tricks for Passing Your Exam 595
Keep studying 595
Topics and scores 596
Need more resources? 597
Facing the exam with the right attitude 598
Failure is an option 599
Schedule it right now! 601
Preparing for the exam 602
Question format 602
The final step 603
Summary 603

Chapter 17: Mock Test A and B 605
Mock Test A 605
Mock Test B 619

Assessments 635

Other Books You May Enjoy 647

Index 651

Preface

When I was a child, I had a few secret wishes:

- **Becoming a great football player**: Given my limited football ability, I soon forgot this one.
- **Becoming a rock star**: Although I love playing drums and piano, I knew this was not my main path.
- **Teaching a computer to do what I want**: I started coding when I was a small child and this dream soon became reality; not by becoming the best coder in the world, but by being able to adapt to new technologies quickly and productively.
- **Being able to draw like a real artist**: No chance here – I've literally no artistic skills.
- **Writing a book**.

Writing a book is something that has always been on the list, but I've never had the skill to be a poet or a novel writer. A few years after the start of my career in the Salesforce world, and a few years before my first Salesforce MVP nomination, I casually started to write my own blog, Nerd @ Work, because I discovered that I had something to tell people: not philosophy, not an amazing drama, but my experience on the Salesforce platform. Who was the audience? The Salesforce Ohana, and I was surprised that people liked what I had to say (again, not art but solid technical stuff). This commitment to the community lead me to the unexpected Salesforce MVP nomination and, at the time of writing, I'm approaching my fifth nomination (fingers crossed).

But writing a blog is not like writing a whole book:

- **With a blog, you don't have the same commitment**: You can write whenever you want.
- **With a blog, you don't need a logical thread**: You can write whatever you want.
- **With a blog, you just keep writing on and on**: There is no end and there are no milestones.

That's why I started to think that I could end up with a whole book about the Salesforce platform, but honestly, I didn't have a clear idea of what to write about or whom the book should be targeted at.

And just while I was compiling a list of possible book titles, the Packt team appeared and proposed that I should write the very book that you are now reading – how strange life is!

Writing this book has been a great challenge that has involved countless weekends and nights passed reading, studying, deepening my knowledge, and writing and reviewing this content.

Although the Packt team and I fixed few mid-term milestones, I only had one milestone in my mind: reach the last chapter, and I was surprised that, chapter after chapter, I really did end up finishing the book.

Childhood dream: check!

As a Salesforce developer and architect with more than 10 years' experience, I always say that any Salesforce technician should have strong administration skills, and I usually suggest that my young colleagues start their career with the Salesforce Advanced Administrator certification rather than the Platform Developer I certification.

Since I was writing about a journey to the Salesforce Advanced Administrator certification, I knew that I had to not only pour all of my experience into the book, but also change my point of view: explaining advanced concepts to trailblazers who have potentially never had the chance to write a single line of code. Believe me, it's not the simplest thing to do, given that I'm a developer at heart who prefers to show code rather than explain how an algorithm works...why? Because it's easier for my brain.

While I was having to cover most of the Salesforce topics required for this certification, I tried to maintain a simple and trivial style to keep the storytelling funny and interesting, more or less like I try to do on my blog, without losing sight of the main target: helping you successfully gain the Salesforce Advanced Administrator certification.

There is no *one size fits all* rule, and I don't have the perfect recipe: study; experiment with configurations; and consolidate your knowledge with the reference links provided to official Salesforce docs, trailblazer's blogs, and Trailhead modules. But, most of all, trust yourself – don't be afraid to schedule your exam and face this certification.

This book has been written to give the Salesforce Ohana another way to master the Salesforce platform and I really hope that, by the end of the last chapter, you'll feel more confident in your increased chances of successfully passing this hard, yet useful, certification and confirming that you are a, `#AwesomeAdmin`.

Who this book is for

This book is suggested to Salesforce administrators who want to maximize their administration skills by having a deeper knowledge of the Salesforce CRM's key features. As a developer at heart, I suggest that you read all the topics that are covered in this book, because I think that a great developer should also have a strong administrator background.

What this book covers

This book covers all the topics of the Salesforce Advanced Administrator certification, comprising 17 chapters contained in 7 sections.

`Section 1`, *Security, Access, and Organization Management*, deals with security concerns, monitoring, and change management.

`Chapter 1`, *Secure Data Access*, discusses how the administrator is the key holder of a Salesforce organization, the guardian of the company's data. As such, their main concern is protecting this valuable asset. The correct object permissions mean that users can only shape data in accordance with the permissions of that user, while planning the right sharing strategy means users will only see the subset of records that they are authorized to read and/or write, thereby delivering coherent and safe business processes.

`Chapter 2`, *Auditing and Monitoring*, is where we will learn how to take control of our organization by monitoring key metrics: user login histories, data usage, setup changes, record field histories, debug logs, and events.

`Chapter 3`, *Change Management*, teaches you about the different Salesforce organization types (such as sandboxes, developer organizations, and production organizations). We will also learn how to master change management with change sets and see what other tools can be used to move organization configurations from one organization to another, and we'll learn how to pull and push data using Data Loader.

`Section 2`, *Data Model Management*, is all about extending custom objects with relations, advanced formulas, and picklist management.

`Chapter 4`, *Extending Custom Objects*, covers the creation of advanced object relationships to support the most complex business cases. You will master validation rules to ensure optimal data quality and consistency, and manage picklist values to increase consistency between objects.

Section 3, *Sales and Service Cloud Applications*, is about delivering sales cloud and service cloud features to unleash sales strategies and service support for your sales reps and service agents.

Chapter 5, *Support Sales Strategies with Sales Cloud Features*, explores how to set up and manage products, customize product scheduling settings for the right payment and delivery constraints, and handle price books to organize prices to deliver to customers. Also, we'll delve into using quotes to deliver product pricing propositions to customers, configuring templates to deliver the right information to customers, and using collaborative forecasts to predict sales revenues and quantities from your opportunity pipeline.

Chapter 6, *Service Cloud Applications*, looks at how to empower service support and use Salesforce Knowledge to create a powerful knowledge base integrated within service processes. Also, we will learn how to use entitlements and milestones to enforce a customer service level agreement. The other topics we'll learn about include delivering efficient service channels with LiveAgent and omnichannel configuration, integrating with your Salesforce console app, and streamlining the way you create, manage, and view cases with case feed configuration.

Section 4, *Data and Content Management*, covers increasing data quality with duplication rules and managing files with Salesforce CRM Content.

Chapter 7, *Improving Data Quality with Duplicate Management*, dives into keeping data clean and accurate to ensure quality: defining duplicate policies for real-time local management, and scheduling duplication jobs for organization-wide management. Also, controlling matching rules to customize how Salesforce identifies duplicates and the way that users are notified when a match is found will be discussed.

Chapter 8, *Salesforce CRM Content Management*, goes into depth on how to use Salesforce CRM Content to organize, share, search, and manage all types of files within our organization. Setting up content, managing the publication of files, organizing files in libraries, searching files, and using content delivery to convert documents into web-optimized versions for online viewing will be the other learning areas of this chapter.

Section 5, *Reports and Dashboards*, introduces you to report creation and how to visualize complex dashboards.

Chapter 9, *Mastering Reports*, teaches you about reports, which give us access to our Salesforce data. Using report types to select targeted objects, selecting the required fields to be displayed, setting up filters to narrow down results, scheduling reports, subscribing to reports to receive notifications, reporting key metrics, and organizing reports to speed up searches will be the key things you will master in this chapter.

`Chapter 10`, *Visualizing Key Metrics with Dashboards,* is where you will learn how to use dashboards to understand changing business conditions so that you can make decisions based on the real-time data that is gathered by reports. Learning how to build dashboards based upon data from reports, displaying data using different kinds of charts, filtering dashboards, running dashboards with different users, managing dashboards, running schedules, and subscriptions will be the main things that are covered in this chapter.

`Section 6`, *Process Automation,* is concerned with implementing Salesforce automation with workflows rules, approval processes, Process Builder, Lightning flows, and custom Apex code.

`Chapter 11`, *Automation with Workflows,* takes you through how to deliver point-and-click automation to your business processes by leveraging workflow rules. Creating different kinds of automated actions, such as field updates, email alerts, outbound messages, and task creation will also be explained in this chapter.

`Chapter 12`, *Automating Record Approval with Approval Processes,* moves on to specifying all the steps required to approve a record, which includes defining the rules and activating the processes. Advanced examples of these concepts will also be present in the chapter.

`Chapter 13`, *Lightning Process Builder,* takes workflow rules to a new level with Process Builder, looking at defining criteria based on objects or platform events to trigger action groups, which consist of immediate or scheduled actions. Troubleshooting a process to understand why errors are arising in order to speed up debugging will also be covered in this chapter.

`Chapter 14`, *Lightning Flows,* will cover flows, which actually collect data and perform actions in our Salesforce organization or an external system. We will also learn about using screen flows to collect data from agents or customers (for example, tutorials or wizards) and explore using autolaunched flows, which are flows that are launched after a record is changed or a button is clicked.

`Chapter 15`, *The Coding Approach,* shows you that when deeper customization is needed, the coding approach is a win-win situation. Understanding how Apex triggers can deliver complex automation for your processes when the point-and-click approach is not enough, and evaluating Visualforce and Lightning component adoption when user experience constraints necessitate coding magic, are the core learning areas in this chapter.

Section 7, Taking Your Certification Exam, prepares you for exam day and tests your skills with two mock tests.

`Chapter 16`, *Tips and Tricks for Passing Your Exam*, teaches you how to really get the most out of this book in terms of passing the exam, preparing you for the Salesforce Advanced Administrator certification, and showing you the best ways to increase your score and get that certification.

`Chapter 17`, *Mock Tests A and B*, contains two complete mock certification exams to help you measure your preparation level.

To get the most out of this book

Although this book covers most of the topics of the exam from scratch, knowledge of the following base concepts is regarded as having already been acquired by the reader:

- The Salesforce Platform architecture
- Standard object definitions and features in Sales Cloud and Service Cloud (accounts, contacts, opportunities, cases, and so on)
- Data model customization (custom objects, custom fields, validation rules, record types, and so on)
- User interface customization (page layouts, Lightning pages, applications and tabs, and so on)
- Basic profiles, roles, and user management
- The basic Salesforce object-sharing model
- Process automation features (workflows, flows, Process Builder, and so on)
- The difference between declarative and programmatic customization

Download the example code files

You can download the example code files for this book from your account at `www.packt.com`. If you purchased this book elsewhere, you can visit `www.packt.com/support` and register to have the files emailed directly to you.

You can download the code files by following these steps:

1. Log in or register at `www.packt.com`.
2. Select the **SUPPORT** tab.
3. Click on **Code Downloads & Errata**.
4. Enter the name of the book in the **Search** box and follow the onscreen instructions.

Once the file is downloaded, please make sure that you unzip or extract the folder using the latest version of:

- WinRAR/7-Zip for Windows
- Zipeg/iZip/UnRarX for Mac
- 7-Zip/PeaZip for Linux

The code bundle for the book is also hosted on GitHub at `https://github.com/PacktPublishing/Salesforce-Advanced-Administrator-Certification-Guide`. In case there's an update to the code, it will be updated on the existing GitHub repository.

We also have other code bundles from our rich catalog of books and videos available at `https://github.com/PacktPublishing/`. Check them out!

Download the color images

We also provide a PDF file that has color images of the screenshots/diagrams used in this book. You can download it here: `https://static.packt-cdn.com/downloads/9781838643898_ColorImages.pdf`.

Conventions used

There are a number of text conventions used throughout this book.

`CodeInText`: Indicates code words in text, database table names, folder names, filenames, file extensions, pathnames, dummy URLs, user input, and Twitter handles. Here is an example: " The `Trigger` keyword comes in handy as well and gives us access to current record values (and even to old ones):"

A block of code is set as follows:

```
trigger OpportunityTrigger on Opportunity (before insert, before update,
before delete, after insert, after update,
after delete, after undelete) {
    //code goes here...
}
```

Bold: Indicates a new term, an important word, or words that you see on screen. For example, words in menus or dialog boxes appear in the text like this. Here is an example: "The **User License** field is one of the mandatory fields of the Salesforce `user` object."

Warnings or important notes appear like this.

Tips and tricks appear like this.

Get in touch

Feedback from our readers is always welcome.

General feedback: If you have questions about any aspect of this book, mention the book title in the subject of your message and email us at `customercare@packtpub.com`.

Errata: Although we have taken every care to ensure the accuracy of our content, mistakes do happen. If you have found a mistake in this book, we would be grateful if you would report this to us. Please visit www.packt.com/submit-errata, selecting your book, clicking on the Errata Submission Form link, and entering the details.

Piracy: If you come across any illegal copies of our works in any form on the internet, we would be grateful if you would provide us with the location address or website name. Please contact us at copyright@packt.com with a link to the material.

If you are interested in becoming an author: If there is a topic that you have expertise in, and you are interested in either writing or contributing to a book, please visit authors.packtpub.com.

Reviews

Please leave a review. Once you have read and used this book, why not leave a review on the site that you purchased it from? Potential readers can then see and use your unbiased opinion to make purchase decisions, we at Packt can understand what you think about our products, and our authors can see your feedback on their book. Thank you!

For more information about Packt, please visit packt.com.

1
Section 1: Security, Access, and Organization Management

In this section, you will learn how to efficiently manage your Salesforce organization by mastering data access security and record sharing, and enhancing monitoring and auditing. You will learn about best practices so that you can handle change management and data across different organizations.

This section includes the following chapters:

- `Chapter 1`, *Secure Data Access*
- `Chapter 2`, *Auditing and Monitoring*
- `Chapter 3`, *Change Management*

1
Secure Data Access

In each Salesforce organization, the administrator is the key holder: they are the guardian of the company's data and thus their main concern is protecting this valuable asset. The right object permissions shape data according to the kind of user who accesses it, while planning the right sharing strategy enables users to see only the subset of records they are authorized to read and/or write, thus delivering coherent and safe business processes.

In this chapter, we will learn about the following topics:

- How data security is handled within the Salesforce platform
- The difference between profiles and permission sets to define what users can do
- Setting up record-level security to restrict/allow access to data depending on the user's shape
- The Salesforce sharing model (from organization-wide default sharing to manual sharing), which determines which objects can be accessed by whom
- Setting up Enterprise Territory Management for a territory-based record-sharing model
- Handling sharing in Salesforce communities to give external users access to data

Controlling who sees what

With tens (or even thousands) of users in your Salesforce organization, choosing the right way to make data visible is an administrator priority: you have to control *who sees what* and you need to be aware of all the options your Salesforce **customer relationship management** (**CRM**) provides.

It's not a coincidence that secure data access is the first subject we are going to study in this book.

In my 10 years' experience, being able to master data access management has always been the key to better data organization, better platform performances, better CRM usability, and of course better customer satisfaction.

Plan the right data sharing and visibility policies at the beginning of your project's journey, along with your data model and business processes. This will prevent your team from strong headaches when the project goes on and no one has ever pictured how users should see data – believe me, doing this important design step at the end of the project is a nightmare.

Data is your number one CRM resource, so use it carefully and with be conscious of it. Let the Salesforce platform take care of it and gently bring your sharing model to life.

Licensing

Like in most applications, every data story begins with a user: they authenticate against the application, they are recognized by their credentials and profile (we're not talking about Salesforce profiles but the generic set of powers a specific kind of user has), and then they are allowed to access the application's features and a subset of the data.

A Salesforce user is identified by their license. The **User License** field is one of the mandatory fields of the Salesforce user object:

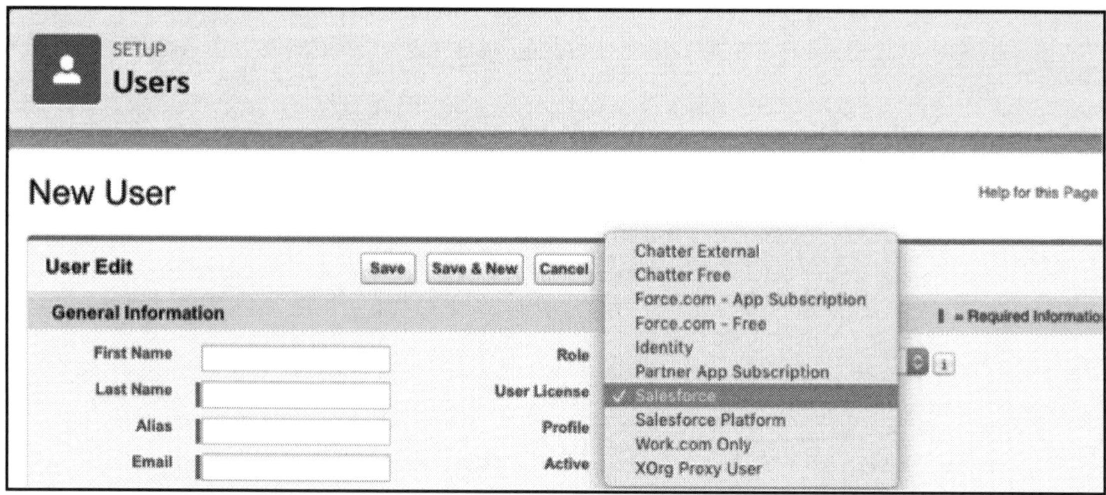

License selection with user creation

The available licenses can be found in **Setup** | **Company Settings** | **Company Information**, in the **User Licenses** section:

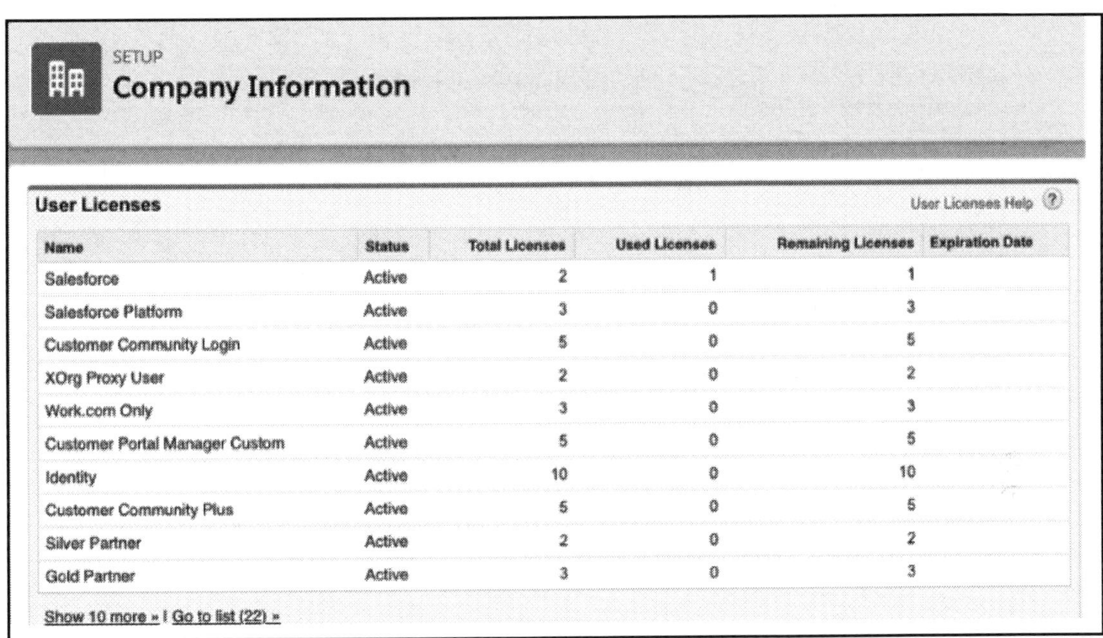
SETUP
Company Information

User Licenses
User Licenses Help

Name	Status	Total Licenses	Used Licenses	Remaining Licenses	Expiration Date
Salesforce	Active	2	1	1	
Salesforce Platform	Active	3	0	3	
Customer Community Login	Active	5	0	5	
XOrg Proxy User	Active	2	0	2	
Work.com Only	Active	3	0	3	
Customer Portal Manager Custom	Active	5	0	5	
Identity	Active	10	0	10	
Customer Community Plus	Active	5	0	5	
Silver Partner	Active	2	0	2	
Gold Partner	Active	3	0	3	

Show 10 more » | Go to list (22) »

Salesforce Company Information – list of available licenses

The number and type of available licenses you have depends on what your company or your customer has agreed to with Salesforce.

For a complete list of available pricing tiers and products, please refer to `https://www.salesforce.com/editions-pricing/overview/`.

We can reasonably divide licenses into three groups regarding data sharing:

- **Full sharing model usage users/licenses**: Users within this category have full access to the Salesforce sharing system. Some objects may not be accessible (for example, the free edition cannot access base CRM objects), but the engine is still there and configurable. This class of users is usually referred to as **internal users**.

- **High volume customer portal licenses**: Users within this category do not have access to the sharing model. Instead, sharing is enabled by matching user fields with other object's relations (for example, the contact lookup on the user is used to provide access to cases with the same contact value). This class of users is generally used in Salesforce communities.
- **Chatter-free license**: This category doesn't have access to the sharing model or any CRM object (standard or custom) and it features collaboration-only access (chatter, groups, and people, to name a few).

For further details on licensing that are out of this scope, have a look at the Trailblazer Community documentation at `https://help.salesforce.com/articleView?id=users_licenses_overview.htm`.

In a few words, the license constrains the kind of powers a user has, which is then delivered with profiles and permission sets. We'll take a look at these in the upcoming sections.

The sharing model

One of the first steps when designing a new Salesforce CRM implementation is to set up data access using the sharing model engine. This specifies who can see what!

To understand how this works, have a look at the following diagram:

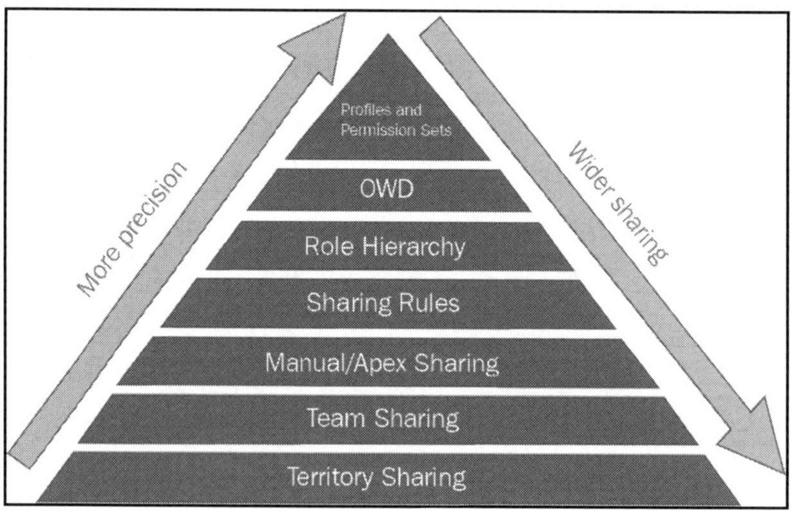

Salesforce sharing architecture

Profiles determine **Object-Level Security** (**OLS**) and **Field-Level Security** (**FLS**). They control which objects a user is allowed to access (right or write capabilities) and which fields are visible and editable. You can create a fine-grained view of what's available for a specific object type.

Your implementation may require that the Sales team shouldn't be able to see the account's billing information. Using FLS, you can hide those fields from the *sales representative* profile. On the other hand, the service team should not be able to access quotes objects: remove any read access to the quote object on the service team profiles.

Permission Sets contains mostly the same attributes as profiles but they are usually added to specific users to provide additional permissions that their sole profile does not grant (it's like giving more powers to selected users). This allows them to create a small set of profiles (that applies to most users, thus reducing the amount of time needed for profile maintenance) and apply permission exceptions to given users without the need to create a brand new dedicated profile.

Supposing you already know what page layouts are, while page layouts define which fields a user can see or write to in that specific view of the record, FLS is org-wide, which means that if a profile cannot access a specific field even though a layout is set to display it, it will never be accessed by that profile.

That's why layouts are used to *organize* data rather than limit its access (for example, a sales user should read the contact fields on a given case with the *Contact Request* record type, even if he is not interested in reading those fields on the *Payment Confirmation* record type, but at the profile level the FLS on those fields are not changed).

After profile configuration, record-level access configuration comes next:

- The **Organization-Wide Defaults** (**OWD**) define how users have access to each other's records: when you want to protect an object, you set up the most restrictive access type (for example, Private) and then use the other available tools to give wider access to specific subsets of users. Let's say a specific profile has access to read and write on the case object: if OWD is set to **Public Read Only**, a user can read all the cases but won't be able to update them unless they are the owner of the record or are allowed to due to the other sharing features.

The OWD is the only configuration that can restrict user access to a record. Remember that this concept is at the base of the Salesforce sharing model.

- **Role hierarchy** represents a hierarchic view of the company's employee structure (such as an organization chart). This level of sharing defines how records are shared across the hierarchy (for example, sales managers can see all the records that are owned by their sales representatives).
- **Sharing rules** are exception rules that can give wider access to records or a group of users who shouldn't actually see those records because of OWD and Role Hierarchy configurations.
- **Sharing sets/groups** are used to share records with Salesforce community users.
- Users can be given the power to share records they own with other users who don't have access to them otherwise. This is called **manual/Apex sharing**, and although it's not an automated configuration, it gives your users the needed flexibility to work with their team members.

Manual sharing is removed when the record's owner changes or when that specific manual sharing doesn't add more access than the default OWD access level.

- Use **team sharing** to grant access to specific records (for opportunity, account, and case objects only): the record's owner (or users who are higher in the role hierarchy or administrators) can create a team granting read-only or read/write access to their team users to access the record. You can only have one team per object.

Developers can create this kind of sharing programmatically.

- **Territory hierarchies** is a feature that's specific for accounts, opportunities, and their child records (records that have a master-child relation with them). You can provide access to records based on specific *one-dimensional* division (for example, business units, zip code, and country) using territory sharing rules, which are recalculated every time the record changes its *territory-linked* fields.
- **Apex sharing** is the most powerful and granular feature that can give your sharing needs the right way to control record access if the previous features are not enough or don't apply to your sharing model. Developers can create algorithms to programmatically share objects with whichever users/groups they need to.

One final kind of sharing is **implicit sharing**, which is related to specifically standard objects and is a native feature that cannot be switched off. **Parent implicit sharing** means that if a user has access to opportunities, cases, or contacts, they also have access to the parent account. **Child implicit sharing** is the opposite; it gives users access to child objects (contacts, opportunities, and cases) to the owner of a given account: the administrator can set up read, write, or no access for child sharing in the role definition.

The following diagram summarizes the previous concepts:

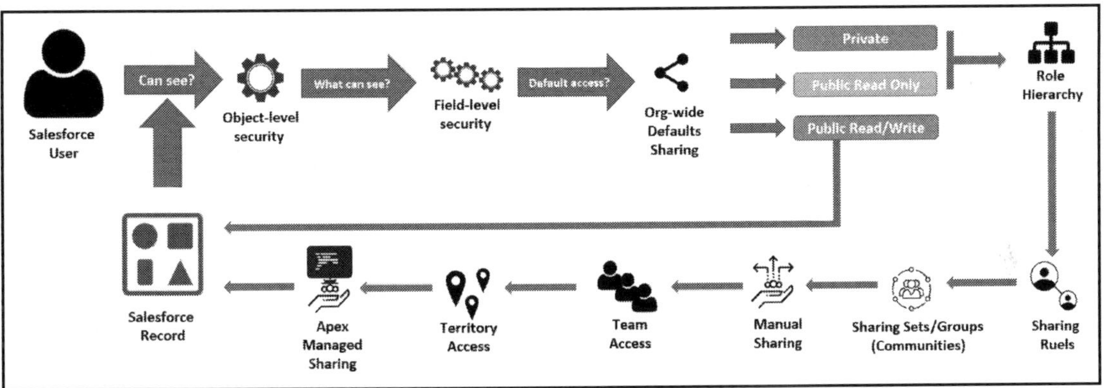

Sharing model flow

Let's dig deeper into each way we can grant access to records.

Profiles, permission sets, and object security

Profiles define how users can access data and the whole Salesforce application.

There should be one profile per user and one license type per profile – easy to remember. Also, more than one user can share the same profile.

Your organization comes with standard profiles that (there are exceptions for some Salesforce editions, such as contact manager, group edition, or essentials edition), you can customize a few permissions for on a standard profile or clone (creating a new custom profile) so that you have full access to its customization (for example, custom object access, field-level security access). The only thing you cannot change is the license type related to a profile.

Permission sets are similar to profiles with a simple difference: you can assign zero or more permission sets to a single user, thus providing additional capabilities that are not set up in the *base* profile. This increases permissions attribution granularity when creating simple profiles with few capabilities and granting users different powers as needed (sometimes, a Salesforce user can have both sales and service capabilities, but you don't want to create a profile with both permissions).

You may ask the following question:

> *"Can I use custom profiles only, instead of permission sets?"*

You definitely can, but only if your users have clear permission needs and their operative role in the CRM is well defined, which is usually not the case. The business can ask for the sales representatives to be able to access and edit cases, though some service agents may be required to edit opportunities, which are a sales representative's unique permission. If you have to take into account any exceptions when setting up permissions, you would end up with tens of custom profiles, a task that can be time-consuming. Instead, you should deliver some base and exclusive profile configuration and provide a *class of permissions* using permission sets to specific users when needed (a user can have only one profile but can be related to multiple permission sets).

To see what features are available in profiles and permission Sets, please refer to `https://help.salesforce.com/articleView?id=permissions_about_users_access.htmtype=5`.

You can edit a profile with two different interfaces: the enhanced profile user interface and the original (or standard) profile interface.

To enable the **Enhanced Profile User Interface**, click on **Setup** | **Users** | **User Management Settings** and enable the **Enhanced Profile User Interface** flag:

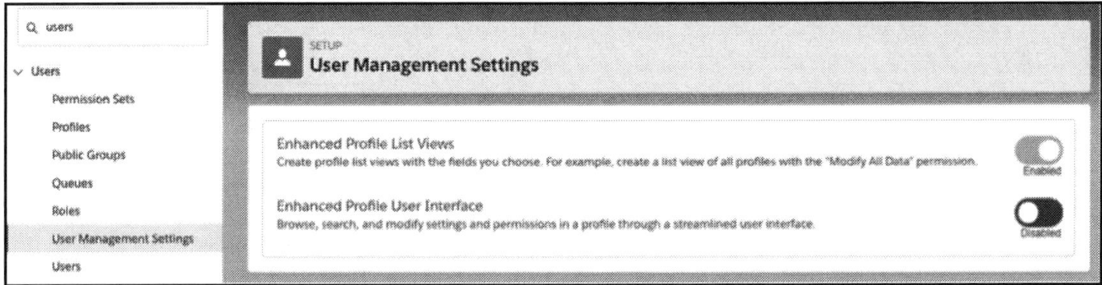

Enabling the enhanced profile user interface

This interface is a more powerful profile editing page that supports all the settings that are provided by the original interface: the main enhancement is the capability to search for settings as opposed to the original interface, where all the main options are in a single page. To switch from a master setting to a child one, you need to browse different pages.

From now on, we'll be using the original interface.

Let's briefly look at every section on the profile editor page:

- **Profile Detail**: This section contains the main details of the profile, including whether it is a standard profile or a custom one. This section is editable on custom profiles only.

A custom profile is a profile that's created upon cloning a standard profile.

- **Console Settings:** Edit layout assignment in Salesforce console apps.
- **Page Layouts:** This section is used to assign layouts to records (and record types if the object has at least one record type).
- **Field-Level Security**: For each object, this defines which fields are visible and editable.

- **Custom App Settings**: This decides which Salesforce applications are accessible by the user and which ones are the default ones.
- **Tab Settings**: Like the **Custom App Settings** section, we can choose which tabs are enabled or hidden.**Record Type Settings**: For any object that supports record types, you can allow users to use them when creating a new record, thus allowing users to have access to specific business processes.
- **Administrative permissions and General User Permissions**: This section contains all the administrative settings and general permissions (such as the **View All Data** and **Modify All Data** superpowers). This section can only be edited for custom profiles.
- **Standard Object Permissions, Custom Object Permissions, and Platform Event Permissions**: These sections define the OLS, that is, CRUD operations and the **View All** and **Modify All** superpowers, which allow the user to view and modify all the records of a given type. Platform events can only be configured with read or create access.
- **Session Settings and Password Policies**: These sections display profile-specific session settings (such as session duration and security level) and everything about password management that overrides the **Setup** | **Security** | **Session Settings** and **Password Policies** org-wide settings.
- **Login Hours**: Define when a user should be able to log in to Salesforce.
- **Login IP Ranges**: Defined the origin IP addresses that are considered safe to access your Salesforce organization (there's a restriction on a company's IP ranges). Within this range of IPs, users won't be asked for an activation pin (this is sent via email or SMS). You can also restrict this to org-wide login so that it's executed from within this range in **Setup** | **Security** | **Session Settings**.
- **Enabled Apex Classes Access and Enabled Visualforce Page Access**: From here, you can enable access to Apex classes (for example, enable a user to access a specific custom Apex web service) and Visualforce pages (for example, access to a specific Visualforce wizard).

- **Other permissions**:
    - **External Data Source Access**: Access to external records (defined in **Setup** | **Integrations** | **External Data Sources**).
    - **Named Credential Access**: Access to specific external web servers (**Setup** | **Security** | **Named Credentials**).
    - **Service Presence status:** Available presence statuses (for example, live chat operator status such as Active, Away, or Offline. Go to **Setup** | **Features Settings** | **Service** | **Omni-Channel** | **Presence Statuses** to do this. Note that you need **Omni-Channel** activation).
    - **Custom Permissions**: Allows profiles to have custom permissions that have been designed to modify a Visualforce or Lightning component's behavior on the developer side and validation rules on the administrator side (**Setup** | **Custom Code** | **Custom Permissions**).
    - **Default Community**: Default Salesforce community (if any).

If you want to create a new custom profile, you only have to jump to the standard profile you want to modify (or choose another custom profile that's already set up) and click the **Clone** button, which brings you to the following page:

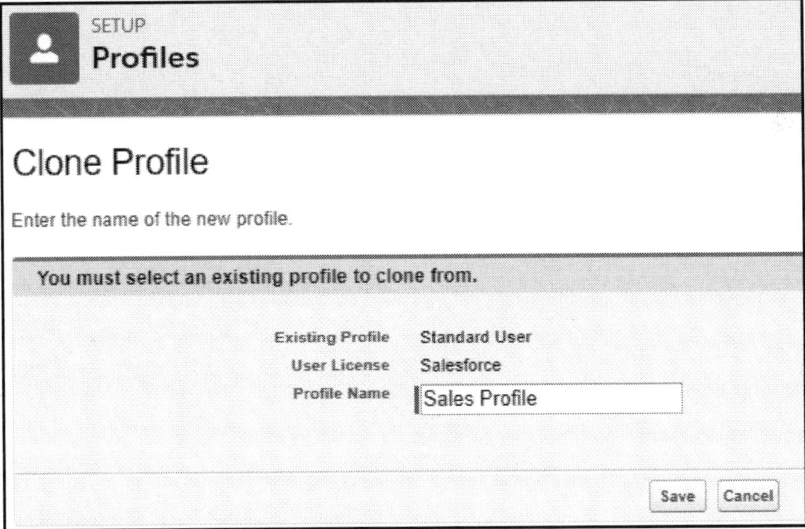

Cloning a standard profile

From now on, the profile will be completely customizable and will be listed as a custom profile on the profile's **Setup** | **Users** | **Profiles** page:

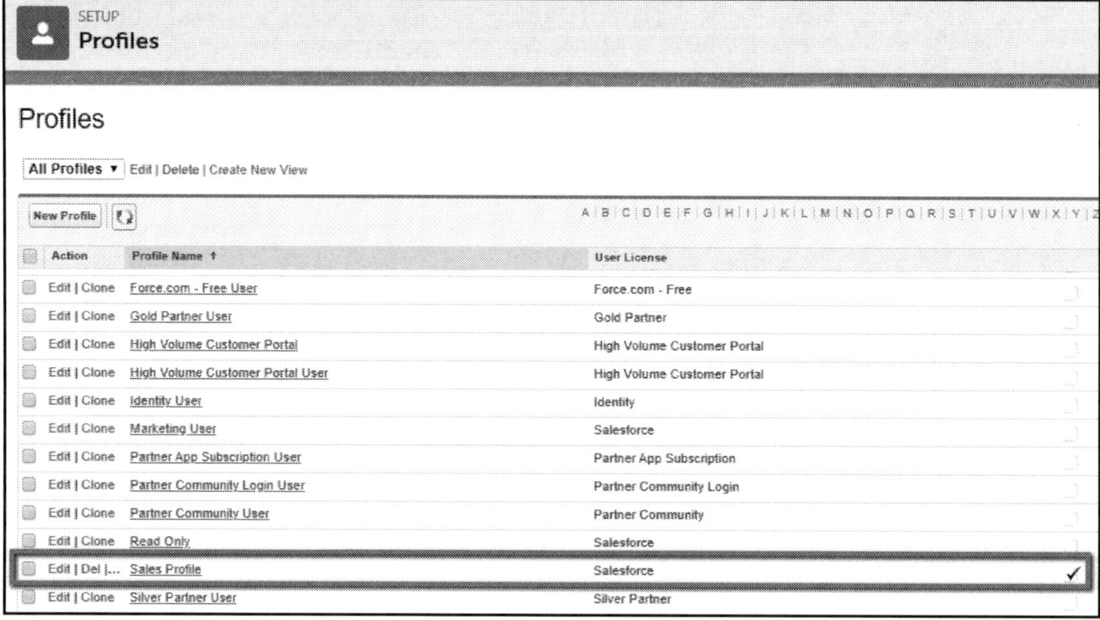

Custom profiles on the Profiles page

Now, let's look at how we can create permission sets.

Permission sets

Permission sets are, as the term suggests, a collection of permissions or settings that give users access to specific platform features/functions.

Permission sets are used to extend application feature access to users without changing their profiles.

Every setting you can apply to permission sets is also found on profiles (but not vice versa). A given user is related to only one profile, but it can be assigned to multiple permission sets.

Permission sets are not used to restrict permissions: you cannot use a permission set to revoke access to a specific object of a field if another permission set or user's profile grants this permission.

Think about a service user who has a service profile (cloned from the standard user profile) and can access only accounts, contacts, and case objects. A selection of service users can also directly contact prospect customers using lead data: using a **Lead Access** permission set, you can give the service user access to read and write leads.

This concept is valid for whatever kind of permission that's available on the permission sets.

You can create a permission set by going to **Setup** | **Users** | **Permission Sets**:

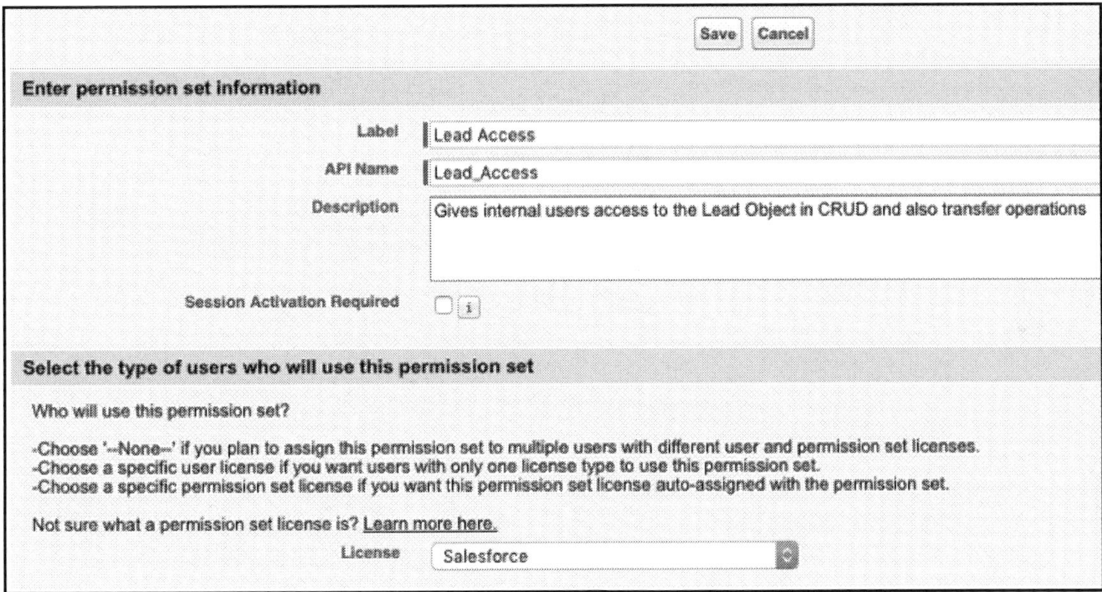

Save Cancel

Enter permission set information

Label: Lead Access
API Name: Lead_Access
Description: Gives internal users access to the Lead Object in CRUD and also transfer operations
Session Activation Required

Select the type of users who will use this permission set

Who will use this permission set?

-Choose '--None--' if you plan to assign this permission set to multiple users with different user and permission set licenses.
-Choose a specific user license if you want users with only one license type to use this permission set.
-Choose a specific permission set license if you want this permission set license auto-assigned with the permission set.

Not sure what a permission set license is? Learn more here.

License: Salesforce

If you don't fill in the **License** field, you won't be able to see all the possible settings. Only use *no license* permission sets when you want to apply them to users whose license is allowed to enable it.

For example, don't create a *no license* permission set with the **Author Apex** setting if you plan to assign it to a chatter-free user.

The permission set editor uses the enhanced profile view:

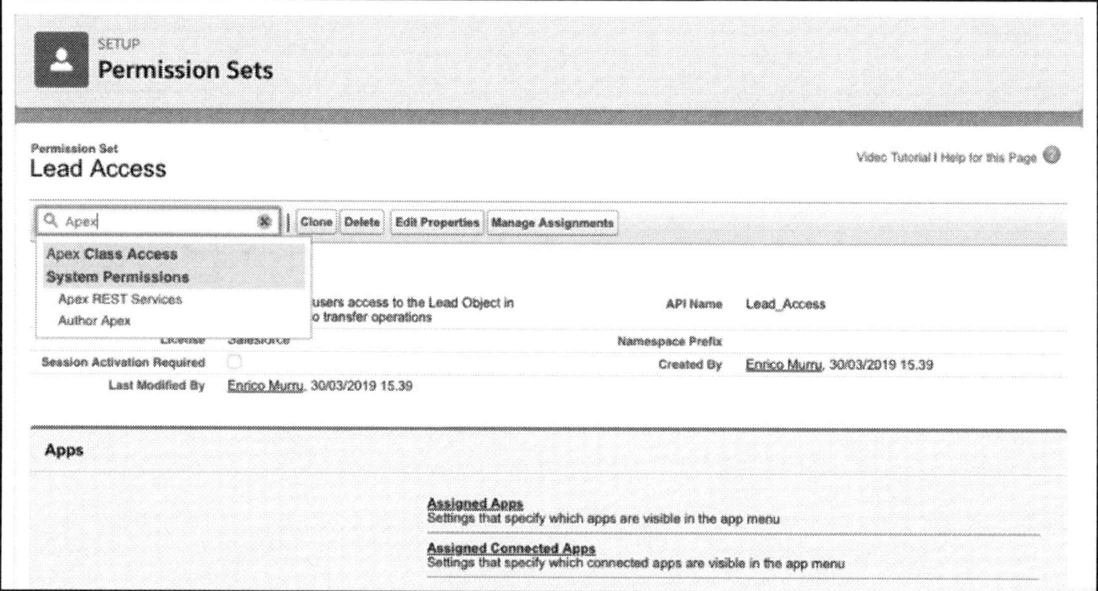

The **Session Activation Required** flag is used to create permissions sets that are associated with specific kinds of sessions.

Let's say you have a mobile app that is capable of creating inventory custom objects (read, create, and edit). However, if the same user accesses the Salesforce application on their desktop, they should not be able to edit any inventory record; session activated permission sets can only be activated if the session has been created from that mobile app. For more information on this topic, please refer to the following Salesforce Help article: `https://help.salesforce.com/articleView?id=perm_sets_session_map.htm`.

The following limitations apply for the maximum number of permission sets that can be created in a given organization:

Personal edition	Contact manager	Group edition	Essentials edition	Professional edition	Enterprise edition	Unlimited and performance edition	Developer edition
N/A	1	5	10	1,000	1,000	1,000	1,000

Object-Level Security (OLS)

The first level of access type is **Object-Level Security** (**OLS**), as we saw previously on the profile edit page:

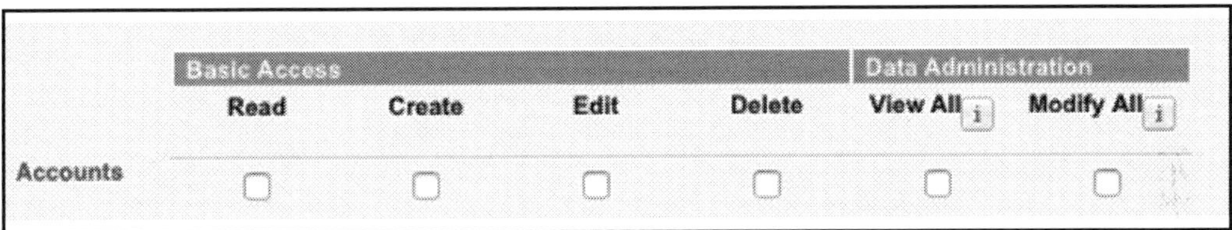

These kinds of operations are usually referred to as *CRUD operations*:

- Create
- Read
- Update (or Edit)
- Delete

Some of them respect sharing configurations while some do not:

- **Read**: Users can view records of this type if the sharing settings allow them to (sharing respected).
- **Create**: Users can create and view records (sharing respected regarding the read operation); that is, you cannot have **Create** without **Read** enabled.
- **Edit**: Users can edit and read records (sharing respected); there can be no **Edit** without **Read**.
- **Delete**: Users can read, edit, and delete records (sharing respected); there can be no **Delete** without **Read** and **Edit**.
- **View All**: Users can see all the records of this object and thus sharing is not respected.
- **Modify All**: Users can read, edit, delete, transfer, and run approval on all the records of this object, thereby overriding the sharing settings.

View All and **Modify All** work like the **View All Data** and **Modify All Data** user permissions on profiles, but there should be a better alternative to convey better access granularity to records.

Object accessibility causes the object's tab to be visible to a given user.

View All Data and **Modify All Data** permissions should be granted to administrators only as they should be the only ones who can view every record in your organization.

Field-Level Security (FLS)

The concept of **Field-Level Security** (**FLS**) is easily pictured in the FLS settings for a given profile's access to an object:

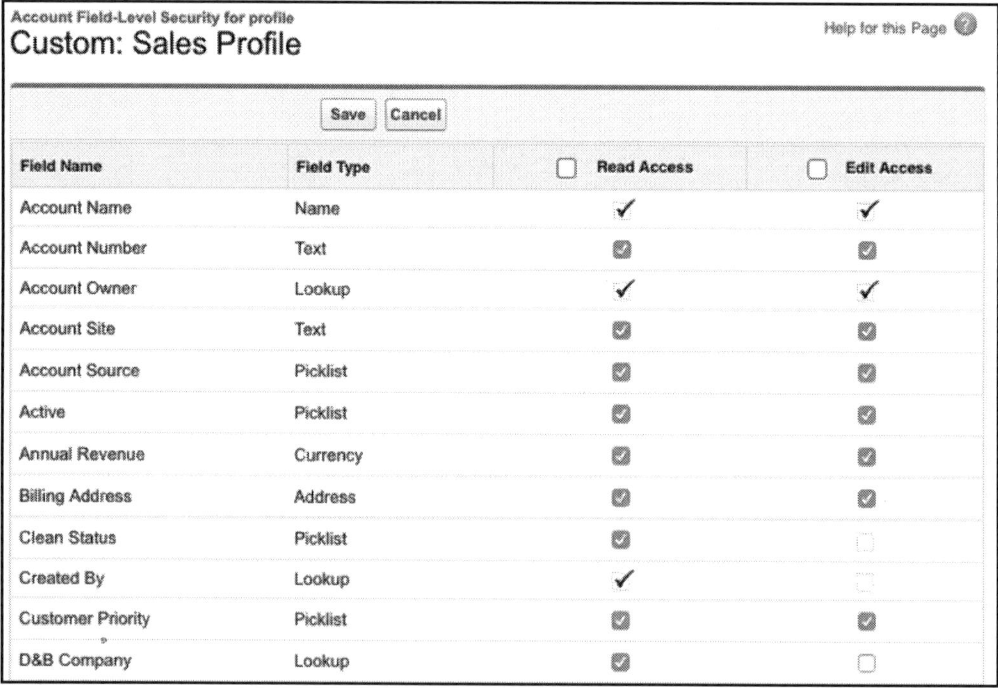

Account Field-Level Security for profile

Custom: Sales Profile

Help for this Page

Save Cancel

Field Name	Field Type	[ ] Read Access	[ ] Edit Access
Account Name	Name	✓	✓
Account Number	Text	[x]	[x]
Account Owner	Lookup	✓	✓
Account Site	Text	[x]	[x]
Account Source	Picklist	[x]	[x]
Active	Picklist	[x]	[x]
Annual Revenue	Currency	[x]	[x]
Billing Address	Address	[x]	[x]
Clean Status	Picklist	[x]	[ ]
Created By	Lookup	✓	[ ]
Customer Priority	Picklist	[x]	[x]
D&B Company	Lookup	[x]	[ ]

You can define **Read Access** and **Edit Access** on fields (**Edit Access** requires **Read Access**). If you remove **Read Access** from a given field, the user won't be able to see that field on the object layout, even if the field has been added on that layout.

The same applies to **Edit Access**. If the record is in edit mode but the current user doesn't have **Edit Access** to that field, the field won't be writable.

Required fields (marked as required or master-detail fields) will always have read and edit access, while system fields (such as **Created By** or **Created Date**) will always be read-only.

> You can enable editing for audit fields for imported records only. Go to `https://help.salesforce.com/articleView?id=000171151` for more details.
>
> You should prefer FLS to layout-specific field configurations since it reduces the number of required layouts and makes field access coherent across profiles and record types.

If you want to see what determines field access, jump to **Setup | Object Manager**, look for any object, click on **Fields & Relations**, select any field, and click on the **View Field Accessibility** button to see the following display:

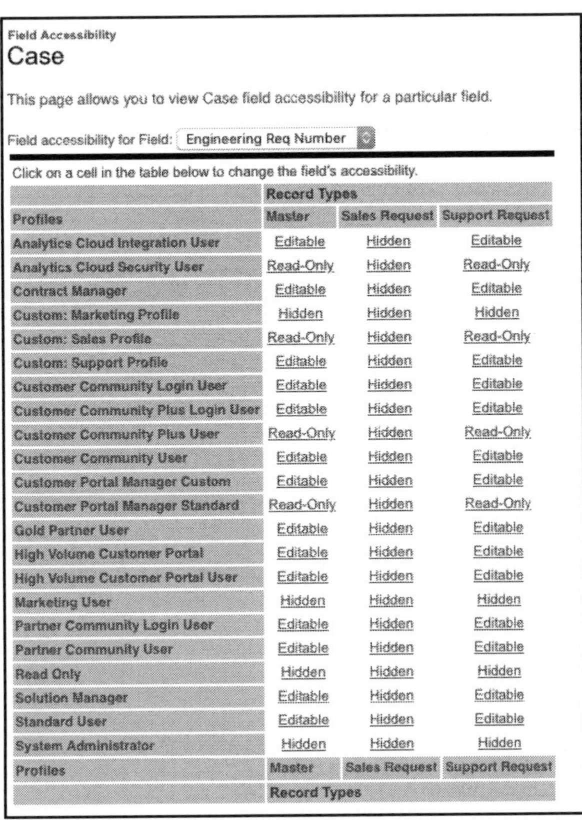

Field Accessibility

Case

This page allows you to view Case field accessibility for a particular field.

Field accessibility for Field: Engineering Req Number

Click on a cell in the table below to change the field's accessibility.

	Record Types		
Profiles	Master	Sales Request	Support Request
Analytics Cloud Integration User	Editable	Hidden	Editable
Analytics Cloud Security User	Read-Only	Hidden	Read-Only
Contract Manager	Editable	Hidden	Editable
Custom: Marketing Profile	Hidden	Hidden	Hidden
Custom: Sales Profile	Read-Only	Hidden	Read-Only
Custom: Support Profile	Editable	Hidden	Editable
Customer Community Login User	Editable	Hidden	Editable
Customer Community Plus Login User	Editable	Hidden	Editable
Customer Community Plus User	Read-Only	Hidden	Read-Only
Customer Community User	Editable	Hidden	Editable
Customer Portal Manager Custom	Editable	Hidden	Editable
Customer Portal Manager Standard	Read-Only	Hidden	Read-Only
Gold Partner User	Editable	Hidden	Editable
High Volume Customer Portal	Editable	Hidden	Editable
High Volume Customer Portal User	Editable	Hidden	Editable
Marketing User	Hidden	Hidden	Hidden
Partner Community Login User	Editable	Hidden	Editable
Partner Community User	Editable	Hidden	Editable
Read Only	Hidden	Hidden	Hidden
Solution Manager	Editable	Hidden	Editable
Standard User	Editable	Hidden	Editable
System Administrator	Hidden	Hidden	Hidden
Profiles	Master	Sales Request	Support Request
	Record Types		

For every record type (if any) and profile, you will have a picture of field accessibility (**Hidden**, **Read-Only**, or **Editable**) on the assigned profile.

The Salesforce sharing model

Once you have selected which objects and fields a user can have CRUD access too, you need to know how to control **record-level** access. We can do this using Salesforce's sharing settings.

OWD sharing

To define the **Organization-Wide Defaults** sharing settings, go to **Setup** | **Security** | **Sharing Settings**:

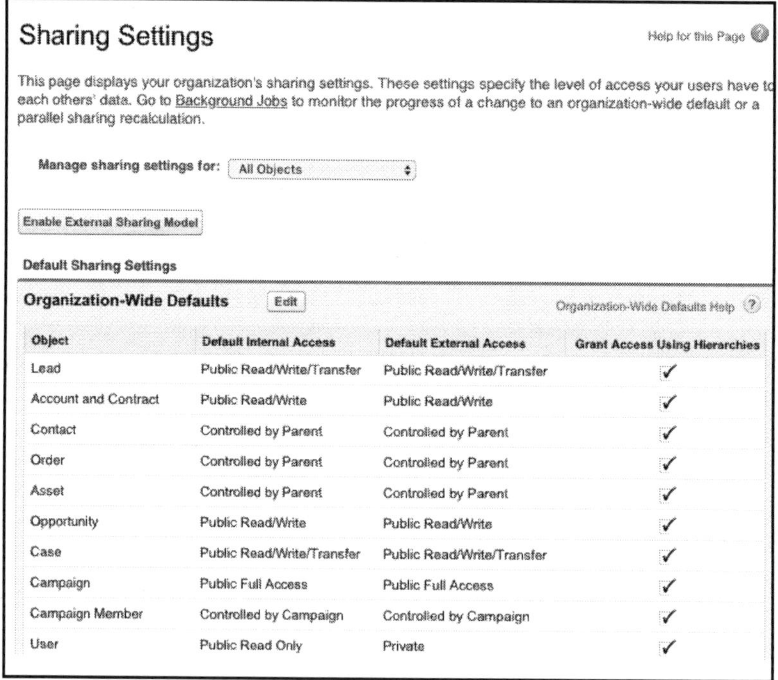

A selection of standard objects and all custom objects can be set in this page.

This OWD page is meant for setting the most restrictive access to a given object. This means that, from now on, you can ask an administrator to only grant additional access and not restrict it.

By default, Salesforce uses role hierarchies to grant access to records to the users that belong to roles above a given user hierarchy. This means that if a user owns a record (whose object is set as Private in the OWD, so it should be only visible to its owner), using hierarchies, the manager user who is above that role can access the record as well.

You can disable hierarchy access by unflagging the **Grant Access Using Hierarchies** flag for custom objects only. Role hierarchy will no longer be enforced, but users with **View All**, **Modify All**, **View All Data**, and **Modify All Data** access will still be able to access that record.

If you change an object's OWD to a wider value (for example, from **Private** to **Public Read-Only**) the *visibility is updated instantly*: users who weren't able to access the records will immediately be allowed to do so.

If you restrict access (for example, from **Public Read/Write** to **Private**), Salesforce will start a recalculation that could take hours to complete, depending on the size of the dataset.

Be smart when planning your OWD changes. Once the calculation has been completed, you'll receive a confirmation system email.

The OWD settings have the following values (a selection object has specific values that differ from this list):

- **Controlled by Parent**: If a record is a *child* of another kind of record (for example, a contact is parented to an account), you can give this record the same access level as its parent. If a user can edit an account, then they're allowed to edit its children contacts as well. When a custom object is a *master-detail* child of a standard object, the only available value is **Controlled by Parent** and it is not editable.
- **Private**: Only the record's owner and users above their role hierarchy can view, edit, and report on the record.
- **Public Read Only**: The record is viewable and reportable by any user, but it can only be edited by its owner and users above the owner's hierarchy.

- **Public Read/Write**: The record is viewable and editable by any user in your organization. Only the owner can delete or manually share the record.
- **Public Read/Write/Transfer**: Available only on cases and leads, the transfer operation allows a record to be transferred of ownership, but only the owner can delete or manually share it.
- **Public Full Access**: Available only on campaigns, this allows all users to read, edit, and delete a campaign, regardless of whether they are the owner or not.

A user object has the following two available values:

- **Private**: A record is accessible by the owner (that is, the same user) and by the users on the hierarchy above it.
- **Public Read-Only**: The record is accessible by any user in the organization.

In order to improve recalculation performance, you can enable **External Organization-Wide Defaults** and change the way records are shared with external users (such as customer community users).

Some types of external users are as follows:

- Authenticated website users
- Chatter external users
- Community users
- Customer portal users
- Guest users
- High-volume portal users
- Partner portal users
- Service cloud portal users

It's good practice to set the **Default External Access** to **Private** and then extend accessibility using, for example, sharing rules or sharing sets for the external users only.

External access can be set for the following objects:

- Account
- Asset
- Case
- Contact
- Individual
- Opportunity

- Order
- User
- Custom objects

Remember that the external access level cannot be more permissive than the corresponding internal access level.

To enable external OWD defaults, click on the **Enable External Sharing Model** button on the **Setup** | **Security** | **Sharing Settings** page. All external default values are matched with the internal settings.

If you want to disable this setting, revert all the external values so that they match the internal ones.

Role hierarchies

With role hierarchies, users can have access to records that are owned by or have been shared with users below their hierarchy. In a few words, the CEO (the person with the highest role) can see any record owned by any user, while the Sales Manager can see records that are owned by or have been shared with sales representatives but cannot see records owned by Service Manager users.

This applies to objects with OWD set to **Private** or **Read Only** because of the principle that *sharing can grant wider access and not restricted access.*

This sharing method can be enabled on the OWD **Grant Access Using Hierarchies** setting and can only be disabled for custom objects.

To set up roles, go to **Setup** | **Users** | **Roles**:

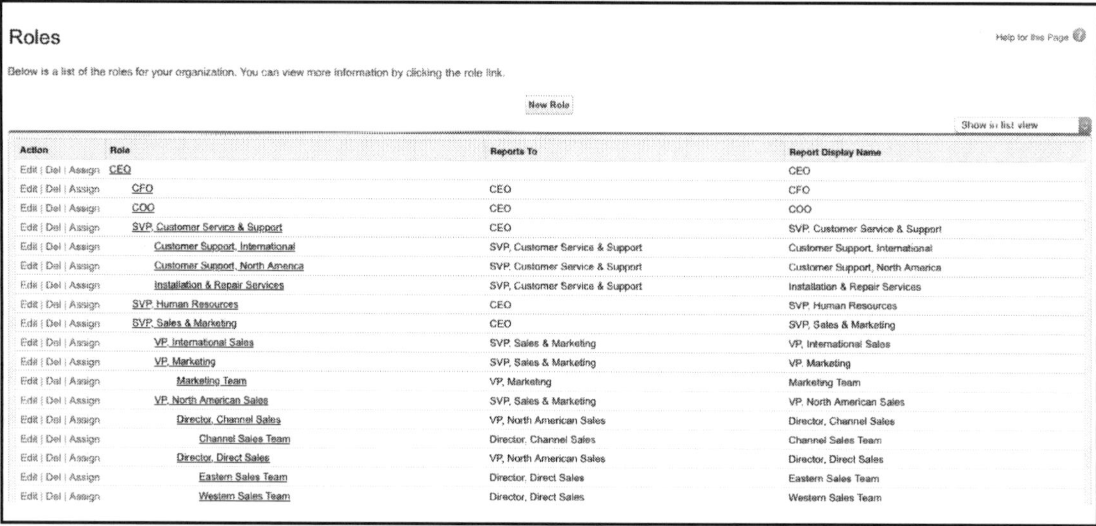
Roles

Help for this Page

Below is a list of the roles for your organization. You can view more information by clicking the role link.

New Role

Show in list view

Action	Role	Reports To	Report Display Name
Edit | Del | Assign	CEO		CEO
Edit | Del | Assign	CFO	CEO	CFO
Edit | Del | Assign	COO	CEO	COO
Edit | Del | Assign	SVP, Customer Service & Support	CEO	SVP, Customer Service & Support
Edit | Del | Assign	Customer Support, International	SVP, Customer Service & Support	Customer Support, International
Edit | Del | Assign	Customer Support, North America	SVP, Customer Service & Support	Customer Support, North America
Edit | Del | Assign	Installation & Repair Services	SVP, Customer Service & Support	Installation & Repair Services
Edit | Del | Assign	SVP, Human Resources	CEO	SVP, Human Resources
Edit | Del | Assign	SVP, Sales & Marketing	CEO	SVP, Sales & Marketing
Edit | Del | Assign	VP, International Sales	SVP, Sales & Marketing	VP, International Sales
Edit | Del | Assign	VP, Marketing	SVP, Sales & Marketing	VP, Marketing
Edit | Del | Assign	Marketing Team	VP, Marketing	Marketing Team
Edit | Del | Assign	VP, North American Sales	SVP, Sales & Marketing	VP, North American Sales
Edit | Del | Assign	Director, Channel Sales	VP, North American Sales	Director, Channel Sales
Edit | Del | Assign	Channel Sales Team	Director, Channel Sales	Channel Sales Team
Edit | Del | Assign	Director, Direct Sales	VP, North American Sales	Director, Direct Sales
Edit | Del | Assign	Eastern Sales Team	Director, Direct Sales	Eastern Sales Team
Edit | Del | Assign	Western Sales Team	Director, Direct Sales	Western Sales Team

You can create up to 500 roles for your organization.

Every user should have a role, otherwise their data won't show up on displays based on their role (such as an opportunities report and forecast rollups).

System administrator users may not have the role set, but it is good practice to fill in this field, especially if these users own records. If a role is not set, it is likely that their records won't appear on reports/views.

You can always set the highest role (for example, CEO) for administrator users and not care about record visibility since system admins should have the **Modify All Data** permission, which grants access to the whole organization's dataset.

To avoid performance issues, no user should be able to own more than 10,000 records. If this is unavoidable (for example, the user is an integration user), assign that user a higher role to avoid complex sharing calculations.

If you have a huge number of roles and users, it is suggested that you use SOAP APIs (for example, a Data Loader) to increase efficiency (at least in the organization setup phase or when users change their role frequently).

Sharing rules

Sharing rules create exceptions for OWD settings and can grant wider access to public groups, roles, and territories.

Before we look at sharing rules in detail, let's talk about **Groups**.

Public and personal groups

Groups are sets of users and can contain users, other groups, and all the users in a given role or territory hierarchy (or even the users below that given role/territory, that is, the so-called **subordinates**).

Your organization supports public groups, which are created by administrators and can be used by any user, and personal groups, which are created by any user and only accessible to them.

Groups can be created for the following reasons:

- For default sharing with sharing rules (only public)
- To share a record with other users (both public and personal)
- To share a Salesforce CRM Content library (only public)
- To assign users to a selected action on Salesforce Knowledge (only public)

Since public groups are involved in sharing calculations to increase system performance, we need to take the following into account:

- Avoid creating groups with few users (use manual sharing instead).
- Don't adopt groups for users that need frequent move in and out.
- Don't nest groups for more than five levels deep.
- Enable **Grant Access Using Hierarchies** on the public group configuration, but only if that group doesn't include a*ll internal users.*

A group can contain the following:

- Users
- Public groups
- Personal groups (available only when creating personal groups)
- Roles (internal and subordinates, or internal and portal subordinates)
- Partner users
- Customer portal users

Working with sharing rules

Like any other sharing method other than OWD, sharing rules cannot restrict access to records.

To create a new sharing rule, go to **Setup** | **Security** | **Sharing Settings**, choose an object in the **Sharing Rules** section, and click the **New** button:

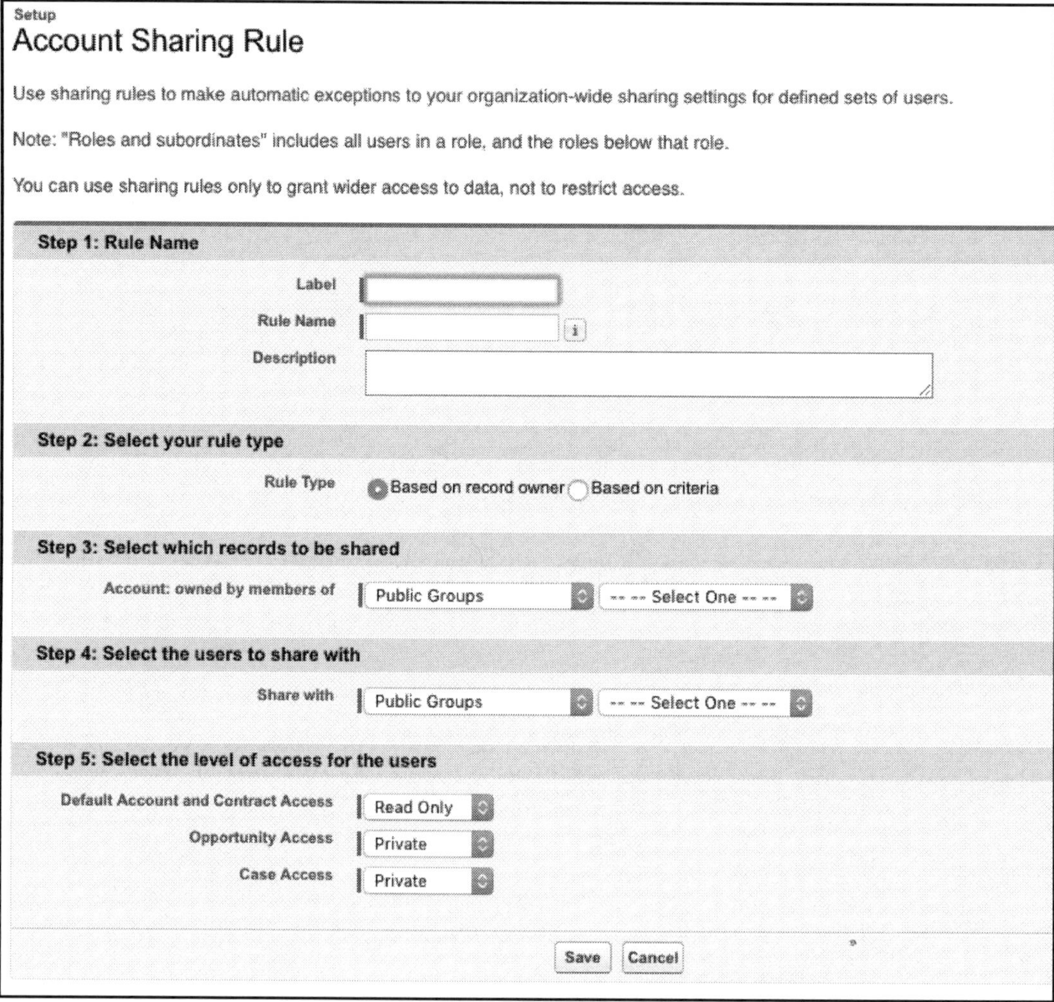

There are two different kinds of sharing rules:

- **Owner-based**: Record identification is based on ownership; for example, you can share an owned record with a given role or group
- **Criteria-based**: Record identification is based on the record's fields; for example, you can share a record that has the **Internal Division** custom field set to **Utilities.**

Criteria-based sharing rules are more expensive in terms of performance, but that's why you are required to create up to 50 criteria-based sharing rules per object. The overall number of sharing rules per object (owner-based or criteria-based) has a limit of 300.

Another thing to remember is that although criteria-based rules use record fields to calculate sharing and not its owner, role and territory hierarchy could still take place (if it's not been disabled for custom objects).

The following field types can be used for criteria calculation:

- Auto number
- Checkbox
- Date
- Date/time
- Email
- Lookup relationship (for the user ID or queue ID)
- Number
- Percent
- Phone
- Picklist
- Text (case-sensitive)
- Text area (case-sensitive)
- URL

You can set different values for the Text and Text area fields by separating them with a comma.
If a field type you need for the criteria is not supported, create a workflow or trigger to copy that value into a text/number field.

You can even apply filter logic to create more complex criteria.

After you have decided which type of sharing rule you want to create, select the categories of users to share with (for example, roles, territories, or groups) and the sharing access level:

- **Private**: This is only available for associated contacts, opportunities, and cases (for example, **Account Sharing Rule**).
- **Read only**: Reads a record.
- **Read/Write**: Reads and updates a record.
- **Full Access**: Reads, updates, deletes, transfers, and shares records (just like its owner).

Once a rule has been created, the **Share with** value cannot be updated.

Here is an example of an **Account Sharing Rule**:

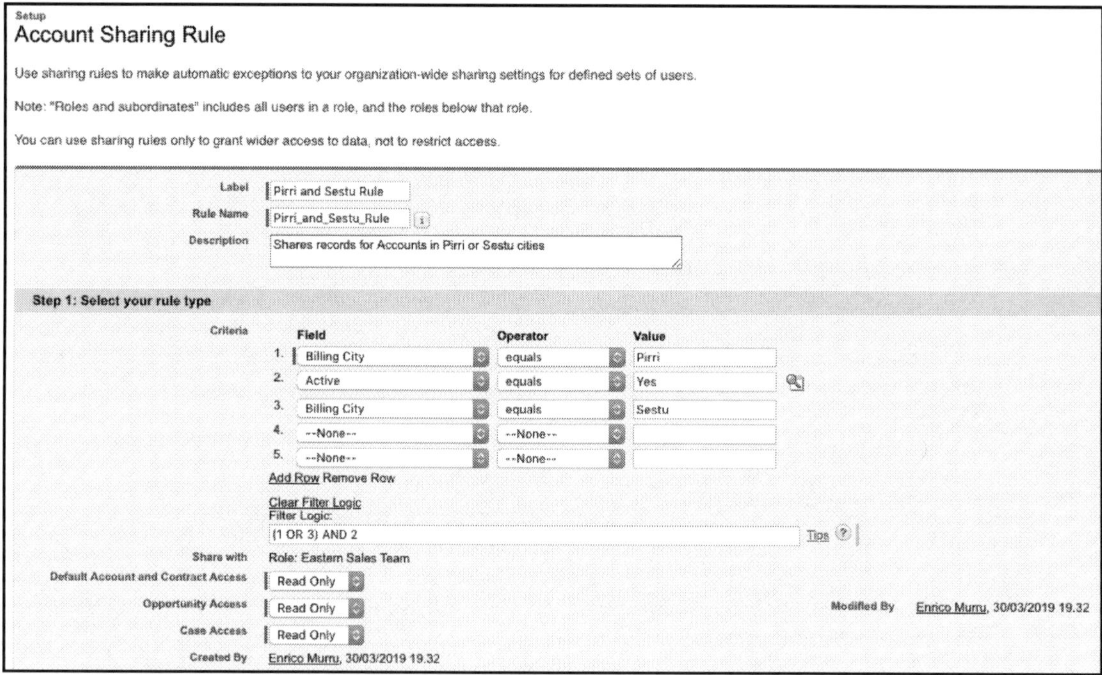

It shares accounts with the **Billing City** of `Pirri` or `Sestu` that are in an **Active** state to users in the **Eastern Sales Team** role, giving them **Read Only** access to the account and the related contact, case, and opportunity objects (they are specific to the account object).

The following are some considerations about sharing rules:

- If you have multiple sharing rules for a given record, the widest rule is actually applied.
- You cannot add high-volume users to sharing rules because they don't have a role.
- Sharing rules apply to all records (new and old) and are applied to active and inactive users.
- Sharing rules are also recalculated every time a user enters/exits a role, a territory, or a group or when a user transfers the record to another user.
- Because sharing calculation can take a while, Salesforce puts in a background calculation job and notifies the user with a system email when the calculation is ready.
- Lead sharing rules don't apply to account, opportunity, and contact objects that are generated after lead conversion.

Manual sharing

Manual sharing is the ability for a record's owner to give access to that record (and also other related records) to other users who are not necessarily included in their hierarchy. If you give another user access to an account record, that user would be able to access cases and opportunities.

At the time of writing, this feature is only available in Salesforce Classic (you can take a look at this at `https://success.salesforce.com/ideaView?id=0873A000000LmluQAC`).

To manually share a record, you must either be its owner, a user above the owner's hierarchy (if **Grant Access Using Hierarchies** is enabled for that object), any user with full access, or a system administrator.

The **Sharing** button can be displayed on a record page if its OWD is set to **Private** or **Public Read-Only**.

In the following screenshot, we can see that the account has a **Public Read Only** OWD:

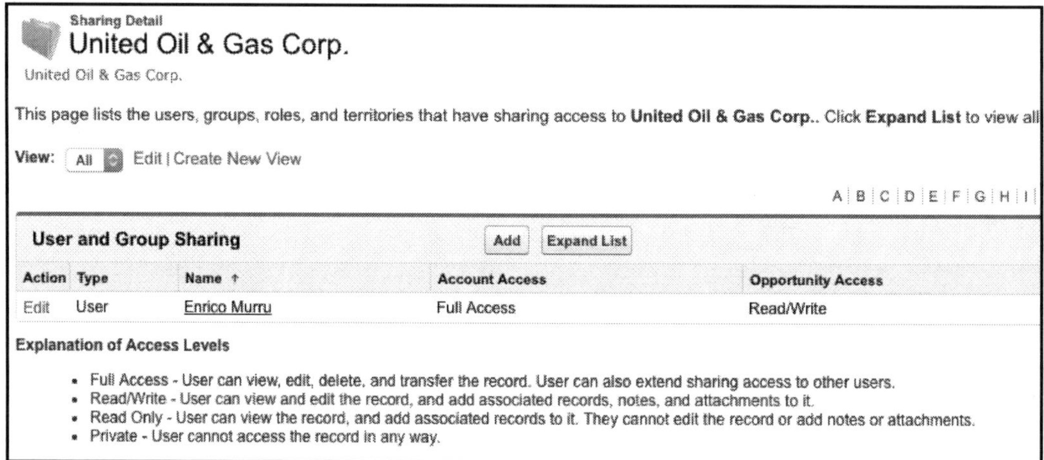

By clicking the **Add** button, you can set up manual sharing for the record:

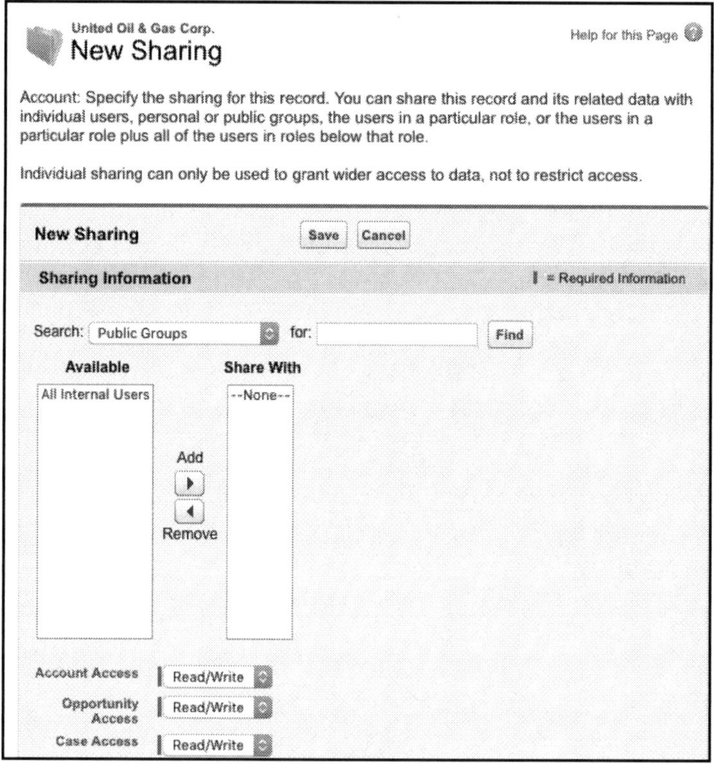

In the **Search** field, you can include the following information (depending on the features in your organization):

- **Manager groups**: All the user's managers
- **Manager subordinates groups**: All the user's managers and their subordinates
- **Public groups**: Groups defined by the administrators
- **Personal groups**: Groups defined by the current owner
- **Users**: All internal users
- **Roles**: All the roles in your organization
- **Roles and subordinates**: All the roles in your organization (not available if portals are enabled)
- **Roles and internal subordinates**: All the roles in your organization and all the users below that role hierarchy (no portal roles considered)
- **Roles and internal and portal subordinates**: Like the previous point, but with portal roles and users
- **Territories**: All the territories defined in your organization (if territory management is enabled)
- **Territories and subordinates**: All the territories with the users below the territory hierarchy

We can use the **Find** button to search for entities to share the record with. Once we have found them, we can move them into the **Share With** select list. Then, we can select the required access level (**Full Access**, **Read/Write**, or **Read-Only**).

Once saved, this is what you will see on the record's **Sharing Detail** page:

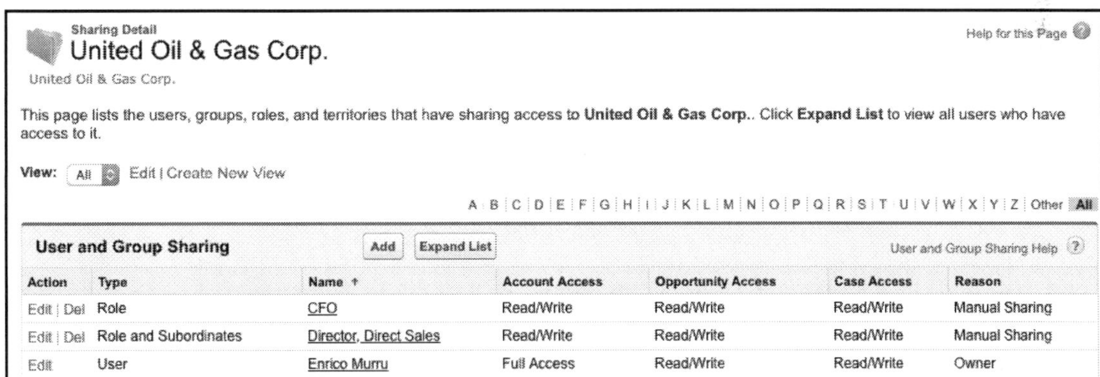

You can't share a record with another user unless they have read permission on the given object, and you can't share a record if the owner is an inactive user.

Apex managed sharing

When the sharing options aren't enough, or you simply need to share a given record automatically with a user or a group without changing its ownership, you can go with Apex managed sharing.

This kind of sharing is close to manual sharing but it is best used with Apex automation or external API calls (that is, the other system's operations directly into Salesforce).

To change an Apex managed sharing record, you need to have a **Modify All Data** permission: that's why this custom sharing is maintained even if the record changes ownership.

How to create Apex managed sharing rules is out of the scope of this book, and you need developers to achieve this kind of custom sharing. However, you may have to consider it when sharing policies are highly complex or the other sharing methods don't deliver the required level of sharing granularity.

Team sharing

You can define account, opportunity, and case teams to ease collaboration on those objects and increase access levels for specific users in the team.

Account teams

An account team groups a number of users that work together to manage a given account record.

To enable account teams, click on **Setup** | **Feature Settings** | **Sales** | **Account Teams**. You'll see a new related list on the account object that lists all the team members.

Each member has a given role (that is, a picklist of the account team objects):

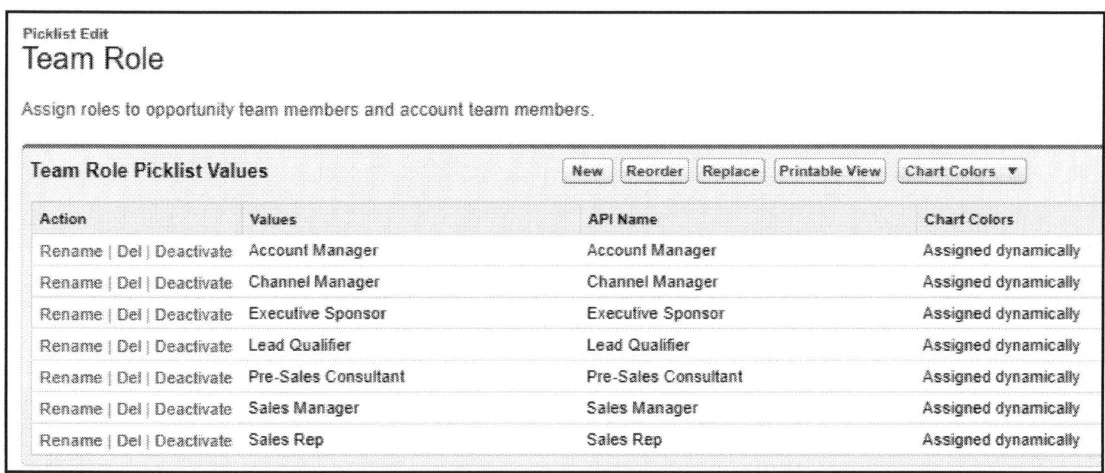

Picklist Edit

Team Role

Assign roles to opportunity team members and account team members.

Team Role Picklist Values

New | Reorder | Replace | Printable View | Chart Colors ▼

Action	Values	API Name	Chart Colors
Rename | Del | Deactivate	Account Manager	Account Manager	Assigned dynamically
Rename | Del | Deactivate	Channel Manager	Channel Manager	Assigned dynamically
Rename | Del | Deactivate	Executive Sponsor	Executive Sponsor	Assigned dynamically
Rename | Del | Deactivate	Lead Qualifier	Lead Qualifier	Assigned dynamically
Rename | Del | Deactivate	Pre-Sales Consultant	Pre-Sales Consultant	Assigned dynamically
Rename | Del | Deactivate	Sales Manager	Sales Manager	Assigned dynamically
Rename | Del | Deactivate	Sales Rep	Sales Rep	Assigned dynamically

By doing this, you can set up any role you need for your business.

Team roles are informational values and don't have anything to do with role hierarchy sharing.

From the account team related list, you can click on the **Add Team Members** button to add account team members:

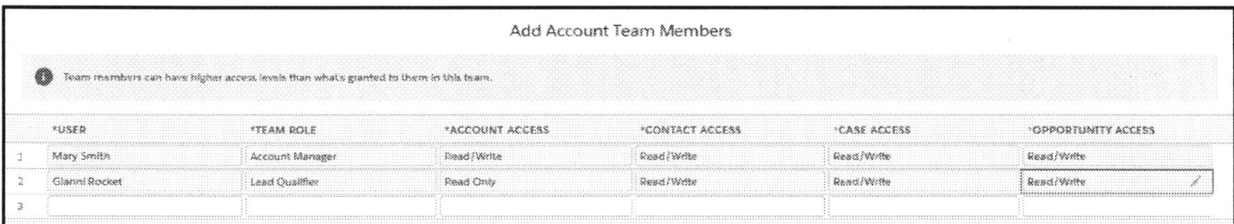

Add Account Team Members

Team members can have higher access levels than what's granted to them in this team.

	*USER	*TEAM ROLE	*ACCOUNT ACCESS	*CONTACT ACCESS	*CASE ACCESS	*OPPORTUNITY ACCESS
1	Mary Smith	Account Manager	Read/Write	Read/Write	Read/Write	Read/Write
2	Gianni Rocket	Lead Qualifier	Read Only	Read/Write	Read/Write	Read/Write
3						

To add members, you need to have edit access on the account, while to edit or delete a member, you need to be the owner, a user above the owner's hierarchy, a user with full access on the record, or an administrator.

The account, contact, case, and opportunity access fields are used to open up access for an account and its related records (and not to restrict it).

Contact access is unavailable if the contact's OWD is set to **Controlled by Parent**.

A user cannot provide wider access to a record they don't actually have (if the owner has read-only access to the account, the added members would at least have read-only access). Instead, administrators can increase the access level.

You can add default teams to set a predefined set of people in your team.

Opportunity teams

The concept behind opportunity teams is the same as account teams: a group of users working together for an opportunity.

Click on **Setup** | **Feature Settings** | **Sales** | **Opportunities** | **Opportunity Team Settings** and flag **Enable Team Selling**.

Member roles have the same values of account teams (**Setup** | **Feature Settings** | **Sales** | **Team Roles**), so consider this when changing the picklist values.

You can add a default team, an account team, or add new users:

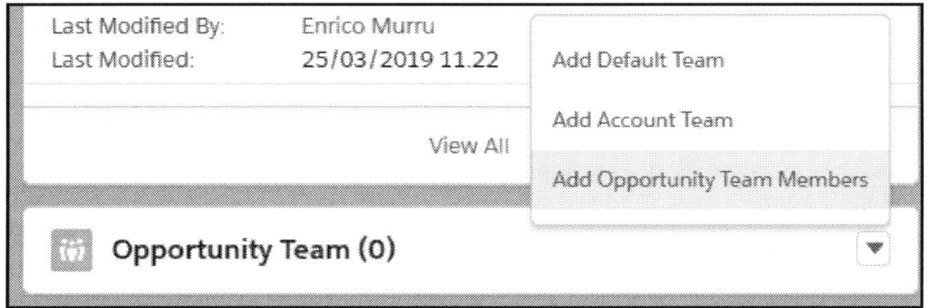

The only access level you can open to the team's members is opportunity access:

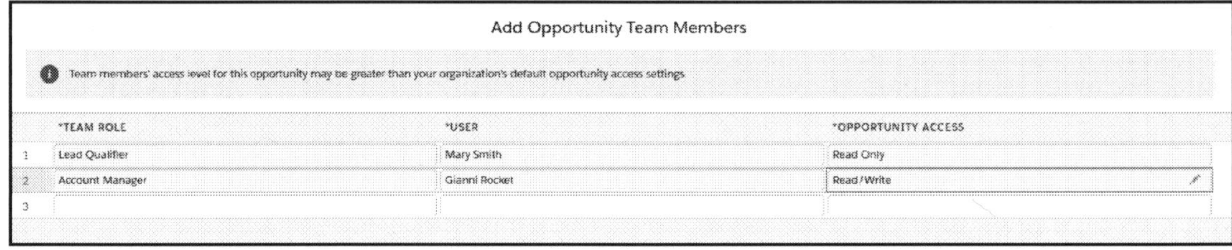

The concepts of member creation and editing are the same as for account teams.

Opportunity teams cannot be used with private opportunities.

Case teams

Like account and opportunity teams, case teams are meant to enhance the service process: define people that can have access to the case.

These people can be actual users or contacts, provided they are customer portal users.

The core of this kind of team is the case team roles configuration (**Setup** | **Feature Settings** | **Service** | **Case Teams** | **Case Team Member Roles**):

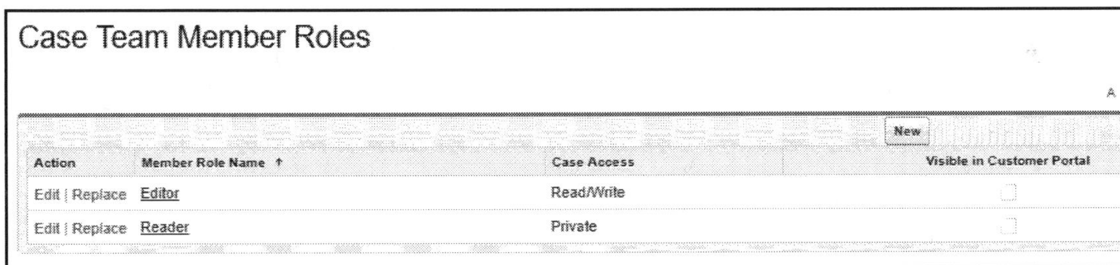

From here, you can define which role has which access level on the case team. You can set **Private**, **Read Only**, and **Read/Write** access levels. **Visible in Customer Portal** allows users from the customer portal to see that member.

From the case related list (you probably need to manually add this related list on the case page layout), you can select users you want to be part of your team:

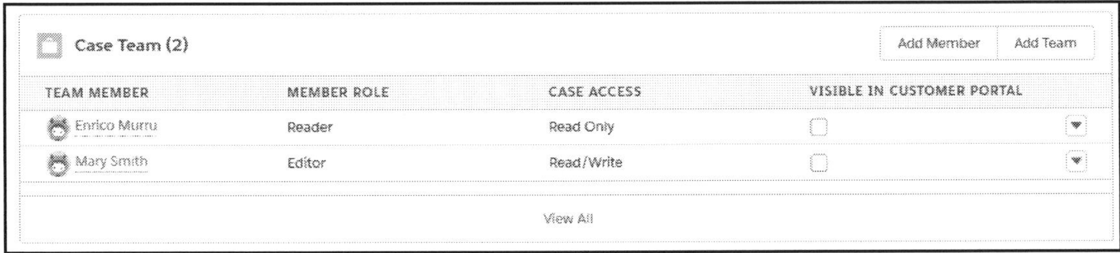

The same sharing considerations apply for case teams as well.

Some considerations about sharing

There are some peculiarities and exceptions regarding the sharing model that you should be aware of.

The following are the peculiarities and exceptions regarding role hierarchy-based sharing:

- Contacts that are not parented to any account are inherently private, so they are visible to their owners and administrators. For this category, contact sharing rules are not applied.
- The same happens for notes and attachments with the **Private** flag enabled, which are visible only to the user who created them (and administrators).
- Events marked as **Private** are only visible to their owners and administrators.
- Role hierarchy is effective on users above them in the hierarchy, but only if they have the **Read** or **Edit** permission on the given object.

Regarding object deletion, a record can only be deleted by its owner, administrator, users above them in the hierarchy, or any user that has been granted full access sharing. For cases and leads, even though a user has public read/write/transfer access, only the owner (and administrator) can delete that record.

To add notes and attachments to a record, you should have read/write access to it and at least read access so that you can create activities or associate a child record with it.

When dealing with large datasets, consider changing the sharing model can have an impact on your system due to it having to recalculate the access level across your organization, which may take several hours to complete.

If you have more than 2 million accounts and have set up account teams and territory management, take a closer look at performance to ensure that you don't have any inherently complex sharing calculations that can cause long-running transactions.

If you need to bulk change the sharing model, you can ask the Salesforce Support team to activate the *defer automatic sharing rule calculations* feature. With this in place, you can make all the changes you need on the OWD/sharing model and then execute the bulk recalculation when administration work has finished.

Avoid having a small number of accounts with thousands of contacts, cases, or opportunities. This is called **data skew**, and it can cause performance degradation. Keep this in mind and make accounts have a children ratio no greater than 1:10,000 (the less the better). This also occurs with **ownership skew**, which is when a few users hold ownership of thousands of objects. If this happens, make sure that the user is out of the role hierarchy (the user's role field is not filled in) or it has a higher role (for example, CEO). This simplifies sharing calculations.

A final suggestion is not to consider account hierarchies related to sharing. If a user owns a parent account, this doesn't mean they can have access to the child accounts; they aren't related to role or territory hierarchies.

Enterprise territory management

The last way to share records is by aligning your company's sales territories hierarchy. This kind of sharing model is applied to account sharing and related opportunities.

At the time of writing, there are currently two different kinds of territory management:

- Original territory management
- Enterprise territory management

For the scope of the Salesforce Advanced Administrator certification, we'll describe the latter since original territory management will be retired in June 2020 (this announcement can be found at `https://help.salesforce.com/articleView?id=000273181&language=en_US&type=1`).

Remember that this sharing option can only be activated if your organization doesn't use the old Customizable Forecast for opportunities that will be retired in June 2020 as well (this announcement can be found at `https://help.salesforce.com/articleView?id=000273188language=en_UStype=1`).

Let's dig deeper into the main concepts of **territory management** (**TM**).

The first element of TM is the **territory type**, which defines the kind of territories you can create. A territory type can refer to geographic zones (for example, EMEA territories) or to account segmentation (for example, utility companies). The label and description of a type should be self-explanatory so that you can avoid misunderstandings when creating territories. They won't be displayed in the hierarchy but will work pretty much like a territory guideline.

With territory type priority, you can define the priority of each territory type according to your sales strategy; for example, you can define a high priority with a value of **001** and a lower priority x with a value of **010**. We suggest that you define priorities that take into account possible future changes in territory type creation (don't start by setting 001 and 002 for your only two territory types if you may have a new territory type in the next year with an intermediate value). When you create a new territory, you'll be able to choose its territory type and see its priority.

The **territory** object is the core of TM since it represents a group of accounts and the Salesforce users who may access those accounts. They can have parent and child territories in order to replicate your sales strategy. They are composed of users, manually assigned accounts, a forecast manager, and the rules to automatically assign accounts to this territory (pretty much like sharing rules). Depending on the territory configurations, an account can be assigned to multiple territories.

The territory model is a complete model for your organization. By using this model, you can create relationships between territories to find the best one that fits your sales strategy. You can have up to four concurrent models and only one active at a time.

The territory model is pictured in the territory hierarchy and shows the relation between territories, as shown in the following screenshot:

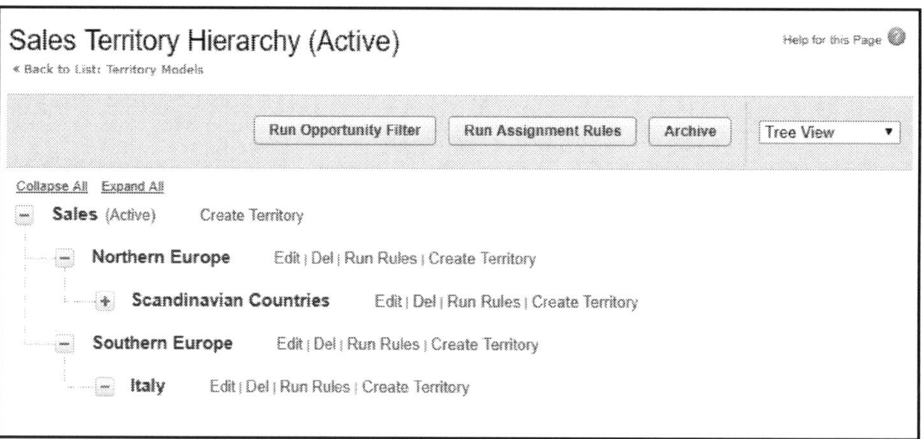

This page is useful if you wish to edit the hierarchy and run all the assignment rules and opportunity filters (this feature requires some custom Apex coding that's out of this scope; please refer to `https://developer.salesforce.com/docs/atlas.en-us.apexcode.meta/apexcode/apex_interface_TerritoryMgmt_OpportunityTerritory2AssignmentFilter.htm` for more details).

The last concept is territory model state. A model can have the following statuses:

- **Planning**: Previews the model before activating it.
- **Active**: There can be only one model in the active state.
- **Archived**: Only an active model can be archived. After a model becomes archived, each reference to the territory (for example, the territory field on the opportunity field) becomes blank.
- **Activation failed**: Something bad happened when activating (see notification email for more details).
- **Archiving failed**: Something bad happened in terms of the archive's state.

To enable TM, go to **Setup** | **Feature Settings** | **Territories** | **Territory Setting** and click **Enable Enterprise Territory Management**:

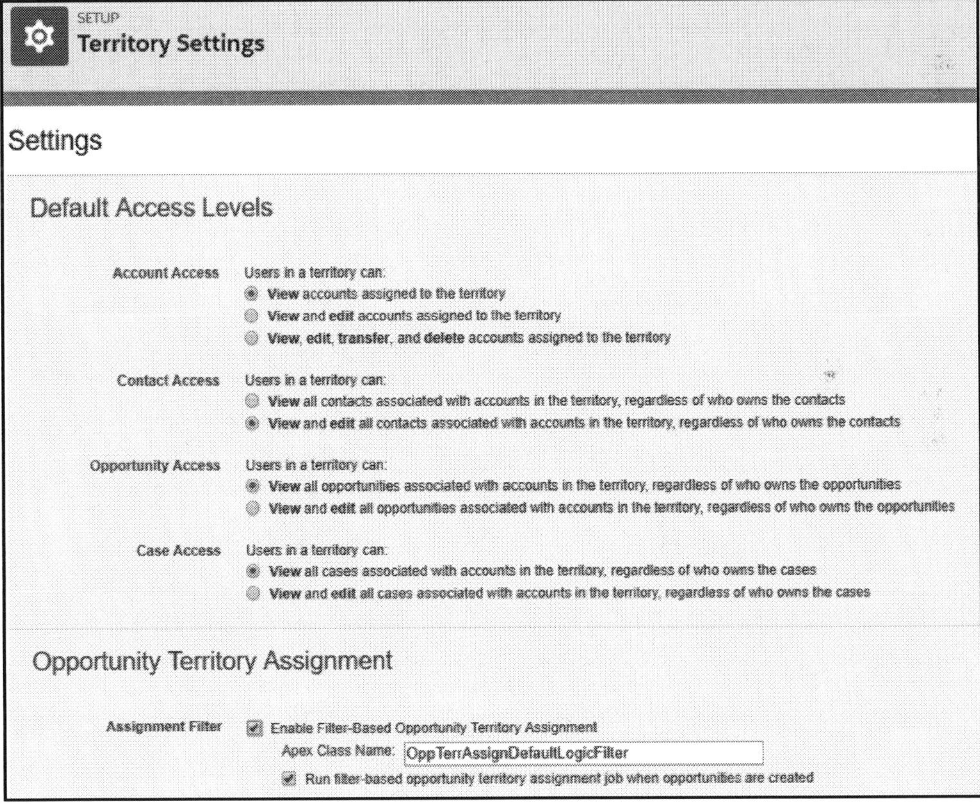

Territory Model's default access settings

In here, you can set up default access to accounts and opportunities for each territory. In addition, you can enable contacts and case access, but only if the OWD for them is set to Private.

From the **Opportunity Territory Assignment** section, you can enable a more detailed filter when setting up territory management for Opportunities. The default `OppTerrAssignDefaultLogicFilter` Apex class can be found in the documentation (see `https://developer.salesforce.com/docs/atlas.en-us.apexcode.meta/apexcode/apex_interface_TerritoryMgmt_OpportunityTerritory2AssignmentFilter.htm`) and is out of scope for this book (ask a developer to help you with the setup).

Each territory has its own default values that are inherited by the parent territories above it, as shown in the following screenshot:

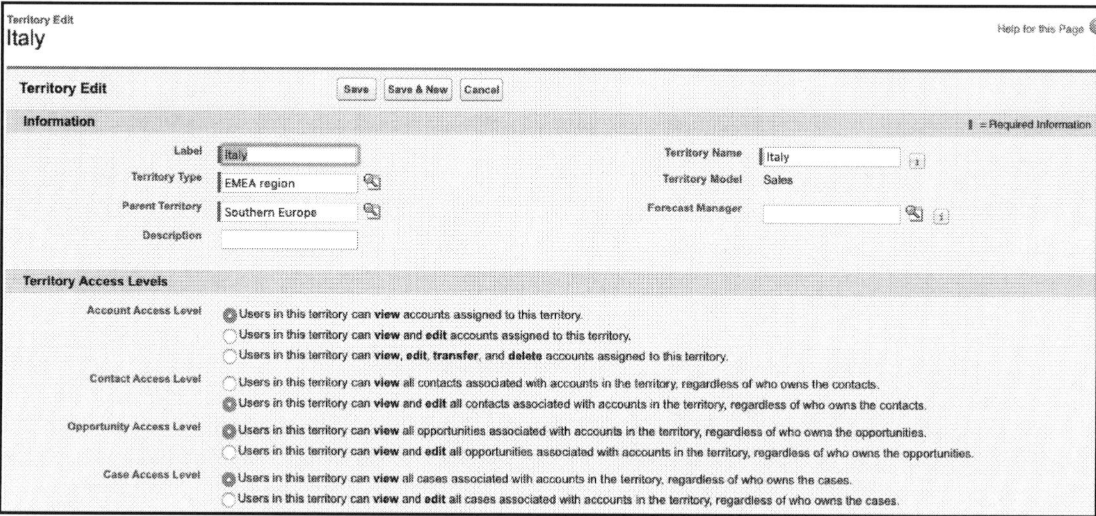

A territory contains assigned accounts and users.

Remember that you can create up to 1,000 territories per model for Developer Edition and Enterprise Edition organizations, while for Unlimited and Performance organizations, you can ask Salesforce support to let you have up to 99,999 territories (more than 20,000 will need a deeper inspection for approval).

The first way you can assign an account to a territory is by using rules that, based on the account's characteristics, can decide whether an account belongs to a given territory or not. These rules apply on account creation and are updated if the Territory Model is in an active state:

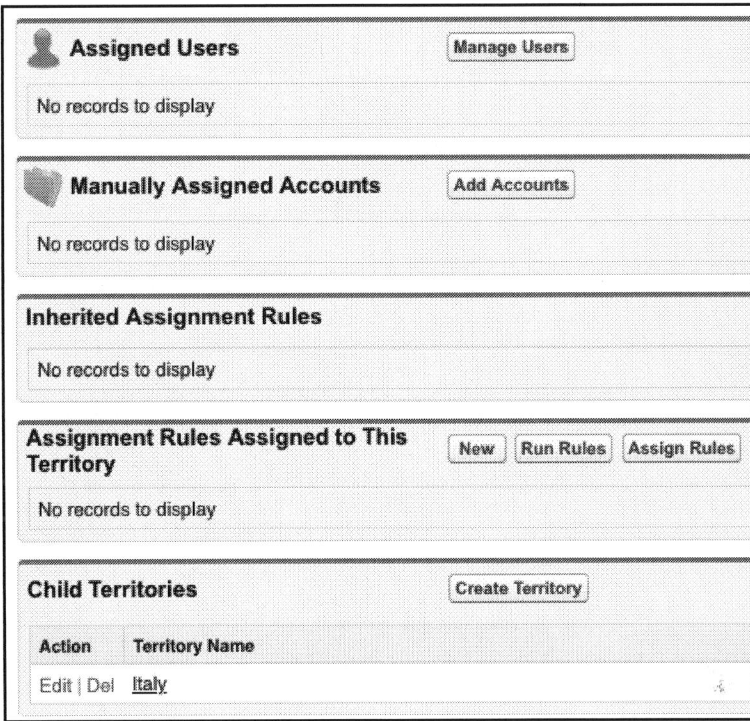

To create a new rule, go to the territory settings page, scroll down to the **Assignment Rules Assigned to This** section, and click the **New** button:

Object Territory Assignment Rule

New Object Territory Assignment Rule

Help for this Page

Object Territory Assignment Rule Edit

Step 1: Enter the name of this rule

= Required Information

Rule Name

Unique Name

Step 2: Enter the selection criteria for this rule

Base your rule on object characteristics such as:

- Industry
- Annual revenue
- Number of employees
- Region

Field	Operator	Value	
--None--	--None--		AND
--None--	--None--		AND
--None--	--None--		AND
--None--	--None--		AND
--None--	--None--		

Add Filter Logic...

Step 3 (optional): Apply to child territories

Apply to child territories — Applies the rule to **Southern Europe** territory and its descendants

Step 4 (optional): Set as active

Active

Learn More

A rule consists of field conditions (for example, **Country equals Italy**, and **Country equals Spain**) that define the account fields to which assignment is based on, the possibility to assign the same rule to the child territories, and the active flag to enable this rule.

Can we assign to child territories? The answer is yes. First, define a generic rule that matches the different territories (for example, **Country equals Italy**, **Country equals Spain**, and **Country equals Greece**, which identifies southern Europe countries) that is used in the Southern Europe territory and then create a territory-specific rule in each child country for internal regions (for example, for Italy, we can have **Region equals Sardinia**, **Region equals Sicily**, and **Region equals Tuscany**). Finally, create specific grand-children territories depending on the postal code values you received.

Remember not to use the same rule on a child if you are already using it on a parent territory. Moreover, if your organization is using country and states picklists, use the `contains` operator and not the `equals` operator.

A territory can have up to 15 assigned rules.

You can exclude an account from the territory rules calculation by setting up the **Exclude from territory assignment rules** flag when updating the record (it is hidden by default on the page layout and its field-level security should be set to visible):

If you change a rule, you need to reassign the accounts that are part of the hierarchy manually by clicking the **Run Assignment Rules** button at the model level or the **Run Rules** link at the territory level:

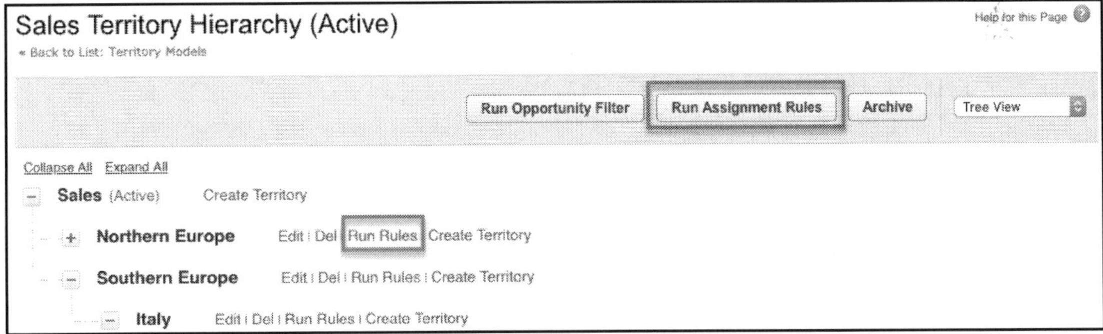

From the territory setting page, you can even add an account manually. This is useful when sharing rules are not enough to identify an account:

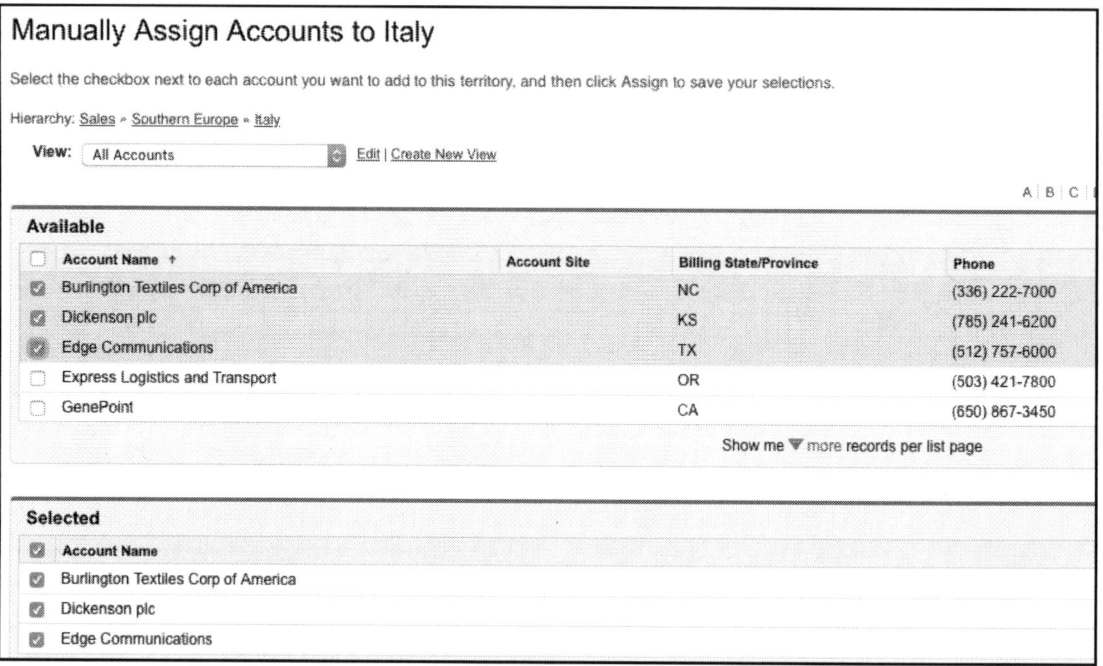

To see all the accounts related to a given territory (if you're using rules or manual assignment), click on the **View Accounts** button on the territory page.

Opportunities can be assigned to territories using an Apex filter (as shown earlier), but you can do this manually as well by using the **Territory** field and checking the **Exclude from the territory assignment filter logic** checkbox (they should be placed on the opportunity layout if needed):

Why is this necessary? Accounts can span multiple territories, and so there is a need to clarify where opportunities have been assigned.

Users can be associated with territories if we use the **Manage Users** button in the **Assigned Users** section of the territory setup page. Using the UI, you can assign up to 1,950 users to the territory. If you have a wider audience per territory, you should use APIs (for example, Data Loader; see the **UserTerritory2Association** object's details at `https://developer.salesforce.com/docs/atlas.en-us.api.meta/api/sforce_api_objects_userterritory2association.htm`).

You can even define territory roles for users that have been assigned to a given territory. Let's go through this now:

1. To define roles, you need to switch to Salesforce Classic (at the time of writing, that is, in Spring 2019), click on **Setup** | **Customize** | **User Territory Associations** | **Fields**, and look for the **Role in Territory** field:

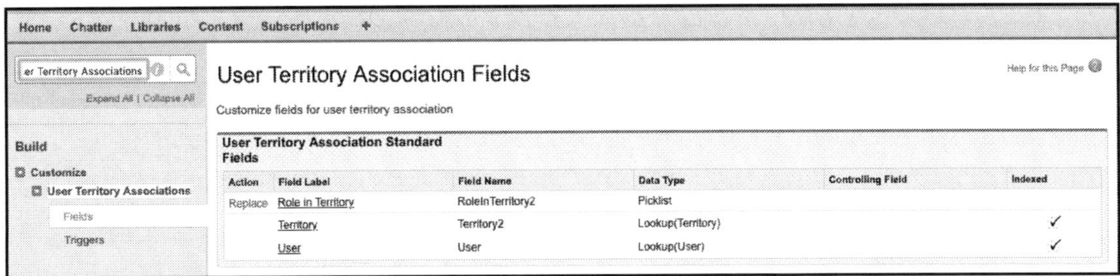

2. Define your roles (here is an example):

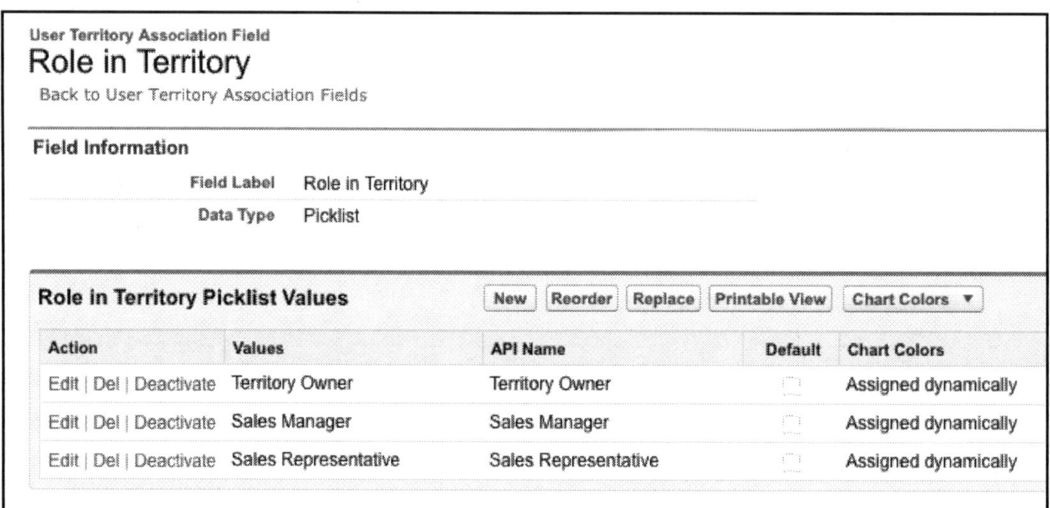

3. Then, go back (in Classic or Lightning Experience) to the territory page and go to the **Assigned Users** section. From here, it is possible to edit the user's role within the territory:

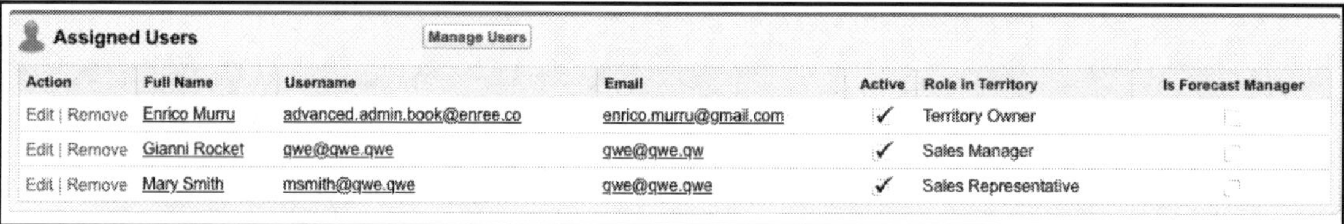

You can even define whether a user is a forecast manager. This option is used in opportunity forecasts so that a user can roll data up or down their territory hierarchy (and even adjust and view forecast data).

Sharing within Salesforce communities

Before closing this chapter, a few words should be said on how sharing is handled in communities. You should already be aware of what Salesforce communities are, but let's provide a brief summary anyway.

Salesforce communities are a way to allow external people to interact and collaborate with your business processes. This includes customers, partners, or even employees. They are an effective way to share Salesforce data with external users and allow internal users to interact with them, reducing the service cost.

Communities are created using point and click features with tools such as the Community Builder with built-in Lightning components ready for admins to use. You can even create your own customizations using Visualforce pages or Lightning components (with your developer's help):

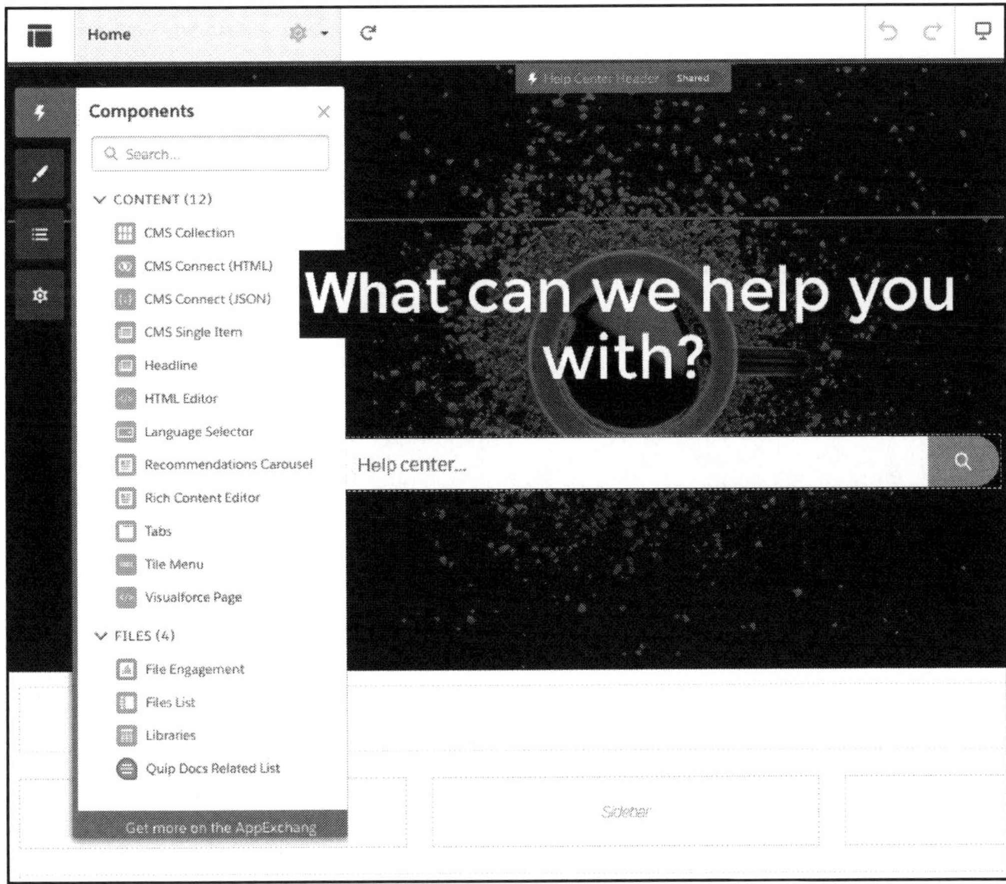

Community builder

An organization can have multiple communities for different uses. Let's look at some examples:

- A customer community where your customers can activate self-service in order to reduce the amount of effort needed for the back office to support your products
- A partner community dedicated to your external sales partners where they can create opportunities and help your internal sales team
- An employee community for dedicated internal activities such as collaboration

Communities are the evolution of the old customer and partner portals feature.

When you create a community, you have to choose a preset template from the available list on the community creator wizard. These templates allow you to expose a certain subset of features of your CRM (Sales- or Service-oriented).

Talking about data sharing, as we saw when we talked about OWD and external sharing, a community's users have a dedicated sharing model. It can be role-based or sharing-set-based, depending on the user licenses in use.

For Partner Community, Customer Community Plus, and Lightning External Apps Plus user licenses, you can define an internal role hierarchy based on the account that each external user is associated with.

You can define how users are hierarchically related within a given account; for example, when you enable an account to be a partner account (at the time of writing, you need to switch to Classic to use the **Enable as Partner** button on the account record).

Go to **Setup** | **Feature Settings** | **Communities** | **Communities Settings** and set the number of partner roles (**Community Role and User Settings**). Let's say we want three roles. When enabling a new partner user, the user creation form displays a role picklist where you can define the role for that given user within the account's hierarchy:

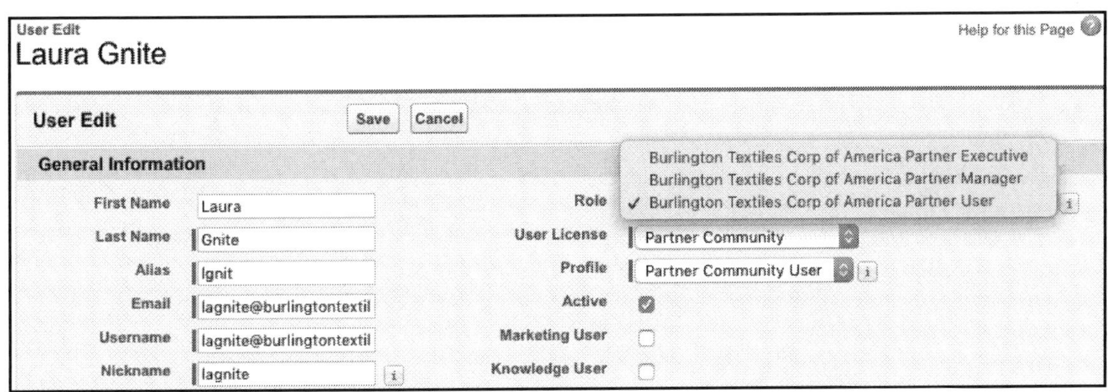

These roles appear in the portal roles or portal roles and subordinates when you've defining sharing. This way, records owned by partner users can be shared using the usual sharing model:

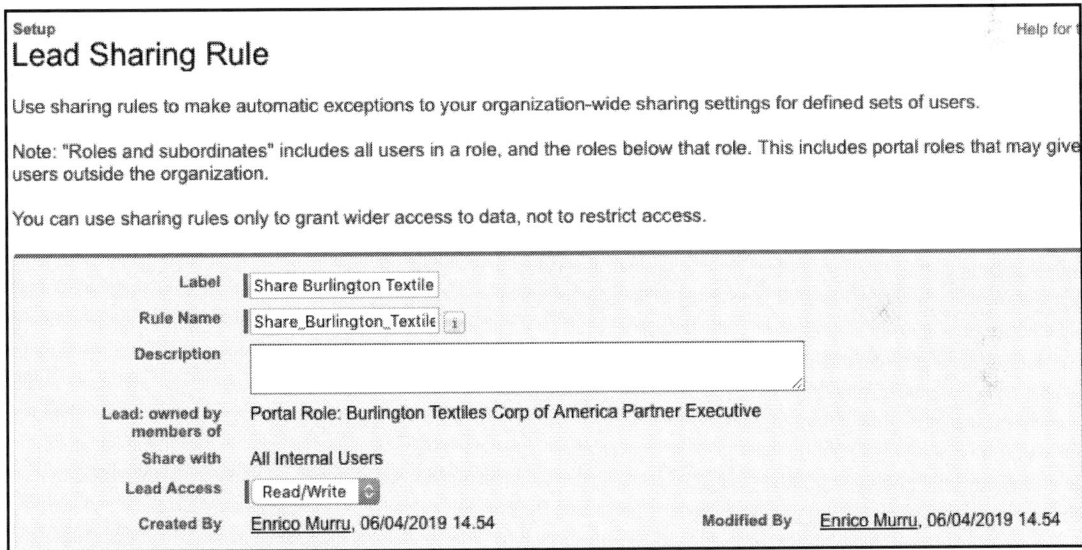

For performance reasons, keep the number of partner/customer roles to one and use partner super user access to grant specific users within the account's hierarchy access to records owned by other community users, including the child of the same account.

To enable this feature, go to the **Communities Settings** page:

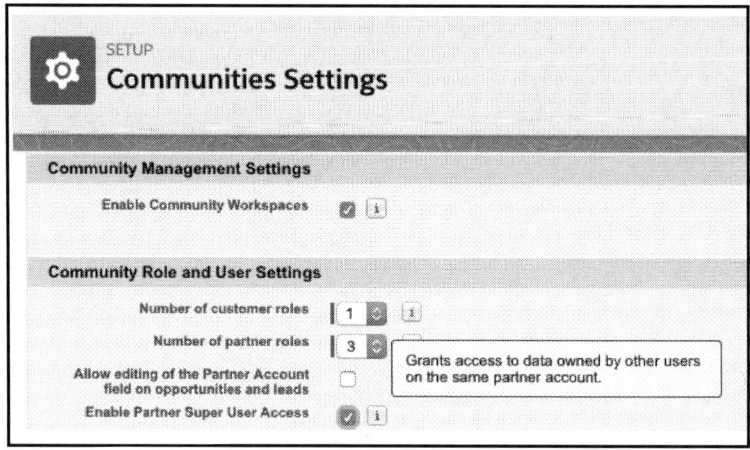

Partner and customer roles in communities

Super user access is enabled for opportunities, cases, leads, and custom objects owned by community users.

To assign this kind of permission, use the **Manage External User** dropdown in the contact layout in classic mode:

Super user access enabled on the contact page

To assign superuser access for customer users, create a permission set (or use a previously created one) with the portal super user permission and assign it to the community users that you want to be superusers.

High-volume community users

High-volume community users do not have roles, which removes any performance degradation related to sharing calculations with external users: they are not affected by the number of roles that are selected in the Communities Settings page.

The related user licenses are **Customer Community**, **High Volume Customer Portal**, and **Authenticated Website**.

But how does sharing work for high-volume users?

They only share the records they own through share groups. Note, however, that they are affected by the following sharing behaviors:

- They can access their own account and contact records with implicit sharing.
- They have read access on their account record.
- They can access a record's parent if the OWD for that record is Controlled by Parent.
- They can access a record if the OWD for that record is Public Read-Only or Public Read/Write.
- They can see other records if sharing sets have been set up.
- They cannot manually share records.
- They can't directly own an account.
- Case teams are not supported if the case owner is a high-volume user.
- They cannot be included in groups, sharing rules, account, opportunity, and case teams, Salesforce CRM content libraries, or territories.

To allow high-volume users to access records, use sharing sets. Every record you want to share with a user should have at least a user, contact, or account lookup related to the same high-volume user.

For example, you can share all the contacts related to the user's account or you can give write access to the Personal Order custom object related to the user's contacts:

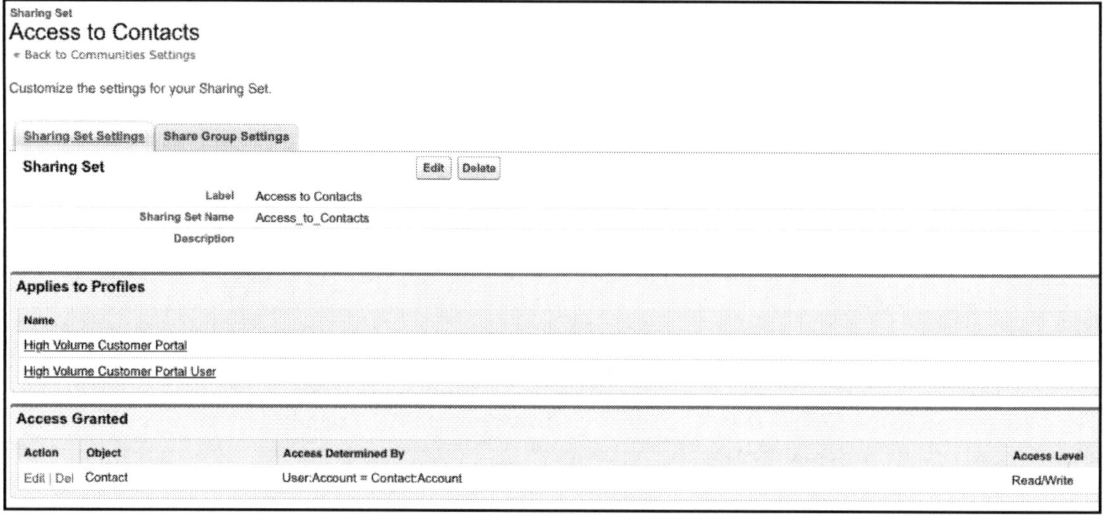

Sharing sets configuration

Once you have created a Sharing Set, you can click on the **Sharing Group Settings** tab to set up who can see the high-volume user records: click on the **Activate** button to enable this feature (this can take a while, and an email is sent upon activation).

From here, you'll be able to specify a set of users who'll be able to access the records that have been defined in this sharing set and that are owned by high-volume users:

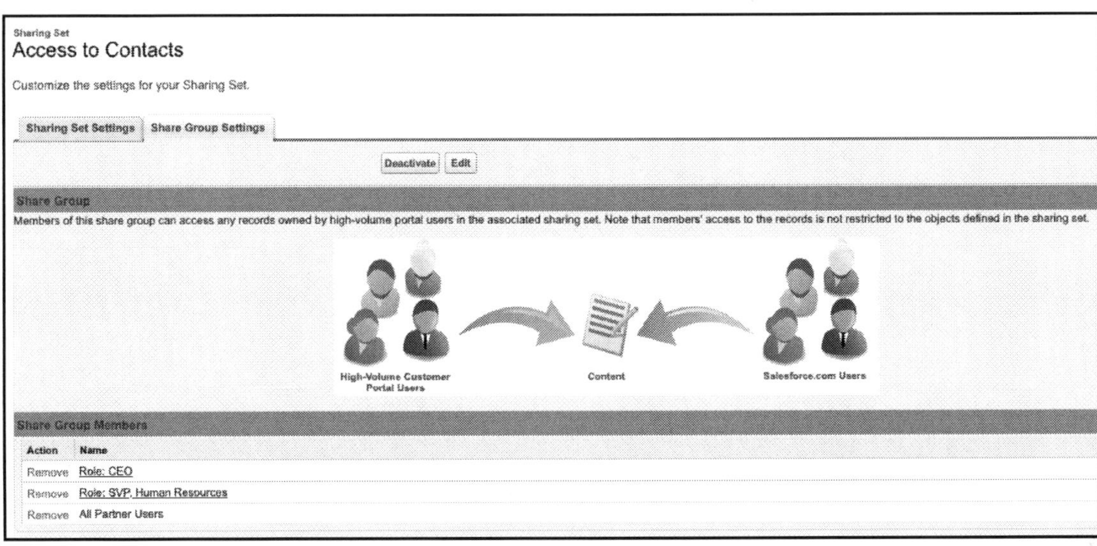

Share group configuration

Summary

Record-level security is one of the most important topics when designing a successful Salesforce implementation. By completing this chapter, we have learned about the power of the Salesforce sharing model and all its possible options, from permissions to org-wide defaults, mastering sharing rules and role hierarchies, segmenting your accounts with Enterprise Territory Management, and controlling how Salesforce communities play a role in oversharing.

The Salesforce platform runs in a multi-tenant architecture, which means our Salesforce organization runs on the same server as other Salesforce organizations, which in turn means that we are all using the same resources. To keep your customization clean and performant, we need to know exactly which resources are used the most so that we don't reach our organization's limits.

In the next chapter, we will cover organization monitoring.

Questions

1. You want to hide the shipping address fields of the account object from all of your sales representative users. What do you do?
    a. Configure field-level security to hide fields from sales representative profiles.
    b. Create a permission set to configure field-level security to hide fields.
    c. Assign no layout to the account object.
    d. Change the org-wide default sharing to Controlled by Parent for the Shipping Address object.
2. You need the sales representative users to be able to do some service-related work. What do you do?
    a. Create multiple profiles and assign them to the sales representative users.
    b. Assign a sales representative profile and the service representative profile to the selected sales representative users.
    c. Use a permission set to enable specific service abilities.
    d. Create a new license and profile to provide the new service features.
3. You want to give Delete access to the account object but not the Edit permission. How can you do this?
    a. Delete access requires **Read** and **Edit** OLS: this requirement makes no sense regarding OLS.
    b. Simply flag the Delete permission on the user's profile and unflag the Edit permission.
    c. Add the Modify All Data permission to the user's profile.
4. Your OWD sharing on the lead object is set to Public Read/Write. How can you restrict its access to **Public Read Only** for a selected role?
    a. Create a permission set and give it the Private OLS permission on the lead object.
    b. You cannot restrict the record-access level except by changing the OWD settings.
    c. Create a sharing rule to restrict access to the Private object level for the given role.
    d. Enable the View All permission on the lead object for the given role.

5. The OWD on the account is set to Private. An SLA custom object, which is the child of a master-detail relationship with the account object, should be able to be edited by the account's owner. How do you set up the OWD on the SLA object?
    a. OWD between master and child objects cannot relate.
    b. Set the OWD on the SLA object to Controlled by Parent .
    c. Set the OWD on the account object to Controlling Children.
    d. Set the OWD on the SLA object to Public Read/Write.
6. The OWD on the Interview custom object is set to Private. HR managers should be able to see their HR reps records. How can they do this?
    a. Change the OWD of the Interview custom object to Public Read-Only.
    b. HR reps should have a role above HR managers and Grant Access Using Hierarchies for the Interview object should be flagged.
    c. HR reps should have a role above HR managers and Grant Access Using Hierarchies for the Interview object should not be flagged.
    d. HR managers should have a role above HR reps and Grant Access Using Hierarchies for the Interview object should be flagged.
7. You are required to create a sharing rule to give read/write access to accounts objects owned by all the sales representatives to all the service managers (OWD on the account is Public Read). How do you do this?
    a. Create a criteria-based sharing rule that shares all the records owned by the sales representatives role with the sales managers role by setting the default access on the account object to Read/Write.
    b. Create an owner-based sharing rule that shares all the records owned by the sales representatives role with the Sales Managers role by setting the default access on the account object to Read/Write.
    c. Create a criteria-based sharing rule that shares all the records owned by the Service Managers role with the sales representatives role by setting the default access on the account object to Private.
8. The OWD on the lead object is set to Public Read-Only. Which statements are true regarding this?
    a. Only the owner can manually share the record.
    b. The administrator can manually share the record, as well as change the lead's ownership.
    c. Users in the role above the current owner can see the record and edit it.

b. The owner cannot change ownership of the record.
c. Any owner or administrator can manually set the lead setting access to Private.
d. Any owner or administrator can manually set the lead setting access to Public Read-Only.
e. Any owner or administrator can manually set the lead setting access to Public Read/Write.

9. You are sharing policies on the account object involves highly complex logic, such as making queries on different related child objects and external system Apex callouts. What can you do to achieve this?
    a. Enable a sharing model that involves criteria-based sharing rules for the child objects queries and manual sharing for the external system Apex callouts.
    b. Set the OWD of the account object to Private or Public Read-Only (depending on the requirements) and deliver Apex managed sharing by implementing custom Apex code with a developer of your team.
    c. Set the OWD of the account object to Private and allow users to use manual sharing with predefined public groups.
10. Service representatives work in groups and share their accounts and related objects (such as cases or opportunities) to provide a better service experience to their customers. While owning an account, a service representative wants to give access to their team. How can they do this?
    a. Enable account teams and instruct the service representative on how to set up an account team and provide read/write access to case and opportunity objects.
    b. Enable opportunity teams and instruct the service representative on how to set up an account team and provide Read/Write access to case and account objects.
    c. Enable case teams and instruct the service representative on how to set up an account team and provide read/write access to account and opportunity objects.
11. You can set up different team roles for opportunity and account teams.
    a. True
    b. False
12. You can set up different team roles for case and account teams.
    a. True
    b. False

13. You found that a lot of contacts are not related to any account. What does this mean?
    a. The account field on the contact object is always required.
    b. Unparented contacts are always considered with OWD set to Private, regardless of the OWD configuration.
    c. Contact sharing rules are not applied to this category of contacts.
    d. Unparented contacts are always considered with OWD set to Public Read-Only, no matter the OWD configuration.
14. Manager users cannot see case records owned by their subordinates. How can we deal with this? The OWD on the case record is set to Private:
    a. The OWD should be changed to at least Public Read-Only.
    b. The OWD on the case records may have the Grant Access Using Hierarchies set to false.
    c. Check the manager profile and see if it doesn't have the case's OLS set to **Read** or **Edit**.
    d. Check the manager profile and see if it doesn't have the case's sharing model set to Owned by Manages.
    e. The OWD on the case records may have the Controlled by Parent value.
15. What is data skew?
    a. A performance degradation issue caused by users that own thousands of records
    b. A performance degradation issue caused by a few accounts with thousands of related children
    c. A performance boost created by the **defer automatic sharing rule calculations** feature
16. Your sales strategy depends on accounts based on the Industry field (for example, utilities, high-tech, software, and food) but also on geographic regions (such as EMEA, north-america, and asia-pacific). How can you configure your organization to match this territory configuration?
    a. Enable Enterprise Territory Management and define territory types based on geography and industry.
    b. Enable Enterprise Territory Management and define territory types based on geography only.
    c. Enable Enterprise Territory Management and define territory types based on industry only.
    d. You cannot mix territories of a different kind in your model.

17. Which statements are true about Enterprise Territory Management?
    a. You can open access to account, contact, opportunity, and case objects but not custom objects.
    b. You can open access to account, contact, opportunity, case, and custom objects.
    c. You can assign accounts and opportunities manually to a given territory.
    d. An account and a related opportunity can belong to different territories at a given time.
    e. An account can belong to different territories at a given time.
18. Your organization has a partner community that's used by sales partners so that they can create opportunities. You want all the opportunities that are used by partner users to be shared with all internal sales representatives. How can you do this?
    a. Enable sharing sets for your community.
    b. Enable share groups for your community.
    c. Enable partner roles on the community's setup and create sharing rules for each partner role that opens up access to sales representative users.
    d. Enable partner superuser access.
19. Which kind of objects can be shared with high-volume users using sharing sets?
    a. All objects, no matter their format
    b. Only objects that are related to the user's account/contact/user object
    c. Only accounts, contacts, and users

2
Auditing and Monitoring

Let's give our organization monitoring skills a boost. Security is Salesforce's number one concern, and we, as administrators, are the security marshals of our organization. In the previous chapter, we saw how to set up secure access to our records using object permissions and the Salesforce sharing model.

In this chapter, we'll have a look at how you can monitor and audit your organization to ensure that everything is working properly and how you can proactively address any issue with your organization. There are different metrics that we can use to keep an eye on our daily administrator work. We'll have a look at some of them to ensure that your implementation is working correctly.

In this chapter, we'll learn about the following topics:

- How to delegate some of your administrative tasks—as a sheriff, you need a deputy
- How to monitor login access—have a look at who is accessing our organization
- How to monitor key metrics of your organization's usage, or how customization lies on your organization's limits
- How to enable debug logs for point-and-click customizations for effective debugging
- How to check the overall security status of your organization
- How to actively monitor all kinds of user events (such as logins, report executions, and Visualforce loading, to name a few) with event monitoring

Delegated administration

Before jumping into monitoring and auditing, we're going to look at a Salesforce CRM feature that has been delivered to ease your daily life as an administrator, concentrating on important tasks such as designing data-sharing policies or implementing business processes rather than unlocking users or creating new ones. If you are a good administrator, then you are good at multitasking, but this skill is not enough when dealing with user-crowded organizations or poorly trained users.

By delegating some administrative powers, we are granting users the ability to handle other users and other administrative tasks. This is especially useful when dealing with organizations with complex role hierarchies or organizations that are distributed worldwide, where it is hard for you to quickly answer user needs from the other side of the world (we are great administrators, but we need to sleep, too).

There are three ways to achieve this delegation:

- Assign selected users a **System Administrator** profile
- Assign a profile with **Manage Users** permission
- Enable **delegated administration**

Using the System Administrator profile is the easiest choice, but it leads to a potential Armageddon: we are giving our (sometimes poorly trained?) users the power to change every aspect of the organization. This is why we should not do this, unless the user in question will be a skilled administrator.

If you are reading this book, you are a trusted administrator in your company. Don't take this recognition for granted; keep learning, but most of all, don't assume that other people will automatically take as much care of your organization as you do. What is our suggestion? Give your sheriff's star only to people you trust.

Another way to delegate is to assign the **Manage Users** permission. We can create a permission set with this system permission and assign it to certain users.

This is not a cool choice at all. In fact, we are giving a user way more than what we actually need them to have. They can now expire all passwords, clone, edit, or delete profiles, edit or delete shared settings, and edit user login hours (I've seen people locking down their profiles with login hours when no other admin was there to help them!).

They can also create new system administrators because there is no restriction on the kind of profiles they can handle: that leads to the Armageddon we mentioned earlier.

The right choice is delegated administration, a safe method for providing delegated user management access by granting limited administrative privileges to a selected set of users.

After delegation, they'll be able to do the following:

- Create and edit users
- Unlock users
- Reset passwords
- Assign specific profiles
- Assign permission sets
- Assign users to public groups
- Log in as another user, for users who granted login access to their admins
- Manage custom objects (except when creating relationships or changing organization-wide sharing defaults)

Everything is role-constrained, which means that they can manage only users within a specific role and its subordinates.

Defining a delegated administration group is straightforward. Navigate to **Setup | Security | Delegated Administration** and click on the **New** button. This will bring up the following screen:

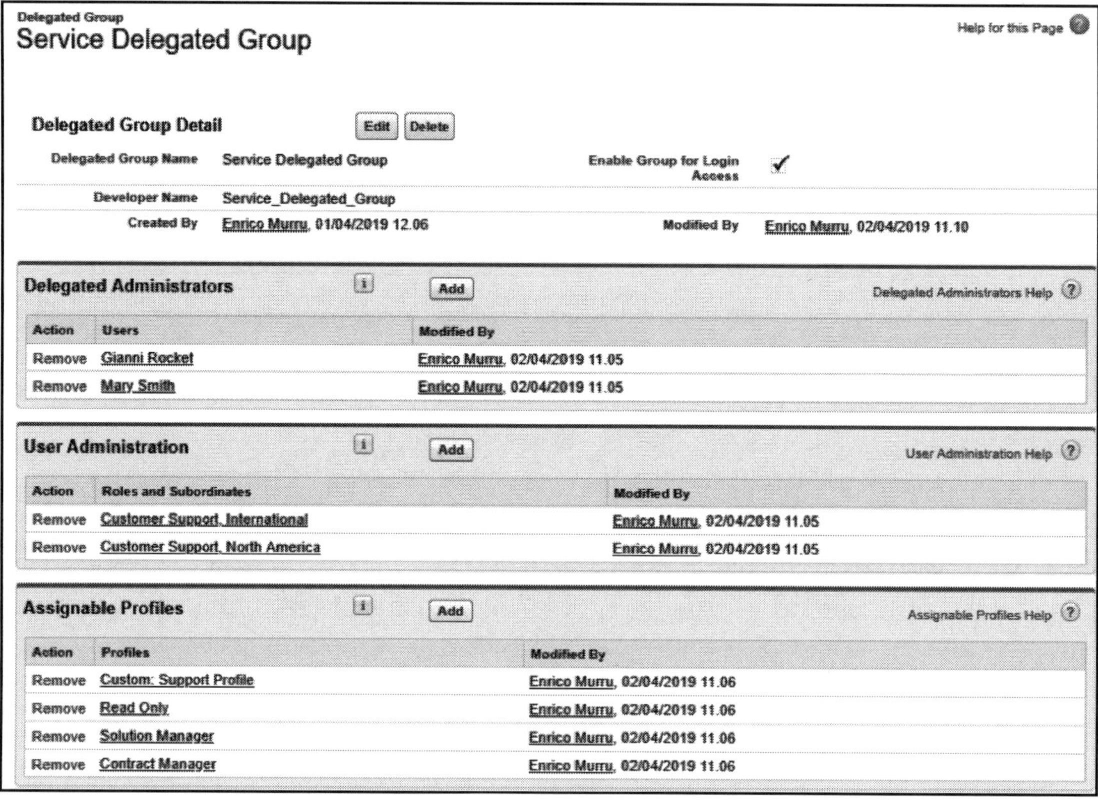

Delegated administrator group

Fill in the following options:

- **Name/developer name**: Identify the group.
- **Enable group for login access**: Users within this group can log in as a user that they manage.
- **Delegated administrators**: Choose the trusted users that you want to be delegates.
- **User administration**: Users within selected roles will be administered by this group.
- **Assignable profiles**: Delegates can only assign users the selected profiles.
- **Assigned permission sets**: The same as assignable profiles, but applying to permission sets.
- **Assignable public group**: The same as assignable profiles, but applying to groups.
- **Custom object administration**: Custom objects that can be partially managed by delegates (for example, page layouts and new custom fields).

Remember that we cannot assign profiles or permission sets with the Modify All Data permission.

Delegates must fill in the **Role** field for the users they are creating, forcing them to put new users in the role hierarchy (as an administrator, when we create a new user, we don't need to fill in the role field). They also cannot modify any permission set.

If you want to delegate data management for only one object, simply assign the delegate the View All or Modify All permissions and skip delegated administration.

Remember that we cannot assign partner and customer portal users to delegated administration. You can instead give a portal administrative duties to portal users.

Once administrative delegation is enabled, we can start monitoring who does what and the status of our precious organization, as shown in the following sections.

Monitoring your organization

The first place that we can use to monitor our organization is the **System Overview** page.

To reach this feature, navigate to **Setup** | **Environments** | **System Overview** to reach a place where we can monitor (in a dashboard mode) our main organization limits, such as the following:

- Schema limits
- API usage limits
- Business logic limits
- User interface limits
- License limits
- Portal roles

When a limit is reached (95% of its value), the item is highlighted with a big warning:

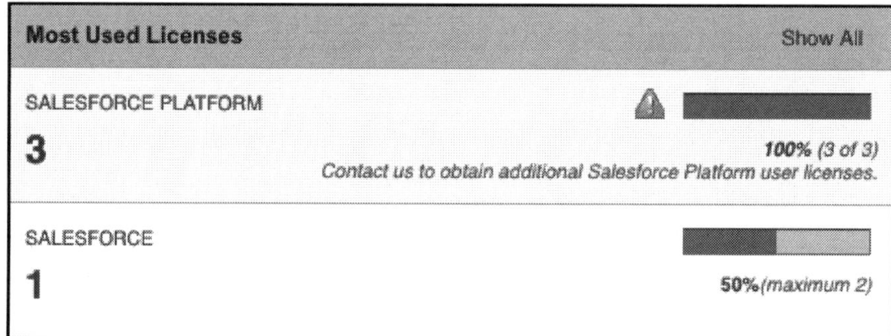

Keep an eye on this page at least daily: you never know when limits may be broken. Keeping on top of this will help you to resolve any issues before they can get worse.

This page shows the following limits:

- **Schema limits**: This monitors custom objects, custom settings limits, and data storage limits. By clicking on each number, we are redirected to the corresponding setup page where these limits can be configured (for example, **Object Manager** for the custom object limit or the **Storage Usage** page for data limits).
- **API usage limits**: This limit is the number of API calls occurring within a time frame of 24 hours. This is an organization-wide usage and is not related to a given user. When you reach this limit, API usage is temporarily blocked until the 24-hour window counts a number of calls that is less than the organization limit.

What does count against API usage limits? We can count, for example, the data loader data extractions or inserts/updates/deletes, external tools for Salesforce integrations, such as development IDEs (such as Visual Studio Code or the Force.com IDE), workbench operations, external systems related to an organization (such as billing services), and middlewares. APIs are used by external systems; the more the organization is connected to external systems, the more the API's count increases.

If an organization has external system integrations, then breaking this limit can give you some headaches because no system can communicate with your Salesforce instance until the API calls counter drops under the limit.

Both you and your developers should take care of this limit to make an accurate estimation of API call usage when implementing business processes that make intensive use of external calls to your organization.

- **Business logic limits**: Monitors the number of active workflow rules, Apex classes, and triggers in place, and the amount of code used (counted against the number of characters in Apex classes and triggers). When this limit is reached, no Apex code can be created until Salesforce support increases it (up to 10 MB; if you need more, Salesforce support requires access to your organization to verify whether you are unable to refactor your Apex code to stay within the limit—more code means more work for the Apex engine.).
- **User interface limits**: Monitors the number of Salesforce custom apps (**Setup | App Manager**), active Salesforce sites, active flows, custom tabs, and Visualforce pages.

- **User license limits**: Monitors the active licenses used in your organization and shows only the three most frequently used licenses, showing an error if you reach a 95% usage. To have a look at all the licenses, click on the **Show All** link, which will bring you to the **Setup** | **Company Settings** | **Company Information** page:

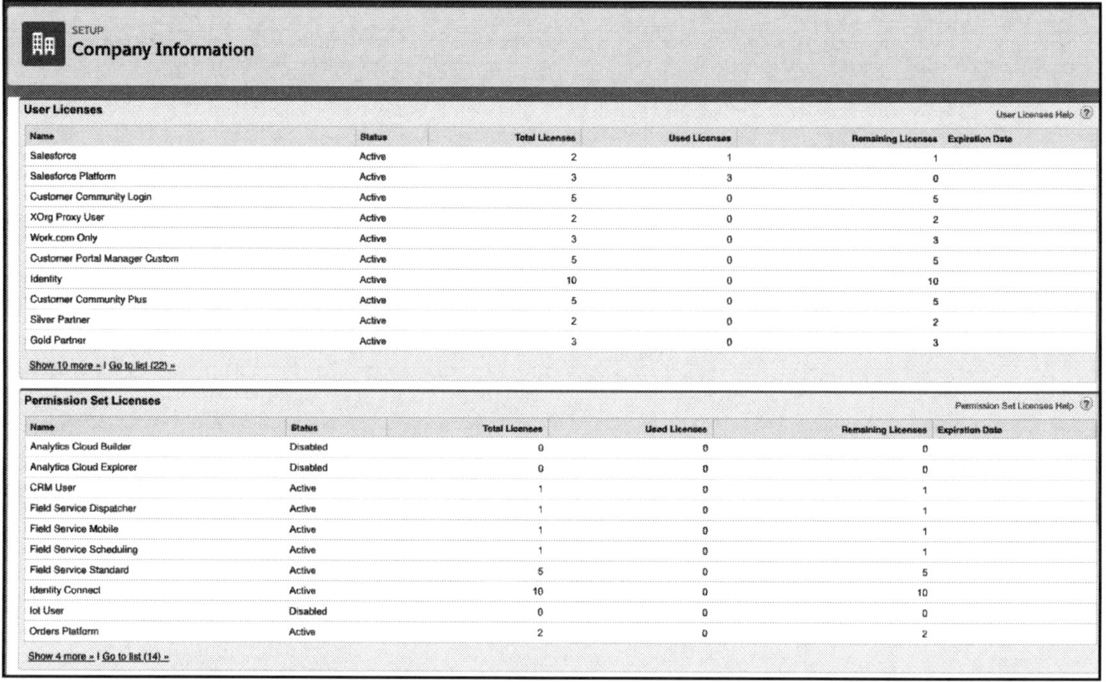

- **Portal roles limits**: Monitors the total number of roles across all your partner portals, customer portals, and communities (have a look at the last pages of the previous chapter to remind yourself what community roles are). We have a prebuilt limit of 5,000 roles that can be used (remember, roles are related to the accounts that partner or customer users are linked with).

You can ask the Salesforce support to increase the limit to up to 100,000 roles and more, but it is highly recommended that you keep the number of roles to a minimum by first removing unnecessary roles. This will increase the platform's overall performance.

This is a high-level section. In the next sections, we'll be covering more monitoring metrics that we should use to check on our daily Salesforce work.

Monitoring object-specific limits

Let's have a deeper look at object limits regarding the Salesforce schema configuration (or metadata).

To access an object's limits, click on **Setup** | **Object Manager** | **Object Limits** to bring up the following page:

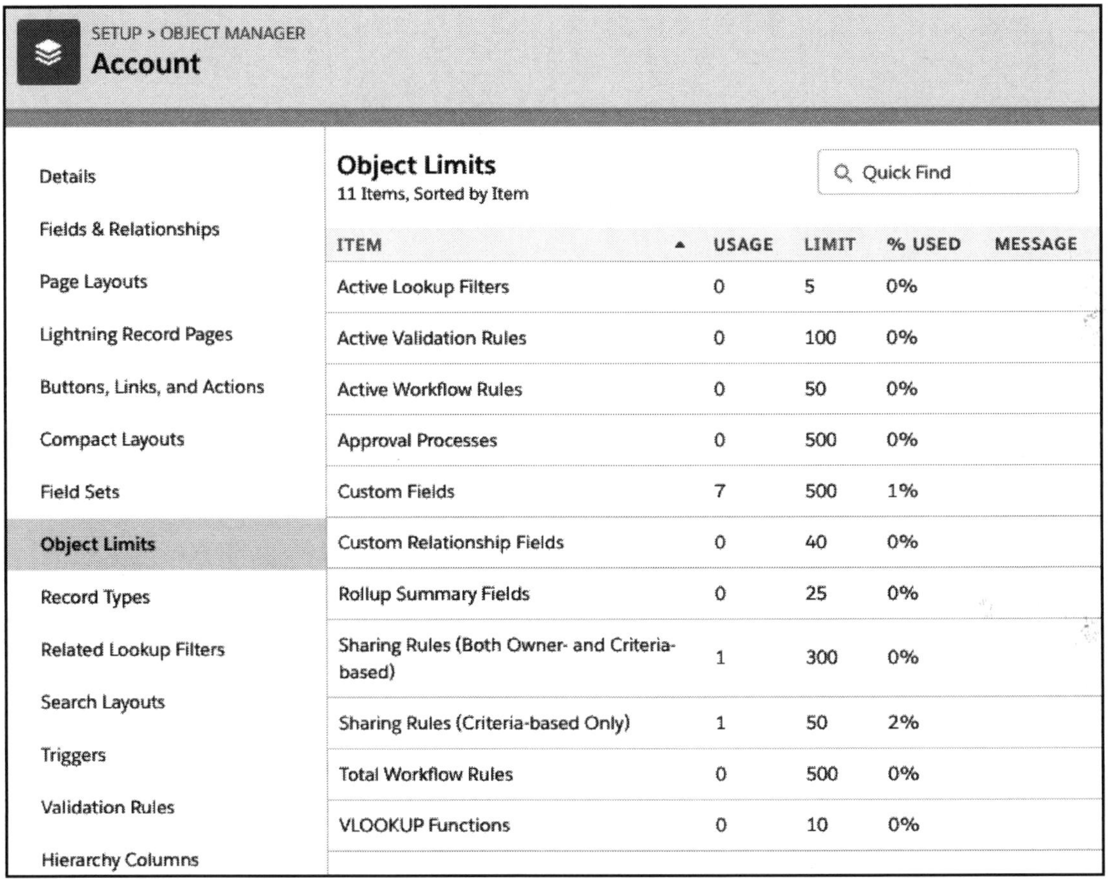

SETUP > OBJECT MANAGER

Account

- Details
- Fields & Relationships
- Page Layouts
- Lightning Record Pages
- Buttons, Links, and Actions
- Compact Layouts
- Field Sets
- Object Limits
- Record Types
- Related Lookup Filters
- Search Layouts
- Triggers
- Validation Rules
- Hierarchy Columns

Object Limits

11 Items, Sorted by Item

Quick Find

ITEM ▲	USAGE	LIMIT	% USED	MESSAGE
Active Lookup Filters	0	5	0%	
Active Validation Rules	0	100	0%	
Active Workflow Rules	0	50	0%	
Approval Processes	0	500	0%	
Custom Fields	7	500	1%	
Custom Relationship Fields	0	40	0%	
Rollup Summary Fields	0	25	0%	
Sharing Rules (Both Owner- and Criteria-based)	1	300	0%	
Sharing Rules (Criteria-based Only)	1	50	2%	
Total Workflow Rules	0	500	0%	
VLOOKUP Functions	0	10	0%	

Object Limits page

As an administrator, you need to have the limits of the Salesforce Objects clear in your mind when customizing your organization, and this is a good place to see where implementations are going.

We can track whether administrators and developers are using too many custom fields or sharing rules, preventing process refactoring, and allowing more structured field usage.

It's common for old organizations to see different custom fields that refer to the same information because the person who created it didn't take care of internal knowledge or process documentation, leading to a useless proliferation of fields. Remember to document all field usage (the **Description** field that you see when you create a new custom field is your friend).

Monitoring storage

Salesforce has three types of storage:

- **File storage:** This includes file storage types, such as chatter files, CRM content, documents, and attachments
- **Data storage**: This includes data records on the CRM, such as accounts, contacts and any other standard object, and all custom objects
- **Big object storage**: This is a particular set of Salesforce objects that are meant to refer to very large datasets (billions of records) and are especially intended for archival purposes

Big objects are beyond the scope of this book. Refer to `https://trailhead.salesforce.com/content/learn/modules/big_objects` for more details.

To access the complete limits for an in-depth analysis, click on **Setup** | **Data** | **Storage Usage**:

Storage Usage

Help for this Page

Your organization's storage usage is listed below.

Storage Type	Limit	Used	Percent Used
Data Storage	5,0 MB	292 KB	6%
File Storage	20,0 MB	13 KB	0%
Big Object Storage	1.000.000	0	0%

Current Data Storage Usage

Record Type	Record Count	Storage	Percent
Opportunities	31	62 KB	21%
Cases	26	52 KB	18%
Leads	22	44 KB	15%
Contacts	21	42 KB	14%
Campaigns	4	32 KB	11%
Accounts	12	24 KB	8%
Solutions	10	20 KB	7%
Case Team Member	2	4 KB	1%
System Streaming Channels	2	4 KB	1%
Rule Territory Associations	1	2 KB	1%
Last Used Setup App	1	2 KB	1%
Last Used App	1	2 KB	1%
Territory Models	1	2 KB	1%
Photos	2	0 B	0%

Current File Storage Usage

Record Type	Record Count	Storage	Percent
Photos	2	13 KB	100%
Content Bodies	1	2 B	0%

File and data storage page

We are granted a base of 10 GB of data storage for the contact manager, group, essentials, professional, enterprise, performance, and unlimited editions (while developer organizations are tied to 5 MB) that can be incrementally increased by contacting Salesforce support (by purchasing more storage or more licenses).

The organization starts with 10 GB of file storage space for the contact manager, group, professional, enterprise, performance, and unlimited editions, while the essentials edition is allocated 1 GB of space. We can get more file storage by purchasing more storage or by acquiring additional user licenses.

The **Percent** column of data or file storage in the previous table is not related to the actual percentage of storage used, but only to the percentage of storage used by that item in the overall count. What does this mean? In the previous screenshot, the **Photos** percent of 100% doesn't mean that the photos are consuming all 20 MB of available file storage, but rather they are consuming 100% of all the consumed file storage (in this example, the photos' percentage has been approximated to 100% because the other items that are consuming the file storage—the content bodies—consume less than 1% of actual storage).

This page also shows the top owners of the records (this allows you to monitor data skew; refer to the previous chapter to refresh your memory of what data skew is):

Top Users by Data Storage Usage

User	Storage	Percent
Enrico Murru	252 KB	86%
Laura Gnite	24 KB	8%
Mary Smith	4 KB	1%

Top Users by File Storage Usage

User	Storage	Percent
Chatter Expert	13 KB	100%
Automated Process	2 B	0%

Top record owners

For comprehensive information about file and data storage allocations for organization type and per-user-license types, refer to Salesforce help at `https://help.salesforce.com/articleView?id=overview_storage.htm type=5`.

Monitoring the login history

Another metric that is useful for security purposes is the monitoring of every login attempt on your organization. With this metric, you know exactly who is logging in, how many times they have logged in, and from where they are logging in—for example, you can check whether your users are logging in from certain locations or using an out-of-policies browser.

Click on **Setup** | **Identity** | **Login History** to bring up the following page:

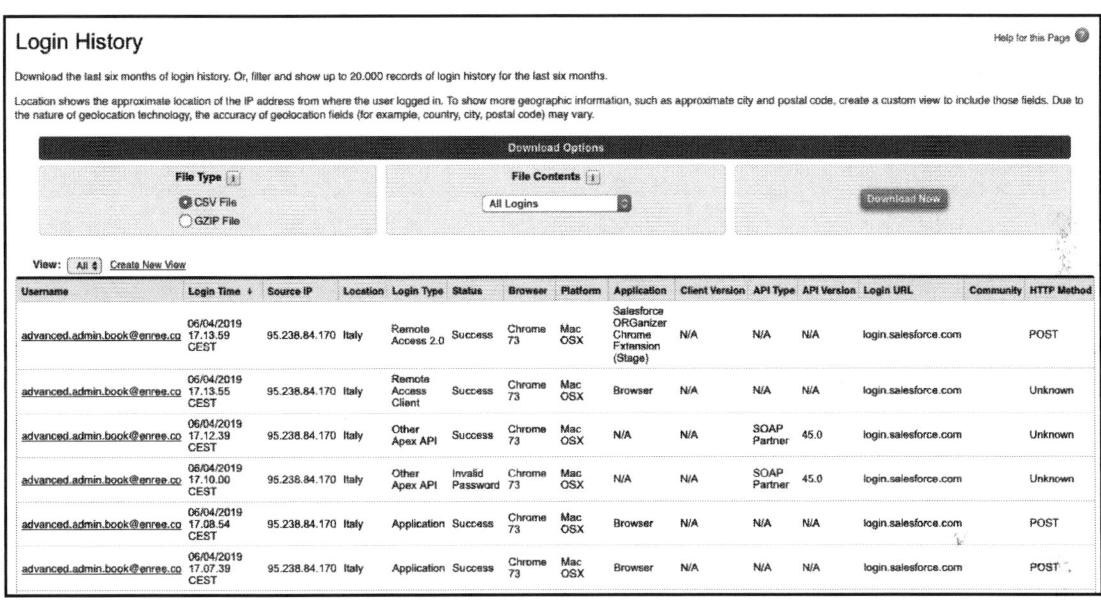

Login History

Help for this Page

Download the last six months of login history. Or, filter and show up to 20.000 records of login history for the last six months.

Location shows the approximate location of the IP address from where the user logged in. To show more geographic information, such as approximate city and postal code, create a custom view to include those fields. Due to the nature of geolocation technology, the accuracy of geolocation fields (for example, country, city, postal code) may vary.

Download Options

File Type: CSV File / GZIP File — File Contents: All Logins — Download Now

View: All — Create New View

Username	Login Time ↓	Source IP	Location	Login Type	Status	Browser	Platform	Application	Client Version	API Type	API Version	Login URL	Community	HTTP Method
advanced.admin.book@enree.co	06/04/2019 17.13.59 CEST	95.238.84.170	Italy	Remote Access 2.0	Success	Chrome 73	Mac OSX	Salesforce ORGanizer Chrome Extension (Stage)	N/A	N/A	N/A	login.salesforce.com		POST
advanced.admin.book@enree.co	06/04/2019 17.13.55 CEST	95.238.84.170	Italy	Remote Access Client	Success	Chrome 73	Mac OSX	Browser	N/A	N/A	N/A	login.salesforce.com		Unknown
advanced.admin.book@enree.co	06/04/2019 17.12.39 CEST	95.238.84.170	Italy	Other Apex API	Success	Chrome 73	Mac OSX	N/A	N/A	SOAP Partner	45.0	login.salesforce.com		Unknown
advanced.admin.book@enree.co	06/04/2019 17.10.00 CEST	95.238.84.170	Italy	Other Apex API	Invalid Password	Chrome 73	Mac OSX	N/A	N/A	SOAP Partner	45.0	login.salesforce.com		Unknown
advanced.admin.book@enree.co	06/04/2019 17.08.54 CEST	95.238.84.170	Italy	Application	Success	Chrome 73	Mac OSX	Browser	N/A	N/A	N/A	login.salesforce.com		POST
advanced.admin.book@enree.co	06/04/2019 17.07.39 CEST	95.238.84.170	Italy	Application	Success	Chrome 73	Mac OSX	Browser	N/A	N/A	N/A	login.salesforce.com		POST

Login History page

This page shows up to 20,000 login attempts over the last six months. If you need more, you can download a CSV or a zipped file.

We can even create a filtered list to show only a subset of the records (for example, only incorrect password login attempts).

Some of the relevant information on this page is as follows:

- **Username**
- **Login Time**

- **Source IP**: This is the IP from which the user has tried to log in. Use this information to find out whether you have a user accessing the organization outside the allowed and authorized locations (for example, check whether they are using the security token from an outside app).
- **Location**: This is the inferred location based on IP address information.
- **Login Type**: The kind of login used (for example, Application, Remote Access 2.0, OAuth, SAML)—that is, which methods are my users using?
- **Status**: Login status (**Success** or the reason for failure, such as **Invalid Password** or **User Locked**).
- **Application**: The kind of application used (**Browser** or any other custom app).
- **Browser**
- **Platform**: The kind of platform (for example, the operating system) used for login.
- **Login URL**: Which login endpoint has been used. You can monitor whether users are using the standard login page or the **My domain** URL.
- **Community**: The originating community.
- **HTTP Method**: Using the GET method should be avoided because it may inadvertently expose the user's username and password.

By creating a new list view, we can show more columns, such as the following:

- **TLS Protocol**: The encryption protocol used by a user's client application.
- **Latitude** and **Longitude**: The accuracy depends on various factors.
- **Country**, **Country Code**, **City**, **Postal Code**, and **Subdivision**: These are inferred from the geolocation:

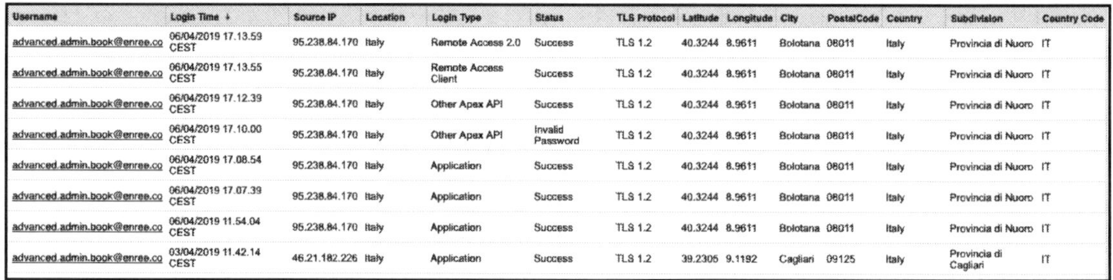

Username	Login Time ↓	Source IP	Location	Login Type	Status	TLS Protocol	Latitude	Longitude	City	PostalCode	Country	Subdivision	Country Code
advanced.admin.book@enree.co	06/04/2019 17.13.59 CEST	95.238.84.170	Italy	Remote Access 2.0	Success	TLS 1.2	40.3244	8.9611	Bolotana	08011	Italy	Provincia di Nuoro	IT
advanced.admin.book@enree.co	06/04/2019 17.13.55 CEST	95.238.84.170	Italy	Remote Access Client	Success	TLS 1.2	40.3244	8.9611	Bolotana	08011	Italy	Provincia di Nuoro	IT
advanced.admin.book@enree.co	06/04/2019 17.12.39 CEST	95.238.84.170	Italy	Other Apex API	Success	TLS 1.2	40.3244	8.9611	Bolotana	08011	Italy	Provincia di Nuoro	IT
advanced.admin.book@enree.co	06/04/2019 17.10.00 CEST	95.238.84.170	Italy	Other Apex API	Invalid Password	TLS 1.2	40.3244	8.9611	Bolotana	08011	Italy	Provincia di Nuoro	IT
advanced.admin.book@enree.co	06/04/2019 17.08.54 CEST	95.238.84.170	Italy	Application	Success	TLS 1.2	40.3244	8.9611	Bolotana	08011	Italy	Provincia di Nuoro	IT
advanced.admin.book@enree.co	06/04/2019 17.07.39 CEST	95.238.84.170	Italy	Application	Success	TLS 1.2	40.3244	8.9611	Bolotana	08011	Italy	Provincia di Nuoro	IT
advanced.admin.book@enree.co	06/04/2019 11.54.04 CEST	95.238.84.170	Italy	Application	Success	TLS 1.2	40.3244	8.9611	Bolotana	08011	Italy	Provincia di Nuoro	IT
advanced.admin.book@enree.co	03/04/2019 11.42.14 CEST	46.21.182.226	Italy	Application	Success	TLS 1.2	39.2305	9.1192	Cagliari	09125	Italy	Provincia di Cagliari	IT

Login History custom list view

The same information can be found on the user's record page in the **Login History** section.

Monitoring the identity verification history

By going to **Setup** | **Identity** | **Identity Verification History**, we can monitor up to 20,000 login verification attempts over the past 6 months.

This page shows information such as two-factor logins or identity verification through email when a user logs in from outside the safe IP ranges setup in **Setup** | **Network Access**:

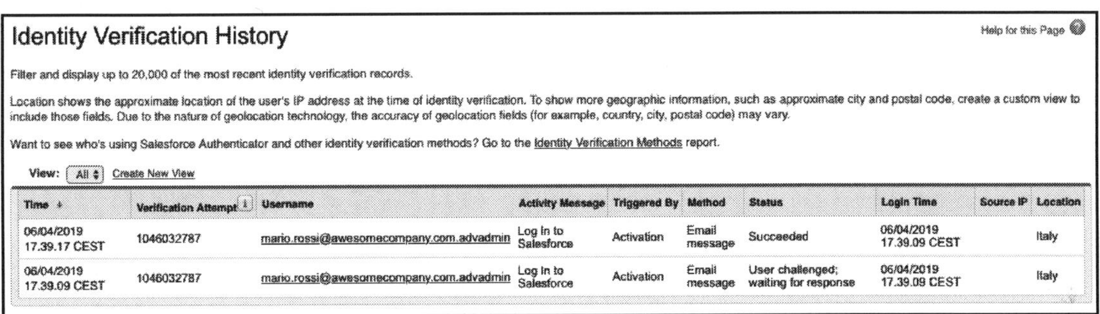

Identity Verification History page

As for login history, you can create your own list view to show other fields, such as geolocation fields.

Monitoring changes: View Setup Audit Trail

You can monitor any setup change on the organization, such as user-related changes (password and email address changes) or any change in your organization's components (from workflow rules to Apex classes, and from login IP ranges to sharing rules).

Go to **Setup** | **Security** | **View Setup Audit Trail** to see a list of the last 20 changes or to download the complete lists from the last 6 months:

The last 20 entries for your organization are listed below. You can download your organization's setup audit trail for the last six months (Excel .csv file).

View Setup Audit Trail

Date	User	Source Namespace Prefix	Action	Section	Delegate User
06/04/2019 17.37.44 CEST	mario.rossi@awesomecompany.com.advadmin		Changed email for user Mario Rossi from mario.rossi@awesomecompany.com to enrico.murru@gmail.com	Manage Users	
06/04/2019 17.37.44 CEST	mario.rossi@awesomecompany.com.advadmin		For user mario.rossi@awesomecompany.com.advadmin, the User Verified Email status changed to verified	Manage Users	
06/04/2019 17.37.44 CEST	mario.rossi@awesomecompany.com.advadmin		Changed email for user Mario Rossi from mario.rossi@awesomecompany.com to enrico.murru@gmail.com	Manage Users	
06/04/2019 17.37.25 CEST	mario.rossi@awesomecompany.com.advadmin		Email change attempted for user Mario Rossi from mario.rossi@awesomecompany.com to enrico.murru@gmail.com	Manage Users	
06/04/2019 17.36.15 CEST	mario.rossi@awesomecompany.com.advadmin		Password changed	Manage Users	
06/04/2019 17.35.48 CEST	advanced.admin.book@enree.co		Password changed	Manage Users	
06/04/2019 17.12.26 CEST	advanced.admin.book@enree.co		Added Login Ip Range to System Administrator from 0.0.0.0 to 255.255.255.255	Manage Users	
06/04/2019 17.11.39 CEST	advanced.admin.book@enree.co		Deleted Login Ip Range to System Administrator from 0.0.0.0 to 255.255.255.255		
06/04/2019 16.08.11 CEST	advanced.admin.book@enree.co		Created new user Mario Rossi	Manage Users	
06/04/2019 15.32.55 CEST	advanced.admin.book@enree.co		Changed membership of Group Access to Contacts share group	Groups	
06/04/2019 15.29.35 CEST	advanced.admin.book@enree.co		Finished activating portal share group for Access to Contacts	Customer Portal	

View Setup Audit Trail page

This page is extremely useful in organizations with multiple admins as anyone can keep track of all the changes.

From this page, we can also track delegated administration operations made by users in the delegated groups (the **Delegated User** column shows a flag). This way, you can monitor the behavior of your delegates and decide whether they are acting as expected (and if your trust is well placed).

To read the full list of available tracked changes, refer to Salesforce Support (see `https://help.salesforce.com/articleView?id=admin_monitorsetup.htmtype=0`).

We can query this information using the `SetupAuditTrail` object via Data Loader or any API client (refer to `https://developer.salesforce.com/docs/atlas.en-us.api.meta/api/sforce_api_objects_setupaudittrail.htm` for more information).

As an example, the following SOQL query returns all recent permission set changes:

```
Select Action, CreatedBy.Username, CreatedDate, DelegateUser, Display,
Section from SetupAuditTrail Where Action = 'PermSetCreate' order by
CreatedDate DESC
```

This leads to the following result:

Action	CreatedBy.Username	CreatedDate	DelegateUser	Display	Section
PermSetCreate	advanced.admin.book@enree.co	2019-03-30T14:39:32.000+0000		Created permission set Lead Access: with User License Salesforce	Manage Users

To run this SOQL query, you can use Data Loader, Salesforce Workbench (read more at `https://trailhead.salesforce.com/en/content/learn/modules/database_basics_dotnet/sql_to_soql`), or tools such as browser extensions.

Field history tracking

After answering the question *Who sees what?*, now we are going to answer the question, *Who did what?*

With field history tracking, we know which user changed which field on a given record. This information is displayed on the history list (that we should add to each page layout that we are using):

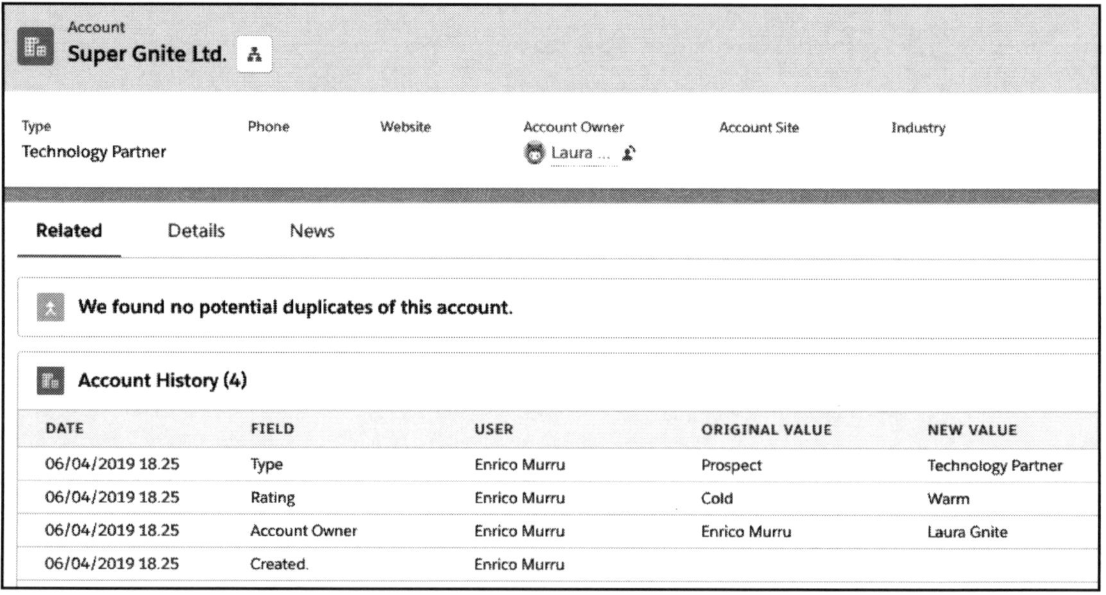

Field History list on the Account object

History data is retained for up to 18 months if we access a record through a browser or 24 months for a record accessed via API (for example, Data Loader, Workbench, or any other tool) by querying the `ObjectHistory` object (for example, `AccountHistory`, or `CustomObject__History` for custom objects).

Here is an example of the SOQL query that delivers the same result as the Account History list of the previous example:

```
Select CreatedBy.Name, CreatedDate, Field,OldValue, NewValue from
AccountHistory Where AccountId = '0011i000007K2LEAA0' Order By CreatedDate
DESC
```

This leads to the following:

CreatedBy.Name	CreatedDate	Field	NewValue	OldValue
Enrico Murru	2019-04-06T16:25:42.000+0000	Type	Technology Partner	Prospect
Enrico Murru	2019-04-06T16:25:33.000+0000	Rating	Warm	Cold
Enrico Murru	2019-04-06T16:25:25.000+0000	Owner	Laura Gnite	Enrico Murru
Enrico Murru	2019-04-06T16:25:25.000+0000	Owner	0051I000000e5QAAAY	0051I000001AZCSAA4
Enrico Murru	2019-04-06T16:25:17.000+0000	created		

Organizations created before June 1, 2011 have perpetual login history retention.

There are a few limitations regarding field history tracking:

- The old value is not tracked for text fields with more than 255 characters.
- Old/new values are not automatically translated—that is, if you have a **Pizza Type** picklist whose value is changed by an Italian user to **Al Salame**, it won't display as **Pepperoni** for an English-speaking user (all translations referred to here are made with the Translation Workbench; for more information, refer to Salesforce Support at `https://help.salesforce.com/articleView?id=workbench_overview.htmtype=5`).
- The field's label is always translated into the current user's language (for example, **Pizza Type** will be shown to an Italian user as **Tipo di pizza**).
- Date, date/time, and number fields are always displayed with the viewing user's locale.
- If an Apex trigger causes a change in a field that the current user doesn't have access to, the change is not tracked. Field history always follows field-level security settings.
- Time fields aren't tracked in the field history list.

To enable field tracking, jump to **Setup** | **Object Manager** | **ObjectType** | **Fields & Relationships** and click the **Set History Tracking** button:

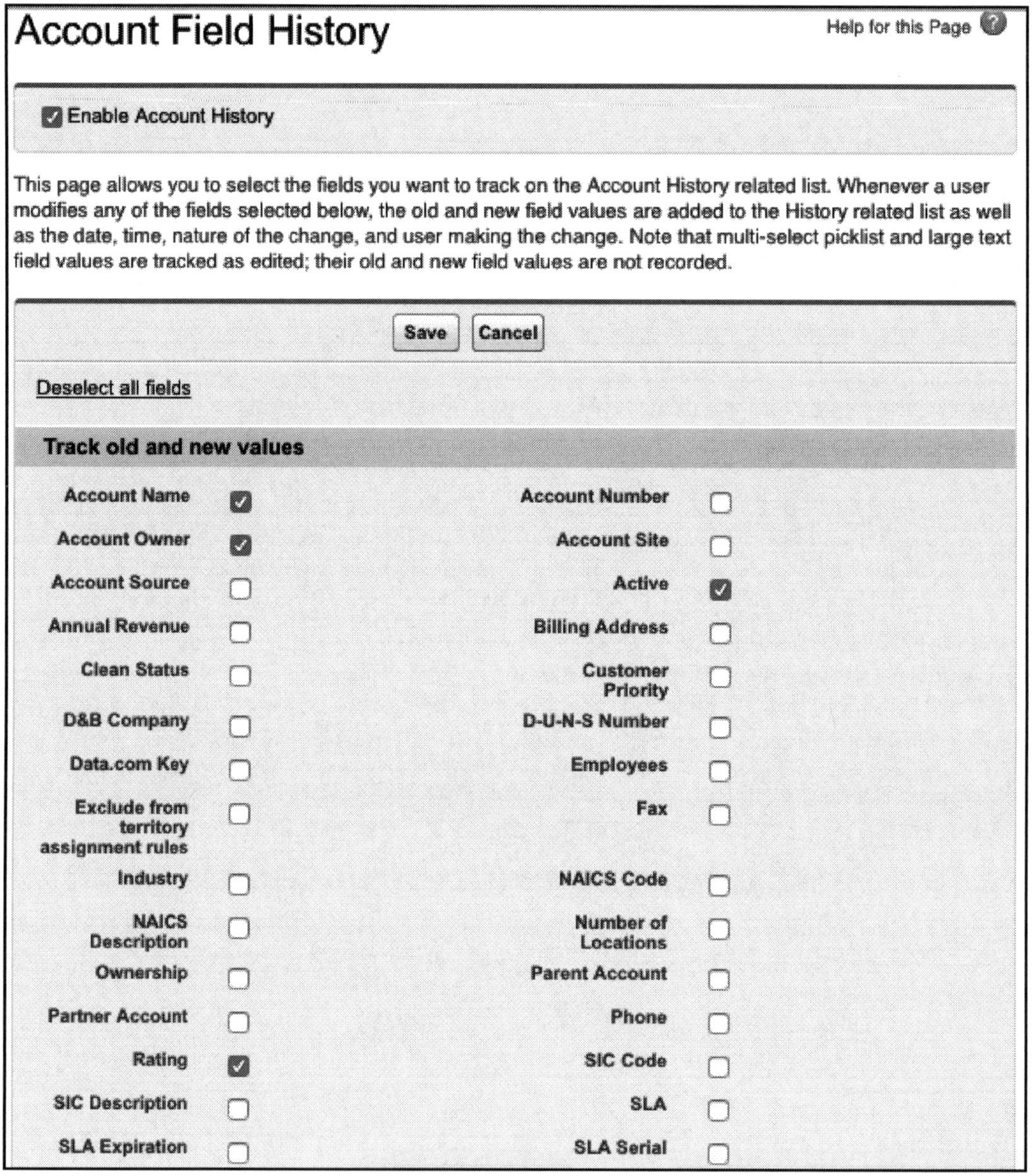

Account Field History

Help for this Page

Enable Account History

This page allows you to select the fields you want to track on the Account History related list. Whenever a user modifies any of the fields selected below, the old and new field values are added to the History related list as well as the date, time, nature of the change, and user making the change. Note that multi-select picklist and large text field values are tracked as edited; their old and new field values are not recorded.

Save Cancel

Deselect all fields

Track old and new values

Account Name
Account Number
Account Owner
Account Site
Account Source
Active
Annual Revenue
Billing Address
Clean Status
Customer Priority
D&B Company
D-U-N-S Number
Data.com Key
Employees
Exclude from territory assignment rules
Fax
Industry
NAICS Code
NAICS Description
Number of Locations
Ownership
Parent Account
Partner Account
Phone
Rating
SIC Code
SIC Description
SLA
SLA Expiration
SLA Serial

Field History tracking configuration

Salesforce Shield (available with additional licensing costs) delivers the **Field Audit Trail** feature, which increases the number of fields tracked and the time they are retained. You can even define customized retention policies to align with legal and administrative regulations, such as the GDPR for the EU, PIPAs for Canada, or APPI for Japan (more information can be found at `https://help.salesforce.com/articleView?id=field_audit_trail.htmtype=5`).

Background job monitoring

When dealing with long-running operations, such as sharing recalculations, Salesforce puts a job in a background queue so that the calculation can be done better using the organization resources. When the job is completed, Salesforce sends a notification to the user who triggered the job, informing them of the completion.

When dealing with large datasets, background jobs can take hours to complete, and we may be asked to monitor its status.

Go to **Setup** | **Environments** | **Jobs** | **Background Jobs**:

All Background Jobs

Help for this Page

Use this page to monitor background jobs. Please contact salesforce.com if you need to abort a job.

View: All Background Jobs Create New View

Action	Submitted Date ↓	Job Type	Job Sub Type	Status	Percent Complete	Errors	Submitted By	Completion Date
	06/04/2019 14.54	Sharing Rule Create	Lead - Owner Sharing Rule	Completed	100%		Murru, Enrico	06/04/2019 14.54
	06/04/2019 0.18	Chatter Unified Digest		Completed	100%			06/04/2019 0.41
	05/04/2019 0.18	Chatter Unified Digest		Completed	100%			05/04/2019 0.20
	04/04/2019 0.18	Chatter Unified Digest		Completed	100%			04/04/2019 0.44
	03/04/2019 0.18	Chatter Unified Digest		Completed	100%			03/04/2019 0.45
	02/04/2019 15.45	Territory Model Activation Chunk Job		Completed	100%		Murru, Enrico	02/04/2019 15.45
	02/04/2019 15.45	Territory Rule Realign Chunk Job		Completed	100%		Murru, Enrico	02/04/2019 15.45
	02/04/2019 12.37	Organization-Wide Default Update	Opportunity - Account Child Access	Completed	100%		Murru, Enrico	02/04/2019 12.37
	02/04/2019 12.37	Organization-Wide Default Update	Case - Account Child Access	Completed	100%		Murru, Enrico	02/04/2019 12.37
	02/04/2019 12.37	Organization-Wide Default Update	Contact - Account Child Access	Completed	100%		Murru, Enrico	02/04/2019 12.37
	02/04/2019 12.37	Organization-Wide Default Update	Case - Insert Record Cluster Rows	Completed	100%		Murru, Enrico	02/04/2019 12.37
	02/04/2019 12.36	Organization-Wide Default Update	Account	Completed	100%		Murru, Enrico	02/04/2019 12.36
	02/04/2019 12.36	Organization-Wide Default Update	Case	Completed	100%		Murru, Enrico	02/04/2019 12.36
	02/04/2019 12.30	Organization-Wide Default Update	Opportunity - Account Child Access	Completed	100%		Murru, Enrico	02/04/2019 12.30

If you need to abort a running job, you need to ask Salesforce Support.

Remember that you can defer the sharing of recalculation jobs by opening a support case with Salesforce Support.

Debug log monitoring

Debug logs are used for live troubleshooting and are usually used by developers when debugging Apex code. There is no reason why an administrator shouldn't also use debug logs for debugging flows, workflows, process builders, or just to better understand why a business process is working in a way that we don't understand.

Debug logs could also be useful for *reverse engineering* scenarios: the lack of documentation might sometimes be a real problem for your organization and you can easily troubleshoot issues by using debug logs.

Let's say we have a workflow rule that sets the account's **Rating** field to `Hot` if its annual revenue is greater than $100,000.

After enabling debug logs (we'll shortly see how logs are enabled), if we create or update an account record by setting its annual **Revenue** field to `$15M`, we will be able to read how the workflow rule evaluation runs and see when the account **Rating** field is updated to `Hot`:

```
45.0
APEX_CODE,NONE;APEX_PROFILING,INFO;CALLOUT,NONE;DB,INFO;NBA,NONE;SYSTEM,DEB
UG;VALIDATION,INFO;VISUALFORCE,NONE;WAVE,INFO;WORKFLOW,INFO
. . .
19:03:01.20
(20286522)|USER_INFO|[EXTERNAL]|0051i000001AZCS|advanced.admin.book@enree.c
o|(GMT+02:00) Central European Summer Time (Europe/Rome)|GMT+02:00

19:03:01.20 (20307561)|EXECUTION_STARTED

19:03:01.20 (20310551)|CODE_UNIT_STARTED|[EXTERNAL]|Workflow:Account

19:03:01.20 (26000808)|WF_RULE_EVAL_BEGIN|Workflow

19:03:01.20 (26040581)|WF_CRITERIA_BEGIN|[Account: Super Gnite Ltd.
0011i000007K2LE]|Set Account Rating |01Q1i000000btDQ|ON_ALL_CHANGES|0

19:03:01.20 (26296080)|WF_RULE_FILTER|[Account : Annual Revenue greater
than 100000]
```

```
19:03:01.20 (26327532)|WF_RULE_EVAL_VALUE|15000000

19:03:01.20 (26333214)|WF_CRITERIA_END|true

19:03:01.20 (26622520)|WF_SPOOL_ACTION_BEGIN|Workflow

19:03:01.20 (30492959)|WF_FIELD_UPDATE|[Account: Super Gnite Ltd.
0011i000007K2LE]|Field:Account:
Rating|Value:Hot|Id=04Y1i000000XZzj|CurrentRule:Set Account Number
(Id=01Q1i000000btDQ)

19:03:01.20 (30526240)|WF_ACTION| Field Update: 1;

19:03:01.20 (30532098)|WF_RULE_EVAL_END

19:03:01.20 (40699861)|WF_ACTIONS_END| Field Update: 1;

19:03:01.20 (40717805)|CODE_UNIT_FINISHED|Workflow:Account

19:03:01.20 (40724015)|EXECUTION_FINISHED
. . .
```

In this (apparently) messy debug log, we can have a look at the following pieces of information about our last account update:

- The user that triggered the update (`advanced.admin.book@enree.co`)
- The code unit about to be executed (`Workflow:Account`)
- The account in the scope of the workflow (`Account: Super Gnite Ltd. 0011i000007K2LE`) and the rule that is going to be evaluated (`Set Account Rating`)
- The criteria (`WF_RULE_FILTER|[Account : Annual Revenue greater than 100000]`)
- The evaluated value (`WF_RULE_EVAL_VALUE|15000000`)
- Whether the criteria have been matched (`WF_CRITERIA_END|true`)
- Any action related to that workflow rule (`WF_FIELD_UPDATE...Field:Account: Rating|Value:Hot`)
- The total number of actions executed (`Field Update: 1;`)

Imagine that you have tens of workflow rules or process builders and you need to understand in which order they are evaluated. This is possible with debug logs, although you need to be used to the log format (don't you want to become a developer-admin, or **dev-min**?).

To be able to retrieve a debug log, you need a **trace flag**, which enables the system to create debug logs for a given user, and a **debug level**, which is needed to filter out the required data.

To create a new trace flag, navigate to **Setup** | **Environments** | **Debug Logs** and then click the **New** button in the **User Trace Flags** section:

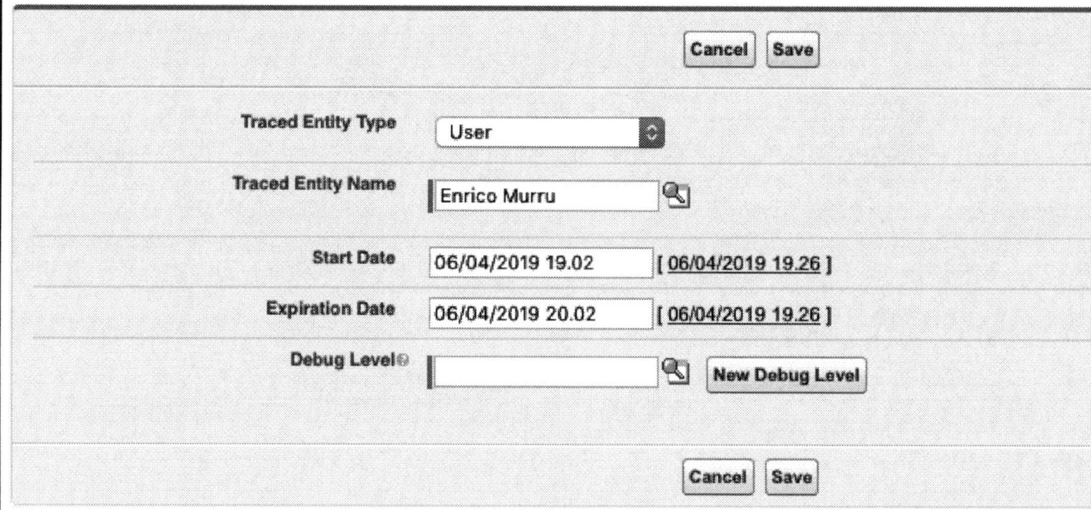

Creating a new trace flag

Look up the user who you want to debug (it could be your user or any other user on your organization), along with the start and end date for tracing, and finally, the debug level. Create your own debug level by clicking on the **New Debug Level** button (or look up one if you have already created it):

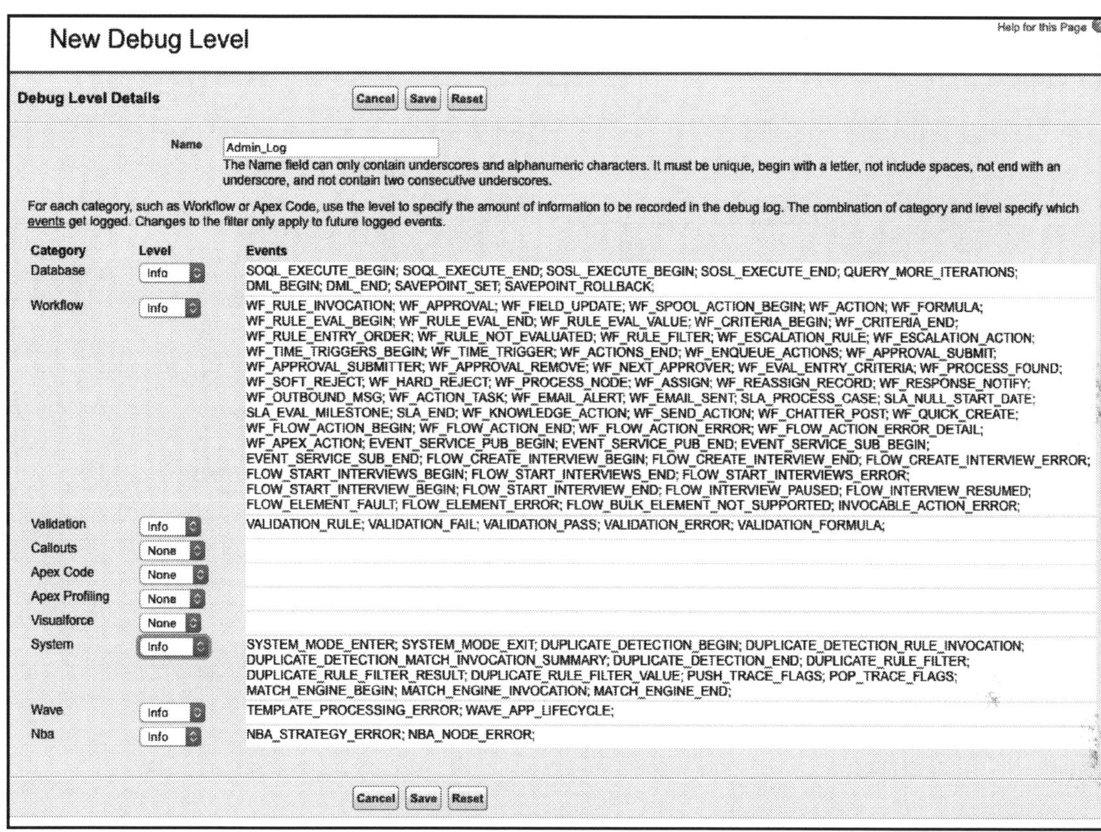

Setting up a new debug level

This complex list simply states what level of verbosity you need in order for each resource to be tracked live. In this screenshot, I've removed anything related to Apex, Visualforce, or Apex Callouts.

Note that enabling debug logs can slow down overall system performance (especially when you have a lot of automation), so activate these features only when needed.

Now that everything is set up, we can start collecting our debug logs from the **Debug Logs** page. Any time we create/update a new record, a new debug log will be created:

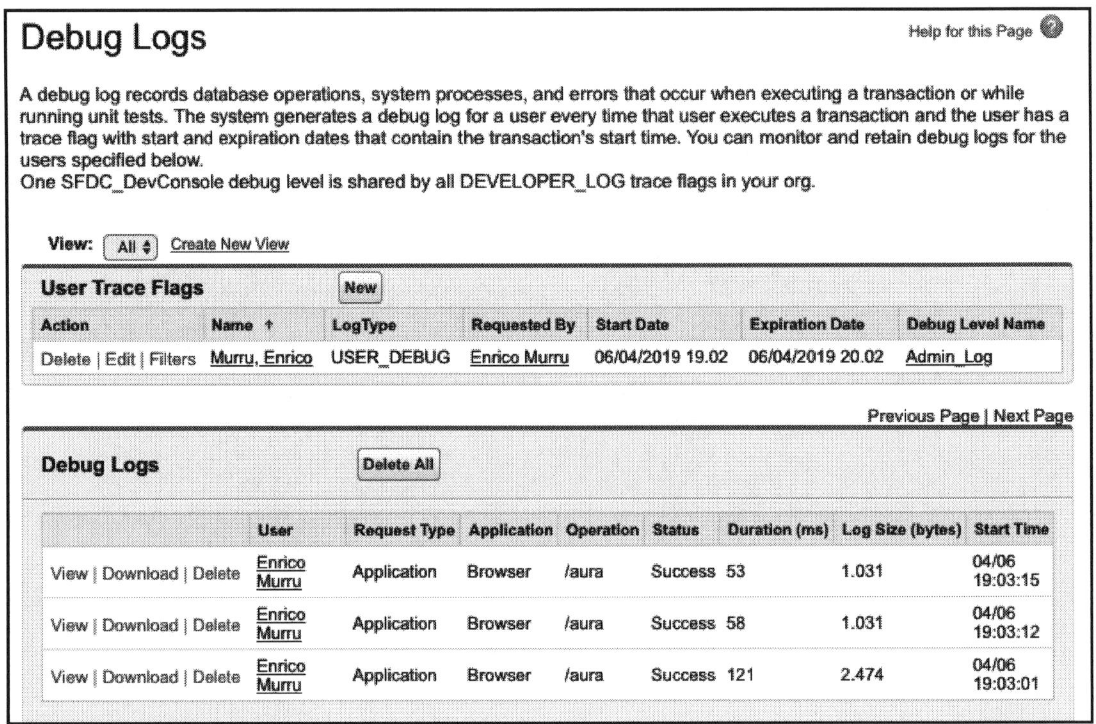

Debug logs list view

Click on the **View** or **Download** link to get a debug log. After every action on the organization by the tracked user, you'll see various entries that are related to Salesforce items that are loaded on your user interface (for example, Lightning components on the record's page that you actually don't want to debug).

If you have different entries for the same start time, open your logs and figure out which debug log you are looking for (for example, by searching for the object's ID or a given workflow rule name you are sure has been triggered).

There are a few limitations regarding debug logs:

- Each log can have up to 5 MB of data. If this is exceeded, Salesforce removes some lines, so the log may not be complete (to avoid this, reduce some of the filter accuracy).
- Logs are retained for 7 days.
- We can have up to 250 MB of debug logs in our organization. To remove them, click on the **Delete All** button in the **Debug Logs** section.
- If a trace flag creates more than 250 MB of logs in 15 minutes, it is disabled, and an email is sent to the last user that changed that trace flag, informing them that it can be re-enabled in 15 minutes.

Don't you feel like a developer now that you know the secrets of debug logs?

When dealing with long debug logs, I suggest using some syntax highlighting text editors, such as Sublime Text or Visual Studio Code, as shown in the following screenshot:

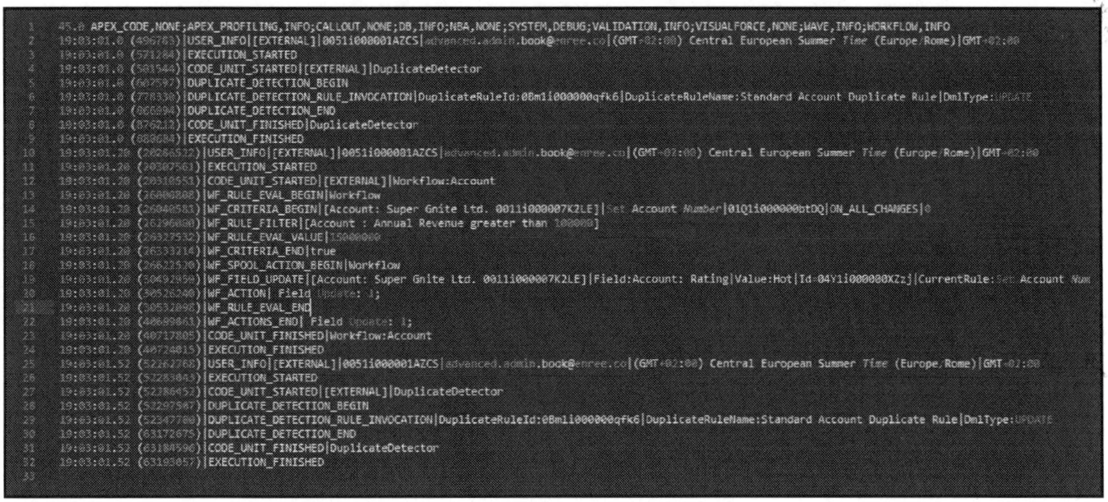

```
[illegible] APEX_CODE,NONE;APEX_PROFILING,INFO;CALLOUT,NONE;DB,INFO;NBA,NONE;SYSTEM,DEBUG;VALIDATION,INFO;VISUALFORCE,NONE;WAVE,INFO;WORKFLOW,INFO
19:03:01.0 ([illegible])|USER_INFO|[EXTERNAL]|0051i000001AZCS|[illegible].book@[illegible]|(GMT[illegible]) Central European Summer Time (Europe/Rome)|GMT[illegible]
19:03:01.0 ([illegible])|EXECUTION_STARTED
19:03:01.0 ([illegible])|CODE_UNIT_STARTED|[EXTERNAL]|DuplicateDetector
19:03:01.0 ([illegible])|DUPLICATE_DETECTION_BEGIN
19:03:01.0 ([illegible])|DUPLICATE_DETECTION_RULE_INVOCATION|DuplicateRuleId:0Bm1i000000qfk6|DuplicateRuleName:Standard Account Duplicate Rule|DmlType:[illegible]
19:03:01.0 ([illegible])|DUPLICATE_DETECTION_END
19:03:01.0 ([illegible])|CODE_UNIT_FINISHED|DuplicateDetector
19:03:01.0 ([illegible])|EXECUTION_FINISHED
19:03:01.20 ([illegible])|USER_INFO|[EXTERNAL]|0051i000001AZCS|[illegible].book@[illegible]|(GMT[illegible]) Central European Summer Time (Europe/Rome)|GMT[illegible]
19:03:01.20 ([illegible])|EXECUTION_STARTED
19:03:01.20 ([illegible])|CODE_UNIT_STARTED|[EXTERNAL]|Workflow:Account
19:03:01.20 ([illegible])|WF_RULE_EVAL_BEGIN|Workflow
19:03:01.20 ([illegible])|WF_CRITERIA_BEGIN|[Account: Super Gnite Ltd. 0011i000007K2LE]|[illegible] Account [illegible]|01Q1i000000btDQ|ON_ALL_CHANGES|[illegible]
19:03:01.20 ([illegible])|WF_RULE_FILTER|[Account : Annual Revenue greater than [illegible]]
19:03:01.20 ([illegible])|WF_RULE_EVAL_VALUE|[illegible]
19:03:01.20 ([illegible])|WF_CRITERIA_END|true
19:03:01.20 ([illegible])|WF_SPOOL_ACTION_BEGIN|Workflow
19:03:01.20 ([illegible])|WF_FIELD_UPDATE|[Account: Super Gnite Ltd. 0011i000007K2LE]|Field:Account: Rating|Value:Hot|Id=04Y1i000000XZzj|CurrentRule:[illegible] Account [illegible]
19:03:01.20 ([illegible])|WF_ACTION| Field [illegible]: 1;
19:03:01.20 ([illegible])|WF_RULE_EVAL_END
19:03:01.20 ([illegible])|WF_ACTIONS_END| Field [illegible]: 1;
19:03:01.20 ([illegible])|CODE_UNIT_FINISHED|Workflow:Account
19:03:01.20 ([illegible])|EXECUTION_FINISHED
19:03:01.52 ([illegible])|USER_INFO|[EXTERNAL]|0051i000001AZCS|[illegible].book@[illegible]|(GMT[illegible]) Central European Summer Time (Europe/Rome)|GMT[illegible]
19:03:01.52 ([illegible])|EXECUTION_STARTED
19:03:01.52 ([illegible])|CODE_UNIT_STARTED|[EXTERNAL]|DuplicateDetector
19:03:01.52 ([illegible])|DUPLICATE_DETECTION_BEGIN
19:03:01.52 ([illegible])|DUPLICATE_DETECTION_RULE_INVOCATION|DuplicateRuleId:0Bm1i000000qfk6|DuplicateRuleName:Standard Account Duplicate Rule|DmlType:[illegible]
19:03:01.52 ([illegible])|DUPLICATE_DETECTION_END
19:03:01.52 ([illegible])|CODE_UNIT_FINISHED|DuplicateDetector
19:03:01.52 ([illegible])|EXECUTION_FINISHED
```

Debug logs displayed with highlighted syntax

Monitoring email logs

There's another debug log we should be aware of—the **email log**. This is required when we want to debug emails sent from Salesforce.

We won't cover the entire email log configuration, but there is something that we sometimes forget to configure when dealing with emails and sandbox organizations: **email deliverability**.

This simple configuration tells Salesforce which kind of email you want to send from your organization (it works in production organizations as well).

Go to **Setup** | **Email** | **Deliverability**:

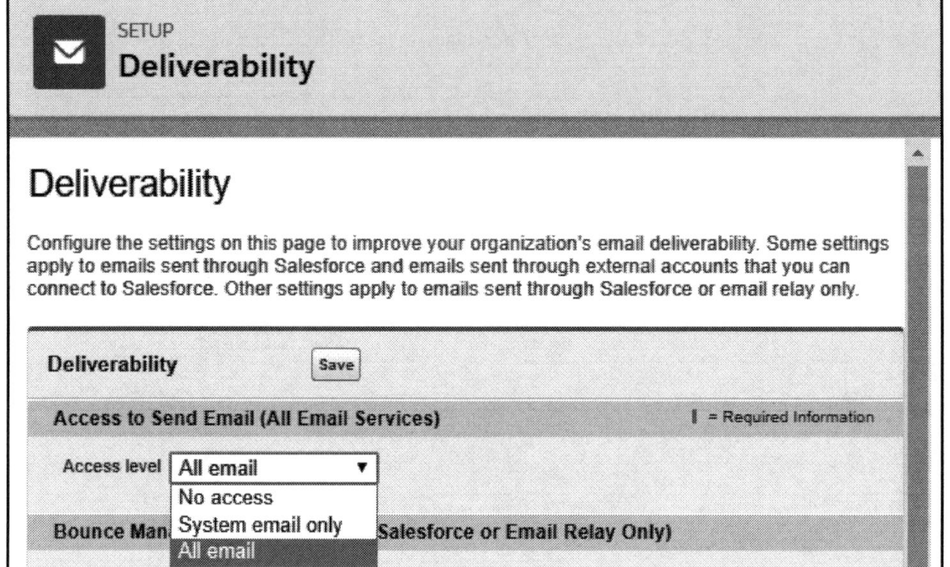

Email deliverability setting

You can set the deliverability to any of the following options:

- **No access**: No email will ever be sent from Salesforce.
- **System email only**: Only system emails will be sent, such as sharing calculations or Apex error notifications.
- **All email**: Every kind of email will pass through the Salesforce email servers.

When refreshing a sandbox, this setting is automatically set to **System email only**, so as to avoid unwanted automations being executed after you have set up your testing environment.

While creating a trial organization (when starting a new Salesforce project for a customer, you start from a trial, which is then promoted to the definitive production organization), this setting cannot be edited, and its default setting is **System email only**. If this happens, don't panic—just raise a case with Salesforce Support.

Now that you are sure that the emails are sent, go to **Setup** | **Environments** | **Logs** | **Email Log Files**, and you will see the following page:

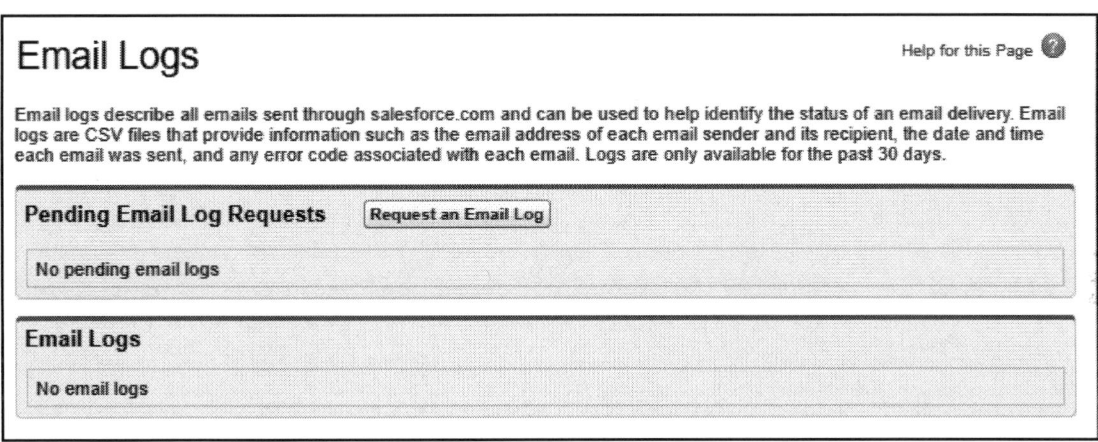

Email Logs page

You can request email logs up to 30 days in the past with no more than 7 days per request. Once you request an email log with the only available button on the interface, choose the correct time frame, set up the domain names or email address for the recipients (if needed), and wait for Salesforce to notify you when the ZIP file is ready.

The ZIP contains a CSV with all the emails sent in the given time frame, which you can use to find out whether emails are not being sent, and for what reason. No body or subject is placed in this CSV, just information pertaining to deliverability.

For more details on how these logs are shaped, refer to Salesforce Help at `https://help.salesforce.com/articleView?id=email_logs_format.htm type=5`.

Health check monitor

Before closing this section, I want to say a few words about the **Health Check** feature, which you can access by going to **Setup** | **Security** | **Health Check**:

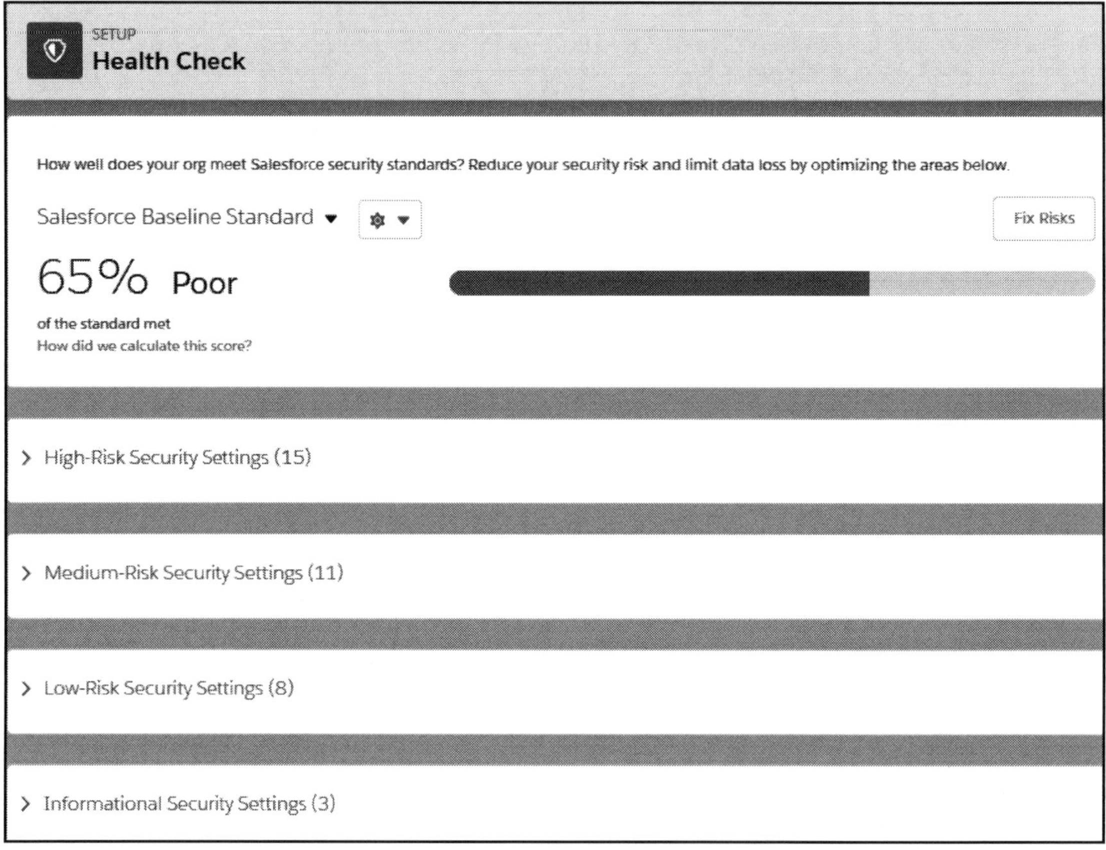

Health Check page

This tool lets us check our security configurations against Salesforce base policies (you can even upload a custom baseline to restrict or extend policies), and it provides an overall security score.

The baseline is composed of different items with a default risk level (high, medium, low, and informational). With custom baselines, you can define which are your actual risk levels.

Here is an *exploded* risk category:

High-Risk Security Settings (15)

STATUS	SETTING	GROUP	YOUR VALUE	STANDARD VALUE	ACTIONS
Critical	Maximum invalid login attempts	Password Policies	No Limit	3	Edit
Critical	Enable clickjack protection for customer Visualforce pages with standard headers	Session Settings	Disabled	Enabled	Edit
Critical	Enable clickjack protection for customer Visualforce pages with headers disabled	Session Settings	Disabled	Enabled	Edit
Critical	Require HttpOnly attribute	Session Settings	Disabled	Enabled	Edit
Critical	Number of Objects with Default External Access Set to Public	Sharing Settings	9	0	Edit
Compliant	Expired Certificate	Certificate and Key Management	0	0	Edit
Compliant	Number of security risk file types with Hybrid behavior	File Upload And Download Security Settings	0 security risk file types with Hybrid behavior	0 security risk file types with Hybrid behavior	Edit

Health Check's risk category items

Each item has a status (**Critical**, **Warning**, or **Compliant**), a grouping column, and the reference and applied values for the given metric. Each row has an **Edit** link that brings you to the proper setup page to mitigate the risk.

Use the **Fix Risks** button to automatically upgrade to the baseline standard values. Not everything can be changed with this button—for elements that can't be changed, proceed manually:

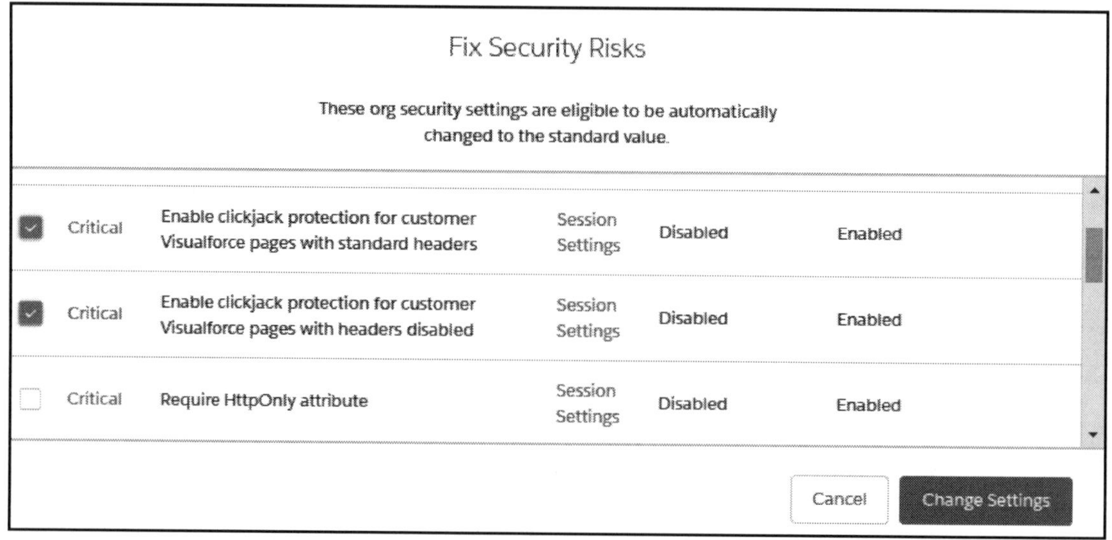

For more information about the items that the baseline tracks, refer to `https://help.salesforce.com/articleView?id=security_health_check_score.htmtype=5#baselinestd`.

To create a new baseline, refer to Salesforce Help (`https://help.salesforce.com/articleView?id=security_custom_baseline_file_requirements.htmtype=5`).

Event monitoring

One last feature that helps us keep our data secure is event monitoring, which is a tool that is meant to get granular details of user activity on our organization. These kinds of actions are called **events**. Tracking events ensures that we can identify abnormal organization usage.

You can monitor a great number of events, including logins (we already covered this information in the *Monitoring the login history* section), Visualforce page loads, API calls, and even report exports.

Protecting data is crucial in our daily work, so what could happen if one of our sales reps, who is going to leave our company, exports a report containing all the leads? This is not good for our security, and it may mean that something bad has just happened.

For a comprehensive list of all supported events, refer to Salesforce Help at `https://developer.salesforce.com/docs/atlas.en-us.api.meta/api/sforce_api_objects_eventlogfile_supportedeventtypes.htm`.

Events are available after 24 hours from when they are created and are readable from **event log files**. If we are using a developer edition organization, we can access all events, but they are limited to 1-day data retention period. If we are in enterprise, unlimited, or performance edition organizations, we have free access to logins, logouts, and insecure external asset event types with a 1-day data retention period. For an additional cost, we can get all event types with a 30-day data retention period.

Do you remember all the information that we can extract from the **Login History** page? Everything about the IPs, geolocation, client, and so on? With event monitoring, we can get a wide view of login events (for example, getting all the logins for a given time frame) and then scale down to get a given user or IP—for example, we can identify an anomaly in the number of logins and attribute it to a specific user, and then we can identify which clients that user is using and thereby find out that he is running buggy software.

Other than logins, we can monitor all sorts of stuff, such as data loss (as we already saw), user adoption (is the number of logins increasing?), or performance issues (Visualforce page loading time, API failures, and so on).

How do we get these files? For this, you have to put your technical hat on. We need to consume Salesforce APIs from the Workbench tool to get the event log files (you can use any other client, but this tool is quite easy to use and configure).

For more information about Workbench, I suggest that you watch this cool webinar by Atul Gupta for the `#SalesforceSaturday` event at `https://www.youtube.com/watch?v=krptf8MHVEE`, titled *How to use Salesforce Workbench like a Pro.*

The steps are as follows:

1. Navigate to `https://workbench.developerforce.com`.
2. Select your organization type (production or sandbox; a developer edition organization is a production-like organization).

3. Click the **Login with Salesforce** button.
4. Enter your credentials.
5. Approve the Workbench app, as shown in the following screenshot:

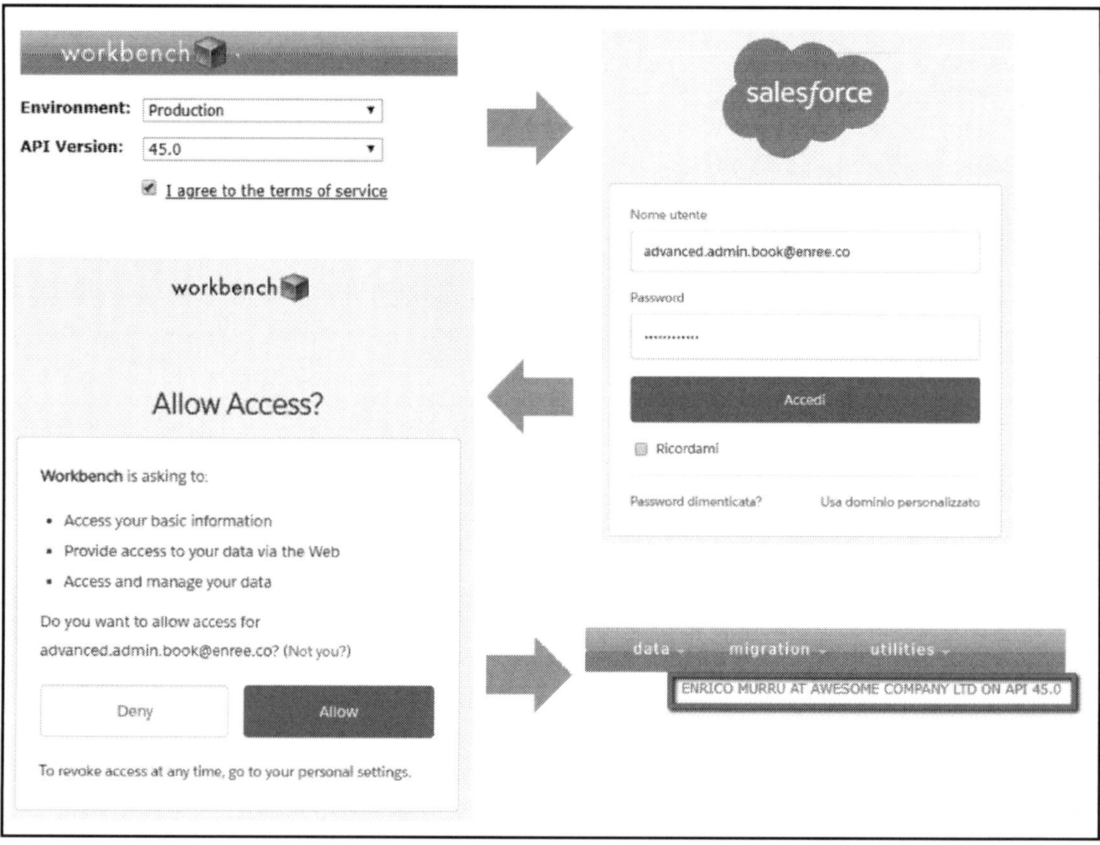

Workbench app enablement

What's happening here? We are unleashing an authentication method called OAuth2. This procedure allows Workbench to use Salesforce APIs on our behalf. By using the Workbench app, we can do all sort of things, such as queries, metadata deployments, and data manipulations. Workbench will take care of the low-level code needed to call Salesforce APIs.

After the successful login with Workbench, a new entry is shown in the **Login History** of our user (as shown in the following screenshot). Even though the user is logging in on their browser from Italy, the Workbench login comes from the USA. Why? Because Workbench servers are not located in Italy as Workbench is a cloud app that anyone can access from anywhere:

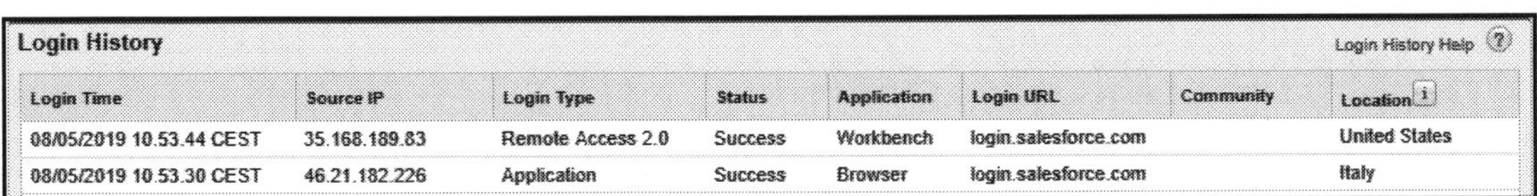

Login History — Login History Help

Login Time	Source IP	Login Type	Status	Application	Login URL	Community	Location
08/05/2019 10.53.44 CEST	35.168.189.83	Remote Access 2.0	Success	Workbench	login.salesforce.com		United States
08/05/2019 10.53.30 CEST	46.21.182.226	Application	Success	Browser	login.salesforce.com		Italy

Login History for the user after Workbench is enabled

To access event log files, ensure that your profile has the **API Enabled** and **View Event Log File** permissions.

In Workbench, click on **Queries** | **SOQL query**, select the `EventLogFile` object, and enter the following SOQL query:

```
SELECT id, createddate, LogDate, EventType, LogFileLength, Interval FROM
EventLogFile
```

The following is what you should get:

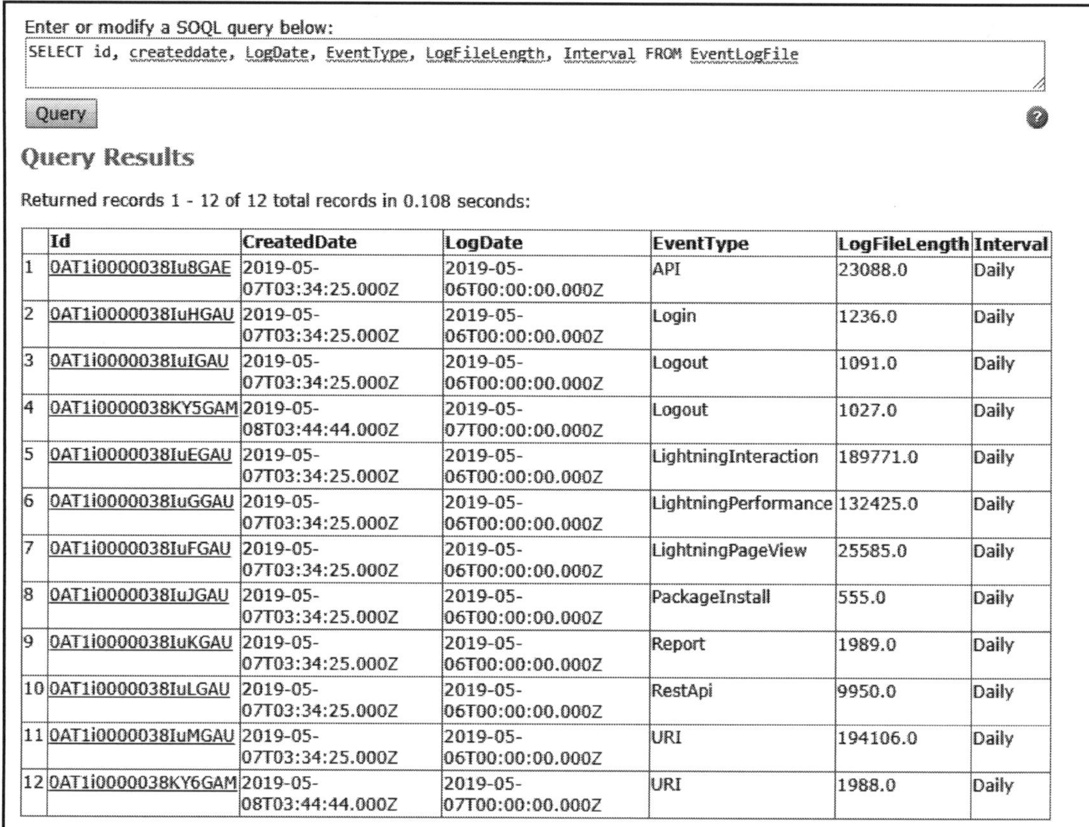

Enter or modify a SOQL query below:

```
SELECT id, createddate, LogDate, EventType, LogFileLength, Interval FROM EventLogFile
```

Query

Query Results

Returned records 1 - 12 of 12 total records in 0.108 seconds:

	Id	CreatedDate	LogDate	EventType	LogFileLength	Interval
1	0AT1i0000038Iu8GAE	2019-05-07T03:34:25.000Z	2019-05-06T00:00:00.000Z	API	23088.0	Daily
2	0AT1i0000038IuHGAU	2019-05-07T03:34:25.000Z	2019-05-06T00:00:00.000Z	Login	1236.0	Daily
3	0AT1i0000038IuIGAU	2019-05-07T03:34:25.000Z	2019-05-06T00:00:00.000Z	Logout	1091.0	Daily
4	0AT1i0000038KY5GAM	2019-05-08T03:44:44.000Z	2019-05-07T00:00:00.000Z	Logout	1027.0	Daily
5	0AT1i0000038IuEGAU	2019-05-07T03:34:25.000Z	2019-05-06T00:00:00.000Z	LightningInteraction	189771.0	Daily
6	0AT1i0000038IuGGAU	2019-05-07T03:34:25.000Z	2019-05-06T00:00:00.000Z	LightningPerformance	132425.0	Daily
7	0AT1i0000038IuFGAU	2019-05-07T03:34:25.000Z	2019-05-06T00:00:00.000Z	LightningPageView	25585.0	Daily
8	0AT1i0000038IuJGAU	2019-05-07T03:34:25.000Z	2019-05-06T00:00:00.000Z	PackageInstall	555.0	Daily
9	0AT1i0000038IuKGAU	2019-05-07T03:34:25.000Z	2019-05-06T00:00:00.000Z	Report	1989.0	Daily
10	0AT1i0000038IuLGAU	2019-05-07T03:34:25.000Z	2019-05-06T00:00:00.000Z	RestApi	9950.0	Daily
11	0AT1i0000038IuMGAU	2019-05-07T03:34:25.000Z	2019-05-06T00:00:00.000Z	URI	194106.0	Daily
12	0AT1i0000038KY6GAM	2019-05-08T03:44:44.000Z	2019-05-07T00:00:00.000Z	URI	1988.0	Daily

Query on EventLogFile records from Workbench

These are all events that occurred on our organization in the **LogDate** (despite the fact that the **CreatedDate** is one day later; remember that we said that events are available 24 hours after their execution).

If you don't have any record, wait for one day for your events to be properly stored.

For a detailed list of the available fields, refer to the `EventLogFile` object reference at `https://developer.salesforce.com/docs/atlas.en-us.object_reference.meta/object_reference/sforce_api_objects_eventlogfile.htm`.

To access the content of one of the records, copy its Salesforce ID (I'm choosing the Report event type), click on **utilities** | **REST explorer**, and input the following URL (be sure to select the **GET** option):

```
/services/data/v45.0/sobjects/EventLogFile/EVENT_LOG_ID
```

Click **Execute** and you'll get something like this:

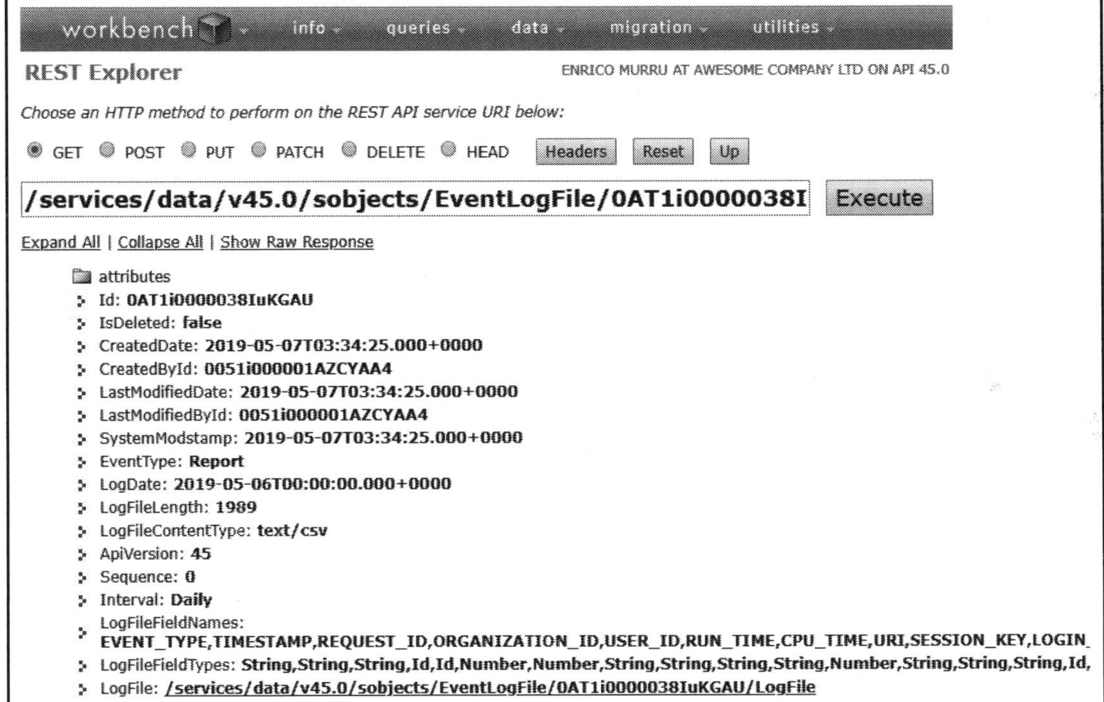

Getting an EventLogFile record using REST APIs

This REST API gets all the information related to a given record. As the **LogFile** field contains all the data of the log, it is not returned on this kind of call, but requires a specific API endpoint to get the content (this is a common behavior for REST APIs dealing with objects).

Click on that link and you'll get the log content:

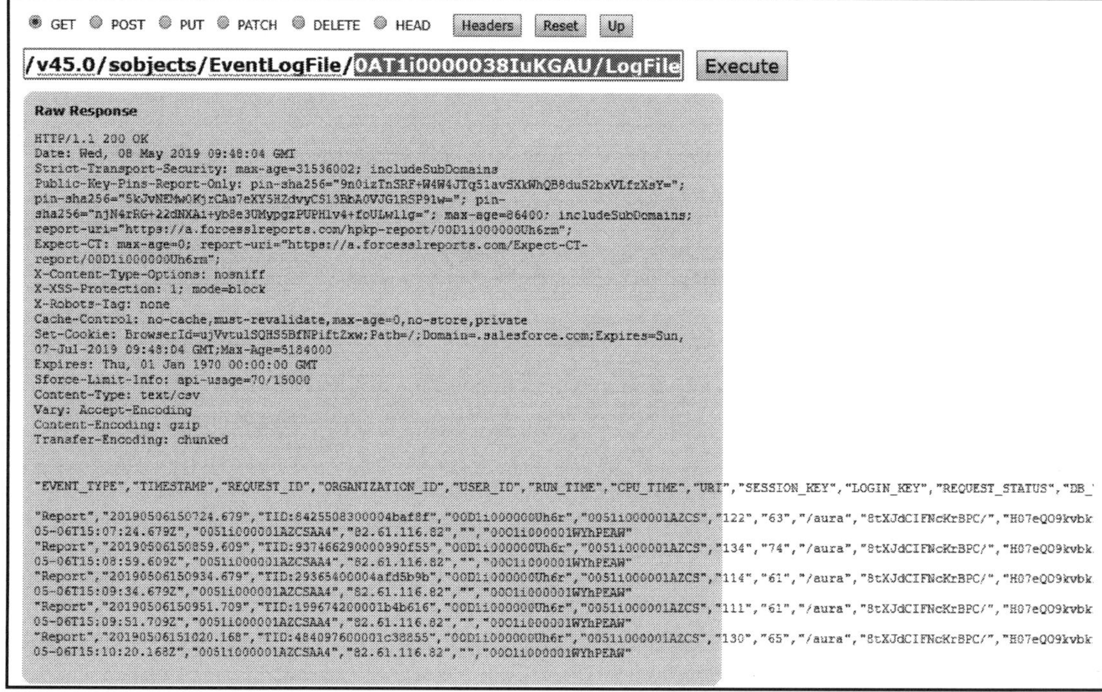

Event log file content

No surprises that it is a CSV file containing all the fields listed on the Report type event definition (you can read more at `https://developer.salesforce.com/docs/atlas.en-us.object_reference.meta/object_reference/sforce_api_objects_eventlogfile_report.htm`).

There's another cool app that you can use to download event log files. Check out the **Salesforce Event Log File Browser** available at `https://salesforce-elf.herokuapp.com`. Log in using the same procedure we used for Workbench and you should see the following result:

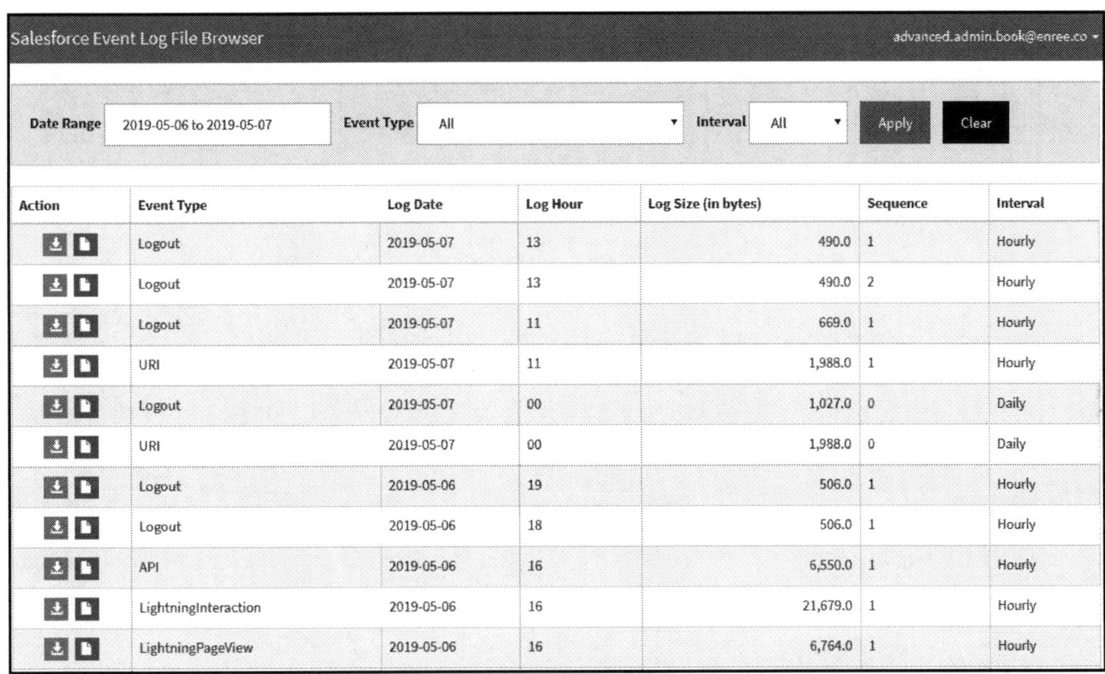

Action	Event Type	Log Date	Log Hour	Log Size (in bytes)	Sequence	Interval
	Logout	2019-05-07	13	490.0	1	Hourly
	Logout	2019-05-07	13	490.0	2	Hourly
	Logout	2019-05-07	11	669.0	1	Hourly
	URI	2019-05-07	11	1,988.0	1	Hourly
	Logout	2019-05-07	00	1,027.0	0	Daily
	URI	2019-05-07	00	1,988.0	0	Daily
	Logout	2019-05-06	19	506.0	1	Hourly
	Logout	2019-05-06	18	506.0	1	Hourly
	API	2019-05-06	16	6,550.0	1	Hourly
	LightningInteraction	2019-05-06	16	21,679.0	1	Hourly
	LightningPageView	2019-05-06	16	6,764.0	1	Hourly

Salesforce Event Log File Browser app

The most useful aspect of this app is the header filter and the one-click download of each CSV.

How do we analyze the data? There's an app for that called the **Event Monitoring Analytics app**, which is available for testing on a dedicated kind of developer edition organization, which comes with all the required data for you to have fun with event logs.

This app is part of the Salesforce Shield platform, which comes with additional costs. More details can be found at `https://help.salesforce.com/articleView?id=salesforce_shield.htmtype=5`.
Refer to the *Event Monitoring Analytics* trail to get a quick start on how to configure the app at `https://trailhead.salesforce.com/content/learn/modules/event_monitoring_analytics/event_monitoring_analytics_get`.

In the following example, we can identify an anomaly on Salesforce Report executions by user (this all comes from the Trailhead trail we referred to earlier):

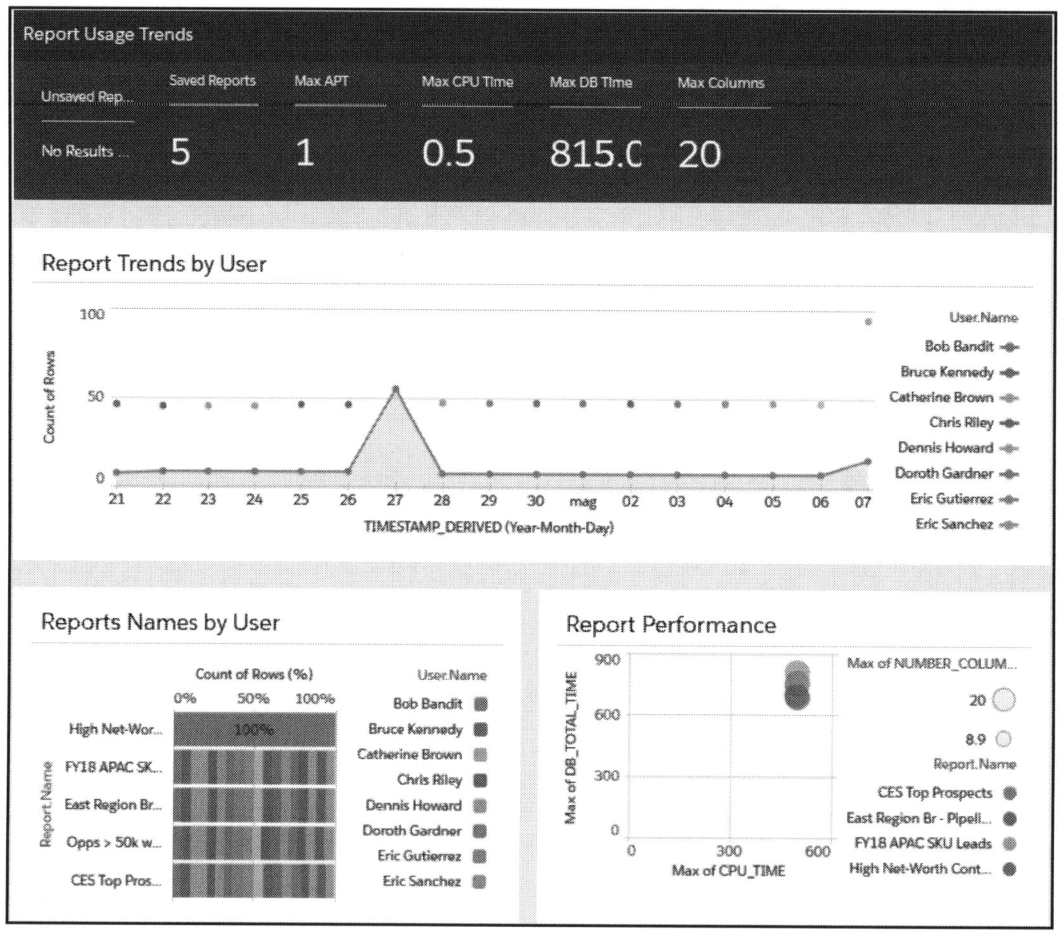

Event Monitor Analytics app on Report type events

It is possible to drill down to any user and see how they are behaving (in the previous screenshot, you can see that Bob is a suspicious user who is constantly running reports), but we also have information about reporting performances (we can spot slow-running reports and proactively inspect them to change filters to allow a quicker runtime).

It is even possible to schedule notification alarms if a certain metric bypasses a given threshold (for example, if the maximum runtime is over a certain number of seconds, or the number of reports downloaded exceeds a safeguard).

Summary

Basic monitoring tools should be a vital part of your administration skills. From login history to setup changes, you are now able to investigate *who did what* on your organization (including delegated administrators).

When a bug occurs, you will even be capable of debugging a record transaction using the debug logs. With the Health Check, you can put down your sheriff's star and put on your medical gown to make the medical diagnosis of your organization.

Now that we have a safe organization, we can talk about how metadata change management is handled in Salesforce and what testing organizations we can use to test out our new implementation.

In the next chapter we will learn about about the different Salesforce organization types (such as sandboxes, developer organizations, and production organizations).

Questions

1. Australian sales reps keep locking their users on a daily basis. You are located in Spain, and sometimes you are not responsive to the unlocking requests. You have been requested to delegate such tasks to selected users. How do you do this?
    a. Assign the users a profile with the **Modify All Data** permission
    b. Assign the users a permission set with the object-level permission **Edit All** on the `User` object
    c. Enable delegated administration to the selected users
    d. Assign the users the delegated administrator profile
2. Your organization makes intensive use of API calls to the billing systems, and the communities have a huge number of partner roles. Where should you go to see how these limits are impacting your org?
    a. **Setup** | **Object Limits**
    b. **Setup** | **API Usage Limits**
    c. **Setup** | **Org Settings** | **Current Limits**
    d. **Setup** | **System Overview**

3. In the last implementation wave for your CRM (Lightning Experience enabled), you can see that you have been requested to create 150 new fields on the `Case` object and 70 new sharing rules based on sparse fields. Before investigating whether the business really needs all those fields and sharing rules, where should you go to tell whether the `Case` object has enough space for new fields and sharing rules?
    a. **Setup** | **Object Manager** | **Case** | **Object Limits**
    b. **Setup** | **Case** | **Object Limits**
    c. **Setup** | **System Overview**
    d. You need to make a SOQL query on the `CustomObjectField` Salesforce object
4. Some users are experiencing long waiting times when loading pages related to, or making SOQL queries on, the `Account` object. You suspect data skew problems. How can you have a look at the top owners of your data storage?
    a. **Setup** | **Object Manager** | **Account** | **Object Limits**
    b. **Setup** | **System Overview**
    c. Make a SOQL query on the `Account` object, grouping all the owners
    d. **Setup** | **Data** | **Storage Usage**
5. From the **Login History** page, what kind of information can you configure?
    a. All users logging in from a given IP range
    b. All users logging in from Italy
    c. All users logging in with a specific port
    d. All users logging in with Chrome
    e. All users logging in with two-factor authentication
6. All your users are required to log in from your company's IP ranges. Remote workers should not be required to stay within this range. How can you check on a daily basis how many users are using the SMS/email activation process for activating their browser?
    a. Go to the **Login History** page
    b. Query the `LoginHistory` object
    c. Use the Setup Audit Trail
    d. Go to the **Identity Verification History** page
7. Someone keeps changing the case layout configuration. Where can you keep track of these changes?
    a. **Login History** page
    b. **Identity Verification History** page
    c. **Setup Audit Trail** page

8. Which of the following sentences are true regarding the **Setup Audit Trail** page?
    a. You can determine what delegated administrators are doing on the organization
    b. You cannot determine what delegated administrators are doing on the org
    c. You can only get the login history of delegated administrators or system admins
    d. You can download setup changes of up to 6 months
    e. You can get the same data from the `SetupAuditTrail` Salesforce objects
9. You want to query all field changes tracked for a specific record of the `Inventory` custom object. Which record would you query against?
    a. `InventoryHistory`
    b. `HistoryInventory`
    c. `InventoryHistory__c`
    d. `Inventory__History`
10. Your organization was created in May 2010 and you are worried about field tracking retention. Which statement is true?
    a. Organizations created before June 1, 2011 have perpetual login history retention
    b. Organizations created after June 1, 2011 have perpetual login history retention
    c. Organizations created between June 1, 2009 and June 1, 2011 have perpetual login history retention
    d. There is no such thing as perpetual field tracking retention
11. You are afraid that an OWD recalculation is stuck because you still haven't received the notification email. What should you do?
    a. Ask the Salesforce Support to abort that job
    b. Monitor background jobs only for sharing recalculation jobs
    c. Monitor background jobs in the **Setup** | **Background Jobs** page
    d. No escape; wait for the completion of the job
12. What is a trace flag?
    a. The way Salesforce enables debug logs for a given user
    b. The way Salesforce filters out relevant debug data
    c. The limit of 250 MB of logs retained

13. What is a debug level?
    a. The way Salesforce enables debug logs for a given user
    b. The way Salesforce filters out relevant debug data
    c. The limit of 250 MB of logs retained
14. Which of the following statements regarding debug logs are true?
    a. You can debug field history tracking
    b. You can have up to 250 MB of debug logs per organization at any given time
    c. You can enable debug logs on all your users to keep track of every operation they make
    d. You can debug most of Salesforce's automation features (workflow, triggers, process builders, and so on)
15. A workflow rule sends an email to a customer when a case is closed, but when testing it on your sandbox, you find that it doesn't work anymore. How can you inspect this issue?
    a. Email cannot be sent from sandbox organizations
    b. In sandbox organizations, email shipping can have a significant delay due to reduced platform resources
    c. Check the email deliverability's setting to be set to **All email**
    d. Request an email log and inspect the results to look for email shipping errors
16. What can you do within the **Health Check** page?
    a. See how well sharing rules perform
    b. Check the number of portal roles
    c. Get an overall status of your organization's security settings
    d. Fix security risks based on your security policies/baseline

3 Change Management

It's important to provide your team with a safe place to implement new features using sandboxes. They should learn to master change management with change sets and learn which other tools can be used to move organization configurations from one organization to another. It is equally important to learn how to pull and push data using the tools the organizations come with.

Once our organization is secure and being proactively monitored, we can move on with the change management of metadata and data by describing different sandbox types that we can use to implement and test our organization's new features, different ways to move configurations between organizations, and finally, how to move data from organization to organization.

In this chapter, we'll learn about the following topics:

- More about Salesforce sandbox types
- Using change sets to move changes from one sandbox to another
- Alternative tools to move changes
- Suggested tools for loading and pulling data from an organization

Testing using sandboxes

Although a popular meme featuring Chuck Norris states that *Testing is for wimps, real men test in production*, believe me when I say this is not a good philosophy!

The ability to develop and test in dedicated and safe environments is key to the success of your efforts, whether it's a 1-year project or a 1-day highly intensive bugfix.

Sandboxes give us and our team the chance to work in an isolated place that mimics (more or less) production, where we can make all sorts of custom configurations and developments and test with production data or even train our users. Everything is done with the different kinds of sandboxes at our service.

Sandboxes can be created, deleted, cloned, and refreshed. Moreover, when a new Salesforce platform release is ready (this happens three times a year, with the winter, spring, and summer releases), sandboxes are the organizations where these major platform releases are first implemented by Salesforce before affecting production organizations, allowing us to test new features or make no regression tests. Depending on your organization instance (that is, the `csXX` in your sandbox's URL, for instance, `https://cs88.salesforce.com/`) and depending on specific limit dates before each release, you can decide to refresh a given sandbox to see the new release as soon as possible or only when production has been upgraded.

When a sandbox is created, it inherits all the metadata configurations from production (or the other sandbox from which it was cloned) and, depending on its type, some, all, or none of the data of the source organization.

Sandbox organizations can only be created from the **Setup** | **Environments** | **Sandboxes** page from production. Here is an example:

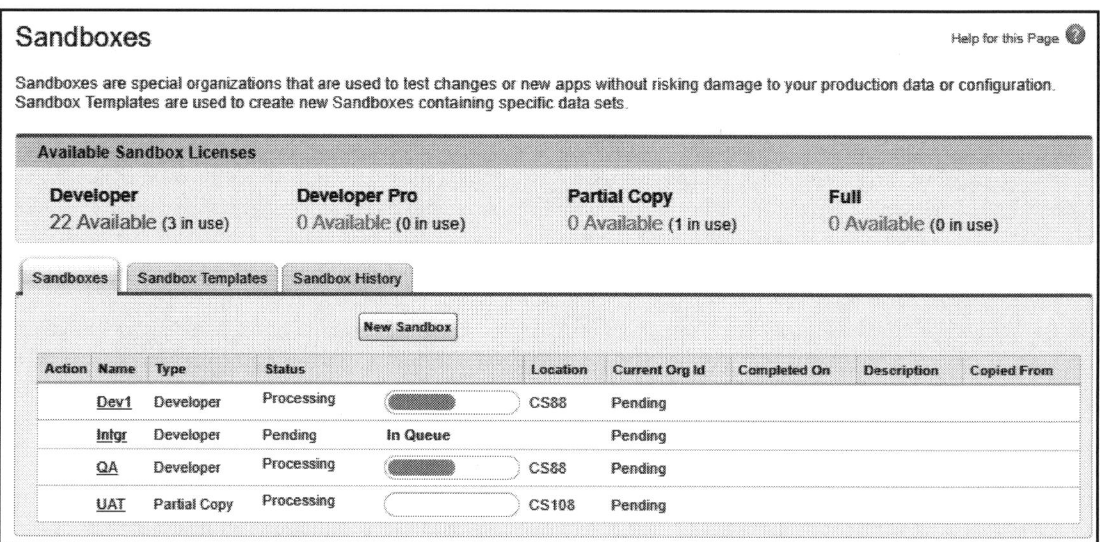

We can have different kinds of sandboxes, all of which we'll be describing shortly:

- Developer sandbox
- Developer Pro sandbox
- Partial Copy sandbox
- Full sandbox

We'll also have a look at how we can put an architecture of diverse sandboxes together so that we can handle changes from one testing organization to the other until production.

Developer sandbox

This sandbox is used mainly for the development process. It contains a copy of all the production metadata but no records at all (exceptions include users, for instance). Having no access to real production data allows administrators and developers to safely develop their features without worrying about how data should be handled.

The Developer sandbox can be refreshed from production once a day and it can hold up to 200 MB of data and 200 MB of file storage. This kind of sandbox is usually assigned to individual developers so that they are free to dismantle an organization without it having an impact on their colleagues.

Developer Pro sandbox

The Developer Pro sandbox differs from the Developer sandbox type regarding the amount of data and file storage that can be held, that is, 1 GB.

This type is generally used for *global* development environments, that is, a sandbox that conveys that all the developers work in a single organization (coming from different Developer sandboxes) and can be used for code base quality assurance (for example, running all Apex tests or validating cross-developer/admin implementations).

Partial Copy sandbox

This is used for testing purposes. It contains all the metadata from production but also a sample of its data, which will have been selected *randomly*. That's why this type is useful for testing the borderline behavior of your implementation.

Partial Copy is often used for user acceptance tests, integration testing, and training. It conveys up to 5 GB of sample data and file storage and can be refreshed every five days.

When you create this kind of sandbox, you need to choose a sandbox template (on the **Sandboxes** page, click on the **Templates** tab):

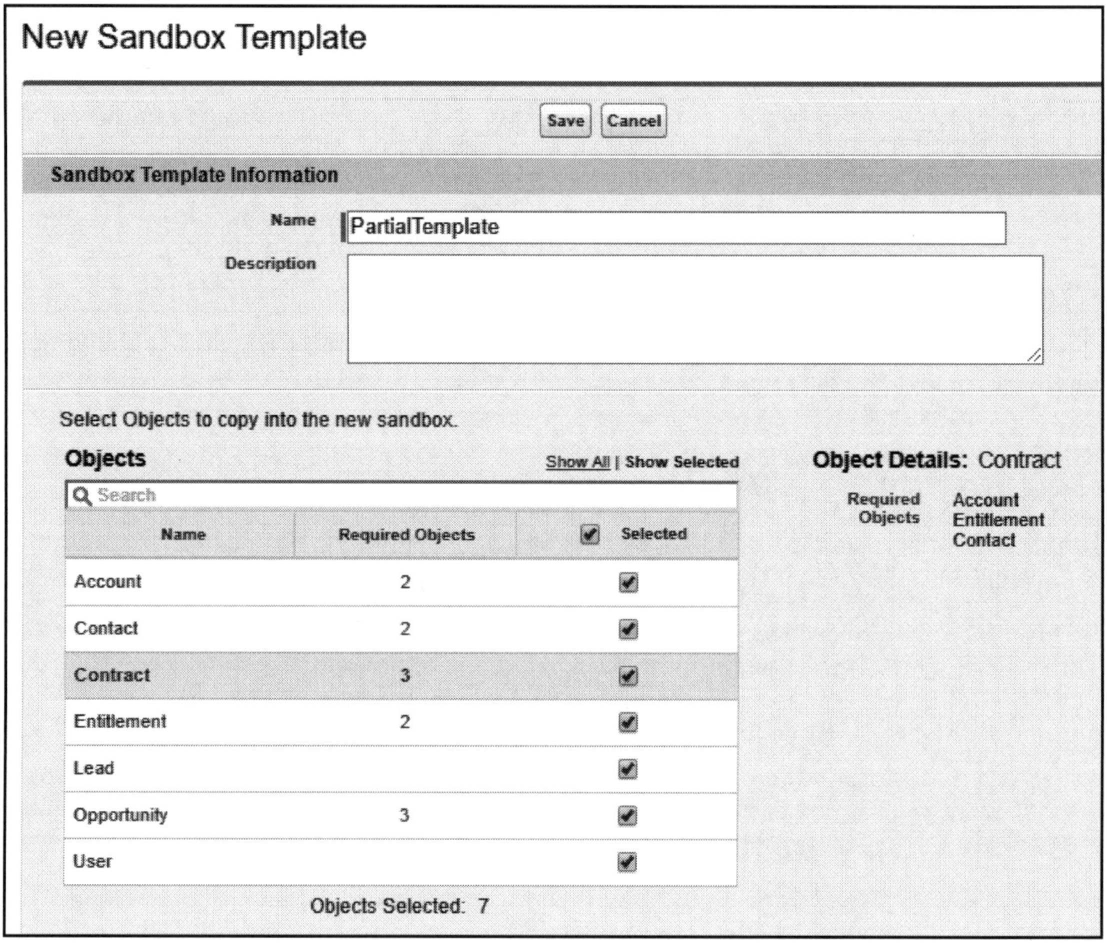

New Sandbox Template

Save Cancel

Sandbox Template Information

Name PartialTemplate

Description

Select Objects to copy into the new sandbox.

Objects Show All | Show Selected

Search

Name	Required Objects	Selected
Account	2	✔
Contact	2	✔
Contract	3	✔
Entitlement	2	✔
Lead		✔
Opportunity	3	✔
User		✔

Objects Selected: 7

Object Details: Contract

Required Objects: Account, Entitlement, Contact

Sandbox template creation

Select all the objects you want to be copied into the Partial Copy sandbox. Considering that Salesforce will copy up to 10K records per object type, up to a total of 5 GB, choose the records almost randomly (there is no way to tell Salesforce which category of records you want to be selected).

Full sandbox

This is the queen of all sandboxes as it reproduces the production environment. Indeed, this sandbox type can be used for performance testing. That being said, it is a full copy of production regarding both metadata and data, and it is aligned with production limits for file and storage quotas. The refresh time is 29 days. However, you can always apply a sandbox template to select the objects you want to be copied.

Why don't you want all the data? There may be certain objects that are useless for your testing.

Copying GBs of data can be time-consuming and you should expect your sandbox creation/refresh time to take several days. The less you need to copy, the faster the copying process is.

When creating/refreshing a Full sandbox, Salesforce asks you what you want to do with field tracking information. You can decide not to include it (faster copy) or you can go up to 180 days back in time (chatter history can be very large).

Because of their nature, Full sandboxes are used for testing external integrations (as external systems expect real production data) or staging for the final validation of your team's work or for production debugging.

For a quick and updated reference on sandboxes, please refer to Salesforce Help at `https://help.salesforce.com/articleView?id=data_Sandbox_environments.htmtype=5`.

About sandbox flow architectures

Partial Copy and Full sandboxes require an additional license to be purchased (contact your Salesforce account manager for more information).

There is no mandatory sandbox configuration setup, but let's have a look at what we can design.

Take a look at the following sandbox architecture, which can be adapted to most projects:

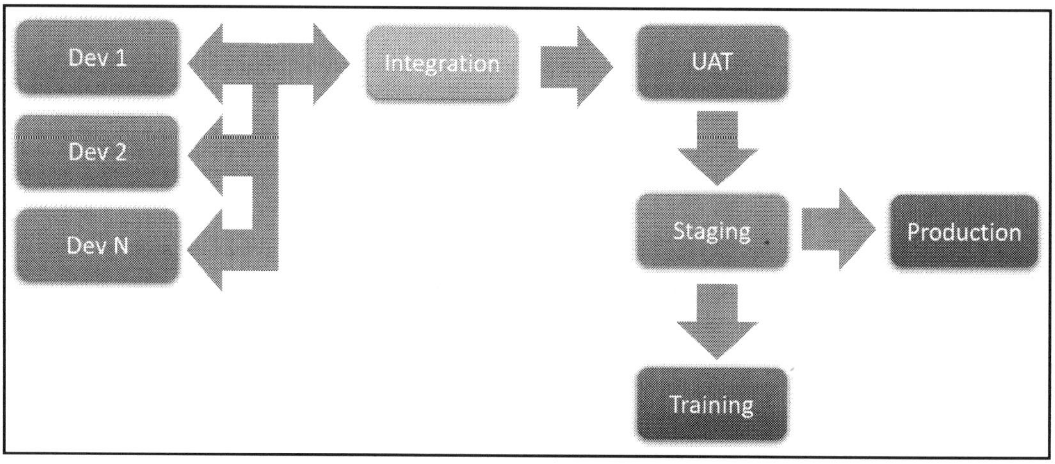

In the preceding diagram, **Production** is the only organization that is not a sandbox.

Dev 1, **Dev 2**, and **Dev N** are part of the **Developer** (**Dev**) sandbox and have been assigned to the three developers that are implementing the following project: due to the kind of job developers do, these sandboxes are full production metadata copies, and no data is received from production, so they are free to mess with the dataset.

Once each developer has a stable code base, the changes are released into **Integration**, which is a **Developer Pro** sandbox, where everything is tested internally in your team to match the requirements.

If legacy systems have a development environment, you can use this sandbox to test the implementation against external systems. In this case, they usually send mock data, so they are not the proper place to validate external integrations, but from here, you can see whether the code/configurations are running as expected. This place is, in fact, the sandbox where the code base is validated with automated testing (UI or backend testing using Apex test suites).

The **Integration** sandbox is also the place where developers bring back their colleagues' changes to their own Developer sandbox.

Once the internal testing has been validated, changes are brought to the UAT (or testing) sandbox. This is typically a **Full** sandbox, but even a **Partial Copy** could be a good fit. The business guys execute their user acceptance tests and validate legacy integrations.

Once everything is OK, changes are deployed to Staging. This should be a **Full** sandbox because this is the last place where you can test with actual production data. This place is optimal for bug testing after a production issue.

Finally, the **Training** organization is used to train your users with these new changes. This is typically a **Partial Copy** sandbox.

Remember that you can ask Salesforce support for a sandbox license when needed for a limited amount of time. This way, you can dispose of multiple instances of Partial Copy or Full sandboxes so that you can support your projects better.

If your company/customer needs a multi-project environment, you can set up a unique Staging instance, which will collect all the developments and use separate Dev-Integration-UAT branches for each project.

Depending on your Salesforce edition, you will have a certain number of sandbox types available. Jump to Salesforce Help for a detailed list at `https://help.salesforce.com/articleView?id=data_Sandbox_environments.htmtype=5`.

When triggering the creation/refresh of a sandbox, you can select an Apex class to be run after the copy has completed. Use this method if you want to create some basic records for your organization (for example, a base dataset for Developer/Developer Pro organizations).

One additional option when handling a sandbox is cloning. You can clone a given sandbox into a new sandbox of the same license type (for example, a Full Copy must be copied into another Full Copy). Cloned sandboxes can be refreshed as well, and they are aligned with their source sandbox.

Remember that when a sandbox is created, usernames are modified and the `.Sandbox-name` suffix is appended (passwords and security tokens remain the same). This means that if a user has a username of `awesomeadmin@mycompany.com` in the new Sandbox called **UAT**, you would log in with `awesomeadmin@mycompany.com.`**`uat`**.

Even users' email addresses are changed by appending the `.invalid` suffix, so no automatic notification is sent after the sandbox is activated. You need to manually change user emails to enable notification. As we discussed in the previous chapter, **Email Deliverability** is also set to **System Email Only** for the same reason.

None of the email fields in your dataset are changed, so take care when using a Sandbox with actual customer data by, for instance, replacing all email addresses by appending an invalidating suffix or using the same fake email address.

Plan your sandbox refresh strategy while taking the following into account:

- Full/partial copy refresh/creation can take days to complete.
- A sandbox is not a copy at a given time; production data and configuration data can change during the copy, so some records may be inconsistent.

For further considerations about sandboxes, please refer to Salesforce Help at `https://help.salesforce.com/articleView?id=data_Sandbox_implementation_tips.htmtype=5`.

A quick note: For companies that have adopted Salesforce DX for release management, the Dev 1-Dev N sandboxes have been replaced with Scratch organizations, which are disposable organizations linked to your production organization (called the Hub). Developers can use SalesforceDX to create and destroy Scratch Orgs in a matter of minutes, so they are able to quickly develop and test their stuff in isolated orgs, thus reducing the maintenance of Dev sandboxes.

For more information about Salesforce DX, refer to the following useful post by Salesforce Ben: `https://www.salesforceben.com/salesforce-dx-mean-admins/`.

Deploying changes with change sets

In the previous section, we talked about the metadata changes that are deployed into a chain of sandboxes until the final production release.

There are different ways to achieve a metadata deployment:

- **Metadata SOAP APIs** (refer to `https://developer.salesforce.com/docs/atlas.en-us.api_meta.meta/api_meta/meta_intro.htm` for more information)
- The **ANT Migration Tool** (sometimes called the Force.com Migration tool—`https://developer.salesforce.com/docs/atlas.en-us.218.0.daas.meta/daas/meta_development.htm`)

- An IDE, such as **Visual Studio Code** (`https://forcedotcom.github.io/salesforcedx-vscode/`) or other popular IDEs
- **Packages**
- **Change sets**

Unlike change sets and packages, the other ways require you to master a developer's attitude. Let's start with change sets.

Change sets is a powerful feature that's meant to help administrators and developers easily deploy metadata from sandbox to sandbox, or from sandbox to production, using a point and click approach.

The following steps are required to unleash change sets:

1. Create an outbound change set on the source organization.
2. Add the changed metadata items to the change set.
3. Upload the change set to an enabled destination organization.
4. Validate the inbound change set on the destination organization.
5. Deploy the change set on the destination organization.
6. Monitor the deployment.

Repeat until you have all green lights!

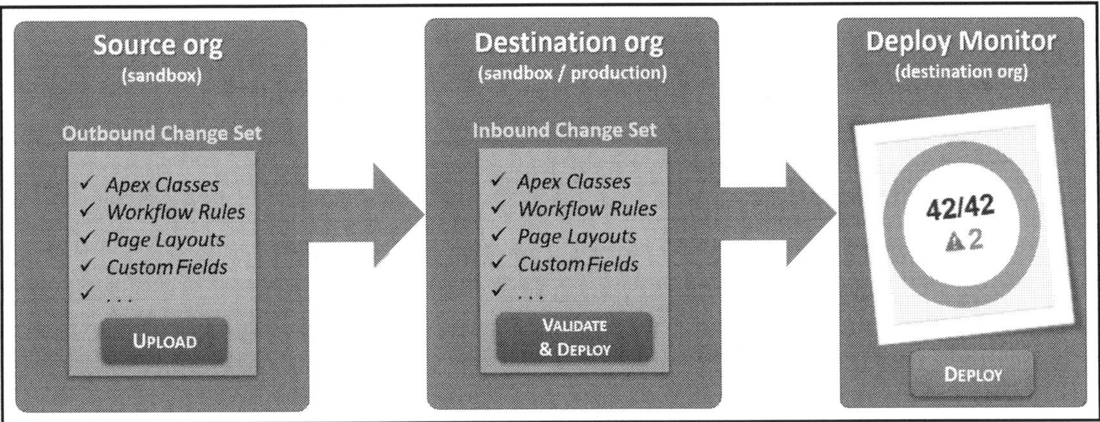

The first thing you need to set up is a deployment connection between the organizations you want to move metadata between. A source organization creates an outbound change set that, while uploaded, becomes an inbound change set on the destination organization.

You can only connect organizations affiliated to a production organization, which means you cannot move metadata using change sets from a Developer Edition organization to a sandbox or production organization. Change sets are enabled only between sandboxes and their production organization.

A connection should also be authorized to send and receive change sets, thus enforcing security on change promotion.

Typically, production will receive changes only when tested and approved. This means we'll have an incoming connection from the UAT sandbox, while Dev and UAT may have a two-side connection because Dev can deploy to UAT. After testing and typically small configuration changes, UAT can bring those changes back to DEV. As we saw in the sandbox architecture earlier, your company may have this particular set of deployment connections.

The following diagram illustrates how connections can be established inside our architecture (as shown in the previous section):

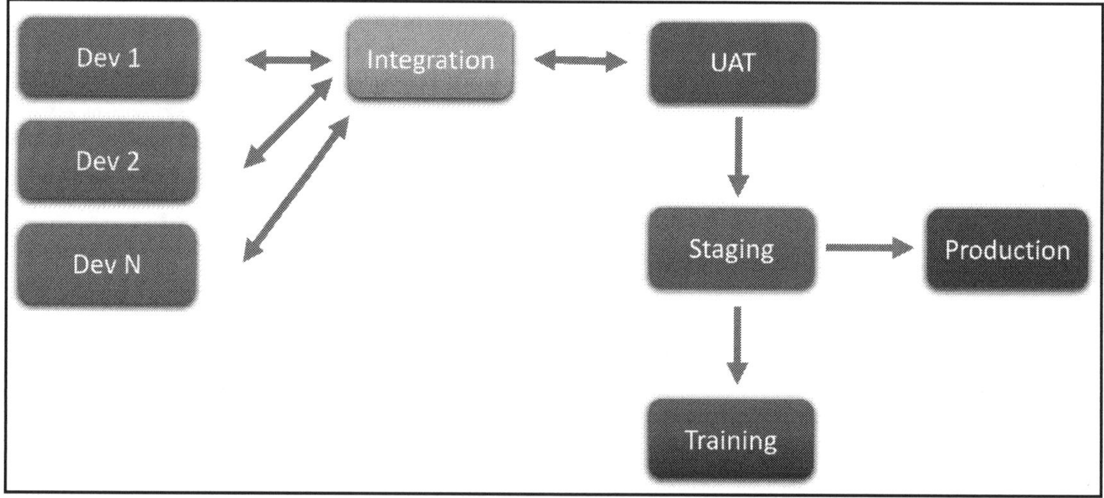

Change set direction on each sandbox

Note that after UAT, the changes only go forward. This may be a requirement of your release management team. Metadata should only be changed until UAT, which becomes the final source of truth for metadata.

There's no one-size-fits-all solution. Design your sandbox structure based on your needs and on your company's policies.

To enable a connection, go to **Setup** | **Environments** | **Deployment** | **Deployment Settings**:

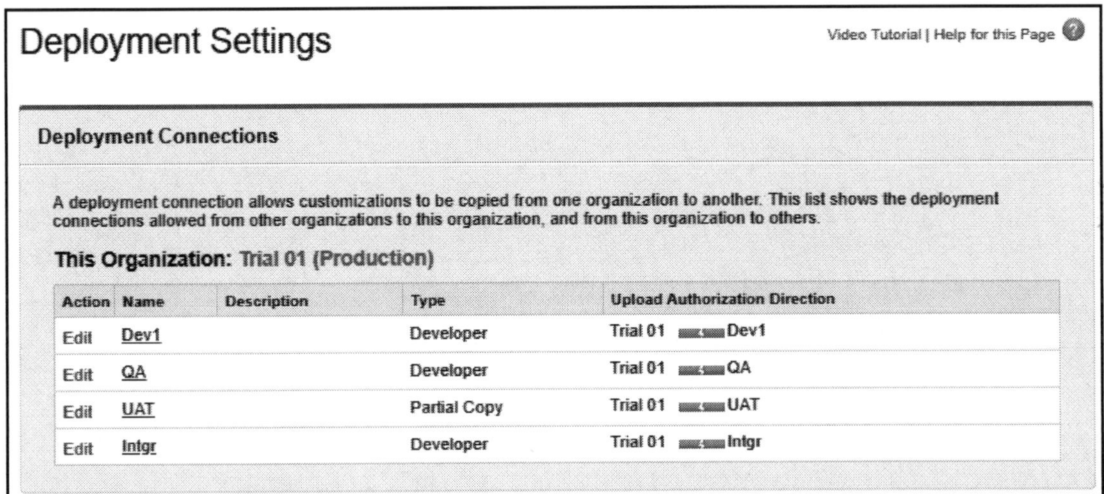

From the list of all your active sandboxes (and production, if you are running the tool in a sandbox), choose a sandbox that you want to establish a connection with by clicking on the **Edit** link:

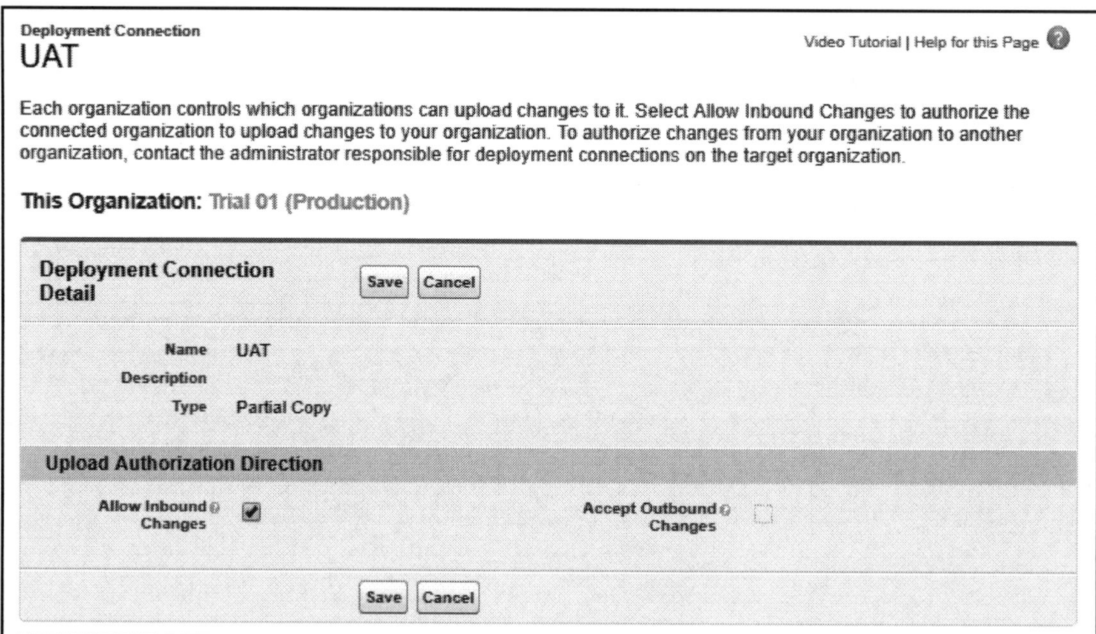

You can enable inbound change sets coming from the selected organization and see if the given organization is accepting inbound change sets from the current organization.

Take a look at the following screenshot:

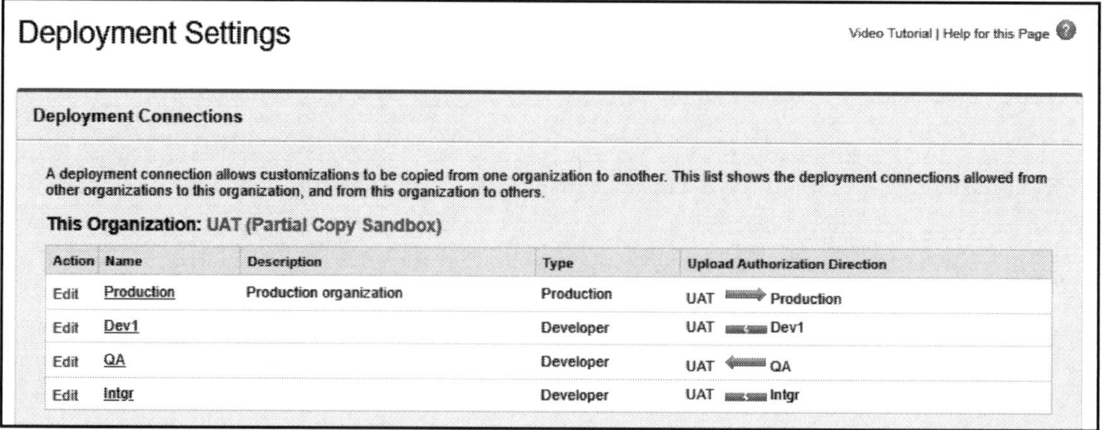

Here, we can see that the **Production** organization can receive inbound change sets from UAT, while UAT has not yet authorized **Production** to send its outbound change sets (**Accept Outbound Changes** is not flagged).

You will see the following screen on the UAT sandbox after configuring some deployment connections. It can deploy to production and accepts deployments from QA.

Once the connections are created, on the source organization, navigate to **Setup** | **Environments** | **Outbound Change Sets**, click on the **New** button, and fill in the **Name** and **Description** fields:

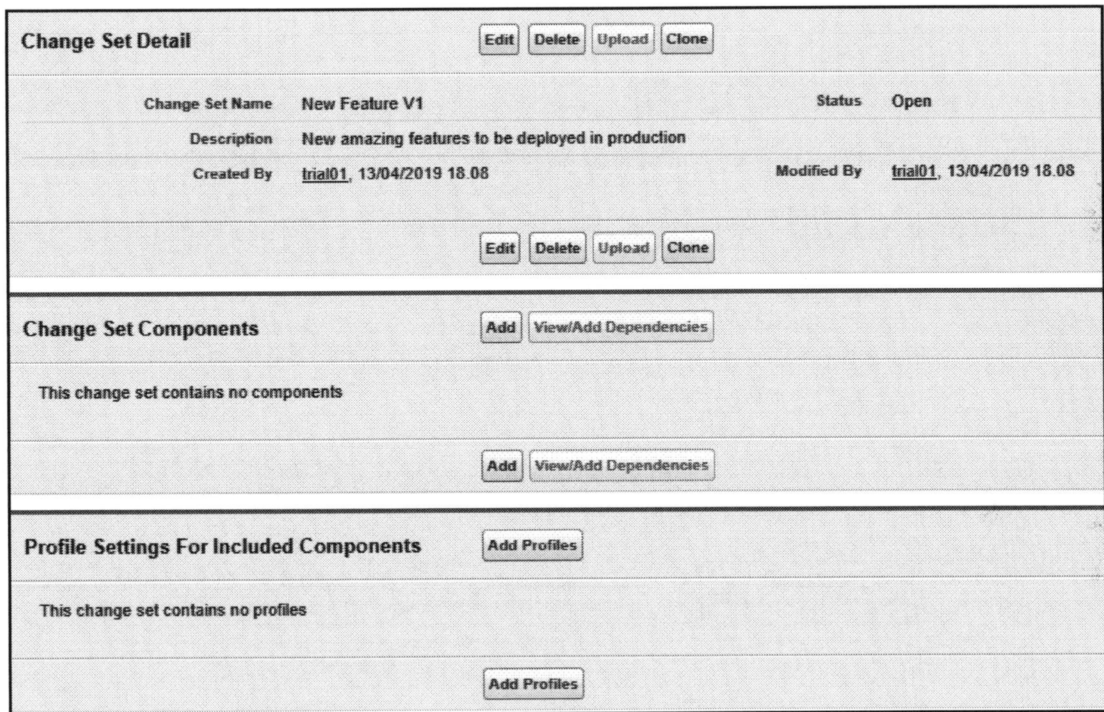

As shown in the previous screenshot, to add a new item, click on the **Add** button in the **Change Set Components** section, choose the component type, and select the changed components. Also, click on **Add To Change Set** to complete the change set's creation:

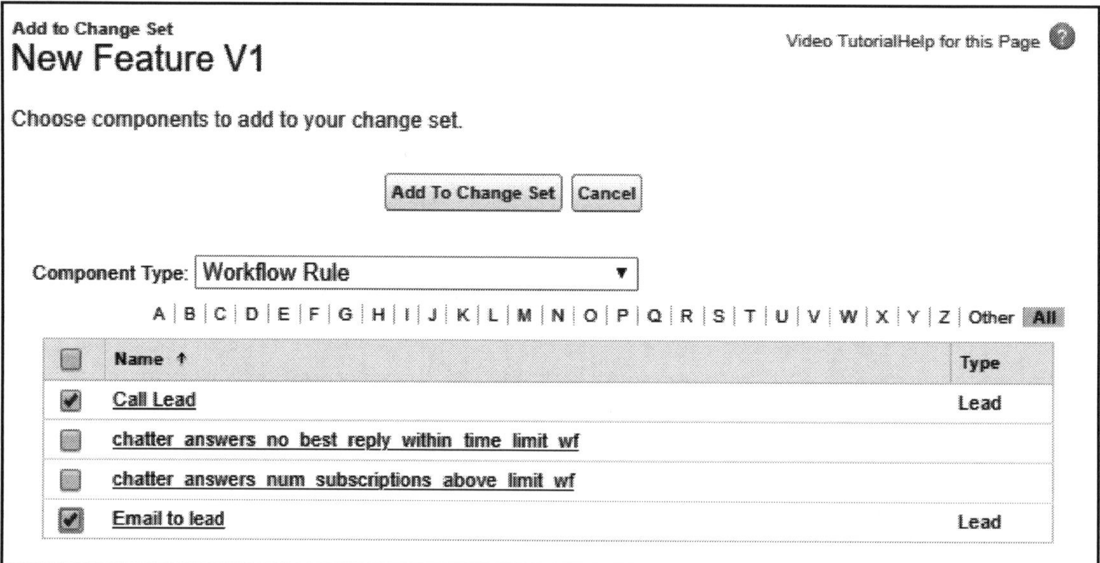

This will open the following view:

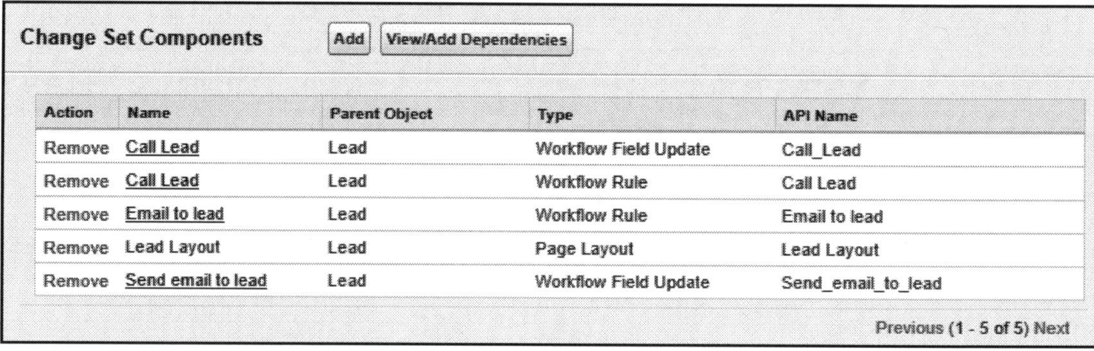

In this example, we have changed some stuff:

- A new custom field on the **Lead** object
- Lead page layout to include the new field
- Two workflow rules that trigger the new field's values
- Two field updates that set the new values on the field according to workflow rules

Not every metadata type is available on change sets. For a comprehensive list, refer to the official documentation at `https://help.salesforce.com/articleView?id=changesets_about_components.htmtype=5`.

Did we forget something? Let's say that everything has been set up (although it hasn't—don't worry, we'll understand why shortly).

Click on the **Upload** button to send the change set to the destination organization:

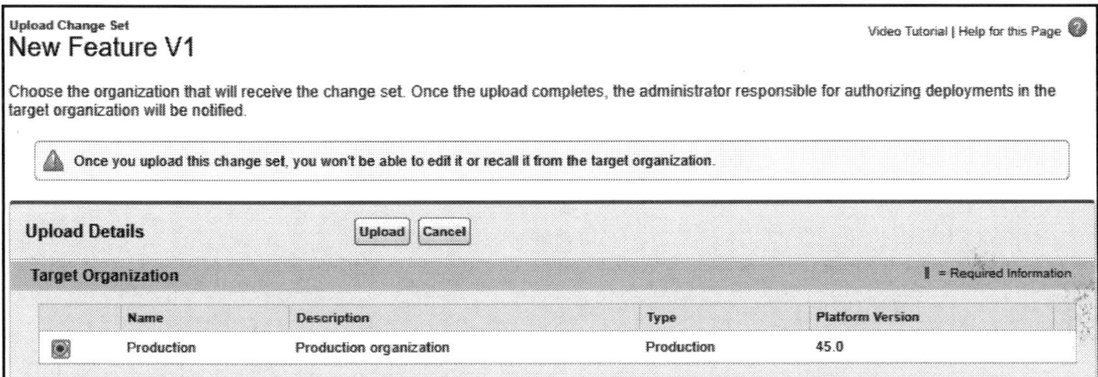

The change set is now being uploaded to the **Production** organization and a notification email will be sent to inform you when the corresponding inbound change set is ready at its destination. This can take a few minutes, so don't panic if you don't see the email instantly.

Once a change set has been uploaded, it's locked. Clone it to create a new change set so that you can add more components.

Jump to the destination organization and navigate to **Setup** | **Environments** | **Change Sets** | **Inbound Change Sets**. Find the new change set and click on it. You may encounter the following message:

Change Set Unavailable

This change set isn't available right now. Change sets are uploaded asynchronously, so a change set that was recently uploaded can take up to 30 minutes or longer before it's available for deployment. Please wait and try deploying your change set again later.

Again, don't panic... it's just that Salesforce still isn't ready to deploy it. Wait for a few more minutes. This is what you will see when the change set is ready to be deployed:

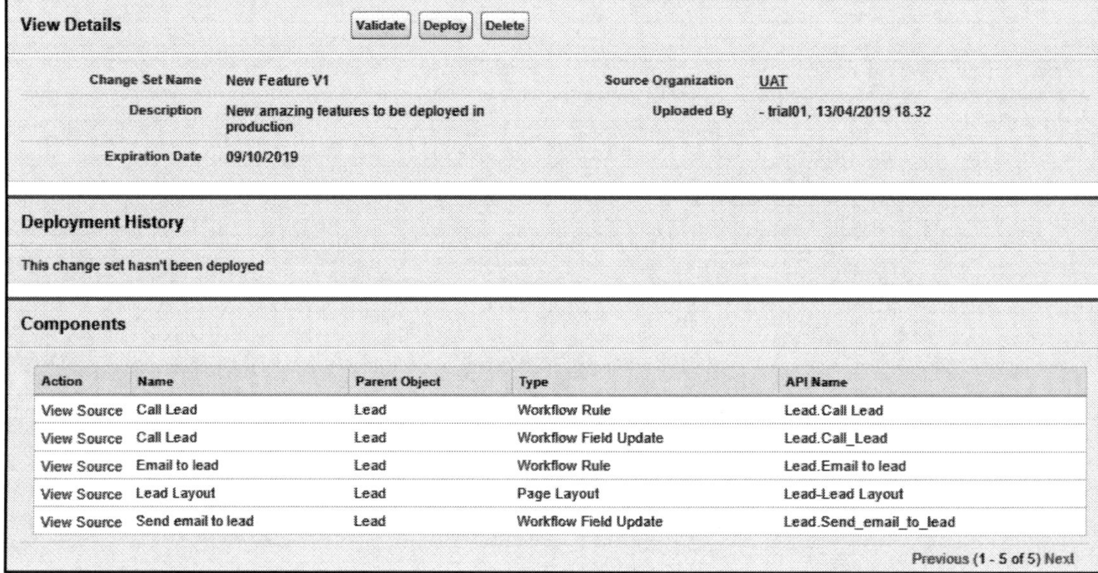

Click on the **Validate** button to validate the change set before deploying it. The system will provide you with a few choices regarding validation on the Apex test's execution:

- **Default**: Depending on the current organization, Salesforce automatically runs all local tests (production) or not (sandbox).
- **Run local tests**: Salesforce automatically runs all local tests (I suggest this for complex change sets, even in sandboxes).
- **Run all tests**: Salesforce automatically runs local and managed tests (this is related to managed/AppExchange packages).
- **Run specified tests**: We can select the Apex test classes to be executed (to speed up deployment times; this is something your developers will tell you to do).

Leave the selection as the **Default** and watch the engine validate your package (from **Setup | Deployment Status**):

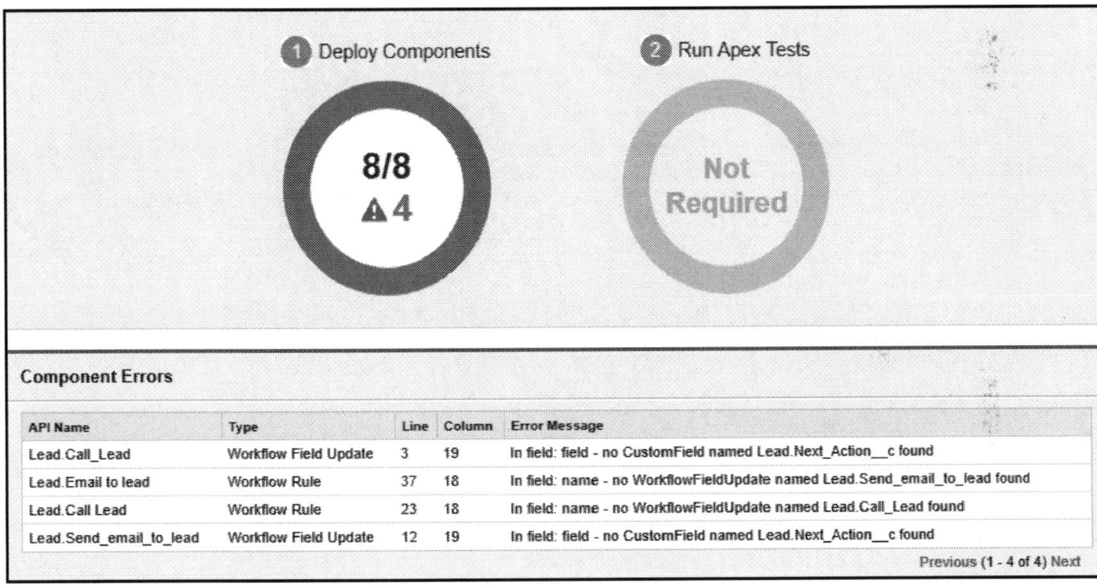

API Name	Type	Line	Column	Error Message
Lead.Call_Lead	Workflow Field Update	3	19	In field: field - no CustomField named Lead.Next_Action__c found
Lead.Email to lead	Workflow Rule	37	18	In field: name - no WorkflowFieldUpdate named Lead.Send_email_to_lead found
Lead.Call Lead	Workflow Rule	23	18	In field: name - no WorkflowFieldUpdate named Lead.Call_Lead found
Lead.Send_email_to_lead	Workflow Field Update	12	19	In field: field - no CustomField named Lead.Next_Action__c found

Previous (1 - 4 of 4) Next

What happened? The new lead field (called **Next_Action__c**) has not been added to the outbound change set on the source organization, and thus Salesforce cannot deploy field updates nor workflow rules. The change set is not valid.

Let's get back to the source organization, jump to the already uploaded change set, and click on the **Clone** button. Lastly, add the new custom field on lead (we called it **Next_Action**):

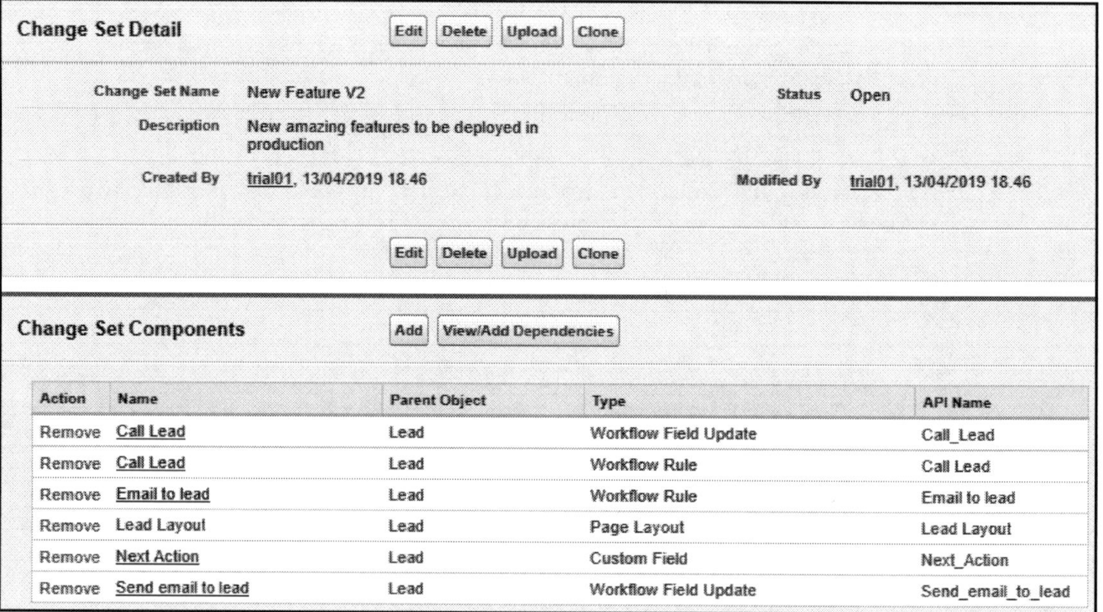

All the other components are still there; we have simply added a new item to the list.

We should not encounter any errors on the destination sandbox when validating the inbound change set.

Before uploading the change set, we also need to include permissions for the new field (so that we don't have to set up an **FLS** (short for **field-level security**) on the new custom field manually).

We can do this in two ways:

- Add a new permission set to the change set components list (if the new features come with a permission set).
- Add the impacted profiles to the **Profile Settings For Included Components** list.

In both cases, only the permissions related to the components list are considered (for example, if you have a permission set that sets FLS for the case's fields, they are not applied to the destination organization along with the change set because the case's fields are not included in the change set. The same applies to profiles). The following screenshot shows that three profiles have been added to the change set:

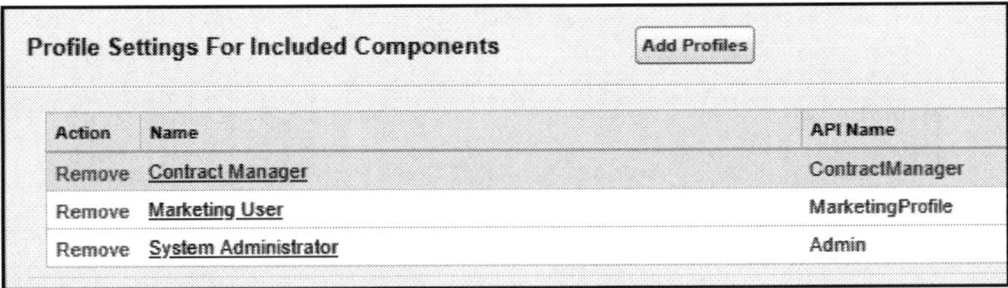

Profile Settings For Included Components [Add Profiles]

Action	Name	API Name
Remove	Contract Manager	ContractManager
Remove	Marketing User	MarketingProfile
Remove	System Administrator	Admin

When cloning a change set, use a different name for the newly created change set (such as an incremental version number) so that you're not confused when dealing with different change sets.

Now, let's upload this to production and validate it again. Go back to the destination organization and click on the **Validate** link next to our new inbound change set version:

Change Sets Awaiting Deployment

Action	Change Set Name	Description	Source Organization	Uploaded By	Uploaded Date
Validate | Deploy | Delete	New Feature V2	New amazing features to be deployed in production	UAT	- trial01 @ UAT	13/04/2019 18.49
Validate | Deploy | Delete	New Feature V1	New amazing features to be deployed in production	UAT	- trial01 @ UAT	13/04/2019 18.32

Previous (1 - 2 of 2) Next

We should get a green light upon validating the change set:

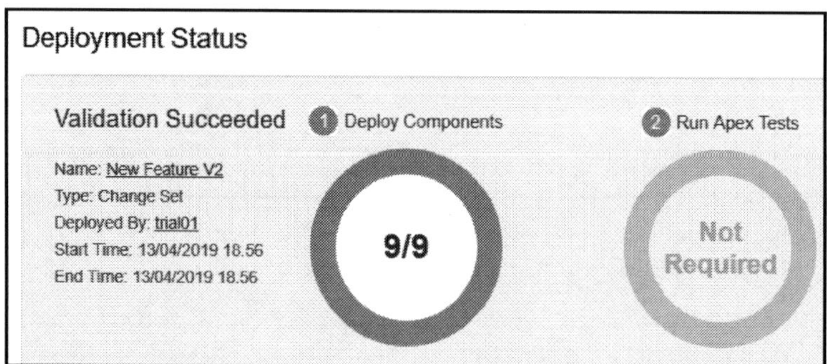

Jump back to the inbound change set details page and click on the **Deploy** button (leaving the **Default** value as it is for Apex tests). You should get a success message:

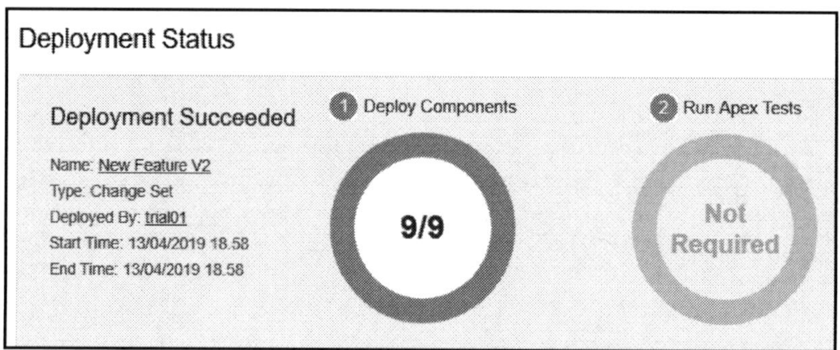

The components are now included in your organization, along with the necessary permissions.

Let's go over some more advice regarding this process:

- Add all the dependent components for a given item (for example, all the custom fields for a given custom object or all the workflow actions for a given workflow rule), otherwise the deployment will fail.
- You can deploy along with validation, but validation is useful when you want to know whether the change set is okay ahead of its actual deployment (depending on release management policies, you may only have a given time frame to deploy a change).
- Limit change sets to 10,000 items to avoid long-running uploads and deployments.

Adding hundreds of items to a change set can be cumbersome, but you can find browser extensions that can help you manage your change sets, such as Organizer for Salesforce (for Chrome and Firefox: `https://organizer.enree.co`), Salesforce Change Set Helper (for Chrome: `https://chrome.google.com/webstore/detail/salesforce-change-set-hel/gdjfanbphogooppaefebaaoohdcigpoi`), and Salesforce Change Set Turbo (for Chrome: `https://chrome.google.com/webstore/detail/salesforce-change-set-tur/dlcjllapchpeedkecmhfnpfenpbglioo`).

Let's move on and discuss using packages to deploy configurations.

Deploying changes with packages

Packages are like change sets but without the constraint that states that organizations should all be children of the same production organization.

This means that change sets are not available on Developer Edition organizations, whereas packages are, and that we can only deploy metadata that is isolated from the destination organization's configuration (packages can be used by ISVs to provide AppExchange general porpoise apps, that's why a package can't be aware of what's already on your organization).

For more information about the ISV partner program, take a look at Trailhead at `https://trailhead.salesforce.com/content/learn/trails/isv_developer_beginner`. Packages can also be used to release basic *libraries* of metadata (such as common formulas, Apex classes, and validation rules) that consultants commonly use on their projects.

To create a new package, click on **Setup** | **Apps** | **Package Manager**. Skip the **Developer Settings** part. This is used to set up the **Namespace prefix**, which is used to isolate your components from another organization's components in order to avoid naming conflicts (this is needed when you're building **managed packages**, which are special kinds of protected packages that are required for AppExchange publication).

Click on the **New** button and give the package a name and description. Then, click on the **Add** button to add components:

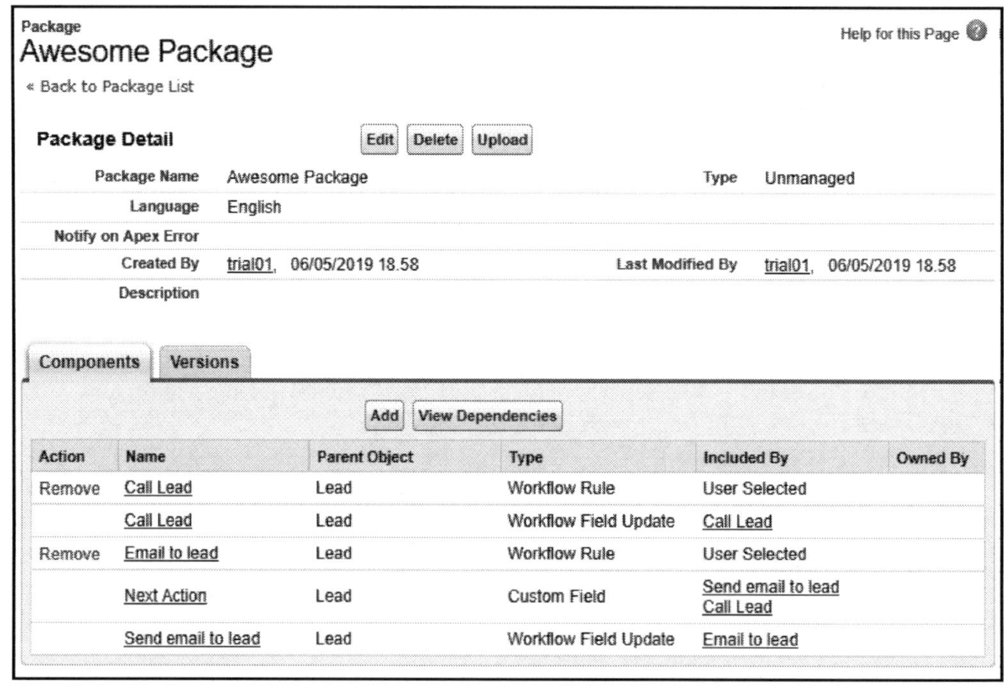

Package editing

The cool thing about packages is that Salesforce automatically adds all the related components to the package. In this example, we have just selected the workflow rules, but we can see that the engine added two field updates and a custom field.

Why do change sets differ in this way? In change sets, you are deploying from a sandbox to sandbox/production organizations, so there is a chance that some components may already be on the destination organization. On the other hand, with packages, we must ensure that everything we need is packed up and ready to be installed anywhere.

When uploading a package, we can define a version name and number (so it's easy to spot which version has been installed in a given organization), as well as an optional password for installation protection (only those who own the password can install this package), a site URL for release notes, post-installation instructions (if any), and features and object requirements.

You can add profiles or permission sets to make the administrator's life easier (only installed components will be affected on the destination organization), just like we can on change sets.

After a successful upload, you'll be granted an installation URL that anyone can use to install this package on any organization.

For a complete guide on package management, please refer to Salesforce Help at `https://help.salesforce.com/articleView?id=package_distribute_apps_overview.htmtype=5`.

Deploying changes with other tools

If we need more control over the deployment process, we can use other tools that are provided by the Salesforce platform.

The first one, which is also at the core of the other methods, is the use of **Metadata APIs**. This is a set of APIs that are used to retrieve, deploy, create, or delete metadata items.

This powerful yet simple set of methods communicate with any Salesforce organization, retrieve all kinds of metadata items, create and update a variety of configurations, and finally deploy those components in a target organization.

Like the other tools that we are going to mention, Metadata APIs don't need source and destination organizations in order to refer to the same production instance. This means you can deploy from a developer edition organization to a Full sandbox, from a developer sandbox to a sandbox, the children of different production organizations, and so on. Metadata APIs are *metadata-centric*, which means they don't need to know who is the original owner of a given item.

For a complete list of all the supported metadata types, please refer to `https://developer.salesforce.com/docs/atlas.en-us.api_meta.meta/api_meta/meta_types_list.htm`.

As an administrator, you typically never get your hands dirty with Metadata APIs; instead, you'll use tools based on these APIs (these tools take care of the communication part of the deployment).

Even though it was discontinued on October 12, 2019, I want to mention an old companion of my days as a junior developer—the **Force.com IDE** (`https://developer.salesforce.com/docs/atlas.en-us.eclipse.meta/eclipse/ide_getting_started.htm`). Even though its support has ended, if anyone has an installed version of it, the IDE can still be used (thanks to the fact that Salesforce keeps supporting old API versions for at least three years after their introduction).

This tool is based on Metadata APIs and on the Eclipse framework (a powerful and free IDE for Java developers). This tool was meant to help developers code their Apex code and Visualforce pages (and Lightning Aura Components ultimately).

To get the Force.com IDE working, all you had to do was the following:

1. Create a new project.
2. Set up the source organization's username, password, security token, and type of instance (for example, production, sandbox, developer organization, pre-release organization, or custom login URL).
3. Select the required metadata components (a developer would typically select classes, triggers, pages, components, and static resources).
4. Wait until the items were retrieved.
5. The developer did their work by changing classes or pages and deploying them to the source organization (it was as easy as hitting *Ctrl* + *S* on your keyboard).
6. Once the change was ready to be released, you selected all the components you wanted to deploy, right-clicked, and selected the **Deploy** menu item.
7. Insert the username, password, security token, and type of instance of the destination organization (that is, a production, developer edition, or sandbox instance)
8. Click on the **Deploy** button to start the deployment.

From the **Setup** | **Environments** | **Deploy** | **Deployment Status** menu, you could watch the deployment work and gather information in the case of a failure.

One of the things that I loved the most was the possibility to create different projects altogether (let's say, one for the Dev sandbox and one for the Test sandbox) and compute differences of the same file on the fly from the two organizations in order to understand what changes have been applied in both instances (when more developers work on the same Apex class, checking for changes can be a mess).

Another thing I loved was the possibility to check the whole project for a given metadata item. Let's say you wanted to know the impact of removing a given custom field. The main question would be, *"Enrico, can you tell me where this field is being used?"* By creating a Force.com project with all the available metadata, you could simply search for a string to get all the matches:

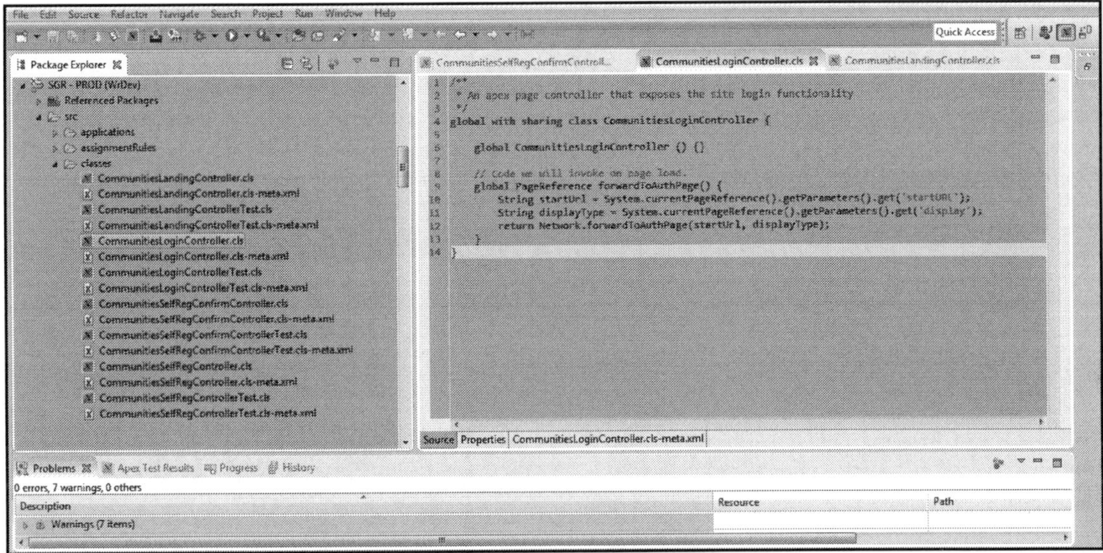

Force.com IDE workspace

Another glorious tool is the **Ant Force.com Migration Tool**. Based on Metadata APIs as well, it is a command-line tool that is meant for automated deploy operations, and due to its nature, it can be used for Continuous Integration, Continuous Deployment, or Continuous Delivery.

But what does this mean? It's a way of saying, *"Hey, when I change something and I approve it, it should be immediately deployed to the destination source."* To do this, developers would generally use a code versioning tool (that is, a tool such as Git or SVN that can keep track of all the changes that have been made to an organization's metadata) and once they had pushed a change to the version control system, an automated script would run and tell the Ant Force.com Migration Tool to activate a deployment.

If you want to find out more about the Ant Force.com Migration Tool, please refer to `https://resources.docs.salesforce.com/sfdc/pdf/salesforce_migration_guide.pdf`.

Another official tool that was created recently (and officially replaces the Force.com IDE) is the **Salesforce Extension Pack for Microsoft Visual Studio Code** (`https://forcedotcom.github.io/salesforcedx-vscode/`). With this, can do all the stuff you could do with the Force.com IDE (and more), but it also supports the new Lightning Web Components framework.

The whole tool was originally meant for **Salesforce DX** development (have a look at the Trailhead trail at `https://trailhead.salesforce.com/en/content/learn/trails/sfdx_get_started` for more information) but it was recently updated to support *project* development (a classic way to develop on Salesforce). The following screenshot shows what Visual Studio Code looks like:

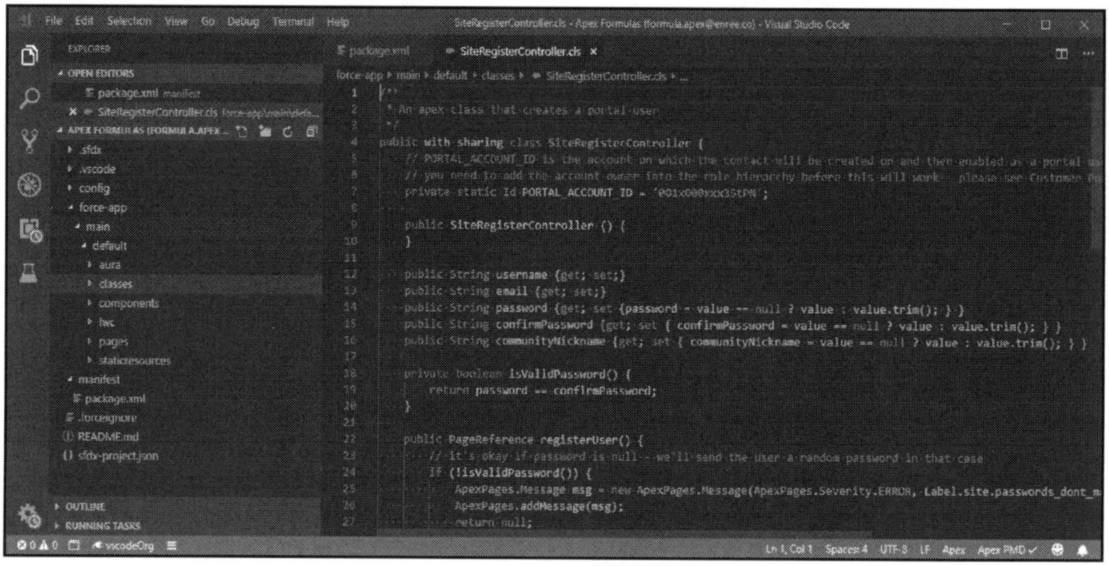

Visual Studio Code workspace

Some other famous but not free Salesforce IDEs are as follows:

- The Welkin Suite (`https://welkinsuite.com/`)
- Illuminated Cloud for the IntelliJ IDE (`http://www.illuminatedcloud.com/`)

Handling data changes

So far, we have talked extensively about how to release metadata changes, but what about data changes?

You may need to cleanse some fields on your records (due to a bug or a change request) or import a new table or even delete a given object from your organization because you don't need it anymore. In the upcoming sections, we will look at how to import and export data. Let's start with importing data using the Data Import Wizard.

Importing data with the Data Import Wizard

Salesforce provides two basic built-in ways to import data into your organization:

- **Data Import Wizard** (in-browser wizard)
- **Data Loader** (external app)

To access the **Data Import Wizard**, navigate to **Setup** | **Integrations** | **Data Import Wizard**, which brings you to the following page:

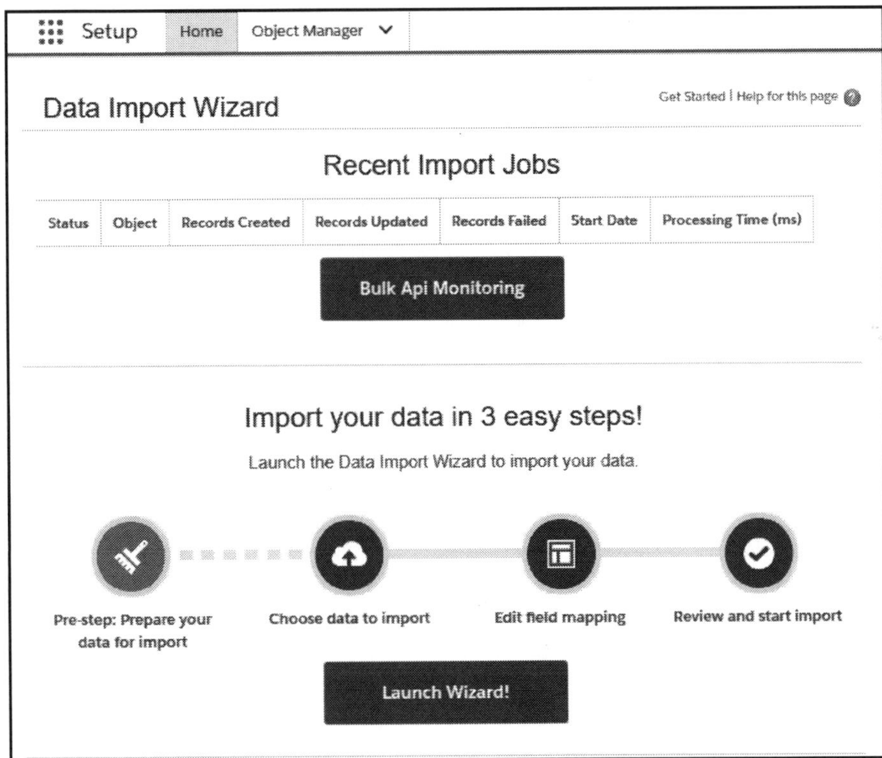

With this tool, you can import up to 50,000 records at a time and easily configure the mapping between the imported file and the objects' fields on Salesforce.

Before importing anything, you will need to load a file in CSV format (up to 100 MB in size).

You can extract a file in this format from any Salesforce report by specifying CSV as the desired format (**Export** is one of the available report object actions you can undertake):

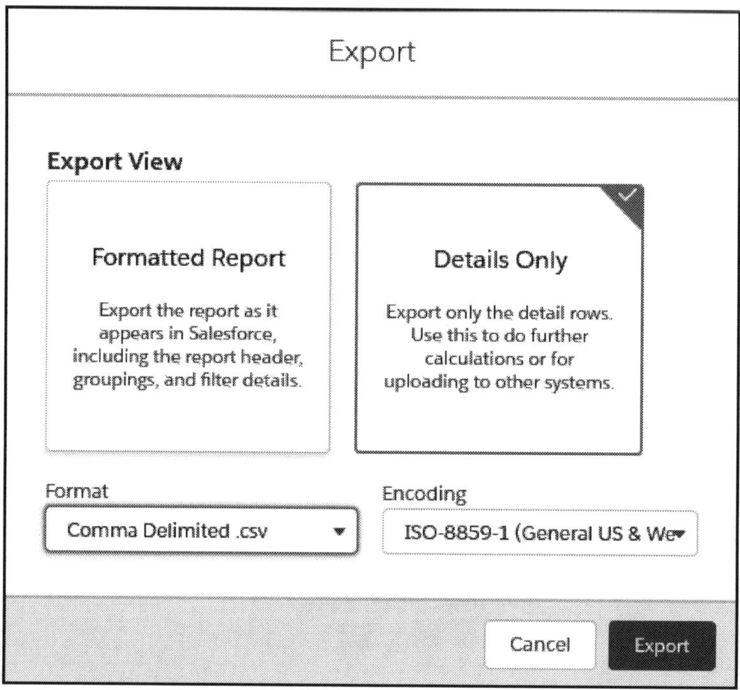

This gives you a file in the following format:

```
"Account Name";"Billing State/Province";"Type";"Rating"
"Super Gnite Ltd.";"";"Technology Partner";"Hot"
"GenePoint";"CA";"Customer - Channel";"Cold"
"United Oil & Gas, UK";"UK";"Customer - Direct";""
```

The preceding code shows semicolon-separated values enclosed in double quotes. To be compliant with the **Data Import Wizard**, replace the semicolon with a comma or tab.

You can export data from whatever source you want (for account, contact, and lead records, you can directly export CSV files from the ACT!, Gmail, or Outlook apps). The important thing is that it's in CSV format.

Before you import anything, you need to clean up your data. Ensure that the necessary header columns are there and that there are some Salesforce field labels that match them so that the import wizard will be able to automatically match the mappings.

If you import a file containing Salesforce IDs for lookup fields, remember that IDs are case-sensitive, which means that if you change the case even for a single character, the IDs won't be recognized, leading to import errors.

Use a column named **Record Owner** to match a Salesforce owner for new records, while valuing it by username, first and last name, or Salesforce ID (the import engine automatically matches the user).

Once the CSV file is ready, click on the **Launch Wizard!** button.

Once the app has been loaded, you'll be required to select the following:

- One of the available standard objects (accounts, contacts, leads, solutions, or campaign members) or a custom object.
- The kind of action you wish to take place:
    - **Add new records**: The file will contain only new records (and if a match is found, no record will be inserted).
    - **Update existing records**: The file will contain only existing records.
    - **Add new and update existing records**: The file will contain both new and existing data that needs to be updated.
- **Match by**: This is the field that is used to understand whether a record is new or already exists.
- **Which User field in your file designates record owners**: Leave this as **none** if you want new objects to be assigned to you. However, you can even use a **Salesforce ID** if you want to use the user's ID, **Name** if you want to use the user's first and last name or full username, or **External ID** if you plan to use some other external ID field for user matching.
- **Trigger workflow rules and processes for new and updated records**: Select this flag to run automations upon a successful record import.
- Select the CSV file to be imported and click **Next**.

Before starting the import wizard, you need to select/change the right field mapping:

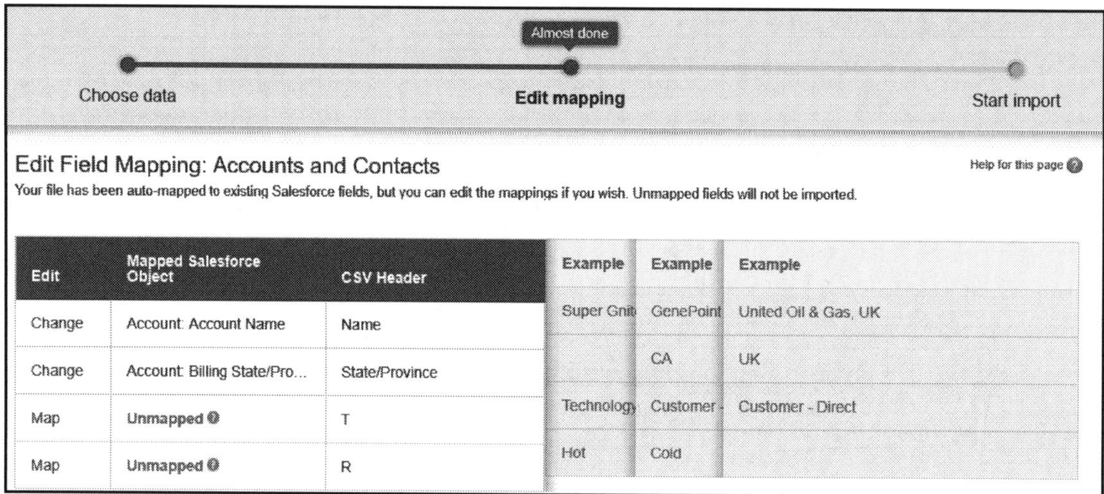

Mapping selection on the Data Import Wizard

Click on **Change** or **Map** to set up different mappings than the ones provided by the wizard.

For Accounts and Contacts, you can set up multiple mappings to refer to both objects. Click on **Next** to review these changes and start the import by clicking on the **Start Import** button (a quick review of what's going on is provided here):

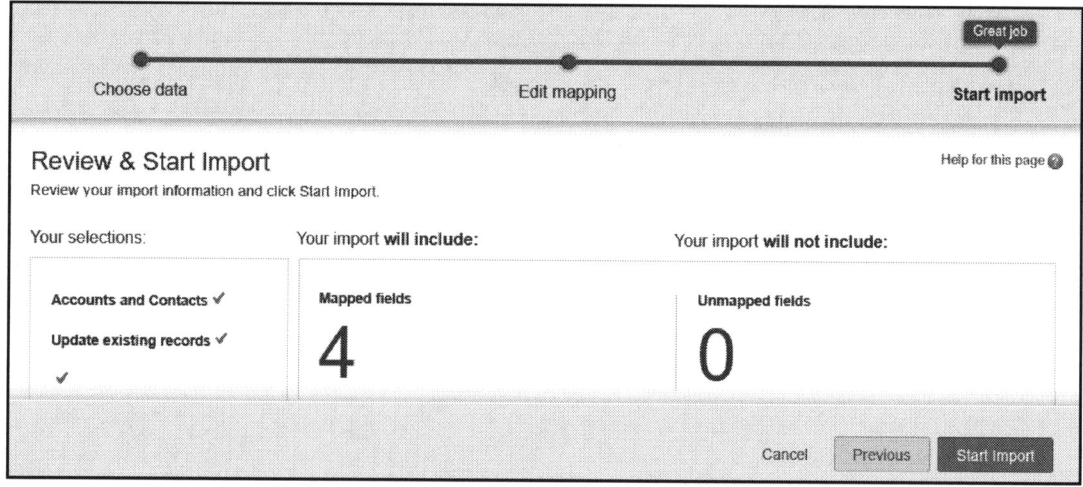

You'll be notified of job completion by email. In the meantime, you can monitor Bulk API jobs (special kinds of APIs that are used to import big data) by going to **Setup** | **Environments** | **Jobs** | **Bulk Data Load Jobs**:

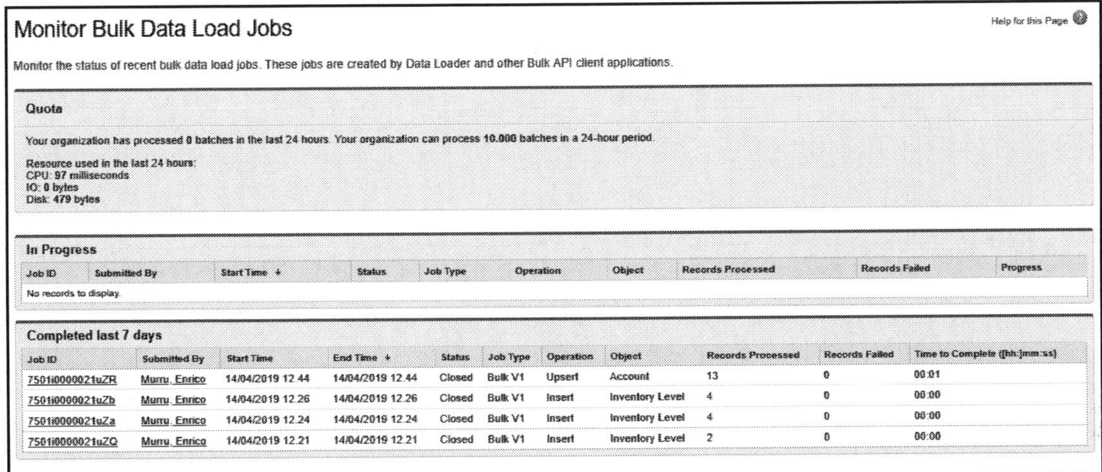

Data Import Wizard job monitoring

Remember that you can only run one import at a time, regardless of the browser or user that triggers it.

Importing data with Data Loader

Data Loader is a standalone application that's used to bulk import (and export) data. It can actually do all kinds of CRUD operations (insert, update, delete, and export).

To download the app, go to **Setup** | **Integrations** | **Data Loader** and select the download link for your operating system (Windows or macOS). The documentation links are also available on this page.

There is even a SaaS version of Data Loader called dataloader.io. It can be downloaded for free, but there will be some limitations regarding what features you can use. Alternatively, you can get the full-featured version if you're willing to pay for additional licensing costs (`https://dataloader.io/`).

Data Loader can be used via its user interface or through the command line to ease the task of automated export/imports. Let's say you have an external billing service that stores in a remote server all the bills created daily, as a CSV file. With a scheduled job on the server, you can enable Data Loader so that it loads this CSV file into Salesforce automatically (supported for servers running Windows only).

You should use Data Loader when you want to load a standard object that is not supported by the Data Import Wizard, or when you want to schedule a lot of data to be uploaded or an export on a regular basis (using the command line).

You may also need to load around 50,000 to 5,000,000 records (you can use it to load one record; there's no limitation on the lower end of the scale), but if you need to bulk update more often, you'll need an external solution, which you can find at AppExchange (`http://appexchange.salesforce.com/`).

We won't talk about this tool extensively in this book, so please refer to Salesforce's official Data Loader guide at `https://resources.docs.salesforce.com/218/latest/en-us/sfdc/pdf/salesforce_data_loader.pdf` if you wish to find out more. If you want a quick glimpse at what you can do with Data Loader, please refer to this awesome post by Salesforce Ben: `https://www.salesforceben.com/introduction-to-the-salesforce-data-loader/`.

Exporting data

In the previous section, we saw that we can export data from Salesforce in the following ways:

- **Reports**: By exporting resulting datasets in CSV (or Excel) format
- **Data Loader**: By using a SOQL query to get a CSV file that contains the results

You can use other tools or even build your own using the SOAP and REST APIs in order to run SOQL and SOSL queries. You can even use Chrome extensions to do this job on the fly (a full list of Chrome extensions, by Salesforce MVP Jitendra Zaa, can be found at `https://www.jitendrazaa.com/blog/salesforce/top-google-chrome-extensions-for-salesforce/`).

Salesforce CRM comes with a backup tool that you can leverage to export data from your organization in CSV format, back it up, and so on. This feature is called **Data Export** and can be found by going to **Setup** | **Data** | **Data Export**.

The tool allows you to do a one-time data export, though it can be scheduled on a weekly or monthly basis, depending on your Salesforce edition (only Enterprise, Performance, and Unlimited deliver the weekly option).

Click on the **Export Now** button to get to the following page:

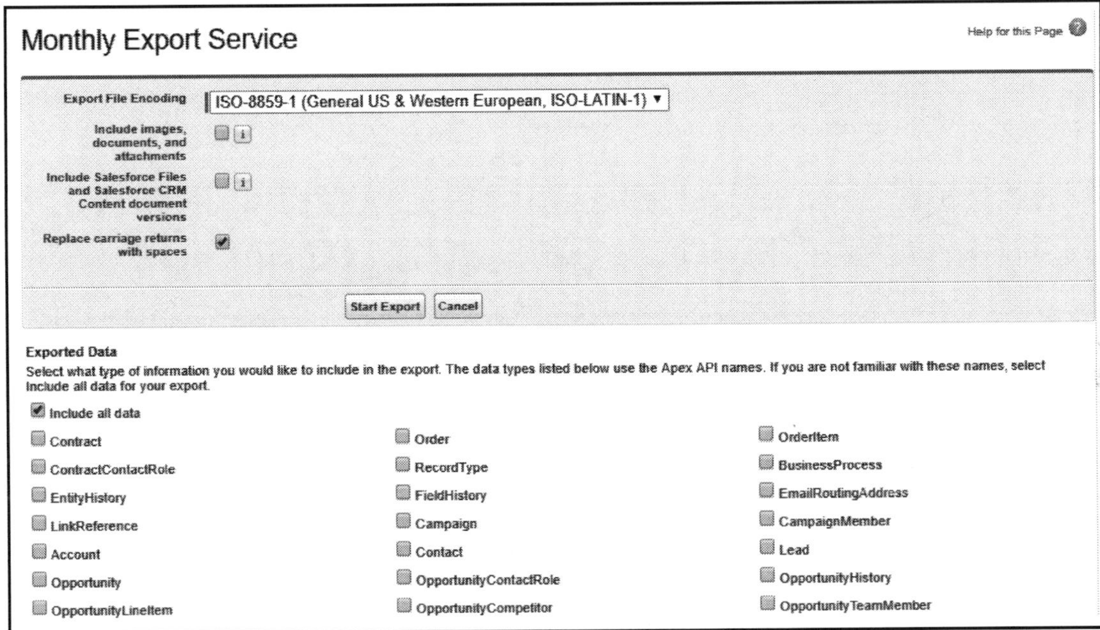

From here, do the following:

1. Choose file encoding.
2. Check the **Include images, documents, and attachments** and **Include Salesforce Files and Salesforce CRM Content document versions** checkboxes, which will create bigger files and increase the export time, respectively.
3. Check the **Replace carriage returns with spaces** box if you want to replace carriage returns/line breaks with a single space (this is useful for certain kinds of integration formats).
4. Select the kind of data you want to export. By selecting **Include all data**, you are, as the option suggests, including every Salesforce object.

The kind of objects that are exported depends on the time you create the export job, so if you are creating weekly/monthly export jobs and you create a new object after their creation, remember to update the export job by selecting **Include all data**.

When you hit the **Start Export** button a job is enqueued and, as usual, Salesforce sends a notification email when the export job has completed:

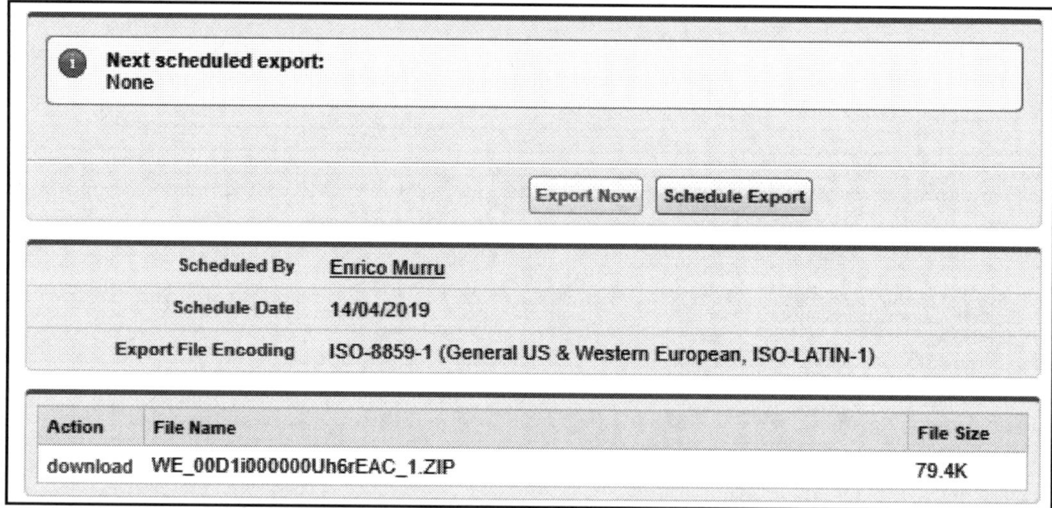

Scheduled Data Export has a similar configuration, except for the scheduled time frame:

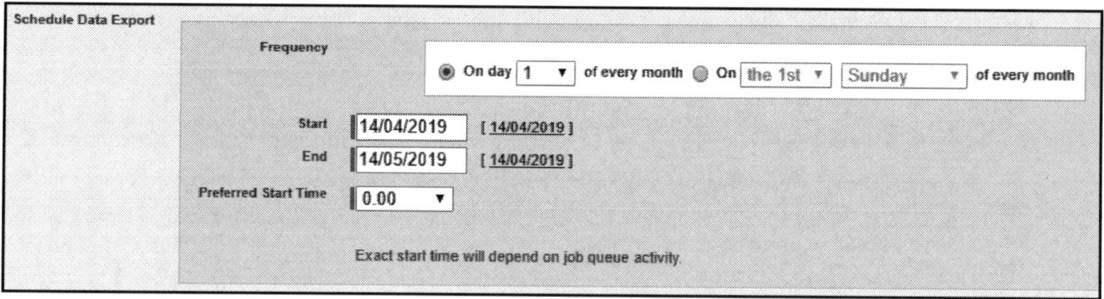

Because jobs are run according to the platform's load, sometimes, export results won't appear on the day the scheduled configuration has specified. If this happens, the job will be scheduled 7 or 29 days after the last executed job (7 for a weekly schedule, 29 for a monthly schedule).

The exported data is saved into a ZIP file that contains all the CSV files for the objects that were exported that are up to 512 MB in size. If the data you've exported is bigger than this, more ZIP files will be created.

You cannot make subsequent executions of Export Now jobs; you have to wait for the minimum time frame allowed for your organization (7 or 29 days). The exported files are available for 48 hours after their creation, after which the files are automatically deleted.

Summary

Planning your delivery strategy in advance using the proper sandbox architecture and knowing the pros and cons of every kind of organization can be critical to the success of your project. Once you and your release management team are satisfied with the strategy, you can deploy changes across organizations using change sets or put automatic delivery in place using tools such as the Force.com Migration Tool (running on Ant).

Once the metadata has been released, you can move data from organization to organization using the Import Wizard or Data Loader. The path to production release can seem hard, but don't worry—you now know about all the tools that can leverage for your Salesforce platform.

In the next chapter, we'll cover some advanced aspects regarding data modeling with relationships, validation rules, and picklist field management.

Questions

1. Some new customization has to be implemented. Where do you make your point and click approach?
    a. In production
    b. In a sandbox
    c. In a Developer organization

2. One of the developers on your team needs a sandbox to do some testing on a newly released feature of the CRM. They want this sandbox to be ready as soon as possible, and there is no need for data or massive data usage. Moreover, once the test has been completed, the sandbox should be refreshed as soon as possible. Which sandbox type would you use?
    a. Developer
    b. Developer Pro
    c. Partial Copy
    d. Full
3. Your developer team has more than 20 developers. They usually deploy on their own Developer sandbox, which is where they also run local tests. There is no particular restriction on the data that's required, nor on the refresh interval required, but you can't wait for days to refresh it. Which sandbox types would you suggest using to merge all the developments into a single organization?
    a. Developer
    b. Developer Pro
    c. Partial Copy
    d. Full
4. Which statements about Partial Copy sandboxes are false?
    a. They can host up to 5 GB worth of files and data.
    b. You need sandbox templates to define which records should be copied.
    c. They are used for development.
    d. They must have no less than 10,000 records per object.
    e. You can use sandbox templates to filter our specific records (for example, record types, picklists, and so on).
5. Where can you do performance testing?
    a. Developer Pro sandbox
    b. Production
    c. Partial Copy sandbox
    d. Full sandbox

6. Which statement is correct about Full sandboxes?
    a. The refresh time is 30 days.
    b. You can select a sandbox template.
    c. They have the same storage as their Production organization.
    d. All field tracking history is automatically copied.
    e. By selecting fewer objects to be copied, you can enhance the copy speed.
7. You want to clone a sandbox. In this situation, which of the following statements is true?
    a. The Destination sandbox must have a *higher* type than its source (for example, if the source is Developer Pro, the destination must be a Partial Copy or Full sandbox).
    b. The Destination sandbox must have a *lower* type than its source (for example, if the source is Developer Pro, the destination must be a developer sandbox).
    c. The Destination sandbox must be the same type as its source.
8. After a sandbox's creation, the Process Builder doesn't send a notification email to a given user. What could be the cause of this?
    a. Email deliverability has been set to **System Email Only**.
    b. Email deliverability has been set to **User Email Only**.
    c. The sandbox is not active.
    d. The Process Builder is not active.
    e. The contact record's email fields have been modified with the `.invalid` suffix.
9. You've developed a Salesforce app with a custom object, page layout, a Process Builder, and a flow on a Developer Edition organization that's been created solely for this development task, and you want to bring the metadata you just created into one of your sandboxes. Which tools can you use for this?
    a. Change sets
    b. The Force.com Migration Tool
    c. An IDE such as Visual Studio Code
    d. Packages
    e. Data Loader
    f. Data Import Wizard

10. You've developed a Salesforce app with a custom object, page layout, a Process Builder, and a flow on a sandbox and you want to deploy this configuration to production. Which tools can you use for this?
    a. Change sets
    b. The Force.com Migration Tool
    c. An IDE such as Visual Studio Code
    d. Packages
    e. Data Loader
    f. Data Import Wizard
11. What is a deployment connection?
    a. The deployment direction of a package
    b. A way to allow inbound change sets from sandbox/production organizations
    c. A way to allow outbound change sets to sandbox/production organizations
12. Which steps are required to deploy a change set?
    a. Activate the deployment connections and then create, upload, validate, and deploy the change set.
    b. Create, upload, validate, and deploy the change set and then activate the deployment connections.
    c. Activate the deployment connections and then upload, validate, and deploy the change set.
    d. Activate the deployment connections and then upload, deploy, and validate the change set.
13. If you want to use an IDE for deployment, which of the following do you need?
    a. Username and password of the origin organization
    b. Login URL of the origin organization
    c. Change set name
    d. Login URL of the destination organization
    e. Username and password of the destination organization

14. You need to export data from your organization. Which tools can you use for this?
    a. Change sets
    b. The Force.com Migration Tool
    c. An IDE such as Visual Studio Code
    d. Packages
    e. Data Loader
    f. Data Import Wizard
15. If you want to upload a file to the Data Import Wizard, what file format should you use?
    a. A CSV file with comma-separated values
    b. A CSV file with tab-separated values
    c. ZIP
    d. PDF
    e. A CSV file with semicolon-separated values
16. You need to insert 40,000 leads. Which tool should you use for this?
    a. Data Loader
    b. Data Import Wizard
    c. dataloader.io
    d. Change sets
    e. The Force.com Migration Tool
17. You need to export all the cases automatically once a day. What should you use for this?
    a. Data Import Wizard
    b. Data Export Wizard
    c. Data Loader

2
Section 2: Data Model Management

In this section, you will learn how to extend the capabilities of Salesforce objects by using advanced relationships, creating effective and reliable validation rules, and understanding master picklist management.

This section includes the following chapter:

- `Chapter 4`, *Extending Custom Objects*

4
Extending Custom Objects

One of the main tasks of a Salesforce admin is the definition of the data model that holds all your CRM data. If you are reading this book, you certainly know how to create new custom objects and fields: mastering data model customization is, without any doubt, a skill you should acquire if you want to be an advanced administrator.

In this chapter, we'll learn the following topics:

- Advanced aspects of object relationships
- An in-depth overview of validation rules
- Advanced aspects of picklist management

Advanced aspects of object relationships

As experienced administrators, we already know the basics of the relationships between Salesforce objects: they are links between different objects that allow you to connect different records all together. The best and easiest way to get a view of all relations between objects is the **Schema Builder**, which can be found at **Setup** | **Objects and Fields** | **Schema Builder**.

When we have a lot of relations, having a whole picture of how the objects relate to each other can be a hard job, and this tool can help to untangle the problem. Be careful! Don't select all the objects in your org; otherwise, all we will see is a plate of spaghetti, as shown in the following screenshot:

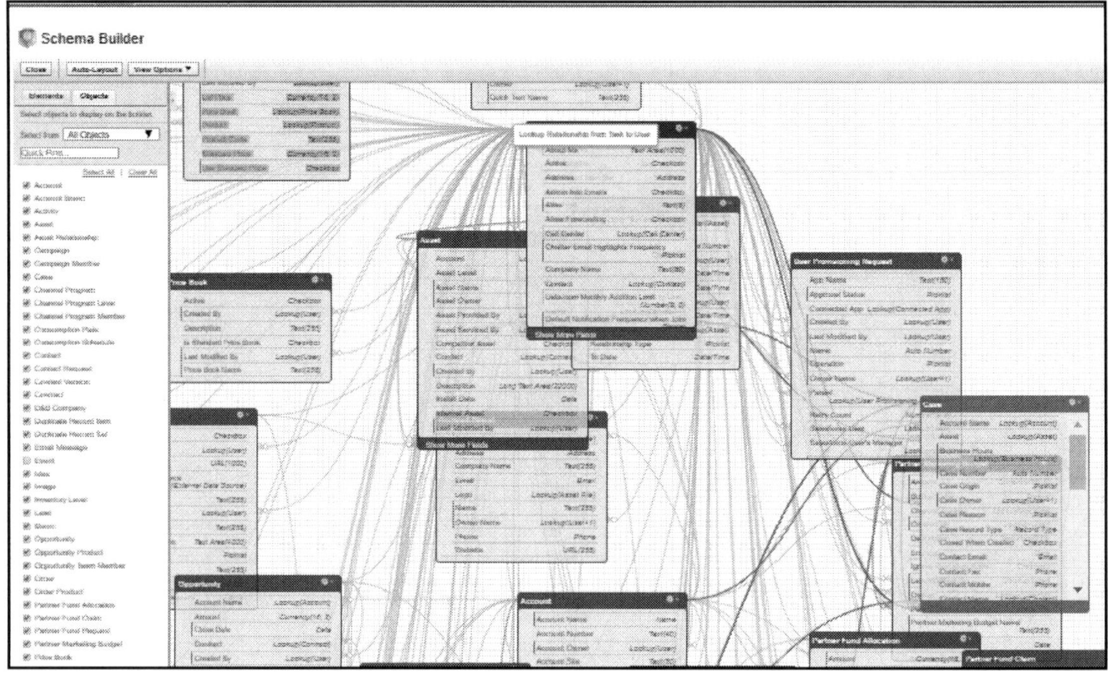

Using Schema Builder to inspect object relationships

On the left sidebar, let's select a few objects, such as `Account`, `Contact`, `Case`, and `Opportunity`. We will get the following view:

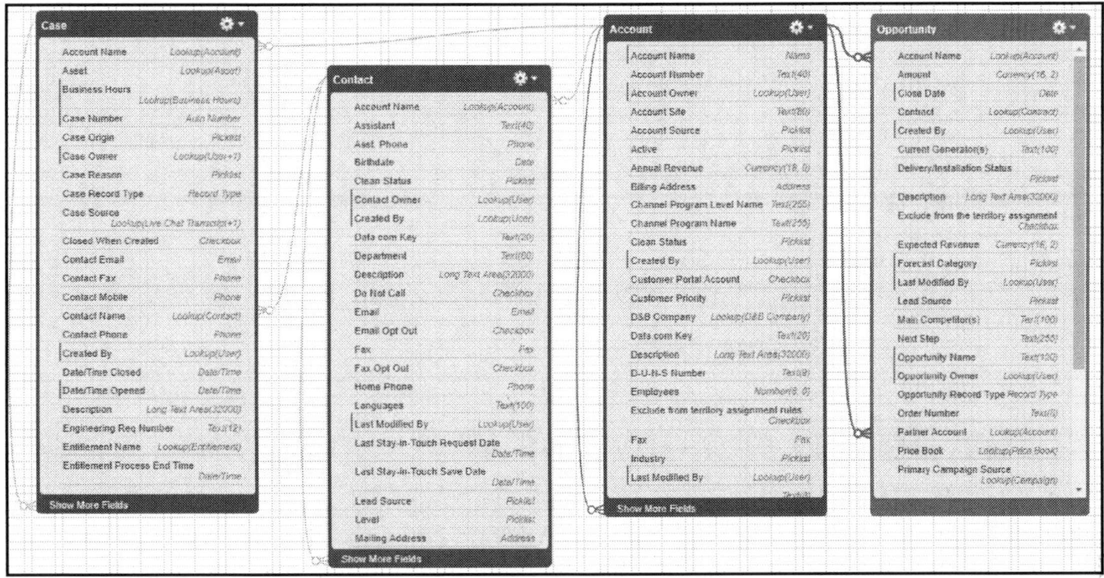

Account-related relations

Each connector starts from the `child` object (the end with the small circle) and ends up on the parent object. We can then deduce the following:

- The `Case` object is related to itself (which means that it is related to another record of the same type), `Contact`, and `Account`.
- The `Contact` object is related to itself (if we have a look at all of the fields belonging to `Contact`, we'll find the `ReportsTo` field, which relates a contact with a parent contact) and to its parent `Account`.
- The `Opportunity` object has two relations with the `Account` object (one is the **Account** field and the other is **PartnerAccount** field).
- Finally, the `Account` object has a single relation with itself (the **ParentAccount** field).

If we add the `User` and `Contract` objects to this picture, the mess becomes excessive, and it isn't so easy to deduce every relation (try it yourself).

And all of this is all about standard relations on the Sales/Service Cloud data model. Imagine how much spaghetti you can add with custom relationships!

Salesforce provides different kinds of relationships between objects. These are as follows:

- Master–detail relationships
- Many-to-many relationships
- Lookup relationships
- Hierarchical relationships
- External relationships

We'll also be covering a special kind of field called a **roll-up field**, and considerations about **formula fields** regarding relationships.

Master–detail relationships

The master–detail relationship links two objects in a strong way: children are close to their parent and are strongly related. So this type of relation is usually used to create a detail record.

Think about adding a `Case Detail` custom object that stores multiple case details, such as multiple products, addresses, or repeated business data (for example, energy readings coming from all contacts' smart home devices) related to the same service request (`Case` record). Those details have no meaning without the original `Case`; that's why we choose a master–detail relationship to design this specific model.

When we create a new master–detail relationship, the first thing to select is the `parent` object.

Note that a master–detail field cannot be created on a standard object. This is a platform limitation that any admin should be aware of.

Let's say we have a `Case Detail` custom object with diverse custom fields, and, as mentioned earlier, we want it to be a child of the `Case` object. Jump to **Setup** | **Object Manager**| **Case Detail object**| **Fields & Relationships** | **New Field** | **Master-Detail relationship**, and then select the parent object as **Case** on the first available picklist with a list of the available objects.

You cannot create a master–detail field on an object that is related to the same object type.

After the `parent` object type is selected, we'll define the relationship details:

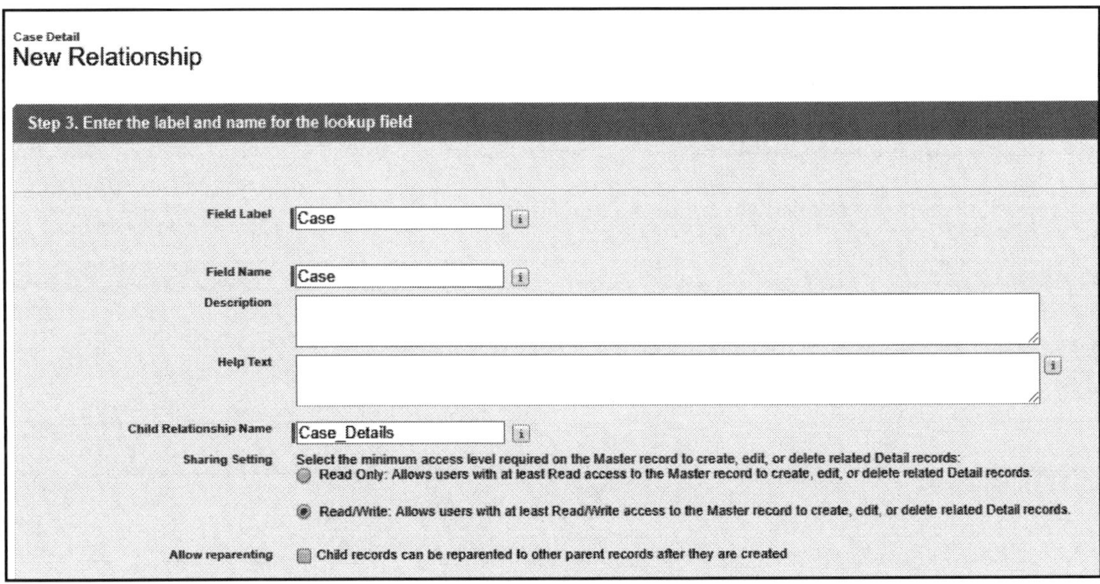

Master–detail relationship options

Given the field name and child relationship name (which is used when SOQL-querying children records directly from the parent), we can define the minimum access level on the master record needed for the users to have complete access to the child object.

Select **Read Only** or **Read-Write** for the minimum access level on the `parent` object. In our scenario, let's leave this to **Read-Write** because we have decided that the `Case Detail` object data should follow the parent record's access.

In this scenario, sales reps who have read-only access to `Case` records will be able to read `Case Detail` objects, but will have no way to create, edit, or delete them.

The `Child` objects should usually strongly relate to their parents, since a few platform releases ago, you could reparent a `child` object. Using the **Allow reparenting** flag facilitates this possibility.

The last section of the master–detail configuration wizard is related to lookup filters. We can choose a filter based on the fields, namely the current object, parent object, current user, current user's profile, current user's role, or applying custom logic (conditions with custom and/or chaining).

A filter may be required or be optional. The user can receive a custom error message if the filter is mandatory or simply a suggestion filter. Users can easily remove filters and select whichever record they want.

Finally, a **Lookup Window Text** field guides the user as to the selection (we are explaining why this filter is in place, but it only works in Salesforce Classic) and the **Active** filter can be used to temporarily disable the filter.

This is what the final configuration looks like:

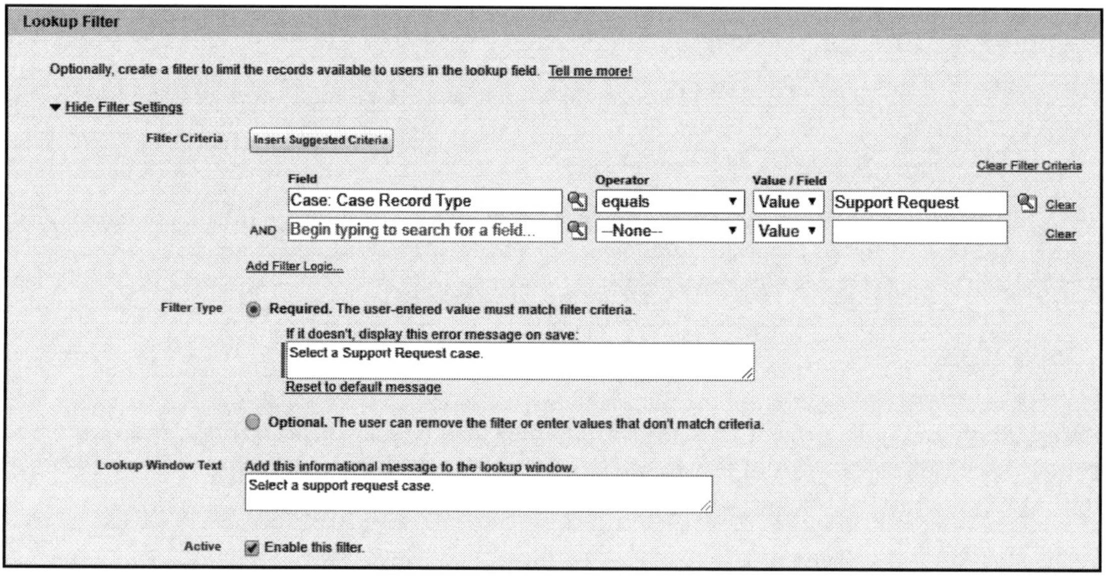

Master–detail filter configuration

Click on the **Next** button at the bottom of the page to jump to the next step. Note that the **Field-Level Security** (**FLS**) for the new object's field defaults to `Visible`/`Writable`, and that the master–detail lookup is a required field by default (after all, you cannot have a child without a master record):

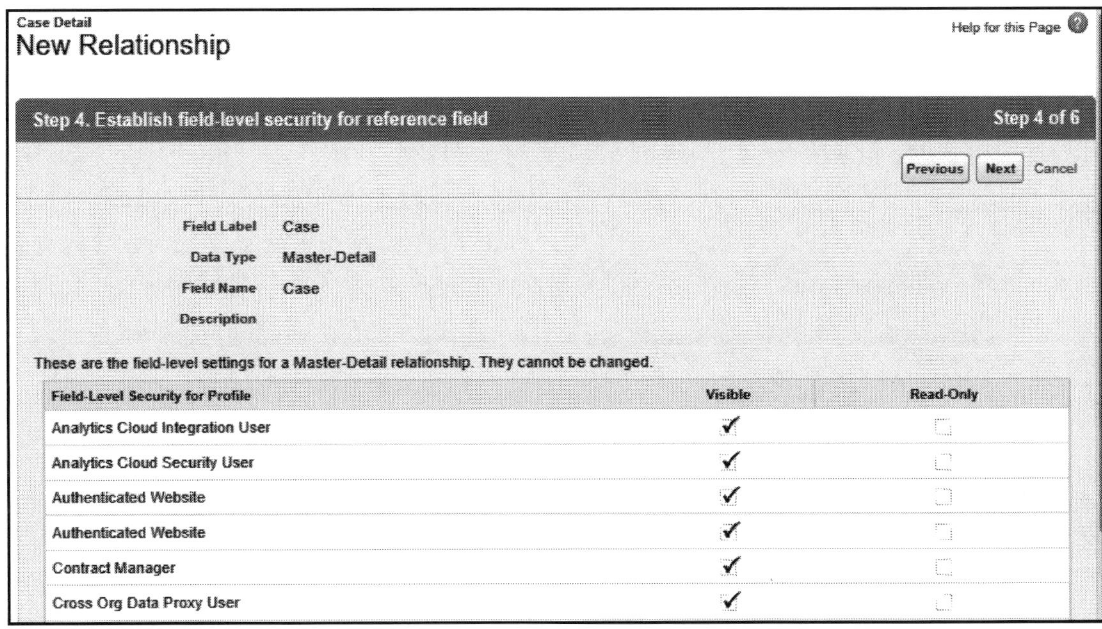

Master-detail field has a fixed FLS configuration

Click on **Next** to select the proper object page layout where the new field must be placed. Even now, the **Case Detail** page layout is mandatorily selected, as the field is required:

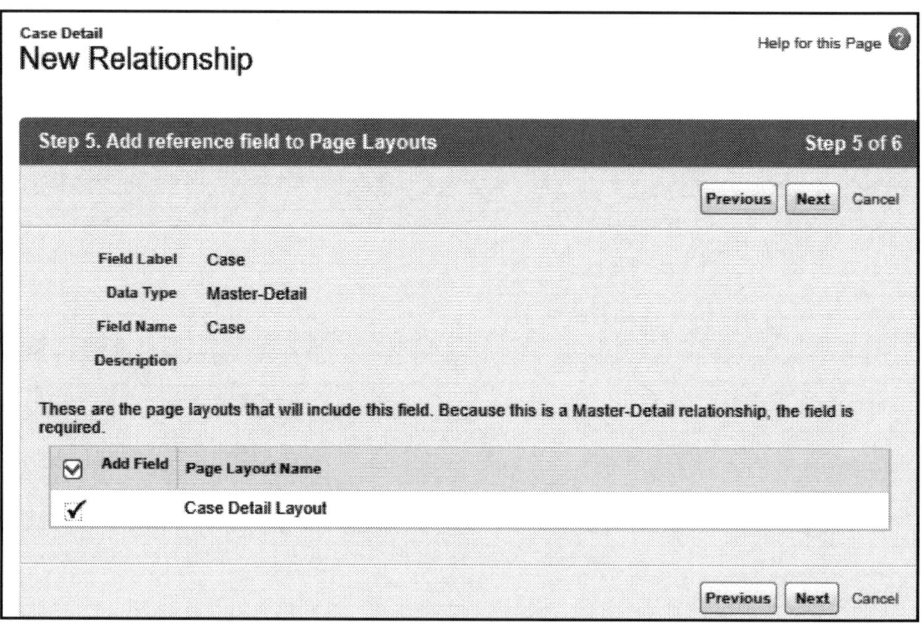

Master-detail field page layout selection

Click on **Next** again and select the `Master` object (`Case`) page layout in which the new **Case Details-** related list should be placed (this last step is only available for relationship field types):

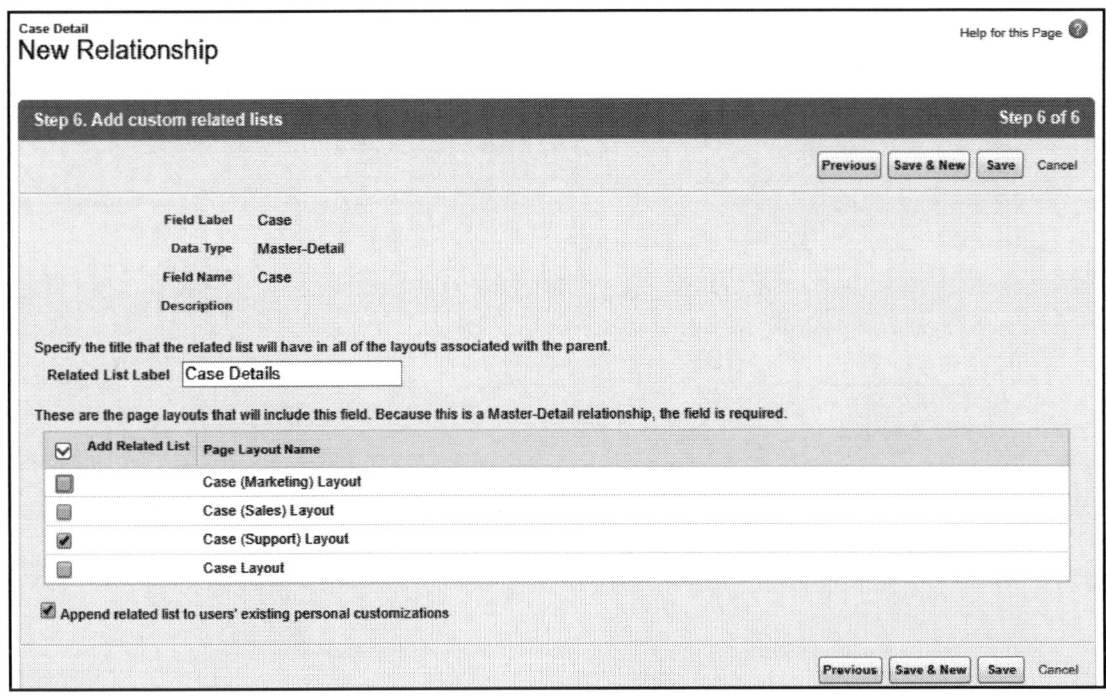

Master–detail related list inclusion on the parent object's layouts

Because we put in place a filter on the relationship that matches only *support* cases, selecting only the **Case (Support) Layout** makes perfect sense.

Create a master–detail relationship only when the object has no records at all (otherwise, Salesforce doesn't know which are the parents of the record already on the dataset). You can create a lookup field instead, populate it for all your current objects, and then convert the field into a master–detail relationship.

To test the relationship filters, let's create a new `Custom Object` tab from **Setup** | **User Interface** | **Tabs** | **New** in the **Custom Object Tabs** section and add it to the **Service (standard__service)** app:

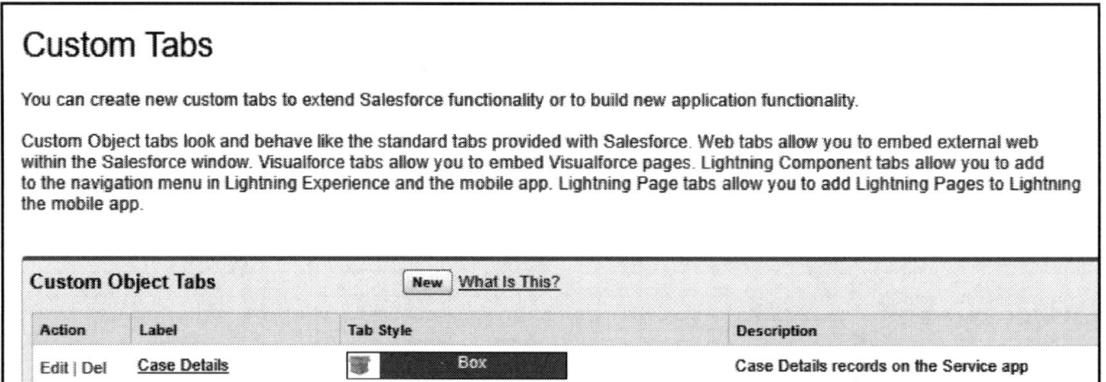

Case Details custom tab

Now, exit the setup and jump to the **Service** app, which looks as follows:

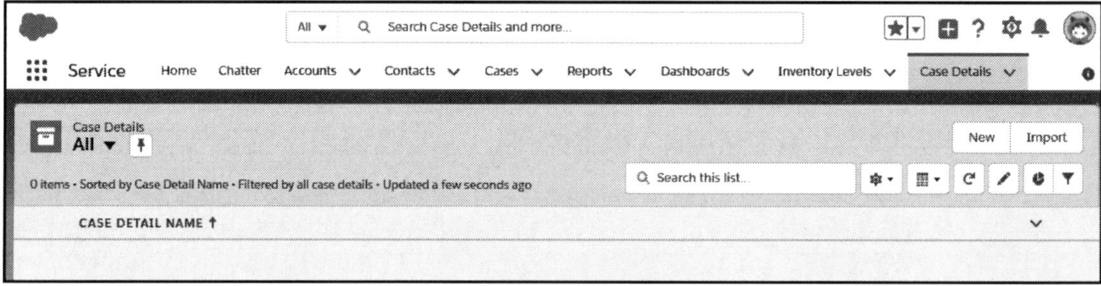

Case Details tab in action

Click on the **New** button and create a new record. The only available field is the **Case** master–detail relationship. Select **+ New Case** and create a new record with the unexpected record type (**Sales Request**):

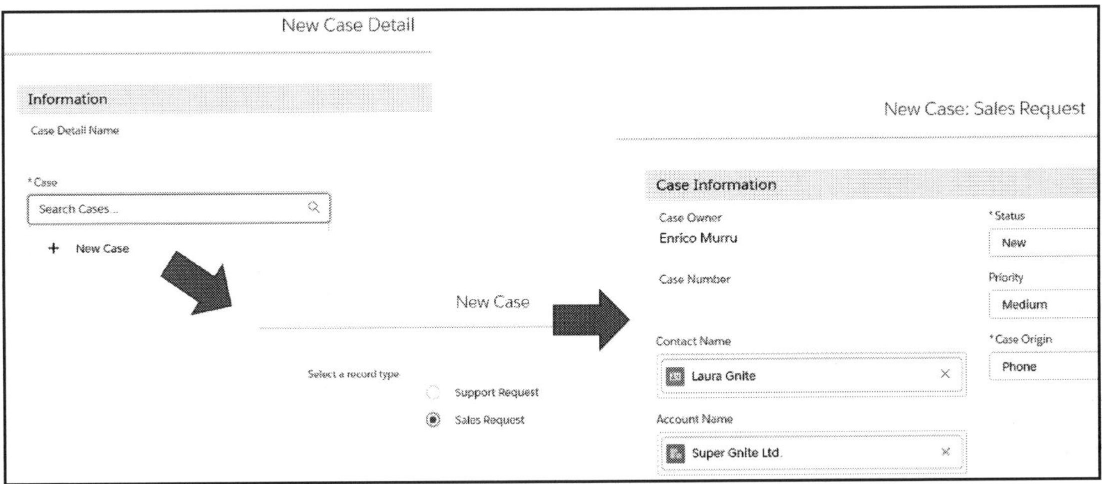

Case creation within a case detail record

Click on **Save** to save the case. The new record should now be related to the case detail record we are trying to create. Hit the **Save** button on the **New Case Detail** wizard to trigger the following error message:

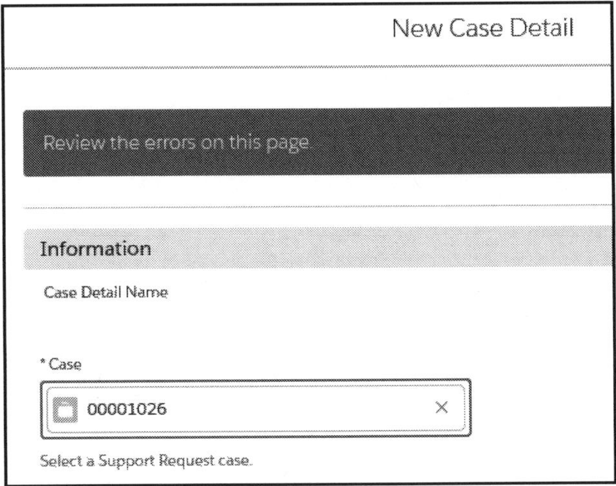

Master–detail filter in action

If we select a **Support Request** record type in the previous step, then the case detail is saved as expected.

This is what you get in the lookup window in Classic mode (have a look at the initial **Select a support request case** message):

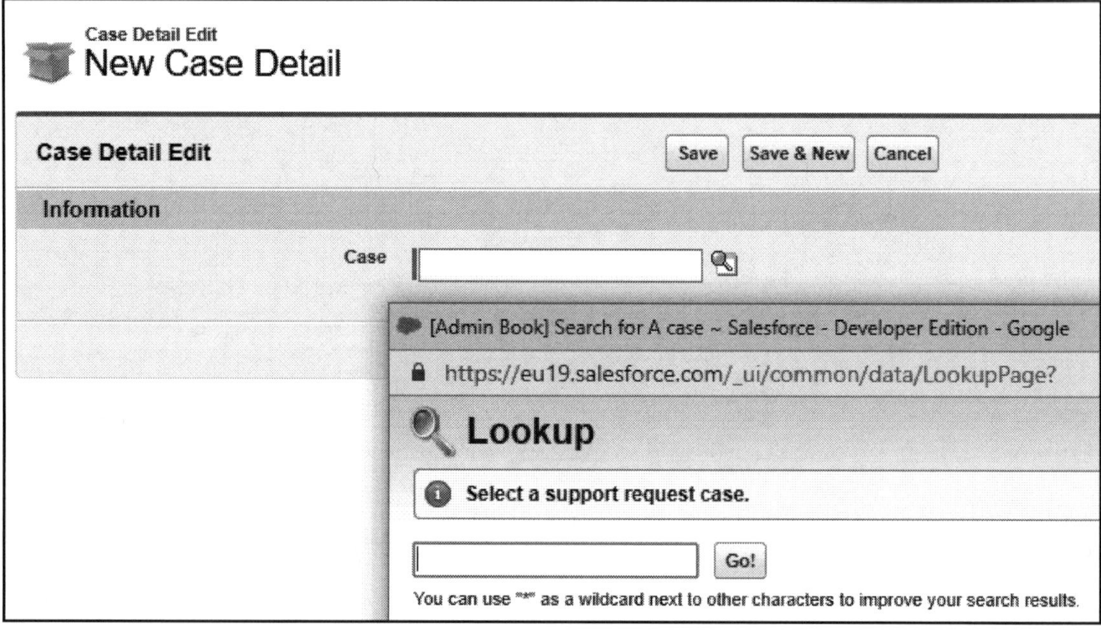

Master–detail lookup window selection in Salesforce Classic

What's peculiar about master–detail relationships? The thing to note is that by deleting the master record, we are deleting its children as well (and when we undelete them—that is, restoring them from the bin—it will automatically undelete the children as well). However, if you delete one of the children first, and then delete the master record and then undelete it, the first deleted child will not be undeleted.

A child record inherits the master record's owner; that's why sharing rules and manual sharing is not available on child records. For the same reason, children inherit their master record's access level.

A custom object can have up to 2 master–detail relationships, up to 40 total relationship fields, and up to 5 active lookup filters (go to **Setup** | **Object Manager** | **Custom Object** | **Object Limits** for a full list). You can have a maximum of three master–detail levels and, within this hierarchy, the records cannot be referenced more than once. If it is a detail record on a given multilevel relationship, then it cannot be the master of another multilevel relationship.

For *data skew* limits, remember not to parent more than 10,000 child records to a master record.

Roll-up fields

A roll-up is a special kind of field that is allowed only on a master object—that is, objects that are on the master side of a master–detail relationship. These fields are used to summarize child fields, such as getting the number of case details parented to a given `Case`, or getting the total amount of invoice records related to an `Account`.

Let's take our `Case Detail` object and add a new custom field called **Invoice Amount** with the `Currency` type, as shown in the following screenshot (you should already have the necessary skills to set up this configuration):

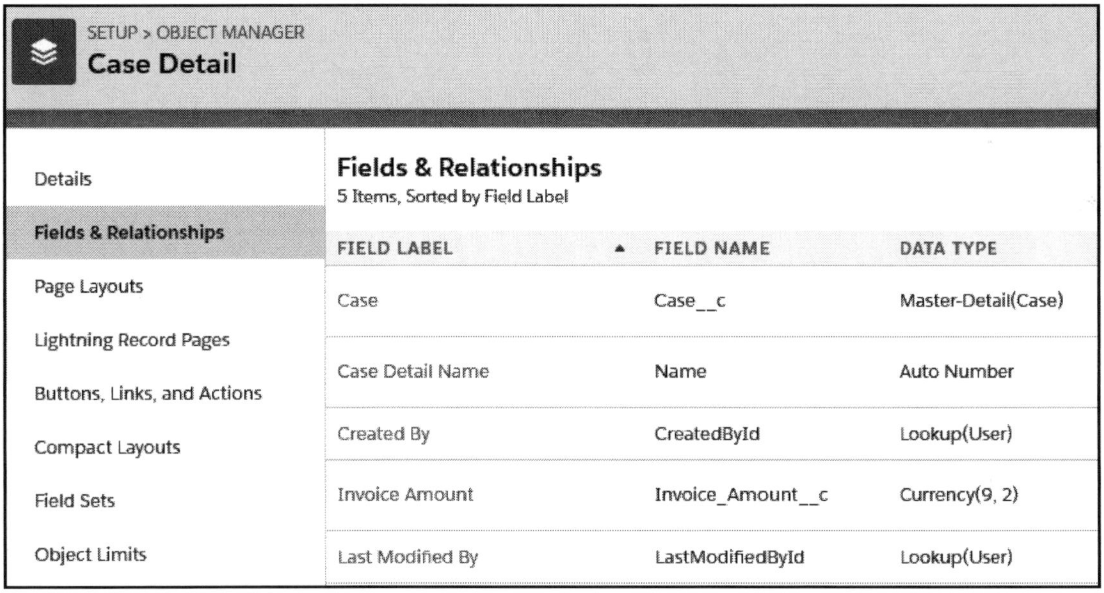

SETUP > OBJECT MANAGER
Case Detail

Details
Fields & Relationships
Page Layouts
Lightning Record Pages
Buttons, Links, and Actions
Compact Layouts
Field Sets
Object Limits

Fields & Relationships
5 Items, Sorted by Field Label

FIELD LABEL	FIELD NAME	DATA TYPE
Case	Case__c	Master-Detail(Case)
Case Detail Name	Name	Auto Number
Created By	CreatedById	Lookup(User)
Invoice Amount	Invoice_Amount__c	Currency(9, 2)
Last Modified By	LastModifiedById	Lookup(User)

Case Detail fields

Let's get back to the `Case` object (the master of the relationship) and create a new **Roll-up Summary** field called Number of details that should show up the number of details related to the current `Case`:

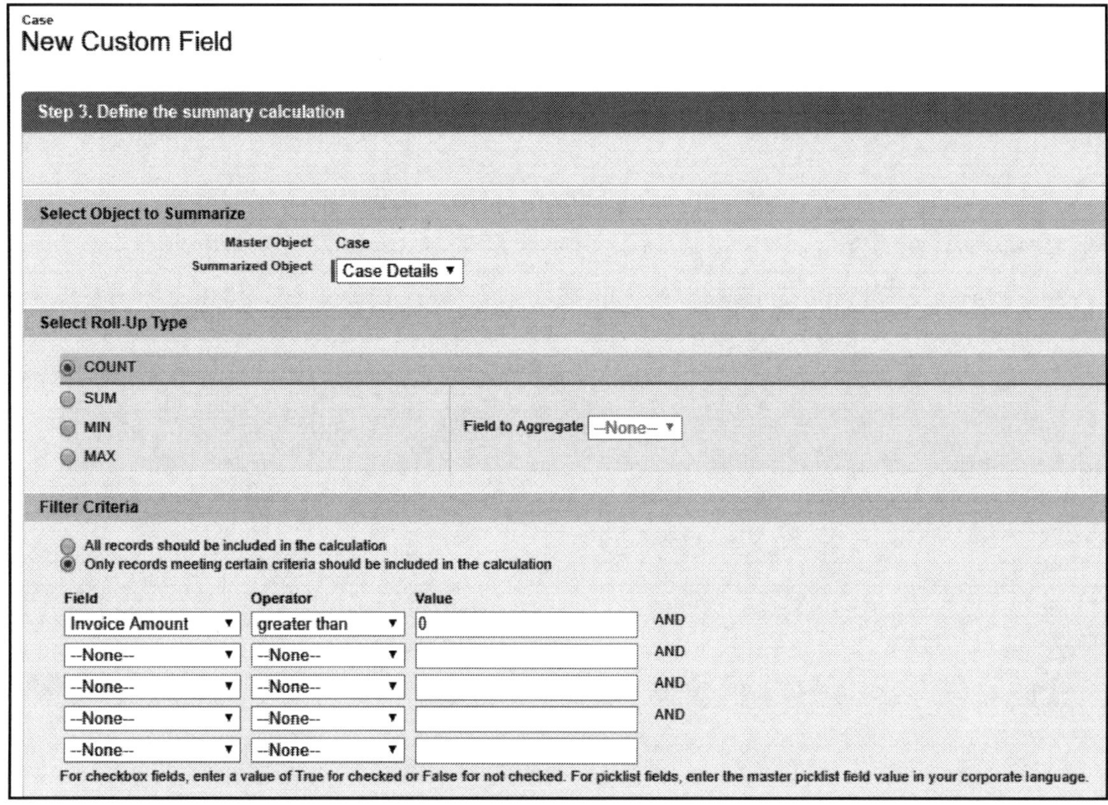

The roll-up field counts the number of child objects

We are selecting the **COUNT** roll-up type and applying a filter so that only case detail records with an amount greater than **0** are selected.

Let's create another roll-up field named **Total Amount** that sums up all the **Case Detail Invoice Amount** fields (using the `SUM` roll-up type with no filter).

Lastly, let's create a new roll-up field called **Maximum Amount** that should display the highest amount among the children objects (let's use the **MAX** roll-up type).

Create a new `Case` and some related children with different **Invoice Amount** values. You should get a result like the following:

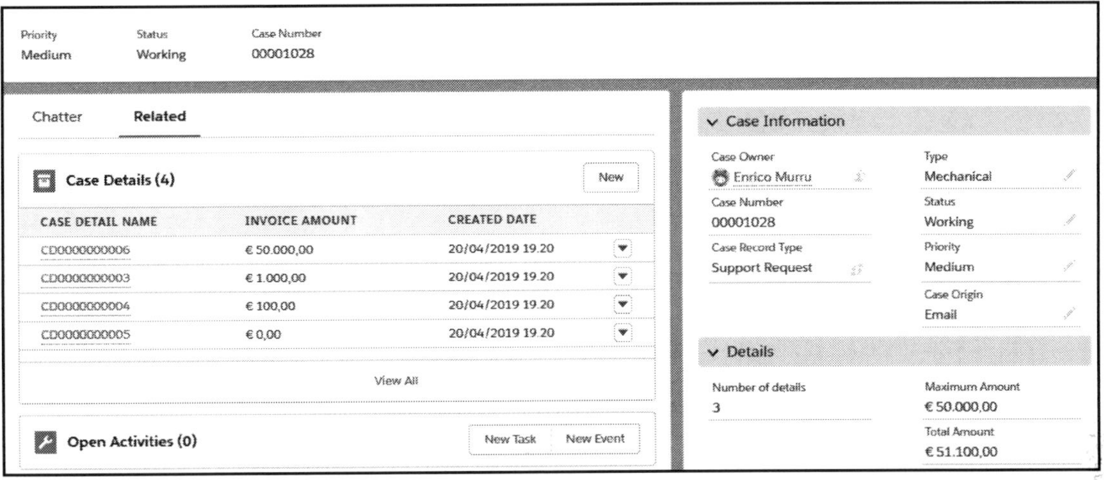

Roll-up fields on the Case object

After a few `Case` layout changes to better highlight the required information, we can see four case details with different **Invoice** amount values (sorted by this value), as well as the following:

- **Number of details** is 3: We have an invoice with an **Invoice Amount** of € 0
- **Maximum Amount** is € 50,000
- **Total Amount** is € 51,100: This is the sum of all invoices, irrespective of the amount

All the calculations are done by the platform in the background.

There is a limitation: if you delete a child record, roll-up fields are not recalculated automatically. For this, you should use the **Force a mass recalculation of this field** option in the **Edit** wizard of the roll-up field.

As a general rule, calculating a new roll-up field can take up to 30 minutes.

You can have up to 25 roll-up fields per object (refer to the **Object Limits** links on the **Object Manager**).

Take care when using roll-up fields and setting up their field-level security. If a user doesn't have access to a child record's field used in a master record's roll-up field, the calculated value is shown anyway despite FLS settings.

We can create special roll-up fields on standard objects, such as `Account` (rolling up to opportunities) or `Opportunity` (rolling up to opportunity products).

For further details and the limitations of roll-up fields, refer to Salesforce Help at `https://help.salesforce.com/articleView?id=fields_about_roll_up_summary_fields.htmtype=5`.

Many-to-many relationships

Using master–detail fields, we can set up the so-called **many-to-many** relationships, which are a way to link a given record to more than one record using `Junction` objects.

When do you need it? Imagine that you want to link a `Case` with multiple `Assets`:

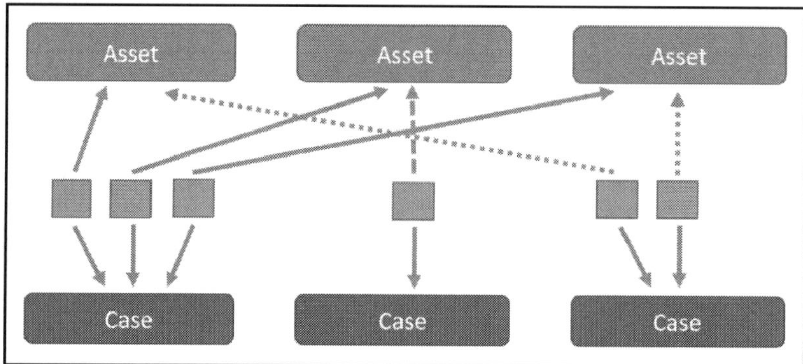

Many-to-many relationships in action

By using a many-to-many relationship, you can link a given `Case` to more than one `Asset` record.

The `Junction` object is a custom object that holds two different master–detail fields: the first master–detail field created is promoted to be the primary relation and the primary master record *masters* deletion, undeletion, and sharing the look and feel (such as the icon and page color) of the child record (in the previous picture, we can say that `Asset` is the primary record). The second master–detail on the `Case` is the secondary relation, which does not *master* any particular behavior.

Lookup relationships

The lookup field is similar to the master–detail relation, as it is used to link two objects without having the same strong binding between the parent and child records.

This means that sharing is not inherited, you cannot have roll-up fields, the child record has its own owner, and if you delete the parent record, then the child is not automatically deleted, and you can look up the same object type.

Creating a lookup field is quite similar to creating the master–detail type:

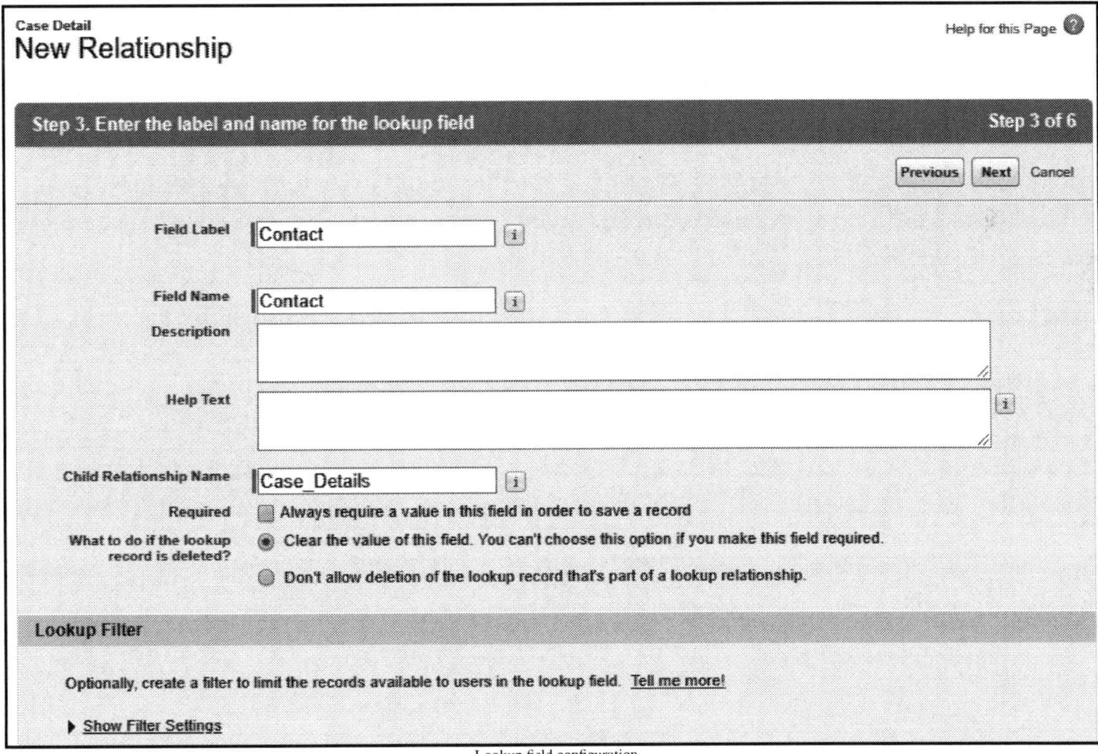

Lookup field configuration

The only difference is that you don't have the `Access` section, just the `What to do if the lookup record is deleted?` option. If the parent record is deleted, you can choose to blank the field or throw an error so that the user is forced to update this relation before deleting the parent.

Field history tracking won't record the lookup field's deletion.

As lookup is not a required field (unlike a master-detail field), you can decide to put it as **Required**.

Filters apply the same way that we saw earlier when we looked at the master–detail field type.

If the main object is a custom object, then you can ask Salesforce Support to enable the **Delete this record also** option, which makes the lookup close to a master–detail relation, at least regarding the deletion behavior: this is called **cascading delete**.

Be aware that cascading delete allows a user to delete a child record they may not have access to.

Lookups can reference the same object type (which is not allowed in master–detail relationships), creating a so-called **self-relationship**: the only limitation is that you cannot look up a record with itself (this is called a **circular reference**).

You can convert a lookup relation into a master–detail relation only if the child records have a field for the master record, whereas you can convert a master–detail into a lookup only if you don't have any roll-up field on the `master` object. A special kind of lookup relationship is the **self relationship**—that is, a lookup that points to the same object type it is originating from. For example, the **Account**, **Case**, and **Campaign** objects all have a `Parent` lookup field that points to the same object type.

Hierarchical relationships

Hierarchical relationships are an exclusive property of the `User` object, and they are used to relate users to each other, following a hierarchy.

When creating a custom field on the `User` object, no other relationship is available other than the hierarchical relationship:

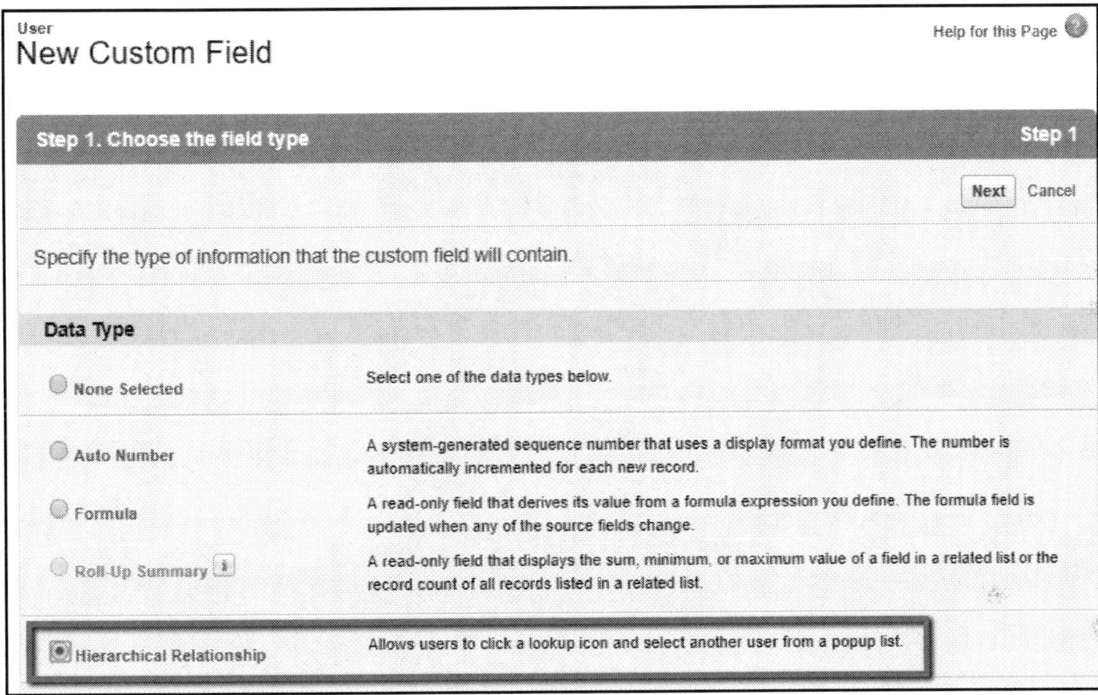

Hierarchical Relationship field type on the User object

This special kind of lookup is used to select only users above a hierarchical level—that is, users who do not directly or indirectly refer to themselves (so my parent user must not be a parent user for one of my child users). The following relation between users is therefore not allowed because **Gustav** is the manager of **Giuseppe**, who is himself the manager of **Gustav**:

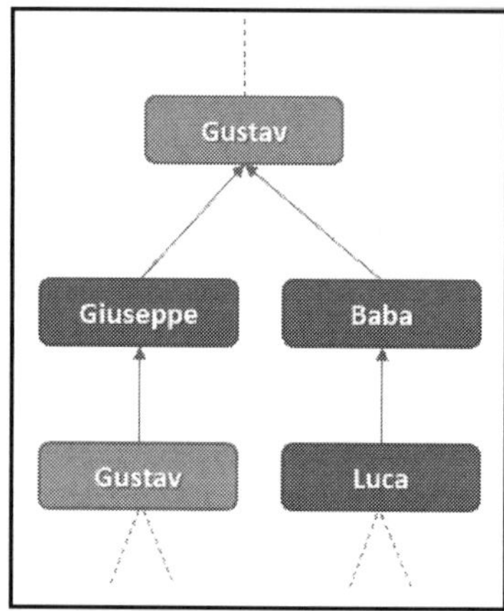

A misconfiguration of a hierarchical lookup setup between users

Formula fields and relations

We can define formula fields that reference related objects (from child to parent only, not vice versa). They are called **cross-object formulas**.

The following is an example of a custom formula field that shows the case's subject on the case detail record:

```
Case__r.Subject + '(' + Case__r.RecordType.Name +')'
```

This formula field will display the parent case's **Subject** field and the case record type's name:

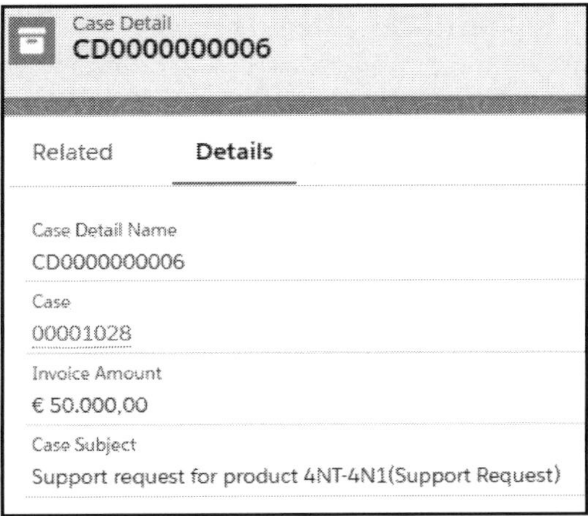

Cross-object formula example

We can reach a grandparent object that is 10 levels away from the current object.

Think about the account's **Parent** field. You can create a hierarchy of accounts and you can reach into a custom formula from a child `Account` to the fields of a parent `Account` that is the fourth parent.

We can create up to 10 unique relations between a child object and related objects.

This means that if you have 15 different lookups on a given record, you can reference at most 10 different object types in the child object formulas. This limit applies to formula fields, but also formulas on rules (such as workflow rules or validation rules) and lookup filters.

External relationships

We're not covering external data sources and external objects in this book, but it is useful to know the concept of external and indirect lookups.

External data sources are a way to define a connection between Salesforce and a legacy system where business data is stored, but it has been decided not to migrate that data inside Salesforce. The reasons behind this choice are that external data may only be historical data that service agents only need to read when necessary (thereby not counting vis-^-vis overall storage limits) or frequently changing data that does not interfere with CRM data, but that is necessary to access when dealing with your customers.

External data sources rely on a technical connection between Salesforce and the legacy system (usually, we talk about the OData protocol) and this is setup to allow Salesforce to access external databases defining external objects, which are a Salesforce representation of those tables within Salesforce (again, data is not stored in Salesforce but using those technical protocol records, which may be accessed in the same way as a normal Salesforce object).

External lookups are then used to link a standard or custom Salesforce object to an external object: this is usually done using an external ID field on the Salesforce object that matches a corresponding field on the external object dataset.

Indirect lookups are lookups defined from an external object that points to a standard or custom Salesforce object, using an external ID/unique field on the parent object to match the link.

For more details about external data sources and external objects, refer to Salesforce Help at `https://help.salesforce.com/articleView?id=external_data_sources.htmtype=5`.

Validation rules

I bet you already know what a validation rule is, but let's discuss them again. A validation rule is a feature that is used to improve data quality. It is checked before a record is saved in the database.

They are defined by the following:

- A name
- An `Active` flag
- A condition (formula) that should trigger the error (a chain of conditions on fields of the object or related objects that triggers an error if evaluated as `true`)
- An error message that is displayed to the user
- A place where the error can be displayed

Here is an example of a validation rule:

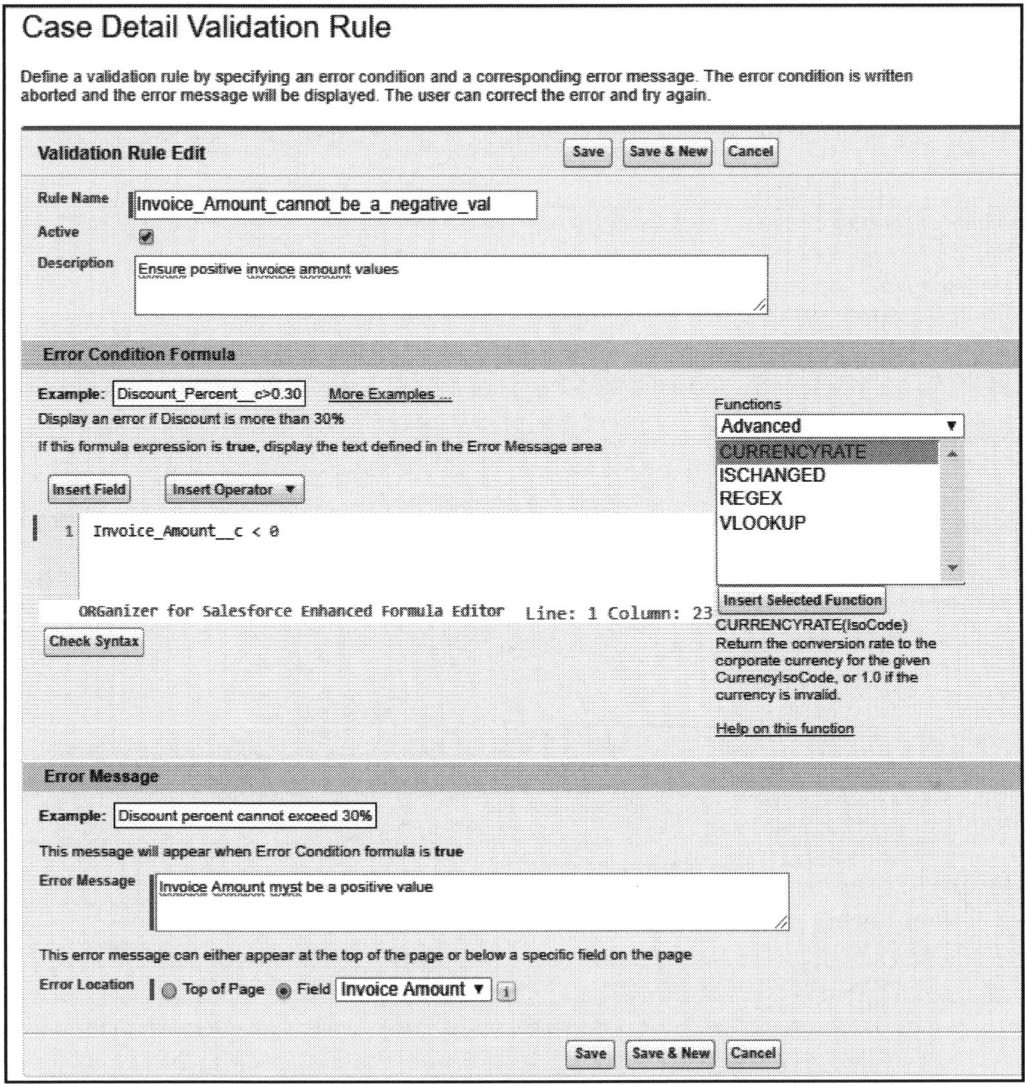

Example of a simple validation rule

This validation rule prevents a user from inserting a negative value in the **Invoice Amount** field:

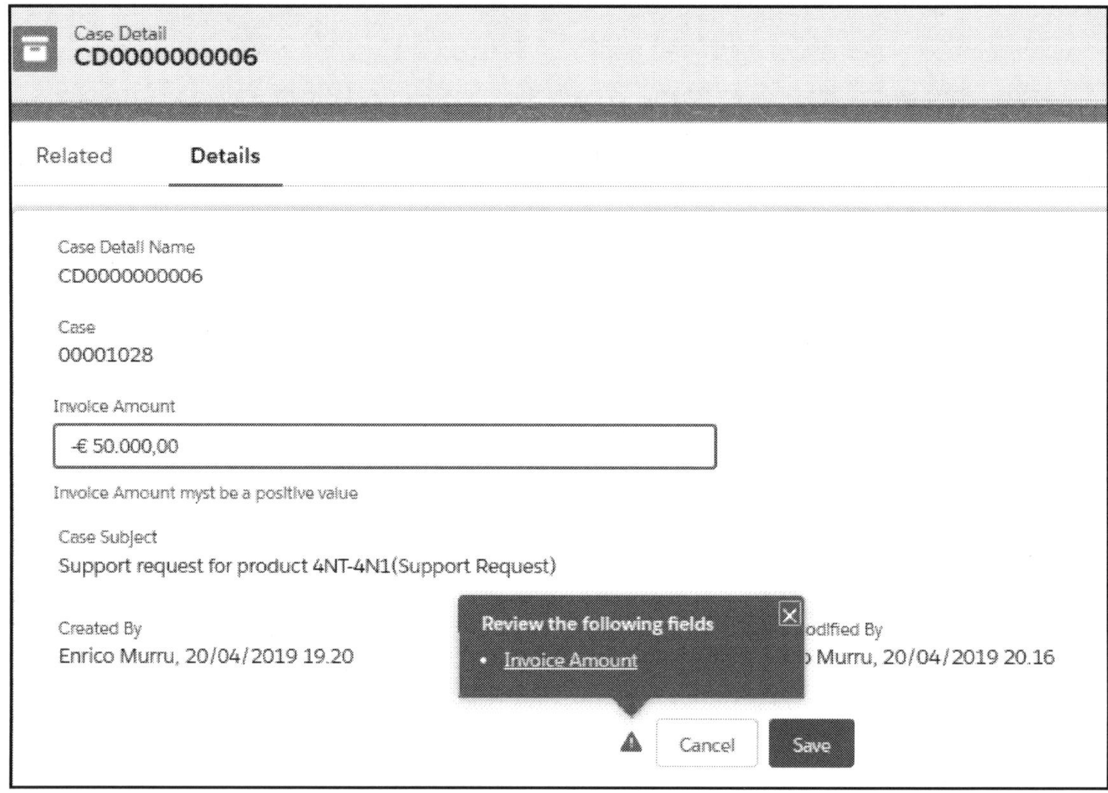

Validation rule triggers if its conditions are met

Some of its configuration fields are easy to understand:

- **Error Message**: Error displayed to the user if a condition is met.
- **Error Location**: Where the error should be placed. This can be set to **Top of Page** or to a specific field (this field must be an editable field, so formulas or roll-up fields are excluded)

As for the condition, we have to use a formula by referencing fields coming from the current object or related objects (we've seen a cross-object formula earlier in this chapter)—that is, the error condition that makes the validation trigger and display the error message to the user.

What if you have more than one validation rule? When saving a record, Salesforce checks all validation rules, and even if a rule triggers an error, all other rules are run so that the user can see all error messages.

Validation rules are executed before any other automation action in the following order:

1. Validation rules
2. Assignment rules
3. Autoresponse rules
4. Workflow rules (with immediate actions)
5. Escalation rules

Note that a workflow rule can update a record, setting its fields to invalid values (against rules defined in the validation rules) just because workflow rules don't trigger validation rules.

At first sight, validation rules overlap with the lookup filter feature. The lookup filter has a much better user experience because it leads the user to a quicker reference selection, anticipating any error.

Use validation rules if you have reached the limit of lookup filters. You can also use validation rules if the logic involved in the rule's condition is way more complex than the one you can create with basic lookup filters.

You don't have to remember any specific field name available; you can use the advanced formula utility (the **Insert Field** button on the validation rule editing page):

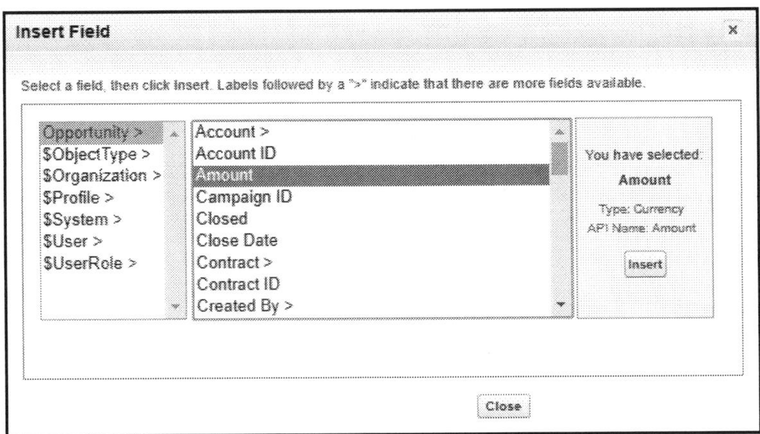

Field selector on a formula editor

You can get the following:

- All current objects' fields and related objects' fields (in this case, we are building a VR for the `Opportunity` object)
- **$ObjectType**: Used to reference specific fields on custom objects (refer to the following *VLOOKUP* section)
- **$Organization**: Current organization fields (such as the name, city, language, locale, everything you can find in the **Setup** | **Company Settings** | **Company Information** | **Organization Detail** section)
- **$Profile**, **$User**, **$UserRole**: Current user, profile, and role details (this can be used to prevent selected users from setting specific fields in various conditions—for example, a portal user cannot close a `Case`)
- **$System**: System fields

Let's have a look at some advanced functions that you can use within rules (and formulas in general):

- `VLOOKUP`
- `REGEX`
- `PRIORVALUE`

For the entire reference of available functions in formulas, refer to `https://help.salesforce.com/articleView?id=customize_functions.htmtype=5`.

VLOOKUP

The `VLOOKUP` function is similar to the Excel function with the same name, and it is used to look up a value inside a specific object's record set.

Let's say we have a custom object that handles all country calling codes.

The object is quite simple:

- **Object's name**: `Call_Prefix__c`
- **Country's full name**: `Country_Name__c` (custom text field)
- **Country's calling code**: `Name` (standard name field)

We want users to manually input the country calling code when creating a new `Contact` (where we are creating the new validation rule) on the `Contact.Phone_Country_Code__c` custom field and check that `Contact.MailingCountry` is equal to the country name found on the `Call_Prefix__c` object with the same code (on its `Name` field).

Using `VLOOKUP`, we can do this easily:

```
VLOOKUP($ObjectType.Call_Prefix__c.Fields.Country_Name__c,
  $ObjectType.Call_Prefix__c.Fields.Name,
  Phone_Country_Code__c) <> MailingCountry
```

That is, if the country name related to the phone country code differs from the `Mailing Country`, an error is triggered.

The first parameter referenced is the field that should be returned, the second parameter is the field to be looked up, and the third parameter is the value to check against (which comes from the validation rule's object). The function returns a value (if more values are found, it returns the first one) that can then be checked against other fields (in our scenario, the `Contact.MailingCountry` field).

We can only use custom objects and the lookup field; the returning field must match their type, and the lookup field must be the `Record Name` field of the custom object.

The `$ObjectType.Object_API_Name.Fields.Field_API_Name` notation is used to reference object fields with no chance of making mistakes (the formula engine will compile against this expression and give an error when saving the formula if something is wrong).

When building formulas, remember that the total number of allowed characters is 3,900, including spaces, line breaks/return characters, and comments. You can chain more formulas (that is, call a *child* formula within another formula), but you cannot exceed the **5,000 bytes** compile size (which includes all children formulas (this limit differs from the characters' size and, if exceeded, the administrator will be notified when saving the rule).

REGEX

The `REGEX` function is used to trigger special checks on the format of a text value, using **regular expressions**. Discussing regular expressions is outside the scope of this book (refer to `https://www.regular-expressions.info/quickstart.html` for a quick start on the grammar of regular expressions), but let's summarize them by saying that you can use a sequence of characters to define a rule that a string should match.

A basic regular expression could be the format of an email address, which can be (simply) written as follows:

```
[a-zA-Z0-9._%-]+@[a-zA-Z0-9.-]+\.[a-zA-Z]{2,6}
```

This matches the example email address, `enrico.murru-1@test-subdomain.domain.it` (letters, numbers and some special characters before the `@` sign, letters, and numbers, and some special characters before the last `.` (dot), and finally only letters for two to six characters).

Email address validation can be way more complex depending on your needs, but `regex` should cover the majority of scenarios.

Let's say we have the need to validate a European VAT code in the `Account.VAT_Code__c` custom field. We don't need what this code represents, but we need to know its structure.

We have been told that we should only validate Italian codes and that the regular expression of this kind of VAT code is `(IT)?[0-9]{11}` (starts with `IT` and ends with `11` digits).

The final regular expression will be the following:

```
AND(
  LEFT(VAT_Code__c, 2) = 'IT',
  NOT( REGEX(VAT_Code__c, "(IT)?[0-9]{11}" ) )
)
```

If the `VAT_Code__c` field starts with `IT` (the first `2` characters on the left-hand side) and it doesn't match the `regex` provided, an error should be triggered. This way, if we input another kind of VAT code, (a German one), no error will be thrown.

You are generally not required to compile the regular expressions, but it's likely you'll be given `regex` to insert a validation rule using the `REGEX` formula.

PRIORVALUE

The `PRIORVALUE` function gets the previous value of a field that is the same value if the record is being created, or the real previous value if the record is being updated.

You could use it to prevent users from updating important fields in specific conditions, such as changing the opportunity amount once it is closed or transition a case to a `Closed` status if the previous status is `Cancelled`:

```
AND(
  ISPICKVAL( PRIORVALUE(Status), 'Cancelled'),
  ISPICKVAL(Status, 'Closed')
)
```

What is the `ISPICKVAL` value? When dealing with picklists, you should use this function to check whether a picklist `list` field equals a certain value:

```
AND(
  PRIORVALUE(Amount) <> Amount,
  IsClosed
)
```

The preceding opportunity's example is simpler as it states that if the `Amount` field value changes and the opportunity is closed, the error is triggered.

This simple control can be replaced with the `ISCHANGED()` function that returns `true` if the value of a given field is changed.

Picklist management

Picklist fields are a basic way to restrict user input: they deliver a default set of allowed values using a select list. From the user interface, it is impossible to set a different value than the ones listed, so you have a guarantee that no invalid value is stored.

This is not technically true, though. The picklist type field is just a *UI-contained* text field, but if it is not enforced, then you can set an invalid value by using other tools (such as REST APIs or Apex code).

Let's try managing a picklist field.

Let's create an **Invoice Type** picklist list field on the `Case Detail` object and uncheck the **Restrict picklist to the values defined in the value set checkbox**:

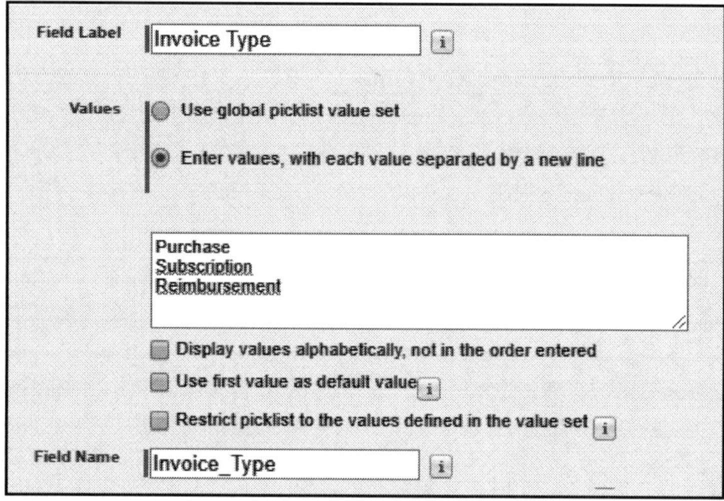

Simple picklist creation

Once the file is created and added to the page layout, you'll be able to create a new **Case Detail** record with the new **Invoice Type** field.

Let's do some developer work now! Open the case detail that we created in the previous chapters and get the Salesforce ID from the URL: your browser URL bar should look something like this:

https://eu19.lightning.force.com/lightning/r/Case_Detail__c/a011i0000075ZkEAAU/view

URL of a Case Detail object

Copy the Salesforce ID to the clipboard; we'll be using it shortly.

Salesforce IDs come with 15 or 18 digits. Don't panic if you see a 15-digit ID if you expect an 18-digit one; most of the features work with both versions of the same value.

If you are in doubt, check whether the first 15 characters have the same characters.

For more information about Salesforce IDs, refer to `https://help.salesforce.com/articleView?id=000004383language=en_UStype=1`.

Let's open the **Developer Console** by going to **Settings** | **Developer Console**:

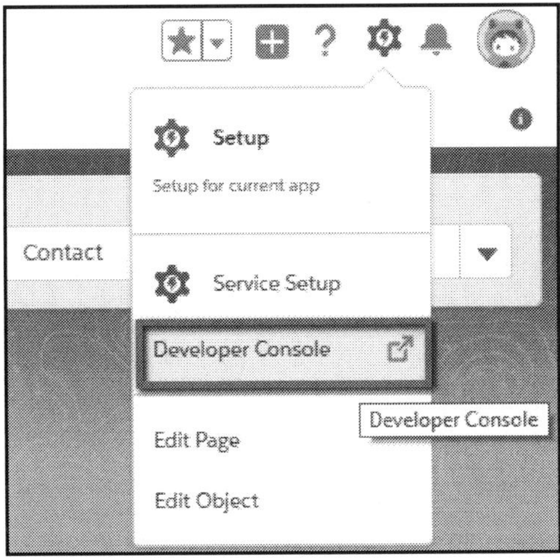

Developer Console link

This will open up the following window:

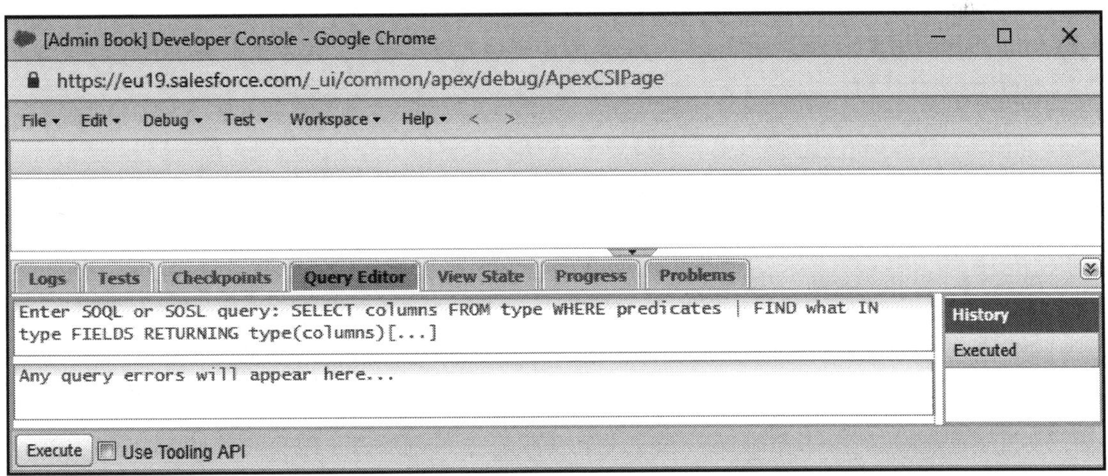

Developer Console window

This magic window is used by developers for quick and dirty stuff, such as Apex classes/trigger creation, query execution, Apex test execution, and more, but there is no reason why an administrator shouldn't use it too.

We want to show that we can update an unrestricted picklist field with whatever value we want.

Go to **Debug | Open Execute Anonymous Window** on the **Developer Console** menu. In the opening text box, let's write the following Apex code:

```
1. Case_Detail__c detail = [Select Id, Invoice_Type__c
2. From Case_Detail__c
3. Where Id = 'a011i0000075ZkEAAU'];
4. detail.Invoice_Type__c = 'Invalid Invoice Type';
5. update detail;
```

What's happening here?

- Lines 1-3 make an SOQL query on the **Case Detail** object, getting the **ID** and **Invoice Type** fields: since we want to update a field, only the **ID** field is necessary for the query, but, for the sake of this example, we are showing how an SOQL query can be composed.
- Line 4 takes the returned record and sets the new value for the **Invoice Type** field.
- Line 5 executes the update of the record.

Think about it. This is exactly what you do using the user interface: open a specific record by its Salesforce ID, click on the **Edit** button, change field values, and click on the **Save** button. The following diagram shows what your script should look like on the **Execute Anonymous** window:

Execute Anonymous Apex script

Are you ready for the magic to take place? Click on the **Execute** button.

If you forget a character or copy the script incorrectly, you may get a pop-up error showing the error message. If that happens, don't worry—you have only mistyped the script.

Don't worry about it. The life of a developer lies between a successful class save and a compilation error because of a forgotten single semicolon character in a thousand lines of code. If everything worked okay, you won't see any message. Go back to your **Case Detail** page and refresh the page to see something similar to the following:

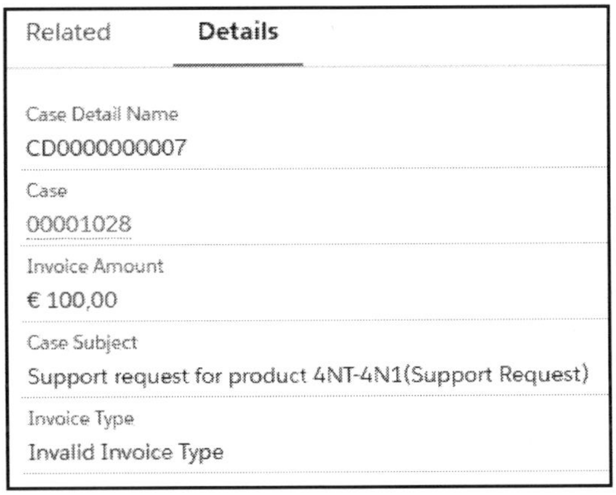

Case Detail updated with an unlisted picklist value

Feeling like a hacker, huh?

If we edit the record and open the **Invoice Type** picklist, we still get the **Invalid Invoice Type** value, but if we select an allowed value and save the record, the disallowed value disappears from the list and everything returns to its default status.

I hope you enjoyed this developer regression. Why would you need this behavior? You want an external system to be able to create a case detail with a specific **Invoice Type** value that shouldn't be allowed for your users (for example, an external system that handles reimbursements).

What if you want the **Invoice Type** field to have the same values as another custom object's picklist (for example, the `Invoice` object with a **Type** field)? You have two choices: replicate the values or use a global value set, the **global picklist value set**.

You can create a global value set by going to **Setup** | **Objects and Fields** | **Picklist Value Sets**, or jump to your newly created picklist field and promote it to a global value set by editing the field and clicking on **Promote to Global Value Set**:

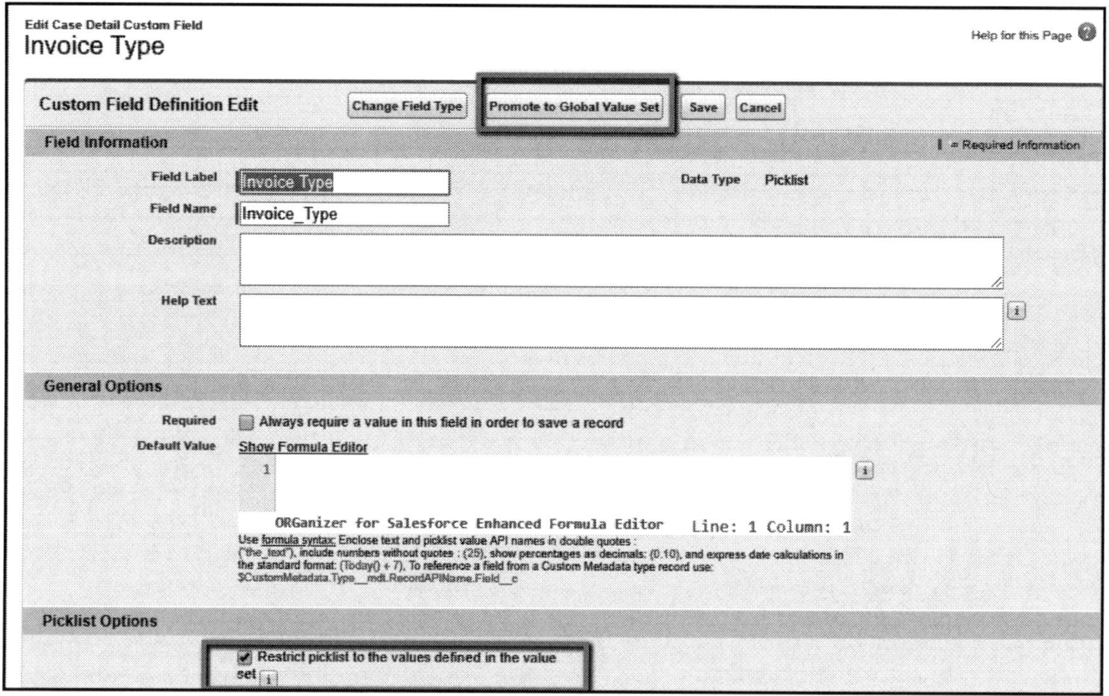

Promoting a picklist list to a global value set

But to promote a global value-set, you need to restrict values to the origin picklist.

Select the **Global Value Set** label/nameed *voilà*, the picklist field will be related to a new global value set:

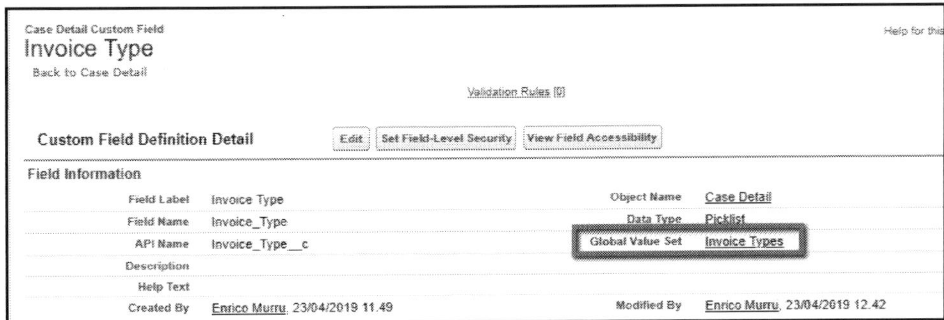

Picklist field related to a global value set

A global picklist is restricted by nature, so no one can add new values using Apex or APIs.

You can have up to 500 global value sets in an org, and each can have up to 1,000 active values. The length per value can be up to 255 characters.

Dependent picklists

Let's spend some time discussing dependent picklists. They are single or multiselect picklists whose values depend on a controlling field that must be a picklist field (with at least one value and fewer than 300 values) or a checkbox field for the same record.

This relation between fields helps keep data accurate and consistent.

Let's say we want a secondary picklist on a `Case Detail` object called **Invoice Reason** whose values depend on the **Invoice Type**. We want this to have the following relations:

Controlling value (invoice type)	Available values (invoice reason)
Purchase	Store purchase Online purchase
Subscription	Monthly subscription Weekly subscription
Reimbursement	Wrong purchase Flawed item

Dependent picklist values example on the case detail object

At first, we create a new picklist field on the `Case Detail` object, and then we click on the **New** link on the **Controlling Field** in the **Picklist Options** section:

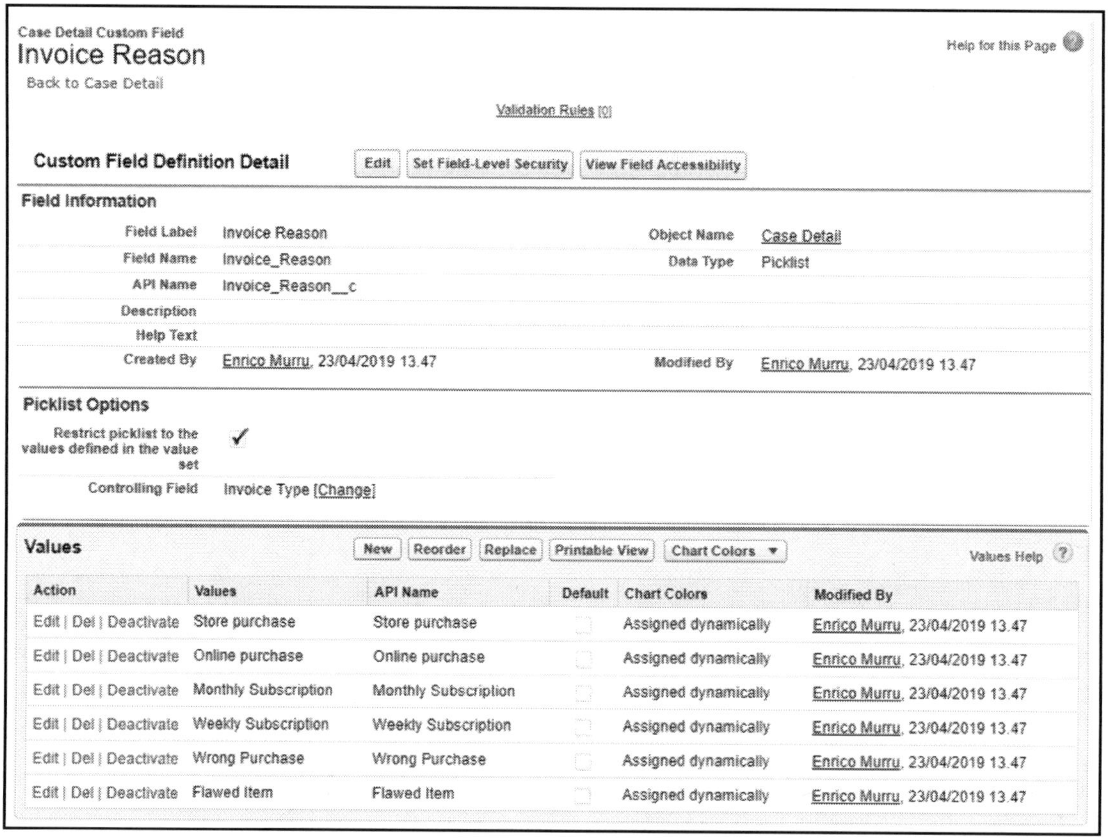

Case Detail Custom Field
Invoice Reason
Back to Case Detail
Help for this Page

Validation Rules [0]

Custom Field Definition Detail Edit | Set Field-Level Security | View Field Accessibility

Field Information

Field Label	Invoice Reason	Object Name	Case Detail
Field Name	Invoice_Reason	Data Type	Picklist
API Name	Invoice_Reason__c		
Description			
Help Text			
Created By	Enrico Murru, 23/04/2019 13.47	Modified By	Enrico Murru, 23/04/2019 13.47

Picklist Options

Restrict picklist to the values defined in the value set	✓
Controlling Field	Invoice Type [Change]

Values New | Reorder | Replace | Printable View | Chart Colors ▼ Values Help

Action	Values	API Name	Default	Chart Colors	Modified By
Edit | Del | Deactivate	Store purchase	Store purchase		Assigned dynamically	Enrico Murru, 23/04/2019 13.47
Edit | Del | Deactivate	Online purchase	Online purchase		Assigned dynamically	Enrico Murru, 23/04/2019 13.47
Edit | Del | Deactivate	Monthly Subscription	Monthly Subscription		Assigned dynamically	Enrico Murru, 23/04/2019 13.47
Edit | Del | Deactivate	Weekly Subscription	Weekly Subscription		Assigned dynamically	Enrico Murru, 23/04/2019 13.47
Edit | Del | Deactivate	Wrong Purchase	Wrong Purchase		Assigned dynamically	Enrico Murru, 23/04/2019 13.47
Edit | Del | Deactivate	Flawed Item	Flawed Item		Assigned dynamically	Enrico Murru, 23/04/2019 13.47

Controlled picklist definition on the case detail object

Then, select the **Controlling** and **Dependent** fields:

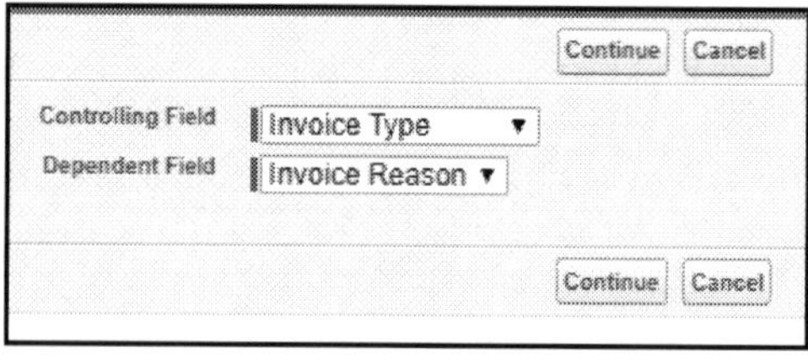

Controlling and Dependent picklist relations

For each controlling value, select one or more (or none) controlled values (click the **Include Values/Exclude Values** button to select/deselect a value):

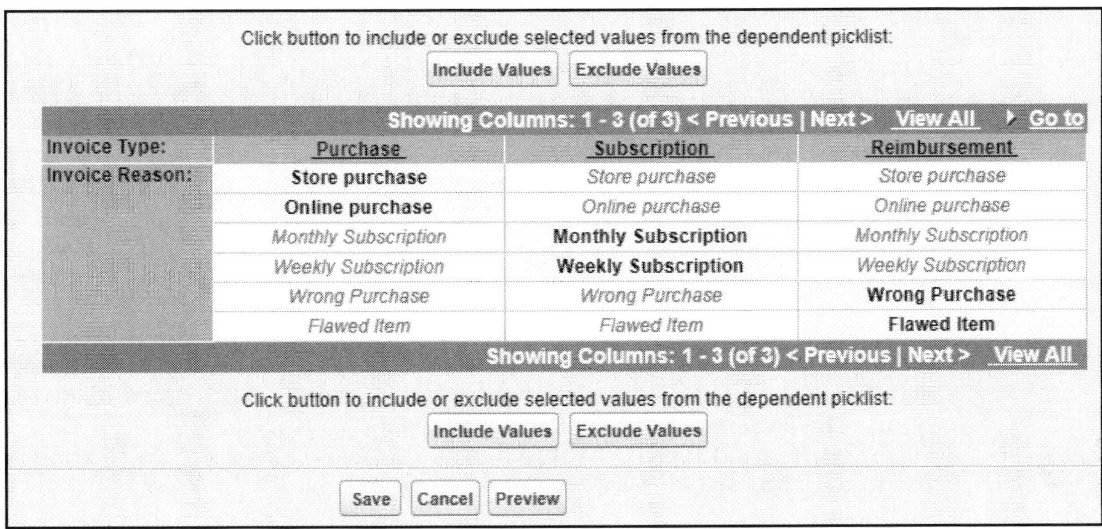

Dependent picklist values selection

Click on **Save** and the magic is done.

Create a new `Case Detail` object and select different values for the **Invoice Type** field to see the **Invoice Reason** field set changes:

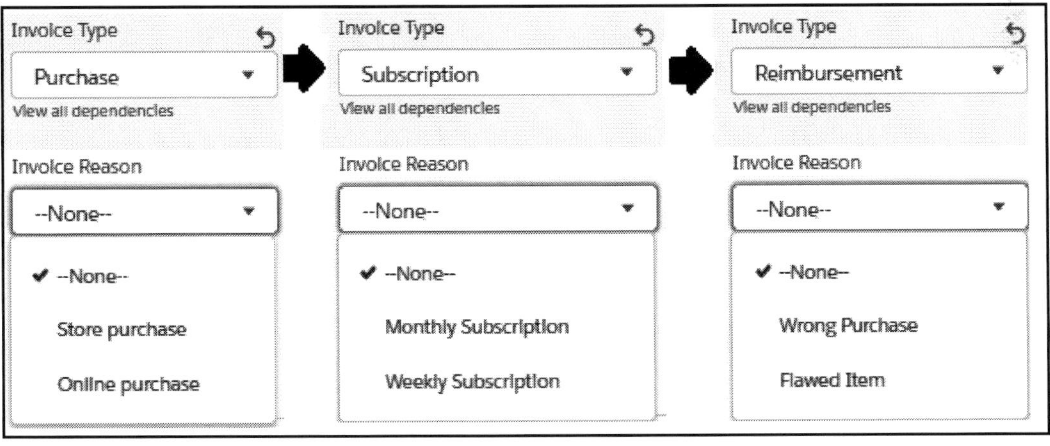

Dependent picklist on page layouts

There are a few things to remember:

- Dependent picklists cannot have a default value
- Standard picklists cannot be dependent picklists
- A controlling picklist field must have from 1 to 300 values
- A dependent field can also be a controlling field for another picklist
- The available dependent values also depend on record type configuration
- Both controlling and dependent fields must be shown on the page layout

Summary

In this chapter, we have learned about the different ways to link Salesforce objects together using diverse kinds of relationships. To ensure better data consistency, we learned about the important aspects of validation rules and some advanced formula functions.

Finally, to achieve even better data quality, we looked at how picklists can deliver a consistent use of global value sets and how dependent picklists can ease user experience with standard page layouts.

In the next chapter, we'll be covering sales and service cloud features that will give your implementation the **wow!** effect.

Questions

1. With the Schema Builder, you can:
    a. Enable workflows
    b. View object relationships
    c. View object fields
    d. View a profile hierarchy
    e. View a sharing model
2. Which is the easiest and best way to relate a parent object with its multiple children detail objects?
    a. A lookup field from child to parent object
    b. A lookup field from parent to child object
    c. A master–detail field from child to parent object
    d. A master–detail field from parent to child object

3. Can you create a master–detail relation with a standard object as a parent?
    a. Yes
    b. No
4. Can you create a master–detail relation with a standard object as a child?
    a. No
    b. Yes
5. By setting the **Sharing** setting to **Read/Write** on a master–detail relation, you are:
    a. Allowing all users who have at least read access on the parent to CRUD a child record
    b. Allowing all users who have read/write read access on the parent to CRUD a child record
    c. Allowing all users who have at least read access on the parent to delete a child record
    d. Allowing all users who have at least read/write access on the parent to delete or create a child record
6. You can filter master records on master–detail or lookup relationship fields on the current user's profile/role:
    a. False
    b. True, but only if the user is a system administrator
    c. True
7. Roll-up fields are created on:
    a. The master object of a lookup relationship
    b. The child object of a master–detail relationship
    c. The child object of a lookup relationship
    d. The master object of a master–detail relationship
8. Which are the avaible roll-up field types?
    a. `Filter`, `Count`, `Max`, `Sum`
    b. `Sum`, `Subtract`, `Multiply`, `Divide`
    c. `Count`, `Sum`, `Min`, `Max`
    d. `Sum`, `Min`, `Max`

9. You need to model a multiple relation between the `Interview` object and the `Interview Question` object so that you can have different questions for a given interview, given that the same question can be related to more than one interview. Which is the recommended solution?
    a. User 2 lookup fields on the `Interview Question` object.
    b. User 2 master–detail fields on the `Interview Question` object.
    c. Create a new `junction` object with two master-detail fields relating to `Interview` and `Interview Question`.
    d. Create a new `junction` object with two lookup fields relating to `Interview Question` and `Interview`.
10. Given a lookup relationship field, you can prevent child deletion by selecting the **Don't allow deletion of the lookup record that's part of a lookup relationship** checkbox under the **What to do if the lookup record is deleted?** option:
    a. True
    b. False; it is related to the parent record deletion
    c. False; this option is not available on a lookup field
11. You can use a hierarchical relationship to:
    a. Relate users to profiles
    b. Relate users to roles
    c. Relate users to users below their hierarchical level
    d. Relate users to users above their hierarchical level
12. Validation rules trigger:
    a. When conditions evaluate to true
    b. When conditions evaluate to false
13. To create a validation rule that looks up to another object's record set, you use the following function:
    a. `REGEX`
    b. `VLOOKUP`
    c. `PRIORVALUE`
14. You need to implement a custom validation in the ZIP code format for the country of India, so you use the following function:
    a. `REGEX`
    b. `VLOOKUP`
    c. `PRIORVALUE`

15. When dealing with the `PRIORVALUE` function on a validation rule and a picklist field, which other function should you use to get the picklist field's value?
    a. `PREV`
    b. `ISPICKVAL`
    c. `VAL`
    d. `VALUEOF`
16. It is possible to set up a value on a picklist field that is not available on its defined value:
    a. True
    b. True, unless it is a restricted picklist
    c. False
17. You can use a global value set to:
    a. Validate picklist values
    b. Define user access on picklist fields
    c. Define picklist values across fields in different objects
18. A dependent picklist field depends on :
    a. A master picklist or checkbox field on the same object
    b. A master picklist or checkbox field on the parent object
    c. A master picklist field on the same object

3

Section 3: Sales and Service Cloud Applications

In this section, you will learn how to power up Salesforce features such as products and quotes management, as well as sales forecasts. Then, you will learn how to increase customer support with Salesforce Knowledge, entitlements, chat, and Omni-Channel.

This section includes the following chapters:

- `Chapter 5`, *Support Sales Strategies with Sales Cloud Features*
- `Chapter 6`, *Service Cloud Applications*

5
Support Sales Strategies with Sales Cloud Features

In this chapter, we'll be dealing with Sales Cloud features. If you are wondering what Salesforce Sales Cloud is, it is the piece of our beloved CRM that is designed to support sales and marketing in both business-to-business and business-to-customer contexts. It supports lead management, campaign creation, deal closing, and product catalog definition. For the purpose of this book, we'll deal with Sales Cloud specifics such as product management, quote management, and opportunity forecasting, which will give you the confidence to implement an effective sales strategy.

In this chapter, we'll focus on the following topics:

- Leveling up product management to better define your selling strategy and see how opportunities are tied to the selling process
- Learning what quotes are and how they can be used along with quote templates to deliver a consistent pricing negotiation
- Configuring forecasts to predict sales revenues and quantities from your opportunity pipeline

Managing products, product schedules, and pricebooks

Products and opportunities are at the core of Sales Cloud features. They identify the deals that a company's sales reps try to close and the products/services involved in the deal.

Before talking about products, let's discuss a few things about opportunities. An opportunity tracks the path of a deal from the first contact with a prospective customer until the deal is closed, and the deal may be successfully closed or lost. The standard fields in opportunities that play a role in tracking the status are shown in the following screenshot:

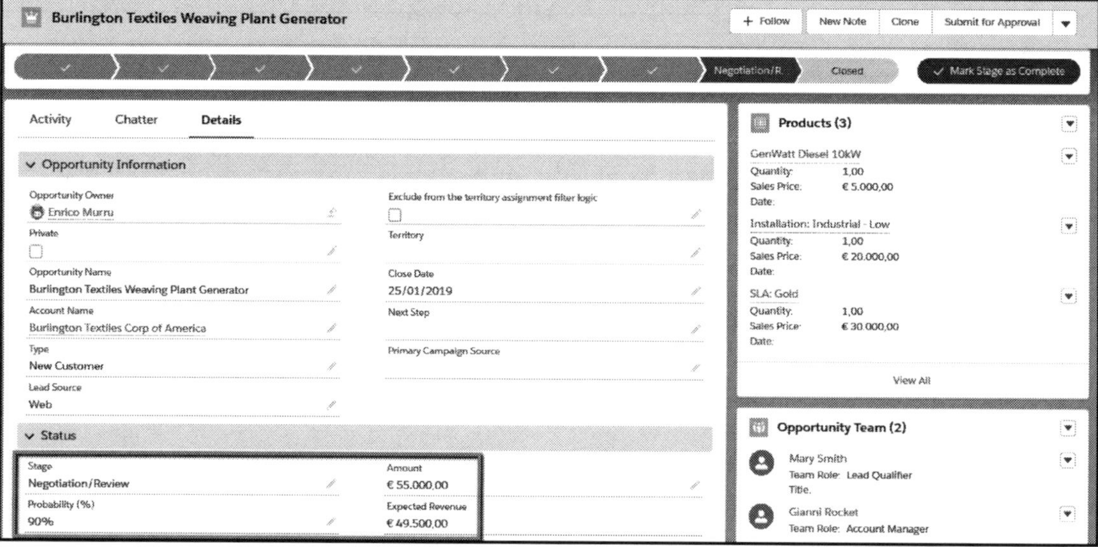

Opportunity stage tracking

The **Stage** states the current status of the opportunity, and it delivers a default probability of closing the deal (which is applied to the total **Amount** in the **Expected Revenue** field).

Every company has its own typical sales process, with typical stage statuses. That's why **Stage** is a picklist that can be customized from **Setup** | **Object Manager** | **Opportunity** | **Fields & Relationships** | **Stage**, as shown here:

Opportunity Stages Picklist Values New | Reorder | Replace | Printable View | Chart Colors ▼

Action	Stage Name	API Name	Type	Probability	Forecast Category
Edit | Del | Deactivate	Prospecting	Prospecting	Open	10%	Pipeline
Edit | Del | Deactivate	Qualification	Qualification	Open	10%	Pipeline
Edit | Del | Deactivate	Needs Analysis	Needs Analysis	Open	20%	Pipeline
Edit | Del | Deactivate	Value Proposition	Value Proposition	Open	50%	Pipeline
Edit | Del | Deactivate	Id. Decision Makers	Id. Decision Makers	Open	60%	Pipeline
Edit | Del | Deactivate	Perception Analysis	Perception Analysis	Open	70%	Pipeline
Edit | Del | Deactivate	Proposal/Price Quote	Proposal/Price Quote	Open	75%	Pipeline
Edit | Del | Deactivate	Negotiation/Review	Negotiation/Review	Open	90%	Pipeline
Edit | Del | Deactivate	Closed Won	Closed Won	Closed/Won	100%	Closed
Edit | Del | Deactivate	Closed Lost	Closed Lost	Closed/Lost	0%	Omitted

Customizing an opportunity's Stage picklist

You can add new values, define whether a given stage is Open, Closed/Won, or Closed/Lost, provide the probability of success, and add a forecast category (which we'll see in the *Predicting deals with forecasts* section).

If the company has more than one sales process, we can use record types on the Opportunity object to segment sales strategies. Before doing this, we have to create one or more sales process configurations from **Setup** | **Feature Settings** | **Sales** | **Sales Processes**. Each sales process is defined by a subset of all stages defined for an opportunity, and we can link a given sales process to more than one opportunity record type.

For example, we may define an **Online Sales Process** that doesn't require much interaction with the customer and can be defined by a small subset of stage values, as shown in the following screenshot:

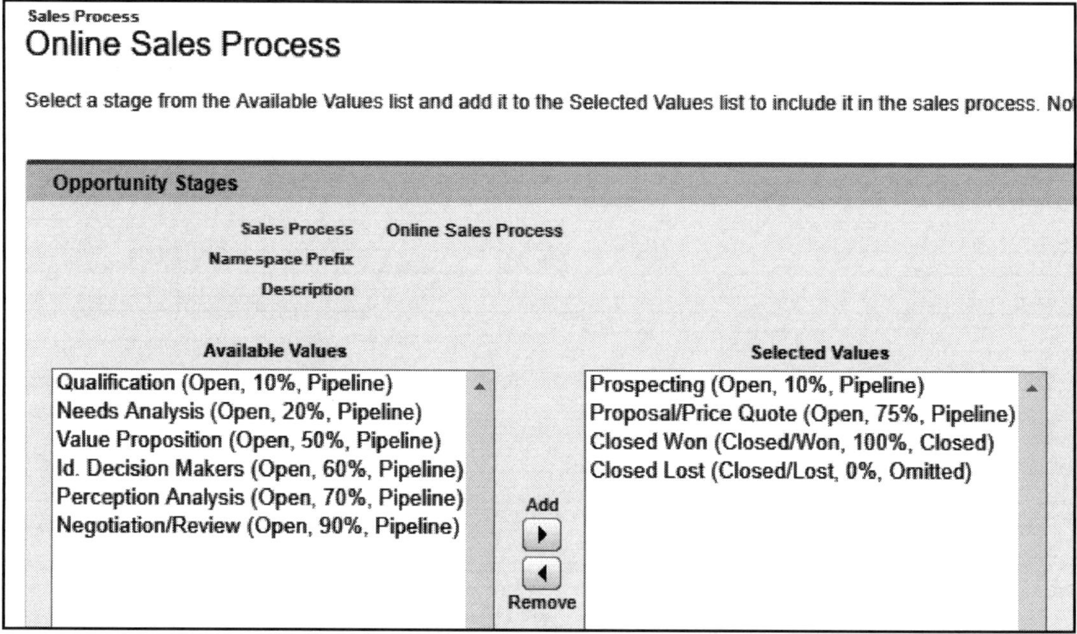

Sales process definition

When we create a new opportunity record type, the related sales process becomes one of the required fields:

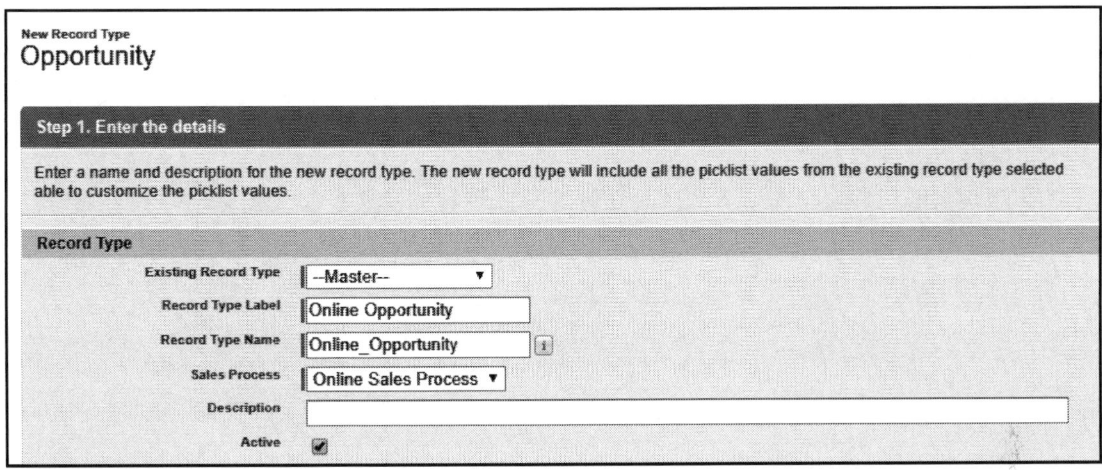

Opportunity record type configuration

Another trait of opportunities is the **Products** list. You can add one or more products to a given opportunity, the only constraint being that they must rely on the same price book:

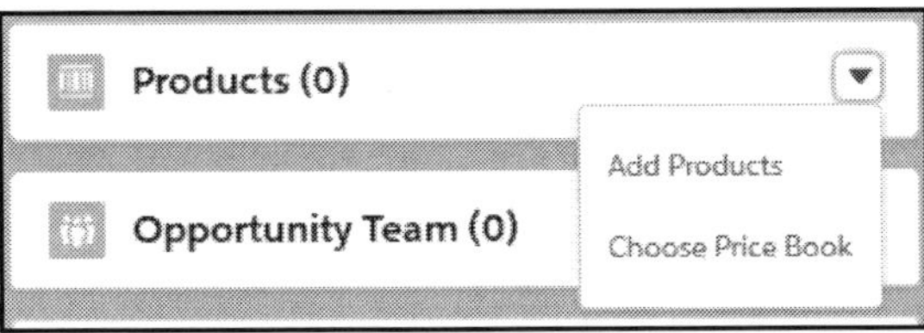

Product and price book selection on the opportunity's Product-related list

If you add a product before selecting the price book, the system will ask for the price book first.

There seem to be many objects relating to products and opportunities. To clarify the relationships, here is a picture taken from the Schema Builder, which shows how opportunities are involved with products and price books (this is something my CTO explained to me in 10 minutes when I was a beginner):

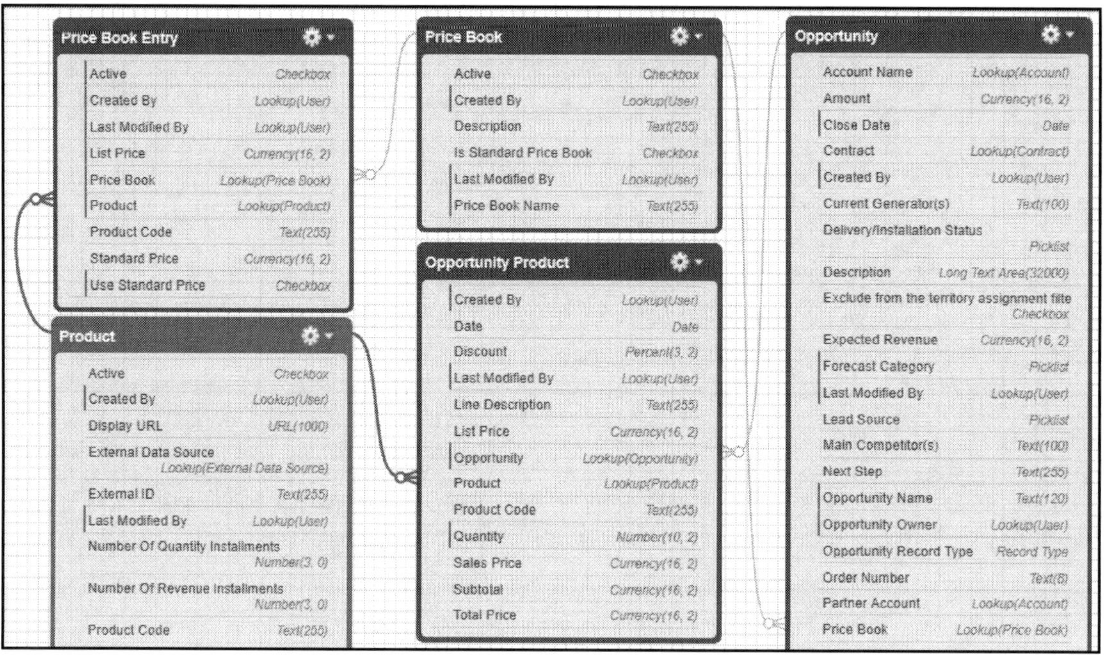

Opportunity and product relations

We can see the opportunity related to a price book, a product related to a price book via a *junction* object called Price Book Entry, and a junction object called Opportunity Product that links a product to an opportunity (at the core, Opportunity Product is also linked to Price Book Entry, because the Price Book constraint must be kept for all opportunity products).

Once you have assigned products to an opportunity, the **Amount** field is not updatable any more because it is calculated as the sum of the quantity of all opportunity products multiplied by their sales price (like a *roll-up* field).

Packing everything up, products are items and services that the company sells to its customers: a product can be linked to different price books with different prices.

Who creates products in our CRM? Administrators or sales managers do this by hand (using the product layout or using mass data creation with tools such as Data Loader) or automatically with external systems called **Product Information Management** (**PIMs**). In this case, the PIM system is the master/owner of the product data, taking care of product activation, pricing, and price book configurations (in this kind of architecture, there is usually an integration between the PIM system and Salesforce that automatically aligns product data).

To create a new price book manually, click on the App Launcher icon and select **Price Books**, and then click **New** to create a new price book. You will get the following box:

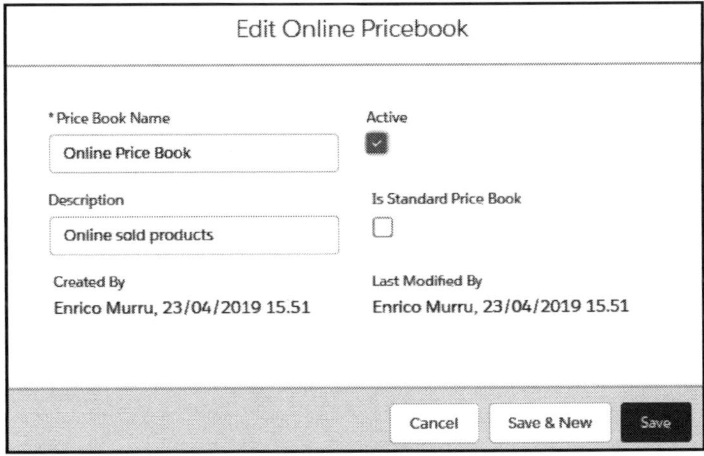

Price Book creation

Then, from the **PRODUCT** list, add one or more products from the **Standard** price book (which should contain all products; consider it as a master product catalog):

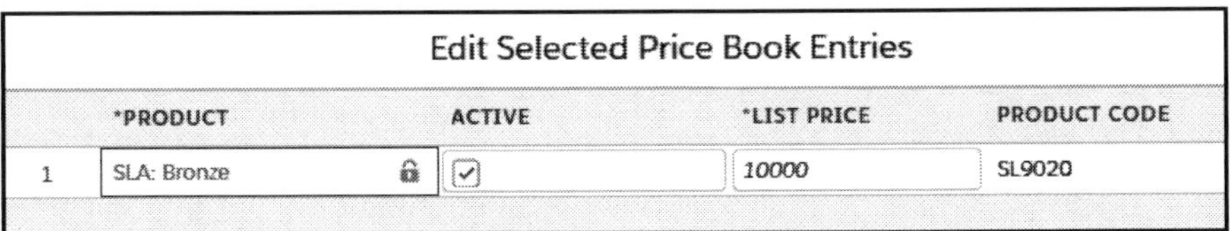

Adding a product to a price book

Each product comes with a standard price (coming from the standard price book), but you can choose a different list price (you may want to define a catalog for a specific country for foreign countries where list pricing suffers from additional taxes).

Sales managers and anyone else who needs to create products must have the **Create** permission on the Product object.

To keep good performances on price books, keep the number of products below 2,000,000.

If we need to create a new product with the same price book configurations and pricing, we can clone a product (use the **Clone** quick action on the product's page layout). Remember that by doing this, any relationships with price books that the user doesn't have access to are not cloned along with the product, and not even fields with read-only access are copied in the cloned record.

To create a new product, go to the **Product** tab and click on the **New** button (it's a standard Salesforce object, after all). Set up a standard price book by clicking on **Add Standard Price** on the **Price Books** list to bring up the following:

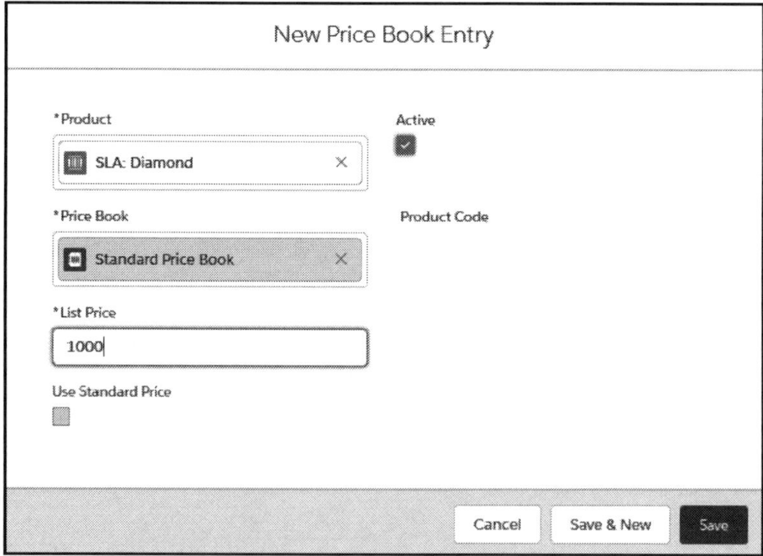

Setting the standard price on a new product

Once the standard price has been set up, we can add the product to other price books:

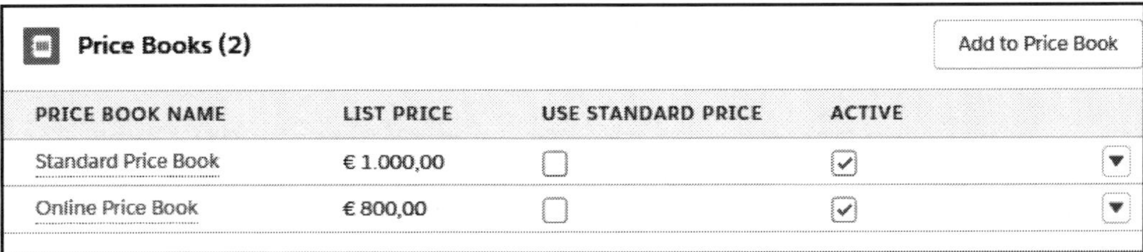

Product added to other price books via the Price Books list

The following pricing can be associated with a product:

- **Standard price**: The base price from the standard price book.
- **List price**: The base price from the picked price book (may or may not match the standard price).
- **Sales price**: The actual price input by sales reps on opportunities (or quotes), which may or may not match the associated price book price.

If you enable **multi-currency** on your organization, for each price, you'll set up different values for each currency.

For more information about multiple currencies, refer to Salesforce Help at `https://help.salesforce.com/articleView?id=admin_currency.htm type=5`.

Regarding product management, you can disable/remove a product within a price book without affecting all the other price book entries, and you can delete a price book without affecting any other product configuration. If you need to completely remove any reference to a product, remove the product from the standard price book.

You can't remove a product or price book if they are used within an opportunity (quote, service contract, or contract line item as well).

Before finishing the product section, we will discuss a special feature of products that delivers a subscription type of product management. It's a repeating product type called **product schedules**.

Product schedules

Product schedules are a feature that define the payment and delivery cycles for your products, provided in the following ways:

- **Quantity schedule**: When the item is delivered, that is, pay once and receive more than once (for example, an annual subscription for a daily newspaper).
- **Revenue schedule**: When the item is paid for, that is, receive once and pay more than once (for example, subscribing to a streaming service and getting the service after monthly payments).
- **Quantity and revenue schedule:** A combination of both configurations. Typically, customers pay in a given schedule and receive the product with a different schedule.
- **Default schedule**: This is the schedule associated with price books that can be further customized by the sales rep on an opportunity, but it's not needed if sales reps usually customize their schedules.

To enable product schedules, navigate to **Setup** | **Feature Settings** | **Sales** | **Products** | **Product Schedules Settings**:

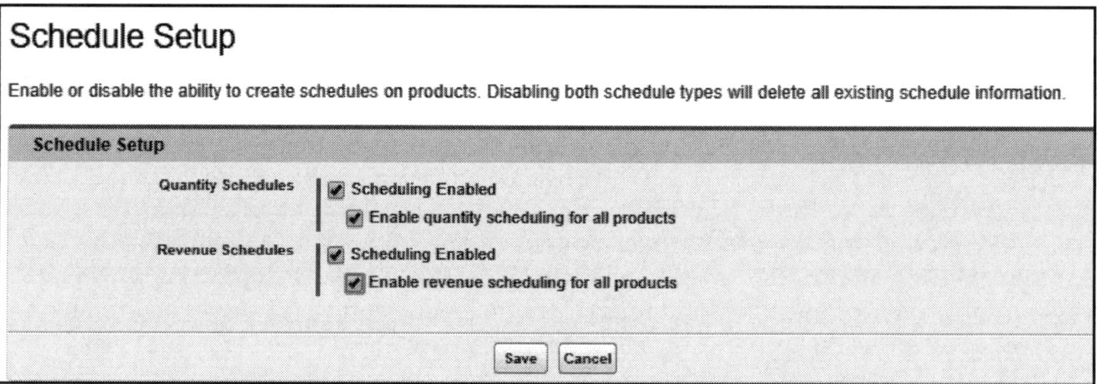

Enabling product schedules

Checking the **Enable quantity/revenue scheduling for all products** checkboxes enables both schedule types on all objects. Leave this unchecked if you want to granularly decide which products have which schedule types.

When this option is enabled, some new fields appear on the product's page layout (you may be required to add them to the product's page layouts):

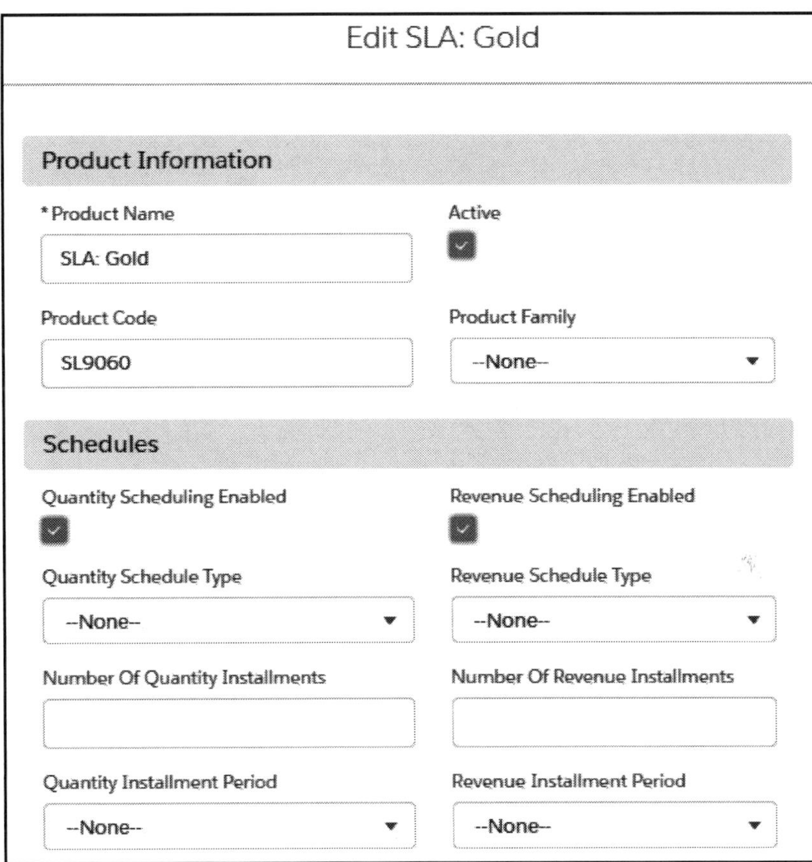

Scheduling options on a product's page layout

Define the standard schedule setup depending on the required product configuration, directly within the product layout, filling in the following fields:

- **Quantity Schedule Type**: You can choose to divide the product amount into multiple installments or repeat the amount on each installment.
- **Number Of Quantity Installments**: Duration of the schedule.
- **Revenue Installment Period:** Frequency of the installment (daily, weekly, monthly, yearly, or quarterly).

Now, go back into an opportunity, choose a scheduled opportunity product, click on the **Related** tab, and, by the new **Schedules** list, click the **Establish Schedule** button:

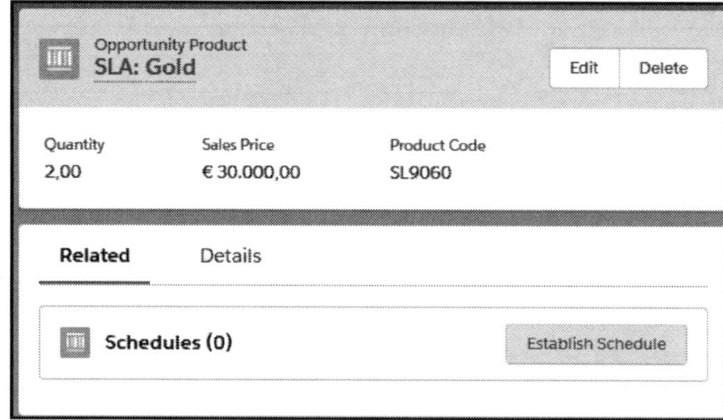

Enabling a schedule on an opportunity

An edit popup will appear and let us set up all the schedule info, with the fields described as follows.

- **Type**, with a value of Quantity, Revenue, or both
- **Quantity Schedule** and **Revenue Schedule** sections (if enabled):

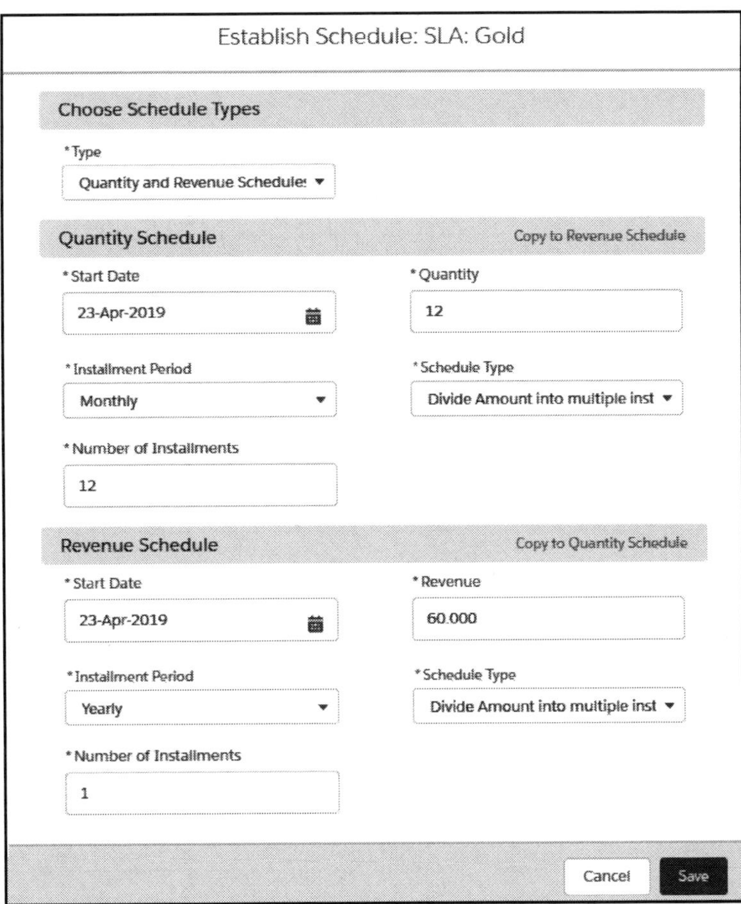

Quantity schedule configuration on an opportunity

After saving the scheduled product, we can see the calculated schedules:

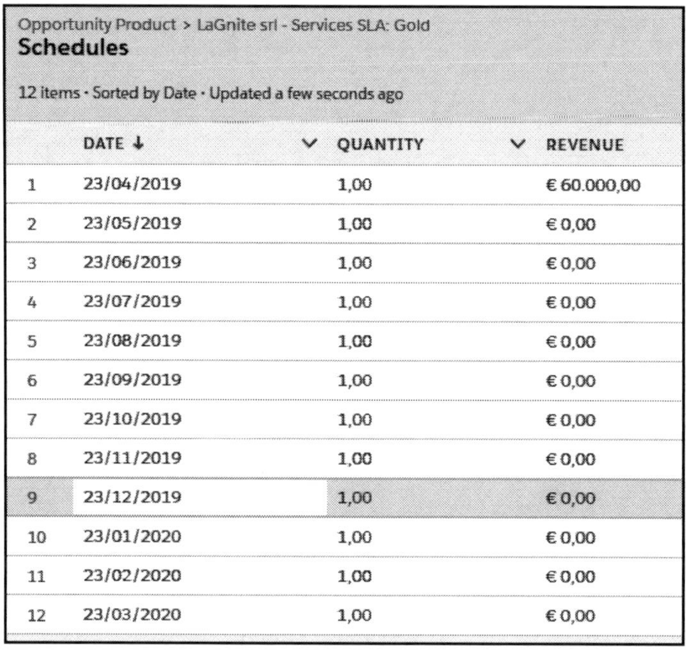

Opportunity Product > LaGnite srl - Services SLA: Gold
Schedules

12 items • Sorted by Date • Updated a few seconds ago

	DATE ↓	QUANTITY	REVENUE
1	23/04/2019	1,00	€ 60.000,00
2	23/05/2019	1,00	€ 0,00
3	23/06/2019	1,00	€ 0,00
4	23/07/2019	1,00	€ 0,00
5	23/08/2019	1,00	€ 0,00
6	23/09/2019	1,00	€ 0,00
7	23/10/2019	1,00	€ 0,00
8	23/11/2019	1,00	€ 0,00
9	23/12/2019	1,00	€ 0,00
10	23/01/2020	1,00	€ 0,00
11	23/02/2020	1,00	€ 0,00
12	23/03/2020	1,00	€ 0,00

Calculated schedules on an opportunity

Click on **Reestablish Schedule** to create a brand new schedule, or click on **Edit Schedule** to manually update the calculated installments.

In the previous example, we have selected 12 monthly installments for a total quantity of 12 (so, once a month) and a unique revenue scheduling for the total amount for this product.

Now that we have seen how products work and how they can be added to opportunities to define the deal's revenue, we'll deal with quotes, which help sales reps to negotiate the deal before its closure.

Managing quotes and quote templates

Quotes contain the proposed prices of items and services sold to customers. They are created after an opportunity, inheriting their products, but quantities and pricing can change. That's why we can have multiple quotes linked to a given opportunity.

No surprises...opportunities pass through various stages (one of them is called **Negotiation/Review**) and so we can have different propositions for our customers. Once a quote is accepted, its products, quantities, and pricing can be synced up with the opportunity.

Quotes are not enabled by default. Go to **Setup** | **Feature Settings** | **Sales** | **Quotes** | **Quote Settings** and click on the **Enable** button. Then, select the opportunities layouts you want to be appended to the **Quotes-**related list:

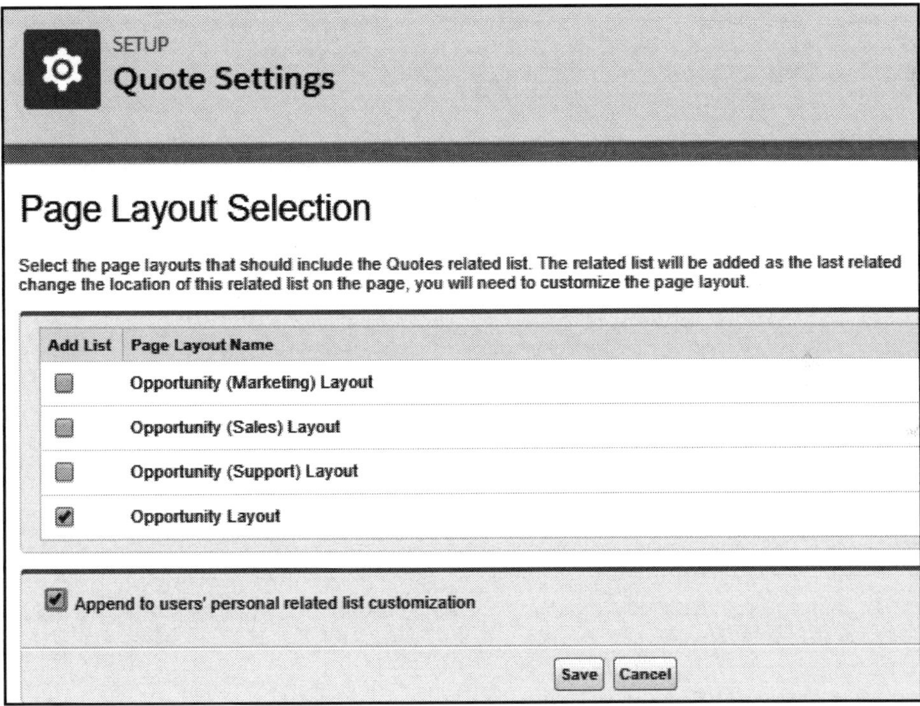

Enabling a Quotes-related list on opportunity page layouts

If you've mistakenly set up the wrong layout, don't worry. We can always set it up manually on each opportunity's page layout.

If you need to disable quotes, click on **Quote Settings** again and click on the **Disable** button. You cannot disable quotes if you have any customizations that refer to quote fields (or quote line items or quote PDFs, which we'll see shortly), such as a formula field, a workflow rule, or a process builder, for instance.

To create a new quote, simply click on the **New Quote** action on the **Quotes-**related list:

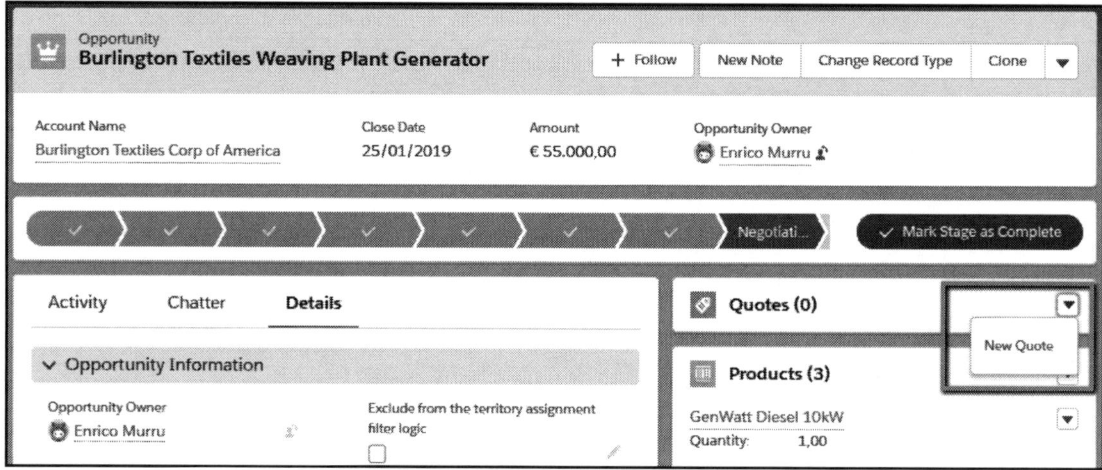

Quote creation from the opportunity-related list

Select all the required fields (such as taxes, contact info, addresses, shipping costs, and expiration date) and hit the **Save** button. We'll get a quote with all the products from the opportunity:

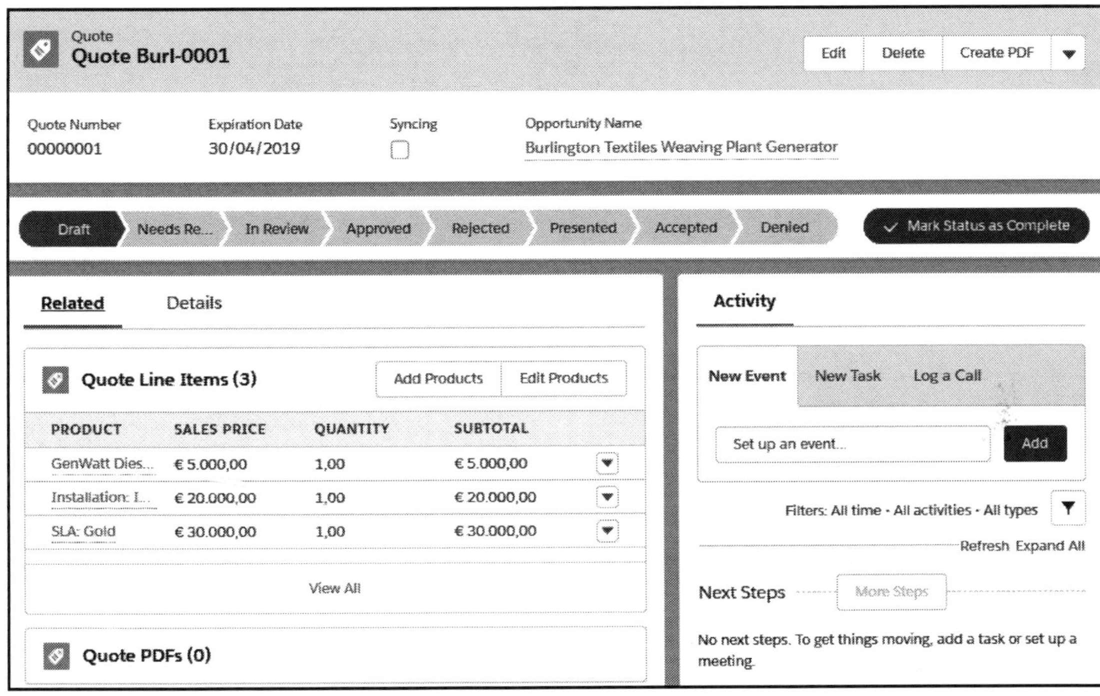

Quote created from an opportunity

You can change any info in the **Quote Line Items** section (these are the quote's products), and you can create a PDF containing all the details of your quote with the **Create PDF** button found on the quote header:

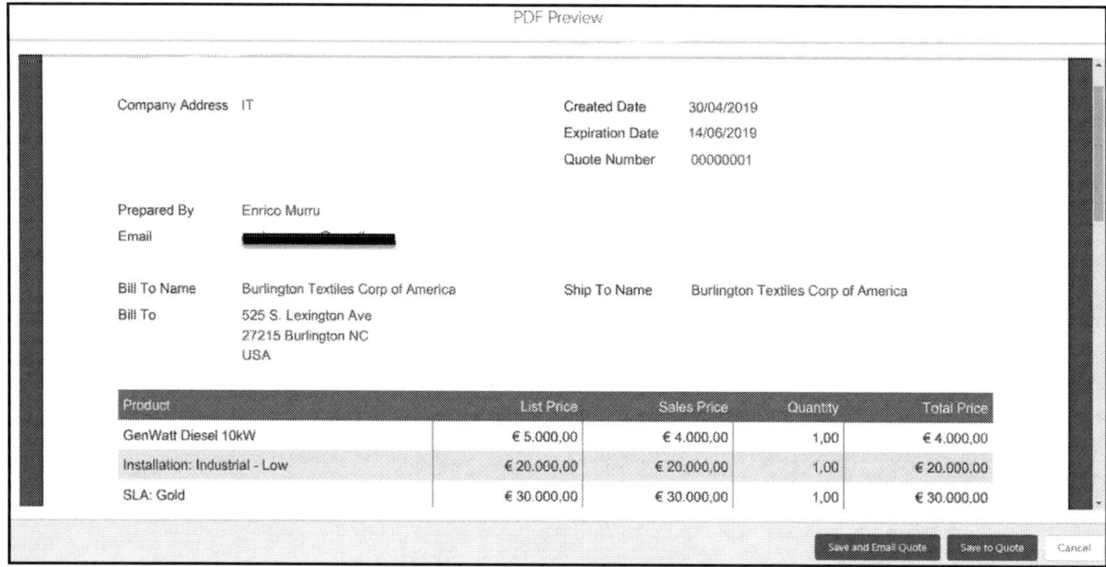

Quote PDF generation

You can save the quote or contextually send an email containing the PDF to the customer. You can send it later if needed from the **Quote PDF-**related list actions.

Quote templates creation

I know what your next question is: what if we want to change the format of a quote's PDF?

Navigate to **Setup** | **Features Settings** | **Sales** | **Quotes** | **Quote Templates** and update the standard template using **Edit**, or create your own template with the **New** button (if you have more than one active template, before printing the PDF, we'll be required to select a template):

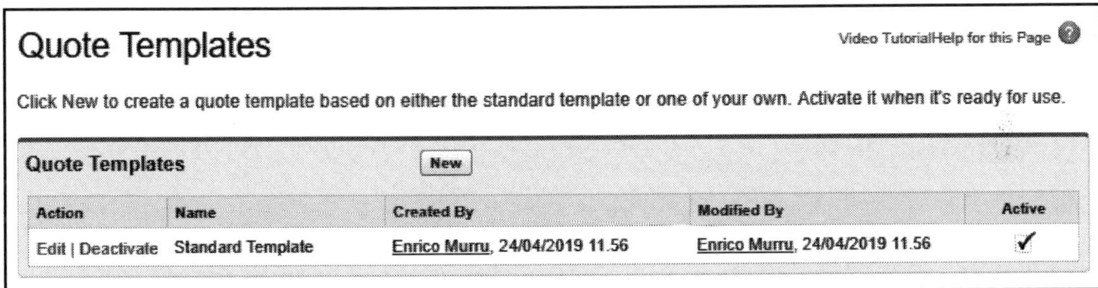

Quote Templates list

When you edit a template, you'll get a page layout-like editor with Header/Body/Footer sections, as shown here:

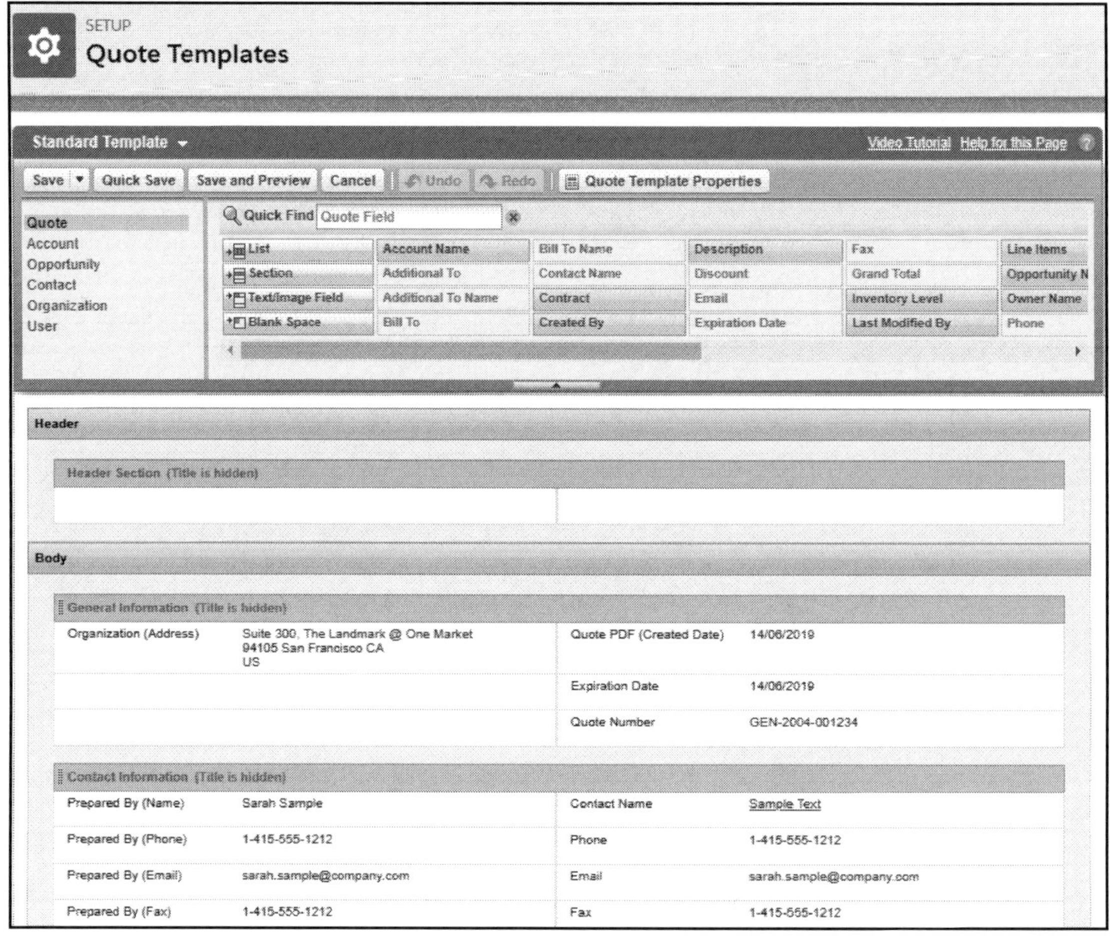

Quote template editor

In any section of the previous template, we can add a **Text/Image Field** to set up some rich text and images to brand your quote's PDF. Use the **List Field** to add a list of any standard or custom object that is related to the quote.

You can even add new sections getting fields from the quote itself, the account, the opportunity, the contact, the organization, and even user-related objects.

Finally, in the footer, let's add a signature section with all required fields using **Text/Image Fields** (this is just a custom text insertion, after all):

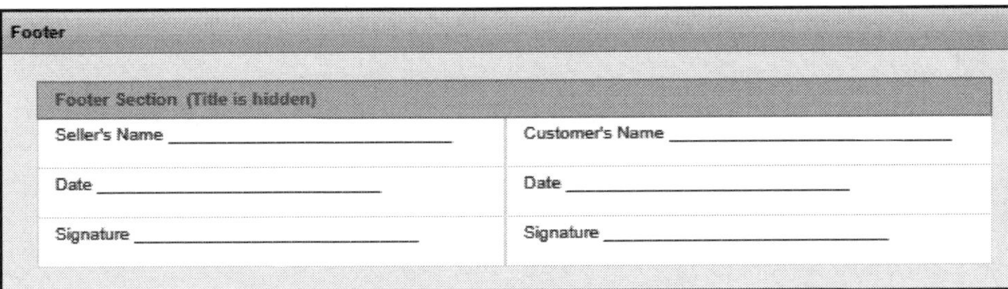

Quote template signature

Quote versus opportunity synchronization

The last important feature of quotes is that we can align a quote's line items to its opportunity's products. To do this, click on the **Start Sync** button (it may be hidden next to the **Create PDF** button).

A message will warn us that any info about opportunity products will be replaced by the quote line items:

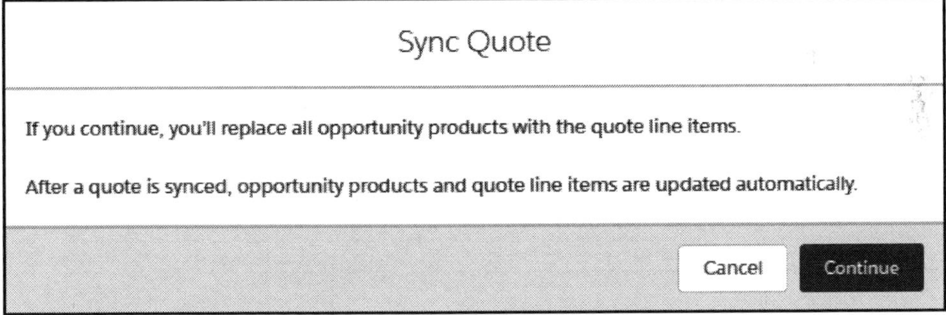

Warning message upon quote sync activation

From now on, until you click the **Stop Sync** action, any change to the quote's products are synced back to its opportunity, and vice versa.

There can be only one synchronized quote at a time.

Once opportunities and quotes are created, the deal proceeds to be, hopefully, closed by all the sales reps of our company. Using forecasts, sales managers can predict the expected revenue for all opportunities involved in their sales department. Let's discuss this in more depth.

Predicting deals with forecasts

A forecast is a prediction of the expected sales revenue of all the deals involved in a defined time frame. They are important for sales managers and, more generally, for the company's business people because they allow proper sales strategy planning.

Opportunities are the core source of data for forecasts because their amounts and quantities roll up over time, depending on their stages and other key data (such as close date, owner, products, and territory). Do you remember the **Probability** and **Forecast Category** fields on the Opportunity object? They are used in forecasts to segment and group opportunity data (no surprise that a 10% probability opportunity has a smaller impact on forecasts than a 90% probability one).

Change forecast categories values from **Setup** | **Object Manager** | **Opportunity** | **Fields & Relations** | **Forecast Category** to align them to the company's sales strategy.

To better understand what forecasts are, let's have a look at the following diagram:

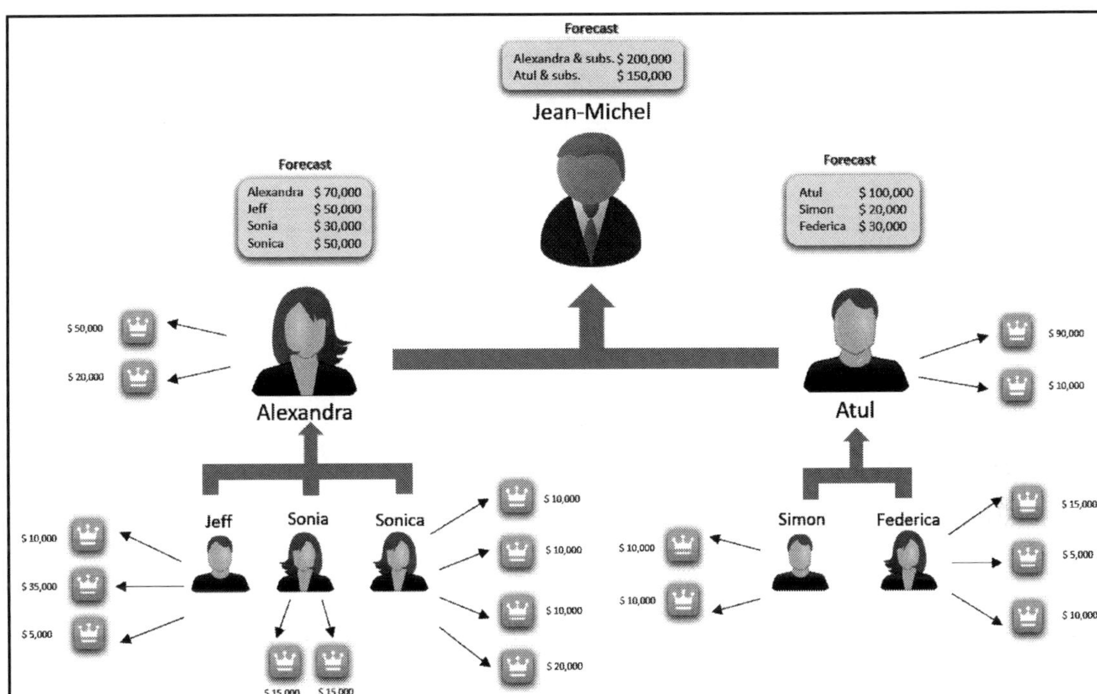

Example of the forecasting hierarchy

This diagram shows a company's hierarchy:

- Jean-Michel is the SVP of Sales
- Alexandra is the VP of International Sales
- Atul is the VP of North America Sales
- Jeff, Sonia, and Sonica are sales reps of the International Sales division
- Simon and Federica are sales reps of the North America Sales division

The following diagram shows an excerpt from the company's role hierarchy:

Role hierarchy example

Forecasts allow each manager to have a look at all their sales opportunities and have roll-up values of all involved revenues.

The Salesforce platform delivers two kinds of forecasting:

- Customizable forecasting
- Collaborative forecasting

Customizable forecasting will be retired in the Summer '20 release. If you want more details on how this feature works, refer to `https://help.salesforce.com/articleView?id=customizable_forecasting_intro.htmtype=5`.

For the differences between collaborative and customizable forecasts, refer to `https://help.salesforce.com/articleView?id=faq_forecasts3_whats_difference_between_versions.htmtype=5`.

In this section, we'll dig into **collaborative forecasting**.

Setting up collaborative forecasting

A picture is worth a thousand words. Let's see what using forecasts is like:

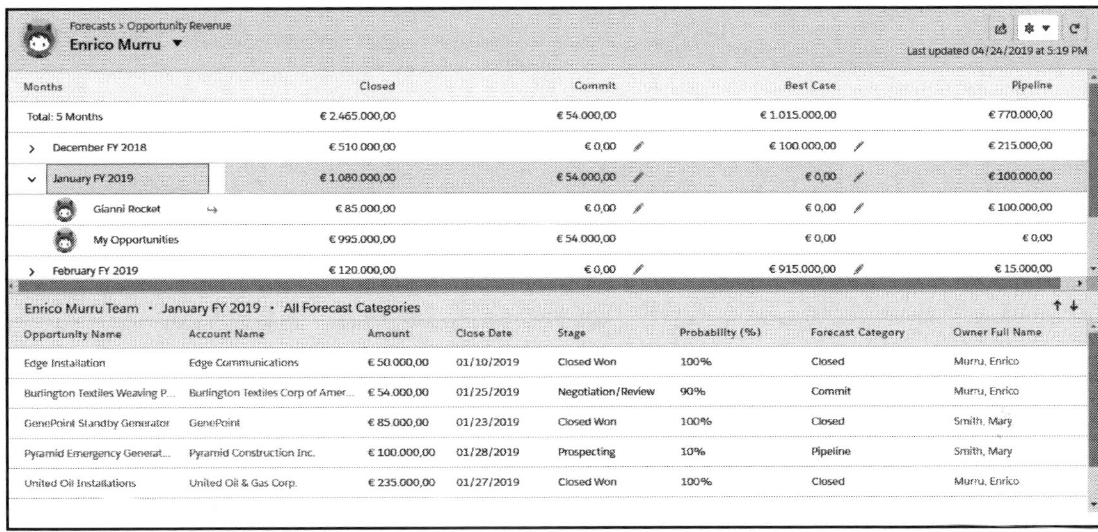

Forecast view of a sales manager

We can see two panels:

- The upper panel shows a cumulative view of all revenues in a 5-month time period, and for each month individually (this is the actual forecast). Each month's row also shows a number of rows related to the users below the current user's role. Each row shows the total revenue for each **Forecast Category** (from left to right, the probability that the deal is closed lowers).
- The lower panel shows the opportunities that concur on the selected time period (on the upper panel).

A manager can have a look at their subordinates' forecast details by clicking on the arrow next to the username:

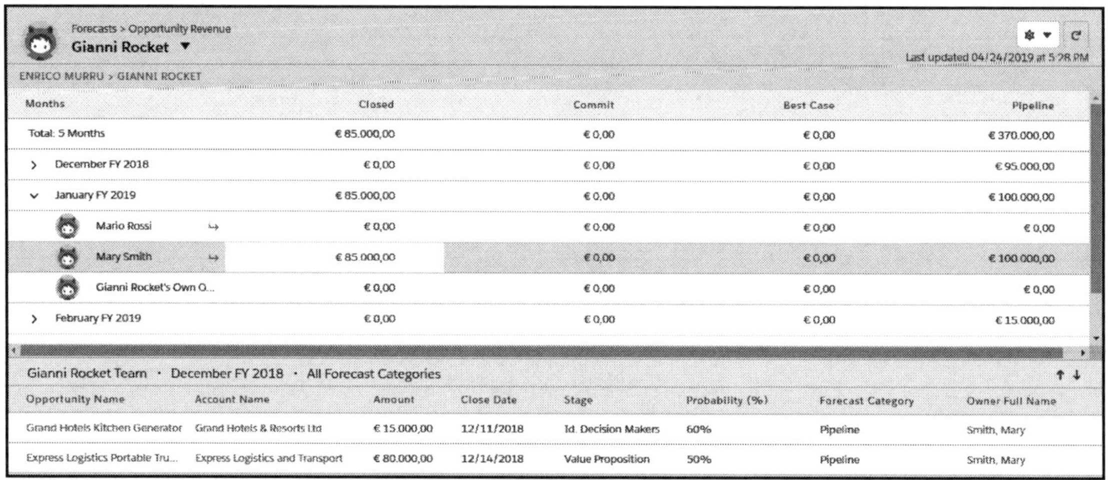

Forecast view of a subordinate sales manager

We can descend to the lowermost users in the hierarchy.

To enable collaborative forecasting, navigate to **Setup** | **Features Settings** | **Sales** | **Forecasts** | **Forecasts Settings** and click on the **Enable forecasts** flag. A list of options will appear.

The first option is the **Forecast Type**, which defines the kind of data that is rolled up for your forecast. You can define up to four forecast types at a time.

Forecast types are defined by the following properties:

- **Forecast Type**: This is the main category on which rolling up opportunities in the forecast (opportunities, product families, opportunity splits, overlay splits, custom opportunity currency field, expected revenue)
- **Forecast Measurement**: This is the kind of metric we want to roll up (revenue or quantity).
- **Forecast Date Type**: This is only for opportunity type, representing the date field used for the time-based roll-up (close date, product date, schedule date, and close date; all other forecast types uses the close date)
- **Fields to show on the List**: This is used to select the list of fields to be shown in the lower panel.

For a comprehensive list of all the value combinations when customizing a forecast type, refer to Salesforce Help at `https://help.salesforce.com/articleView?id=forecasts3_forecast_types_overview.htmtype=5`.

Now, let's discuss forecast types in more detail:

- The **Opportunities** type returns a forecast based on the amount or quantity (the sum of all opportunity product quantities).
- The **product families** type roll-up is based on the Product Family field, which is displayed as an additional level for each period:

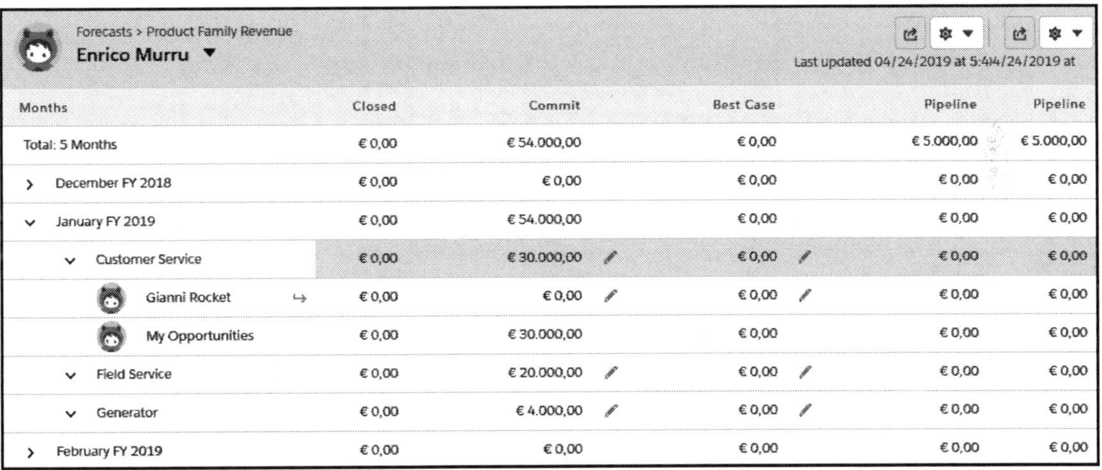

Months	Closed	Commit	Best Case	Pipeline	Pipeline
Total: 5 Months	€ 0,00	€ 54.000,00	€ 0,00	€ 5.000,00	€ 5.000,00
December FY 2018	€ 0,00	€ 0,00	€ 0,00	€ 0,00	€ 0,00
January FY 2019	€ 0,00	€ 54.000,00	€ 0,00	€ 0,00	€ 0,00
Customer Service	€ 0,00	€ 30.000,00	€ 0,00	€ 0,00	€ 0,00
Gianni Rocket	€ 0,00	€ 0,00	€ 0,00	€ 0,00	€ 0,00
My Opportunities	€ 0,00	€ 30.000,00	€ 0,00	€ 0,00	€ 0,00
Field Service	€ 0,00	€ 20.000,00	€ 0,00	€ 0,00	€ 0,00
Generator	€ 0,00	€ 4.000,00	€ 0,00	€ 0,00	€ 0,00
February FY 2019	€ 0,00	€ 0,00	€ 0,00	€ 0,00	€ 0,00

Product families forecast type

- The **opportunity splits** type rolls up on opportunity splits, a feature that is linked with opportunity teams, allowing each member of the team to get credit for a percentage (called a split) of the opportunity amount.

For more information on opportunity splits, refer to `https://help.salesforce.com/articleView?id=teamselling_opp_splits_overview.htmtype=5`.

- The **overlay splits** type tracks the revenue of sales team members who helped to close the deal but were not responsible for the actual closing.
- The **custom opportunity currency fields** type relies on a custom currency field on the Opportunity object.
- The **expected revenue** type uses the opportunity's expected revenue field, which is the amount multiplied by the stage's probability.

Opportunity splits, overlay splits, custom opportunity currency fields, and expected revenue types need team selling and opportunity splits to be enabled, even if they are not actually used.

You can use territories to forecast opportunities and product families. This way, it rolls up on territories assigned to opportunities.

No role hierarchy is used to roll up in this configuration:

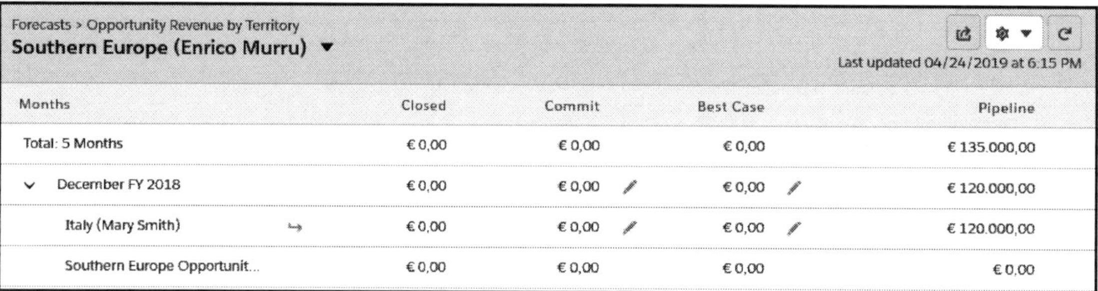

Forecasts > Opportunity Revenue by Territory
Southern Europe (Enrico Murru)
Last updated 04/24/2019 at 6:15 PM

Months	Closed	Commit	Best Case	Pipeline
Total: 5 Months	€ 0,00	€ 0,00	€ 0,00	€ 135.000,00
December FY 2018	€ 0,00	€ 0,00	€ 0,00	€ 120.000,00
Italy (Mary Smith)	€ 0,00	€ 0,00	€ 0,00	€ 120.000,00
Southern Europe Opportunit...	€ 0,00	€ 0,00	€ 0,00	€ 0,00

Example of opportunity forecast with territories

A manager can drill down to the child territories. To configure a territory, the manager needs to go to **Setup** | **Feature Settings** | **Territories** | **Territory Models** | **View Hierarchy** on your model, click on the **Edit** link next to a territory, and fill in the **Forecast Manager** box:

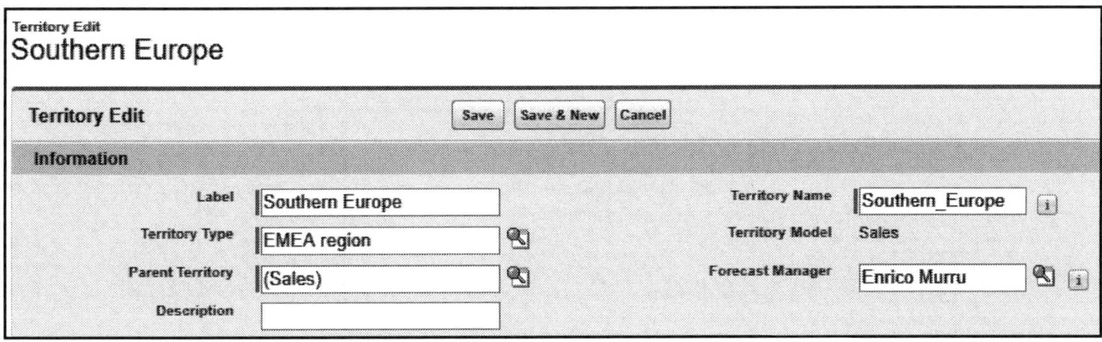

Filling in the Forecast Manager box

Do you remember the territory hierarchy in `Chapter 1`, *Secure Data Access*? The forecast manager of the **Southern Europe** territory can have a look at all the opportunities in the Southern Europe territory and below the territory hierarchy, as a practical example.

Now, let's get back to the **Forecast Settings** page and see that we have so far enabled the following forecast types:

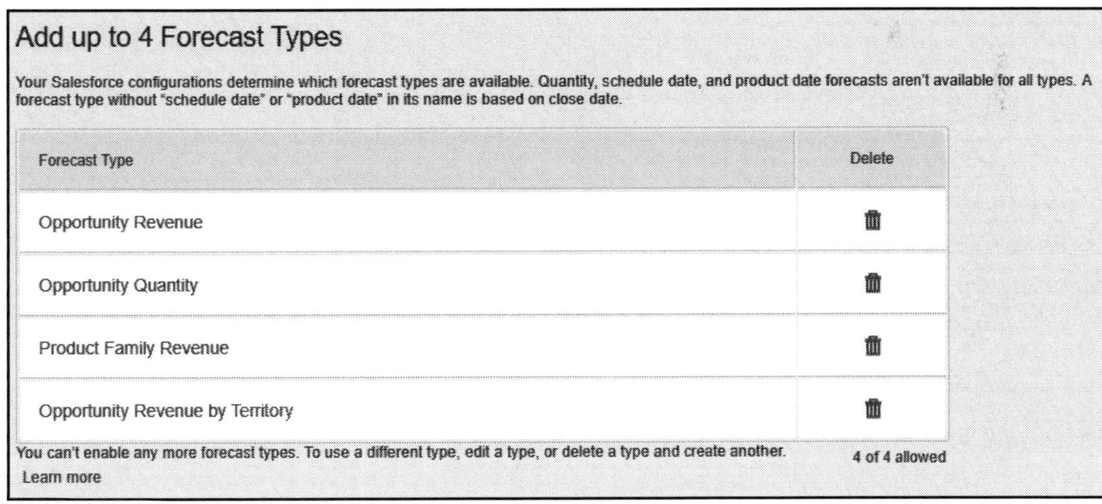

Example of forecast types enabled

To enter the forecast page, click on the **App Launcher** and search for **Forecasts** (you can add the **Forecasts** tab to any Lightning app) and the forecast types can be chosen from the settings icon on the right-hand side:

Forecast types selection on the Forecast view page

From this menu, you can remove rows with no results and set up a custom time range that differs from the default one.

The default forecast time is set up on the **Forecast Settings** page in the **Configure the Default Forecast Display** section:

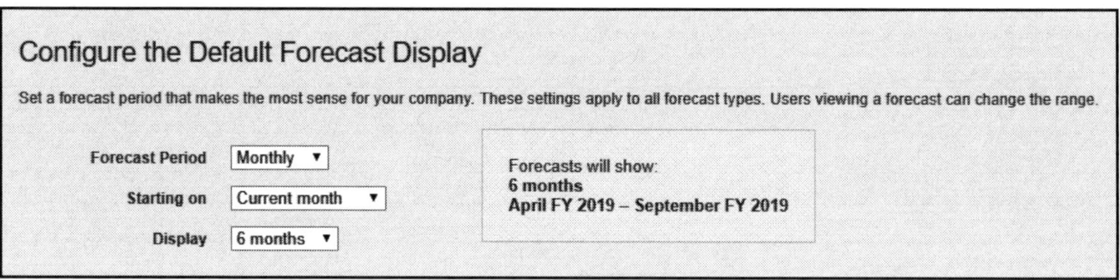

Forecast default time frame selection

Use a period of **Monthly** or **Quarterly**, a start period (+/- 15 months or +/- 8 quarters), and a display window (1-15 months or 1-8 quarters).

Enable **forecast adjustments** for both manager and owner. This way, a manager/opportunity owner can change the expected revenue/quantity by adding or subtracting an amount, using the pencil icon next to a quantity/revenue roll-up cell (this is useful when managers know that their sales reps are too conservative or confident in their opportunity's closing probability):

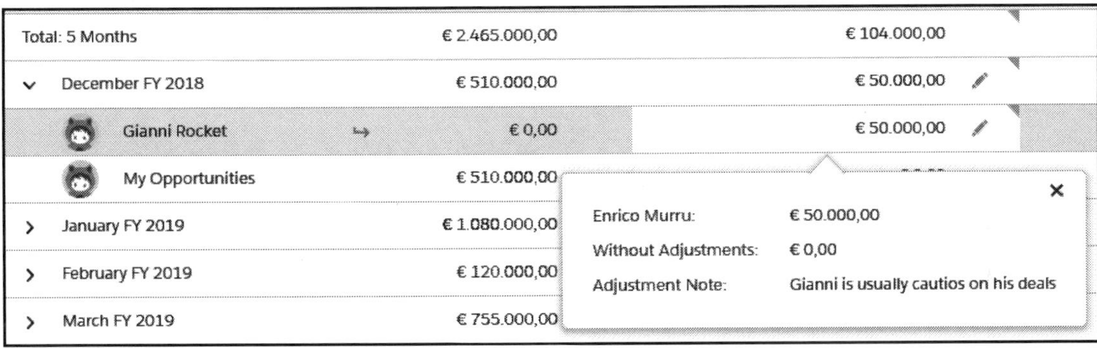

A manager can adjust a forecast category with a comment

Finally, we can set up **cumulative forecast roll-ups**, which allow a cumulative roll-up on each forecast category (rather than showing the sum of all the cells in a column):

- Closed shows only the closed deals
- Commit shows committed and closed opportunities
- Best Case shows best case, committed, and closed opportunities
- Open Pipeline shows pipeline, best case, and committed opportunities

Here is what the cumulative forecast roll-up looks like:

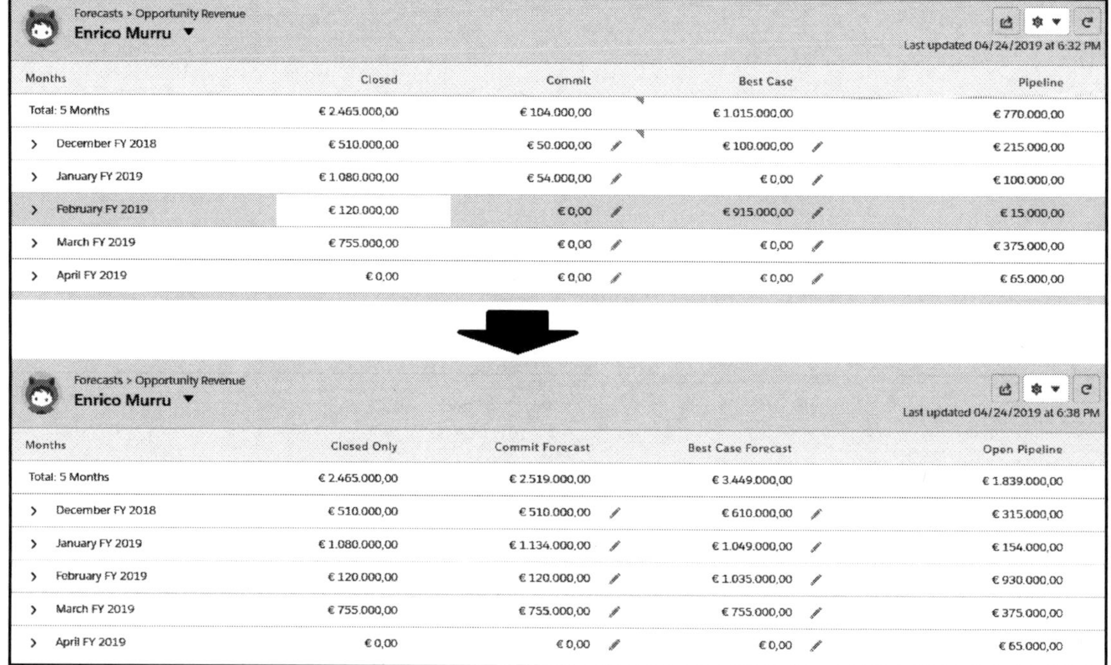

Months	Closed	Commit	Best Case	Pipeline
Total: 5 Months	€ 2.465.000,00	€ 104.000,00	€ 1.015.000,00	€ 770.000,00
December FY 2018	€ 510.000,00	€ 50.000,00	€ 100.000,00	€ 215.000,00
January FY 2019	€ 1.080.000,00	€ 54.000,00	€ 0,00	€ 100.000,00
February FY 2019	€ 120.000,00	€ 0,00	€ 915.000,00	€ 15.000,00
March FY 2019	€ 755.000,00	€ 0,00	€ 0,00	€ 375.000,00
April FY 2019	€ 0,00	€ 0,00	€ 0,00	€ 65.000,00

Months	Closed Only	Commit Forecast	Best Case Forecast	Open Pipeline
Total: 5 Months	€ 2.465.000,00	€ 2.519.000,00	€ 3.449.000,00	€ 1.839.000,00
December FY 2018	€ 510.000,00	€ 510.000,00	€ 610.000,00	€ 315.000,00
January FY 2019	€ 1.080.000,00	€ 1.134.000,00	€ 1.049.000,00	€ 154.000,00
February FY 2019	€ 120.000,00	€ 120.000,00	€ 1.035.000,00	€ 930.000,00
March FY 2019	€ 755.000,00	€ 755.000,00	€ 755.000,00	€ 375.000,00
April FY 2019	€ 0,00	€ 0,00	€ 0,00	€ 65.000,00

Cumulative forecast roll-up before and after

To enable users to access forecasts, enable the **Allow Forecasting** flag on the user object.

If we are using role-based forecast types, we can add users from **Setup** | **Features Settings** | **Sales** | **Forecasts** | **Forecast Hierarchy**. This page shows all roles in the organization and highlights managers:

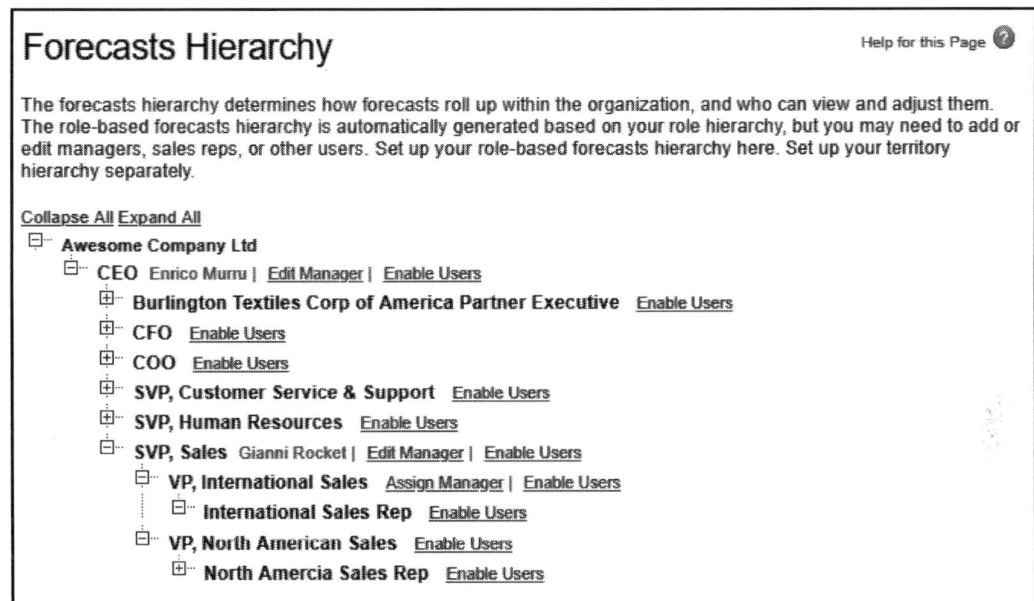

Forecast role hierarchy configuration

You can enable users from this page using the **Enable Users** link, which shows all users within that role and that have the **Allow Forecasting** flag enabled.

If the current organization has multi-currency enabled (refer to the previous section), on the **Forecast Settings** page we can set up the default currency (users can forecast on their preferred currency from the settings of the Forecast view page):

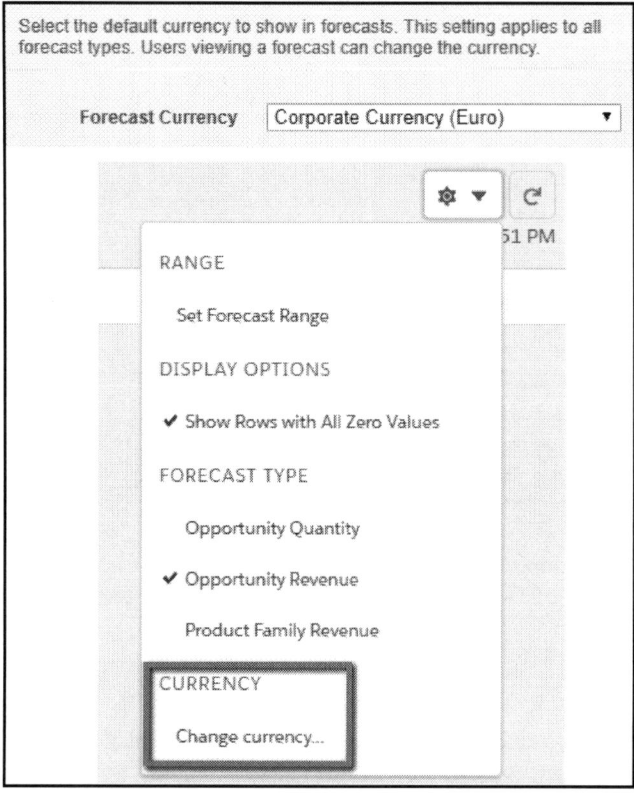

Default currency and custom currency selection on the forecast settings and view page

Another feature related to forecasts is **quotas**, that is, a monthly/quarterly goal assigned to a sales team or territory. A manager's quota is the sum of his subordinates' quotas and is related to a given forecast type. This feature originally required manual configuration with Data Loader or APIs (to load quota data), but with the Summer '19 release, administrators can finally define quotes with point and click from the CRM setup.

For more information on how to load quotas, refer to Salesforce Help at `https://help.salesforce.com/articleView?id=forecasts3_quotes_intro.htmtype=5`.

Summary

In this chapter, we discussed some advanced Sales Cloud features. We saw how to configure products, price books, and product schedules, and how they are related to opportunities, the source of all the deals.

With quotes, we learned how to propose a deal to a customer, create different proposals, export them in PDF format with quote templates, and sync quotes line items with opportunity products.

Finally, we discovered what forecasts are and how collaborative forecasts can give sales managers a preview of how sales activities are delivered in order to adjust and plan the right sales strategy.

The next chapter will be dedicated to some cool Service Cloud features that will enhance the service support experience.

Questions

1. Which standard opportunity fields are used to track the status and likelihood that the deal will be closed?
    a. Status
    b. Stage
    c. Probability
    d. Type
    e. Forecast category
2. How can you define a new sales strategy for your opportunities?
    a. Configure a new sales process with its own stage values and assign them to a new opportunity record type
    b. Create a new opportunity record type and assign it a specific set of stage picklist's values
    c. Create a new sales team and assign it to new opportunities
    d. Create a new sales territory and assign it to new opportunities
3. The Amount field on the opportunity:
    a. Can no longer be updated once products are added to an opportunity
    b. Is related to the likelihood that a deal is closed
    c. Is related to the Stage field
    d. Is the sum of all opportunity products' prices

4. What is a PIM?
    a. A Probability Info Messaging system
    b. A Product Identity Master system
    c. A Product Information Management system
5. When cloning a product:
    a. All price books are cloned as well
    b. Only owned price books are cloned with the product
    c. Only price books the current user has access to are cloned with the product
    d. Only updatable product fields are copied in the cloned product
6. Which prices are related to a product?
    a. Sell price, standard price, and global price
    b. Standard price, list price, and sales price
    c. Standard price, list price, and selling price
    d. Standard price and multi-currency price
7. Which kind of product schedule can be read as *Pay once and receive more than once*?
    a. Quantity schedule
    b. Revenue schedule
    c. Default schedule
8. Which kind of product schedule can be read as *Receive once and pay more than once*?
    a. Quantity schedule
    b. Revenue schedule
    c. Default schedule
9. What is true about quotes?
    a. We can have more quotes for the same opportunity
    b. We can have only one quote for the same opportunity
    c. We can sync more than one quote up to the same opportunity
    d. We can sync only one quote up to the same opportunity
10. In a quote template, we can add:
    a. Quote fields only
    b. Quote fields and opportunity fields only
    c. Quote fields and related records fields
    d. Text and image branding

11. Which is the most recent forecasting type in Salesforce?
    a. Customizable forecasting
    b. Collaborative forecasting
12. Which of the following are forecast types?
    a. Opportunities
    b. Product families
    c. Territories
    d. Overlay splits
    e. Amount field
13. If we enable forecast based on opportunity amount and territory:
    a. Role hierarchy is enforced
    b. Role hierarchy is no longer considered
14. To enable users to forecast:
    a. Enable the Allow Forecasting flag on the User object
    b. Enable the Allow Forecasting flag on the profile
    c. Enable the Allow Forecasting flag on the permission set
    d. Enable the Forecasting User permission on the User object
15. If a sales manager knows his sales reps, behavior regarding closing opportunities, which feature can the manager use to adjust forecasts?
    a. Forecast alignments
    b. Forecast corrections
    c. Forecast adjustments

6
Service Cloud Applications

In the previous chapter, we learned how our business can leverage Salesforce sales capabilities to enhance our chances of closing a deal. When a deal is made, we need to build a strong relationship with our customers using our platform features. This is known as **Customer Relationship Management** (**CRM**).

What's CRM without a proper service center? Salesforce Sales Cloud provides great tools that we can use to set up a fully functional service center. In this chapter, we'll use Salesforce Knowledge to create a powerful **knowledge base** (**KB**) that will be integrated within service processes, entitlements, and milestones to enforce a customers' **service-level agreement** (**SLA**), allow the Live Agent to deliver an efficient service chat, and provide Omni-Channel configuration so that we can smartly route our incoming service requests.

In this chapter, we'll cover the following topics:

- Salesforce Knowledge
- Configuring Omni-Channel
- Live Agent chat and communities
- Entitlements for SLA management (and more)

Salesforce Knowledge

An ancient Sanskrit proverb says that *there is no comparison between a King and a scholar, as the king is celebrated only in his country, whereas a scholar is celebrated everywhere*. This is a concept that a Latin aphorism summarized in *scientia potentia est*, or *knowledge is power*: this applies to any aspect of life, including Salesforce.

We are not planning to rule the world or win a battle; all we want to do is speed up and enhance customer service using knowledge.

As we discussed in `Chapter 1`, *Secure Data Access*, data is the focus of business processes and extracting knowledge from it can be a win for a company.

The kind of knowledge we are actually talking about is related to customer services. Think about this book: isn't it a compilation of useful information that we can use to administer our CRM? This is knowledge.

How many times have you been asked to add a field to a page layout? When you did this, did you take the time to explain a quick *how-to* on page layouts to your junior intern, or did you do it yourself because you could do it quicker? Or did you write a few Trailhead references to help people learn from your knowledge? This is knowledge.

Have you ever assisted your service representatives when they were answering a question and kept telling them the same suggestion/answer over and over? Or do you keep sending them that old email thread where they can find the answer for themselves? This is knowledge as well.

These are great examples of knowledge processes: if I know something that can be of public use, I write it down and share it with my team because *verba volant scripta manent*, or *words fly, writing remains*.

Let's apply this concept to Service Cloud:

- Customers keep creating cases (via web-to-case forms or by contacting the call center) and asking for a specific procedure regarding a product the company sells. Use your knowledge to send an article containing all the necessary details.
- A new intern has just joined your company. All the important policies and guidelines for their first few days of work may be accessible on our company's internal KB.
- Known issues about a software product are listed on a public KB, which is accessible through the company's customer community. Customers don't even need to contact the call center to get their answers (until the problem is well-defined and harder to solve than simply reading the FAQs you provide).
- Your sales partners need constantly updated data sheets about the company's new products. A shared KB allows your sales partners to know what they are selling, as well as the company's business, to ensure that everything about their brand-new product is up to date.

At the time of writing, Salesforce provides two types of knowledge:

- Classic Knowledge
- Lightning Knowledge

For the sake of this guide, we'll deal with Lightning Knowledge, but we'll summarize the main differences later on.

For more information about Classic Knowledge, please refer to Salesforce Help at `https://help.salesforce.com/articleView?id=knowledge_setup.htmtype=5`. Alternatively, take a look at the Trailhead module at `https://trailhead.salesforce.com/content/learn/modules/knowledge_essentials?trail_id=service_cloud`.

If you come from Classic Knowledge and plan to migrate to Lightning Knowledge, use the **Lightning Knowledge Migration Tool** (more details can be found at `https://help.salesforce.com/articleView?id=knowledge_migration_tool.htmtype=5`).

The following are the main concepts of Lightning Knowledge:

- Articles are stored in the knowledge standard object (we can customize this like any other standard object).
- Different article types are related to different record types (in Classic, each article type was a standalone custom Knowledge object with its own fields and layouts).
- Articles are grouped into category groups and data categories (to ease search and categorization capabilities).
- Users can search for articles and post them on Chatter or attach them to cases.
- Users can read articles (depending on the kind of user and article configuration).
- Users can create, edit, and publish articles (the so-called publishers).
- Users can delete or archive articles (higher administrators).

Once you turn on Lightning Knowledge, you can't go back, so plan the activation carefully.

Setting up Salesforce Lightning Knowledge

The easiest way to set up Salesforce Lightning Knowledge is by using the Lightning Knowledge Setup flow, which is accessible from **Settings** | **Service Setup** | **View All** | **Knowledge Setup**:

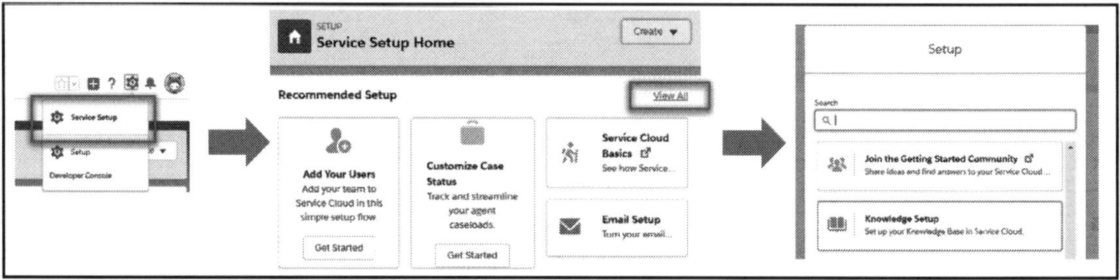

Lightning Knowledge Flow activation

This wizard executes the following actions:

1. Enables Lightning Knowledge.
2. Selects the users who will be the authors (the ones with create and publish permissions).
3. Creates data categories and groups (for example, the **Southern Europe** group, with **Italy**, **Germany**, and **France** as categories). Don't worry about setting up categories at this stage; you can set them up later.

After completing the wizard, go to **Setup** | **Object Manager** and look for the Knowledge object that has just been enabled on the organization. Its API name is different from the other standard or custom objects because it ends with the `__kav` suffix.

A record type called **FAQ** will have been created for you (along with a dedicated page layout), as well as the **Question** and **Answer** custom fields (feel free to remove them and create your own custom fields if you wish to).

The users you selected in the first step of the wizard will have the **Knowledge User** user's permission (you can always add this permission manually to other user records).

This permission grants the user access to the knowledge authoring actions (if we go to the **Knowledge** tab from **App Launcher** without the **Knowledge User** permission, we will be able to see all of the available articles, but we won't see a **New** button so that we can create more).

The user also gets the Knowledge LSF permission set, which grants edit and publish permissions on articles, as well as object-level and field-level permissions on the Knowledge object.

Assigning the permission set without activating the **Knowledge User** setting is not enough to enable an author. This is because the number of licensed knowledge users is limited by your organization's license limits. You can find your organization's limits by going to **Setup** | **Company Settings** | **Company Information** in the **Feature Licenses** section:

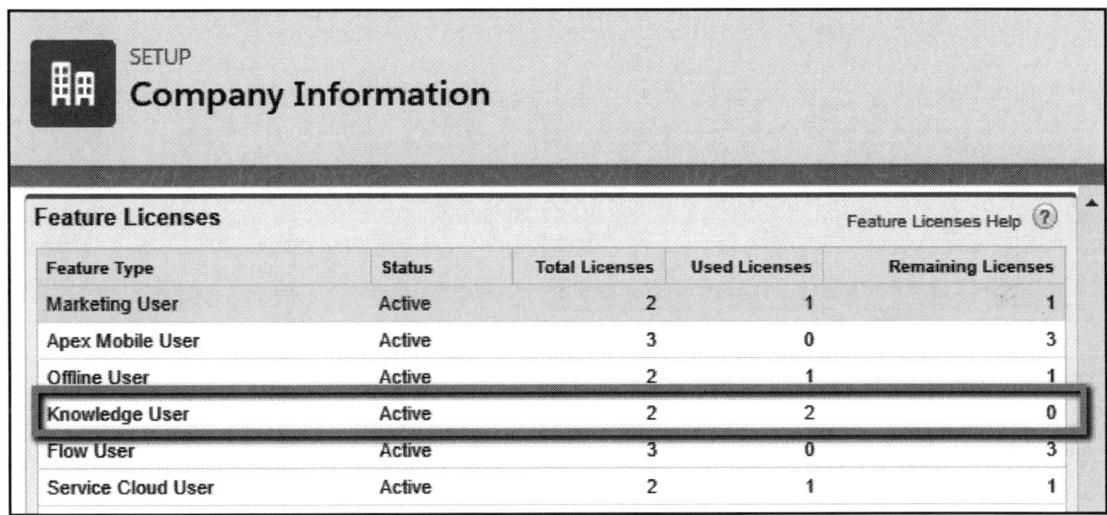

Knowledge User feature license

As a general rule, only selected users can access authoring capabilities, but all internal users get automatic access to knowledge articles in read-only mode (unless their profile has been configured so that they can't access the Knowledge object).

Lightning Knowledge uses user permissions to grant access to authoring actions. On the other hand, Classic Knowledge uses public groups and article actions.

Handling articles

Knowledge home is a simple object list page where we can configure list views, as we do with any other object. To access this page, click on **App Launcher** and look for **Knowledge**.

Click on a specific article (or create a new one) to access the article record page:

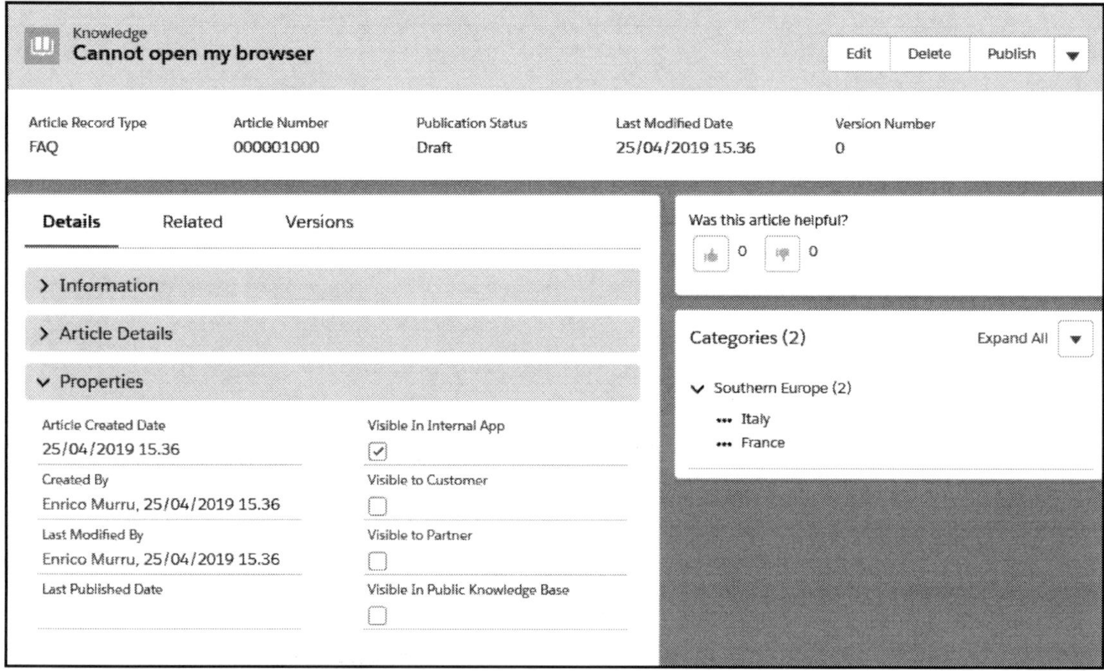

Article view

From here, we can configure the following:

- The main page layout, along with all the available actions (such as **Edit**, **Publish**, **Change Record Type**, and so on) that are linked to one or more record types
- A compact layout for the header section
- The **Details/Related/Versions** tabs
- The rating component (uses the Lightning App Builder to add/remove components)
- The article data categories component (if the user has the **Manager Categories** permission, they'll be able to change the article's categories)

When creating a new article, we need to set the following:

- The article's title and URL (these are required fields)
- Any custom field we want to be a part of the current article's record type
- Visibility flags to control who sees what on your organization:
    - **Visible Internal App**: Visibility to internal users (the default is true; this cannot be unchecked)
    - **Visible to Partner**: Visibility to partner community users
    - **Visible to Customer**: Visibility to customer community users
    - **Visible In Public Knowledge Base**: Visibility in public communities

The article's life cycle can be summarized as follows:

1. Create an article (draft version 1).
2. Approve the article (draft version 1).
3. Publish the article (published version 1).
4. Update a new version of the article (draft version 2).
5. Approval of the article (draft version 2).
6. Publish the article (published version 2).
7. Archive the article.
8. Delete the article.

Step 4 and *step 5* can be repeated as many times as needed, whereas steps 7-8 require specific permissions on the user's profile (the archive articles and delete Knowledge object-level permissions should only be given to high-level/trusted users).

Approval steps 2 and 5 can optionally use standard approval processes to ensure high-quality levels of knowledge content.

The publish action can be executed immediately or at a given time, that is, when it's been scheduled:

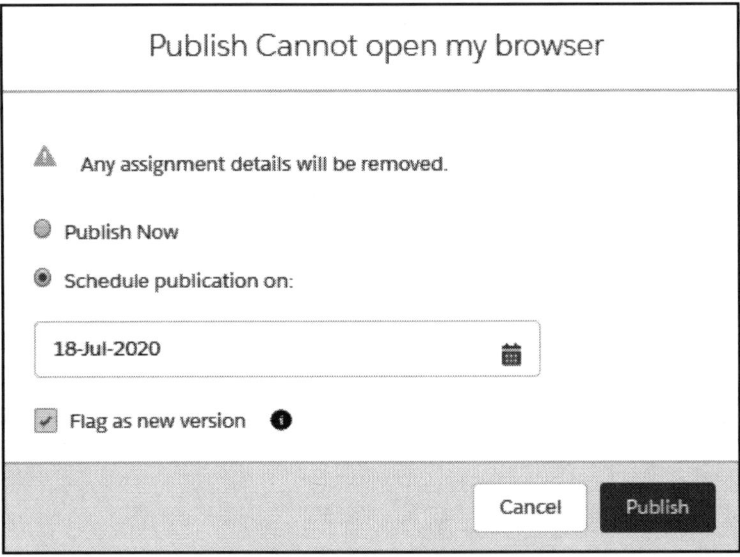

Article publish modal

When using **Publish Now**, we can publish the modified article without generating a new version of it.

There can only be one published article version at a time (see the **Publication Status** field of the Knowledge object). By using the **Restore** action, we can take an older version and make it the active one. This creates a new draft article version that can be published to override the latest version.

Other than publish, there are more actions we can perform (available from the **Mobile & Lightning Actions** section of the Knowledge object page's layout editor):

- **New**: Create an article (available on Knowledge home only).
- **Edit**: Edit a draft article.
- **Edit as Draft**: Only appears if the article has been published; it creates a new draft.
- **Assign**: Change owner.
- **Delete**: Delete the record.
- **Change Record Type**: By changing the article's record type, a new page layout may be linked to it.

- **Archive**: Archive a published article.
- **Restore**: Creates a draft from an archived version of the article.
- **Submit for Approval**: If approvals are enabled, the article is submitted to be approved by a manager.
- **Submit for Translation**: If multiple languages are enabled, this submits a translation.

One of the coolest additions to the Salesforce Knowledge family is the Knowledge component, which is available in the Lightning Service Console:

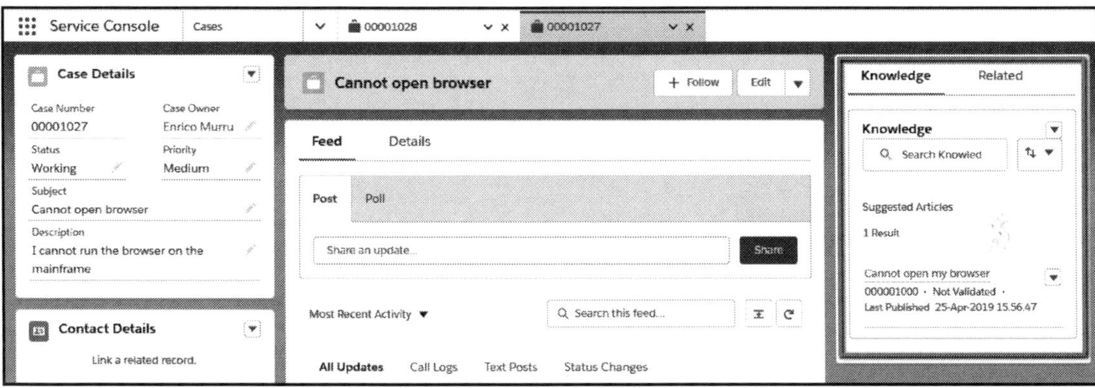

Knowledge Lightning Component

We can add this component by using the **Settings** | **Edit Page** link, which opens the Lightning App Builder.

This component does the following:

- Suggests articles based on the case's details
- Allows you to search knowledge articles
- Allows you to create new articles
- Attaches/removes articles from the current case

You can even use this component outside the Service Console by adding it to a record page using the Lightning App Builder.

Managing data categories

In the previous sections, we looked at how we can limit access to Knowledge with object-level security, field-level security, and record types through profiles and permission sets.

If we want to restrict access to specific articles in a more granular way, we need to use data categories. By using these, we can categorize articles into a structured hierarchy of categories.

Let's say our company sells products to North America, Asia, and Southern Europe. We may need to categorize our knowledge based on these macro-territories for specific countries (for example, power supply specifications change from country to country, as well as regulations).

Let's define the data category structures:

- North America:
    - Canada
    - USA
- Southern Europe:
    - Albany
    - Greece
    - Italy
    - Spain
- Asia:
    - China
    - India
    - Japan

Articles may be linked to all the categories, to a subset of them, or none of them.

You can define data categories by going to **Setup** | **Feature Settings** | **Data Categories** | **Data Category Setup**:

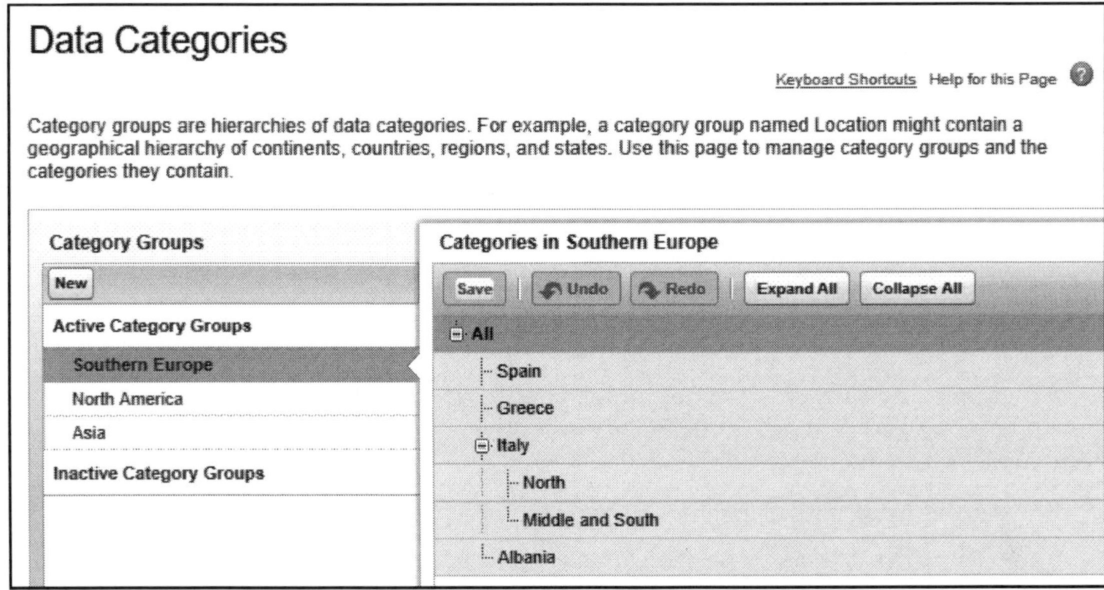

Data Categories setup

You can have a maximum of 5 category groups and only 3 activated at a time, 100 categories in a group, 5 levels of nested categories, and up to 8 data categories from a data category group assigned to an article (as of summer 2019).

Categories are assigned on the right-hand side of the article page (if you can't see the categories component, add it with the Lightning App Builder). From this component, we can select a whole group of category groups or single child categories, but not both.

Data categories can even be mapped to a case's fields. We can do this by going to **Setup** | **Feature Settings** | **Service** | **Knowledge** | **Data Category Mappings**. This way, cases are automatically assigned to specific categories groups, thereby filtering knowledge articles to a greater extent.

One of the cool features of categories is that they can handle visibility at the profile or role level. But how does this work?

If a user doesn't have access to a category (depending on their profile, permission sets, or role), they won't be able to attach it to a case, and the Knowledge component won't be able to suggest any of the articles in those categories. If an article has more than one category assigned to it, the user should be able to access to at least one category per group among the selected categories.

You can select the default category group's visibility by going to **Setup** | **Feature Settings** | **Service** | **Data Categories** | **Default Data Category Visibility**:

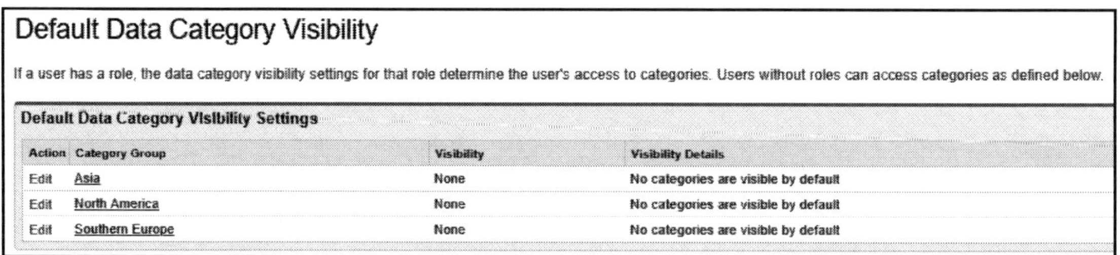

Default Data Category Group Visibility setup

From here, we can define the following:

- **All Categories** (by default, all the categories are accessible)
- **None** (by default, no category is accessible)
- **Custom** (you can select default accessible categories, as shown in the following screenshot)

The following screenshot shows the **Category Group Visibility** edit form:

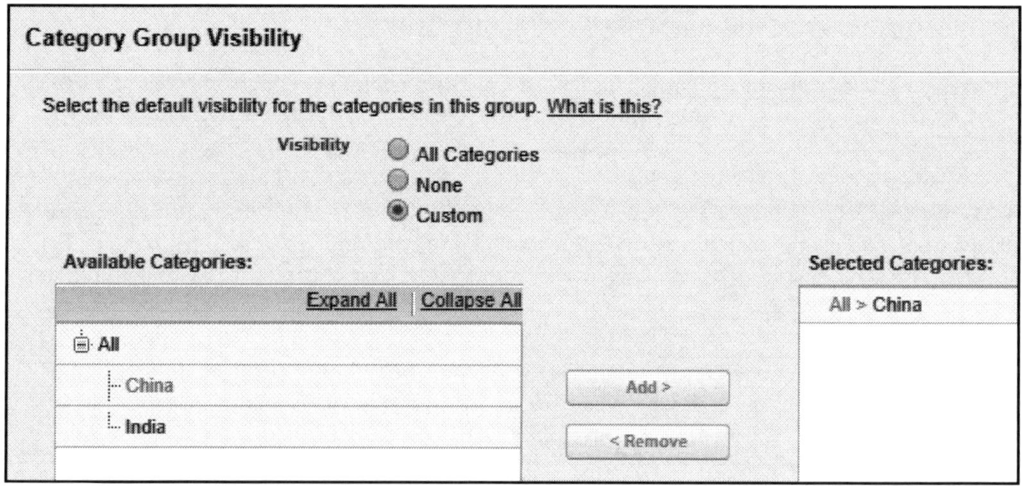

Default category visibility custom setup

That being said, you go to **Profiles | Permission Sets | Roles** to get a more granular category definition. When setting up roles, visibility is inherited by the child roles and, despite common Salesforce sharing behavior, we can restrict further access using roles. That's why we can set the CEO role so that it has full access to categories while selecting different roles with custom or no access. If the parent role doesn't have access to a category, then the child roles won't be able to see them either.

The same configuration can be made at the profile or permission set level, but no inheritance is in place here.

It is not possible to restrict access to profiles. Please refer to Salesforce Help at `https://help.salesforce.com/articleView?id=000268329 language=en_UStype=1` for more details.

If you are interested in setting up Knowledge with communities, please refer to Salesforce Help at `https://help.salesforce.com/articleView?id=networks_knowledge_access.htmtype=5`.

Importing external knowledge

Before ending this section, let's spend a few minutes talking about how we can import articles into Salesforce Knowledge that come from external sources (that is, an old knowledge system or an external website).

The process of importing articles involves creating a ZIP file containing all the required information. To do this, follow these steps:

1. Create a CSV file that holds the first row of all the fields that will be imported into Salesforce (for example, `Record Type`, `Title`, `Language`, `Data Categories`, and so on—basically, any custom field), as well as all the article's information on the following rows. If a field is typed as *rich text* or *file*, the corresponding HTML files, images, or generic file formats can be added as a relative path from the ZIP's content structure.
2. Define a property file (it has to be named with the `.properties` extension) that contains the key import parameters (such as date/time format or CSV encoding/separator).

3. Add the required extra content (such as HTML files and images for rich text fields or generic files for file type fields) to subfolders (for example, `data/html`, `data/images`, and `data/files`). Remember to respect the relative folder paths when creating CSV files. For example, if the `Description__c` custom field is a **Rich Text** field and it contains some HTML formatted data, in the CSV on the row of the `KN001` article, just fill in the corresponding column with the `data/html/art_desc_KN001.html` value, which refers to the path on the ZIP file we're going to create. If the HTML file contains a reference to the `KN001-01.png` image, that image should be linked with an `<IMG/>` tag within the HTML file, pointing to the relative path of the image within the ZIP, that is, `data/images/KN001-01.png`.
4. Create a ZIP file, which must contain the root folder of the CSV file, the properties file, and all the required subfolders.
5. Import the file from **Setup** | **Data** | **Import Articles** and monitor the import process from **Setup** | **Environments** | **Monitoring** | **Article Imports**.

The following are some limitations to consider (these are just a few):

- There can only be one CSV file and one properties file, and they must be in the root directory of the ZIP file.
- Filenames must not contain any special characters.
- The ZIP process must preserve the folder's structure (which is natural since CSV and HTML may have local references to other files).
- A ZIP file must be under 20 MB in size and each uncompressed file must be under 10 MB in size.
- A CSV file must have less than 10,000 data rows (1 header and 9,999 article detail rows).
- Each row must have less than 400,000 characters and any cell in the CSV file must be smaller than 32 KB.
- An article can have up to 49 translations inside a given CSV file.

Refer to Salesforce Help at `https://help.salesforce.com/articleView?id=knowledge_article_importer.htmtype=5` for more details about the import feature of Knowledge articles.

If you need to import translations of articles that are already on the CRM, please refer to Salesforce Help at `https://help.salesforce.com/articleView?id=knowledge_translation_import.htmtype=5`.

Configuring Omni-Channel

Customer happiness is a key success factor in CRM. If your customers are not satisfied with the support they are receiving, they may give your services and products a bad review, and that's not good for business.

Even if a customer has a problem with a product or service, being able to solve the issue quickly changes the customer's perception of the issue; they know that the business' support has prioritized them and that the issue will be fixed soon.

While multi-channels give the customer the freedom to choose their preferred channel (web, SMS, phone, chat, a email), Omni-Channel featured services allow agents to be delivered to the most important cases from all the channels. That's why we say that the Omni-Channel is an agent-facing feature.

The following diagram shows how Omni-Channel works:

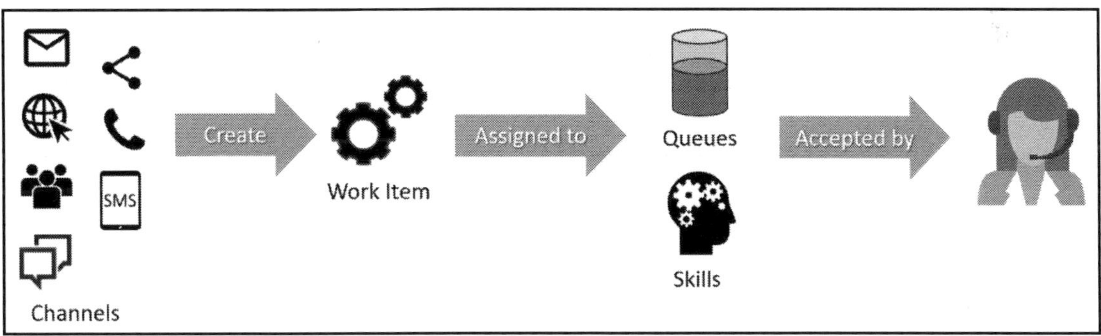

Omni-Channel flow

Here's how it works:

1. Requests come from multiple channels.
2. Work items are created (cases, leads, chats, incoming calls, and more).
3. Work items are assigned to queues or skills.
4. The Omni-Channel engine routes the work items to the proper agents, who may be awaiting in a specific queue that corresponds to their skill set.

The cool thing about Omni-Channel is that agents don't have to pick their work items anymore because the Omni-Channel engine decides what they can handle automatically. This is a great improvement in call center efficiency.

To enable Omni-Channel with default values, go to the **Service** app from the **App Launcher**, click on the **Setup** icon, and then click on **Service Setup**. From here, go to the **Recommended Setup** section, click on **View All**, and look for **Omni-Channel Setup**.

The wizard will ask for the following information:

- A queue name to handle the work items and the agents to be added (depending on the available Service Cloud licenses)
- The work item's cost (or size) and total capacity for each agent (how many work items they can handle concurrently)

Let's go over what this flow does in the background:

1. Enables Omni-Channel (**Setup** | **Omni-Channel Settings**).
2. Creates a Service channel for cases (**Setup** | **Service Channels**), which states which object should be routed.
3. Creates presence statuses for the agent (**Setup** | **Presence Statuses**), which state whether users are online or not.
4. Assigns presence statuses to users (using the **Omni Setup Flow** permission set).
5. Adds the Omni-Channel utility to the standard Service Console (this is the console utility where agents accept incoming work items).

If you open the Service Console using the **App Launcher**, you will see something similar to the following screenshot:

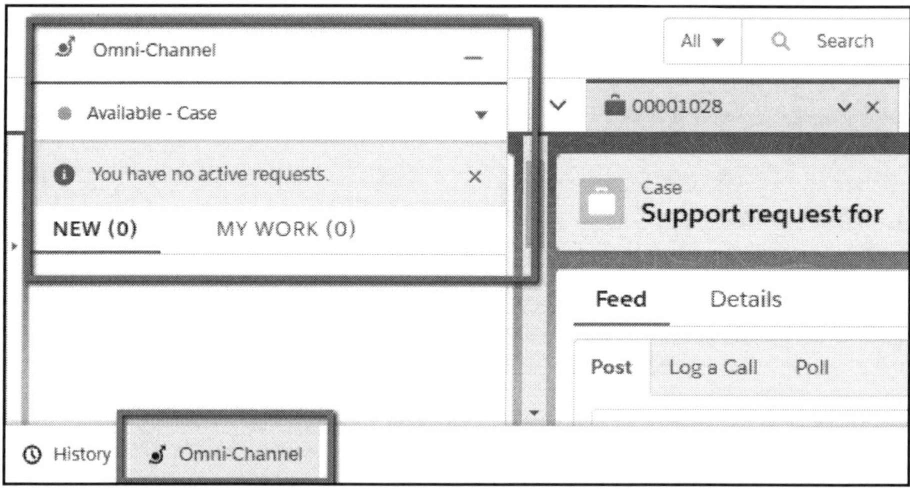

Omni-Channel utility component on the Service Console

By changing the presence to **Available - Case**, our user is now ready to accept incoming work items. If we want to add more users to the high-priority cases queue, go to **Setup** | **Queues** | **High-Priority Cases** and add the required users.

In the Omni-Channel setup flow, we set the following:

- Work item size to 5
- Agent capacity to 10

This tells Omni-Channel that, given an agent's capacity to handle work items (10 is just a number; we could have put 100, 1,000, or anything else), a single work item (1 case, in our scenario) consumes 5 unit of capacity.

These values are stored in the **Routing Configuration** (go to **Setup** | **Routing Configuration**; this holds the work item's size) and **Presence Configuration** (go to **Setup** | **Presence Configurations**; this holds the agent's total capacity).

There is one more thing you need to know about routing decisions: the **Routing Configuration** holds the **Routing Model** and **Priority** fields. Let's go over these now:

- **Priority** (an integer number, where 1 means higher priority) tells Omni-Channel which work items should have priority in routing (a chat may have higher priority than cases because we have a customer that is waiting for an agent's response).
- **Routing Model** can be set to **Least Active** or **Most Available**; that is, routing is made to the agent with the least amount of open work or to the agent with the least amount of work item capacity compared to open work items.

What happens when a new work item joins the queue? Agent Francesca has just started work (she arrives to work early; she's all alone in her company's big open space) and activated the online presence status so that she's ready to receive new work items. At this time, she has a full capacity of 10.

A new work item comes in and she is notified about the new item in the queue. She takes charge of the new case. At this time, she has received a size 5 work item, so her total capacity is now 5 (if the case is closed, she'll have a capacity of 10 once more).

Then, another case joins the queue; she's notified of this and she accepts it. Her capacity is now 0, which means she cannot receive work items until her capacity has been reduced.

If another work item comes in, she won't be notified about it, and Omni-Channel will try to notify another agent or wait until Francesca has closed at least one of her cases.

To try this out, go back to the **Service Console** app, click on **Cases**, and then click the **New** button to create a new case. Put in whatever information you want and click **Save**. You'll notice that nothing happens; why? This is because our user already owns the record.

Click the **Change Owner** case button and move the case's ownership to our high-priority cases queue.

A sound notification should warn you that a new work item is incoming (the Omni-Channel components will start blinking).

Click the Omni-Channel and accept the case:

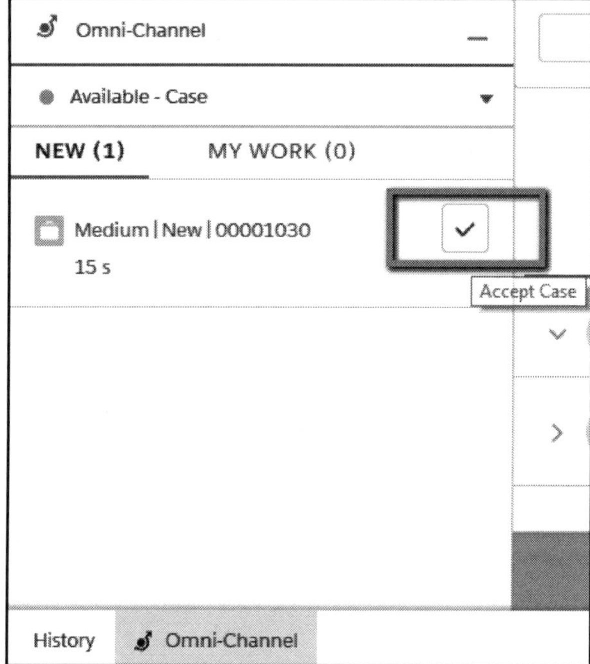

Incoming work item on the Omni-Channel utility component

By accepting this case, its ownership goes back to the current user and it is now listed on the **MY WORK** tab of the Omni-Channel component.

Repeat these steps again and accept another case; you will see that you have no capacity.

If we try this for the third time, no notification will be sent, but once we close one of the two cases we own (the capacity will become 5), the components will start notifying you about the third item. This is because you have enough capacity to accept new cases.

Let's summarize all the configuration steps:

- A Service channel turns (almost) any Salesforce object into a work item.
- Routing configuration is used to determine how work items are routed to agents.
- Presence configuration tells us how many work agents can take cases from Omni-Channel's engine (a user can only be assigned to one presence configuration; being assigned to a new presence configuration overrides the previous one for that given user).
- A queue is created as a waiting room for incoming work items and users are related to queues, so they are allowed to receive new work items (the queue object is related to the Routing configuration; in this case, from the queue edit form).
- Presence statuses state whether the user is available to receive new items, or whether they're busy or offline (each presence status can also be enabled for specific Service Channels). We can customize Presence statuses from **Setup** | **Presence Statuses** and they must be assigned to users using profiles or permission sets.

What if I have high-priority cases and low-priority cases? Create a new Routing configuration with lower (higher in number) priority, create a new low-priority cases queue, and then use automation (workflows, the Process Builder, Apex triggers, external API integrations, and so on) to assign incoming cases to the right queues.

So far, we've looked at **queue-based routing**. This is suitable for smaller Omni-Channel setups with a few users and queues, but if we need more fine-grained tuning, we can use **skill-based routing** or **external routing**. We'll cover these in the upcoming sections.

Skill-based routing

Rather than sending work items to the first available user in a queue, skill-based routing matches the most expert user in terms of the characteristics of an incoming work item. Users should have the necessary skills to handle the item.

Having a skill is one of the key metrics of an agent's expertise and can be something such as language proficiency, product knowledge, certifications handled, or account history. Each skill can have a proficiency level from 0 (none) to 10 (maximum).

Skills are assigned to users via the **Service Resource** object and to work items via the **Skill Requirements** object. Matching the skill means matching the right agent. If we have multiple skills, the item is routed to an agent that handles all of the required skills.

With queue-based routing, a queue represents a single skill (such as a product or spoken language), so it is not possible to assign a work item to more than one queue. Skill-based routing helps with more complex scenarios where multiple skills are needed.

If no users with the required skill(s) are found, the item is not routed until the right user is available. To enable skill-based routing, go to **Setup** | **Omni-Channel Settings** and check the **Enable Skills-Based Routing** flag.

You can define the required skills by going to **Setup** | **Omni-Channel** | **Skills**. Don't assign users within the skill configuration as this is not related to Omni-Channel setup.

To assign skills to users, use the **Service Resource** object (you can find this tab from the **App Launcher**):

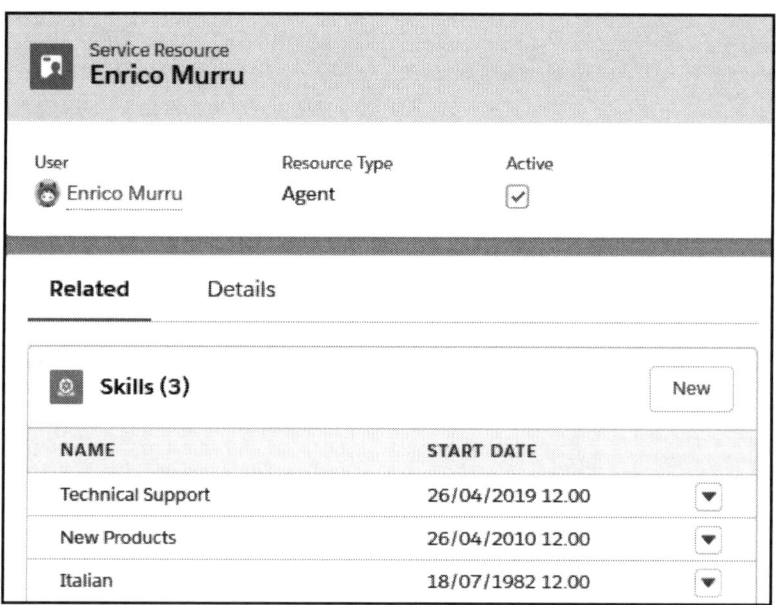

Omni-Channel skills related to a user

But how can we relate skills to incoming work items? We can do this using custom Apex code and a Process Builder or Apex trigger in order to execute custom routing. Please refer to Salesforce Help at `https://help.salesforce.com/articleView?id=omnichannel_skills_based_routing_route_work_items_using_skills.htmtype=5` or the following Trailhead module for more information: `https://trailhead.salesforce.com/content/learn/modules/Omni-Channel-lex/understand-sbr`.

External routing

If Salesforce is a new addition to the overall application layer and you cannot use Salesforce's routing engine, external routing allows work items to be routed based on an external application, which will decide which agents have enough capacity and the skills to handle a work item.

To find out more about this routing model, and if you feel you want to join the developer side of things, please refer to the Omni-Channel developer guide at `https://developer.salesforce.com/docs/atlas.en-us.218.0.omni_channel_dev.meta/omni_channel_dev/omnichannel_developer_guide_intro.htm`.

Omni-Channel Supervisor app

Let's talk about another cool feature that comes with Omni-Channel: the **Omni Supervisor** app.

You can access this from the **App Launcher**. It provides us with an effective way to monitor an agent's work in real time, as well as their queues backlog and assigned work and skills backlog:

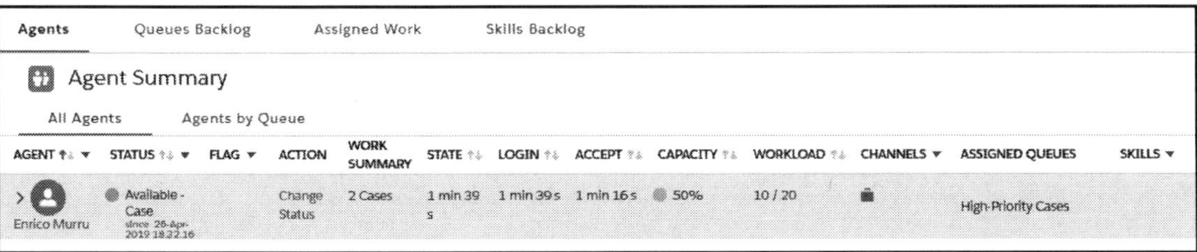

Omni-Channel Supervisor agents view

By clicking on an agent, we can look at all the details of their work:

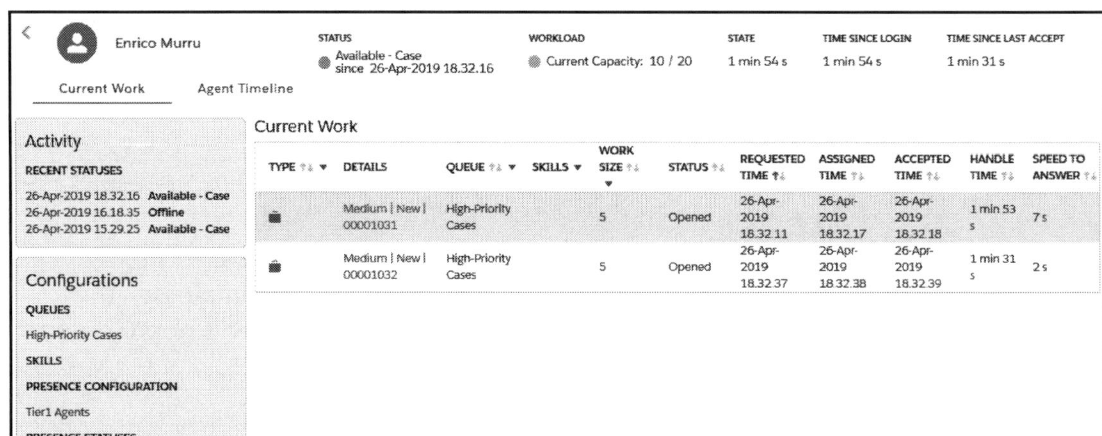

Agent capacity details on the Omni-Channel Supervisor page

For a detailed list of what we can review from this page, please refer to Salesforce Help at `https://help.salesforce.com/articleView?id=omnichannel_supervisor_intro.htmtype=5`.

One of the most effective channels that speeds up case resolution is live chat. We'll explore this in the next section.

Live Agent chat and communities

In the previous section, we saw how work items can be automatically routed to agents, and live chats are similar to work items. Live Agent lets customers chat in real-time with support agents.

Using Live Agent, supervisors can even inspect their agent's chat and assist them by whispering messages (these messages can only be seen by agents). Let's think of them as live suggestions.

Live Agent can be fully customized using point and click; however, the platform delivers a set of APIs that can be used by developers to empower the chat experience.

Salesforce Community setup

Before talking about the Live Agent's configuration, let's spend some time talking about Salesforce Communities. This is a big topic and we would need to write an entire book to cover everything, but there's no reason why we shouldn't provide a quick overview.

We talked about communities in `Chapter 1`, *Secure Data Access*, but now, we are going to show the steps that are required to create a new community.

We are introducing communities at this point because we'll be using the web chat from within a community to enhance the service support experience.

To get started:

1. click on **Setup** | **Feature Settings** | **Communities** | **Communities Settings**
2. check the **Enable communities** flag
3. choose a domain name that will be used to look up your communities.

I've chosen **adv-admin-community-01**, which translates to `https://adv-admin-community-01-developer-edition.eu19.force.com`. This is where the Developer Edition has been added (because it is a Developer Edition organization); `eu19` is the instance name (in production, we won't have this). Click on **Check Availability** to check whether the domain has already been taken by someone else. Click **Save** to start creating a new community.

Click on **New Community** to start the community wizard.

The first thing you need to choose is the community template. We have the following options:

- **Help Center**: A public self-service community where we expose the KB.
- **Customer Account Portal**: A help center that's designed for customers. Here, they can access their data and update it.
- **Customer Service**: A responsive self-service template with multiple prebuilt themes. It provides questions and allows us to search for articles, collaborations, and case access.
- **Aloha**: A base app launcher that supports single sign-on (including social logins) for quick application access.
- **Visualforce and Tabs**: A template where developers can completely customize any page using Visualforce technology. This is not Lightning-based and doesn't work with the Community Builder.

- **Partner Central**: A sales partner-dedicated template.
- **Build your own**: A base template with all the basic features (login, home, password management, record/record list base pages, and so on). We can customize these using themes and branding.

Each community template can access specific prebuilt pages/components and features. For a complete list, please refer to Salesforce Help at `https://help.salesforce.com/articleView?id=rss_component_reference_table.htmtype=5`.

Choose **Help Center** as our community template. A new quick setup wizard will open up.

Fill in the community's name (for example, `Awesome Service Site`), as well as the community's URL, though this is optional (let's say we want to use `awesomeservice`. In our example, the final URL will be `https://adv-admin-community-01-developer-edition.eu19.force.com/awesomeservice`). Check the **Publish my help center after completing setup** flag to automatically publish the community once the wizard is completed.

Because we have set up the required knowledge, the wizard asks for data categories to be used as community topics (we'll leave this blank; we don't need it. You can skip the next step as well, which is where we can select knowledge authors). The wizard should terminate upon success and we should see **Community Workspaces**, which is where we can administer the community.

From here, we can access the following features:

- **Builder**: This is a point-and-click app where we can set up security, branding, themes, and configure all the pages in our community, as well as add standard and custom Lightning components. After making changes, hit the **Publish** button to publish your changes.
- **Administration**: Sets up various preferences, such as community state (active, not active), template type, allowed members for authenticated access (with profiles and permission sets), login branding, email settings, and much more.
- **Moderation**: This is all about discussion moderation.
- **Content management**: Articles, topics, and recommendations.
- **Gamification**: From here, you can set up gamification to increase engagement.

For an in-depth Salesforce Communities study on this topic, please refer to Salesforce Help at `https://help.salesforce.com/articleView?id=networks_overview.htmtype=5`.

This is all we need for the Live Agent's configuration. Now, let's look at how we can set up the Live Agent.

Chat (Live Agent) Setup flow

Let's start with the **Chat (Live Agent) Setup** flow (we are accustomed to these kinds of flows since we have already used them for Knowledge and Omni-Channel setup).

Go to **Service Setup** | **Recommended Setup** | **View All** and look for **Chat With Customers**. The wizard will guide you to the following steps:

1. Add a new queue and an agent group (name the queue `Incoming Web Chats` and the agent group `Chat Agents`) and assign users to the group (we can add them later). This step sets up the presence and queue for the chat work items (as we have already seen in Omni-Channel). Users need to have an additional Live Agent license and they are assigned the **Live_Agent_Setup_Flow** permission set for presence.
2. Add new routing configuration for the web chat (set the priority to 1 and change the high-priority cases to 2).
3. Adjust the agents' workload by setting a proper chat work item size and the agent's capacity. Leave the agent's capacity as it is (10, in this case, like the previous configuration) and set the work item size to 2 (agents can easily take care of more than one chat at a time).
4. Live Chat will be used outside the CRM or at least on a customer community. If you don't have a Salesforce Site or a community already set up, this step also creates a new empty site. Fill in the **Website URL** textbox with the community domain we set up earlier (`https://adv-admin-community-01-developer-edition.eu19.force.com`) and select our community as the **Salesforce Site Domain**.
5. Now, we'll be asked how we want to link chats to our CRM data, such as lead (if the chat is meant for sales), case and contacts, or only contacts (for service purposes). Let's select **Cases and Contacts** (select a record type for the contact and case if requested).
6. Let's leave the offline support as disabled (this creates a form that the customer can fill in if the chat is not available).

Voilà—the chat is almost ready. A snippet of code will be displayed (you can get it from **Setup** | **Chat (Formerly Live Agent)** | **Chat Buttons and Invitations**) and it should only be used outside Salesforce (if we plan to add the web chat feature to a custom website and not a community).

The setup flow will have created a new queue (go to **Setup** | **Routing Configurations** and select **Incoming Web Chat**). Here, we'll see the **Incoming Web Chat**-related queue.

There is also a new **Presence Configuration** called **Chat Agents**. As we mentioned in the previous section, users can only be linked to one presence configuration at a time (the old **Tier1 Agents** configuration has no user associated with it now and can be safely deleted).

Go back to your community. Now, we want to add a new component called the **Embedded Chat** (formerly **Snap-In**) so that we can use the chat from within the community.

Click on **Setup** | **All Communities** and select the **Builder** link next to the **Awesome Service Site** community. Now, click on the Lightning icon (components) on the left-hand side of the toolbar, search for the embedded chat standard component, and place it in the lowermost section of the template, as shown in the following screenshot:

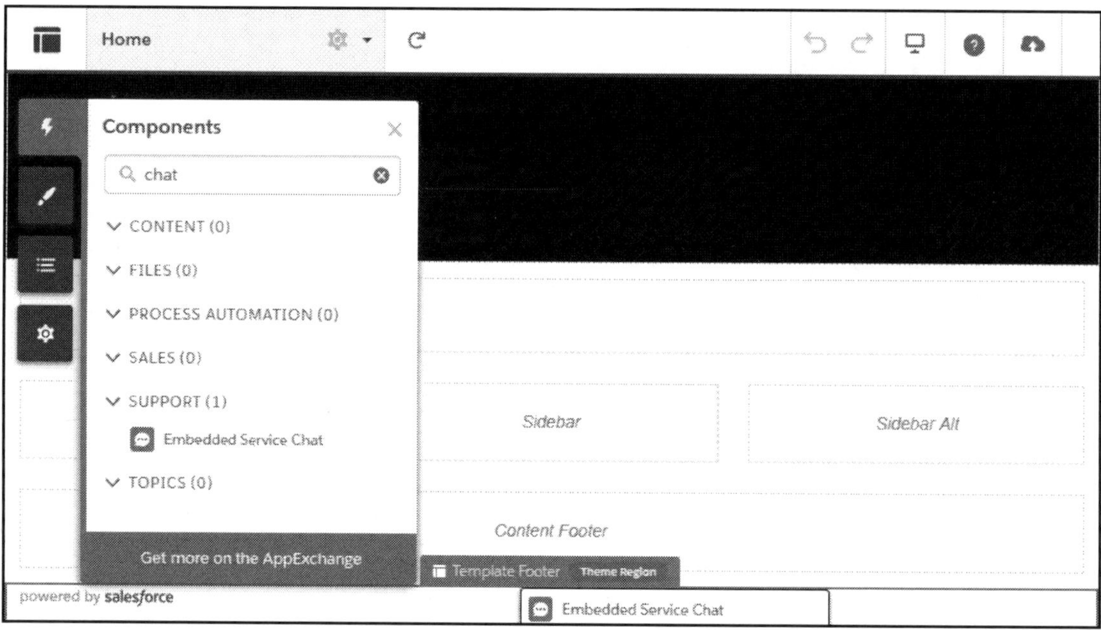

Adding the snap-in component to the community template

If you refresh the page, you'll get a scary error:

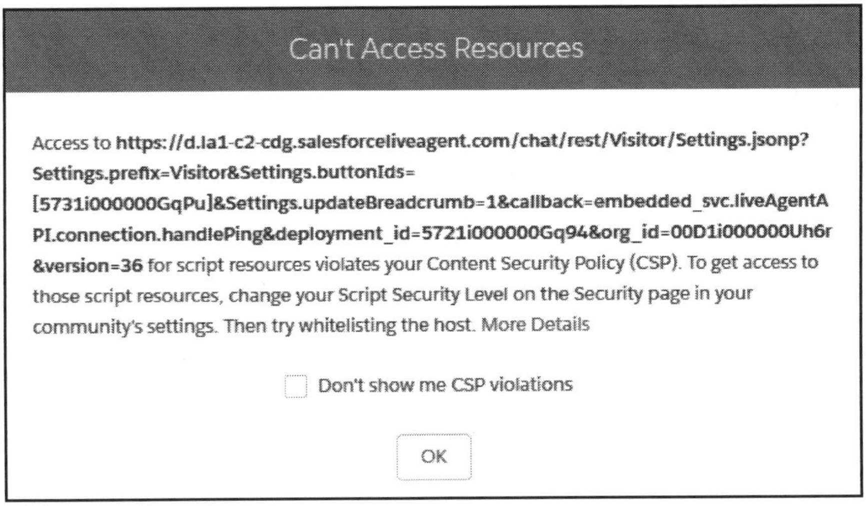

Can't Access Resources

Access to **https://d.la1-c2-cdg.salesforceliveagent.com/chat/rest/Visitor/Settings.jsonp?Settings.prefix=Visitor&Settings.buttonIds=[5731i000000GqPu]&Settings.updateBreadcrumb=1&callback=embedded_svc.liveAgentAPI.connection.handlePing&deployment_id=5721i000000Gq94&org_id=00D1i000000Uh6r&version=36** for script resources violates your Content Security Policy (CSP). To get access to those script resources, change your Script Security Level on the Security page in your community's settings. Then try whitelisting the host. More Details

Don't show me CSP violations

OK

Snap-in error for the Content Security Policy

This is something slightly technical, but it is a safeguard so that only trusted domains can be used from within a community. The Live Agent channel uses a parallel HTTP domain for the chat requests, so we need to explicitly tell Salesforce that this domain is safe to use.

Copy the domain part of the URL from this message (in this example, it is `https://d.la1-c2-cdg.salesforceliveagent.com`; you can get it from **Setup** | **Live Agent Settings**).

We are almost there, so don't panic. This stuff is more developer-oriented and you won't need to set it up by yourself in most cases, but it's important to know all the steps involved in Live Agent snap-in activation.

Click the **Settings** icon (the gear icon), go to the **Security** tab, and select the **Allow Inline Scripts and Script Access to Whitelisted Third-party Hosts** value from the **Content Security Policy** (**CSP**) section (click **Allow** on the confirmation modal). Then, click on the lower **+ Add Trusted Site** button and add the Live Agent domain. This should be our final configuration:

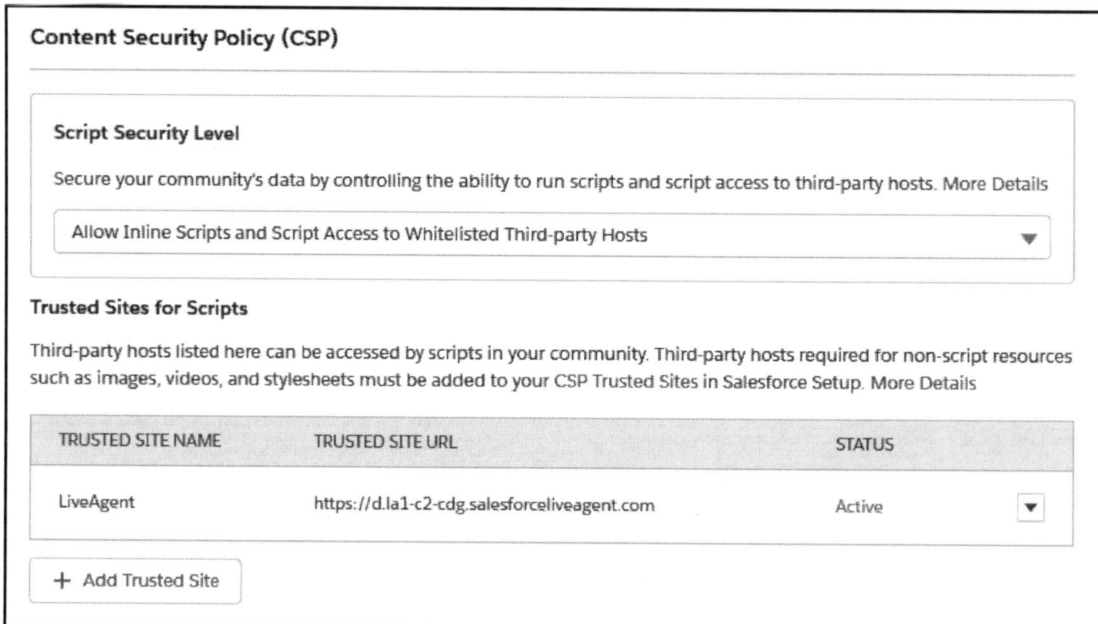

Content Security Policy set up for Live Agent

On the lower part of your template, a new **Agent Offline** component will appear. Click on it to view its settings:

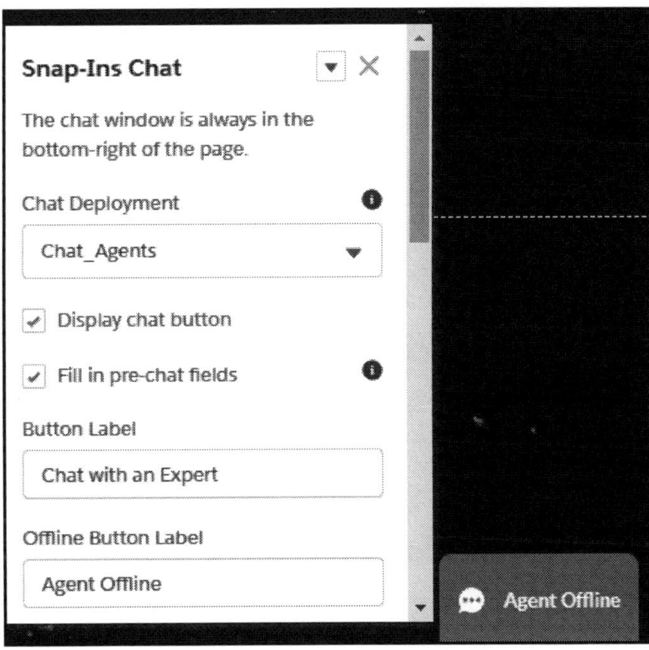

Snap-in component configuration

Click on the **Publish** button at the top of the builder and wait until you receive an email notification stating that the community has been published. Let's test it.

Open the community in a new tab and the **Service Console** app in another one.

On the **Service Console** app, open the Omni-Channel component and set the presence to **Available - Chat** (you may see the **Available - Case** presence status, which won't trigger the availability of the chat). After a few seconds, the snap-in component on your console should change its label to `Chat with an Expert` (text labels can be changed from the snap-in component's configuration settings).

Click on the community component. A form should appear, asking for the customer's data:

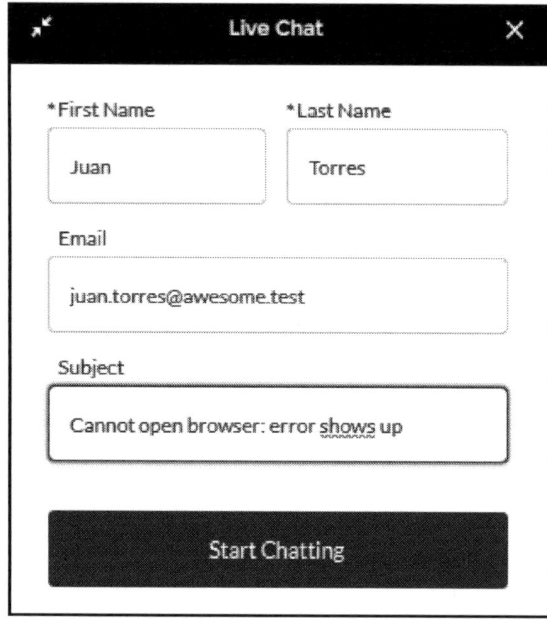

Live Chat's pre-chat form

This is called the **pre-chat** form, and it is can be configured from **Setup | Embedded Service** (formerly **Snap-Ins**).

Once we click on the **Start Chatting** button, the magic happens. On the console, the agent is notified about the incoming chat by the Omni-Channel; a new case and contact are automatically created using the pre-chat form, and the chat can flow instantly between the agent and the customer (try it yourself). The system searches for any contact that matches the email address the user entered on the pre-chat form. If no exact match is found, a brand-new contact is created with the details of the pre-chat form.

If you create a new case using the same procedure that we used in the Omni-Channel section (changing case ownership to a high-priority case queue), you'll see that no case is sent to the agent's work queue.

This is because the **Available - Chat** presence status is not related to the case's configuration. Let's say that an agent is available to chat; they can handle cases as well (but not the contrary). Go to **Setup** | **Omni-Channel** | **Presence Statuses** and edit the **Available - Chat** status. From here, add a reference to the Service channel configuration we created for the case work items:

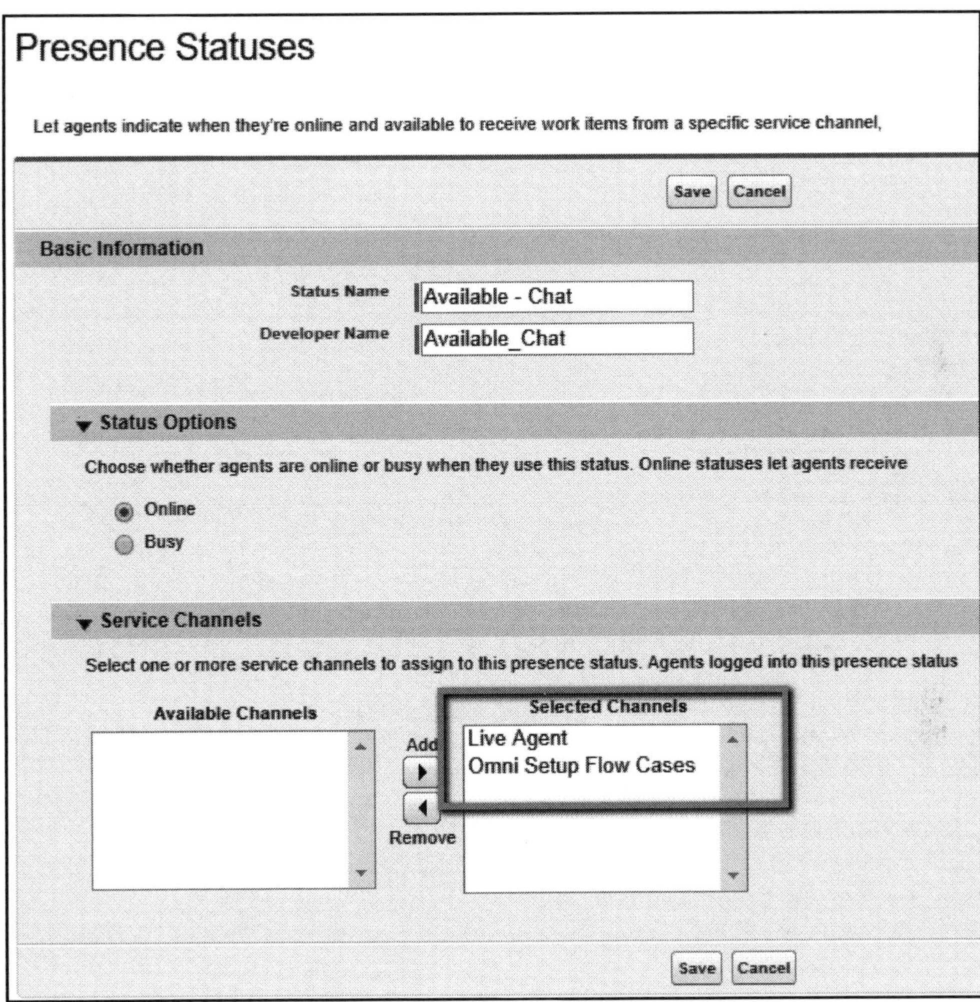

Presence Statuses configuration for two different Service channels

If you have created a new case and successfully managed to handle it with the Omni-Channel component, go to the **Omni Supervisor** app so that we can monitor the capacity status:

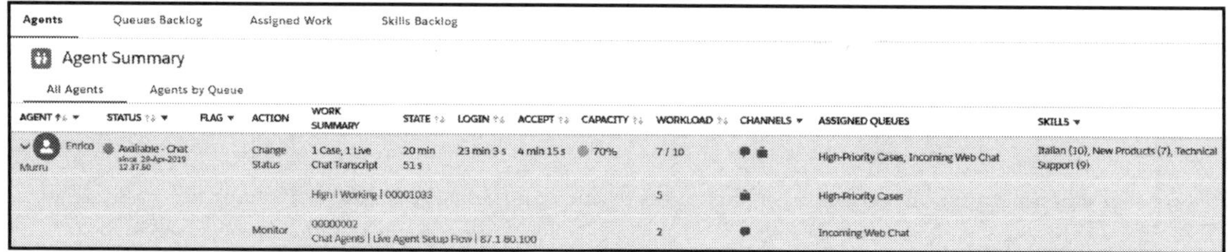

Agent's capacity during a chat and case management session

For more details about snap-ins, please refer to Salesforce Help at `https://help.salesforce.com/articleView?id=snapins_chat_setup.htmtype=5`.

Einstein Bots

Although this is beyond the scope of this book, I want to spend a few minutes talking about **Einstein Bots**. Einstein Bots, which is an add-on for Live Agent (Chat), provides us with an automated way to interact with customers without using one of the precious resources of our call center: the agent's time.

With a point and click configuration (Apex customization is also possible), any Live Agent (Chat) chat can be put in charge by an automated bot so that it can answer a customer's questions in a human-like fashion, thus solving the easiest issues a customer may have (for example, a product specifications list, common questions, store opening hours, order status inquiries, and more).

Whenever the customer doesn't receive the right answer or wants more information on a certain subject, *fail-safe* mode is activated, which directly transfers the chat to a human agent.

Do not pretend your bot is a human.

Bots can also be used to help the customer identify issues, while the real answer will be given by a human agent after the issue has been addressed.

Einstein Bots is a relatively new feature, so expect it to become feature-rich in the upcoming releases of Salesforce.

For a deep dive into Einstein Bots, please refer to Salesforce Help at `https://help.salesforce.com/articleView?id=bots_service_intro.htmtype=5`, or follow the awesome trail at `https://trailhead.salesforce.com/content/learn/trails/service_einstein`.

Entitlements for SLA management (and more)

Our call center is ready to achieve its potential, but before we close this chapter, let's add the last piece of the puzzle.

Let's talk about SLAs. If we are building service processes, we are giving our customers a way to contact us if something is wrong with their product.

Our company sells highly specialized software: if a software license is purchased, the customer receives email and chat support, but if they purchase, let's say, 10,000 licenses, we can provide 24/7 phone support.

In Salesforce, SLAs are handled with entitlements. In this scenario, we can create an entitlement object related to the customer's account.

If the customer calls the call center, the agent can have a look at the account's related list to see whether phone call support is available. If it isn't, the agent can suggest a new deal so that the customer can upgrade their service experience. If the SLA is okay, the agent can answer the customer and create a case for support if needed.

Because these features are not fully supported in Lightning, let's switch to Salesforce Classic to configure them and then go back to Lightning Experience to see the differences between them.

You can enable entitlements from **Setup** | **Entitlement Settings**.

The standard entitlement object is now enabled, the Entitlements related list is available on accounts, assets, and contacts (Lightning Experience does not support contacts at the time of writing, that is, Summer 2019), and the entitlements tab can be added to your apps.

For a detailed list of all the required permissions so that you access every entitlements feature, please refer to Salesforce Help at `https://help.salesforce.com/articleView?id=entitlements_giving_users_access.htmtype=5`.

Add the entitlements-related list to the account object (this will work in LEX as well) and create a new entitlement:

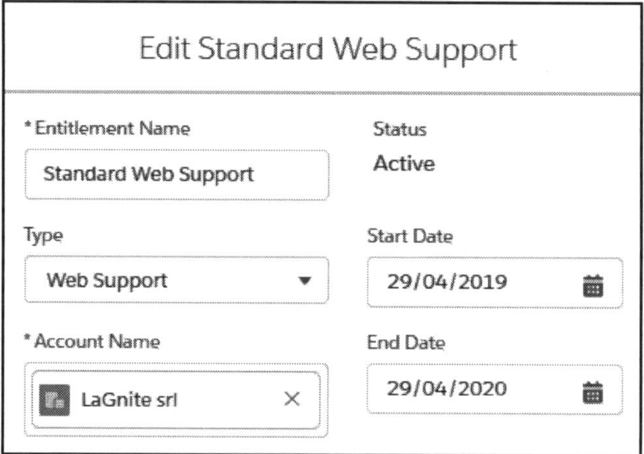

New Entitlement on account

We can add new custom fields to the Entitlement object that make sense for your company's support processes (I would customize the **Type** picklist field first by adding my company's entitlements types).

Note that if the **END DATE** expires, the status will expire as well:

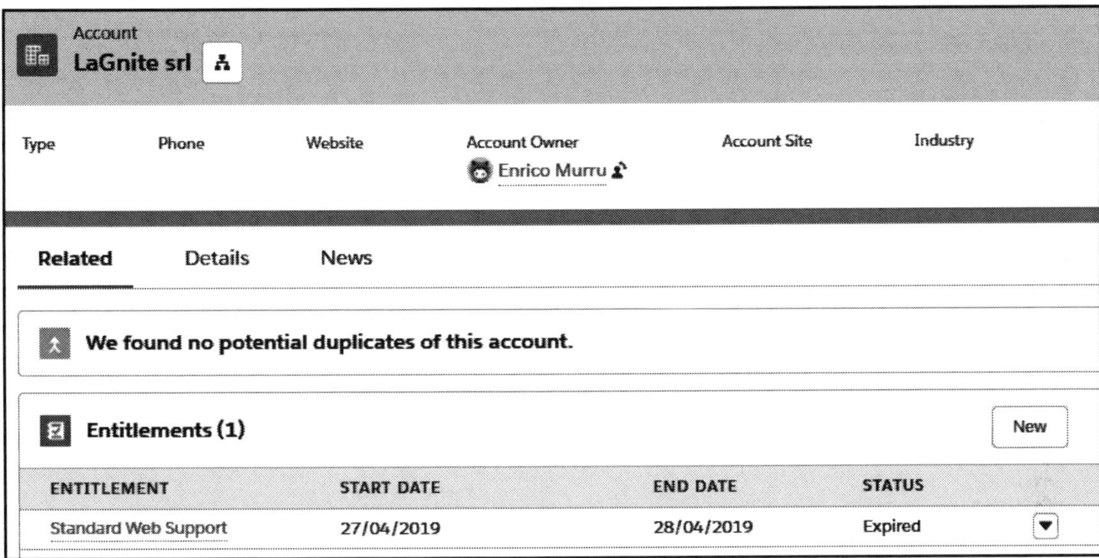

Entitlement status modification on SLA expiration

Entitlements can be added to accounts, assets, service contracts, and contacts by hand (you have a loyal/strategic customer that you want to take care of and so you'll want to manually add an entitlement).

If you want to link an entitlement to a product (we sell 1-year support with our new software), we can use Entitlement Templates.

Create a new template by going to **Setup** | **Entitlement Templates**:

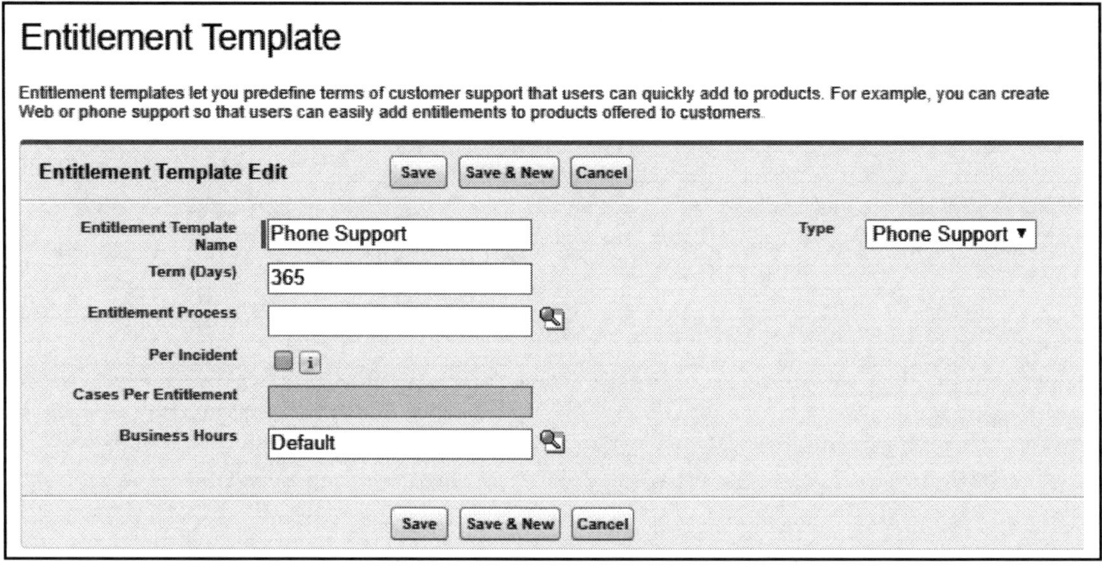

Entitlement Template creation

Now, we can define an entitlement that is automatically assigned to an asset when its product field is associated with it.

The Entitlement Template's lookup is not available on Lightning Experience (as of summer 2019), so go back to Classic and add the template to our product:

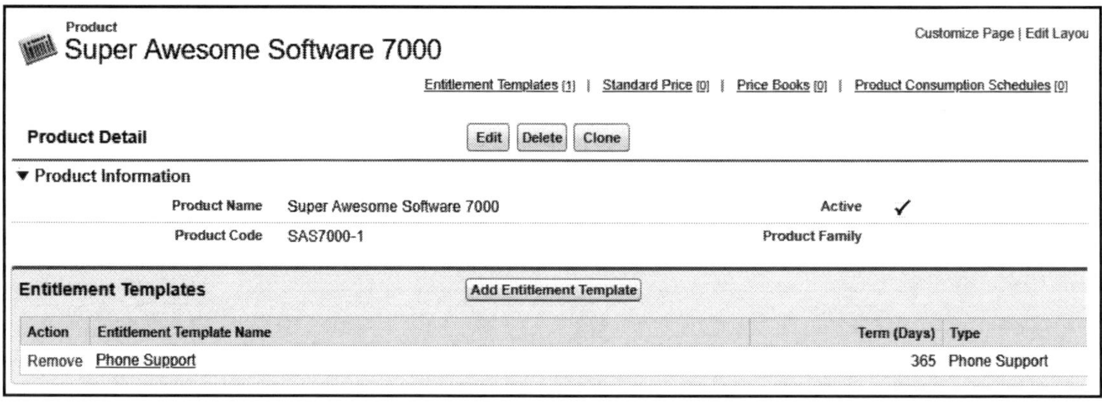

Entitlement Template on a product

Now, let's create a new asset by filling in its product lookup:

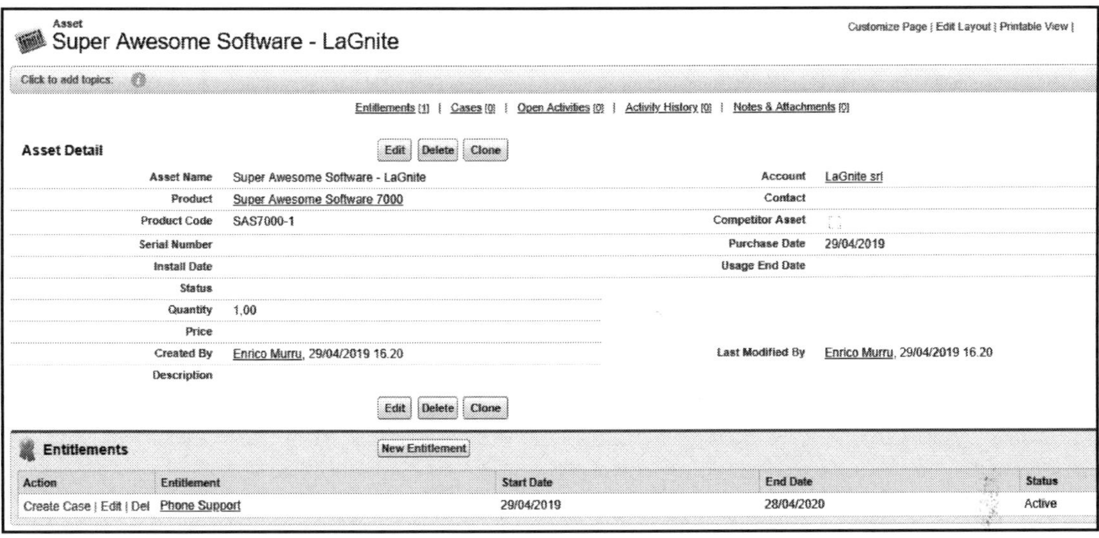

Entitlement created automatically after the Entitlement Template

A new entitlement is automatically created based on the Entitlement Template's configuration.

SLAs can be as easy as checking whether a customer has support for their contract, though they can be more complex if we need to enforce case resolution within a given amount of time.

Entitlement processes configure the timeline with steps (called **Milestones**) that the support team has to complete to resolve a case (or work order).

Let's say that our high-priority cases must be solved within 2 hours, while medium and low-priority cases must be solved within 1 day.

Let's start by creating a new **Milestone** by going to **Setup** | **Milestone**:

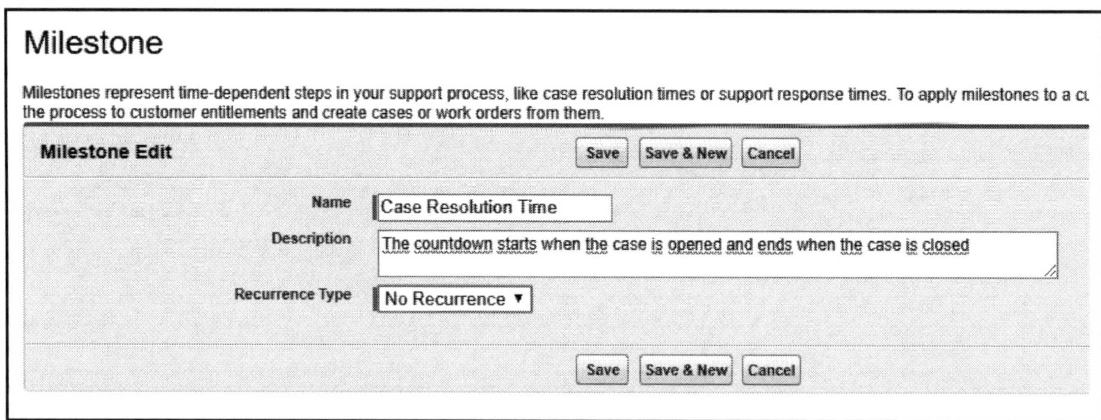

Milestone creation form

Recurrence Type states that this milestone will occur once per case.

Now, let's create a new entitlement process by going to **Setup** | **Entitlement Processes Edit**. Select the case process type and fill in the other fields:

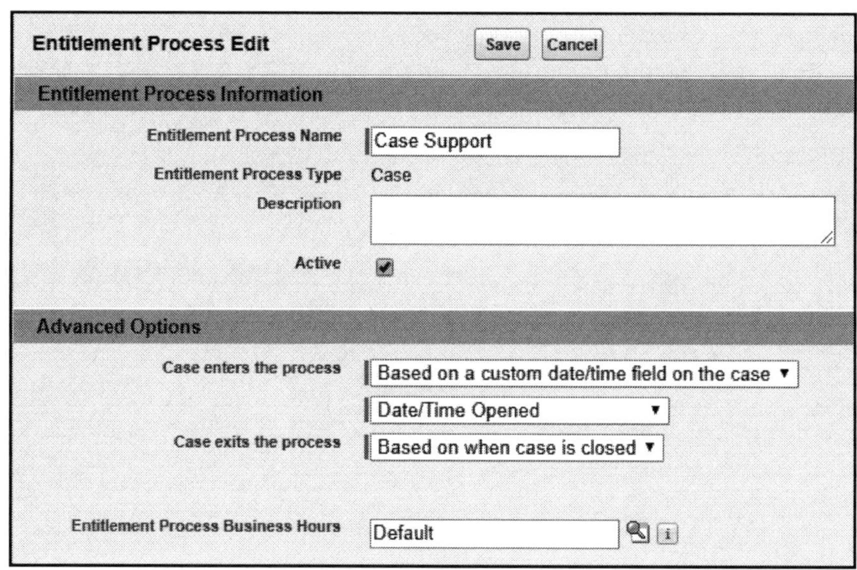

Entitlement process creation form

We have chosen to start the process based on the **Date/Time Opened** field and chosen to end it when the case is closed. Business Hours are required if you have more than one set of Business Hours defined (this is when your agents usually work on cases).

Now, we will add a new milestone based on the one we created earlier:

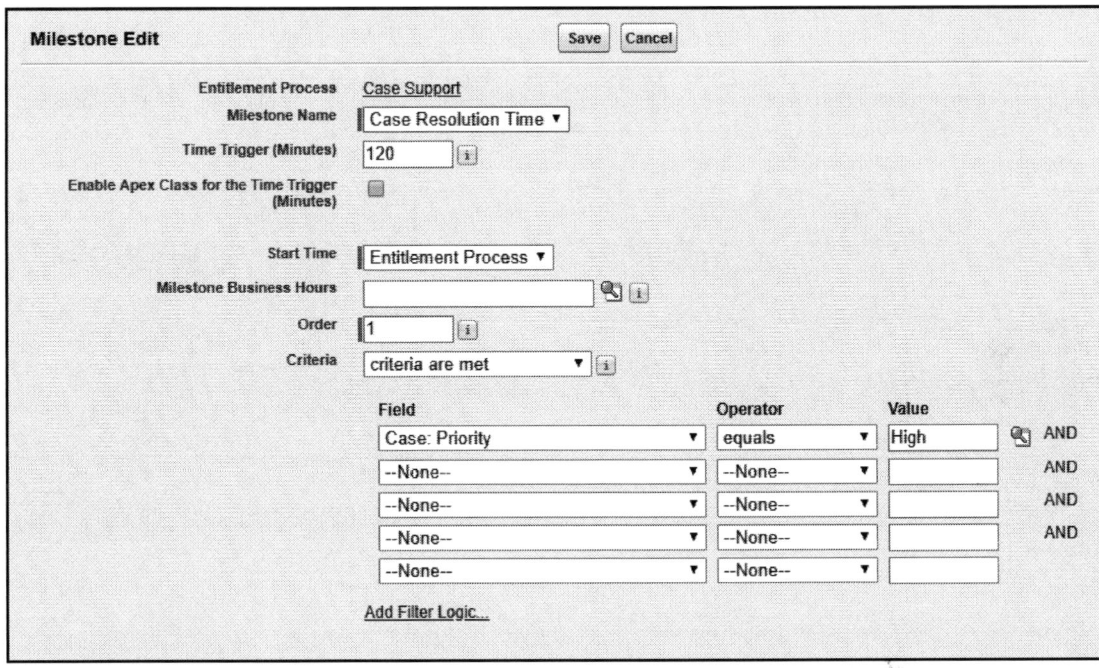

Milestone creation form on the entitlement process

This is quite easy to understand: here, we need to trigger the milestone after 120 minutes (2 hours) for high-priority cases.

Let's add one more for medium and low-priority cases:

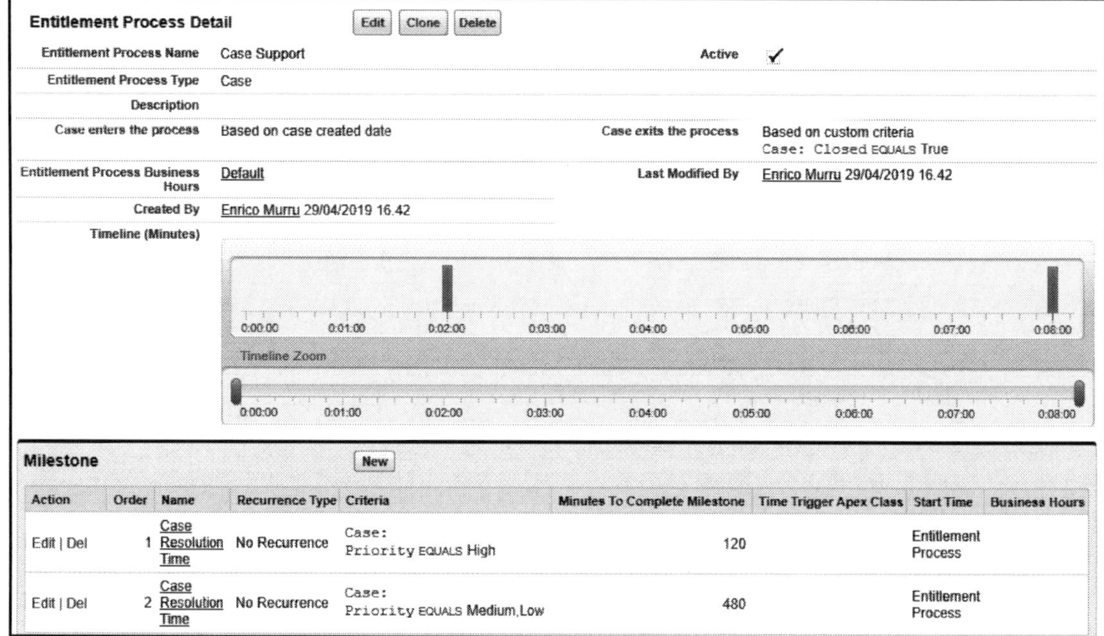

Entitlement process timeline view

What we get is a timeline that shows us how the entitlement is configured. We are almost there! Now we are going to apply actions to the milestones. On the Milestones-related list, click on the **Case Resolution Time** link next to the high-priority item. From here, we can define success, warning, and violation actions.

Success actions are triggered as soon as the milestone is completed, while for warning and violation actions, we can set up a time-triggered action.

We want to warn the user when an hour has passed but the case hasn't been closed. Let's create a quick email template by going to **Setup** | **Classic Email Templates**:

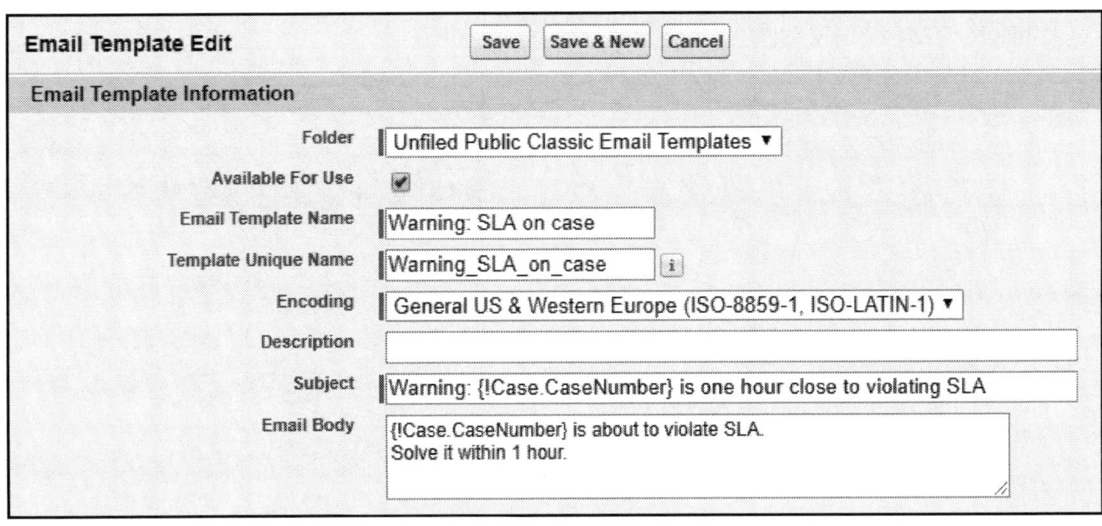

Email template to warn the user about violating the SLA

Click on **Add Time Trigger**, select **1 Hours**, and click **Save**. Then, click on **Add Workflow Action** and select **New Email Alert**:

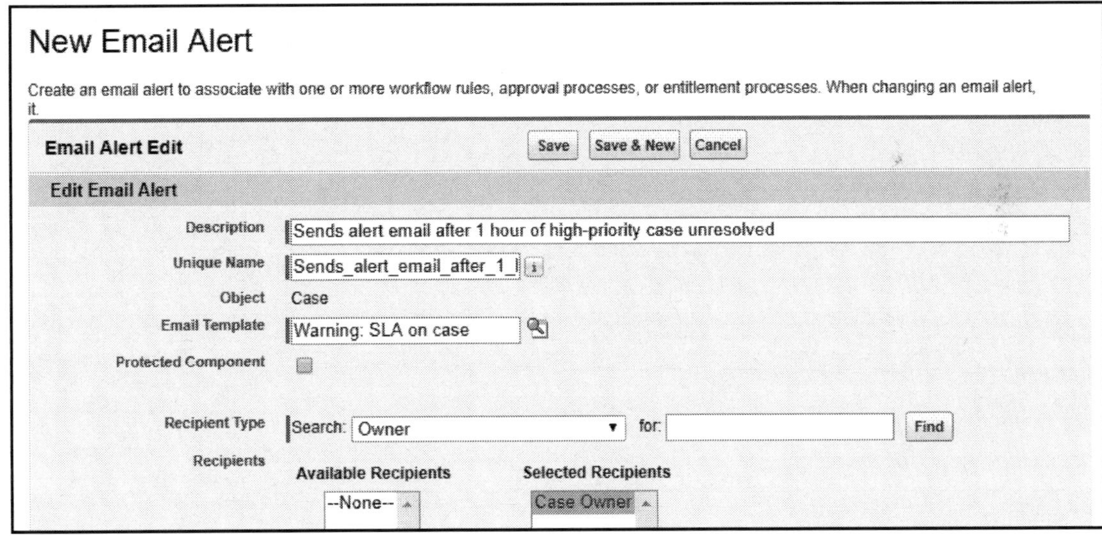

Email alert action

Add another email as a violation action:

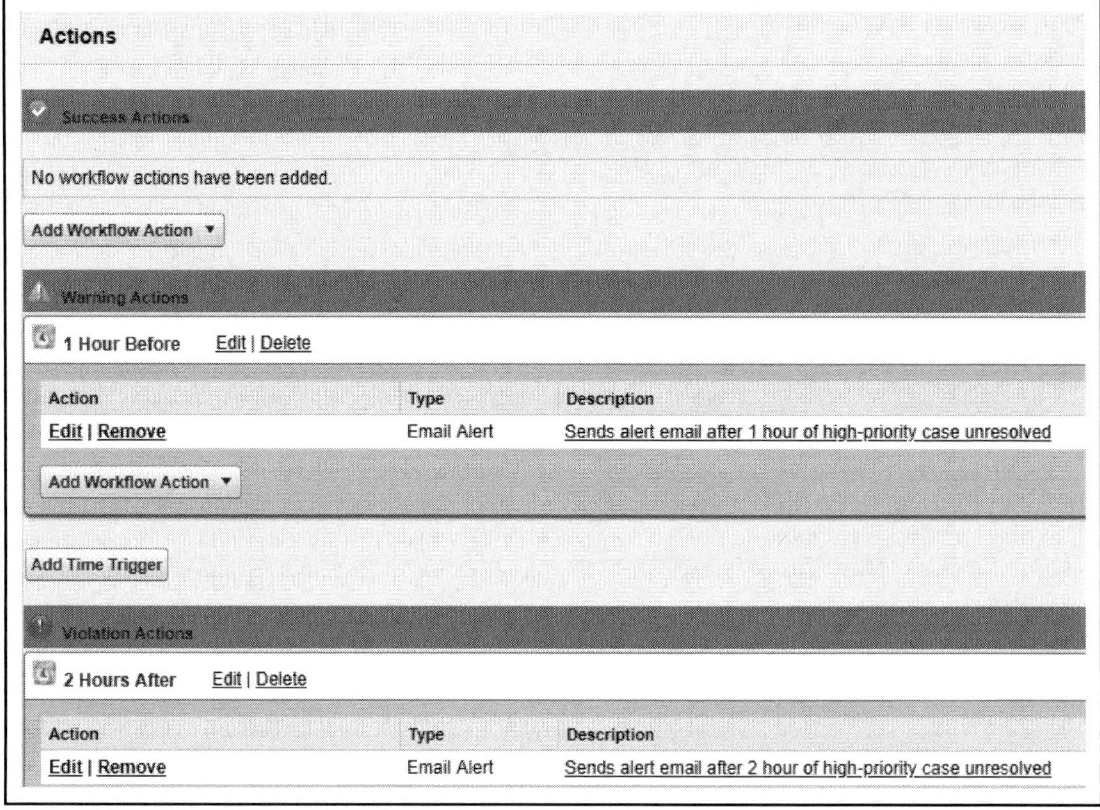

Milestone actions configured for warnings and violations

This entitlement process can be now linked to any entitlement (or entitlement process) we've created:

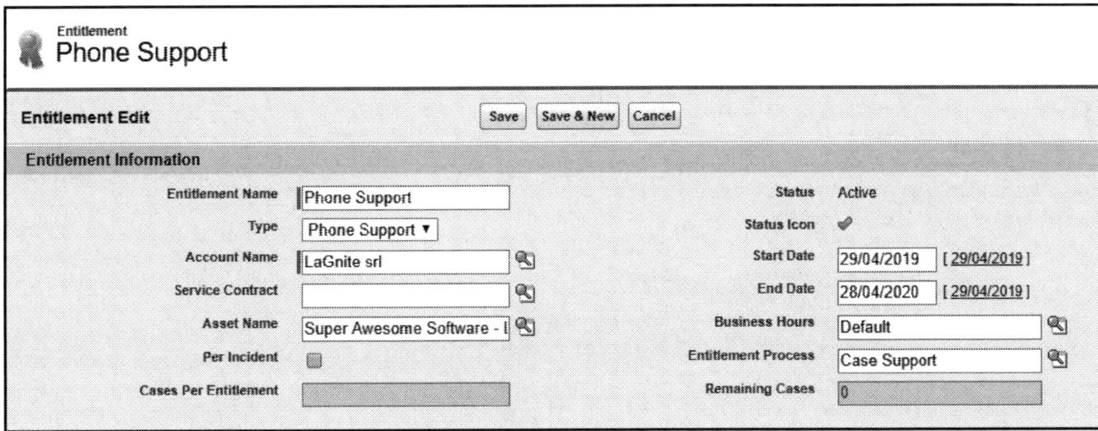

Adding an entitlement process to Entitlement

Now, any agent can create a new case using the Entitlement-related list on the account, contact, service contract, or asset object:

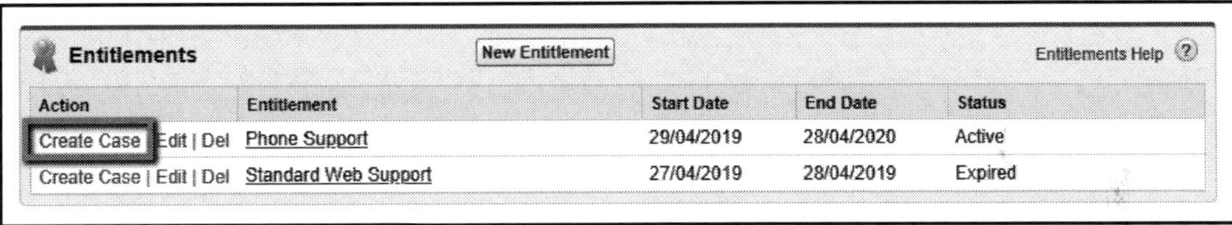

Creating a case from the Entitlements-related list

The **Entitlement Name** field on the case object is automatically populated (you can update it manually if you wish; you can even add validation rules or automation with the Process Builder or custom Apex trails to set it up automatically based on your service process policies). Remember to set the right FLS on the case's Entitlement fields; otherwise, the Entitlement lookup won't be filled in:

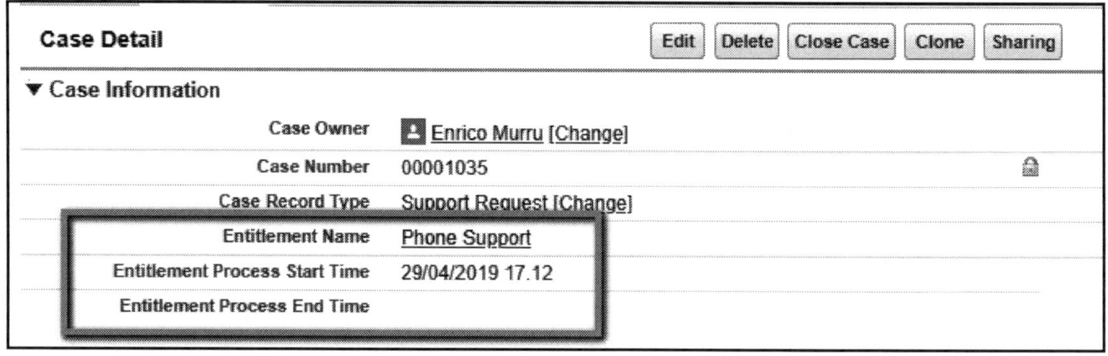

Entitlement fields on the case

How's the timeline doing? A cool widget called Milestone Tracker is available on case feeds and can be added to layouts from the layout page editor. To do this, go to **Feed View** | **Other Tools and Components** | **Milestone Tracker**:

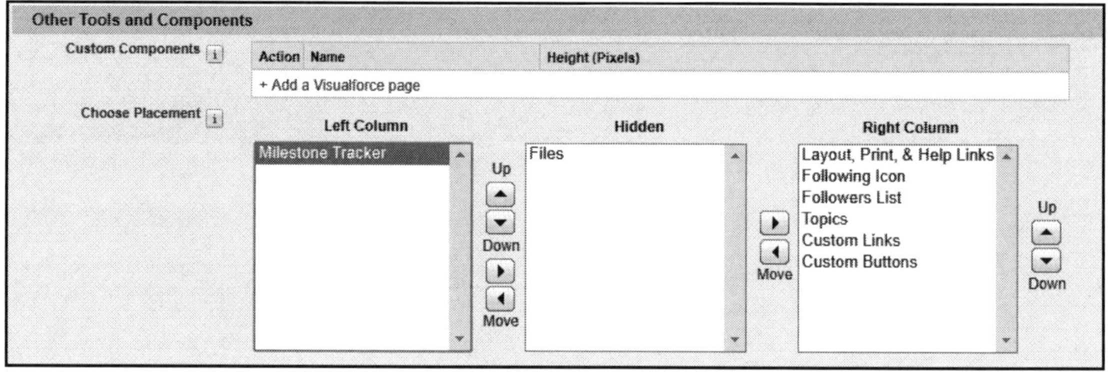

Milestone Tracker case feed's component

Now, we'll see something similar to the following screenshot:

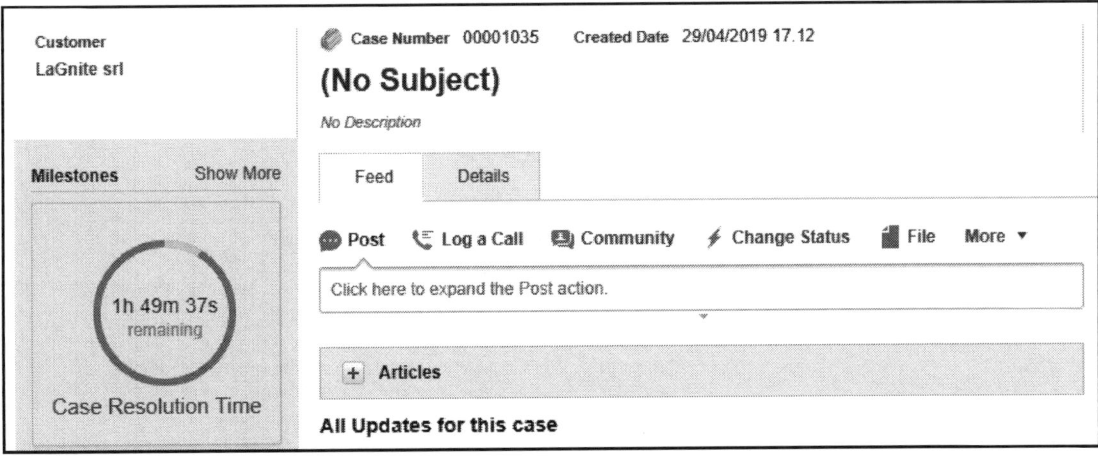

Milestones tracking on the case's feed in Salesforce Classic

You can add more than one milestone per entitlement process in order to track different SLA metrics.

In Lightning Experience, we need to add the **Milestones** standard Lightning component to the case's record page (though it's not available on console apps yet, as per the summer 2019 release):

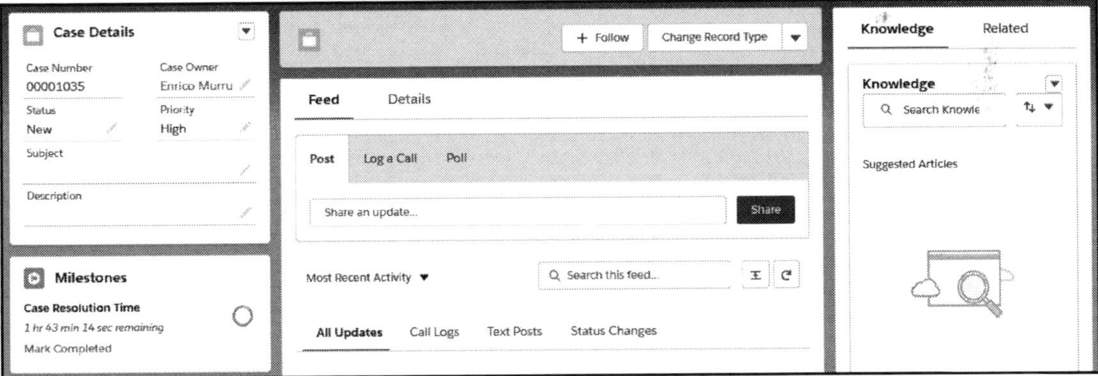

Milestones Lightning component for Lightning Experience organizations

We can monitor all ongoing entitlement processes (time-triggered actions) by going to **Setup | Monitor | Entitlement Processes**:

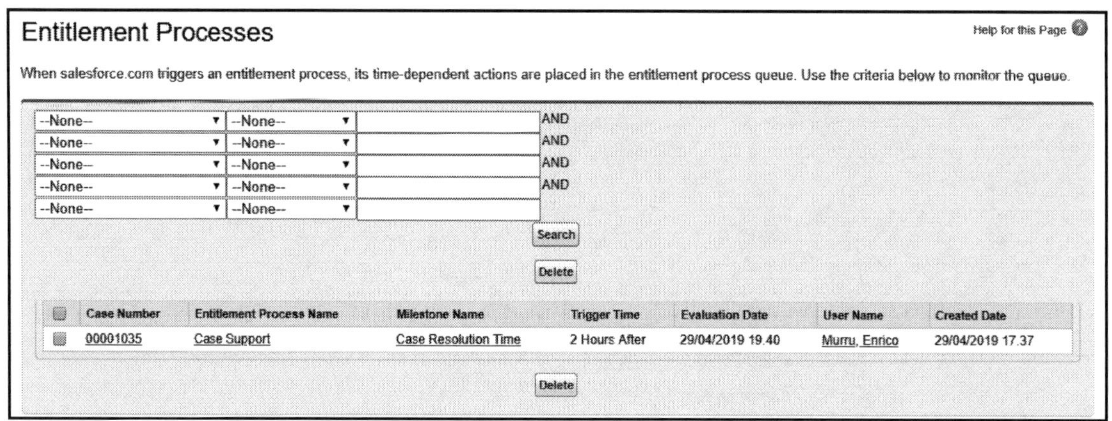

Monitoring entitlement processes

When dealing with objects that entitlements could be attached to, we can use service contracts. We can use these to track all the SLAs, warranties, and subscriptions related to a given account.

Please refer to Salesforce Help for more information about service contracts: `https://help.salesforce.com/articleView?id=entitlements_service_contracts_parent.htmtype=5`.

For more information on entitlements, please refer to Salesforce Help at `https://help.salesforce.com/articleView?id=entitlements_best_practices.htmtype=5`.

To find out more about entitlements on Salesforce Communities, please go to `https://help.salesforce.com/articleView?id=entitlements_impl_partportal.htmtype=5`.

Summary

In this chapter, we learned how to empower our service support. Lightning Knowledge can be used to create a KB that can help internal agents speed up case resolution or even allow customers and partners to self-service their support needs (allowing agents to spend more time on more complex tasks).

Omni-Channel lets agents concentrate on case resolution rather than deciding on whether an incoming request can or cannot be handled (and if they have the required skills to solve it). With the Live Agent, customers are directly linked to agents using the live chat, thus delivering a real-time service experience.

Finally, we talked about entitlements, which relate your customers to the proper service level agreements. With entitlement processes, no agent will ever lose a case resolution time constraint.

In the next chapter, we'll talk about data and content management.

Questions

1. Your company is using Classic Knowledge to handle its internal KB, but you have been asked to migrate to Lightning Knowledge. How can you achieve this?
    a. Turn on Lightning Knowledge and migrate all the articles manually
    b. Delete Classic articles and reimport them in Lightning Knowledge format with a Data Loader.
    c. Use the Lightning Knowledge Migration Tool.
2. How can you differentiate between an article's type in Lightning Knowledge?
    a. Use Knowledge object record types.
    b. Use article object record types.
    c. Use article type configuration.
3. What are Knowledge data categories used for?
    a. To call the Lightning Knowledge record types
    b. To categorize roles and profiles for article publication
    c. To categorize articles and allow access to selected roles/profiles or a subset of articles

4. What happens if a queue-based Omni-Channel has been configured where an agent has a capacity of 10, but they are the only agent online and are handling 2 cases that have been configured as work items where the size is 4?
    a. They will be notified about any incoming cases by the Omni-Channel component.
    b. They won't be able to accept the new case until one of their cases is closed or another agent with a capacity greater than 10 comes online.
    c. They won't be able to accept the new case until one of their cases is closed or another agent with a capacity greater than or equal to 4 comes online.
    d. They will be notified by the Omni-Channel component of an incoming case but they won't be able to accept it.
5. What is external routing?
    a. A Live Agent feature that's used to transfer a chat to another agent
    b. An Omni-Channel feature that's used to route work items to agents using an external system
    c. A mechanism for sharing work items across an organization
6. Can a chat be configured so that it can be used alongside an Omni-Channel?
    a. No, the chat is a standalone feature.
    b. Yes, but the chat work item's capacity is set to 2.
    c. Yes, and you can set up a chat capacity for your agents.
7. Where can a chat be embedded?
    a. On a Salesforce Community
    b. On an external portal
    c. Only on a Salesforce site
8. Your products are covered by 2-year on-site support. How can you configure this feature?
    a. Enable entitlements, create a new entitlement template, and add it to the selected product.
    b. Enable entitlements, create a new milestone template, and add it to the selected product.
    c. Enable milestones, create a new entitlement template, and add it to the selected product.

9. What is a milestone?
    a. A time trigger that starts a workflow action when a case hasn't been closed within a certain amount of time
    b. Another way to call an entitlement process, which involves steps
    c. A step that the support team needs to complete in order to close a case
10. What happens when a milestone is not completed?
    a. The case is automatically closed.
    b. The case is automatically escalated.
    c. Depending on the entitlement process configuration, different workflow actions may be triggered when the milestone is not completed.

4

Section 4: Data and Content Management

In this section, you will learn how to handle data deduplication by delivering matching and duplication rules. You will also handle file libraries that include Salesforce CRM content.

This section includes the following chapters:

- `Chapter 7`, *Improving Data Quality with Duplicate Management*
- `Chapter 8`, *Salesforce CRM Content Management*

7
Improving Data Quality with Duplicate Management

After looking at key sales and service features, let's go back to data quality. In this chapter, you'll learn how to provide data consistency using duplicate management for standard and custom objects by defining duplicate and matching rules.

Using duplicate record management, we can keep data clean and accurate and thereby ensure quality. We can use duplicate policies for real-time duplicate management (users can be notified if a duplicate record is found) or schedule duplication jobs for org-wide management of duplicates.

In this chapter, we will cover the following topics about duplicate management:

- Understanding duplicate management
- Exploring customizing rules

Understanding duplicate management

Data quality is one of the key factors for any company because it ensures that business strategies rely on accurate information (you know exactly where you are and where you want to go).

In the previous chapters, we learned some ways to ensure data quality:

- Using data access configurations to grant proper access to records (avoiding unauthorized access to sensible information)
- Using validation rules to keep coherence
- Using picklist fields to ensure proper field completion
- Using custom relations to correlate data

But there is another platform feature that can be of great help with data accuracy: **duplicate management**. This feature applies to accounts, contacts, and leads (but also custom objects), and is meant to limit the amount of duplicate records by our sales team.

Let's say a big event is hosted at a local business center and our company has booked a booth (like companies do at Dreamforce). Our sales reps collect leads on the field using the Salesforce application from their smartphone. They meet lots of people, and it's impossible for them to remember whether they already met the same company/lead.

With duplicate management, we can allow them to spot whether a lead or account has already been added to our CRM and even whether they have the permission to merge these duplicates into a single entity (they may have got different information about a company or lead at different events; by merging, they create a more accurate record).

Let's see how this feature works.

If an org is created after summer 2017, the standard duplicate rules are activated by default for accounts, contacts, and leads. If you need a person account, the rules must be activated after the person account feature is enabled on your org.

Local duplicate management

Local duplicate management is the part of duplicate management that is related to how the user interacts with duplicates. To have a look at the standard rules, navigate to **Setup** | **Data** | **Duplicate Management** | **Duplicate Rules** to bring up the following page:

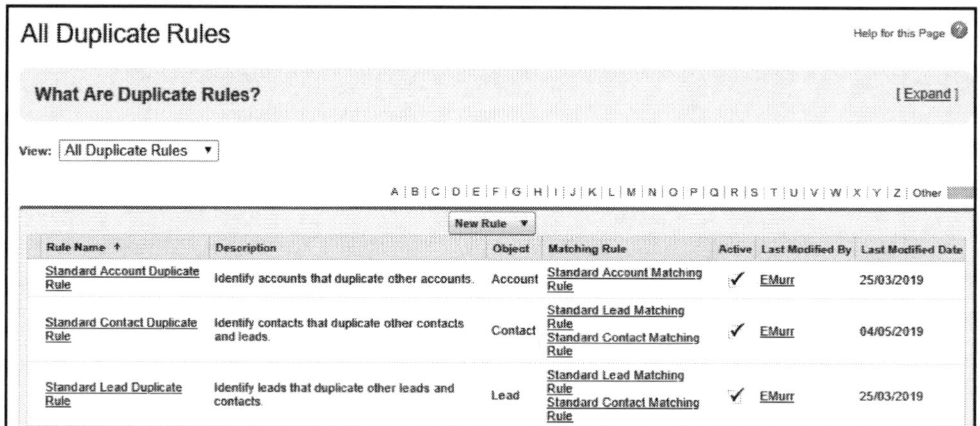

Duplicate Rules main page

Let's edit the **Contact** rule and make sure the configuration is the same as that shown in the following screenshot:

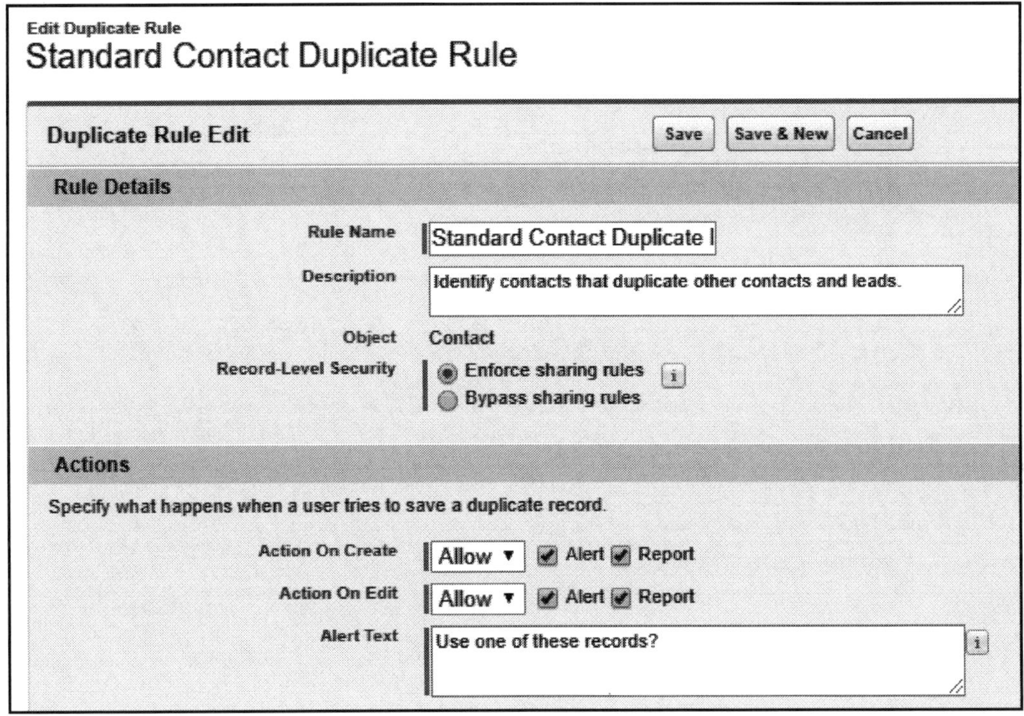

Duplicate rule editing

If you scroll down on this form, you'll see information about matching rules, as shown in the following screenshot:

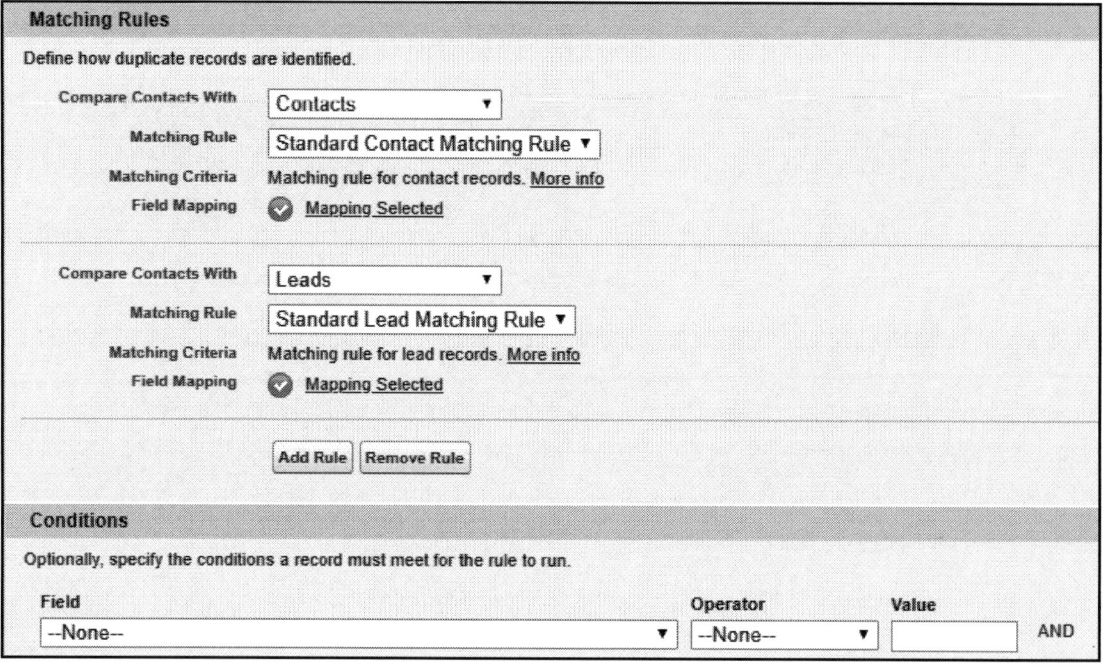

Matching rules section on duplicate rules editing

As the name clearly states, matching rules are the rules used to match duplicates (we'll learn more about matching rules later on).

With this configuration, the rule checks for potential duplicates enforcing sharing rules (only accessible contacts are notified to the current user), but it also allows the creation and updating of a record despite duplicates being found (the other option is Block, which prevents creation and updating). By selecting the Alert flag, Salesforce displays the potential duplicate information on the page layout.

So, what happens if we create two contacts with the same first and last name? Before saving, we get the following information on the upper part of the creation/editing panel:

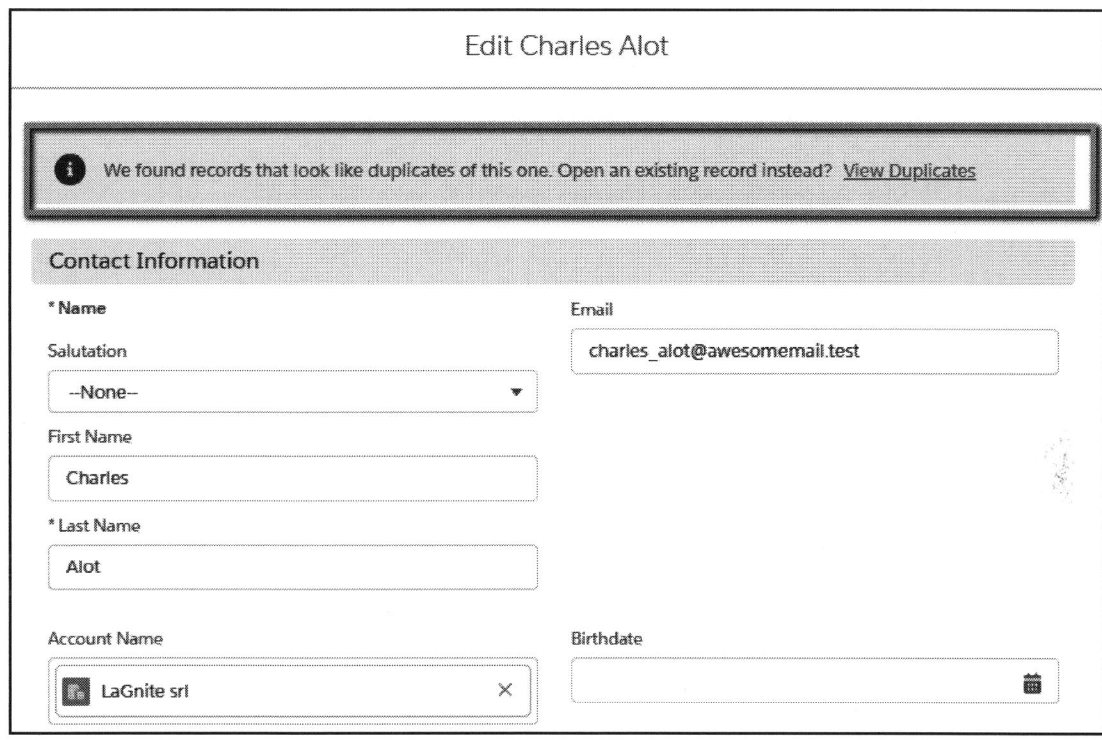

Duplicate record alert

If we ignore this message, we still get an information toast after saving:

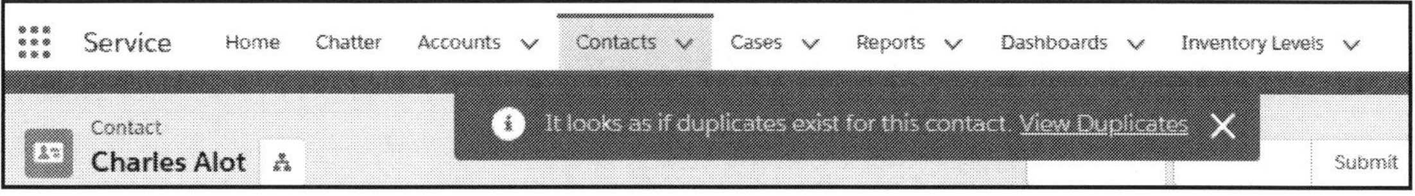

Duplicate alert on record save

On the **App Builder**, we can add the **Potential Duplicates** standard Lightning component, which will tell us the condition of the duplicates on the record at any time:

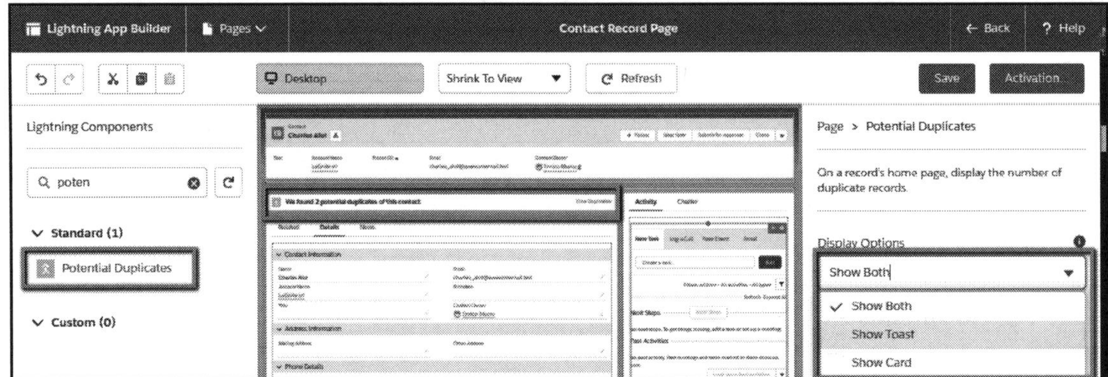

Potential Duplicates components on the App Builder for the Contact record page

You'll now receive both the toast notification and the card highlight:

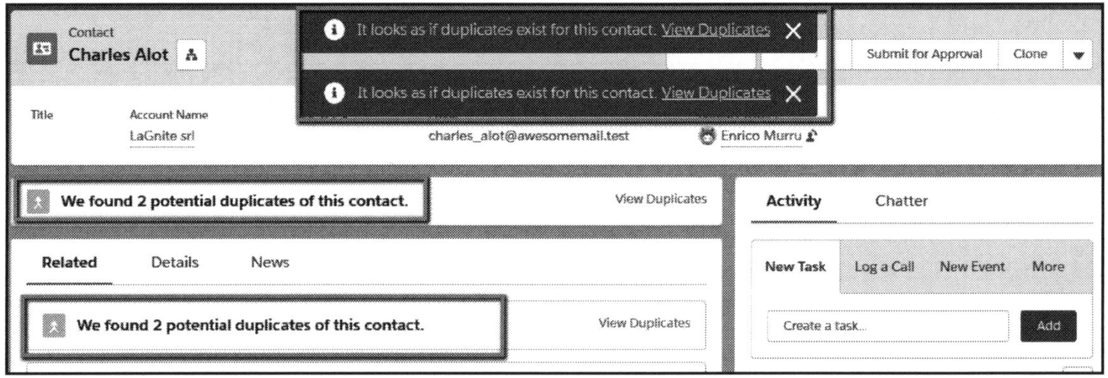

Potential duplicate alerts on contact's record page

There's a chance you will get two toast notifications. That's because you already have the **Potential Duplicates** component by default as a **Related** list. Decide whether you want the component in both places or not, and if so, configure the **Related** list to display only the card using the component configuration shown in the previous **Potential Duplicates** component screenshot.

Let's click on the **View Duplicates** link, which will show the following screen:

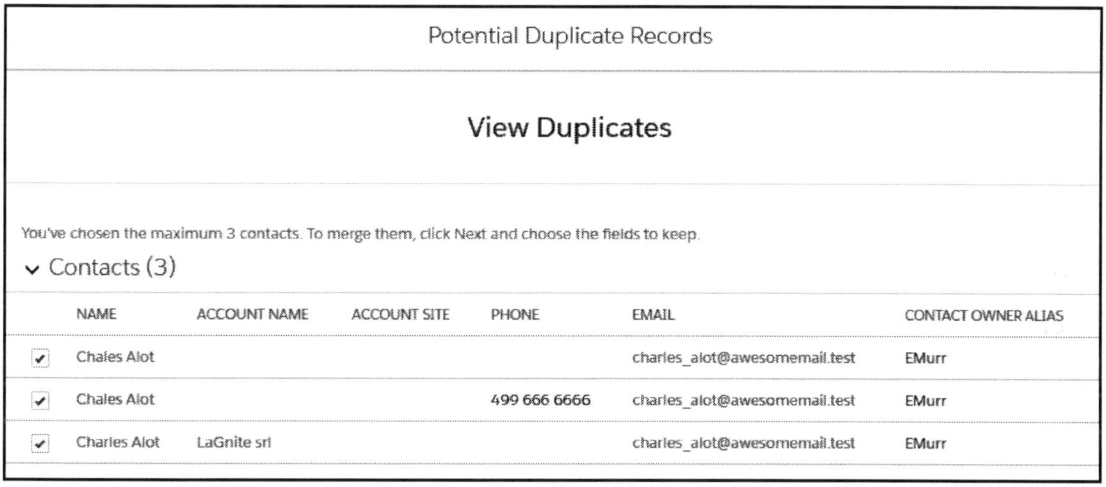

Potential Duplicate Records

View Duplicates

You've chosen the maximum 3 contacts. To merge them, click Next and choose the fields to keep.

Contacts (3)

	NAME	ACCOUNT NAME	ACCOUNT SITE	PHONE	EMAIL	CONTACT OWNER ALIAS
✔	Chales Alot				charles_alot@awesomemail.test	EMurr
✔	Chales Alot			499 666 6666	charles_alot@awesomemail.test	EMurr
✔	Charles Alot	LaGnite srl			charles_alot@awesomemail.test	EMurr

Potential duplicates selection for merging records

We can now merge all potential duplicates by selecting all the required records, then click the **Next** button to get a matrix with all of the different fields to choose from:

Potential Duplicate Records

Compare Contacts

When you merge, the master record is updated with the values you choose, and relationships to other items are shifted to the master record.

	Chales Alot Select All	Chales Alot Select All	Charles Alot Select All
MASTER RECORD	Use as master	Use as master	Use as master
NAME	Chales Alot	Chales Alot	Charles Alot
ACCOUNT NAME	[empty]	[empty]	LaGnite srl
TITLE	[empty]	Marketing Mananager	[empty]
MAILING ADDRESS	[empty]	[empty]	Via Cagliari 09028 Sestu CA ITALY
PHONE COUNTRY CODE	[empty]	[empty]	+39
PHONE	[empty]	499 666 6666	[empty]
MOBILE	399 666 6666	[empty]	[empty]
ASSISTANT	[empty]	Gianni	[empty]

Field selection of duplicate records for merging

Select all the fields you want to merge into a single record. Once the merge is completed, you get a unique record that will replace old duplicates:

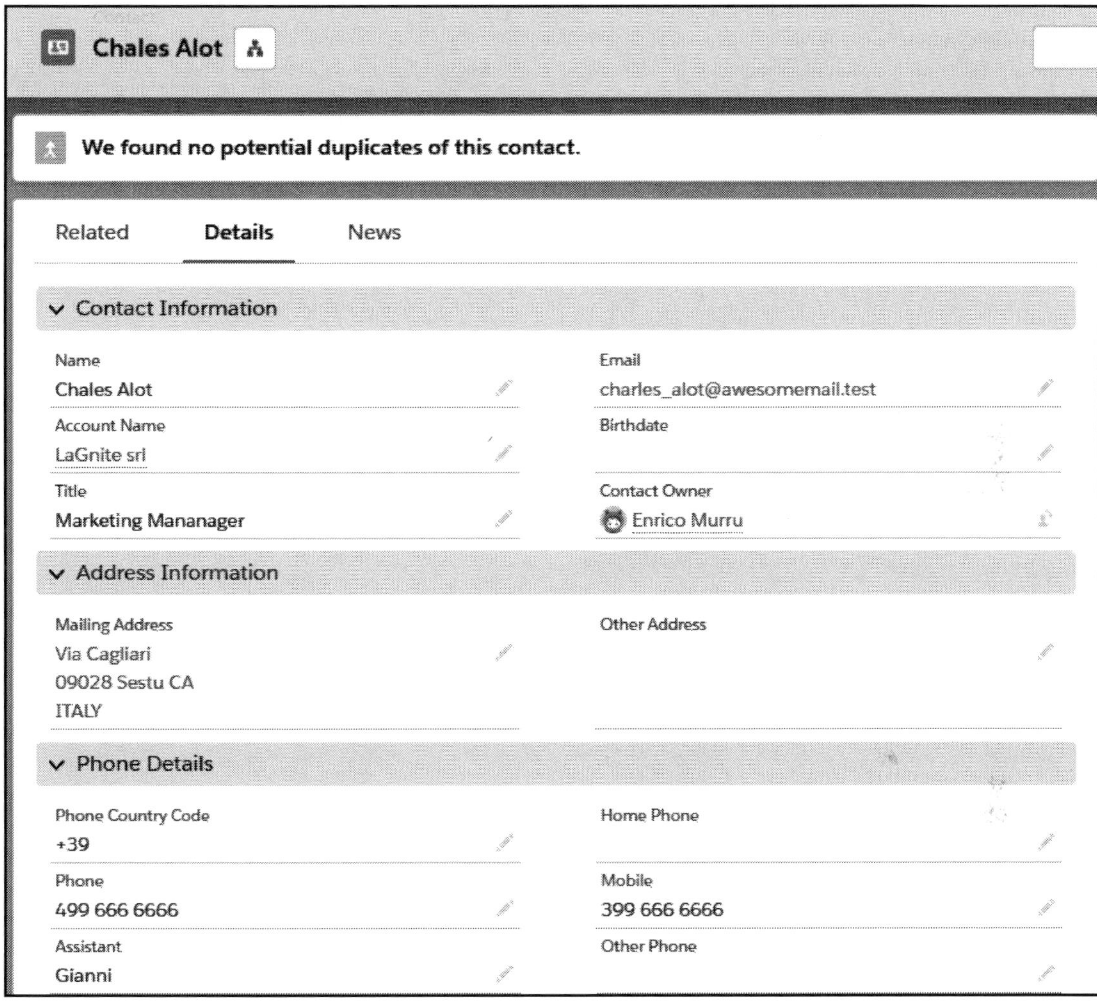

Merged contact from duplicates

No potential duplicate will be found.

What happens if we select **Block** on the **Action on Create/Edit** options for the **Potential Duplicates** rule? The user is blocked from creating the record, but receives a warning instead:

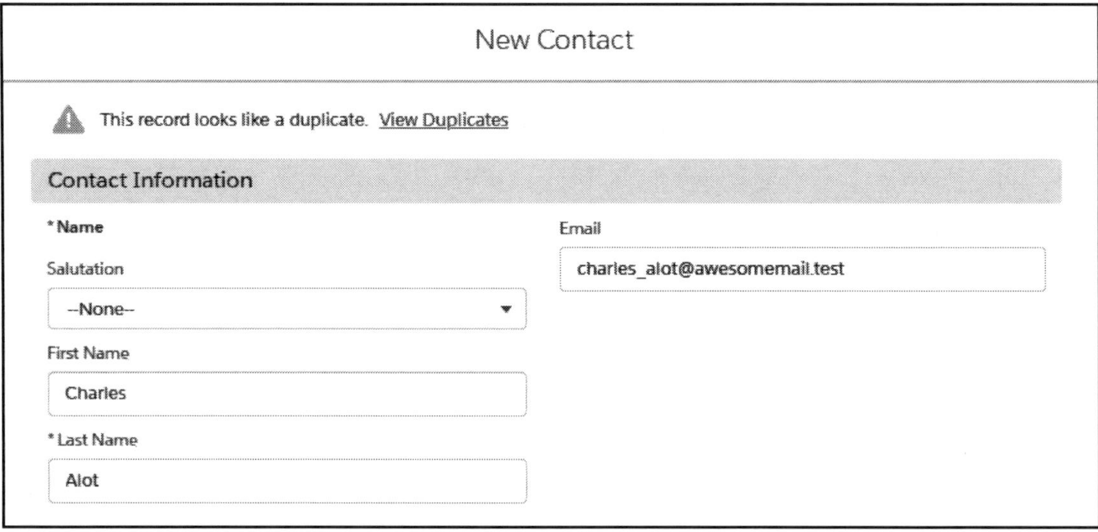

Blocking the duplicate rule prevents record creation

Click on **View Duplicates** to get a list of all potential duplicates. No merge operation is now available; instead, we can only jump into the records found:

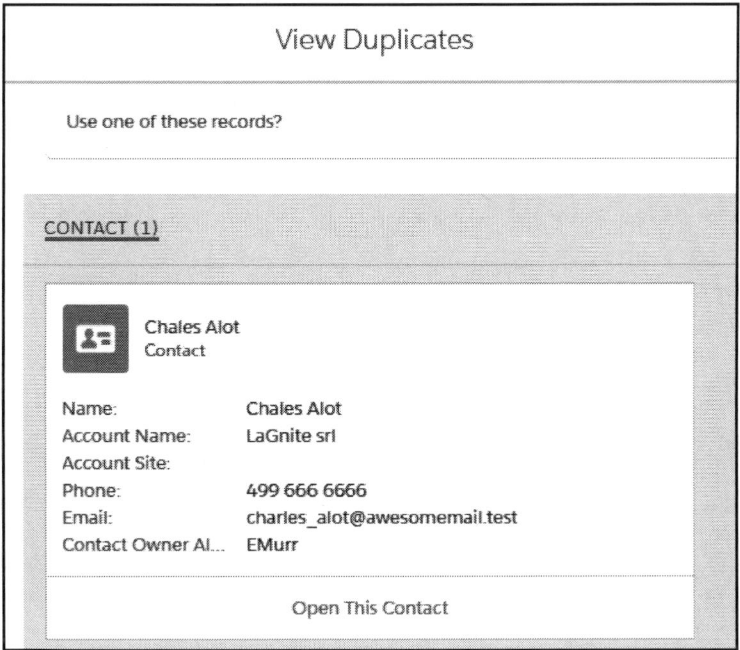

Duplicate record selection on blocking potential duplicates rule

This is the same link you can reach from the information alert when the rule is configured with the **Allow** option and you are creating a new record or editing one without using inline editing on the record page.

Local duplicate rules can be applied to accounts, contacts, leads, and custom objects as well, but the **Potential Duplicates** Lightning component is only available for accounts, contacts, and leads.

Global duplicate management

What if we decide to activate duplicate management after our sales reps have already created lots of leads? We cannot ask all our sales reps to open leads one by one to check duplicates and merge them; that will definitely be a waste of time.

For this purpose, we can use duplicate jobs with standard or custom matching rules to scan accounts, contacts, or leads for duplicate matching. This feature is only available on the **Performance** and **Unlimited** editions; that's why this feature is not available in Developer edition orgs.

If you can access an org of this kind, navigate to **Setup** | **Duplicate Management** | **Duplicate Jobs** and select **New Job** to create a new duplicate-matching job:

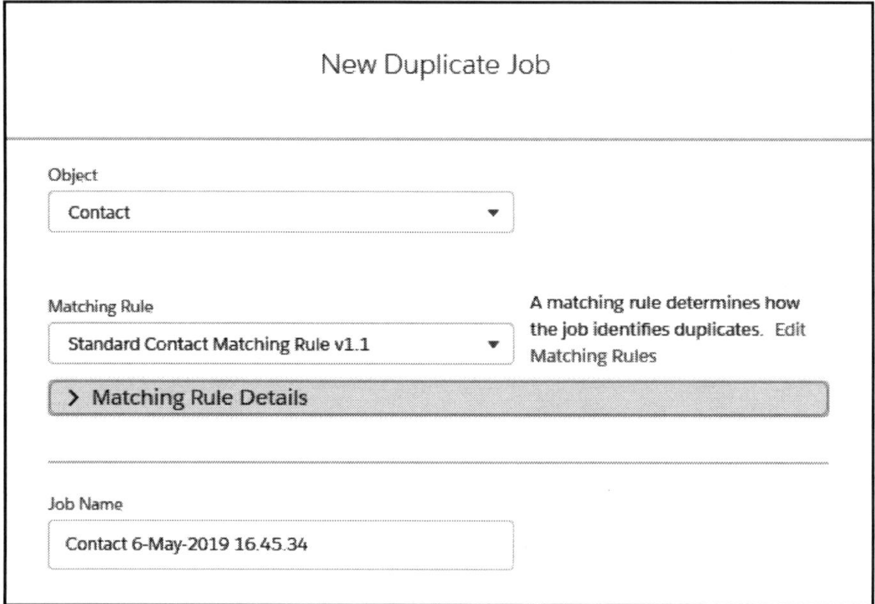

Create a new duplicate job

Select the object you want to inspect, the matching rule (it can be a standard or a custom rule), and finally the job's name. Hit **Run** to run the job and wait for it to be completed (a notification email will be sent).

This is how duplicate job results are displayed (you get all the duplicate records set on the org from **App Launcher** | **Duplicate Record Sets**):

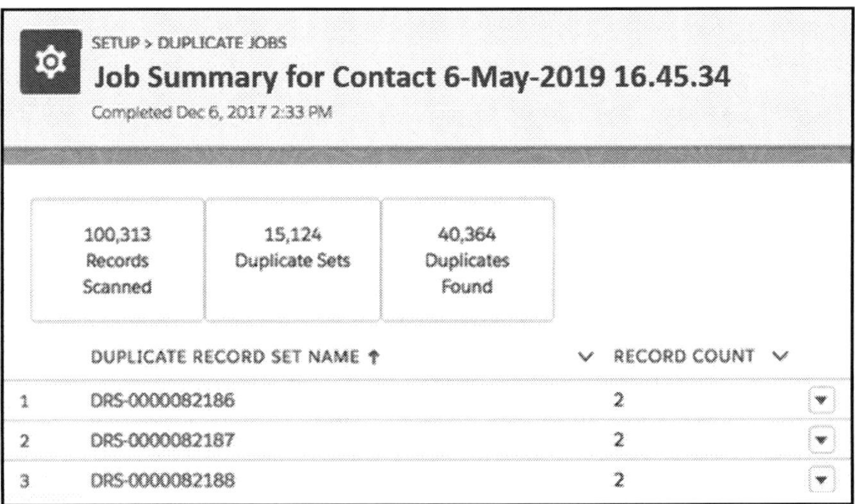

Duplicate job result

Each record set represents a set of records that are potential duplicates. To see which records those are, jump to the **Duplicate Record Items** list on the **Duplicate Record Set** record. Use the **Compare and Merge** quick action to start the merge activity that we saw in the previous section:

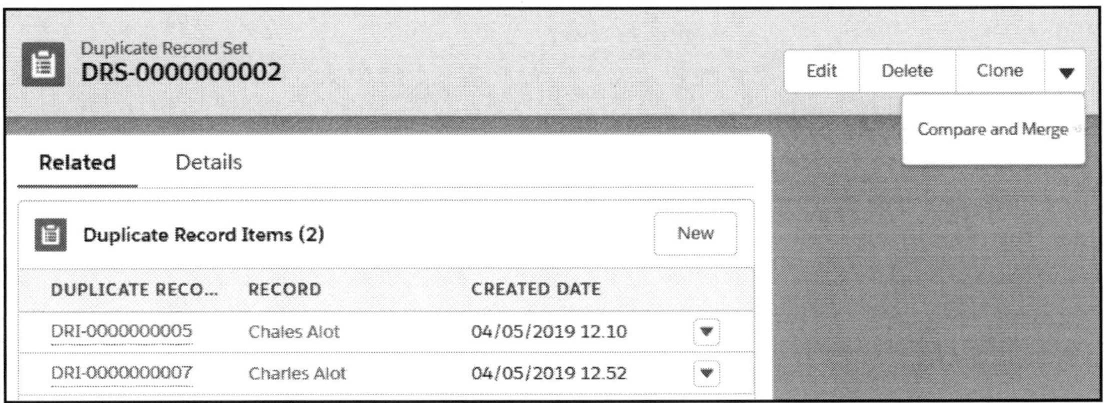

Compare and Merge action from the Duplicate Record Set layout

To let users merge these duplicate sets, give them access to the object. If we want to share the results of a job, we can run a report on the duplicate record generated by our job.

It is possible to run duplicate jobs on custom objects, but the duplicate record set cannot be merged.

There are a few things to remember:

- If you create a new job with the same configuration (object and matching rule), the new job overwrites any earlier job of the same kind
- If a matching rule is updated, all results of previous jobs are deleted once a new job with the same matching rule is run
- If the total number of duplicates found reaches 1,000,000, then no new job can be run (you will have to delete some of the results)
- If the org contains too many records, the job can fail (there will be no more information available on this point; just use it as a warning and ask Salesforce Support in the case that jobs are constantly failing)
- Even if we delete all the results of a job, its status is retained (such as the time of the run, the number of records, the duplicates that were found, and so on)
- Do not use an encrypted field on a matching rule; otherwise, the job will fail

Reporting on duplicate job results returns the following:

- Duplicate records generated by user direct creation/editing (using the **Allow** configuration of the duplicate rule)
- Records generated by duplicate jobs
- Records added manually to a record set (yes, you can manually create a duplicate record set)

Although reporting is a subject that we'll be exploring in the following chapters, you should already be aware of how reporting works and how report types are used.

To report on duplicate record set records, we need to create a new report type from **Setup** | **Features Settings** | **Analytics** | **Reports & Dashboards** | **Report Types**, by selecting a **Lead**, **Account**, **Contact**, or **Duplicate Record Set** as the primary object and adding a secondary object as the **Duplicate Record** items:

- If we choose **Account**, **Lead**, **Contact**, or a **Custom Object** as primary objects, we want to inspect how many duplicates there are for a specific object.
- If we choose **Duplicate Record Set** as the primary object, we simply want to know if our brand-new duplicate rules are working as expected:

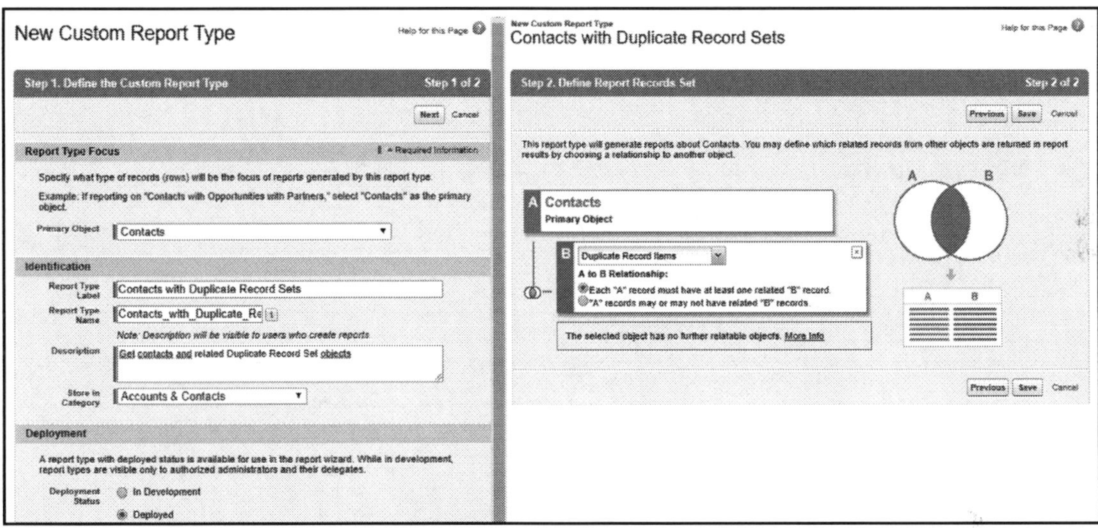

Report type configuration for duplicate management

Enable users to access the **Duplicate Record Set** and **Duplicate Record Items** objects to make them access the new report type. The following screenshot is an example of a report on the contacts and their related duplicate report items:

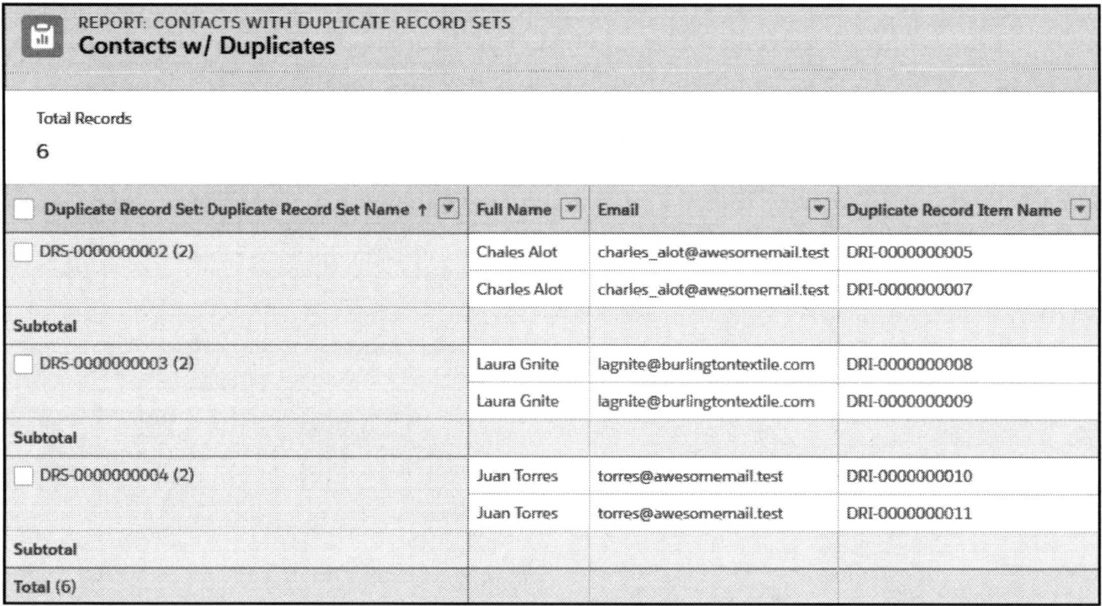
REPORT: CONTACTS WITH DUPLICATE RECORD SETS
Contacts w/ Duplicates

Total Records

6

Duplicate Record Set: Duplicate Record Set Name ↑	Full Name	Email	Duplicate Record Item Name
DRS-0000000002 (2)	Chales Alot	charles_alot@awesomemail.test	DRI-0000000005
	Charles Alot	charles_alot@awesomemail.test	DRI-0000000007
Subtotal			
DRS-0000000003 (2)	Laura Gnite	lagnite@burlingtontextile.com	DRI-0000000008
	Laura Gnite	lagnite@burlingtontextile.com	DRI-0000000009
Subtotal			
DRS-0000000004 (2)	Juan Torres	torres@awesomemail.test	DRI-0000000010
	Juan Torres	torres@awesomemail.test	DRI-0000000011
Subtotal			
Total (6)			

Reporting on duplicate record items and contacts

To troubleshoot errors that prevent duplicate or matching rules, you can jump to **Setup** | **Data** | **Duplicate Management** | **Duplicate Error Logs**.

Errors can arise if the engine that calculates duplicates is temporarily down or if a required custom field on the **Duplicate Record Set** or **Duplicate Items** objects is not populated (you can customize these objects from **Setup** | **Object Manager** as you would do with any other standard object). Let's test this out.

We will create a custom field on the **Duplicate Record Item** object (marked as required):

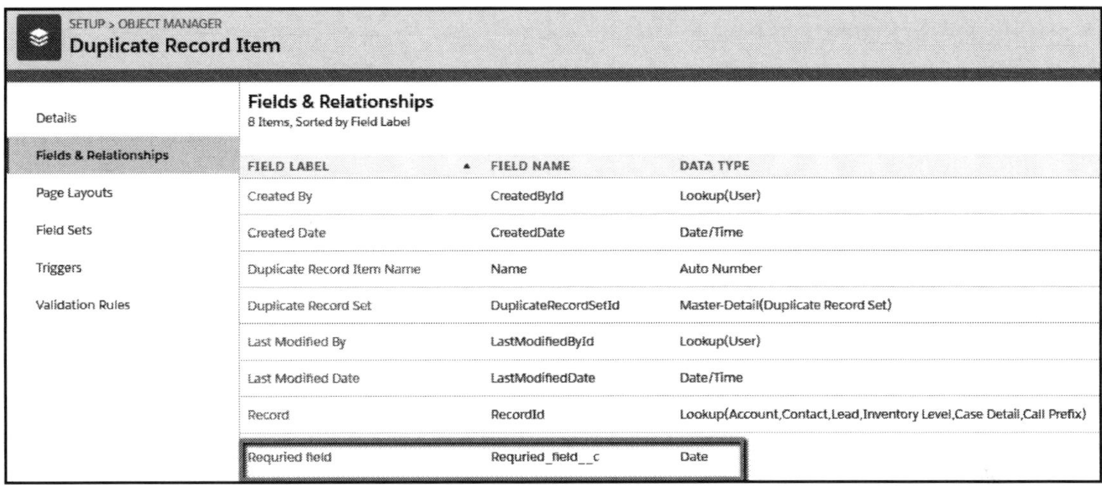

New custom field on the Duplicate Record Item object

Now let's create a new contact using the same name and email address. Nothing happens on the page layout (other than the duplicate alert), but if we go to the **Duplicate Error Logs** page, then this is what we will see:

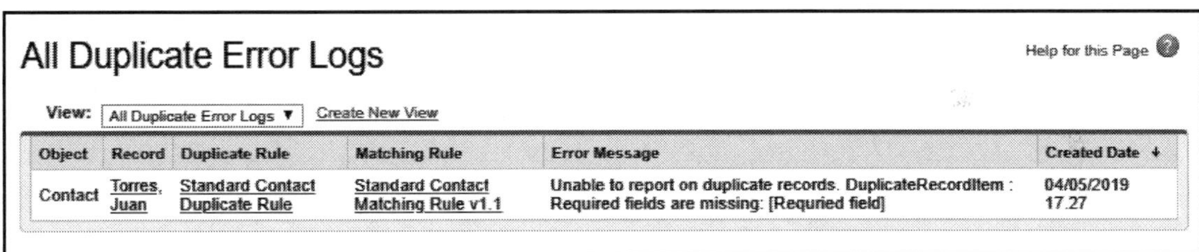

Reporting a duplicate calculation error

As you can see, no duplicate record item has been created (and therefore cannot be reported). Logs are retained for 90 days.

Exploring and customizing rules

In this section, we will learn how to customize the duplicate and matching rules.

Customizing duplicate rules

As we have already seen in the previous sections, duplicate rules are used to alert on potential duplicates or prevent potential duplicates for a given record (if it is used on objects other than **Account**, **Contact**, and **Lead**, the **Potential Duplicates** component cannot alert the user in real time, but the **Duplicate Record Set** object will be created anyway).

To create a new duplicate rule, jump to **Setup** | **Duplicate Management** | **Duplicate Rules** and click the **New Rule** | **Contact** button. Select the object you want the rule to be created on:

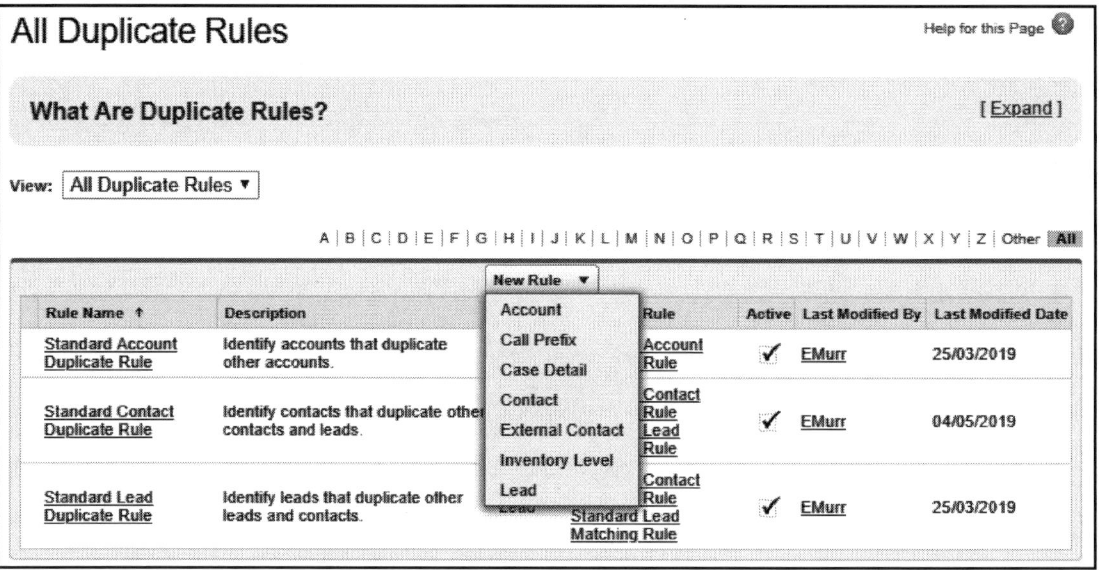

Duplicate rule creation

Before creating everything, let's design our scenario. We have a custom object called **External Contact** that comes from an external system and represents thousands of contacts on an external system that the business guys decided not to migrate into **Contacts** (because there is too much data inconsistency). But despite this, this table should be used when creating new contacts on the system to enrich data.

This object holds the following custom fields:

- **First Name** (text, 80)
- **Last Name** (text, 80)
- **Company** (text, 80)
- **Email** (email type)
- **Phone** (phone type)

Let's also create a new tab and add it to our app (and create our first record manually):

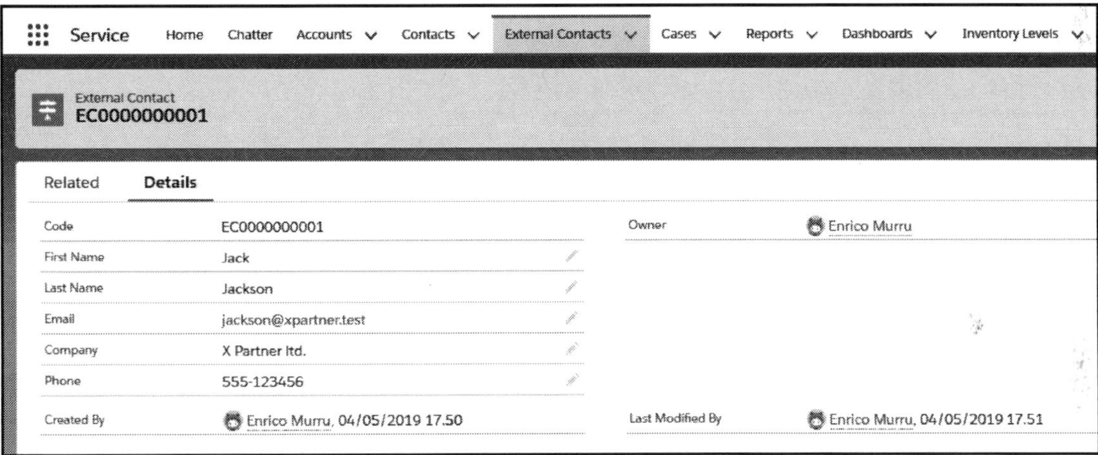

Custom object to handle external contact data

Let's go back to the **Duplicate Rule Edit** creation page. We have already seen how these sections work:

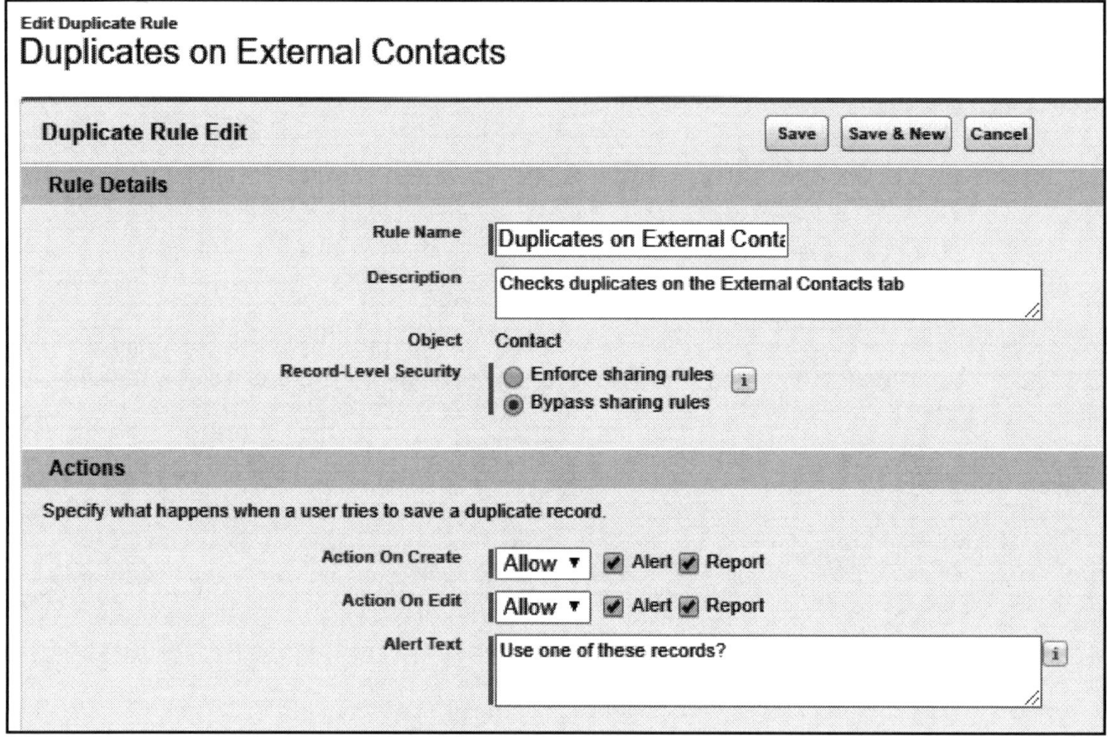

Custom duplicate rule creation

The section below **Actions**, not shown in the previous screenshot, is about matching rule selection. We haven't created a custom matching rule yet, so leave this section empty (it will be populated with one of the standard matching rules on the **Contact** object (we'll get there shortly).

The last section is called **Conditions** and it can be used to select specific conditions on the record that should be checked (for example, conditions on fields of the contact, account or current user records). Hit **Save** to save the new rule (if it is not yet active).

If we want to reorder the rules on the same object, click on the **Reorder** link on the rule page and select the required order:

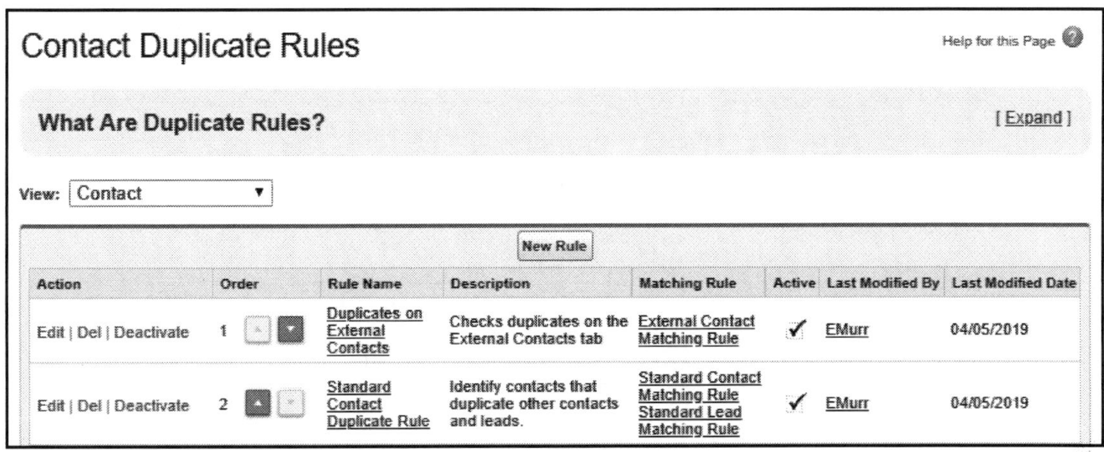

Duplicate rule sorting on the same object

If a match is found on the first rule, the second one is not evaluated at all.

Customizing matching rules

A matching rule defines how duplicate records are identified. We have predefined standard matching rules, but we can create new matching rules by going to **Setup** | **Duplicate Management** | **Matching Rules** and clicking on **New Rule**. Select the **External Contact** object.

Let's create a rule with the following configuration:

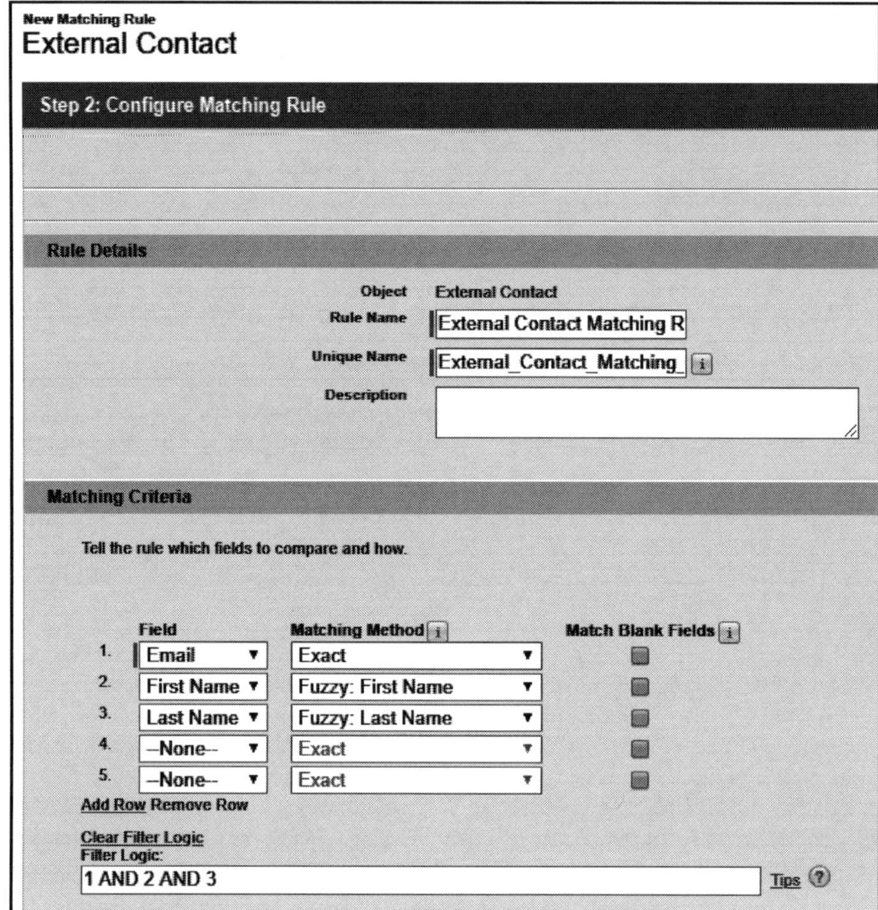

Matching rule creation

The **Matching Criteria** section states which conditions should trigger the potential duplicate match. Matching methods define the algorithm used to compare values and can be set to **Exact** to be triggered only if we have the same value or **Fuzzy:** ***type*** to provide specific data type algorithms (match for first/last names, company, and so on). Select the **Match Blank Fields** if blank field matching can be a valid filter. Activate the matching rule with the **Activate** button.

For a deeper understanding of matching methods, refer to Salesforce Help at `https://help.salesforce.com/articleView?id=matching_rules_matching_methods.htmtype=5` and `https://help.salesforce.com/articleView?id=matching_rules_matching_algorithms.htmtype=5`.

Let's go back to the duplicate rule in the external contacts we created in the previous section, edit it, and compile the **Matching Rules** section (you can add more than one rule) and select your brand new matching rule:

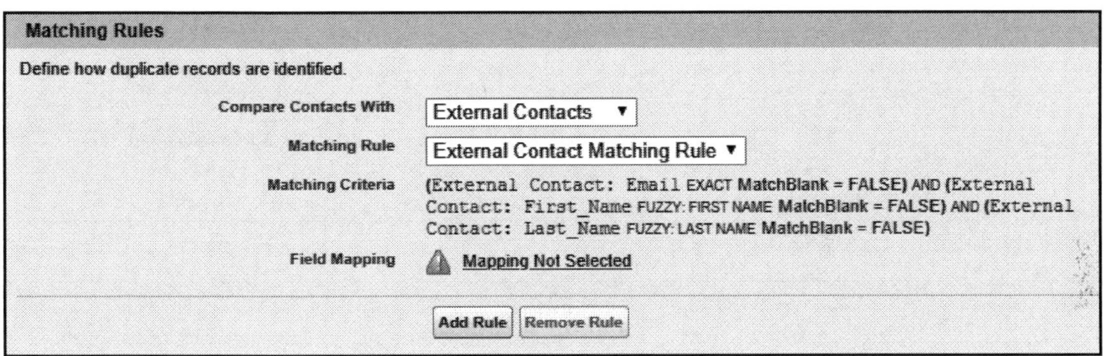

Matching rule selection on a duplicate rule

The last thing to do is map the fields to the custom **External Contact Field** object so the algorithm can properly match records. Click on the **Mapping Not Selected** link next to the small warning icon:

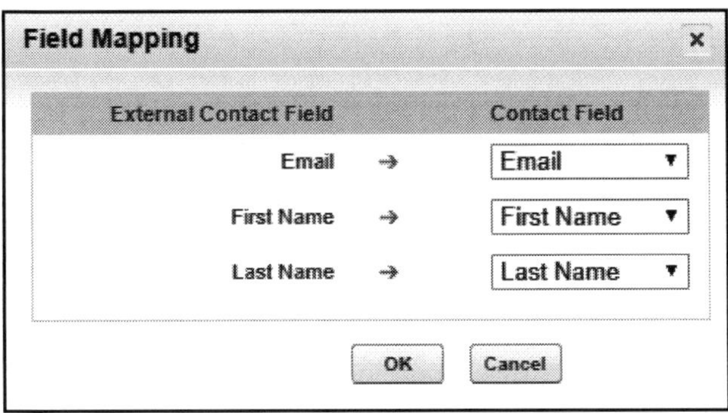

Mapping selection on duplicate rule

Save the rule and click on the **Activate** button.

Now let's create a new contact record with the same **First Name**, **Last Name**, and **Email** of the external contact we created earlier:

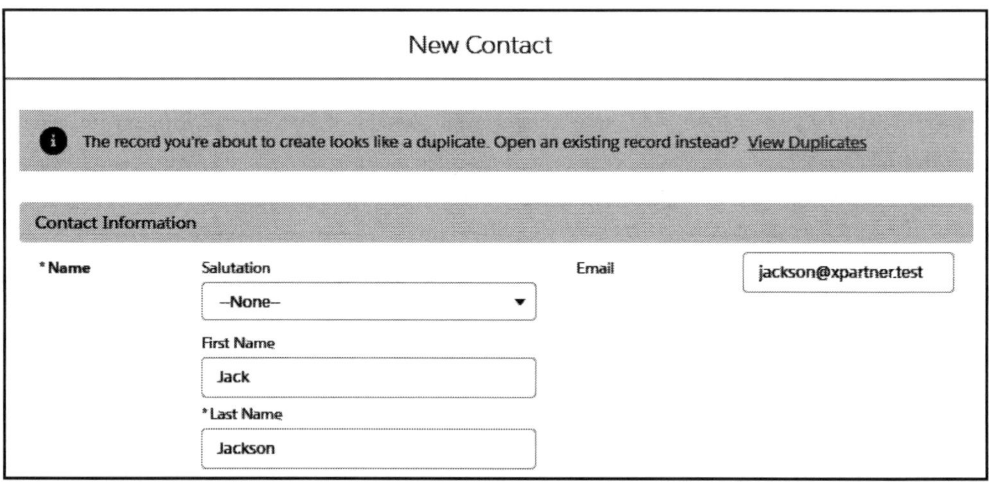

Duplicate rule running on custom object

The only difference is that once we save the contact record and click on the **View Duplicates** link on the potential duplicates component, we cannot merge records as they are different objects:

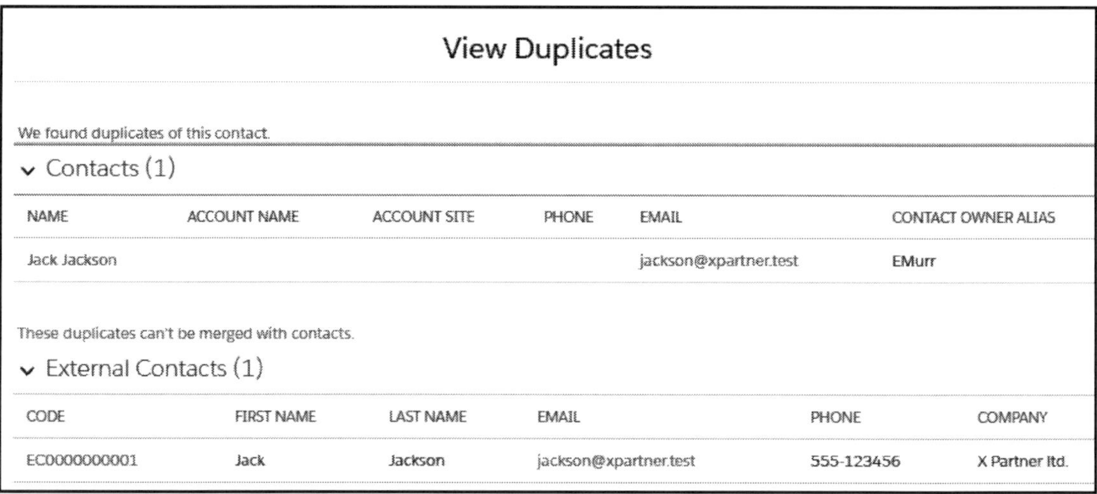

Duplicates found on custom object

Now we can use the external contact fields to enrich our new contact, and then delete the record once the data has been manually merged (this is just an example that doesn't have the best user experience, but it gives your fantasy a boost!).

This is only a simple way to implement cross-object duplicate rules; you can define any kind of duplicate rules with custom objects. The only limitation is that the **Potential Duplicates** component will only work with **Account**, **Contact**, and **Lead** objects; to have a look at all duplicates for a custom object, use duplicate jobs instead.

Considerations regarding duplicate management

We can have up to 5 active duplicate rules per object and up to 3 matching rules on each duplicate rule (and 1 matching rule per object).

We can also have up to 5 matching rules (active or not) per object, a total of 25 matching rules (active) on all objects, and up to 100 matching rules (active or not). A matching rule can have only one lookup relationship.

Global picklists are not supported in duplicate rules and custom picklists cannot be used in cross-object duplicate rules.

Another interesting behavior is that a duplicate rule, when editing a record, is triggered only if the user changes one of the fields mapped on the rule.

When duplicate rules won't run, the following happens:

- Records are created with the **Quick Create** tool (for more details, go to `https://help.salesforce.com/articleView?id=basics_creating_records_with_quick_create.htmtype=5`) or using Community Self-Registration.
- Leads are converted to accounts or contacts and the **User Apex Lead Convert** flag is disabled (you can find more details at `https://help.salesforce.com/articleView?amp;language=en_USid=000214462type=1`).
- The record is restored with the **Undelete** button.
- The records are manually merged.
- If we have rule conditions on related objects and the corresponding lookup field is not filled in on the record we are creating/updating, the rule is not triggered.

- The duplicate alert is not shown when records are imported with data import tools or through Salesforce APIs (as with Data Loader) or a person account is converted into a business account (and the new business account matches another duplicate).
- If two potential duplicate records are saved simultaneously, they are compared only with records already on the database, so users are not alerted/blocked. If the **Report** option is set on the rule, then duplicate record sets will correctly include simultaneous records.

For a detailed list of standard duplicate rules, refer to Salesforce Help at `https://help.salesforce.com/articleView?id=duplicate_rules_standard_rules.htmtype=5`.
For a detailed list of standard matching rules, refer to Salesforce Help at `https://help.salesforce.com/articleView?id=matching_rules_standard_rules.htmtype=5`.
For some interesting matching rule examples, refer to Salesforce Help at `https://help.salesforce.com/articleView?id=matching_rule_matching_examples.htmtype=5`.

Summary

In this chapter, we learned about duplicate management on standard and custom objects to increase data consistency across our CRM database.

We used matching rules to define the objects, fields, and algorithms to be checked when detecting duplicates; duplicate rules to alert or block users when creating new account, contact, or lead records; and duplicate jobs to make an org-wide analysis of all duplicates for standard and custom objects. Now you know another great instrument to ensure data integrity for your business data.

In the next chapter, we'll deal with content management to organize, share, search, and manage files within our org.

Questions

1. What objects can duplicate management be applied to?
    a. Only contacts and leads
    b. Accounts, contacts, leads, and custom objects
    c. Accounts, contacts, and leads
    d. Leads and contacts
2. True or false: local duplicate rules rely on record visibility across the org.
    a. True; the algorithm identifies duplicates among the records the current user can view.
    b. False; the algorithm identifies duplicates among all the records, despite the sharing settings.
    c. It depends on the duplicate rule configuration **Record-level security** setting.
3. What does the **View Duplicates** link on the **Potential Duplicates** component do?
    a. Automatically merges all identified duplicates.
    b. Selects the identified duplicates to be merged.
    c. It only gives a list of identified duplicates: the user should merge them from the **Merge Duplicates** wizard on the lead object.
4. A business wants to stop sales reps from creating potential duplicate leads. Which duplicate action should be set up on record creation or edit?
    a. Block.
    b. Allow.
    c. Notify.
    d. Validate.
5. Will the user be notified if a duplicate is found upon the creation of a custom object?
    a. No, because the **Potential Duplicates Lightning** component is only available for account, contact, and lead objects.
    b. Yes, it works for any standard and custom object.
    c. No, because matching rules cannot be created for custom objects.
6. What is global duplicate management meant for?
    a. To display a duplication alert when a new record is created.
    b. To run a background job for duplicate record set creation on account, contact, lead, and custom objects (for further reporting).
    c. To run a background job for duplicate accounts, contacts, and leads.

7. The setup item that defines the Salesforce object type we want to identify duplicates on is:
    a. The duplicate rule.
    b. The matching rule.
8. When defining a matching rule, you can define:
    a. Matching criteria and filter logic to identify duplication rules on the account, lead, and contact objects.
    b. Matching criteria and filter logic to match null values on the same record.
    c. Matching criteria and filter logic to identify which objects fields should be used to identify duplicates.
9. If you define a duplicate rule on object X, which uses a matching rule on object Y, which of the following is true?
    a. Object X records can be merged with object Y records with a custom mapping.
    b. You need to configure the proper mapping on the duplicate rule to match object Y's fields defined in the matching rule with the object X fields on which the duplicate rule is defined.
    c. You cannot merge records of type object X with duplicates records of type object Y.
    d. You can merge object X's records with object Y's records only if matching fields have the same API name.
10. Which of the following is true about duplicate management?
    a. Duplicate rules run on a record restored with an undelete.
    b. Duplicate rules run on a record restored with a delete.
    c. Cross-object duplicate rules cannot use custom picklist fields.
    d. When editing a record, a duplicate rule is triggered if the user changes any field on the duplicate rule's object.
    e. When editing a record, a duplicate rule is triggered only if the user changes one of the fields mapped.

8
Salesforce CRM Content Management

In this chapter, we'll analyze a way to handle data in a documented format, using the Salesforce CRM Content feature.

We will learn how to use Salesforce CRM Content to organize, share, search, and manage all types of corporate files within our organization. We will also learn how to set up content, manage the publication of files, organize files into libraries, search files, and use content delivery to convert documents into web-optimized versions for online viewing.

In this chapter, we'll cover the following topics:

- Setting up Salesforce CRM Content
- Managing content libraries
- Adding files to libraries
- Delivering content externally
- Searching for content files

Setting up Salesforce CRM Content

Salesforce CRM Content is a feature that is aimed at simplifying content (file) management in our org.

There are other ways to manage files within an org, for example, through files, Salesforce Knowledge, documents, and attachments. For more details on the differences between them, refer to Salesforce Help at `https://help.salesforce.com/articleView?id=collab_files_differences.htmtype=5`.

The main features of Salesforce CRM Content are as follows:

- Files can be organized into libraries and administrators can configure access to these libraries in order to grant the correct sharing, visibility, and security policies. By using private libraries, users can even create their own libraries to better organize their own files.
- Files can be searched either using metadata information (such as the author, title, format, or tags) or the full body of the content (file).
- Users can subscribe to content in order to be notified of changes to their metadata or version.
- Files can be previewed without downloading.
- Files are tracked depending on the number of thumbs up/down, subscriptions, previews, and downloads.

As of summer 2019, Salesforce CRM Content is only available on Salesforce Classic (which is where we'll be doing most of this chapter's exercises); however, files from libraries are available on Salesforce Lightning Experience as well.

To set up Salesforce CRM Content, click on **Setup** | **Salesforce CRM Content** and then click on the **Enable Salesforce CRM Content** flag. Optionally, you can also flag **Autoassign feature licenses to existing and new users** in order to assign content licenses automatically to internal users.

To enable a given user manually, select the user from **Setup** | **Users**, and then flag the **Salesforce CRM Content User** flag. Optionally, flag **Receive Salesforce CRM Content Email Alerts** for real-time email alerts on any updates about subscribed content, and flag **Receive Salesforce CRM Content Alerts as Daily Digest** to receive updates that are grouped into daily emails.

Aside from the System Administrator profile, make sure that your users have the following profile permissions depending on their content management role:

- **Manage Salesforce CRM Content**: Create, edit, and delete libraries and their membership (this permission includes all other permissions).
- **Create libraries**: Create libraries only.
- **Manage Content Permissions**: Create, edit, or delete library permissions.
- **Manage Content Properties**: Create, edit, or delete custom fields on Salesforce CRM Content.
- **Manage record types and layouts for files**: Create, edit, or delete record types and page layouts on Salesforce CRM Content.

As content is composed of a file and some metadata, we can create custom fields in the **Content Version** standard object just like we do with any other object (**Setup** | **Object Manager** | **Content Version**), such as a **Source** custom field that handles the origin of the file (for example, the business department, IT, or AMS). These custom fields appear on the file page layout when you upload a new file.

We can even define **Content Version** record types to further segment content types.

Further Salesforce CRM Content options

We can define multilanguage support in **Setup** | **Salesforce CRM Content** | **Enable multilanguage search and contribute**. With this option, a new **Language** picklist is shown when editing and searching for content in the **Content** page:

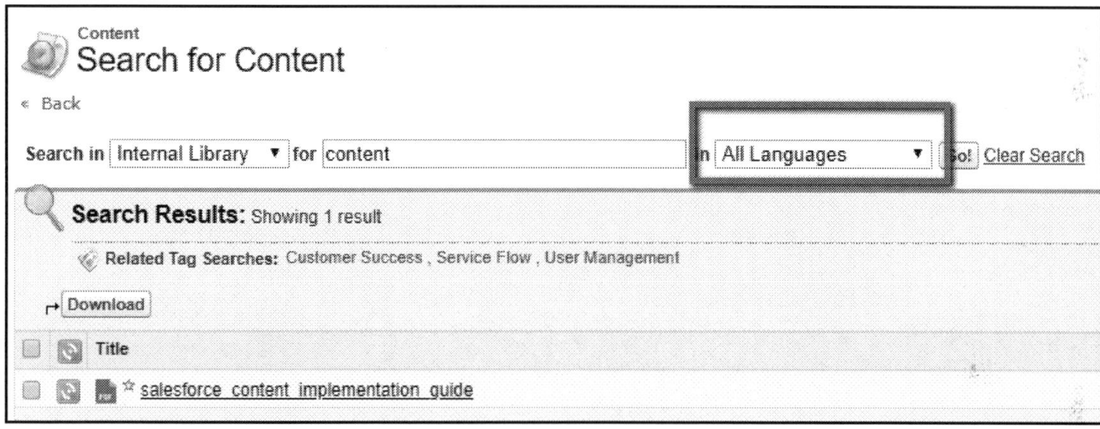

The language search filter for multilanguage setup

Moreover, libraries can be displayed on communities using branded images to speed up library identification (with Lightning Experience only).

For more information about setting up branded images, refer to Salesforce Help at `https://help.salesforce.com/articleView?id=collab_files_customize_libraries.htmtype=5`.

With the setup complete, we can now create and manage the content libraries in order to organize our content files. Let's see how this is done in the next section.

Handling content libraries

The first step to enabling Salesforce CRM Content for your users is to set up a library, which is the control panel for storing, sharing, and managing files.

Each org can host up to 2,000 libraries (as of the winter 2020 release).

Perform the following steps to complete the setup:

1. Let's switch to Salesforce Classic and search for the **Libraries** tab:

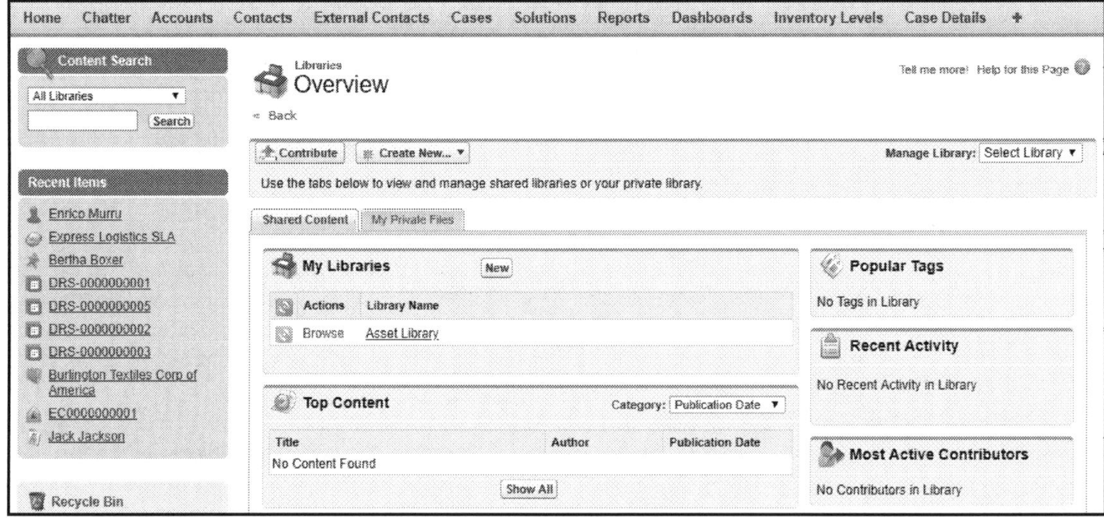

The Content Libraries tab

2. In the **My Libraries** section, click on the **New** button to create a new library. Fill in the **Name**, **Unique Name**, and **Description** fields, and then add new members in the **Save and Add Members** step:

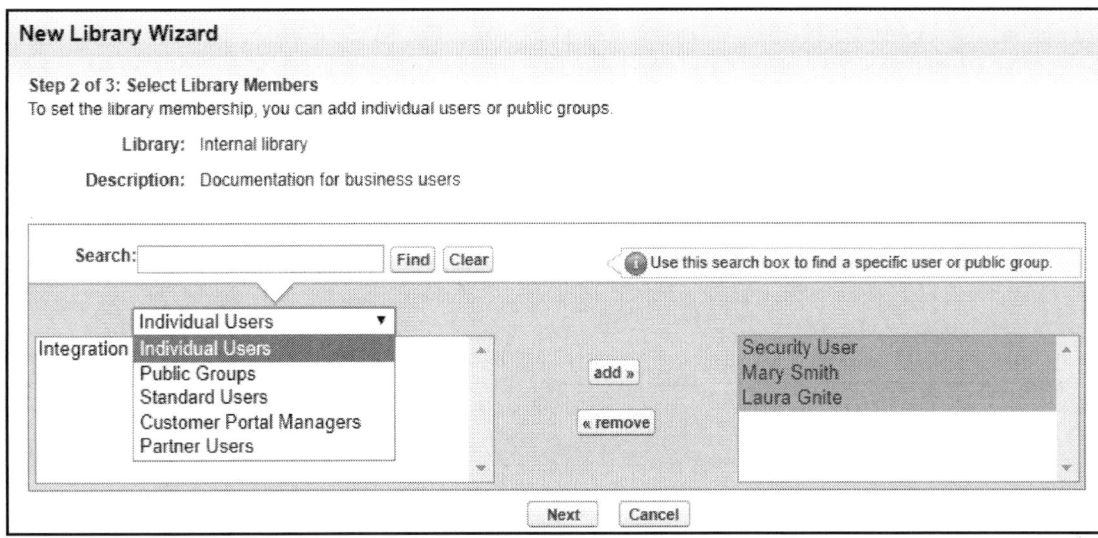

Adding members to a library

3. Click on **Next** to add permissions to each member:

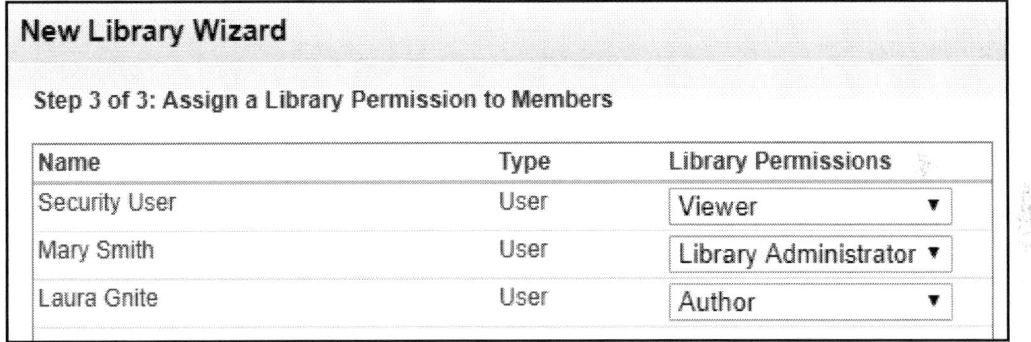

Setting up library permissions for library members

This setting gives a specific role to each user by providing **Library Permissions**. These determine the type of tasks a member can do in a particular library so that the same user can have different permissions within each library.

4. Navigate to **Setup** | **Salesforce Files** | **Content Permissions** and click on any preset permission (there should be three default permissions available: **Library Administrator**, **Author**, and **Viewer**):

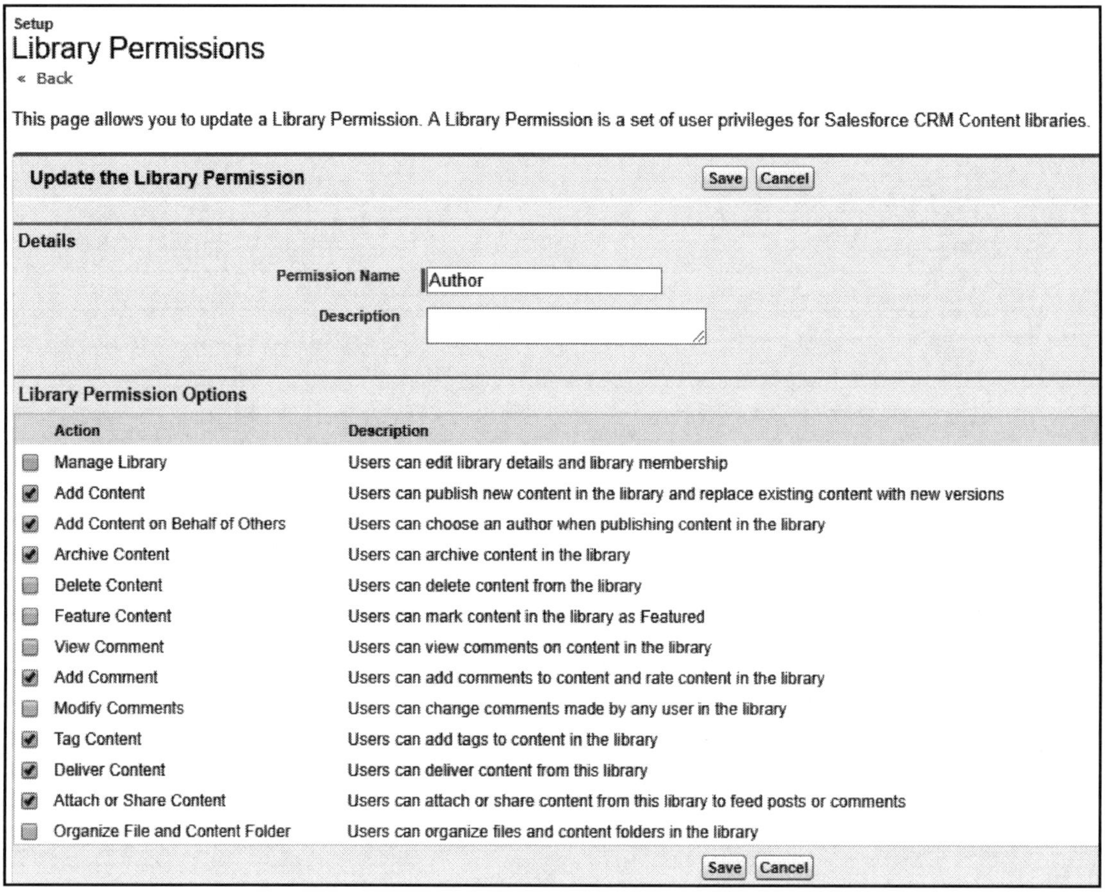

Setup

Library Permissions

« Back

This page allows you to update a Library Permission. A Library Permission is a set of user privileges for Salesforce CRM Content libraries.

Update the Library Permission Save Cancel

Details

Permission Name: Author

Description:

Library Permission Options

	Action	Description
☐	Manage Library	Users can edit library details and library membership
☑	Add Content	Users can publish new content in the library and replace existing content with new versions
☑	Add Content on Behalf of Others	Users can choose an author when publishing content in the library
☑	Archive Content	Users can archive content in the library
☐	Delete Content	Users can delete content from the library
☐	Feature Content	Users can mark content in the library as Featured
☐	View Comment	Users can view comments on content in the library
☑	Add Comment	Users can add comments to content and rate content in the library
☐	Modify Comments	Users can change comments made by any user in the library
☑	Tag Content	Users can add tags to content in the library
☑	Deliver Content	Users can deliver content from this library
☑	Attach or Share Content	Users can attach or share content from this library to feed posts or comments
☐	Organize File and Content Folder	Users can organize files and content folders in the library

Save Cancel

Salesforce CRM Content library permissions

For a detailed explanation of each option, refer to Salesforce Help at `https://help.salesforce.com/articleView?id=content_workspace_perm_add.htmtype=5`.

This is the status of our newly created library:

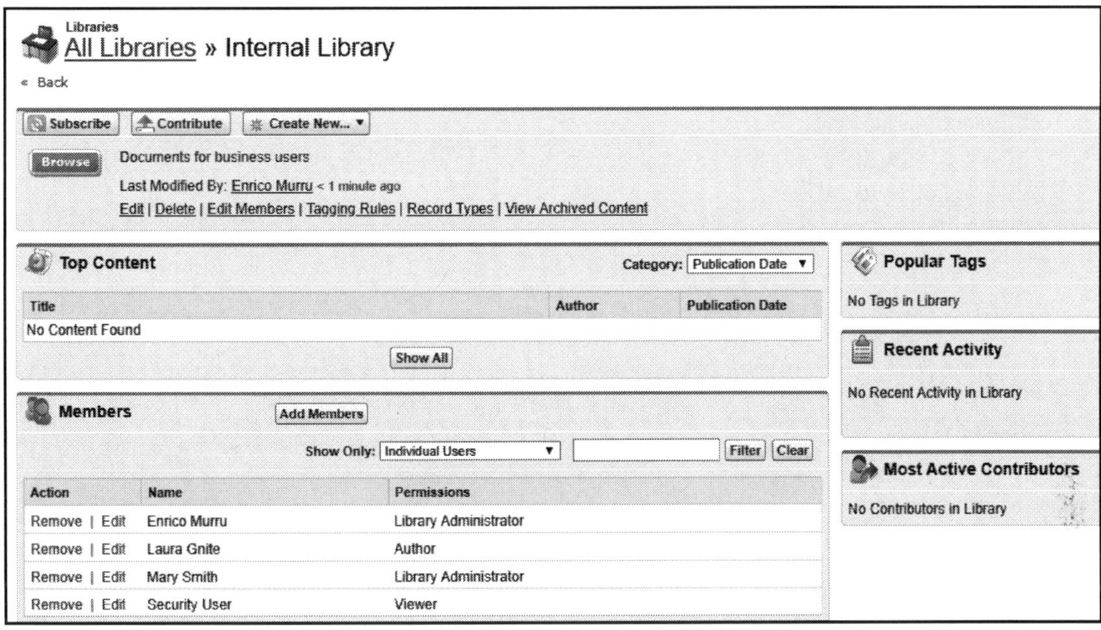

The Library layout

Another important feature of libraries is the ability to add tags to content files (which is also a way to filter out files when searching).

At the library level, we can define the following tagging rules (click on the **Tagging Rules** link in the library header):

- **Open tagging**: Contributors can add whatever tag they want on content. Salesforce will autosuggest tags based on a user's recent activity and the **Popular Tags** list.
- **Guided tagging**: Contributors can always add whatever tag they like, but the system will guide them with a list of suggested tags, which we have to set up after setting up this rule's value (you can refer to the following screenshot as an example).
- **Restricted tagging**: Contributors can only choose from suggested tags.

The following is an example of setting up **Guided Tagging**:

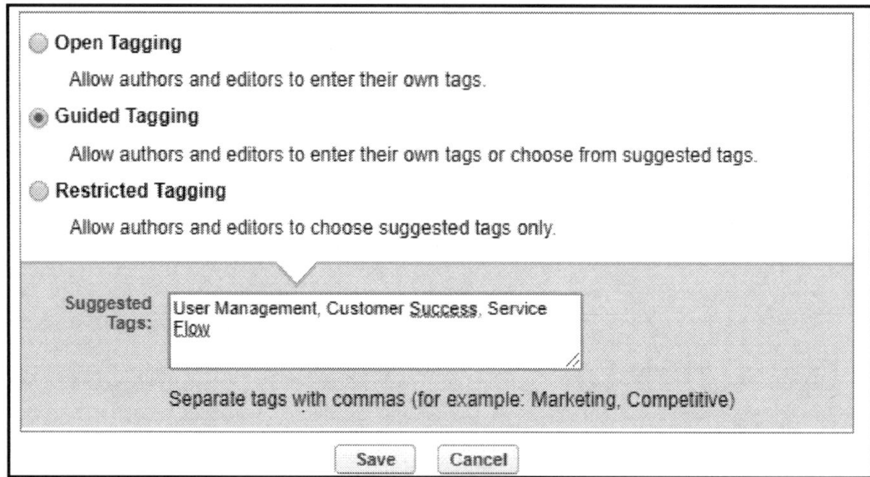

The Guided Tagging rule in the library

Remember the following:

- You can move content from one library to another and you will get an error if you move from a wider tagging rule library to a stricter tagging rule library and the content has unsupported tags.
- If a restricted tagging rule is applied after content has been added, invalid tags are still attached to the content (though not visible) and removed only when a new version of the content is published or tags are edited.
- A tag name cannot be edited or deleted; we can remove a tag from the content, but the tag will remain in the database.
- Tags are case insensitive.
- Try to limit the number of tags: they are used to segment search engine results and users can subscribe to them, so too many of them can cause clutter.

Another option to restrict the type of content available in a library is through record type restrictions, which are available by clicking on the **Record Types** link in the library record layout header:

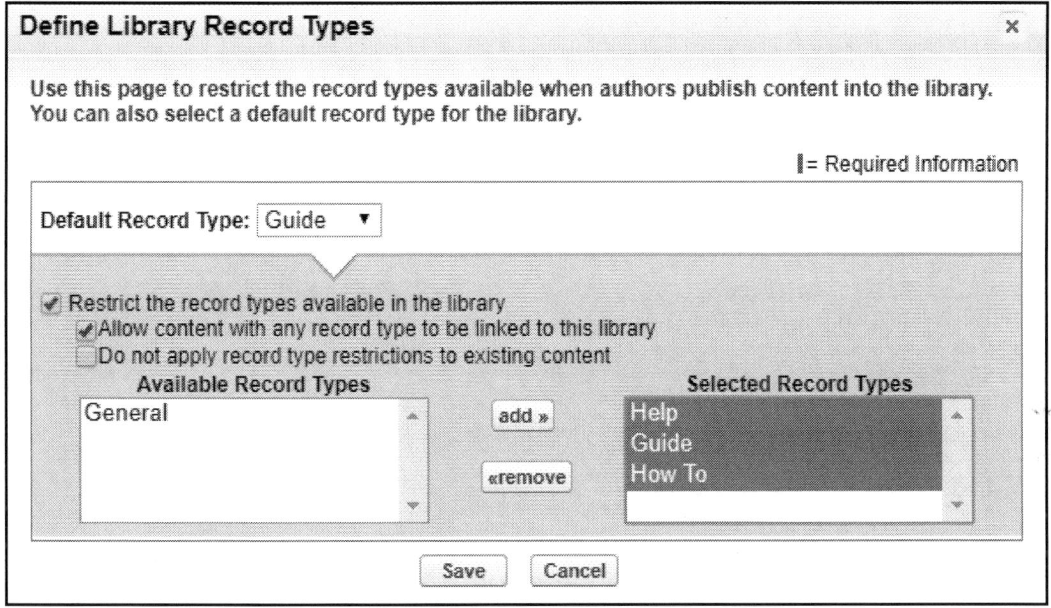

Restricting content with Record Types in a library

With this option, we can define the default record type given to content created from the following library. Flag the **Restrict the record types available in the library** checkbox if you want to actually restrict content types, flag the **Allow content with any record type to be linked to this library** checkbox to allow shared content from other libraries to be linked to this library without any record type restriction, or flag the **Do not apply record type restrictions to existing content** checkbox to apply restrictions to existing content as well (record type restrictions can be applied after the library has been created, so it may not be necessary to apply restrictions onto old content).

You can access **Libraries** from Lightning Experience via the **Files** tab:

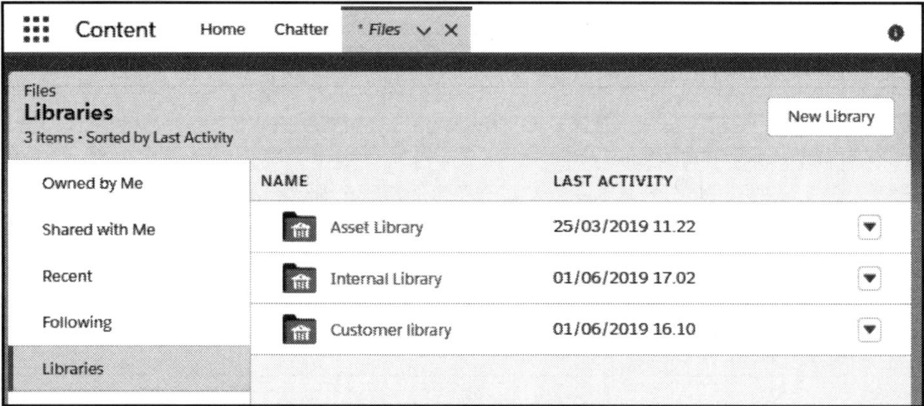

Library records accessible from Lightning Experience

From Lightning Experience, we can only set up membership (as demonstrated in the following screenshot) but no other setting (as of winter 2020):

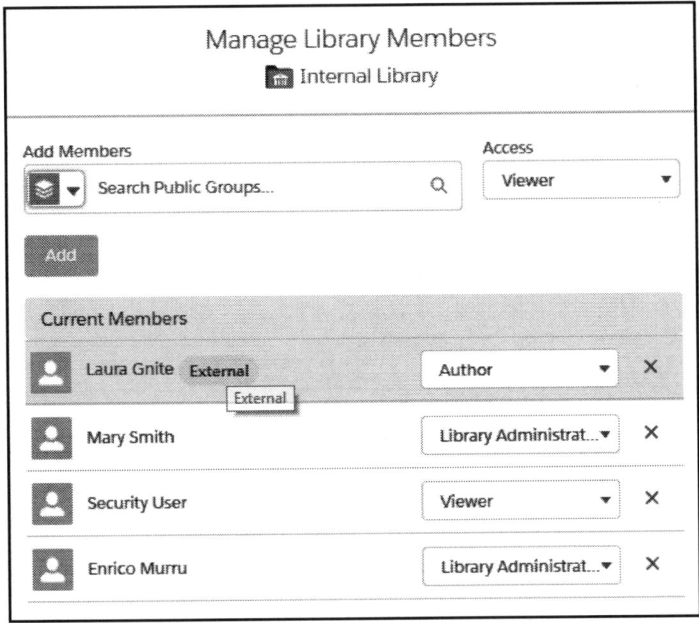

Membership editing on a library from Lightning Experience

In Lightning Experience, we can also create folders (and subfolders) to organize files within a library (not supported in Lightning Experience) using the **New Folder** button:

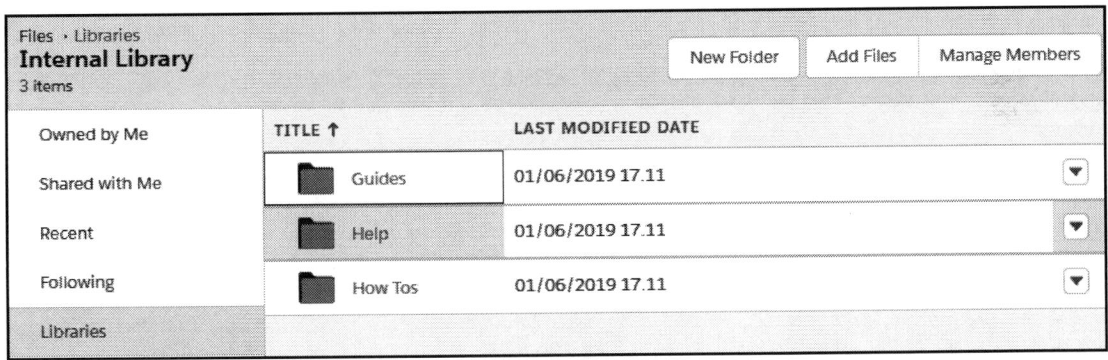

Folder setup in Lightning Experience in libraries

In the preceding screenshot, the **Internal Library** library has been configured with three subfolders: **Guides**, **Help**, and **How Tos**. In this way, content file organization becomes more organic and easy to browse.

Now it's time to see how you can add files to libraries.

Adding files to libraries

Add a new file using the **Add Files** button in Lightning Experience. You can upload a new file to a given library's folder/subfolder. After a file is created, you can view most of its metrics:

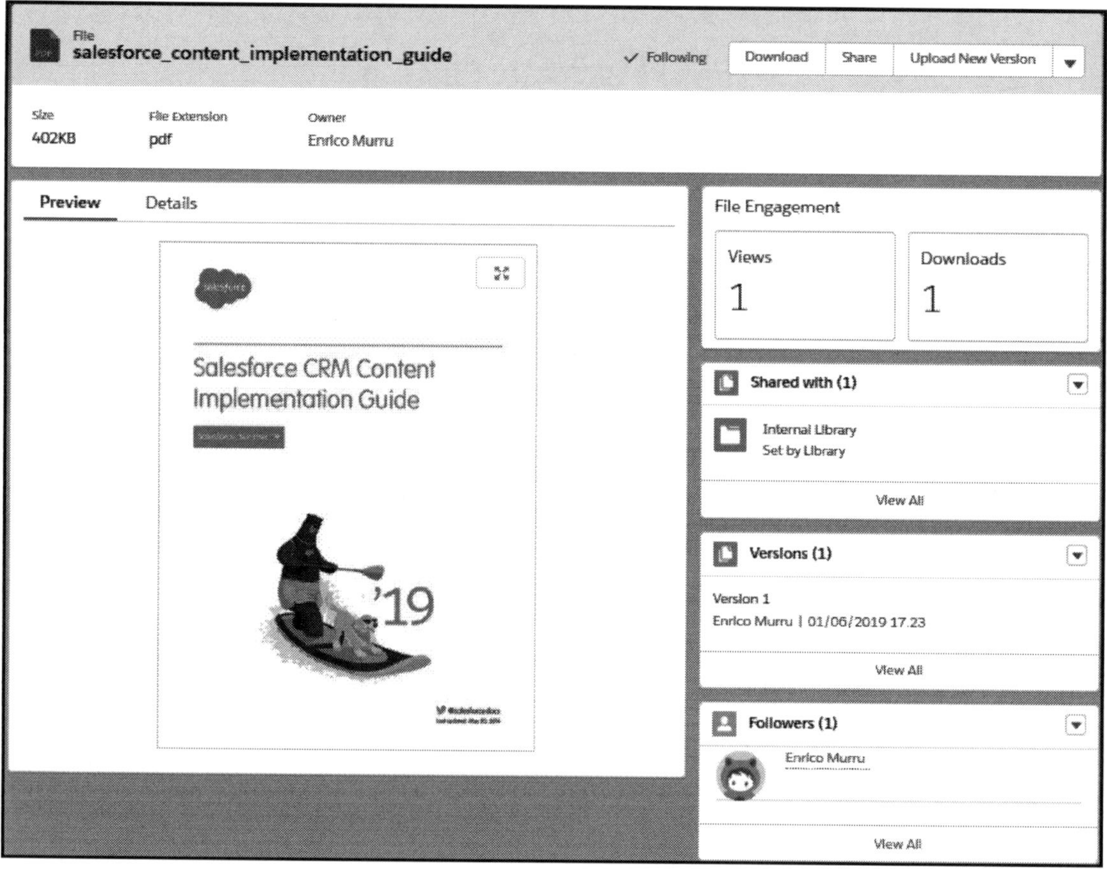

File details on Lightning Experience

There no such thing as tagging. Let's switch back to Salesforce Classic. You should already be familiar with switching to Salesforce Classic; just click on **Switch to Salesforce Classic** on your user's icon, as illustrated here:

Enrico Murru
advanced-admin-01-dev-ed.my.salesforce....
Settings
Log Out
DISPLAY DENSITY
Comfy
Compact
OPTIONS
Switch to Salesforce Classic

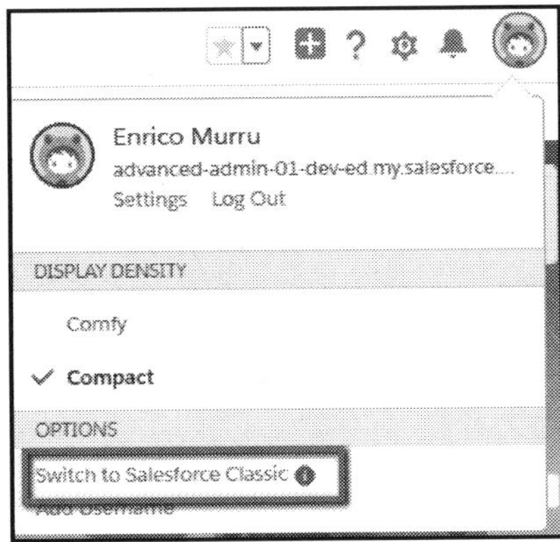

Jump to the **Salesforce Content** tab and select the library and the content just uploaded using Lightning Experience. Then, click on the **Edit** drop-down and choose **Edit Content Details**:

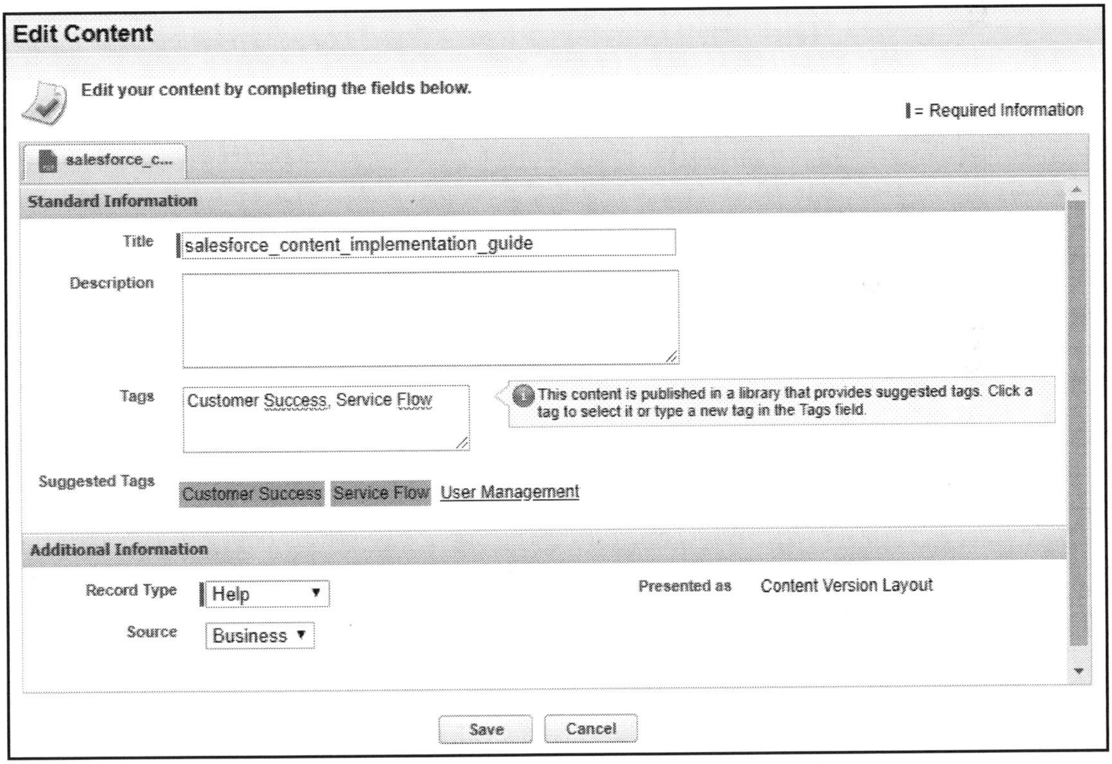

Edit Content
Edit your content by completing the fields below.
= Required Information
salesforce_c...
Standard Information
Title
salesforce_content_implementation_guide
Description
Tags
Customer Success, Service Flow
This content is published in a library that provides suggested tags. Click a tag to select it or type a new tag in the Tags field.
Suggested Tags
Customer Success
Service Flow
User Management
Additional Information
Record Type
Help
Presented as
Content Version Layout
Source
Business
Save
Cancel

Content details in Classic view

The **Standard Information** section contains the title, description, and tags used (with the suggested ones included), while the **Additional Information** section displays **Record Type** (the **Help** record type has been automatically assigned, as per the library configuration we saw earlier) and any custom field that the current layout contains (in the preceding screenshot, this is **Content Version Layout**).

Another difference is that while in Lightning Experience we can follow a file using the **+ Follow** button, in Classic, we can subscribe to a content item using the **Subscribe** button (and receive the necessary updates as per the user record configuration, which we saw previously).

In Lightning Experience and Classic, content files can be versioned by uploading a new version. The difference between Lightning Experience and Classic is that, in Classic, it is possible to update all information on the fly, including tags:

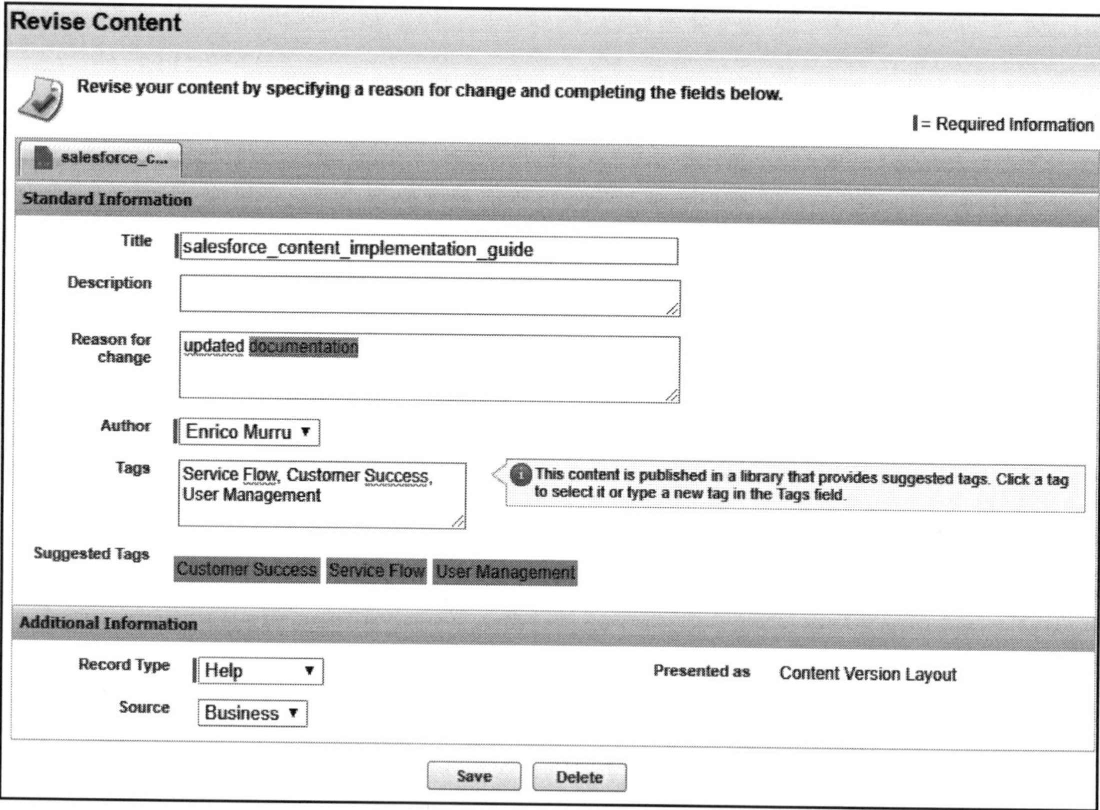

Uploading a new content file version in Classic

The last thing to note is that, in Classic, we can flag a content item as **Featured Content** (click on the **Feature Content** link on the content's detail page), so we can put content in the **Featured Content** section of the library's page:

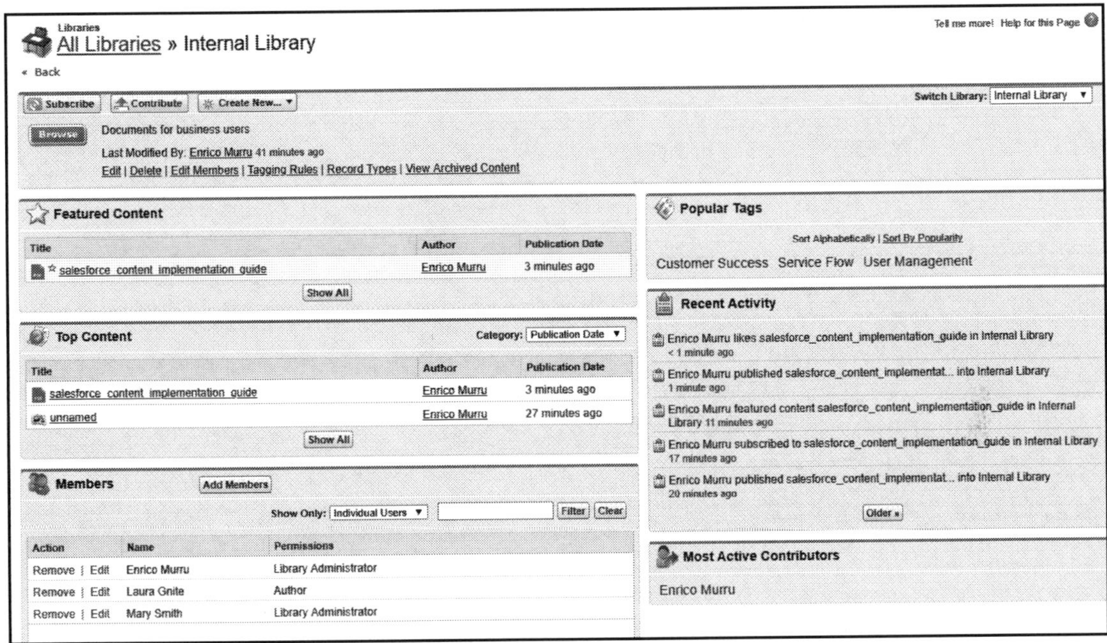

The library main page with all the sections filled

Note that all the right-hand column sections are populated automatically as well (for example, **Popular Tags**, **Recent Activity**, and **Most Active Contributors**).

Enabling Google Docs

If your company uses Google Apps, you can link your Salesforce to Google Docs to get instant access via Salesforce CRM Content to your cloud docs.

To enable **Google Apps** access, jump to **Setup** | **Google Apps Settings**:

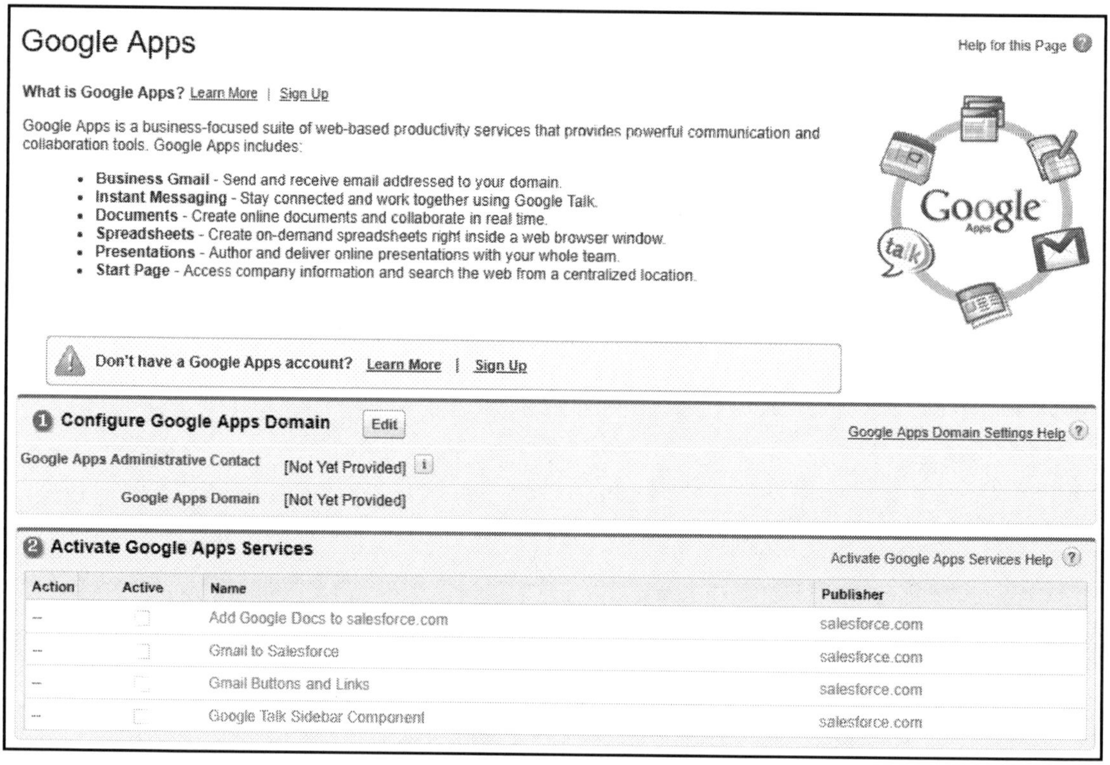

Google Apps

Help for this Page

What is Google Apps? Learn More | Sign Up

Google Apps is a business-focused suite of web-based productivity services that provides powerful communication and collaboration tools. Google Apps includes:

- **Business Gmail** - Send and receive email addressed to your domain.
- **Instant Messaging** - Stay connected and work together using Google Talk.
- **Documents** - Create online documents and collaborate in real time.
- **Spreadsheets** - Create on-demand spreadsheets right inside a web browser window.
- **Presentations** - Author and deliver online presentations with your whole team.
- **Start Page** - Access company information and search the web from a centralized location.

Google Apps

talk

Don't have a Google Apps account? Learn More | Sign Up

1 Configure Google Apps Domain Edit

Google Apps Domain Settings Help

Google Apps Administrative Contact [Not Yet Provided]

Google Apps Domain [Not Yet Provided]

2 Activate Google Apps Services

Activate Google Apps Services Help

Action	Active	Name	Publisher
--		Add Google Docs to salesforce.com	salesforce.com
--		Gmail to Salesforce	salesforce.com
--		Gmail Buttons and Links	salesforce.com
--		Google Talk Sidebar Component	salesforce.com

Google Apps configuration

With the **Add Google Docs to salesforce.com** service enabled, we can add any Google Doc to our content and deliver the features of Salesforce CRM Content to Google Docs, while keeping our org free of files.

If your company owns a Google Apps account, follow Salesforce Help at `https://help.salesforce.com/articleView?id=google_apps_parent.htmtype=5` for more details on configuration.

Content packs

A content pack is a collection of related content items that are stored as a group within Salesforce CRM Content (for example, product-related documents or generic company policies).

Using the **Create New... | Content Pack** button on the library main page, we can create a new content pack (note that Adobe Flash is required for the wizard to run) and select content documents from all our accessible libraries. Additionally, that content pack can be published in a personal library or in a public library.

Each content pack is equivalent to a content document (you can set up tagging, the language, description, title, record type, and custom fields). Additionally, you can execute all other actions (such as versioning, flag as a feature, subscribe, or deliver content), as illustrated in the following screenshot:

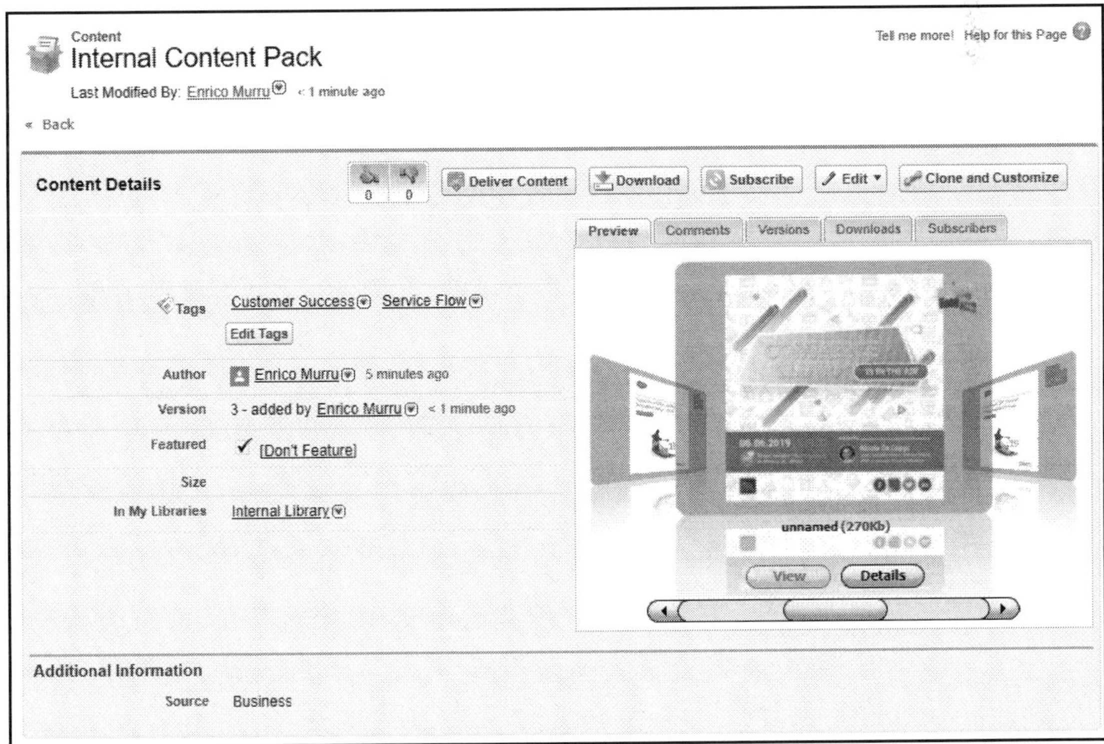

The content pack details page

The content pack feature is enabled by default in **Setup** | **Salesforce CRM Content** | **Enable content pack creation**. If you disable this feature after content packs have already been created, the content packs continue to exist and users can still modify their metadata information; however, there's no way they can customize the content (with the **Clone & Customize** or **Edit** | **Content Pack** buttons).

Content delivery

A content delivery is another interesting feature of Salesforce CRM Content. It allows content files to be shared for online viewing (such as sharing with colleagues or customers) in a web-optimized version using an encrypted URL that can be safely shared. Here, *web-optimized* simply means that the files are automatically optimized by Salesforce in order to be viewed directly on the browser without any further configuration required on the administrator's part.

This feature is available on Salesforce Classic only as of summer 2019.

To enable this feature, jump to **Setup** | **Content Deliveries and Public Links**, which leads to the following configuration page:

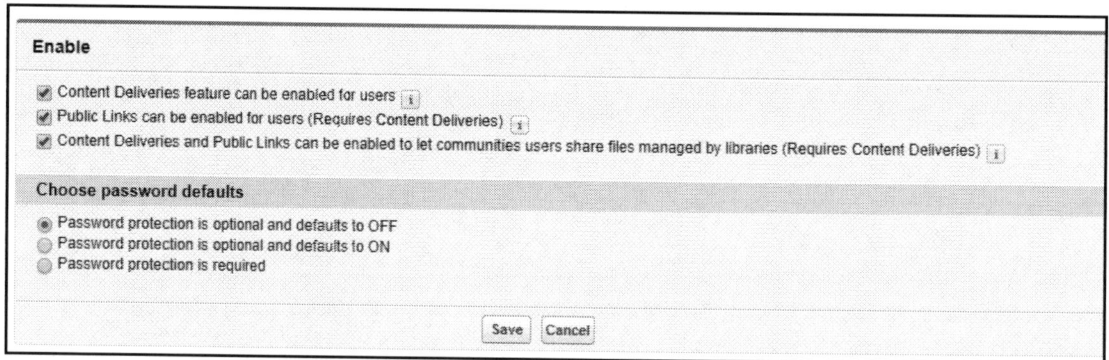

Content delivery configuration

The first flag enables the content delivery feature, while the other two allow for the creation of public links to be shared with/without password protection by internal users or community users.

In addition to this, users must have the **Create Content Deliveries** or **Create Public Links** permission (either on their profile or with a custom permission set). In addition to this, users within a library must have the **Deliver Content** option on the library's permission.

Choosing password protection when using content delivery is an optimal choice, especially when sharing confidential data with leads or customers.

When setting **Password protection** to **ON**, password protection defaults when creating a public link, but a user can unflag this option, making the link accessible to the public. Using the **required** password protection makes the flag *unflaggable* during content delivery creation.

If a password is required, it is generated upon content delivery creation, and it is up to the user to send the link along with the password so that the customer/lead can open the content.

If we have the **Deliver Content** permission on a given library, the **Deliver Content** button appears on each document, which triggers a quick delivery wizard:

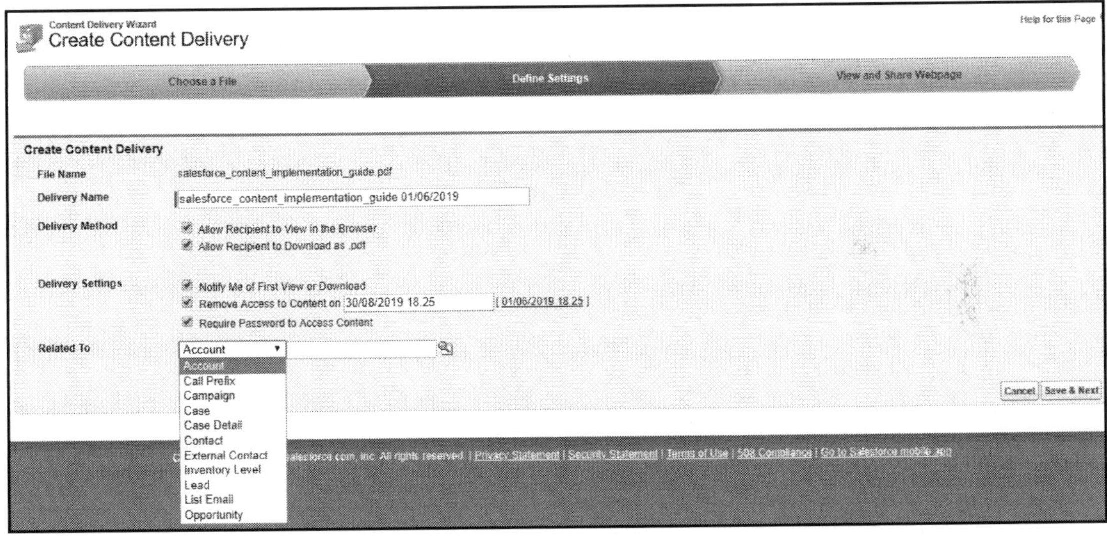

Content Delivery wizard

We can set up the way the document can be accessed (through the browser and/or direct download), a notification email upon first view/download, content access expiration, and password restriction. Moreover, we can relate the content to a standard object (**Account**, **Contact**, **Lead**, **Campaign**, **Opportunity**, or **Case**) or a custom object (a **Content Delivery** related list can be added to those objects' layouts).

Let's click the **Next** button to trigger the generation of the delivery link:

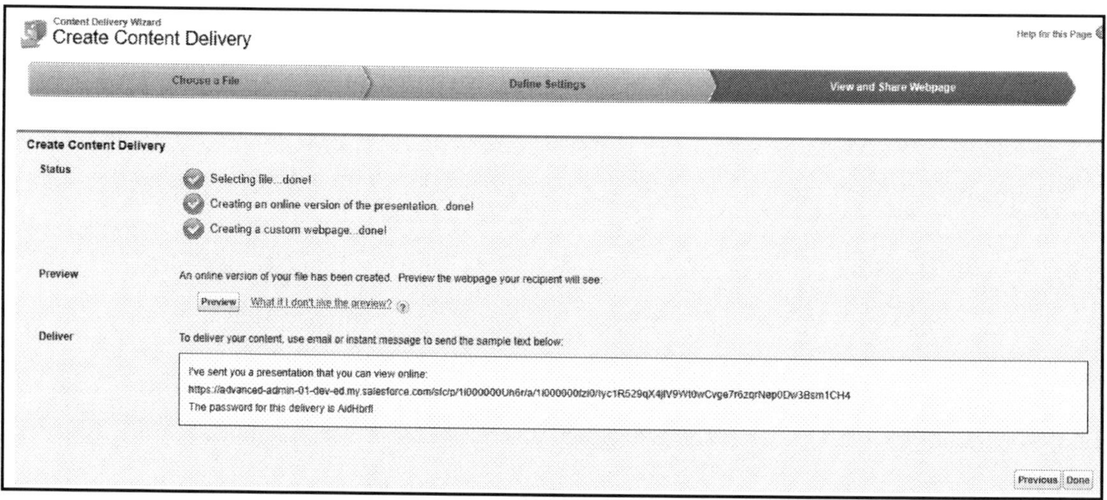

Last step of the Content Delivery wizard

If you have selected password protection, the password is displayed in the yellow box. If you try to open the provided link, a modal window will mandatorily ask for the delivery password.

There are a few limitations to this feature:

- A maximum of 20,000 views of content delivery in a 24-hour window is supported and a total of 20 GB bandwidth is allocated. If a recipient tries to access the content when the limits are reached, they are encouraged to try again later.
- Supported formats include PNG, JPG, BMP, GIF, Adobe PDF (not copy-protected), and Microsoft® Office 97-2007 Word, Excel, and PowerPoint files. Other file formats can be created but they are not displayed on the browser (only the download option is available).
- Any file greater than 25 MB cannot be displayed online but can only be downloaded.

You can view statistics on the **Show Content Deliveries** choice of the **Content Delivery** button as follows:

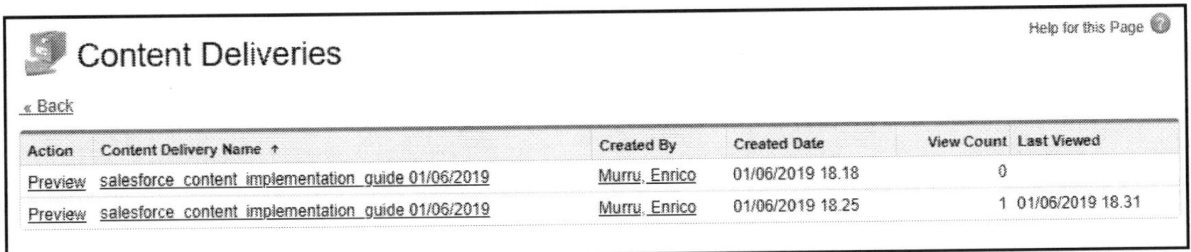

Content Deliveries created for a given content file

In this example, we can see a list of content deliveries that have been created for the given content along with the number of views and the **Last Viewed** date. Note that the first content document here has never been accessed, while the second one had one view.

Content search

Users can search for content documents using the **Search for Content** tab (this is available in Classic only):

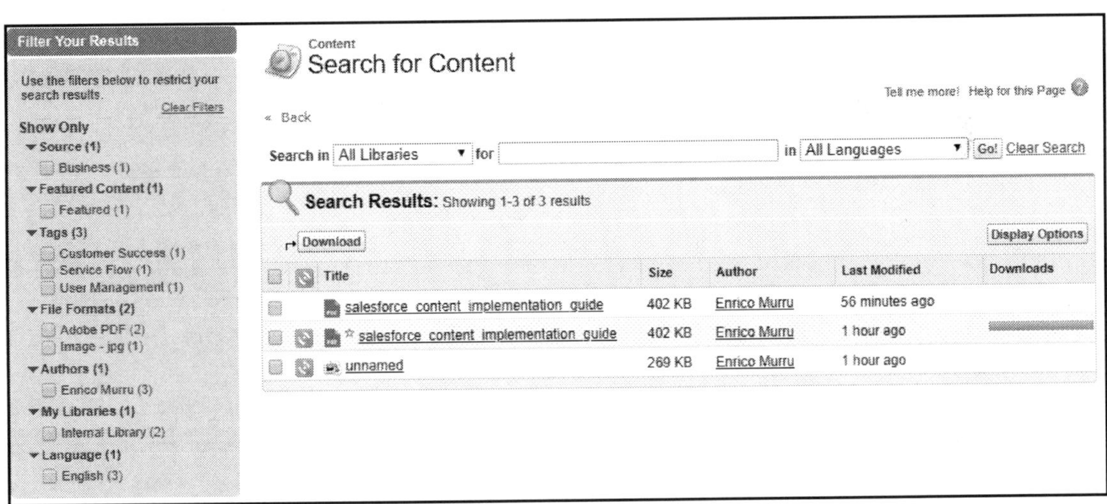

The Salesforce CRM Content search tab

You can filter content documents according to the following:

- Custom fields (in this example, **Source** is a custom field)
- Whether the content is featured or not
- **Tags**
- **File Formats**
- **Authors**
- Library
- **Language**

We can cumulatively download files in ZIP format and even customize the data shown using the **Display Options** button:

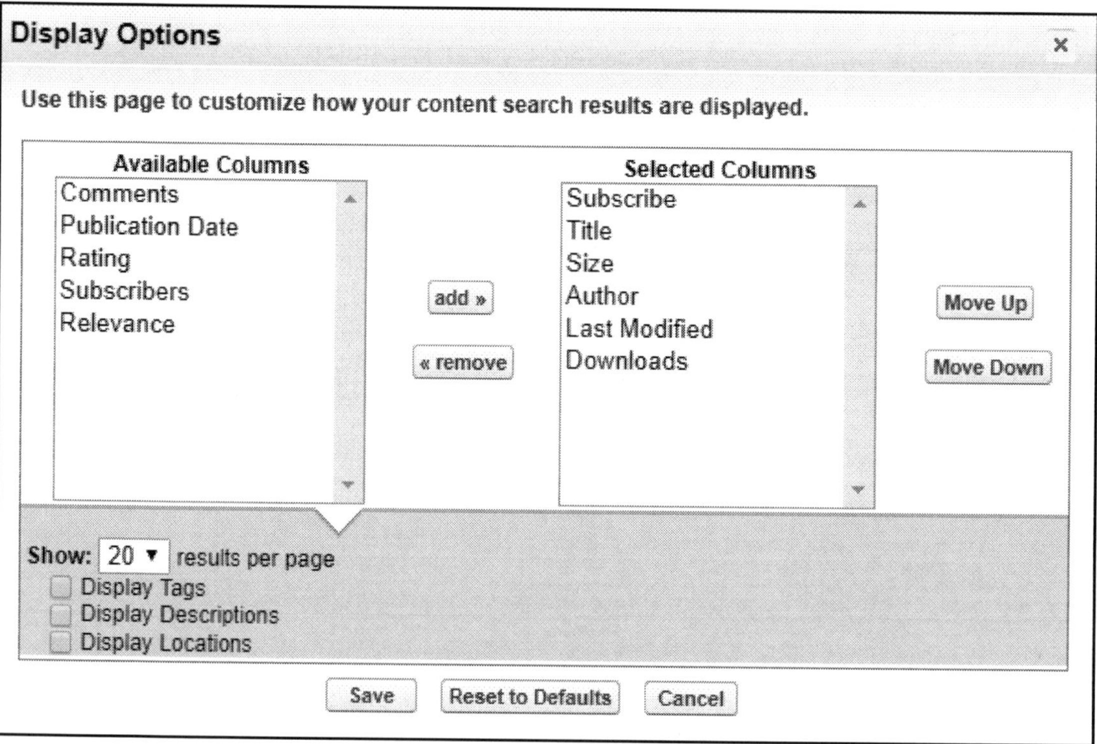

Display Options for content search

In the previous example, we configured the **Search for Content** page to show the fields of **Subscribe**, **Title**, **Size**, **Author**, **Last Modified**, and **Downloads** (with 20 records per page).

Summary

In this chapter, we looked at using the Salesforce CRM Content feature for organizing internal documents into libraries and allowing users to access specific content depending on their permissions. With **Content Delivery**, documents can be shared with external recipients using encrypted links, allowing our leads and customers to consume internal documents (increasing security by setting up a password).

You should now be able to create libraries that can put together corporate documents, give users the proper permissions to access, edit, and administer libraries and their content, efficiently share (more or less) critical content to your customers and partners, and configure content searches for the ease of your users.

In the next chapter, we'll be talking about reporting and dashboards, a task that can take a significant amount of an admin's time.

Questions

1. What is Salesforce CRM Content?
    a. A special kind of Salesforce edition
    b. A feature to simplify file management in libraries
    c. Another way of referring to the documents and attachments feature
2. How can you enable a user to use Salesforce CRM Content?
    a. Enable the **Salesforce CRM Content User** user permission.
    b. Enable the **Enable Salesforce CRM Content** flag on the **Salesforce CRM Content** page.
    c. Enable libraries in your org.
3. What is a content file composed of?
    a. A file
    b. A library
    c. Standard metadata (such as **Author**, **Description**)
    d. Custom fields on the **Content Version** object
4. What is a library?
    a. It can only contain text files.
    b. It contains one or more files.
    c. It can be assigned to users, groups, and/or portal users.
    d. It can be restricted to contain certain ContentVersion record types.

5. What are library permissions?
    a. Another way of referring to ContentVersion record types
    b. Another way of referring to ContentVersion object-level security
    c. A set of specific permission options to be assigned to users that have access to a library
6. What do content tags allow you to do?
    a. Allow you to tag content files on Chatter
    b. Allow you to add filtering options when searching for content files
    c. Allow you to tag content files to the Knowledge component for Console apps
7. What is restricted tagging?
    a. Contributors can add specific tags only.
    b. Contributors are given suggestions of specific tags but they can add new tags if they want.
    c. Contributors can add whatever tag they want.
8. What feature is not available in the File layout of Lightning Experience?
    a. Tags
    b. Adding a new file version
    c. File subscription
    d. The **+ Follow** button
9. What is a content pack?
    a. A collection of files, treated as a single content document (with its own metadata and version).
    b. The collection of all the versions for a given file.
    c. The collection of all the libraries in your org.
10. What is true about content delivery?
    a. You can preview any file format.
    b. It is available on Salesforce Classic only.
    c. It can be related to a Salesforce record (such as Accounts, Contacts, and Leads) and be accessed from the object's **Content Delivery** related list.
    d. You can share a content document to external users by providing an encrypted URL and, optionally, a password.

5
Section 5: Reports and Dashboards

In this section, you will learn about Salesforce's reporting features, such as custom reports, snapshots, complex charting, summary formulas, joined reports, and others.

This section includes the following chapters:

- `Chapter 9`, *Mastering Reports*
- `Chapter 10`, *Visualizing Key Metrics with Dashboards*

9
Mastering Reports

Reports give you access to your Salesforce data and can be used as an important metric for your company's business. With reporting, you can look at all the open cases and see which agent is taking longer to close a case (thereby understanding whether you need to share internal knowledge to make users more productive). With reporting, you can instantly look at ongoing opportunities and find out who is closing more deals. Also, reporting helps you look at how many leads have been created but not converted into customers. In summary, reporting lets you have a deeper look at what's going on in your organization. This is why mastering reporting is a crucial skill for any good administrator.

In this chapter, we'll cover the following topics:

- How to build, format, and chart reports
- How to track historic values on reports
- Define custom report types to shape reports on business needs
- How to filter reports and subscribe to a scheduled run

Building reports

Reporting is at the core of your company's strategy: being able to examine data with infinite formats and display combinations makes us aware of what's happening and what may be the outcome of our company's business, whether that's talking about service support or opportunities that have been sold (we've already talked about forecasting, which is one way of reporting on opportunities).

We're not going to explain every single feature about reporting in this chapter since you will already be familiar with the basic concepts of this important feature. Also, if you are a developer, you may not be very enthusiast about deepening your reporting knowledge. You may think that this is not as fun or creative as developing but, believe me, creating reports can be creative as well.

To build a report, we have to go to the **Reports** tab. If we are on Lightning Experience, for example, we can create reports with the **Lightning Report Builder** or the **Classic Report Builder**, as shown here:

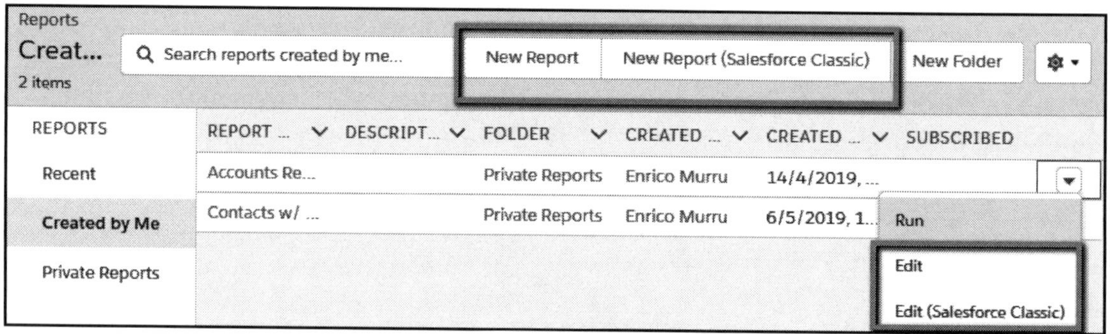

Different ways to create/edit reports

At the time of writing (Summer 2019), these are the main difference between the two tools:

- When grouping data, you need to select the report format (such as tabular, summary, or matrix report) before grouping, while in Lightning Experience, the format is automatically selected (but you can always change it afterward).
- The row limit filters and dashboard settings menu features are not available on the **Lightning Report Builder**.

Don't panic: if something is not available on the Lightning Report Builder, edit the report on the Classic Report Builder (you can switch between the two builders at any time).

Also, remember that, as of Winter 2020, the Lightning Report Builder is in beta version and may be subject to unexpected behavior when creating/editing reports.

When creating a new report, the first thing you'll need to select is a report type, which identifies the kind of data you are going to report on. We have standard and custom report types: the first group is built-in and depends on standard objects, while the second group can already be on our CRM (built-in but customizable) or created by other administrators (with both standard and custom objects).

Report types

The Salesforce platform provides some predefined standard report types that involve diverse objects and conditions (which cannot be modified) and a huge list of custom prebuilt custom report types that are free to use.

An exhaustive list of built-in report types can be found at `https://help.salesforce.com/articleView?id=reports_report_type_reference.htm type=5`.

To create a new report type, go to **Setup** | **Features Settings** | **Analytics** | **Reports & Dashboards** | **Report Types**. A quick how-to guide is shown on the main report type page, that is, if you haven't hidden it yet.

Click the **New Custom Report Type** button and select the **Primary Object**, which is the main object the report type refers to.

Remember the following key points:

- We can choose any object, even ones we don't have access to
- Once the report type has been saved, you cannot change its primary object

Then, choose the **Deployment Status** (use the **In Development** value to prevent other users from using the view report type while it is being built and leave the **Deployed** status as it is if the report type can be used by other users). You will see something like the following:

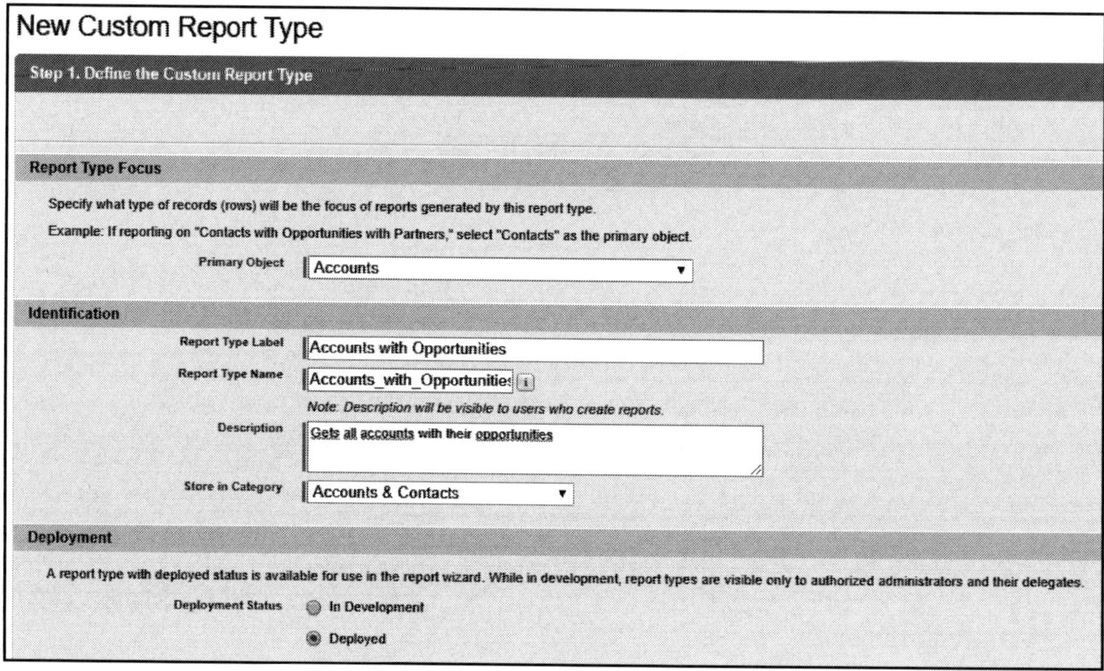

Report type creation form

Click the **Next** button to choose the record set. Now, you will see the following form:

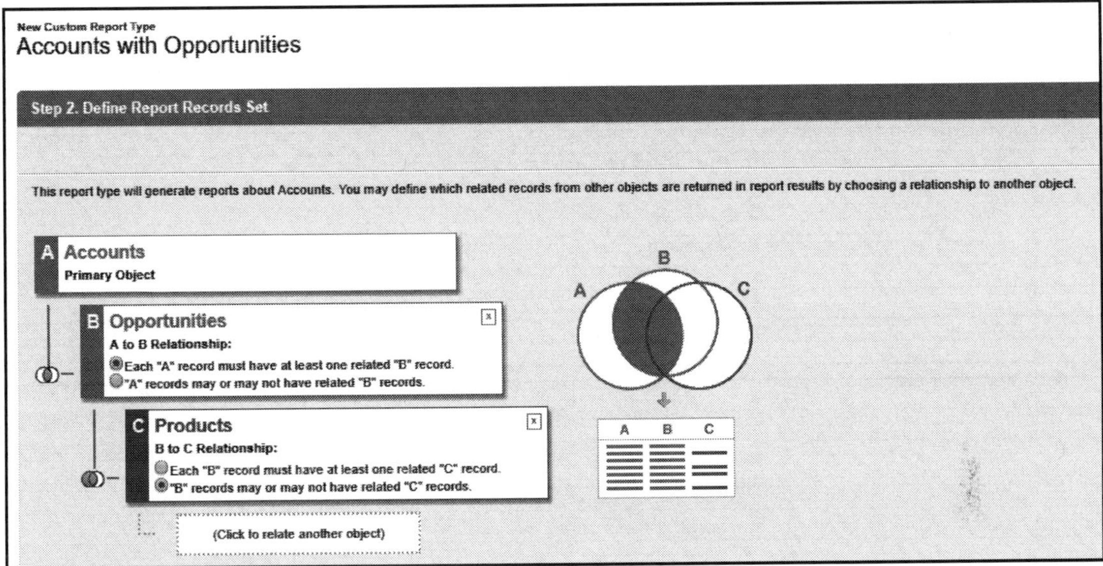

Record set selection on the report type

With this set up, we can set other objects to be retrieved by the report using the primary object, which is the main entity.

In this configuration, we can get the following information:

- All the accounts that have at least one opportunity record associated with them
- All the products for each opportunity, regardless of whether they are related or not

Once the record set has been selected, we need to select all the fields that we can use when the report type is used within a report. We can do this by clicking the **Edit Layout** button in the **Fields Available for Reports** section of the **Report Types** main page:

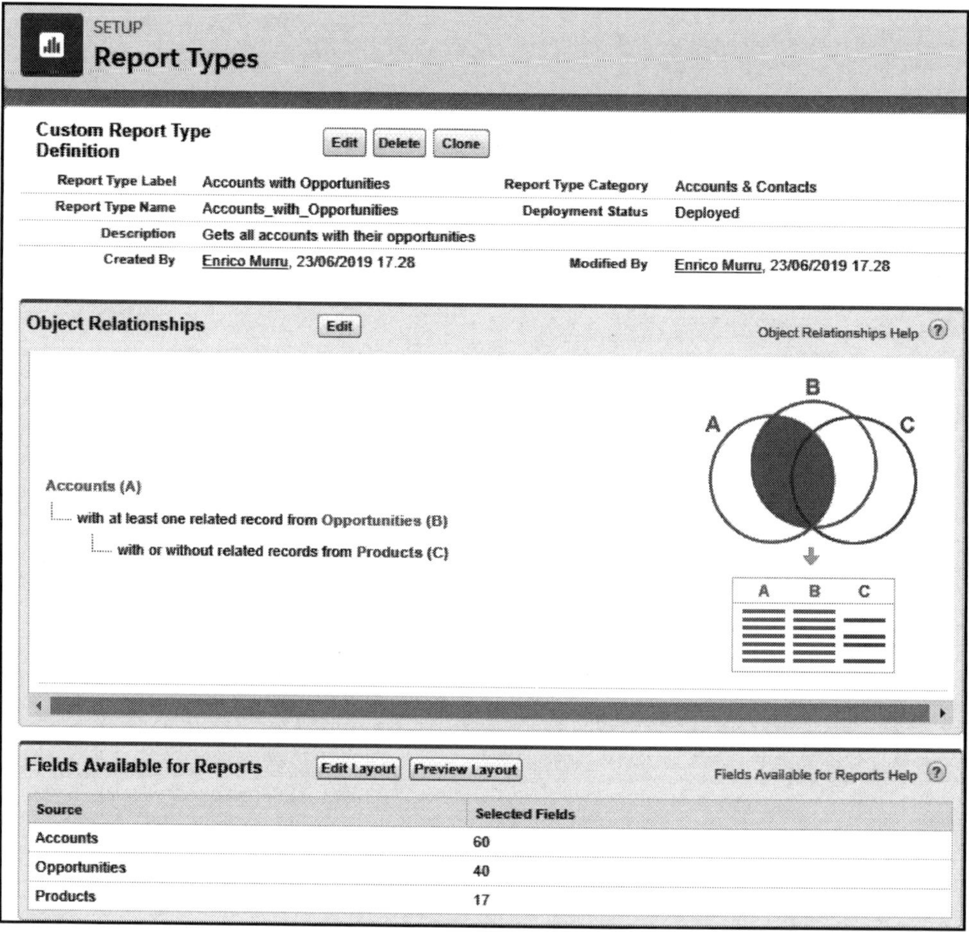

Report Types main page

To add more fields and more related objects (such as owner record fields or any other record from a record related to a lookup field), click the **Edit Layout** button. You will see the following page:

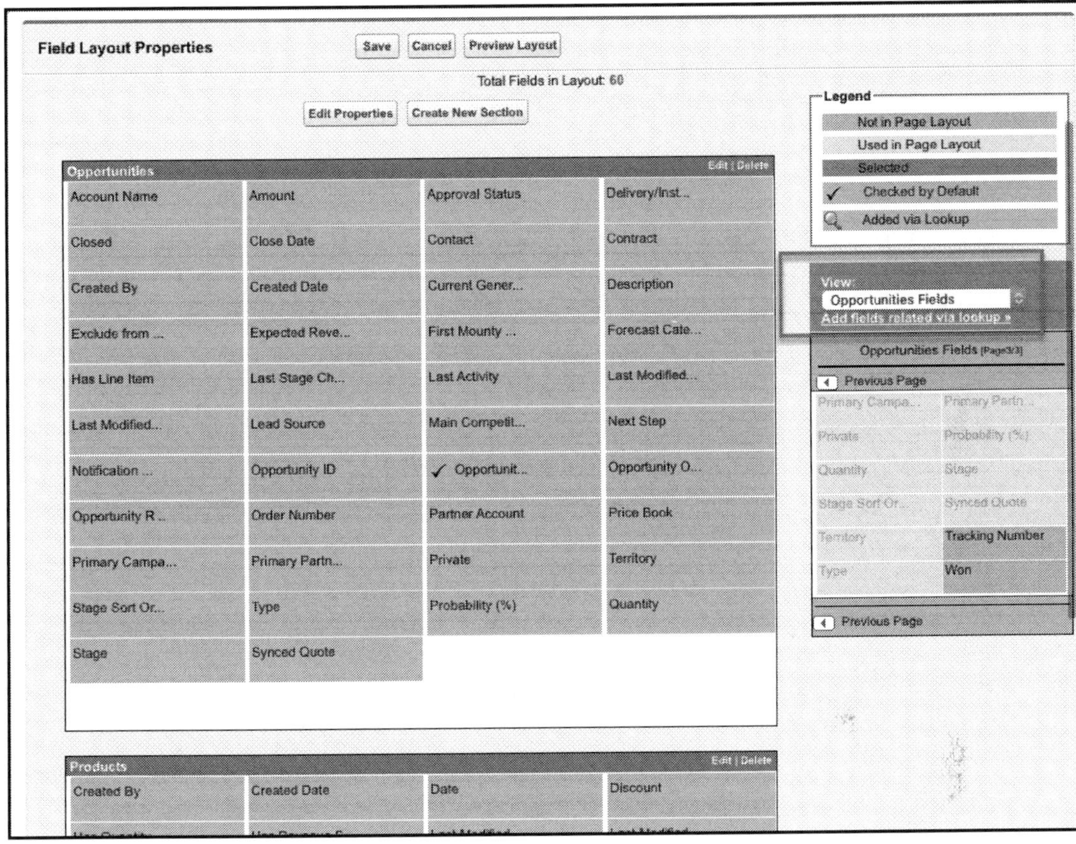

Editing the layout to add more fields to the report type

Here, it is possible to organize fields into sections (to ease field selection on reports). With the **Add fields related via lookup** option, you can select any other field coming from a related lookup (that's held in the object type that was selected on the **View** picklist field, as shown in the previous screenshot).

Once you've set up field selection, you can run a new report using this new report type.

However, there are some limitations regarding this process:

- 1,000 is the upper limit for the number of fields you can have
- You can have up to four object relationships when defining the record set
- You can select up to 56 additional objects via lookup fields, but these fields can only come from up to 20 objects when you're creating a report for the given report type

For a complete list of guidelines, please refer to Salesforce Help at `https://help.salesforce.com/articleView?id=reports_report_type_guidelines.htmtype=5`.

Report formats

The second option we have when creating a new report is selecting the report format. Here, we can choose between the following types:

- **Tabular**: This is a simple list of records with fields displayed in columns, similar to a spreadsheet. This format cannot be used to group data or used with charts or within dashboards (unless you limit the number of rows):

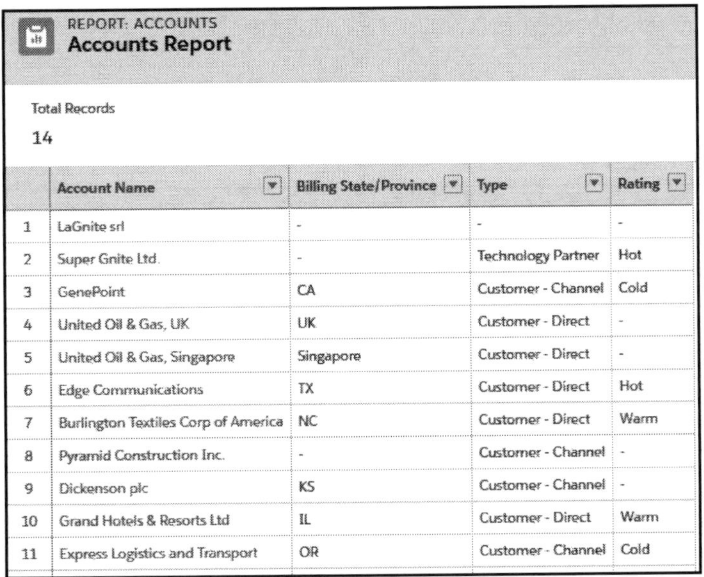

REPORT: ACCOUNTS
Accounts Report

Total Records
14

	Account Name	Billing State/Province	Type	Rating
1	LaGnite srl	-	-	-
2	Super Gnite Ltd.	-	Technology Partner	Hot
3	GenePoint	CA	Customer - Channel	Cold
4	United Oil & Gas, UK	UK	Customer - Direct	-
5	United Oil & Gas, Singapore	Singapore	Customer - Direct	-
6	Edge Communications	TX	Customer - Direct	Hot
7	Burlington Textiles Corp of America	NC	Customer - Direct	Warm
8	Pyramid Construction Inc.	-	Customer - Channel	-
9	Dickenson plc	KS	Customer - Channel	-
10	Grand Hotels & Resorts Ltd	IL	Customer - Direct	Warm
11	Express Logistics and Transport	OR	Customer - Channel	Cold

Tabular report example

- **Summary**: Similar to tabular reports, we can group rows of data (with subtotals) based on a given field and create charts on those groupings (for example, group cases on the Status field and read the subtotals for each status):

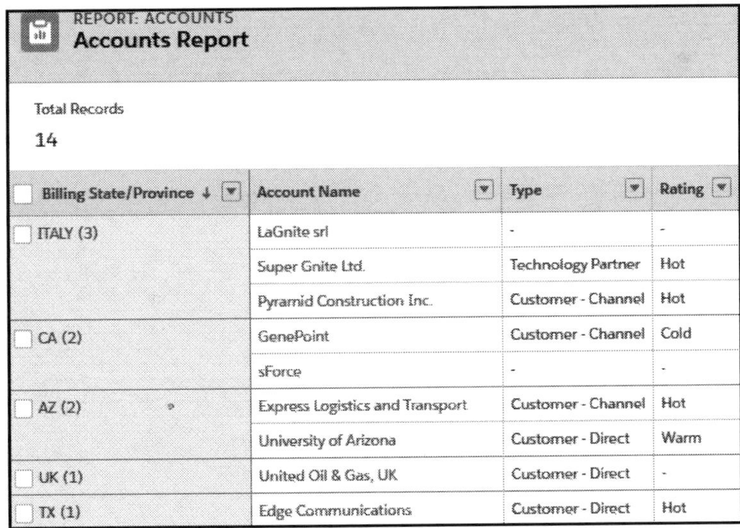

REPORT: ACCOUNTS
Accounts Report

Total Records
14

Billing State/Province ↓	Account Name	Type	Rating
ITALY (3)	LaGnite srl	-	-
	Super Gnite Ltd.	Technology Partner	Hot
	Pyramid Construction Inc.	Customer - Channel	Hot
CA (2)	GenePoint	Customer - Channel	Cold
	sForce	-	-
AZ (2)	Express Logistics and Transport	Customer - Channel	Hot
	University of Arizona	Customer - Direct	Warm
UK (1)	United Oil & Gas, UK	Customer - Direct	-
TX (1)	Edge Communications	Customer - Direct	Hot

Summary report example

- **Matrix**: Like the Summary report format, this format is used to summarize the rows and columns of the given fields. This is useful when you need to compare data from several fields:

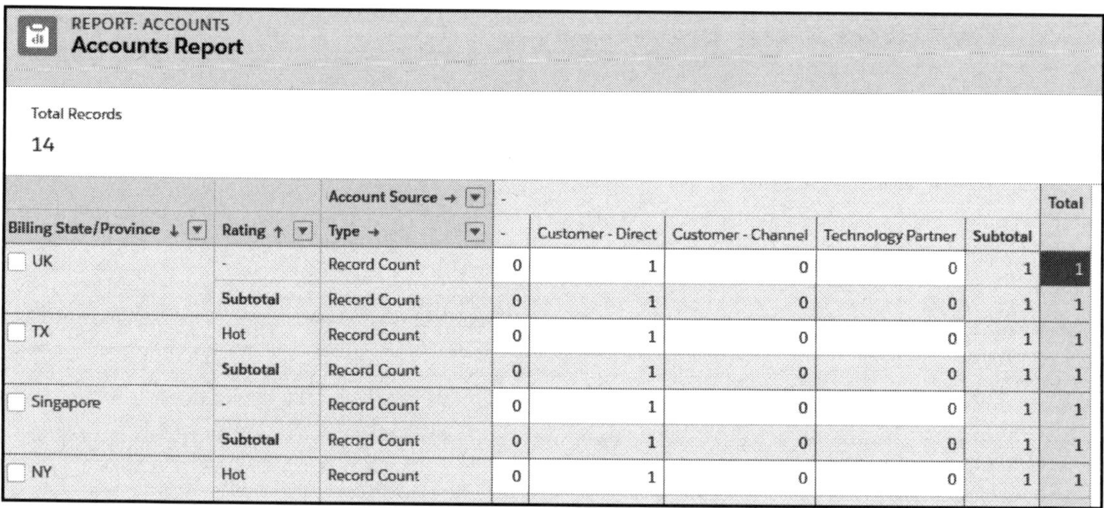

REPORT: ACCOUNTS

Accounts Report

Total Records

14

		Account Source →	-					Total
Billing State/Province ↓	Rating ↑	Type →	-	Customer - Direct	Customer - Channel	Technology Partner	Subtotal	
UK	-	Record Count	0	1	0	0	1	1
	Subtotal	Record Count	0	1	0	0	1	1
TX	Hot	Record Count	0	1	0	0	1	1
	Subtotal	Record Count	0	1	0	0	1	1
Singapore	-	Record Count	0	1	0	0	1	1
	Subtotal	Record Count	0	1	0	0	1	1
NY	Hot	Record Count	0	1	0	0	1	1

Matrix format example

- **Joined**: This format is used to combine reports (even from different objects and report types). For example, you can report **Accounts w/ Opportunities** to get a glimpse of what's going on with each of your customers:

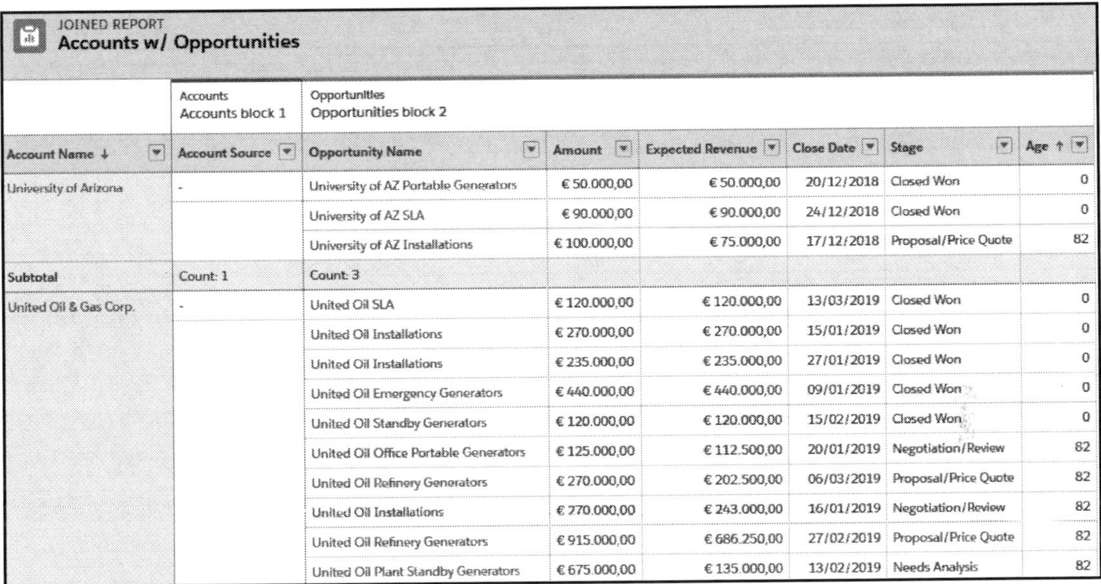

JOINED REPORT
Accounts w/ Opportunities

	Accounts Accounts block 1	Opportunities Opportunities block 2					
Account Name ↓	**Account Source**	**Opportunity Name**	**Amount**	**Expected Revenue**	**Close Date**	**Stage**	**Age ↑**
University of Arizona	-	University of AZ Portable Generators	€ 50.000,00	€ 50.000,00	20/12/2018	Closed Won	0
		University of AZ SLA	€ 90.000,00	€ 90.000,00	24/12/2018	Closed Won	0
		University of AZ Installations	€ 100.000,00	€ 75.000,00	17/12/2018	Proposal/Price Quote	82
Subtotal	Count: 1	Count: 3					
United Oil & Gas Corp.	-	United Oil SLA	€ 120.000,00	€ 120.000,00	13/03/2019	Closed Won	0
		United Oil Installations	€ 270.000,00	€ 270.000,00	15/01/2019	Closed Won	0
		United Oil Installations	€ 235.000,00	€ 235.000,00	27/01/2019	Closed Won	0
		United Oil Emergency Generators	€ 440.000,00	€ 440.000,00	09/01/2019	Closed Won	0
		United Oil Standby Generators	€ 120.000,00	€ 120.000,00	15/02/2019	Closed Won	0
		United Oil Office Portable Generators	€ 125.000,00	€ 112.500,00	20/01/2019	Negotiation/Review	82
		United Oil Refinery Generators	€ 270.000,00	€ 202.500,00	06/03/2019	Proposal/Price Quote	82
		United Oil Installations	€ 270.000,00	€ 243.000,00	16/01/2019	Negotiation/Review	82
		United Oil Refinery Generators	€ 915.000,00	€ 686.250,00	27/02/2019	Proposal/Price Quote	82
		United Oil Plant Standby Generators	€ 675.000,00	€ 135.000,00	13/02/2019	Needs Analysis	82

Joined format example

Grouping data is quite simple in Classic: just drop your field onto the grouping section that's highlighted with the **Group a field here to create a grouping** label in the summary format or with the **Drop a field here to create a row/column grouping** label in the matrix format.

Remember that, when grouping by a date field, you can select the grouping time frame, such as day, week, month, quarter, and year, as shown in the following screenshot:

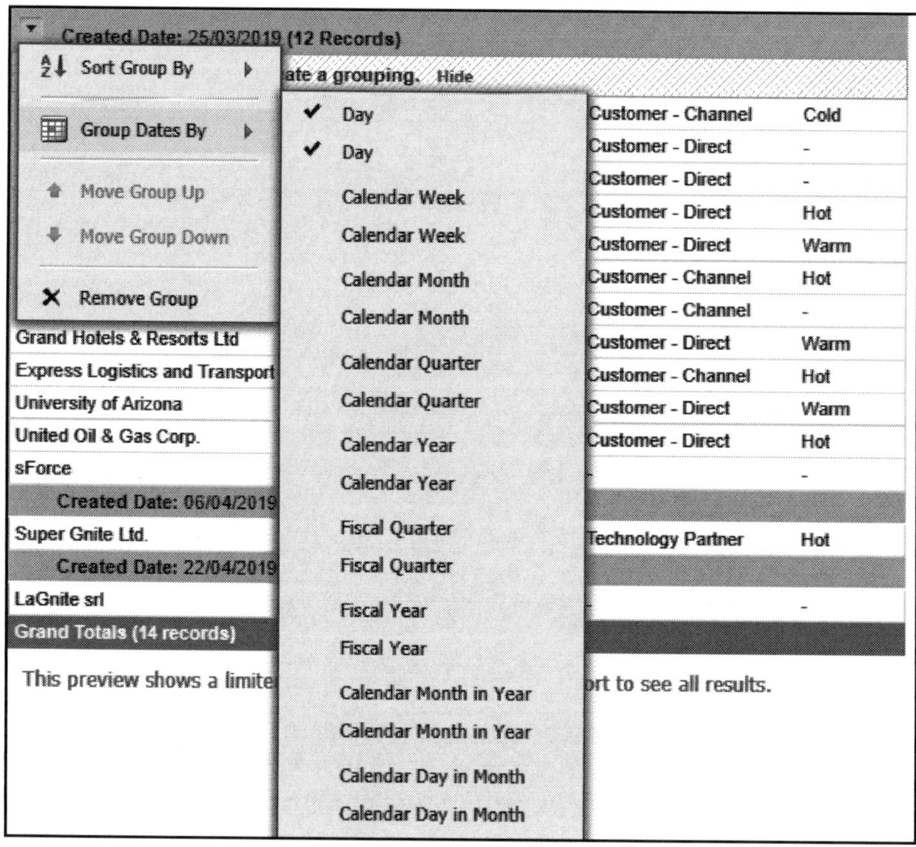

Date field grouping options in Classic

The Lightning Report Builder works in the same way (take a look at the grouping section in the right-hand sidebar to see how grouping differs in Lightning):

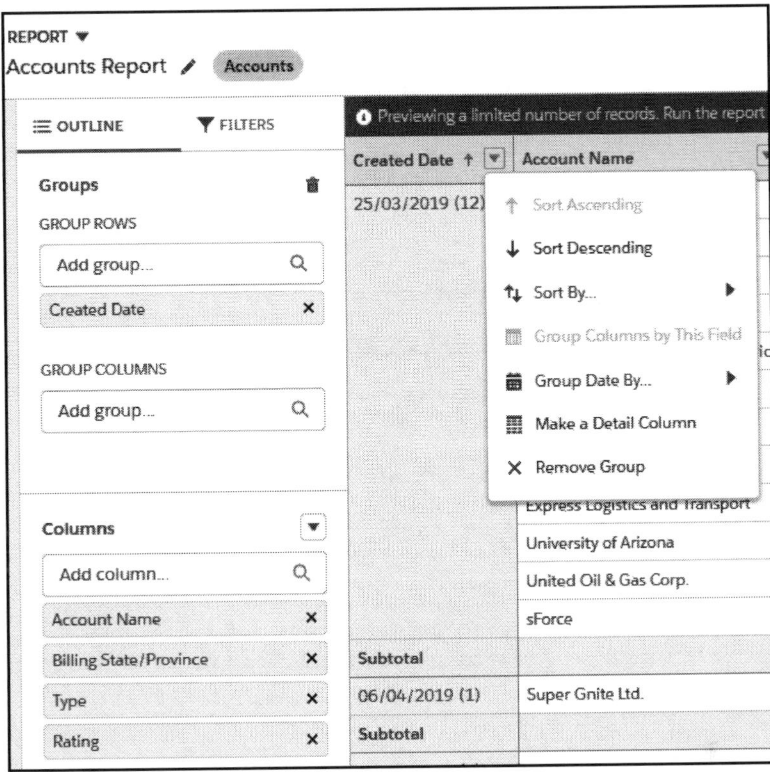

Date field grouping options in Lightning

Regarding grouping, summary and joined reports can have up to three grouping levels, while matrix reports can have two row and two column groupings. In matrix reports, you cannot use the same fields as row and column grouping.

When dealing with joined reports, your reports (known as **blocks**) may be linked using fields in the **Common Fields** category (in Classic) or the **Group Across Blocks** section (Lightning), such as **Account Name** when joining accounts and opportunities reports.

Sometimes, grouping is not enough to understand the report's results. In this case, we add a chart.

Filtering reports

If you are reading this book, then you already know how reports are built, so how a report can be filtered is not a secret to you. However, I bet there are some configuration options that you are not aware of or that you may have never used before. One of them may be the filter by role hierarchy. As the name suggests, it is possible to filter the results based on the roles of the users who own the records.

To access this option, on the Report Builder, click on **Filters** | **Show Me** and select the role you want to narrow:

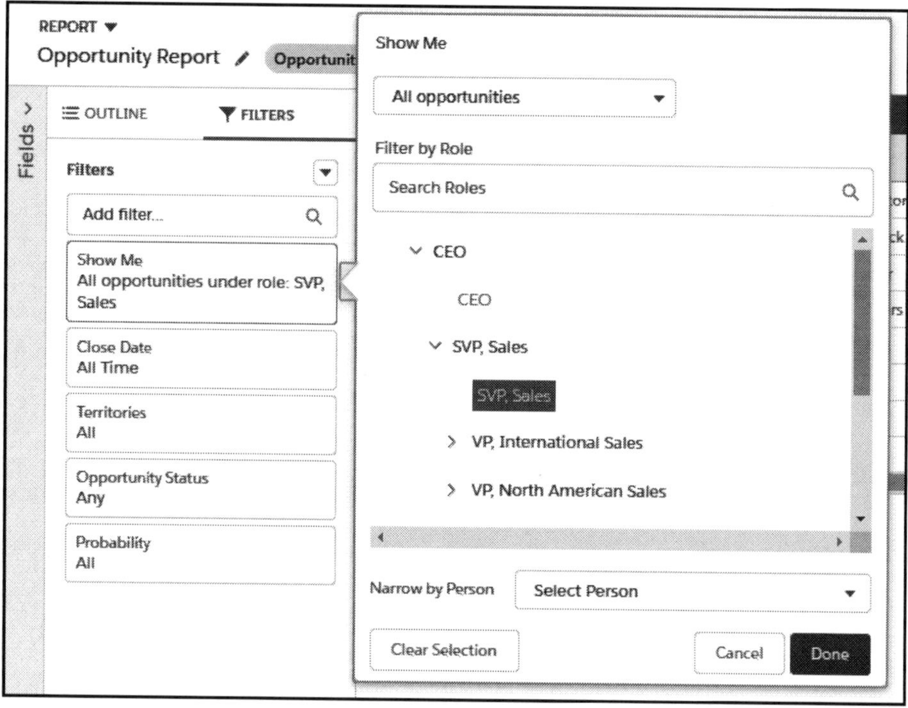

Filtering reports by hierarchy role

Another important option is the cross filter feature. With this feature, you can filter with a condition on a related object.

If we are creating an opportunity report, for example, we can decide whether we wish to host records that have products with a quantity greater than 1.

To achieve this, click on the **Filters** menu and choose **Add Cross Filter**. This will set up filters on opportunities with products that have a quantity greater than 1:

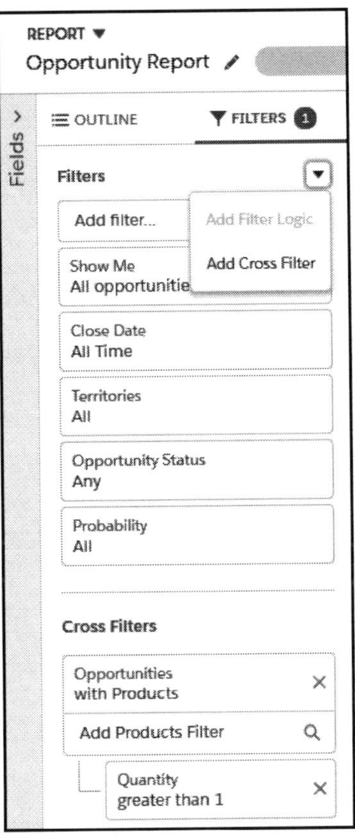

Cross-filter selection

Great power comes with great responsibility, so be cautious when you're using these kinds of filters as it will slow down your report's performance.

Moreover, you can only choose the related objects that have been set up on the report type, so choose your report type wisely.

We can use no more than three cross filters per report and five subfilters per cross filter.

Charting report data

To add a chart (you can only have one chart per report), use the **Add Chart** button (both in Classic and Lightning). Remember that your report must be in summary or matrix format before you can add charts:

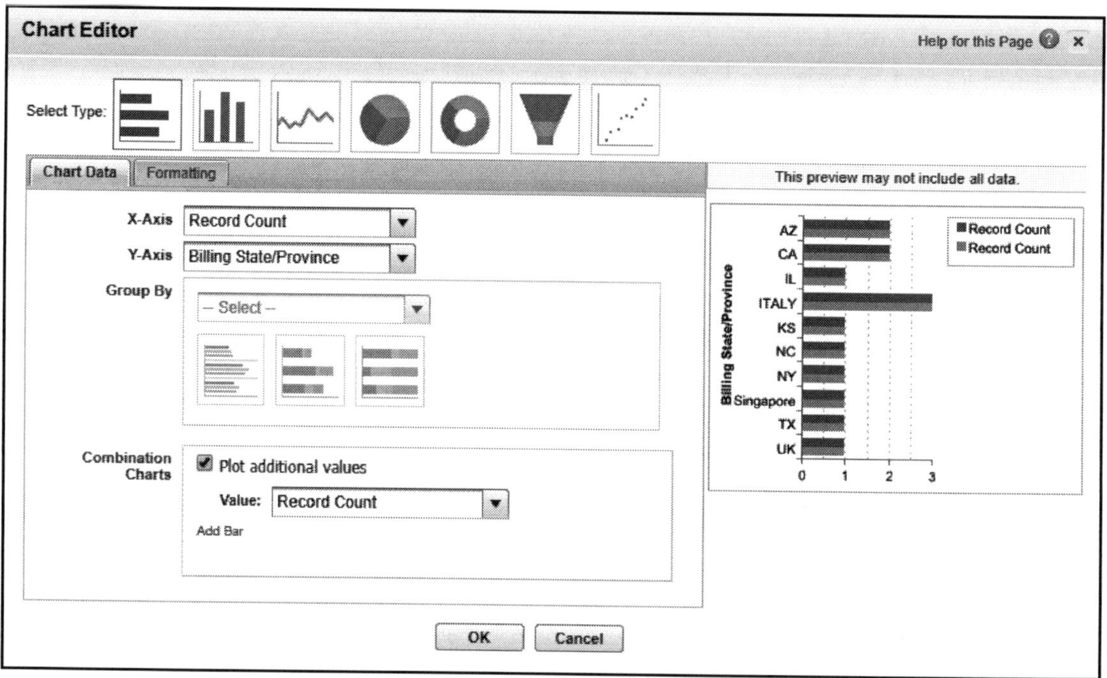

Adding a chart

The following are the settings that we can configure:

- **Chart type**: Decides on the type of display (such as bar, line, pie, funnel, scatter, and so on), which may depend on the report format.
- **X-Axis/Y-Axis**: Decides on which metrics to show in each axis by the record count, groupings, or summary fields.
- **Combination Charts**: We can plot additional values on the chart if the chart supports this feature (for example, we can add the number of employees of a given account, along with the number of locations where the account makes sales). When displaying values with different scales, you can add another *y* axis to the chart so that values are displayed accordingly and in a readable way:

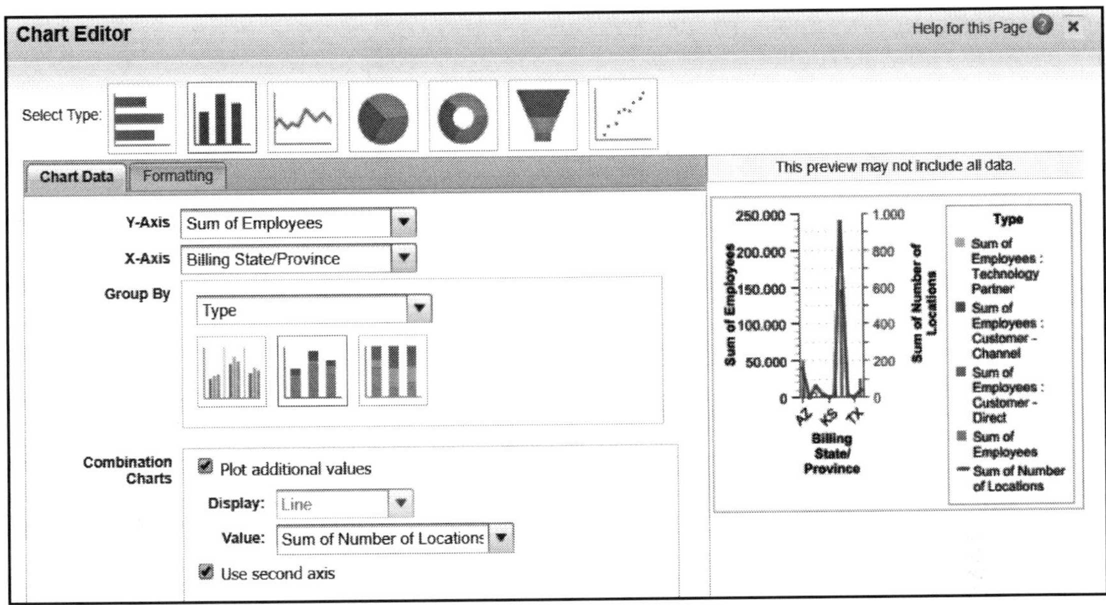

Combination example

* **Grouping**: If we have more than one grouping (for example, accounts by country and then by type), we can chart how each grouping contributes to the overall count:

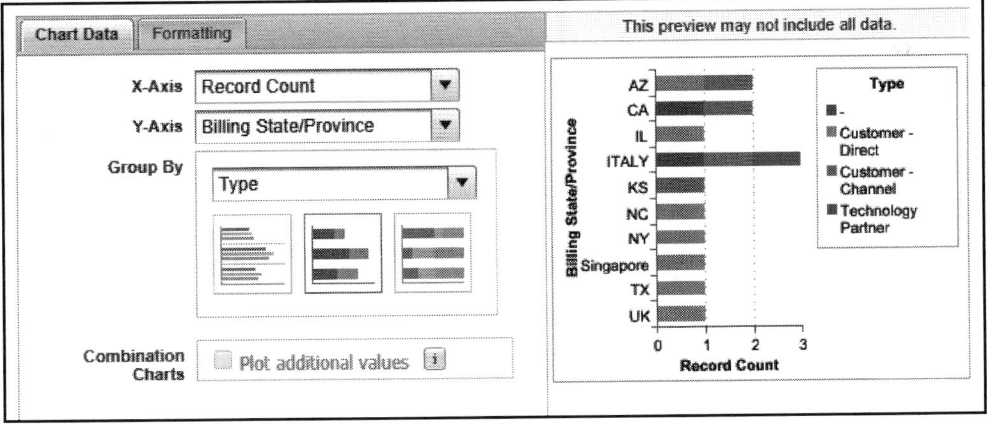

Grouping example on charts

- **Values/wedges/segments**: Which values and wedges are displayed depends on the kind of chart you use (pie, donut, or funnel chart).

We can format the chart with various settings, all of which you can find on the Salesforce Help page at `https://help.salesforce.com/articleView?id=reports_chart_formatting.htmtype=5`.

There are some considerations that we need to be aware of when adding a chart to a report (as of Summer 2019):

- We can have up to 250 groups or 4,000 values in a chart. If we go over these limits, you will receive an error when running the report.
- If a running user loses access to a given field being used in a chart, another field of the same report may be used; otherwise, the record count is used.
- Numeric and currency fields should be rounded up to two decimal places, while percentages should be rounded to one decimal place.
- Negative values are displayed in bar and line charts but not in funnel/pie/donut charts.

Advanced highlighting for report data

Another interesting feature that's used when displaying report data is the possibility to highlight numeric data ranges. However, the report must have at least one summary or custom summary formula field:

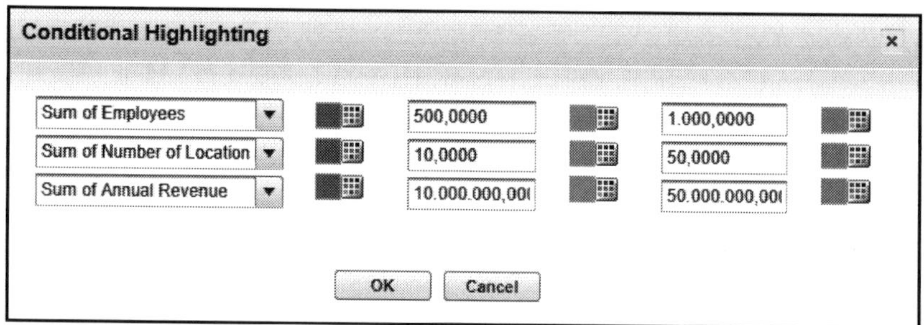

Conditional highlighting in summary fields

Fill in the range of colors and the threshold values shown in the preceding screenshot to highlight the critical values for your report. You should receive the following output:

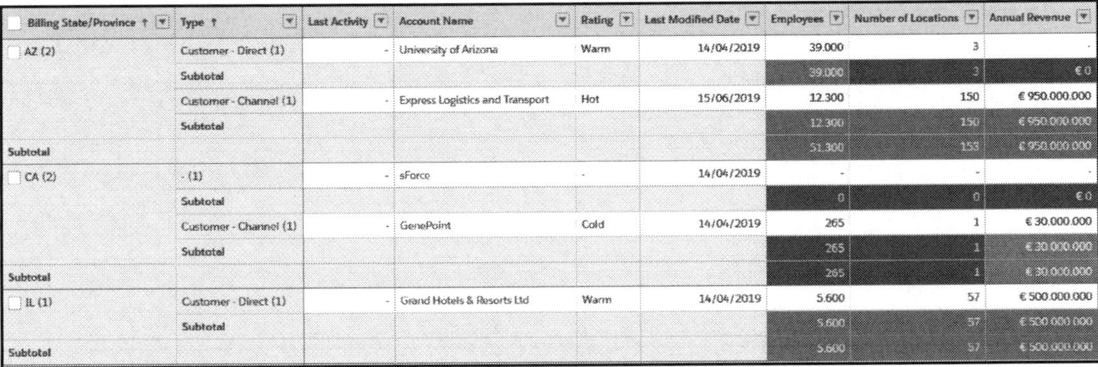

Billing State/Province ↑	Type ↑	Last Activity	Account Name	Rating	Last Modified Date	Employees	Number of Locations	Annual Revenue
AZ (2)	Customer - Direct (1)	-	University of Arizona	Warm	14/04/2019	39.000	3	-
	Subtotal					39.000	3	€ 0
	Customer - Channel (1)	-	Express Logistics and Transport	Hot	15/06/2019	12.300	150	€ 950.000.000
	Subtotal					12.300	150	€ 950.000.000
Subtotal						51.300	153	€ 950.000.000
CA (2)	- (1)	-	sForce	-	14/04/2019	-	-	-
	Subtotal					0	0	€ 0
	Customer - Channel (1)	-	GenePoint	Cold	14/04/2019	265	1	€ 30.000.000
	Subtotal					265	1	€ 30.000.000
Subtotal						265	1	€ 30.000.000
IL (1)	Customer - Direct (1)	-	Grand Hotels & Resorts Ltd	Warm	14/04/2019	5.600	57	€ 500.000.000
	Subtotal					5.600	57	€ 500.000.000
Subtotal						5.600	57	€ 500.000.000

Conditional highlighting display

In the Lightning Report Builder, we can set up to five highlight rules. If we apply more than three rules, conditional highlighting will only be editable from the Lightning Report Builder.

Bucket fields

Numeric, picklist, and free-text fields can be further grouped into a kind of ranged formula called the **bucket column**. We can use bucket columns to group similar values into the same category, such as the level of interest of an account based on its annual revenue field or industry type (such as manufacturing or technology) when given the industry field of accounts.

To create a new bucket column, click on the down arrow icon on the column of the report preview panel you wish to alter and select **Create Bucket Column**. Then, create the buckets for the numeric field, as shown in the following screenshot:

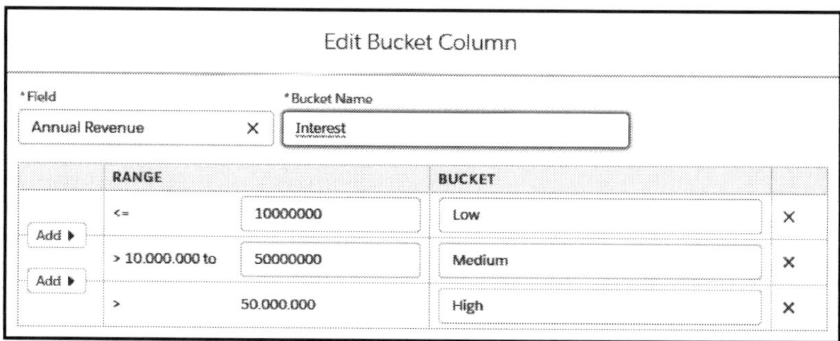

Bucket column configuration of a numeric field

We can also create a bucket column for picklist fields, as shown in the following screenshot:

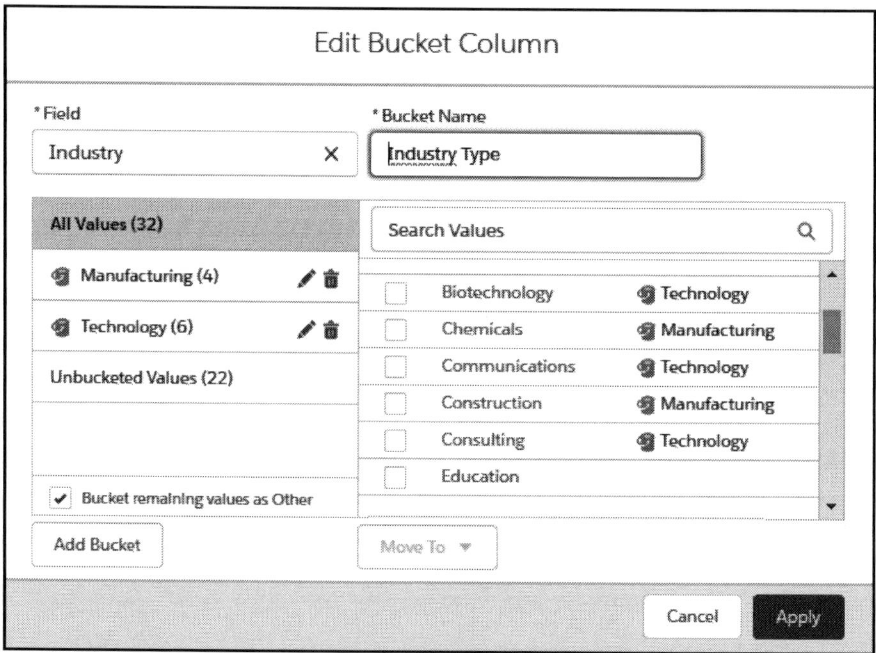

Bucket column configuration of a picklist field

For picklist fields, you can select the **Bucket remaining values as Other** option to categorize unbucketed values into another category.

This is the result of the bucket columns we configured earlier:

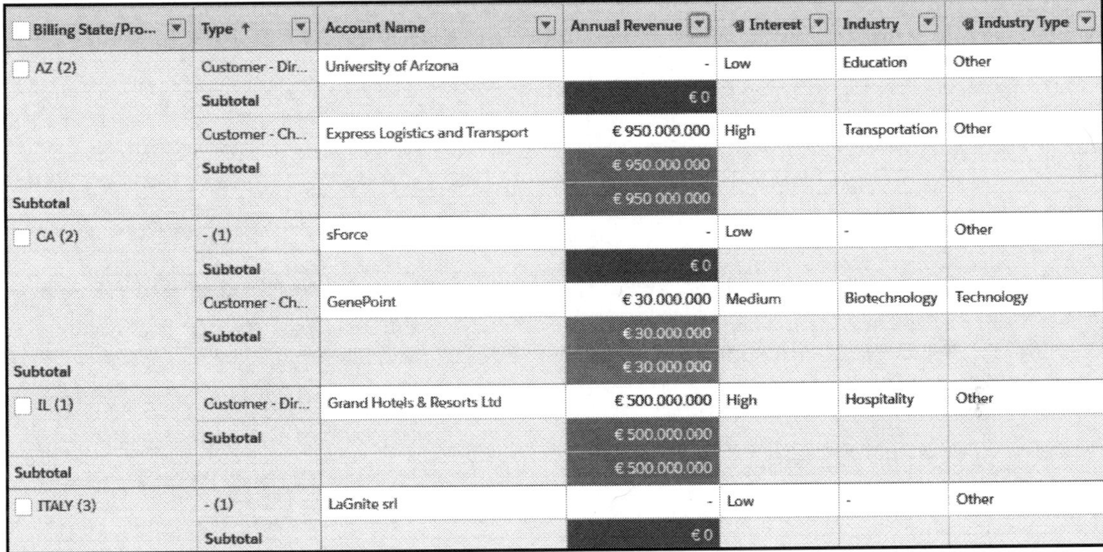

Billing State/Pro...	Type ↑	Account Name	Annual Revenue	Interest	Industry	Industry Type
AZ (2)	Customer - Dir...	University of Arizona	-	Low	Education	Other
	Subtotal		€ 0			
	Customer - Ch...	Express Logistics and Transport	€ 950.000.000	High	Transportation	Other
	Subtotal		€ 950.000.000			
Subtotal			€ 950.000.000			
CA (2)	- (1)	sForce	-	Low	-	Other
	Subtotal		€ 0			
	Customer - Ch...	GenePoint	€ 30.000.000	Medium	Biotechnology	Technology
	Subtotal		€ 30.000.000			
Subtotal			€ 30.000.000			
IL (1)	Customer - Dir...	Grand Hotels & Resorts Ltd	€ 500.000.000	High	Hospitality	Other
	Subtotal		€ 500.000.000			
Subtotal			€ 500.000.000			
ITALY (3)	- (1)	LaGnite srl	-	Low	-	Other
	Subtotal		€ 0			

Bucket columns displayed after configuration

Bucket fields behave like any other field on our report: we can group by bucket fields, chart them, or filter them.

The following limitations apply to bucket fields (as of Summer 2019):

- You can only have up to five bucket fields per report
- You can only have up to 20 buckets per field
- You can only have up to 20 values per bucket

Formulas in reports

Do you miss using formula fields? Regardless of whether the answer is yes or no, reports come with some useful formula options:

- Column summaries
- Summary formulas
- Row-level formulas (beta, as of Winter 2020)

Using column summaries is the least complex way of creating a summary formula out of a numeric field. This is achieved by opening any numeric field options on the corresponding report's column header:

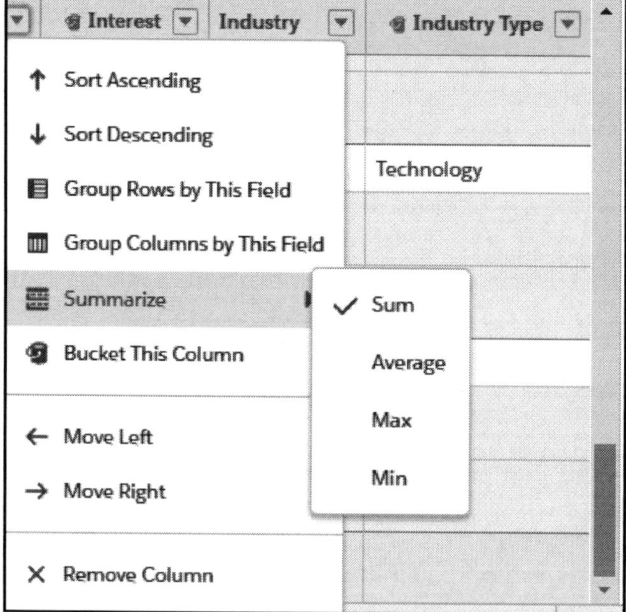

Creating summary fields

We can do one or all of the following operations:

- Sum
- Average
- Max
- Min

You can even click on the **Columns** sidebar to open up the **Summarize** popup:

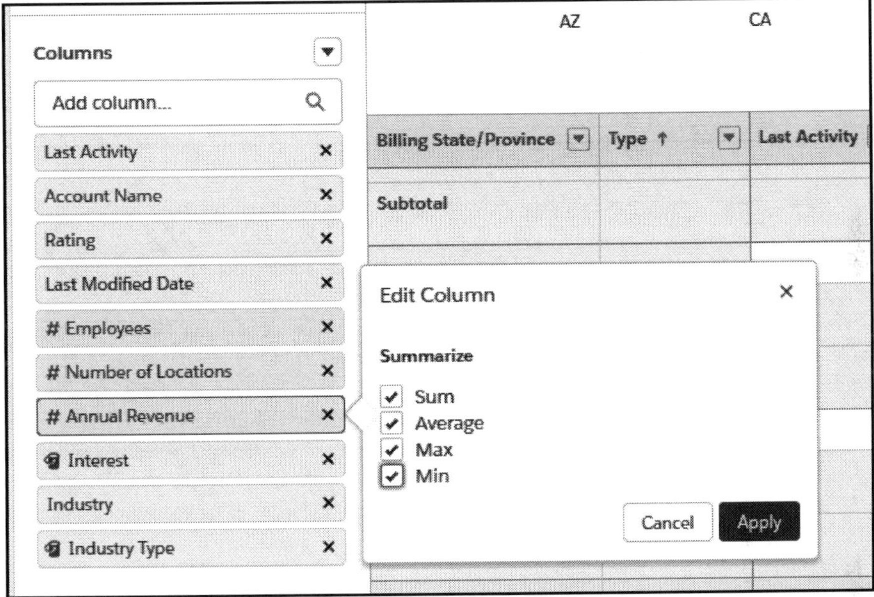

Summarize popup from the Columns sidebar

In this example, we can see the subtotals and the summarized total:

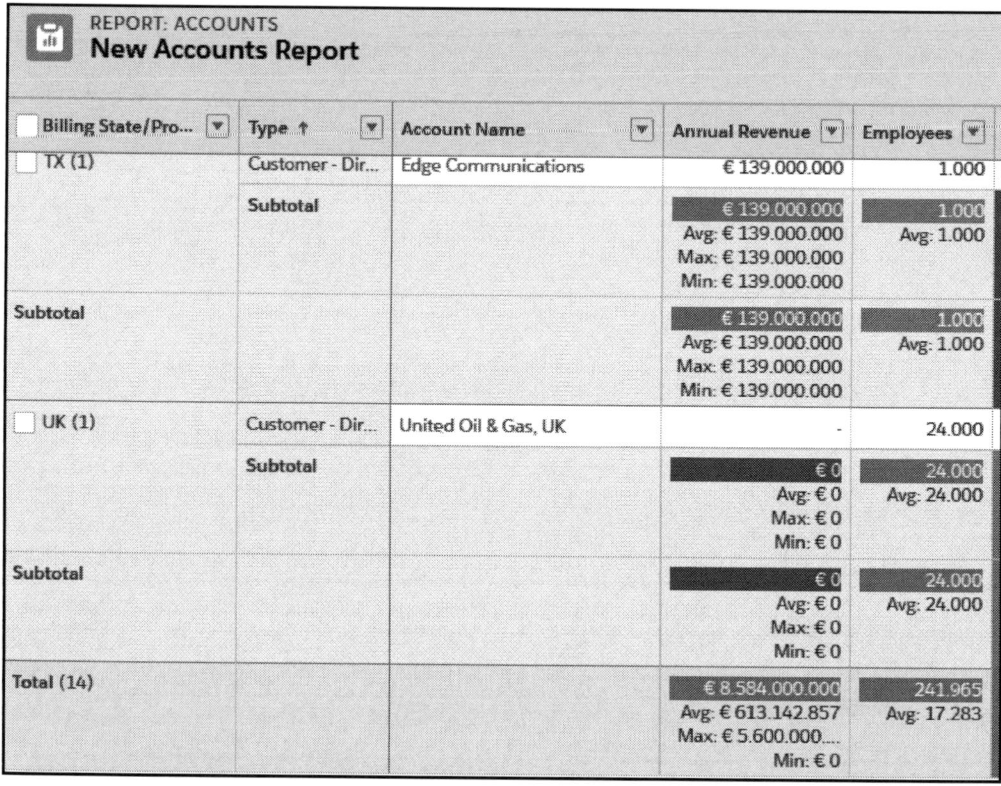

REPORT: ACCOUNTS
New Accounts Report

Billing State/Pro...	Type ↑	Account Name	Annual Revenue	Employees
TX (1)	Customer - Dir...	Edge Communications	€ 139.000.000	1.000
	Subtotal		€ 139.000.000 Avg: € 139.000.000 Max: € 139.000.000 Min: € 139.000.000	1.000 Avg: 1.000
Subtotal			€ 139.000.000 Avg: € 139.000.000 Max: € 139.000.000 Min: € 139.000.000	1.000 Avg: 1.000
UK (1)	Customer - Dir...	United Oil & Gas, UK	-	24.000
	Subtotal		€ 0 Avg: € 0 Max: € 0 Min: € 0	24.000 Avg: 24.000
Subtotal			€ 0 Avg: € 0 Max: € 0 Min: € 0	24.000 Avg: 24.000
Total (14)			€ 8.584.000.000 Avg: € 613.142.857 Max: € 5.600.000.... Min: € 0	241.965 Avg: 17.283

Report summary displaying the subtotal and total

This information is also available on the report's header:

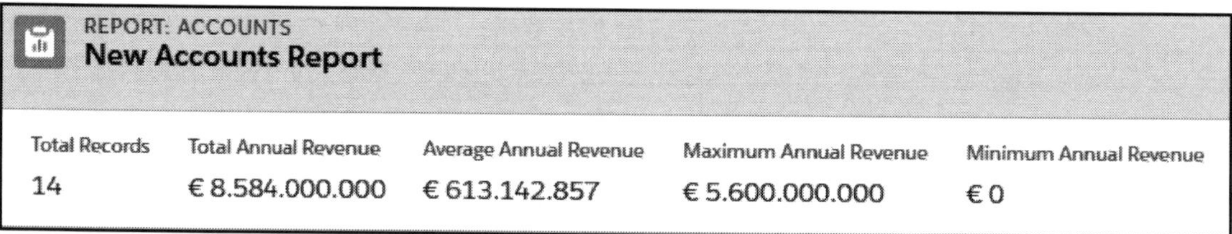

REPORT: ACCOUNTS
New Accounts Report

Total Records	Total Annual Revenue	Average Annual Revenue	Maximum Annual Revenue	Minimum Annual Revenue
14	€ 8.584.000.000	€ 613.142.857	€ 5.600.000.000	€ 0

Summaries on the report's header

Let's go a step further. With summary formulas, we can evaluate a report's group subtotals and grand totals, such as their tax application or fixed margin calculation. This feature is available in both Lightning Experience and Salesforce Classic.

To create a new summary formula (in Lightning), click on the column's sidebar options and choose **Add Summary Formula**. The following popup will appear:

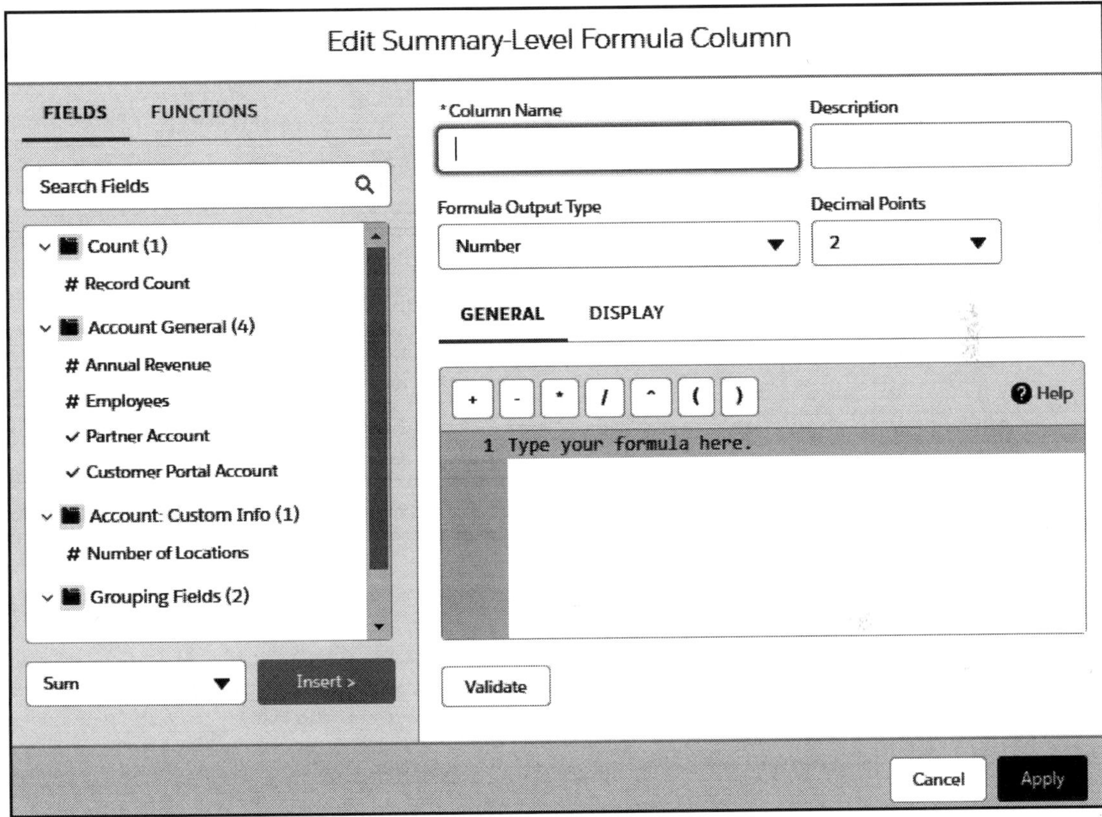

Summary of the formula editor

The editor is divided into different sections:

- The left-hand side shows the fields that were used on the report and a list of available functions (mostly logical and math functions)

- The header displays the details of the formula (such as the return type, only numeric values, and name and description)
- The body of the formula and the chance to display the result of the formula at all summary levels, on the grand total only, or in specific groups (click on the **Display** tab for these options)

Finally, a field is referenced by its sum, average, max, and min values (we are not going to create a row-level formula that applies to any row of the report; instead we will focus on the summary parts of the report, that is, the total and subtotals).

Let's say we want to get the average revenue per employee (given that the employee number is greater than `0`; otherwise, we output `-1`), we can use the following formula:

```
IF(EMPLOYEES:AVG > 0, SALES:AVG / EMPLOYEES:AVG, -1)
```

This results in the following output:

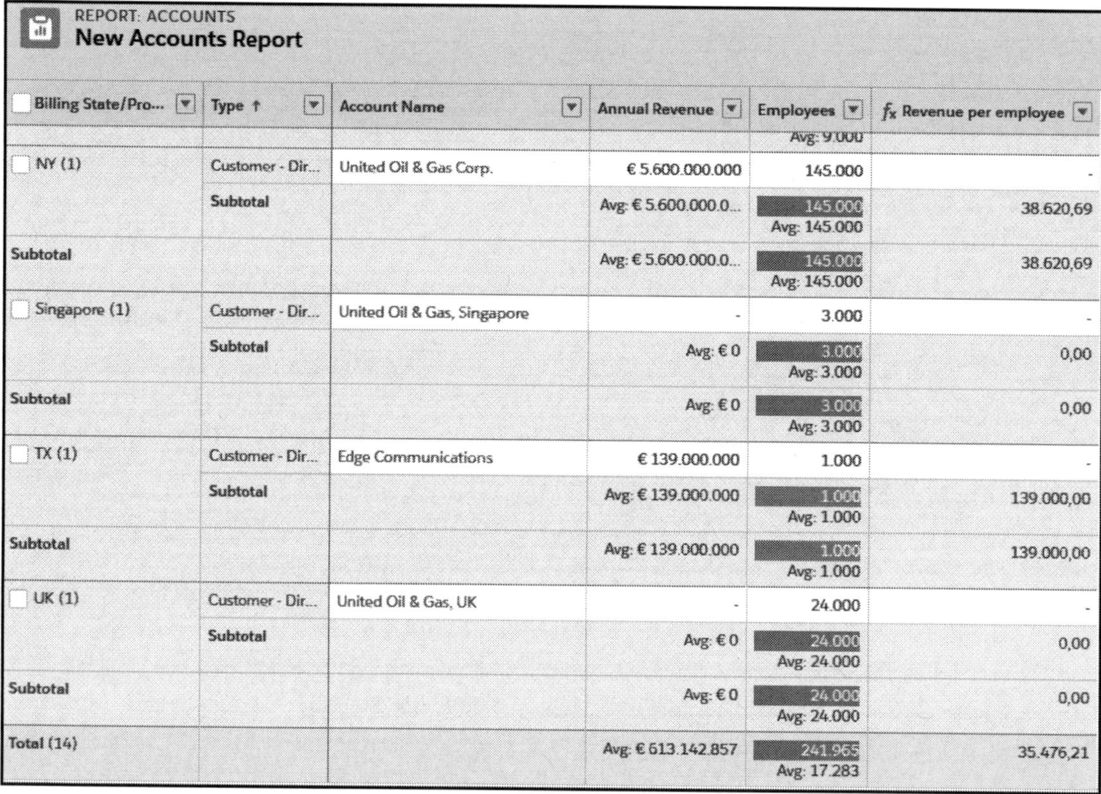

REPORT: ACCOUNTS

New Accounts Report

Billing State/Pro...	Type ↑	Account Name	Annual Revenue	Employees	fx Revenue per employee
				Avg: 9.000	
NY (1)	Customer - Dir...	United Oil & Gas Corp.	€ 5.600.000.000	145.000	-
	Subtotal		Avg: € 5.600.000.0...	145.000 Avg: 145.000	38.620,69
Subtotal			Avg: € 5.600.000.0...	145.000 Avg: 145.000	38.620,69
Singapore (1)	Customer - Dir...	United Oil & Gas, Singapore	-	3.000	-
	Subtotal		Avg: € 0	3.000 Avg: 3.000	0,00
Subtotal			Avg: € 0	3.000 Avg: 3.000	0,00
TX (1)	Customer - Dir...	Edge Communications	€ 139.000.000	1.000	-
	Subtotal		Avg: € 139.000.000	1.000 Avg: 1.000	139.000,00
Subtotal			Avg: € 139.000.000	1.000 Avg: 1.000	139.000,00
UK (1)	Customer - Dir...	United Oil & Gas, UK	-	24.000	-
	Subtotal		Avg: € 0	24.000 Avg: 24.000	0,00
Subtotal			Avg: € 0	24.000 Avg: 24.000	0,00
Total (14)			Avg: € 613.142.857	241.965 Avg: 17.283	35.476,21

Summary formula example

This way, we have acted on the report without creating a custom formula field on the account object. If your sales reps are smart enough, they can be trained to create their own reports.

The following are some things you need to take into consideration regarding summary formulas (if you want to go deeper, check out Salesforce Help at `https://help.salesforce.com/articleView?id=reports_csf_tips.htmtype=5`):

- Date and date-time fields are not supported.
- A summary formula cannot reference another summary formula.
- We cannot group/filter on summary formulas.
- We need at least one grouping to use summary formulas.
- We can get an `#Error!` result on a formula, for example, when dividing by zero.

Finally, let's have a look at the latest addition to the reports formula (as of Winter 2020): row-level formulas.

Row-level formulas are available on Lightning Experience only and, as of Summer 2019, they are in their beta version.

To enable this feature, go to **Setup** | **Feature Settings** | **Analytics** | **Reports and Dashboards Settings** and click on the **Enable Row-Level Formulas** (Lightning Experience only) flag.

To create a new formula, use the **Columns** options menu, as shown in the following screenshot:

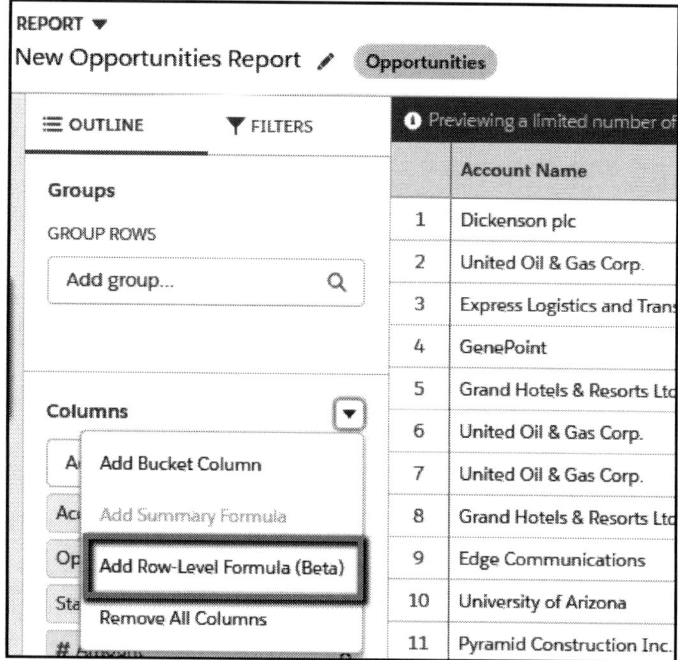

Creating a row-level formula

Now, you should be able to see the row-level formula editor:

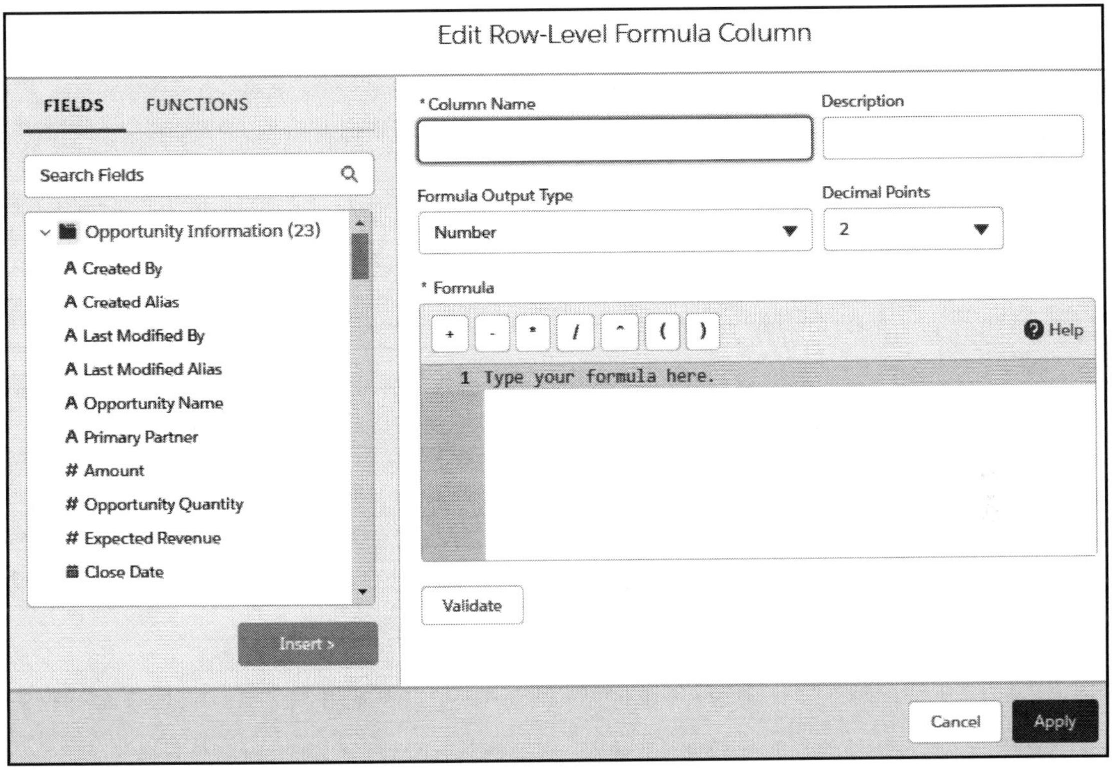

Row-level formula editor

As we saw in the previous summary formula, we have a list of available fields and functions, main formula details, return types, and the body. This time, the return type supports the date, date-time, and text types.

We want to create a formula that counts the number of days it takes for an opportunity to be closed and, given the expected revenue, the average revenue per day (this is just an example and should not be taken as a real KPI for opportunities).

This formula can be written as follows:

```
'€ ' + TEXT(ROUND(AMOUNT / (CLOSE_DATE - DATEVALUE(CREATED_DATE)),2) )
```

Here, **Close_Date** and **Created_Date** are evaluated together by subtracting one date from the other (we used the **DATEVALUE** function to convert the date-time of the **Created_Date** into a simple date value), which gives the difference in days between the dates. Then, the opportunity amount is divided by the number of days. We round the result to two decimal places, convert it into text, and append the Euro symbol to create something that pretends to be a currency field (at the time of writing, that is, Spring 2019, the currency output type isn't supported).

This is the result:

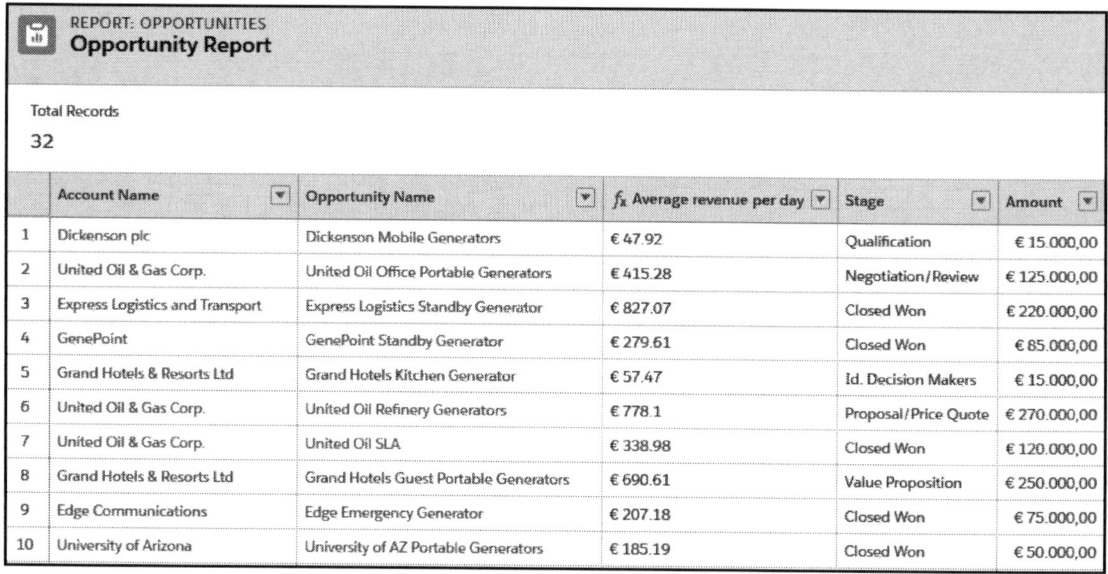

REPORT: OPPORTUNITIES
Opportunity Report

Total Records
32

	Account Name	Opportunity Name	Average revenue per day	Stage	Amount
1	Dickenson plc	Dickenson Mobile Generators	€ 47.92	Qualification	€ 15.000,00
2	United Oil & Gas Corp.	United Oil Office Portable Generators	€ 415.28	Negotiation/Review	€ 125.000,00
3	Express Logistics and Transport	Express Logistics Standby Generator	€ 827.07	Closed Won	€ 220.000,00
4	GenePoint	GenePoint Standby Generator	€ 279.61	Closed Won	€ 85.000,00
5	Grand Hotels & Resorts Ltd	Grand Hotels Kitchen Generator	€ 57.47	Id. Decision Makers	€ 15.000,00
6	United Oil & Gas Corp.	United Oil Refinery Generators	€ 778.1	Proposal/Price Quote	€ 270.000,00
7	United Oil & Gas Corp.	United Oil SLA	€ 338.98	Closed Won	€ 120.000,00
8	Grand Hotels & Resorts Ltd	Grand Hotels Guest Portable Generators	€ 690.61	Value Proposition	€ 250.000,00
9	Edge Communications	Edge Emergency Generator	€ 207.18	Closed Won	€ 75.000,00
10	University of Arizona	University of AZ Portable Generators	€ 185.19	Closed Won	€ 50.000,00

Row-level formula example

Cool, right?

As of Summer 2019, we have severe limitations for row-level formulas (for the complete list, please refer to Salesforce Help at `https://help.salesforce.com/articleView?id=reports_formulas_row_level_limits.htmtype=5`), some of which are as follows:

- We can only have one row-level formula per report
- We can only reference up to three fields per formula
- Some field types are not supported (such as Boolean and picklist)
- We cannot use row-level formulas on joined reports
- The **Edit** (Salesforce Classic) option for editing a report is not available on any report containing a row-level formula

Joined reports

In this section, we will take a close look at joined reports.

As we've already mentioned, the joined reports format allows us to merge different report types into a single report so that we get a single report that contains data from different *sources*.

We can merge up to five different report types (standard or custom), called blocks, where each block can return up to 2,000 records. The only limitation is that they must share common fields (for example, Account Name).

With joined reports, we can, for instance, show all the opportunities for a given account, along with different details (for example, new opportunities, closed opportunities, and lost ones).

In this configuration, the first report type that's added is the principal report type. This report type controls how common fields are named (sometimes, different report types on the same account fields hold different labels).

Joined reports are available on both Lightning Experience and Salesforce Classic. In Lightning Experience, create a new report, choose the first report type you wish to create (which becomes the principal), and then click on the **REPORT** quick menu at the top left of the Report Builder:

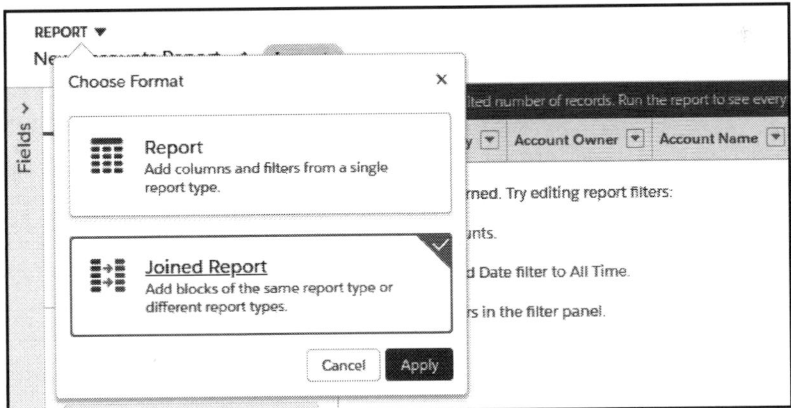

Creating a joined report on Lightning Experience

Now, click the **Add Block** button next to the report name to add new blocks (I'm adding the **Opportunities** report type twice, one for won and one for lost opportunities):

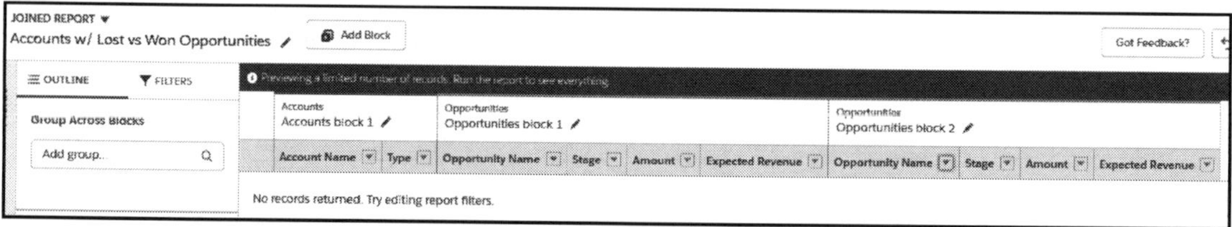

Adding blocks to the joined report

If we run the report at this step, we will get three reports, one next to the other, without any correlation.

Let's add a grouping from the **OUTLINE** section by choosing the **Account Name** field (which represents the account lookup; you can add further groupings if needed, but only up to three):

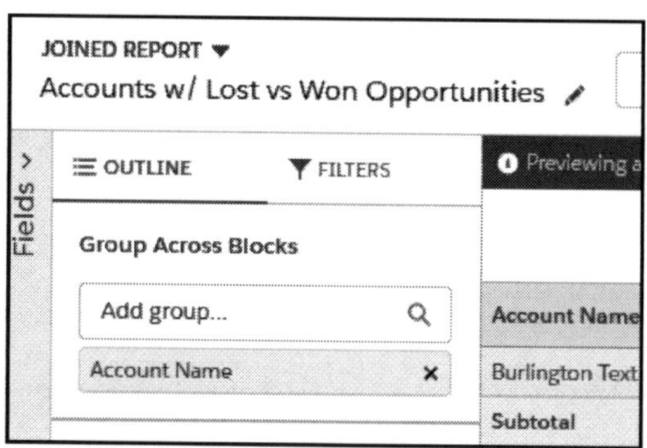

Block groupings on a joined report

Now, the report correctly groups the results by the same account. However, you can see all the opportunities in both blocks since we haven't set up a filter yet.

Let's filter the opportunity reports to get won opportunities displayed first and lost opportunities last (filtering is configured in the **FILTERS** section):

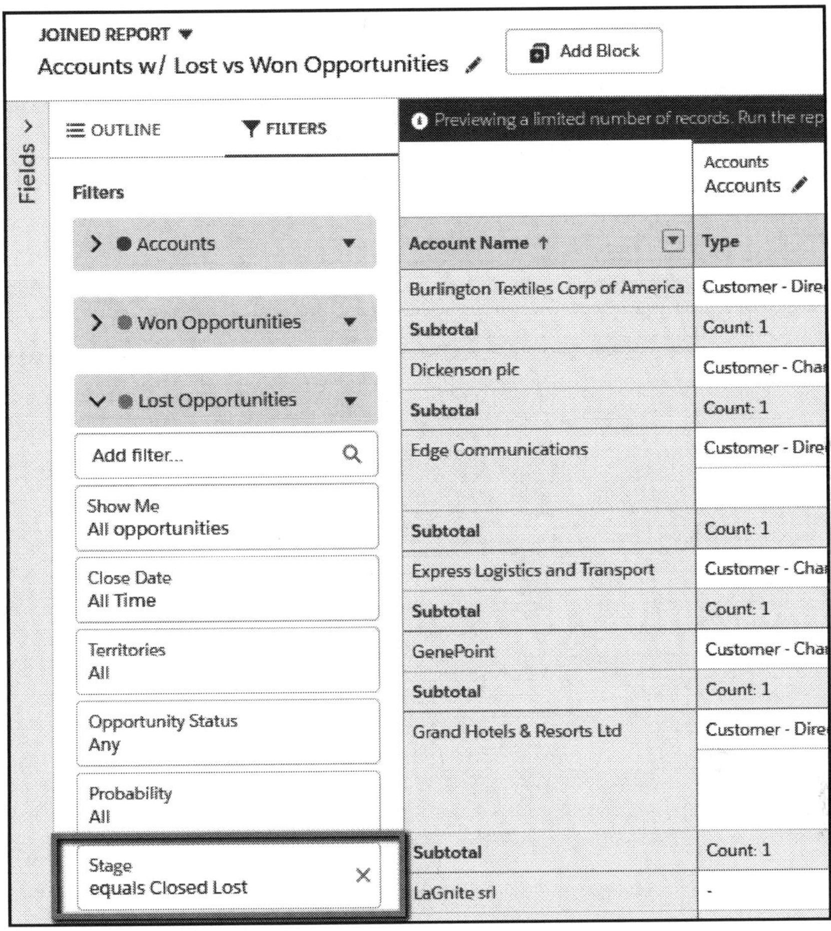

Filtering blocks on joined reports

You can filter with a different stage value for the won opportunities and lost opportunities blocks.

After all this hard work, you will see the following output:

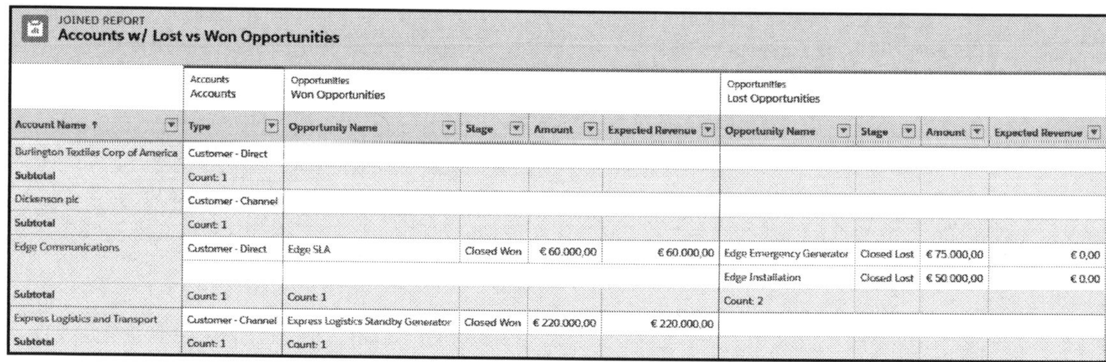

Joined report example completed

Now, we have a bird's-eye view of which opportunities have been lost and which have been won for each account. As you can see, you can customize each block name, add a filter or column, as well as subtotals and even summary formulas.

Tracking history on reports

Reporting on current values is cool, but sometimes, we need to know the trends of certain fields.

As an example, it may be necessary for our call center to find out how the statuses of the cases change day by day or how the opportunity amount and stage vary from week to week.

Historical Tracking Reports

We can implement this kind of insight with **Historical Trend Reporting** or **Historical Tracking Reports**. If enabled, Salesforce stores certain fields value for up to 3 months (plus the current month).

Go to **Setup** | **Feature Settings** | **Analytics** | **Reports & Dashboards** | **Historical Trending** and enable historical trending for opportunities and any other objects you want to track. Here, we have set up an example:

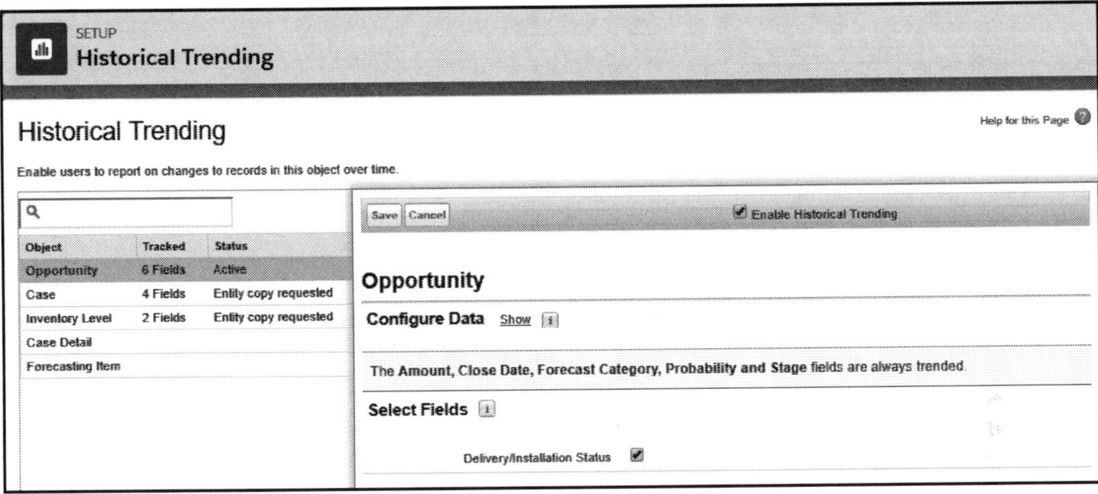

Historical Tracking Reports set up

The result is that you get a custom report type when creating a new report called **Opportunities with Historical Trending** (it depends on the enabled object).

Enablement can take a while (wait until you receive a confirmation email stating that historical tracking has been enabled). When it's ready, you can create a new report with the previous report type.

As we can see, it differs from a typical report:

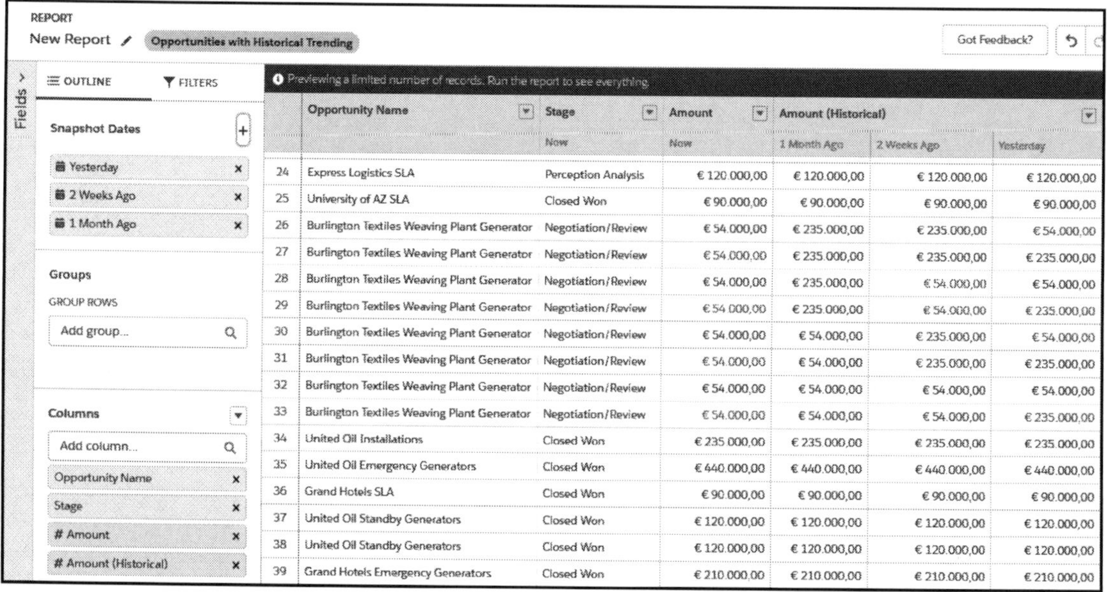

	Opportunity Name	Stage	Amount	Amount (Historical)		
		Now	Now	1 Month Ago	2 Weeks Ago	Yesterday
24	Express Logistics SLA	Perception Analysis	€ 120.000,00	€ 120.000,00	€ 120.000,00	€ 120.000,00
25	University of AZ SLA	Closed Won	€ 90.000,00	€ 90.000,00	€ 90.000,00	€ 90.000,00
26	Burlington Textiles Weaving Plant Generator	Negotiation/Review	€ 54.000,00	€ 235.000,00	€ 235.000,00	€ 54.000,00
27	Burlington Textiles Weaving Plant Generator	Negotiation/Review	€ 54.000,00	€ 235.000,00	€ 235.000,00	€ 235.000,00
28	Burlington Textiles Weaving Plant Generator	Negotiation/Review	€ 54.000,00	€ 235.000,00	€ 54.000,00	€ 54.000,00
29	Burlington Textiles Weaving Plant Generator	Negotiation/Review	€ 54.000,00	€ 235.000,00	€ 54.000,00	€ 235.000,00
30	Burlington Textiles Weaving Plant Generator	Negotiation/Review	€ 54.000,00	€ 54.000,00	€ 235.000,00	€ 54.000,00
31	Burlington Textiles Weaving Plant Generator	Negotiation/Review	€ 54.000,00	€ 54.000,00	€ 235.000,00	€ 235.000,00
32	Burlington Textiles Weaving Plant Generator	Negotiation/Review	€ 54.000,00	€ 54.000,00	€ 54.000,00	€ 54.000,00
33	Burlington Textiles Weaving Plant Generator	Negotiation/Review	€ 54.000,00	€ 54.000,00	€ 54.000,00	€ 235.000,00
34	United Oil Installations	Closed Won	€ 235.000,00	€ 235.000,00	€ 235.000,00	€ 235.000,00
35	United Oil Emergency Generators	Closed Won	€ 440.000,00	€ 440.000,00	€ 440.000,00	€ 440.000,00
36	Grand Hotels SLA	Closed Won	€ 90.000,00	€ 90.000,00	€ 90.000,00	€ 90.000,00
37	United Oil Standby Generators	Closed Won	€ 120.000,00	€ 120.000,00	€ 120.000,00	€ 120.000,00
38	United Oil Standby Generators	Closed Won	€ 120.000,00	€ 120.000,00	€ 120.000,00	€ 120.000,00
39	Grand Hotels Emergency Generators	Closed Won	€ 210.000,00	€ 210.000,00	€ 210.000,00	€ 210.000,00

Historical trending report example

In the **Snapshot Dates** section, you can select up to five different times, while in the **Columns** section, you can choose the enabled fields with the *historical* versions, which will give you the trending scenario of that value (in red or green).

For a complete list of features related to Historical Trend Reports, please refer to Salesforce Help at `https://help.salesforce.com/articleView?id=reports_historical_concepts.htmtype=5`.

Reporting Snapshots

Besides Historical Tracking Reports, **Reporting Snapshots** is another feature that we can implement when we want to report data in a deeper and more customized way.

With Reporting Snapshots, you can map tabular or summary reports to a custom object so that you can work on a report's results in the same way as you would work with any other Salesforce object.

When I was first introduced to Reporting Snapshots, they appeared to be magical—at least from my junior developer point of view. I used them to track day-to-day status changes on changing records on our customer business flows.

For Reporting Snapshots to work, we need a custom report where all the required columns will be tracked, a custom object where the tracked data will be loaded and, of course, custom fields, which will receive actual data when the reports are run.

We are doing this because we want to track the case age by status to see how cases are handled in their life cycle (until they are closed) and check how many days each status stays still.

You can create a simple report that shows open cases by using the following details:

- **Columns**: `Case Number`, `Case Owner`, `Status`, and `#Age`
- **Filter**: **Status not equal to Closed, Cancelled**

This is how it may appear:

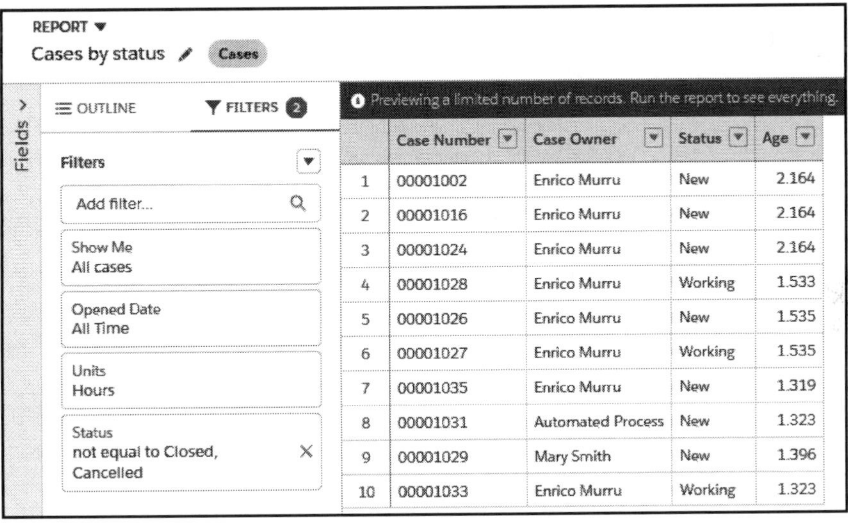

Open cases tabular report

Now, create a new custom object with the following shape:

- Object name: **Open Case Lifespan**
- Custom fields:
    - `Case Number`: Text (20)
    - `Age`: Number (0 decimal places)
    - `Status`: Text
    - `Case Owner`: Text

Remember to set the field-level security for your user (you may run into problems when snapshots are collected if your user doesn't have access to those fields).

To define a new **Reporting Snapshot**, go to **Setup** | **Feature Settings** | **Analytics** | **Reports & Dashboards** | **Reporting Snapshots**, click on the **New Reporting Snapshot** button, select **Running User** as your user, select the previously created report, and then select the **Open cases lifespan** custom object:

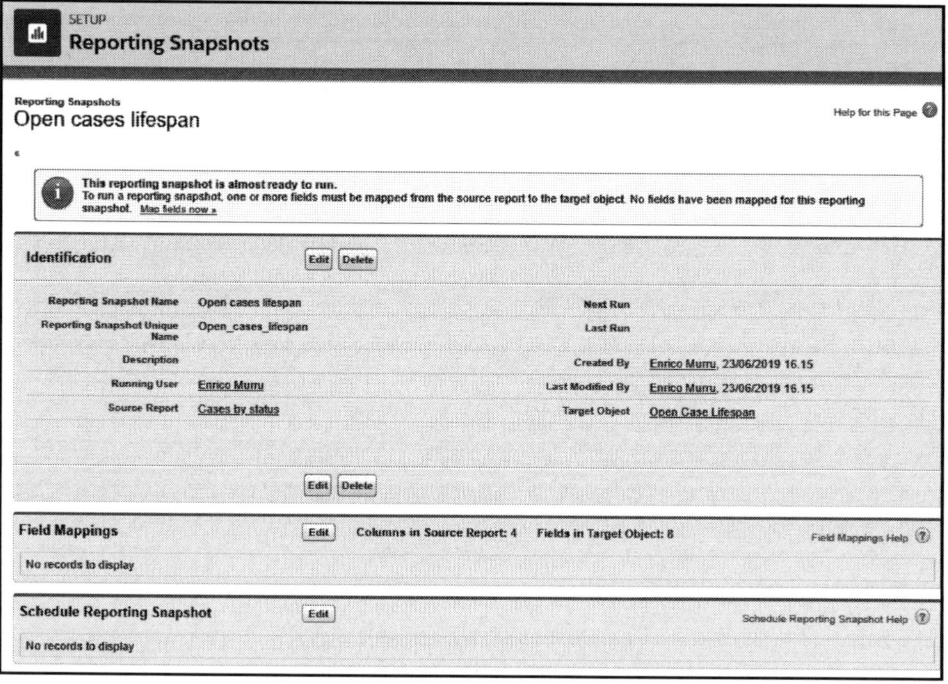

Creating a Reporting Snapshot

Now, click on the **Edit** button on the **Field Mappings** section and select the correct mapping. You should see the following output:

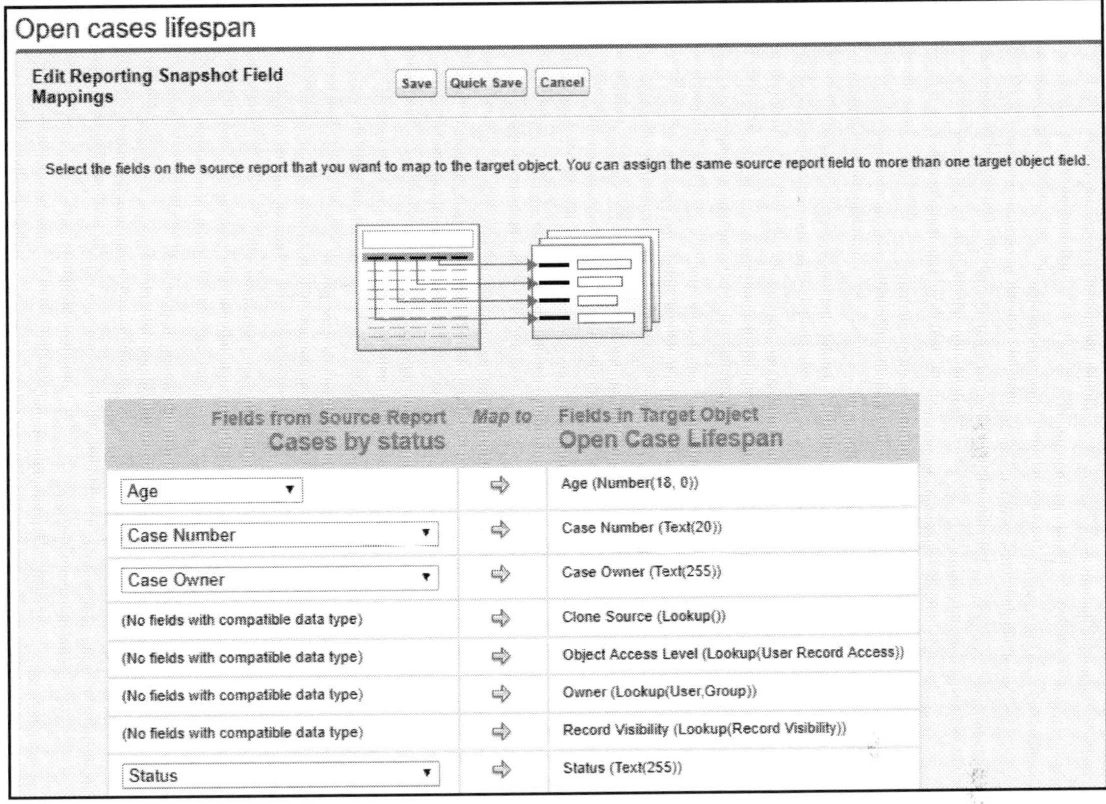

Mapping a Reporting Snapshot

Click on the **Save** button to save your work. Then, click on the **New** button of the **Scheduling Reporting Snapshot** section to select a schedule configuration, as follows:

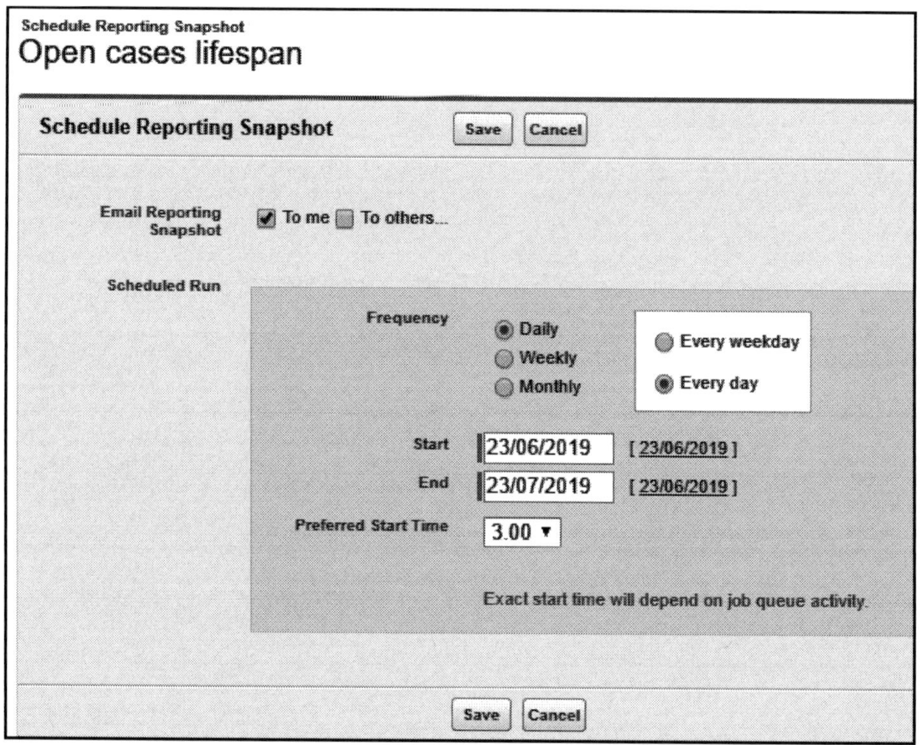

Scheduling a snapshot

You can even select to be notified when the snapshot is executed.

Now, you are all set—all you have to do is wait until the first run.

Unfortunately, there is no way to force a snapshot to run immediately (vote for this idea if you believe in it at `https://success.salesforce.com/ideaView?id=08730000000BpnI`).

After the first run, you can query the **Open Case Lifespan** object, like you would any object.

We can even report on this object to find out more about it.

We've created a new report on the **Open Case Lifespan** object with the following configuration details:

- Grouped by **Case Owner**, **Case Number**, and **Status**
- **Age** column
- Average summary on the **Age** column
- Bar chart with a status on the y axis, `Case Owner` for the bar color, and `Average Age` on the x axis

The previous configuration gives us the following results (this is just an extract that's been divided into two different images and merged into one to show both owners):

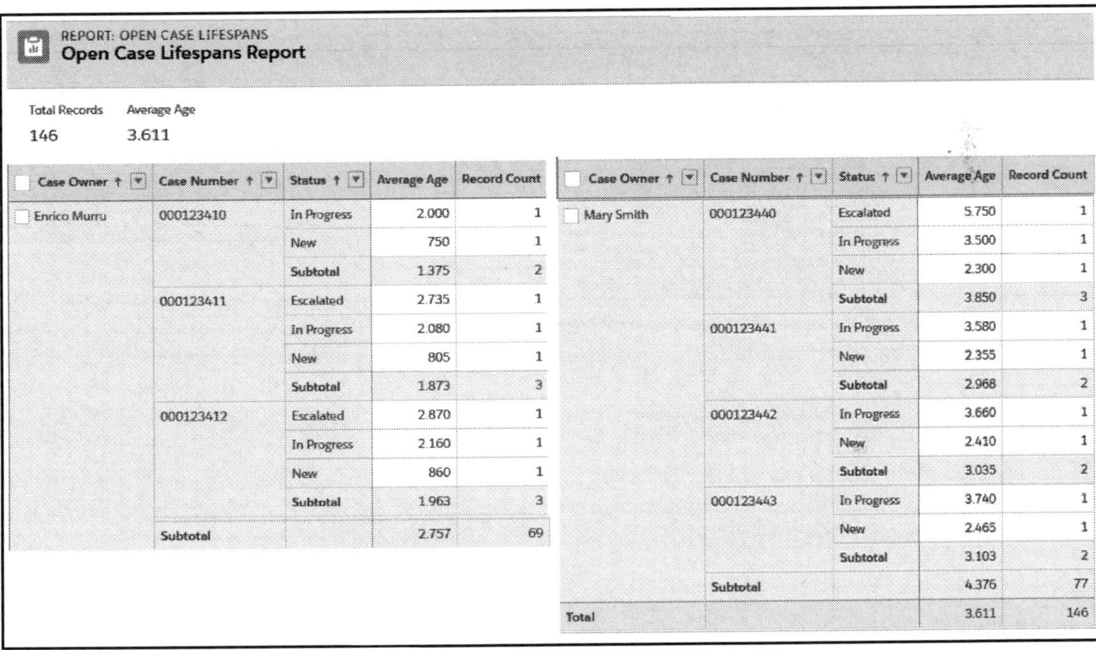

REPORT: OPEN CASE LIFESPANS

Open Case Lifespans Report

Total Records: 146

Average Age: 3.611

Case Owner	Case Number	Status	Average Age	Record Count
Enrico Murru	000123410	In Progress	2.000	1
		New	750	1
		Subtotal	1.375	2
	000123411	Escalated	2.735	1
		In Progress	2.080	1
		New	805	1
		Subtotal	1.873	3
	000123412	Escalated	2.870	1
		In Progress	2.160	1
		New	860	1
		Subtotal	1.963	3
	Subtotal		2.757	69

Case Owner	Case Number	Status	Average Age	Record Count
Mary Smith	000123440	Escalated	5.750	1
		In Progress	3.500	1
		New	2.300	1
		Subtotal	3.850	3
	000123441	In Progress	3.580	1
		New	2.355	1
		Subtotal	2.968	2
	000123442	In Progress	3.660	1
		New	2.410	1
		Subtotal	3.035	2
	000123443	In Progress	3.740	1
		New	2.465	1
		Subtotal	3.103	2
	Subtotal		4.376	77
Total			3.611	146

Reporting on Snapshot records

We also receive the following chart:

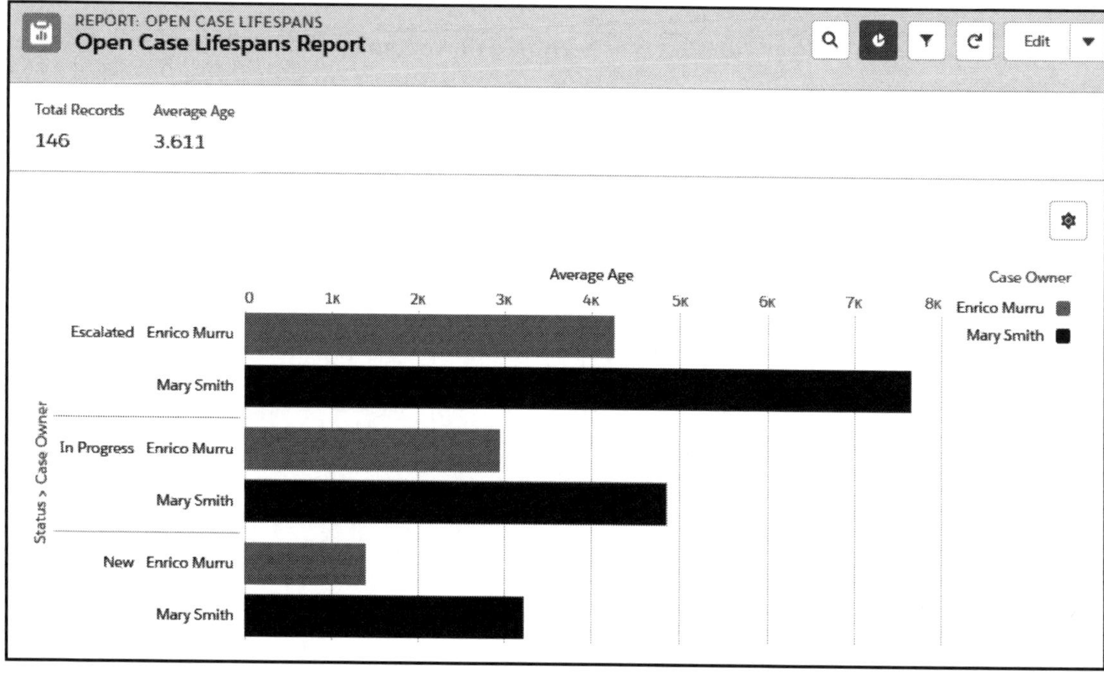

A chart of the reporting snapshot's results

This seems to clearly state that **Enrico Murru** has the best average age case on a status by status grouping.

This may not be the best use case for using snapshots, but it may be a good starting point for your next report.

For more details and considerations regarding Reporting Snapshots, please refer to Salesforce Help at `https://help.salesforce.com/articleView?id=data_about_analytic_snap.htmtype=5`.

Subscribing to reports

In order to complete this chapter, we need to briefly mention report scheduling. We can set up a report so that it runs at a given time and apply a filter so that we receive notifications about it.

To access this feature, click on the **Subscribe** (in Lightning Experience) action on the report page to get to the following modal:

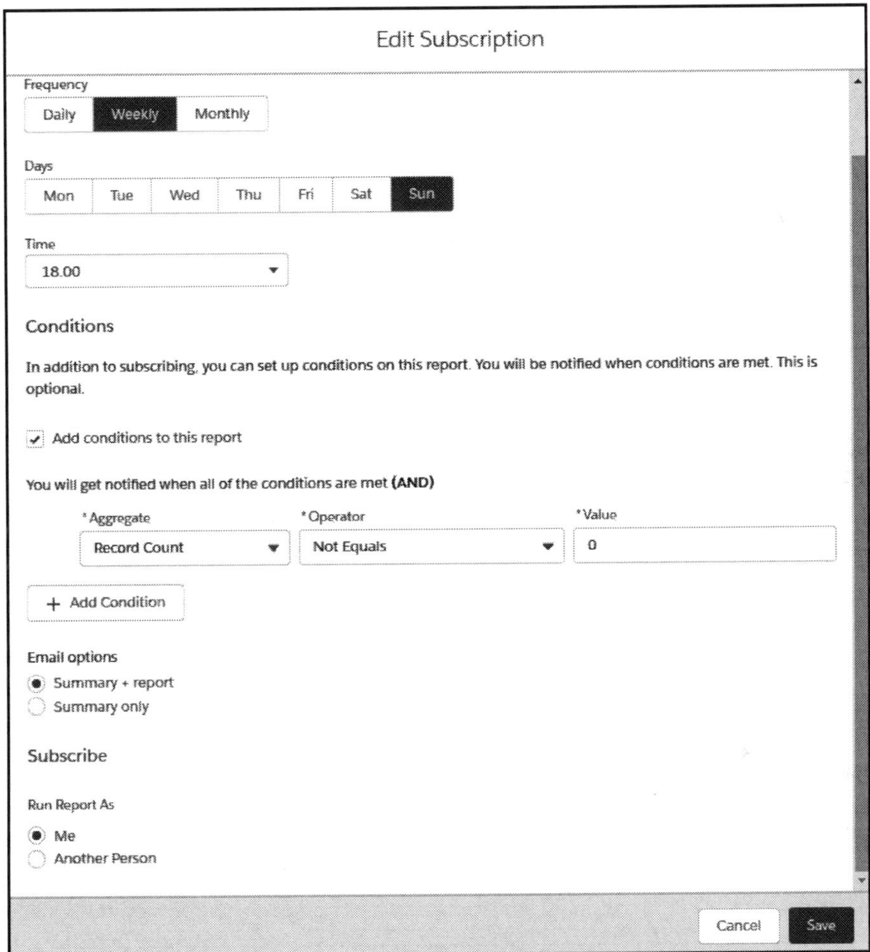

Report subscription

Here, you can set up the following configuration details:

- Frequency configuration and details (such as days, months, and time)
- A special condition to be applied to the notification (in this example, the filter is telling Salesforce to notify us only if the record count is greater than 0)

- The email options (get a summary or a summary and report in CSV format)
- Which user the report has to be executed by, that is, either **Me** or **Another Person**

The following limitations apply:

- Each user can only subscribe to five reports
- You cannot subscribe to a historical tracking report or joined report

Further considerations

Mastering reports isn't easy—you need to master all the reporting features that are available on the platform (and this book will help you achieve those skills), and also be able to properly translate business needs into report specifics (and it can be all but uncommon that your business needs don't fit with the available reporting features). This is where experience will help you out.

For a detailed list of limits and considerations when it comes to reporting, take a look at Salesforce Help at `https://help.salesforce.com/articleView?id=rd_reports_limits.htmtype=5`. The common troubleshooting FAQs at `https://help.salesforce.com/articleView?id=rd_reports_troubleshoot.htmtype=5` will also help you with this.

Summary

By completing this chapter, you have a clear view of how reporting works in the Lightning platform, as well as the features and tools you can use to implement an effective reporting system. In this chapter, we learned how to create reports using standard and custom report types and how to properly format the results using advanced filtering. We also learned how to chart reports using different configurations. Finally, we learned how to get historic trends using historical reports and Reporting Snapshots, as well as how to subscribe to reports to get periodic insights into our organization's data.

In the next chapter, we'll complete the analytics section of this book by covering dashboards so that we can organize reports into full-featured views that tell us what's going on in our organizations.

Questions

1. What can you use to create a report?
    a. Use the Lightning Report Builder
    b. Use the Classic Report Builder only
    c. Use the Classic Report Builder
    d. Use the Lightning Report Builder only
2. Can standard report types be modified?
    a. No, they are built in and cannot be changed.
    b. Only if they're related to custom objects.
    c. No, because they are related to standard objects.
3. Which is true about the tabular report format?
    a. It can be used with charts.
    b. It can be used to group data.
    c. It can be used within dashboards.
    d. It can be used within dashboards, but only when limiting the number of rows.
4. What is the matrix report format used for?
    a. To group related reports together
    b. To group data on rows and columns
    c. To list records in rows
    d. It cannot be related to standard objects
5. Regarding charting, we can have:
    a. No charts for tabular reports
    b. More charts per column
    c. Only one chart per report
    d. Only summary or matrix reports can have a chart
6. Which of the following is true about bucket fields?
    a. They can be created from numeric fields
    b. They can be created from picklist fields
    c. They have no limitations in reports
    d. They can be grouped or used in charts

7. Formulas in a report are:
    a. Bucket fields
    b. Columns summaries
    c. Summary formulas
    d. Row-level formulas
    e. Advanced highlighting
8. Which of the following is true about joined reports?
    a. They are used to display summarized values.
    b. They can have reports with different report types.
    c. They are used to merge different source reports together (whether they have common fields or not).
    d. They are used to merge different source reports together (they should be linked with common fields).
    e. They are available on the Lightning Report Builder only.
9. What does enabling historical trending on a Salesforce object do?
    a. It enables a dedicated report type for Reporting Snapshots
    b. It enables a dedicated report type for historical trending
    c. It can take some time to implement, and historical data is kept for up to 3 months
10. Reporting snapshots records:
    a. Does not go toward Salesforce's data storage limits
    b. Go toward Salesforce's data storage limits
    c. Can be reported
11. When filtering a report:
    a. Standard fields cannot be used in cross filters
    b. We can narrow down the record set based on the role hierarchy
    c. Cross filters can slow down a report's performance

10
Visualizing Key Metrics with Dashboards

In this chapter, we'll dig into dashboards, a graphical representation of Salesforce reports: with Dashboards we can understand the changing business conditions and key metrics that are useful for us to know when making decisions, everything based on the real-time data gathered with Salesforce Reports. We'll see how to create a Dashboard and organize Reports and Dashboards into folders, how to plot each Report within a Dashboard using a specific set of charts (depending on the report type). Then we'll understand how to filter out dashboards, that you can configure to obtain a unique view of reported data, how to subscribe to Dashboards to refresh its data on specific schedules and finally some considerations about Dashboards Salesforce limits.

In this chapter, we'll look at the following topics:

- Organizing reports and dashboards using folders
- Setting up dashboards
- Choosing the right charting options
- Filtering and subscribing to a dashboard
- Limits on dashboards

Let's go through each objective of our chapter one by one.

Building dashboards

As the adage says, *"A picture is worth a thousand words."* That's the concept behind report charts. By properly visualizing data results, you increase the chances of spotting something unusual and can then take the right actions to correct that abnormal trend.

Dashboards are a collection of charts that come from (more or less) related reports. If anyone in your company needs further details of a given chart, they can click on the chart to get to the actual report and all its details (if they have access to them).

Before we start creating a dashboard, let's talk about folders and how you can use them to enable users to access dashboards (and reports).

Reports and dashboards folders

For orgs created after summer 2013, **enhanced folder sharing** is automatically enabled. If you are not in Classic, jump to **Setup** | **Folder Sharing** and flag **Enable access levels for sharing report and dashboard folders** (once enabled, it cannot be reversed).

This feature allows the following:

- Sharing the reports/dashboards folders with users, roles, and groups
- Different permissions to be set at the folder level for both reports and dashboards

With enhanced folder sharing, we get the following permissions:

- **Viewer**: Users with this permission can view folders, run reports, and refresh dashboards
- **Editor**: This grants the same permissions as the viewer permissions, as well as the power to add items for the folders and edit its contents
- **Manager**: This grants the same permissions as the editor permissions, as well as the power to manage folders (create, update, and delete) and manage sharing

A private folder (and all its contents) is hidden from all users (except for administrators) until it is shared with other users.

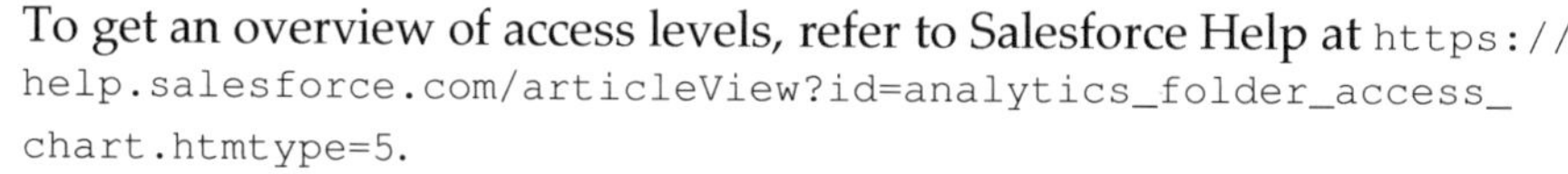
To get an overview of access levels, refer to Salesforce Help at `https://help.salesforce.com/articleView?id=analytics_folder_access_chart.htmtype=5`.

A list of all the user permissions that are needed to share reports and dashboards can be found at Salesforce Help at `https://help.salesforce.com/articleView?id=analytics_sharing_permissions.htm type=5`.

To create a new folder, jump to **App Launcher** | **Dashboards**, click the **New Folder** button, and select the folder's label and unique name. The folder will now be on the **Created by Me** view of the **Folders** subview:

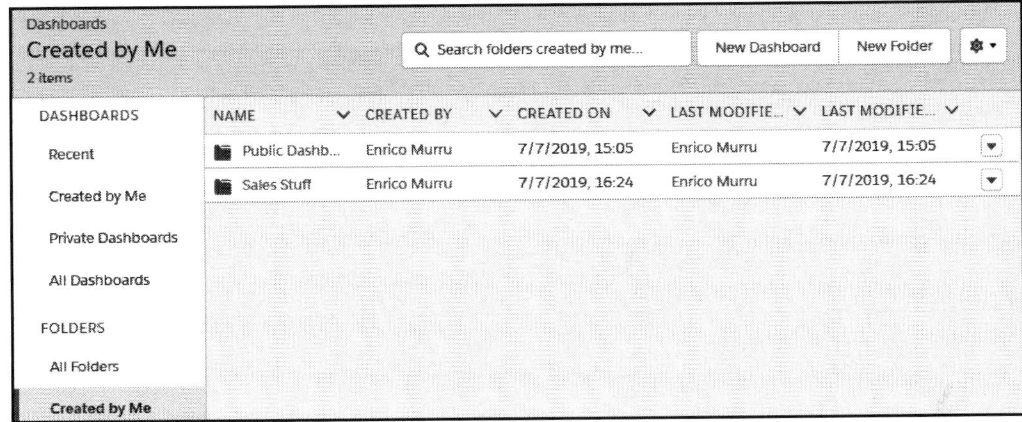

Created by Me folders view

You can create subfolders to better organize dashboards and reports.

To move a report or dashboard within a report/dashboard folder, use the **Move** action when you view reports/dashboard lists or do it directly from the properties panel of each report/dashboard.

To give the right permission to a folder, click on the **Share** action:

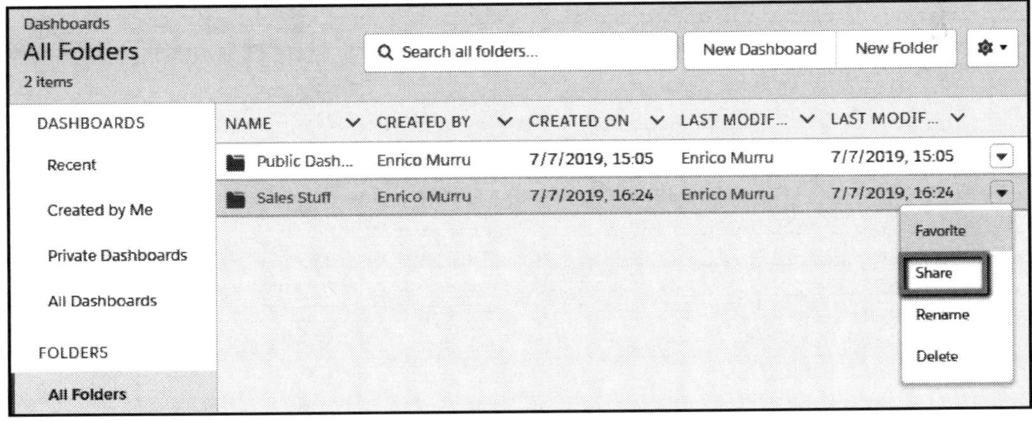

Share action on the folder list view

We can define users, roles, and groups with all kinds of permission granularity, as shown in the following screenshot:

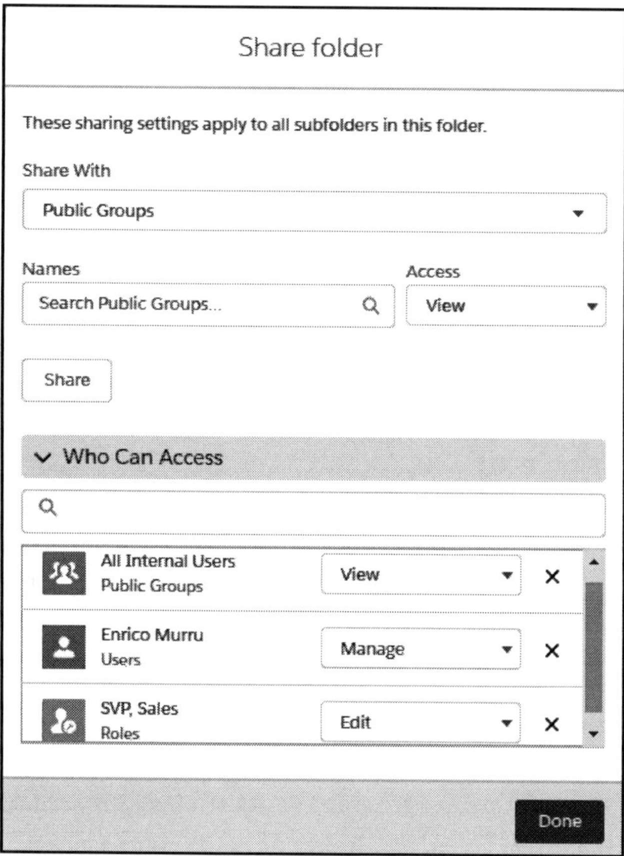

Folder access configuration

In this example, only the administrator user has access as a manager; the entire group of internal users are only viewers and the **SVP, Sales** role has editor-level access.

After this folder regression, let's move on to creating our dashboard.

Setting up a dashboard

Dashboards can be created in Lightning Experience and Salesforce Classic, but in this chapter we'll be digging into Lightning Experience.

For all the details on how to deal with Classic Dashboards, refer to the Salesforce Help at `https://help.salesforce.com/articleView?id=dashboards_create.htmtype=5`.

Before creating a dashboard, make sure you have at least one source report (refer to the previous chapter for more information on them).

Navigate to **App Launcher | Dashboards** and click on the **New Dashboard** button. If you're using a brand-new Developer Edition org, you won't see any dashboards.

Next, add the name and description of your new report (as shown in the following screenshot), but and leave the **Folder** field as the default (or choose your own folder):

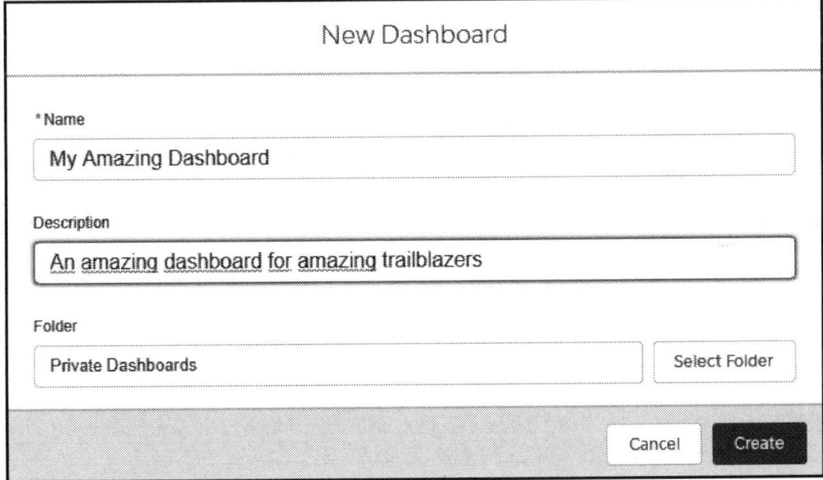

New Dashboard page

Once you have selected a name and a folder for your new dashboard, jump to the dashboard edit panel. If you are used to Classic **Dashboards**, you will be a bit surprised by the dashboard editor's layout:

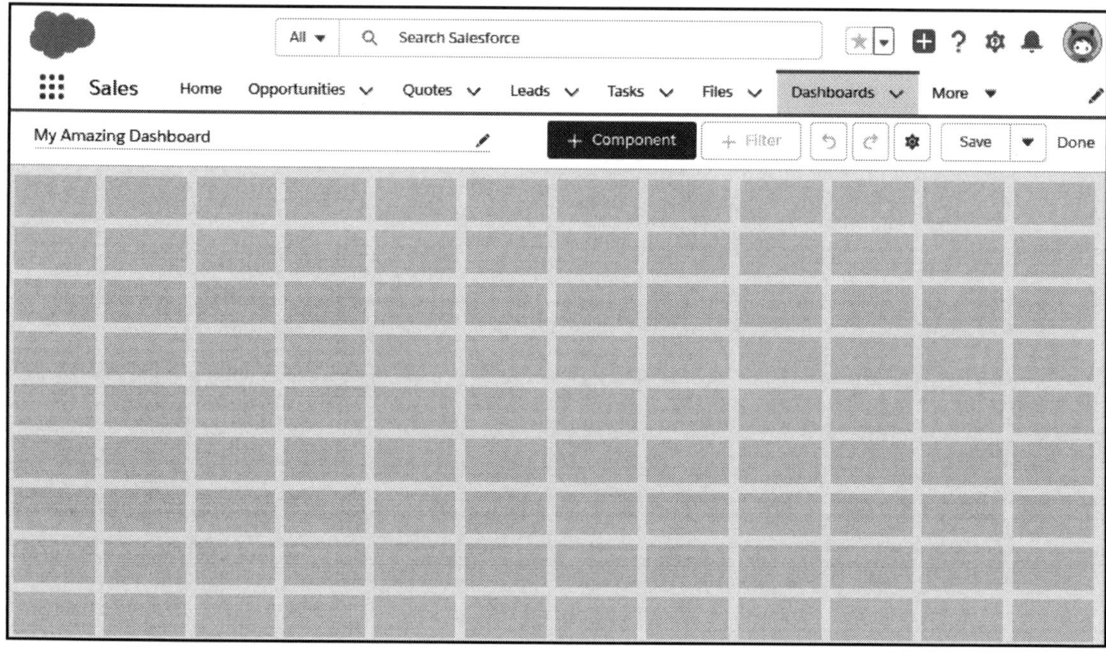

Dashboard editor

You can add up to 12 components per row, but I strongly suggest that you don't do this, as the dashboard will become completely unreadable.

To proceed with adding components, go through the following steps:

1. Click **+ Component** to add a new component to the dashboard, and in the upcoming modal, choose a source report (a component is just the way we identify a report charted within the dashboard. More than one component can refer to the same source report):

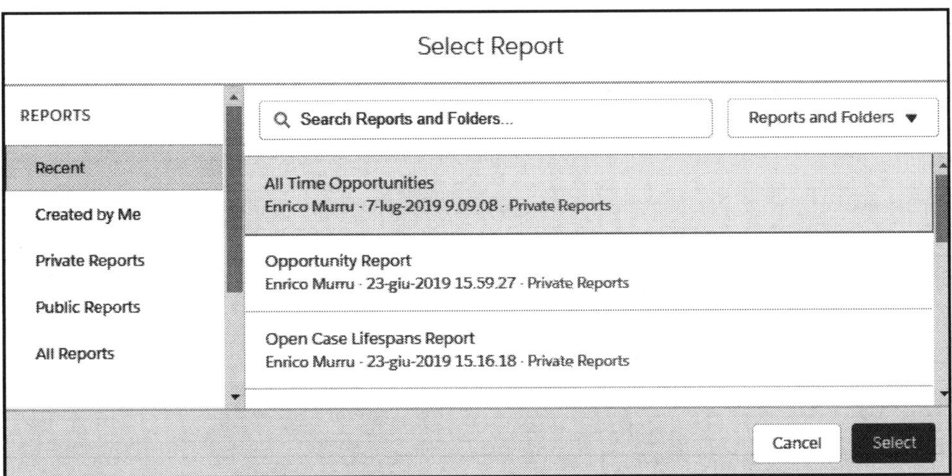

Source report selection

In this example, the **All Time Opportunities** reports show opportunities records grouped by account.

2. Click **Select** and then choose the component properties (i.e. charting options):

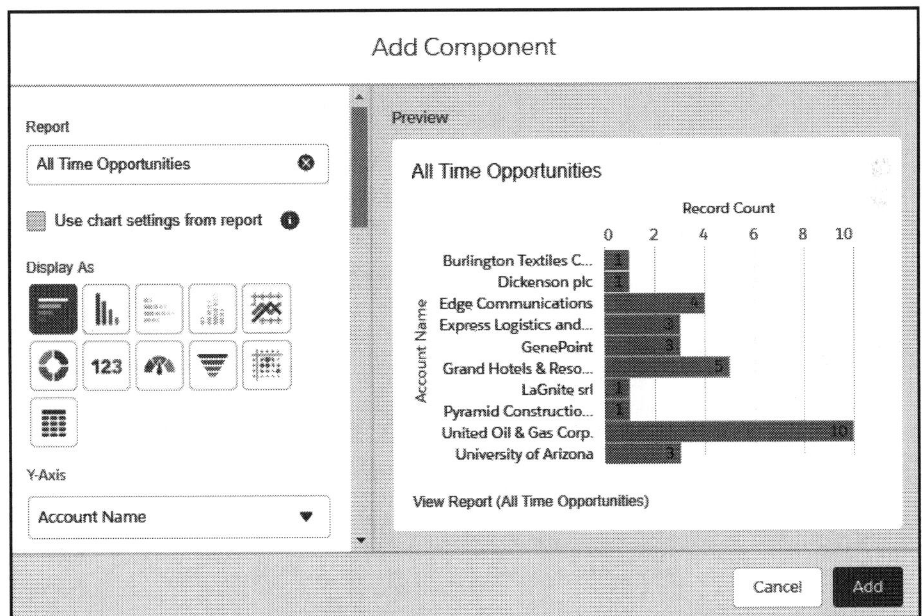

Configuring a dashboard component's chart

3. Click **Add**, and the chart will appear on your dashboard:

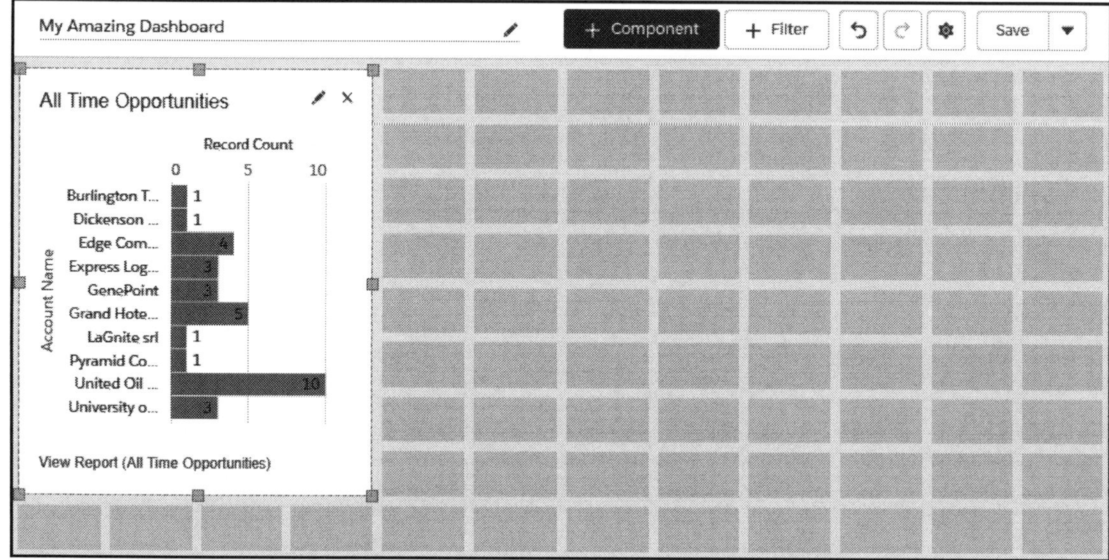

Component added in the dashboard editor

The component can now be resized to fit your needs.

4. Now click on the gear icon next to the **Save** button to configure more settings:

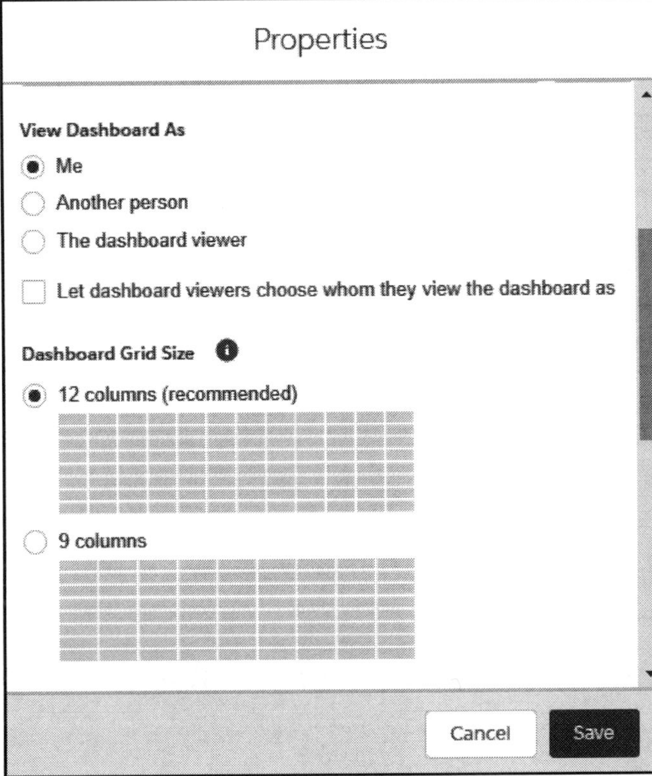

Further settings for the current dashboard

Other than the report name, description, and folder (not shown in the previous screenshot), we can select the *running user* of the dashboards, which means that data will be shown according to the selected user's level of access.

We can choose the following values:

- **Me**: The dashboard is always run with your user's level of access (anyone will actually see the dashboard as you do).
- **Another Person**: Choose any other user (the default is your current user).
- **The dashboard viewer**: This is called a **dynamic report**, which has a few limitations. We can have up to 5 dynamic dashboards for Enterprise Edition, 10 for Unlimited/Performance Edition, and 3 for Developer Edition, and other editions don't support this feature.

The **Let dashboard viewers choose whom they view the dashboard as** flag lets users manually select another user to view the dashboard as: you can let users view dashboards as any other user. If they have the **View My Team's Dashboards** permission in their profile, then they can select any user below their role hierarchy; if they have the **View All Data** permission, then they could select any other user in the org.

Other options refer to the number of columns in the dashboard grid (12 or 9), and if you scroll down the **Properties** modal, you'll also get a dashboard theme and palette customization.

Add some other components, then click the **Save** button and then click **Done** to have a look at your new dashboard:

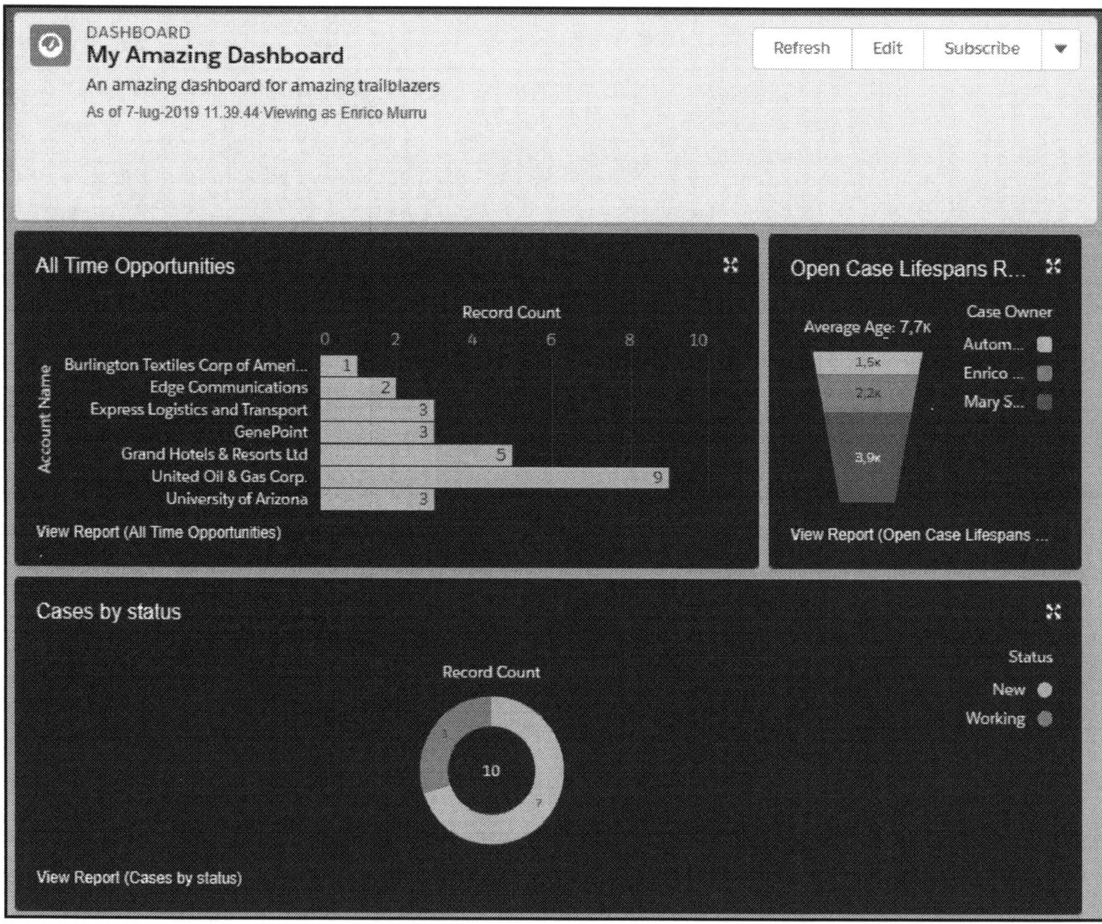

New dashboard

Let's look in more details at component customization and charting.

Selecting the right charting option

In the previous chapter, we saw some different ways to create a chart, and dashboard charts are no different. Indeed, we can create bar charts, stacked bar charts, line charts, donut charts, funnel charts, and scatter charts. **Gauge** and **Metric** charts are not available on the report charting options.

The **Gauge chart** is used to have a precise look at how your metric is performing against a given range.

Create an opportunity report that shows the current year's opportunities and summarizes the **Expected Revenue** field. Now add a new component to your field and select an appropriate range on the **Component Range** property:

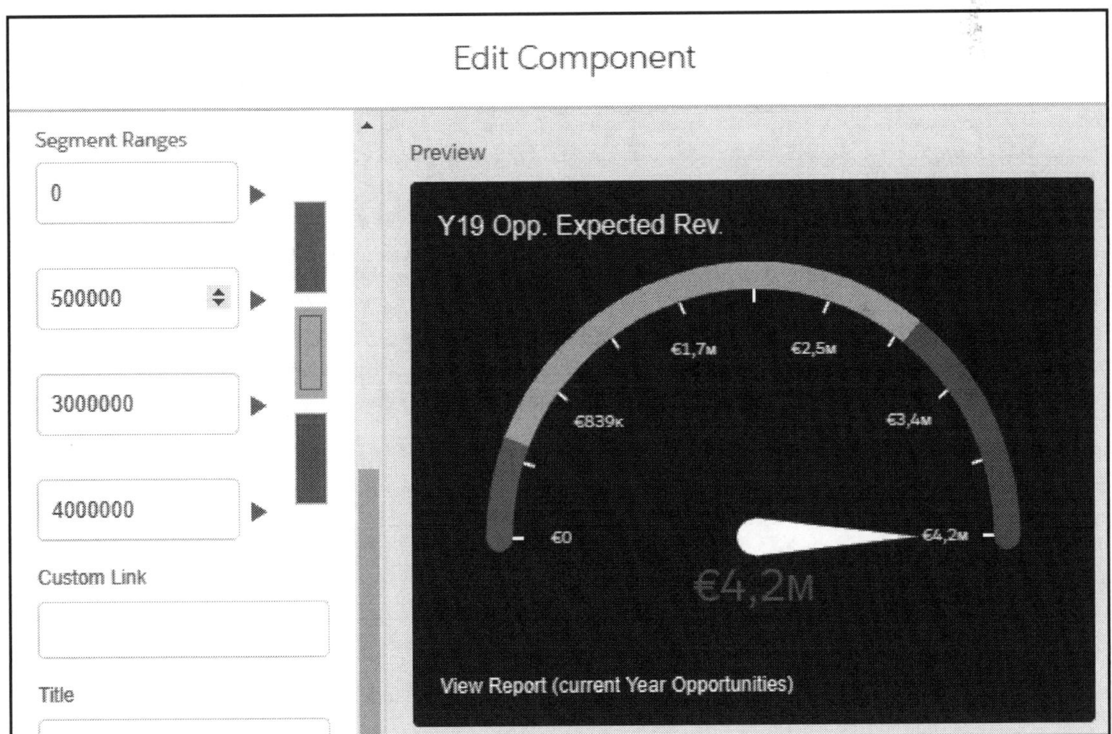

Gauge chart configuration

The **Metric chart** is easier than the gauge chart because it simply displays a number that is the most important metric to be evaluated: it can be customized with show different colors based on a given range.

By using a simple case report that displays the number of open cases (a single filter on the **Closed** field filtered by the false value) and inverting the range colors (our error condition is when there are too many open cases), you get to the metric chart configuration:

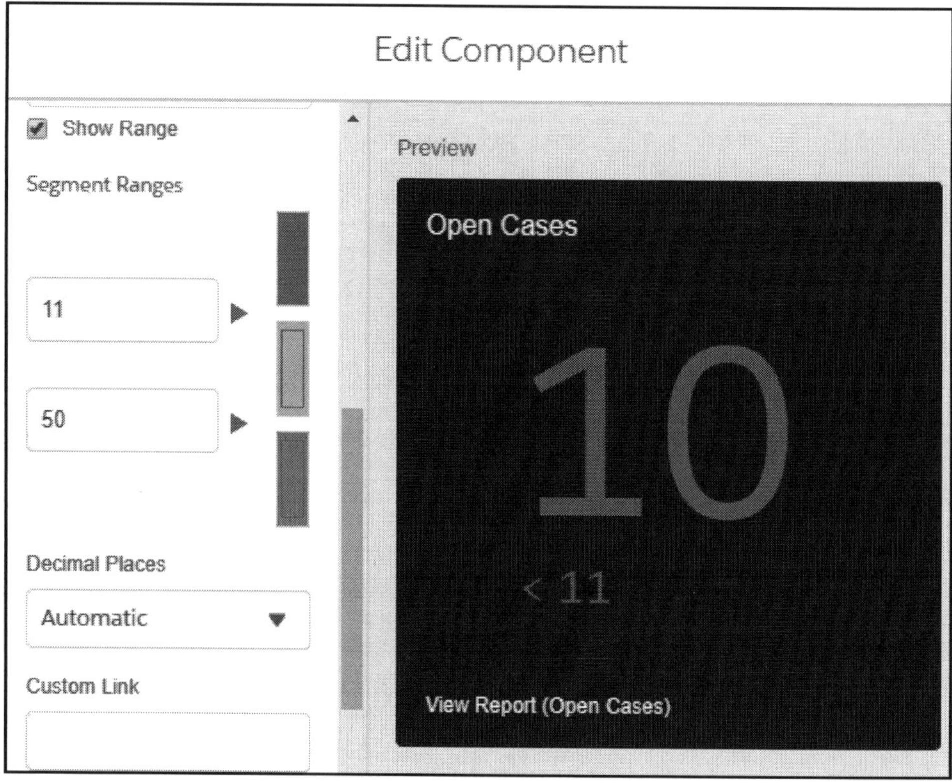

Metric chart configuration

Rearranging components on our new dashboard and putting sales reports and service reports in line, we'll get to the following production-ready dashboard:

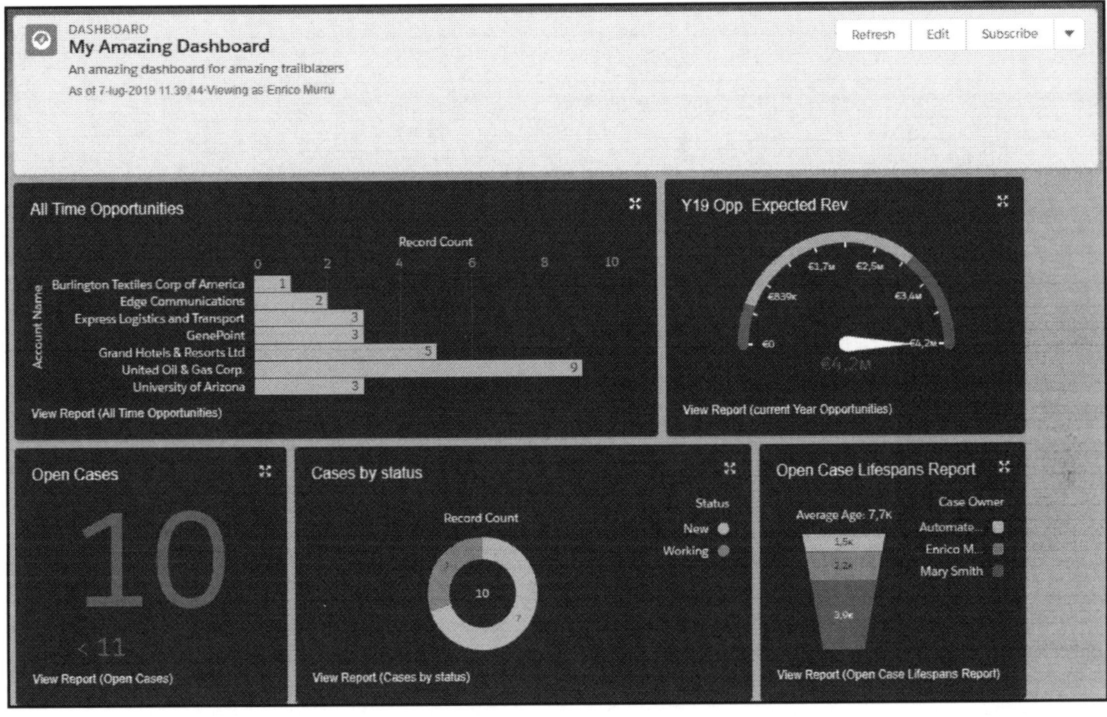

Dashboard example with different components

Remember that if you have already created a chart on a given report, you can use that chart instead of configuring it at the dashboard component level by selecting **Use chart settings from report** on the component editor panel.

If you want to explore all available components settings in more detail, refer to Salesforce Help at `https://help.salesforce.com/articleView?id=dashboards_components_edit_lex.htmtype=5`.

Another option when building a dashboard component is the chance to add a **tabular view** to your report by using the **lightning table** display format (in the following example, the source report is a simple account report):

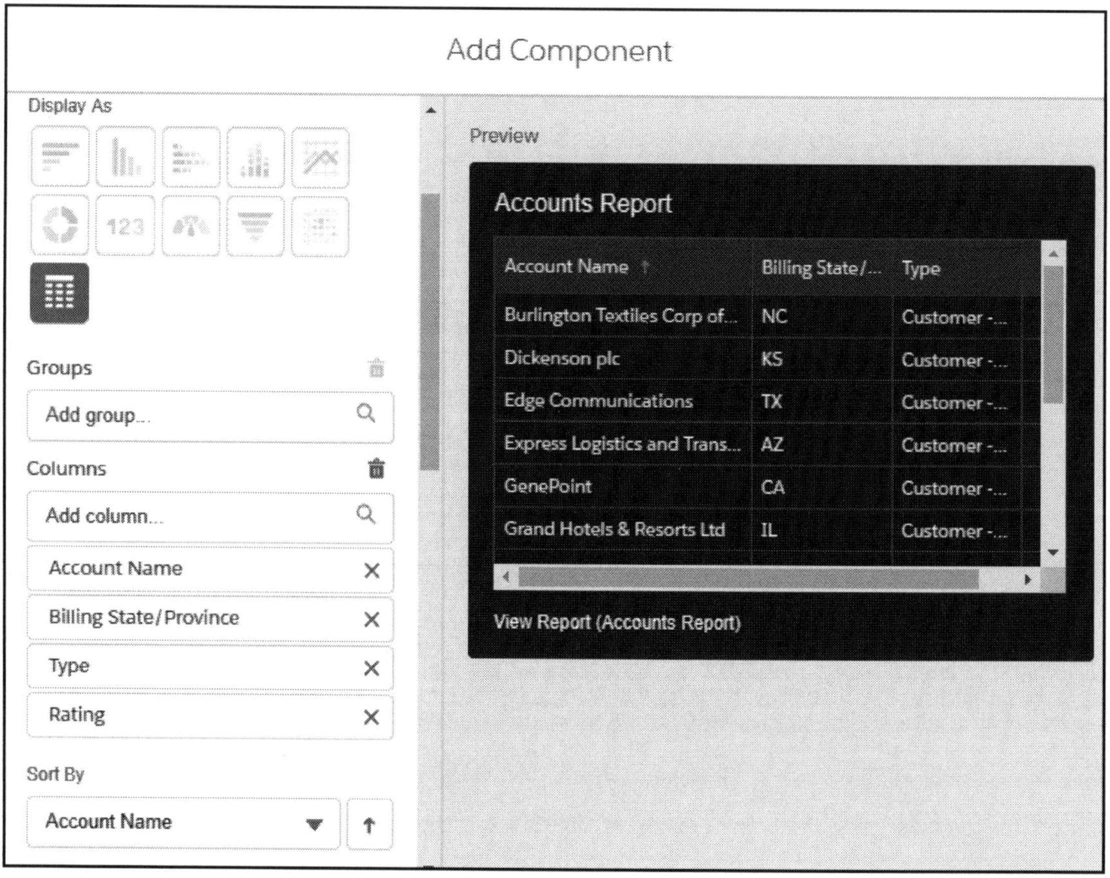

Lightning table component format

The table can show up to 200 records and 10 columns from the source report type.

You can select the columns and sort order for ungrouped reports, but you can also group by a field (in the following example, by **Billing Country**) and add measure fields (such as the min/max of the accounts' **Annual Revenue** field in the following example), or even formula columns defined in the report:

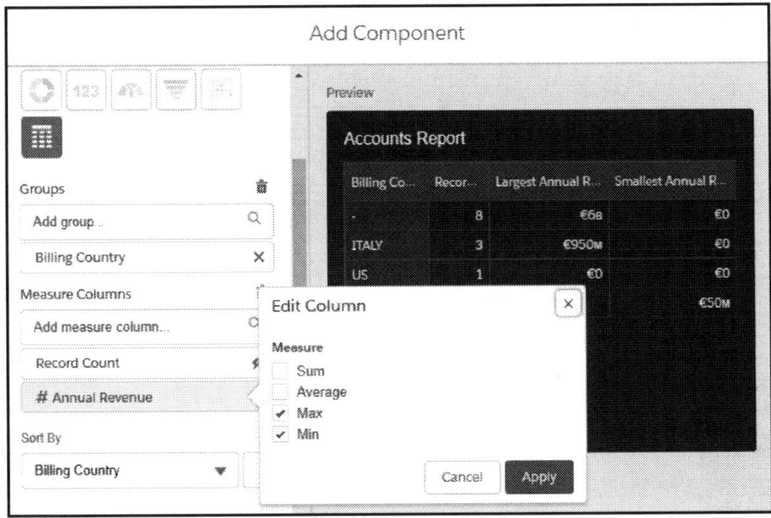

Lightning table example

One last thing to note is a great integration with **Chatter**: you need to enable **Feed Tracking** from **Setup | Features Settings | Chatter | Feed Tracking**, choose **Dashboard**, and click **Enable Feed Tracking** (and select any other field change you want to see on the dashboard's related Chatter).

Once tracking is enabled, to access the dashboard's Chatter, click on the new feed icon left of the **Refresh** button (we can also see that a **+ Follow** button has just appeared):

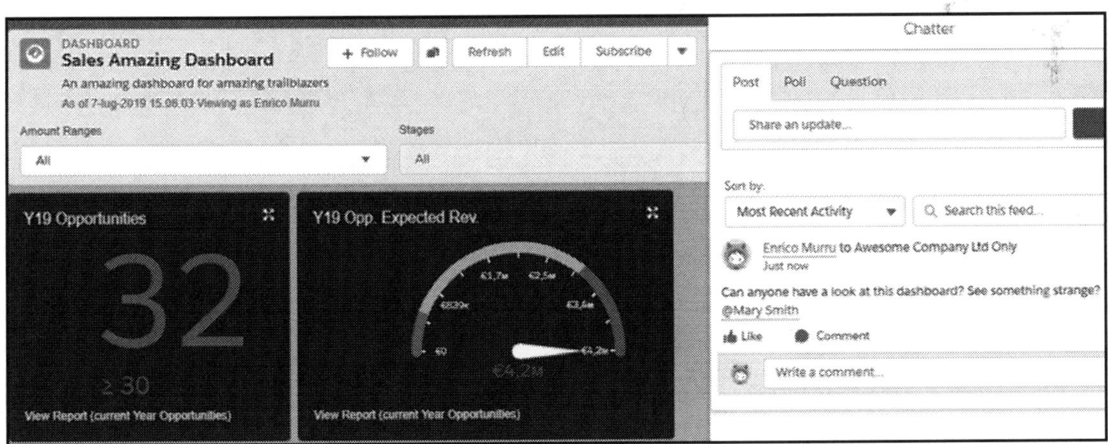

Chatter feed on dashboards

The cool thing is that by clicking the four-arrowed icon in the top-right corner of each component, we can download locally or share the component image on the Chatter feed to start collaboration on dashboards too:

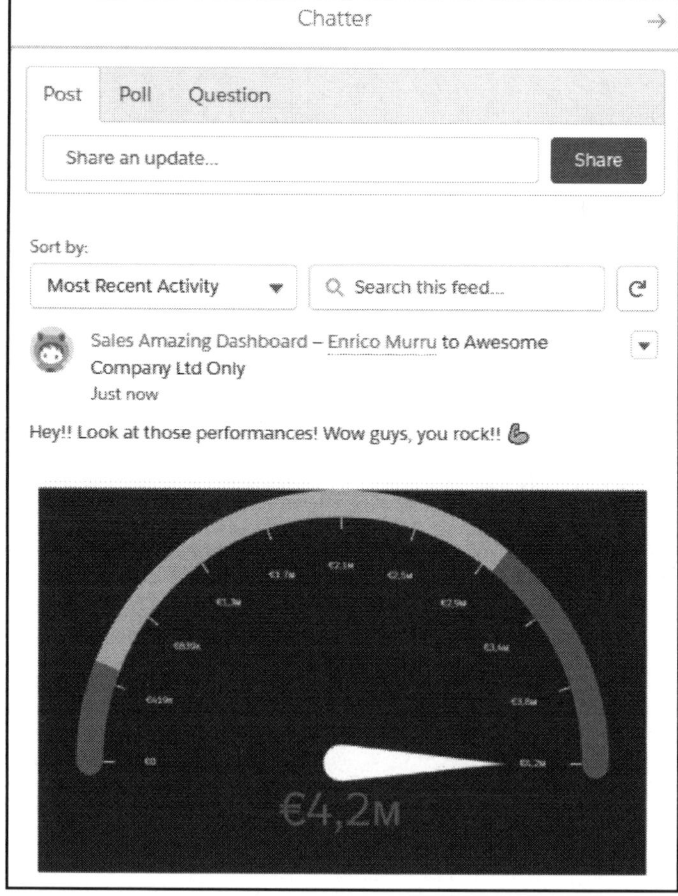

Sharing a dashboard component's image on the dashboard's Chatter feed

Lastly, you can embed dashboards on any app and home lightning page by using the **Lightning App Builder** and the **dashboard** standard lightning component. Simply add the component to your page and select the dashboard to be embedded (it has to be in a public folder):

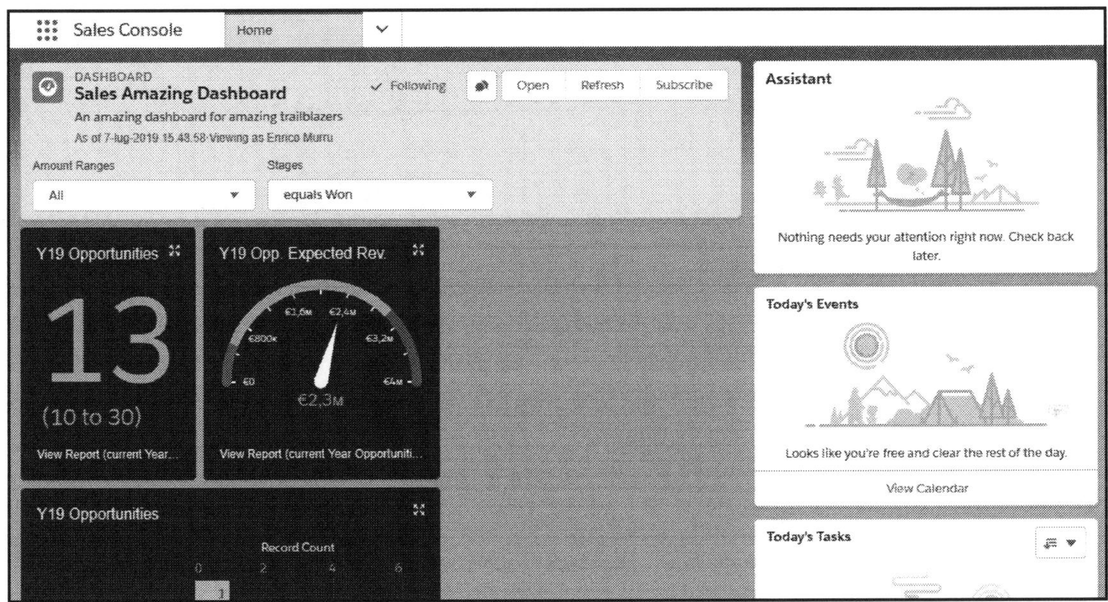

Embedded dashboard on a home lightning page

So far, we have learned how to build a dashboard and configure most of its features. In the next section, we'll be talking about how to filter dashboards.

Filtering dashboards

Before talking about filtering a dashboard, let's see the previous dashboard from the **Save As** action. Create a new **Sales Amazing Dashboard**, which will cover only opportunity-related stuff (I've added a simple metric component that shows the number of opportunities for the current year):

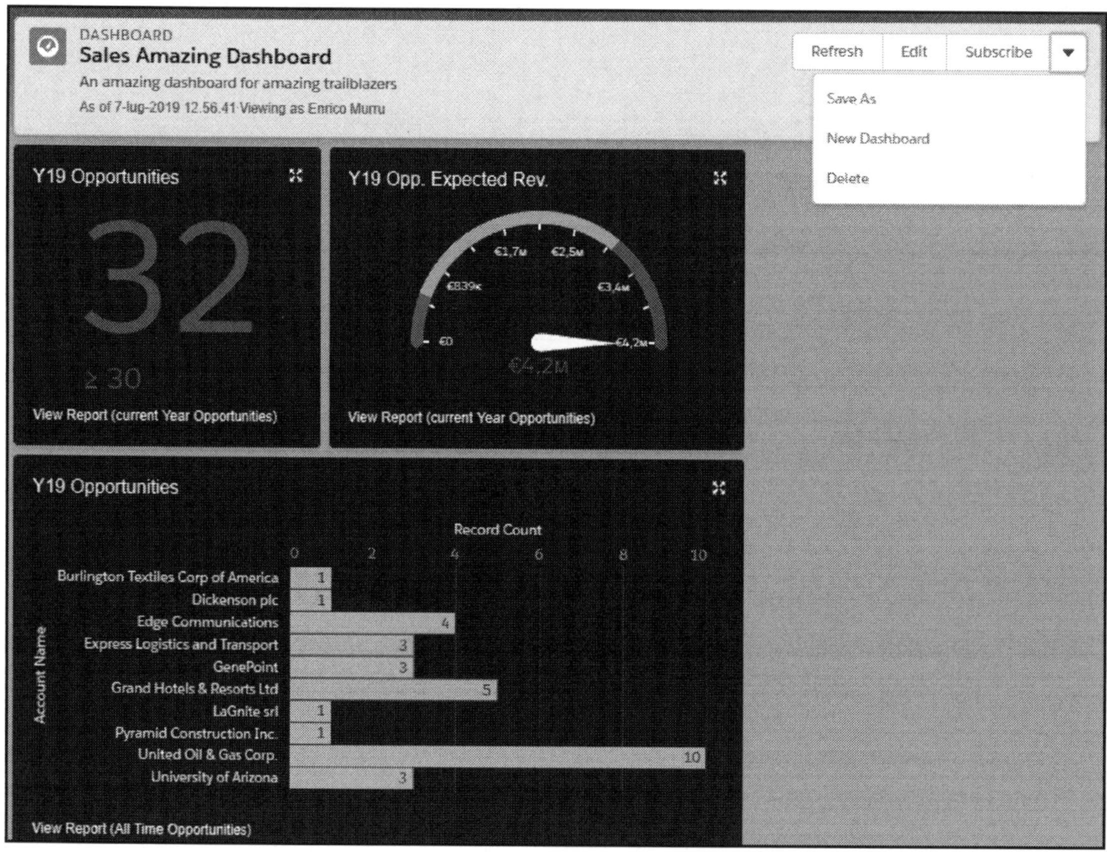

Dashboard created by cloning another dashboard using the Save As action

This feature is very useful because it allows us to create a new dashboard without starting from scratch.

Now click **Edit** on this new dashboard and then the **+ Filter** button to create a new filter:

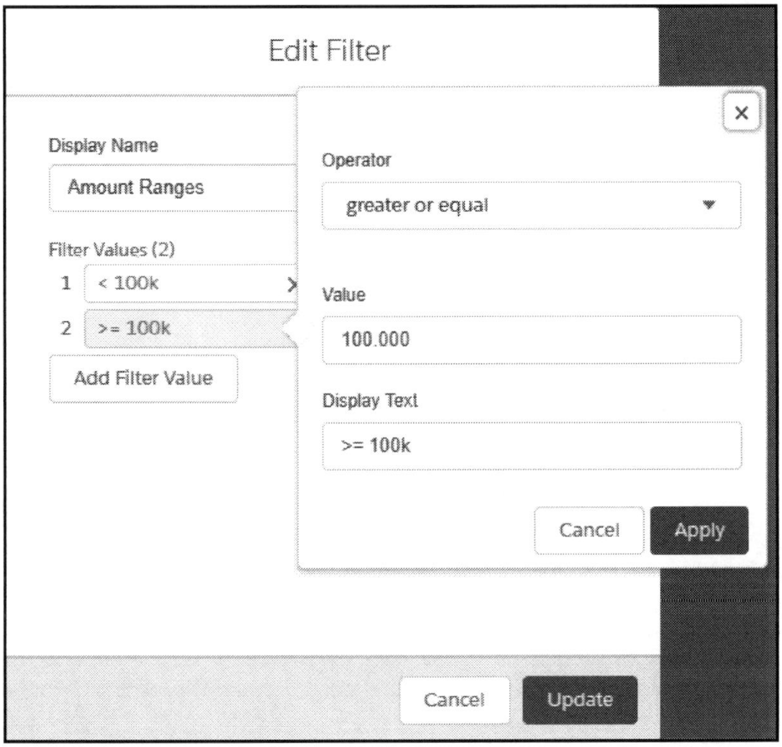

Adding a dashboard filter on a currency field

This filter is based on the **Amount** field and supports two different values:

- Amount >= 100k
- Amount < 100k

We can create another filter on opportunity stages:

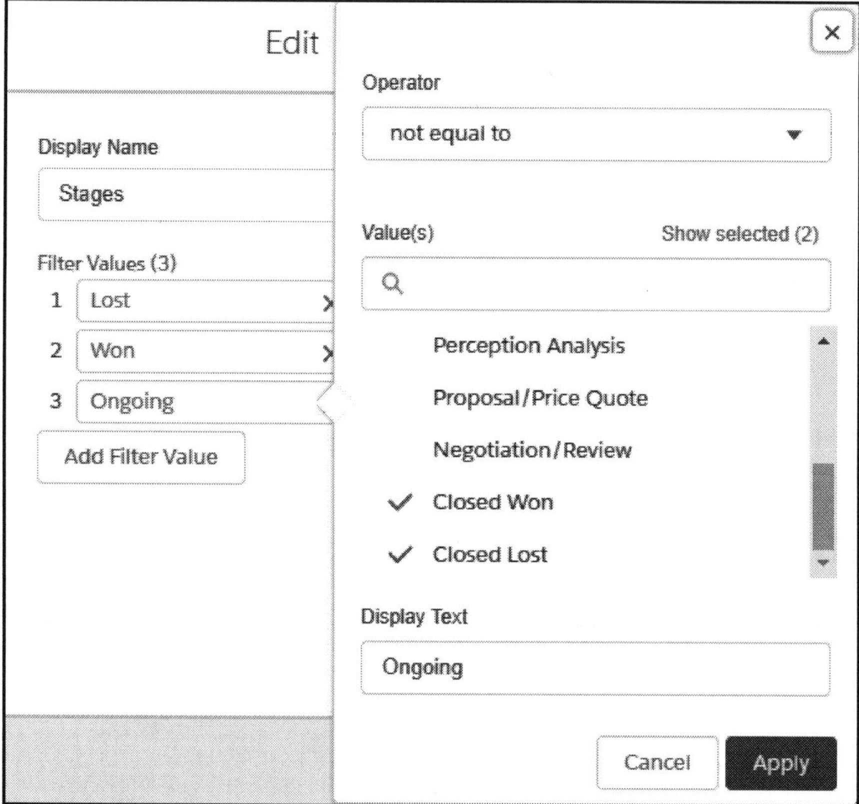

Adding a dashboard filter on a picklist field

This filter filters out the following:

- Lost opportunities
- Won opportunities
- Any other opportunity (opportunities whose stage name is not equal to **Closed Lost** or **Closed Won**)

Once you save the filter, you get a nice filter header at the top of your dashboard where anyone can filter out the results. The following screenshots show how a filter can alter the overall dashboard charts

- Given the dashboard is without any filter:

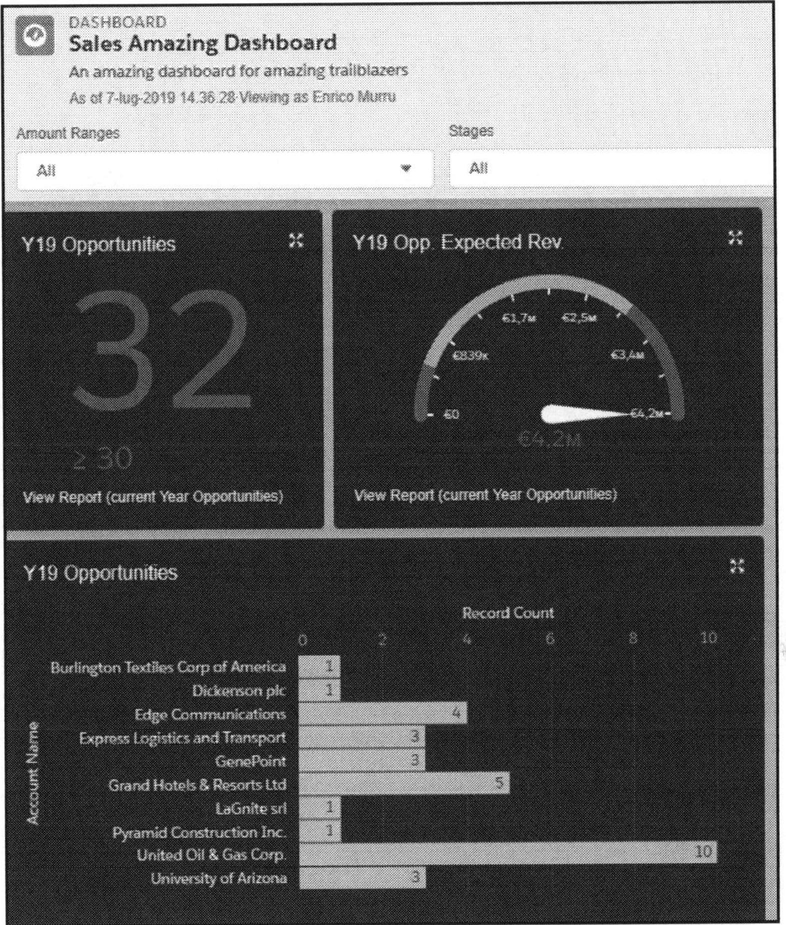

- By applying a filter on Amounts greater or equal then $100k and Stages not equal to "Ongoing" the dashboard instantly updates all the charts:

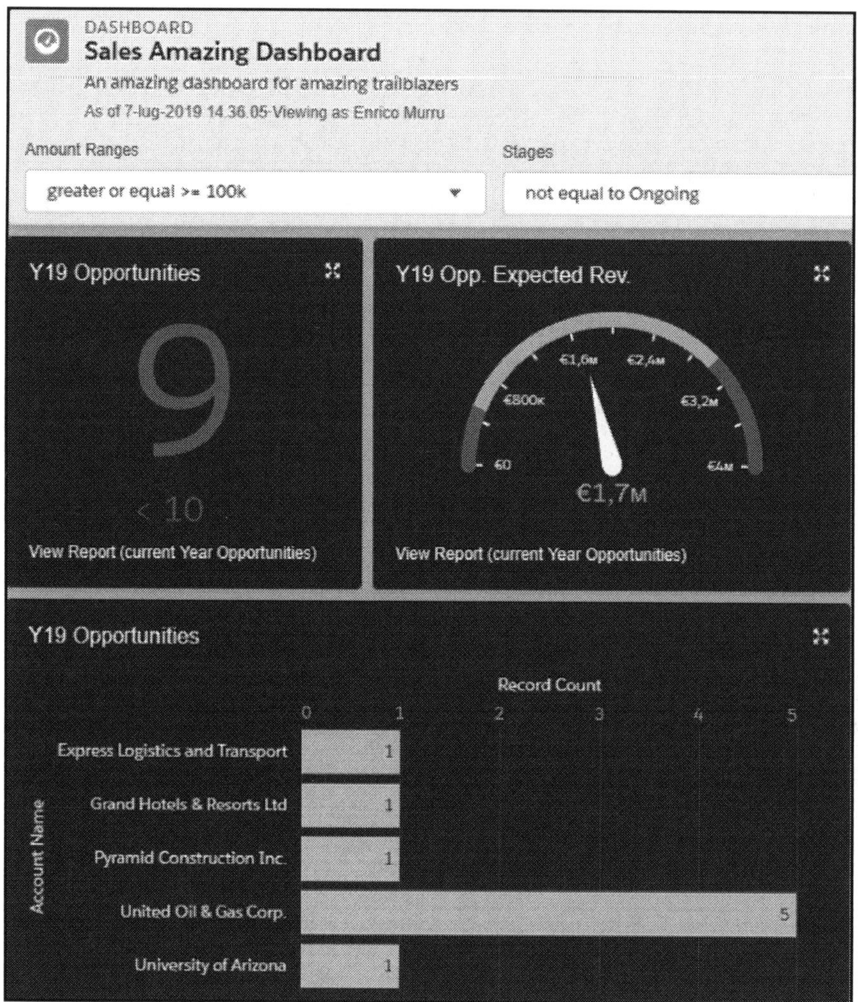

- Adding another kind of filters for Amounts less then $ 100k but with "Won" stages we can see that the dashboards changes again:

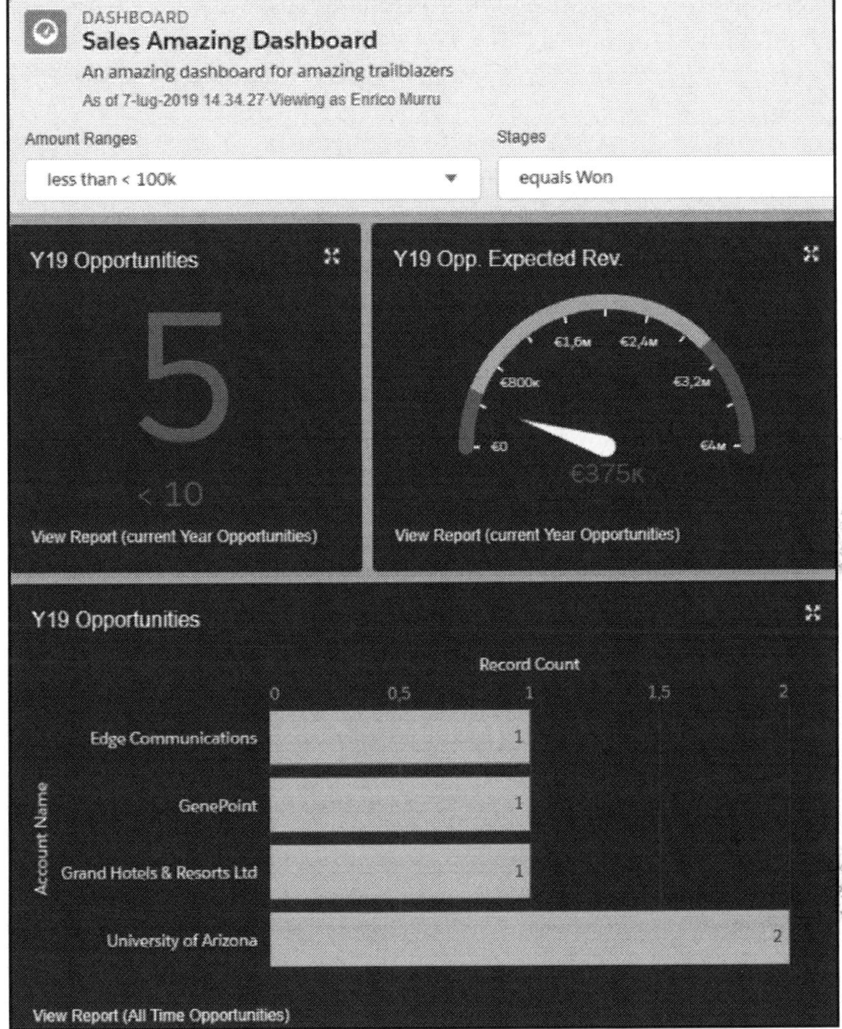

Example of the dashboard filters application

Setting up the right filters will give your users the right way to inspect insights on their org dashboards.

When selecting a field on the filter editing panel, the dashboard editor gives you a dropdown with all the fields that are common to all the reports inside the dashboard.

If you add components within a dashboard that are coming from unrelated objects, you can get an awful error message if filters are already set up that are not usable within the new component. The error message states that `The component can't be displayed because the field(s) you chose for the filter are unavailable`. Either remove the filter or the component.

Filters can be made out of picklists, lookups, and checkboxes using text, numeric, and date/datetime fields, and each filter can have up to 50 values (as of summer 2019). Filters cannot be made out of summary formulas or bucket fields.

When a filter is changed, it can take few seconds for the refresh operation to happen, and cached data is used. If you don't see the expected results, click the **Refresh** button (you can click it once every 60 seconds) or refresh the page.

The filter application is cached, so every time you run a dashboard, you get all of the previously selected filters.

Another interesting feature about filters is that we can click on chart segments to view the details of that segment on a report format, filtered by the aggregation of dashboard filters and segment filters:

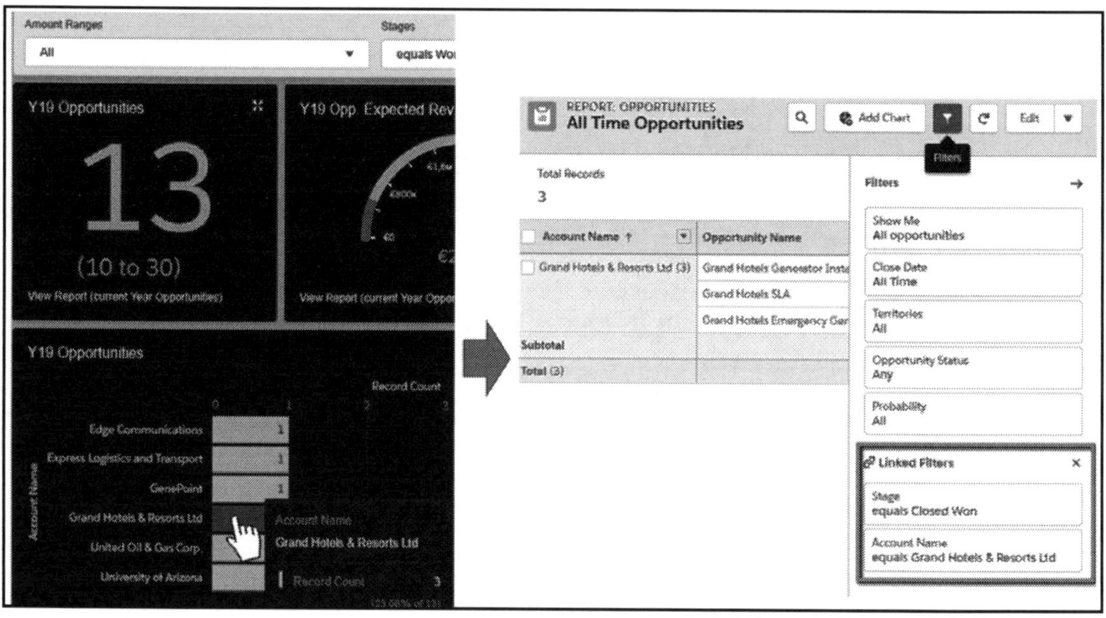

Viewing segment details on a filtered report

The **Filters** button on the report page shows all of the filters applied to the current report's view. To open the report details from the dashboard on a new tab, hold down *Ctrl/cmd* and left-click the mouse.

Subscribing to a dashboard

Dashboards are not refreshed every time we open them; that's the reason behind the refresh button.

Like reports, we can enable users to subscribe to the dashboard to refresh them automatically and receive the results by mail. We can create a daily recap of the status of the call center (unclosed cases, escalated cases, expiring SLAs, and so on) or a weekly review of ongoing deals.

Click the **Subscribe** button on the top header of a dashboard to enable a subscription; the following modal shows up:

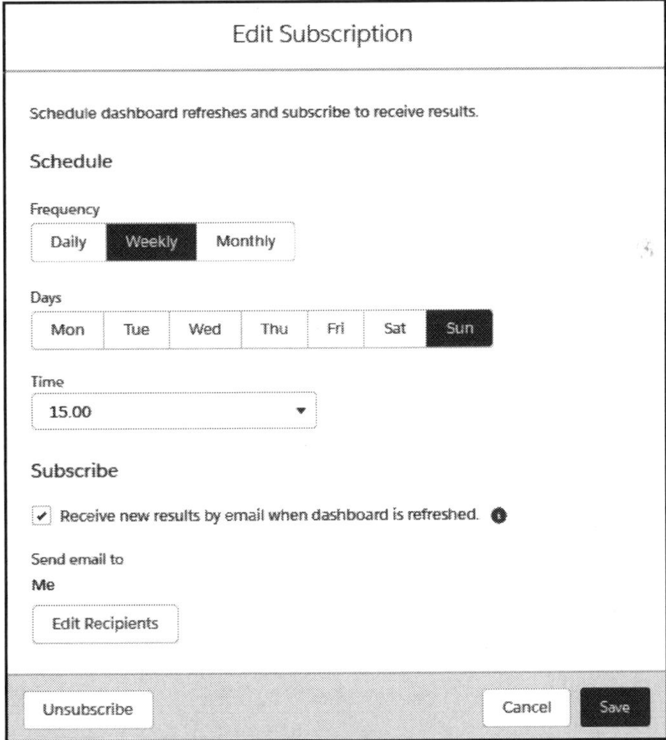

Subscription to a dashboard

We can subscribe to up to five dashboards and refresh on a daily, weekly, or monthly basis. It is possible to subscribe to our own user or other users, groups, or roles, but the dashboard must be placed inside a non-private folder (otherwise the **Edit Recipients** button will not be shown). The kind of entities you can subscribe to (users, roles or groups) depends on the folder sharing settings (which we'll see in the next few section).

Filters aren't applied when you schedule or email a dashboard. You can't schedule subscriptions for dynamic dashboards: they must be refreshed manually.

Limitations with dashboards

One of the most important limitations when dealing with dashboards is that they don't support localization, which means you cannot translate report names, filter names, or component descriptions. Take this into account when developing a multilanguage org.

Many of the limitations have already been described in the previous sections, but some (or all) of them may be upgraded on the next Salesforce releases.

For an up-to-date and detailed list of all limits that apply to dashboards and reports, refer to Salesforce Help at `https://help.salesforce.com/articleView?id=rd_dashboards_limits.htmtype=5`.

For an up-to-date and detailed list of unsupported reports and dashboard differences between Classic and Lightning Experience, refer to Salesforce Help at `https://help.salesforce.com/articleView?id=lex_gaps_limitations_analytics.htmtype=5`.

Summary

In this chapter, we have reached the end of our discussion regarding reports and dashboards. We learned everything there is to know about creating useful dashboards and reports in a way that enables your users to see how a business is going at a glance. By building new dashboards, you can create an engaging and effective view of what's happening in your org and highlight any issues in your processes' data, giving a quick overview for you to highlight pertinent information and execute the right actions to improve your business. We've seen how dashboards can be organized into folders, to limit users level of access, how they are created and configured, how reports can be charted using components, how dashboards are filtered and how users can subscribe to dashboards to get scheduled notifications upon data refresh.

In the next chapter we'll look at how to enhance our business processes using process automation features. They provide more complex data flows within our CRM and automate complex data model needs, allowing our agents to solve custom issues rather than lose time creating or updating related records one after the other, making our data even more coherent with business needs.

Questions

1. What is a dashboard?
    a. It's a collection of report tables
    b. It's a report with a chart
    c. It's a report chart
    d. It is a collection of charts that come from different reports
2. What is a dashboard component?
    a. It's a collection of report tables
    b. It's a report with a chart
    c. It's a report charted within a dashboard
    d. It is a collection of charts that come from different reports
3. A component:
    a. Can have more than one source report
    b. Can be replaced with a lightning component
    c. Can be added anywhere in the dashboard grid
    d. Can be resized within the dashboard grid
4. A dashboard viewed as **Me**:
    a. Means that any user running the dashboard will see components results as if the current user is running it
    b. Means that any user running the dashboard will see components results as if they are running it
    c. Means that any user can change the running user and see data as any other user in the org
5. It is possible to use the chart on a source report instead of creating a new chart from the dashboard component:
    a. True; you can do this using the **User chart settings from report**
    b. False; source reports cannot have a chart

6. All available charting types for reports are available on dashboard components:
    a. True
    b. False
    c. False; some are not available (such as gauge or metric charts)
    d. True; plus gauge and metric charts and lightning tables that are specific to dashboard components
7. Regarding Chatter feeds and dashboards:
    a. You can use Chatter within dashboards
    b. You can post a component's picture as a Chatter post
    c. Chatter feed is not available for the dashboard object
    d. Only reports can be shared on Chatter
8. Any dashboard can become an embedded dashboard on a lightning page unless:
    a. It is stored on a private folder
    b. It is stored on a public folder
    c. Reports are not viewable by the current user
    d. Reports are not manageable by the current user
9. Dashboard filters are applied to any component, unless:
    a. The filter has been created before the component was created and it refers to fields that are not available for that source report
    b. The filter has been created after the component was created and it refers to fields that are not available for that source report
    c. The folder is not shared with the running user
    d. The folder is shared with the running user
10. You should subscribe to a filter if:
    a. You want to automatically refresh it on a daily/monthly/weekly basis.
    b. You want to notify viewers by Chatter on a daily/monthly/weekly basis
    c. You want to notify editors by Chatter on a daily/monthly/weekly basis
    d. You want to receive a recap by email on a daily/monthly/weekly basis
11. Dashboard and report folders can be shared with:
    a. Profiles
    b. Roles
    c. Users
    d. Groups
    e. Queues

6
Section 6: Process Automation

In this section, you will learn how to deliver the best solution for process automation using the declarative tools that the Salesforce platform provides. You will also learn about the programmatic approach.

This section includes the following chapters:

- `Chapter 11`, *Automation with Workflows*
- `Chapter 12`, *Automating Record Approval with Approval Processes*
- `Chapter 13`, *Lightning Process Builder*
- `Chapter 14`, *Lightning Flows*
- `Chapter 15`, *The Coding Approach*

11
Automation with Workflows

Before closing this book, we'll dive into process automation and show the main features for providing a highly efficient process design.

In this chapter, we'll see what process automation is and which tools the Salesforce platform delivers for an administrator to enhance process automation; then we'll focus on workflow rules, a platform feature that delivers point and click automation, meant to automatically execute actions (such as field updates, and emails) on records based on specific conditions for the field, just like a programmer would do while coding, but without any code!

In this chapter, you'll learn the following:

- What process automation is
- How to build workflow rules
- How to apply different automated actions
- How time-based workflows can be set up

What is process automation?

Users are humans and so they can make mistakes, forget how things have to be done, get sick, or be affected by other impediments.

Moreover, certain business process tasks can be executed by the Customer Relationship Management system (CRM), leaving agents free to execute more brain-intensive actions—this is the scope of business process automation.

Salesforce offers more than one way to implement automation in your CRM:

- **Workflows**: Execute a different kind of action when the given criteria (field conditions in record fields) are evaluated on a given object.
- **Approvals**: Act like workflows, but the kinds of action (which are mostly the same as we'll shortly discover for workflows) are limited to record approval (for example, discount approval to an opportunity).
- **Entitlement process**: We covered this kind of automation in `Chapter 6`, *Service Cloud Applications*.
- **Lightning process builder**: This tool assists in the evolution of workflows, making more actions available (even Apex actions) and increasing criteria complexity.
- **Flows**: A point and click framework for creating multi-step wizards (to gather user data) or for creating complex and automated logic to manipulate data without user intervention for the most complex business requirements.
- **Custom code** (Apex, Lightning framework, and Visualforce): This is the developers' realm, custom code to manage both the user interface (Visualforce and Lightning framework) and automated actions (Apex triggers).

Which tool should you choose?

As David Liu (Google engineer, Salesforce MVP, and creator of the **Salesforce Coding Lessons for the 99%**, `www.sfdc99.com`) wrote in one of his greatest posts (refer to `http://www.sfdc99.com/2018/01/22/workflow-process-builder-flow-apex/`), a golden rule states that *you have to use the simplest tool for the job*, but with Lightning Experience this is no longer the case. The rule is now that it depends on the kind of environment and business type in which your organization is working.

He identified 10 categories used to classify automation tools:

- **Simplicity**: Is this tool simple enough to configure?
- **Functionality**: What kind of things can it do?
- **Limits**: Which limits may I encounter when I am running the tool?
- **Scale**: How much can the tool be extended?
- **Debugging**: Can I easily debug the tool?
- **User experience/error handling**: How does error handling work?
- **Testability**: Are out-of-the-box testing tools available?

- **Speed**: What is the speed of execution of the tool?
- **Time to deploy**: How long does it take to deploy this tool in production?
- **Risk**: What is the risk of using this tool?

Each category is given a value in a range from *Bad* to *Excellent*.

In this analysis, you won't find approvals as their features can be related to workflows.

As an example, considering complexity versus functionality, the result we obtain is as follows:

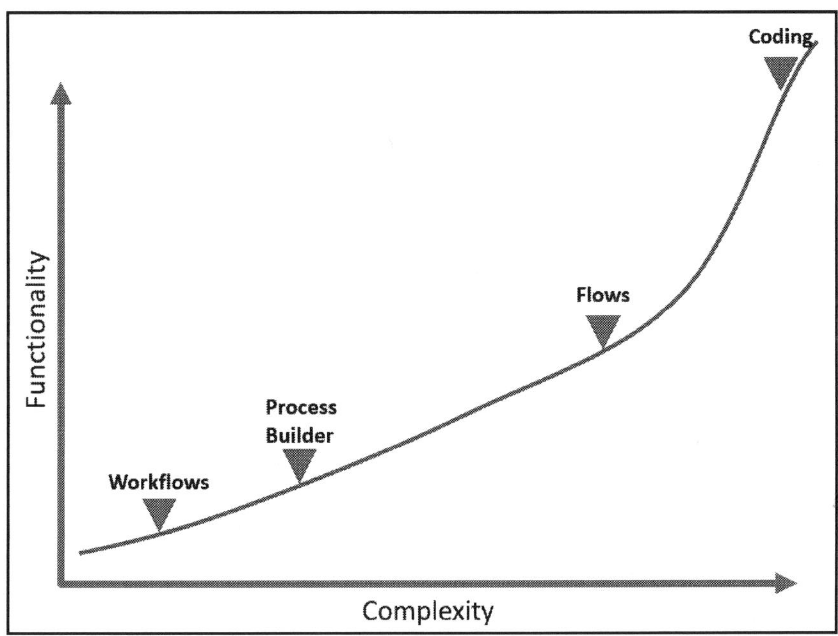

Automation tools compared over functionality versus complexity

This means that if you need high-level features with easy configurations, you need to go for workflows, while if you need complete control over what you are doing, accepting an increased level of complexity (you need to learn Apex and Visualforce/Lightning framework), go for custom coding.

Trust your team's level of experience as well: charts and graphics can give you guidance, but it will always be you, as an advanced administrator, who will have the whole picture of how your CRM is going to be built.

For an overall view of process automation tools, refer to Salesforce Help at `https://help.salesforce.com/articleView?id=process_which_tool.htmtype=5#table_intro` and scroll down to the Automation Tool Features table.

Building workflow rules

If you are on your path to become an **advanced** administrator, I assume you are already familiar workflows.

As a quick reminder, workflows are the *oldest* tool available on the Salesforce platform to run automations in an organization.

This feature is a so-called `if/then` statement tool, which means that **if** a condition is evaluated, **then** an action is performed, just like programmers code every day; for example, **if** an opportunity has an amount greater then $10 million, **then** send an email to the CEO, or **if** a case is not closed within two days, **then** set the Priority field to High—we could make list of examples.

As an example, a statement can be *if a new lead is created, then a task has to be assigned to the record owner to start a sales call;* it's easy to identify the conditional part (a lead is created) and the action part (task assignment).

Since the birth of the Lightning Process Builder automation tool, it is suggested to use it in place of workflows.

But because workflows were introduced many years ago, it is more than likely that your organization will contain workflow automations, so it is mandatory to understand how they work and what their pros and cons are.

We generally talk about workflows, but they are actually composed of two parts:

- **Workflow rule**: This is the actual workflow identified by a criterion on a given record that should trigger actions.
- **Workflow actions**: These are the actions that are performed if a criteria is matched; they can be immediate actions (for example, create a task when the case is closed) or time-dependent actions (for example, sending an email on the contact's birthday).

To create a new workflow rule, click on **Setup** | **Process Automation** | **Workflow Rules**; we already created a workflow rule called **Set Account Rating** in `Chapter 2`, *Auditing and Monitoring*, when we talked about debug logs, so you should already have a configured workflow rule on your organization. The following screenshot shows a list of current workflows in your org:

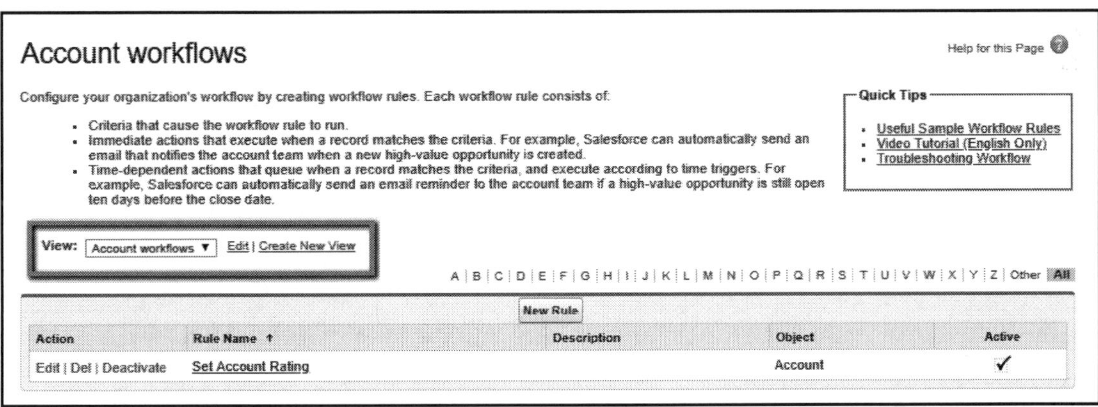

Workflow rules list

Especially when our organization is full of rules across diverse objects, creating a new list view can be more than helpful (in the previous screenshot, the **Account workflows** view was chosen).

When we create a new workflow rule, after object selection, you can select the **evaluation criteria**, which are the conditions under which the rule is evaluated regarding record creation/update. The available values are as follows:

- **Created**: The rule is evaluated only when a record is created, which means the record update is ignored. This kind of evaluation criteria guarantees that the workflow rule is triggered only once per record.
- **Created and every time it's edited**: This evaluation type runs the workflow every time the record is created and updated as long as it meets the rule conditions. This means that if you update the record without changing any field (for example, you edit and save the record without changing any field on the record layout), the workflow executes every time (if the rule matches). With this configuration, no time-dependent action can be related.
- **Created and any time it's edited to subsequently meet criteria**: This is the default evaluation criteria, and it is executed when the record is created or when it's updated, but its field values go from not meeting criteria conditions to meeting them. This time the rule can run multiple times but not if an update is done to fields unrelated to the rule criteria. As an example, if the rule criteria is based on the **Lead Status** field to equal **Open - Not Contacted**, when the record is created with this value the rule runs. If we change the value of **Working - Contacted** the rule doesn't fire, but if we change the value back to **Open – Not contacted** the rule fires again.

Along with evaluation criteria type, we can choose the actual rule criteria, which can be a simple *field-operator-value* list with an and/or logic or a formula that should be evaluated to *true;* use the second format if you need complex logic and access to related objects (for example, accessing **Account** fields from contact objects or record type related logic).

The following screenshot shows a simple lead-based workflow rule configuration:

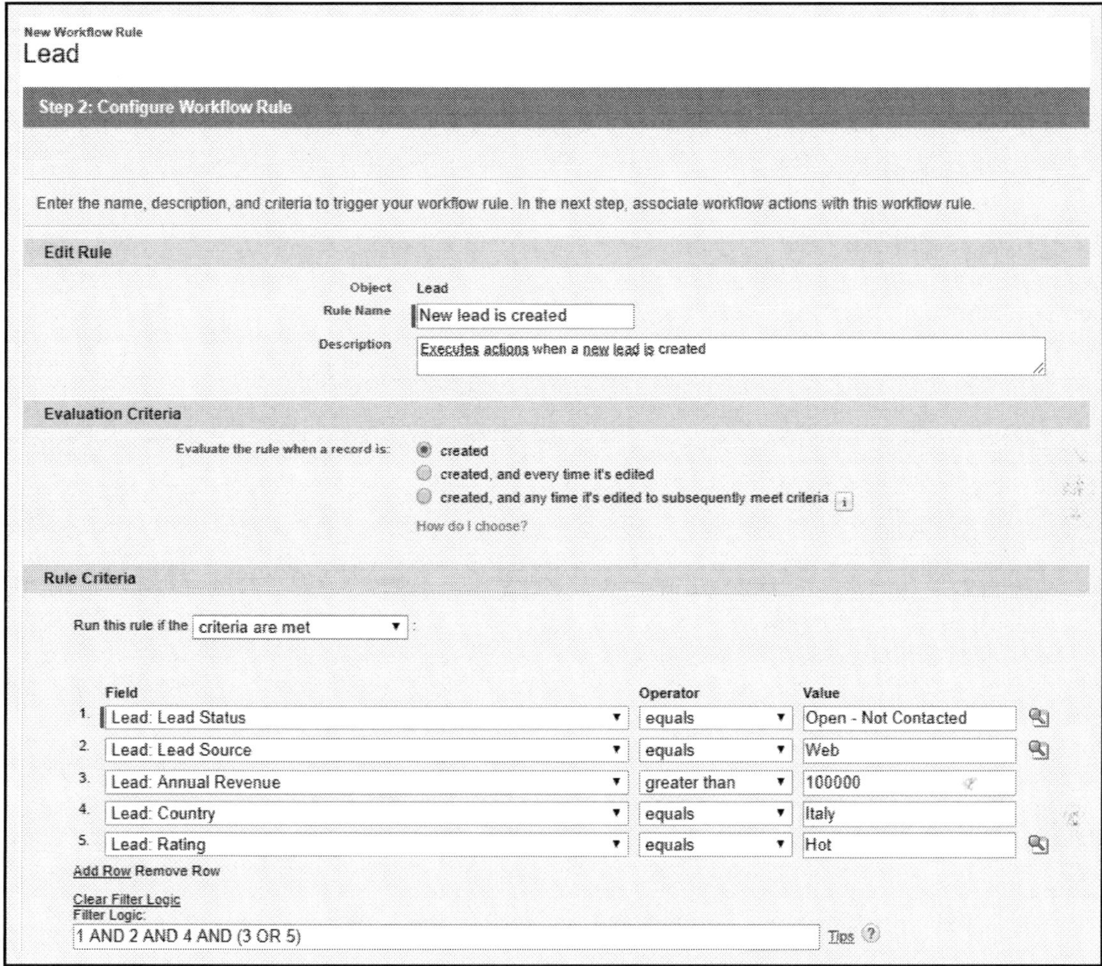

Example of a lead workflow rule with simple criteria conditions

In this example, the rule triggers the lead object when it is created and evaluates to the following criteria:

- **Lead: Lead Status** is `Open - Not connected`.
- **Lead: Lead Source** is `Web`.
- **Lead: Country** is `Italy`.
- **Lead: Annual Revenue** is greater than `100000` or its **Rating** is `Hot`.

You can add up to 25 filter criteria with up to 255 characters each.

Using the formula criteria, this should have been written as follows:

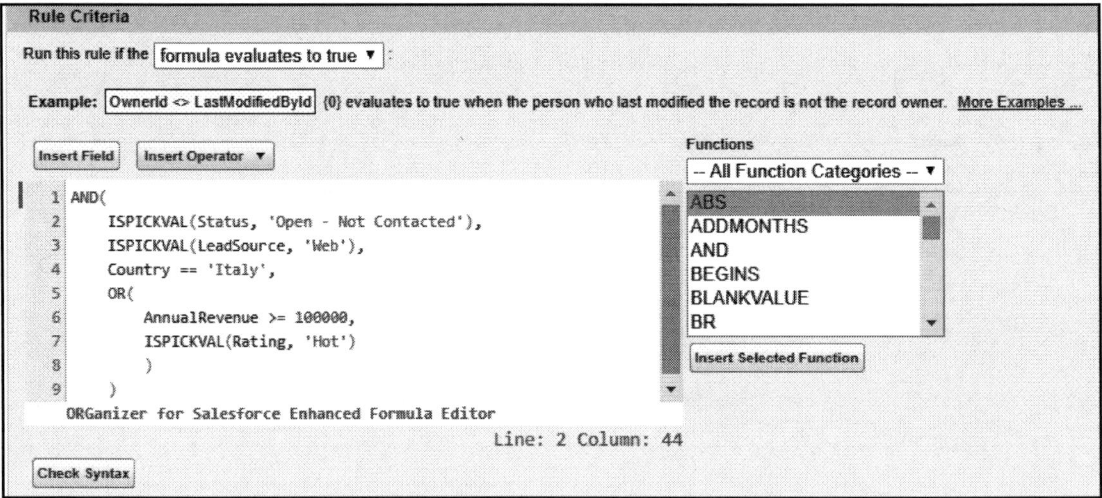

Example of formula criteria for workflow rules

Once you click the **Save and Next** button, the workflow is saved (though inactive) and you are required to add actions (we can add existing actions or create new ones):

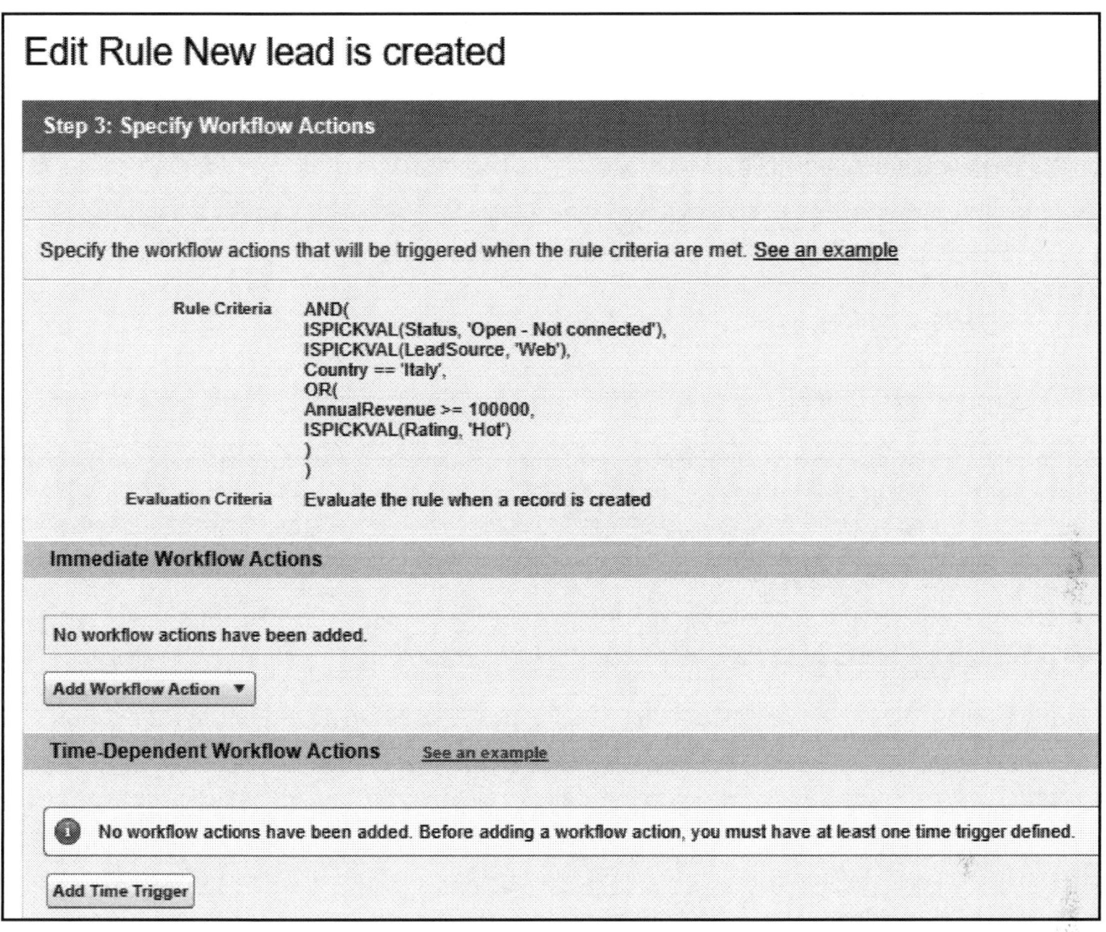

Action selection on workflow creation

As we've said, we can now add immediate actions (that is, actions executed in the same *context* as the record creation event) or time-dependent actions (that is, based on some time-dependent condition, which we'll discover later), but before adding actions, let's look at the kind of actions we can add to a workflow rule.

Automated actions

When a workflow rule's criteria is matched, the related actions (called **automated actions**) are executed: they can be built and reused whenever necessary, meaning that more than one workflow can trigger the same actions.

Workflows can use the following actions:

- Field update
- Task creation
- Email alert
- Outbound message

All these actions can be used on the approval and entitlement processes as well. Only email alerts can be used in flows and the Lightning Process Builder.

We'll see them in the following sections.

Field updates

Field update action is self-explanatory: it can be used to update a field of the target object of the workflow (and even other related objects, as we'll see shortly).

Let's say that our company mostly sell to Italian customers with an high annual revenue, so if a lead comes from Italy and the web source and the annual revenue is up to $100,000, it should automatically be promoted to a **Hot** rating. This is a valid configuration for the example field update:

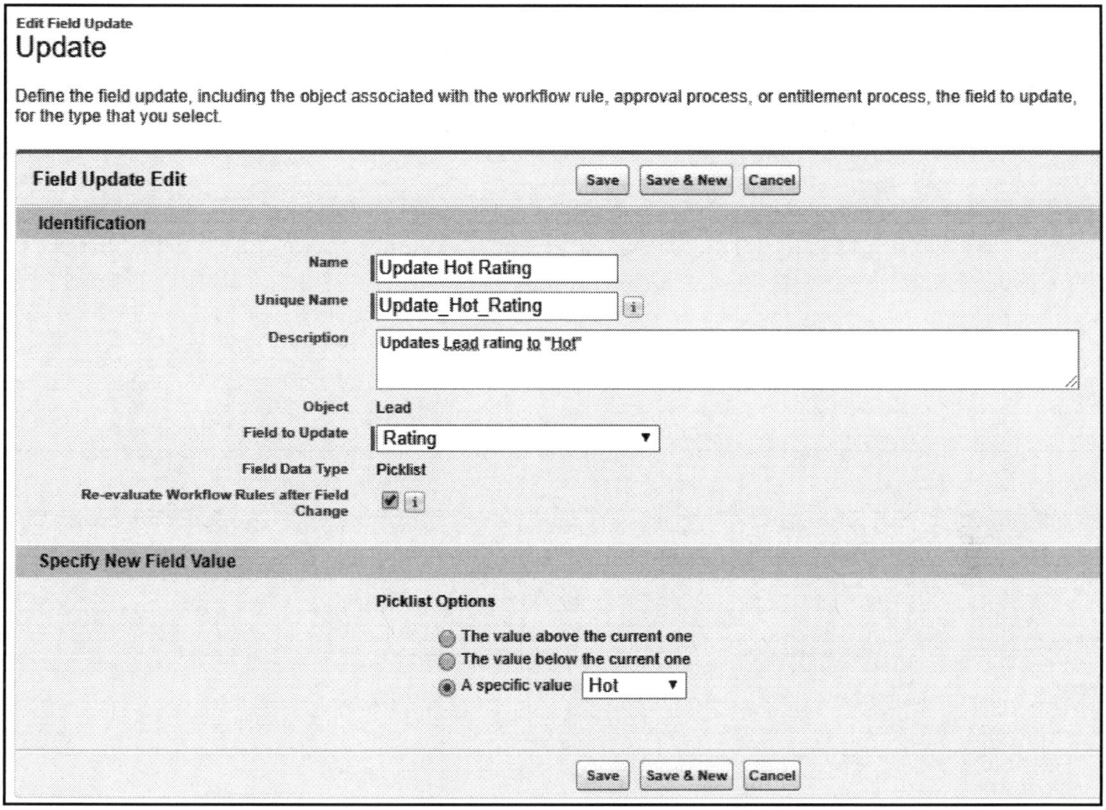

Field update configuration

Besides the usual name and unique name system fields, the object type is already filled in (**Lead**) and the **Field to Update** box has to be filled in with the chosen field, **Rating** in our example.

Being a picklist value, you can select listed values only (you cannot set unlisted values with a field update action); you can even tell the action to choose the previous value or the next value in the picklist, given the current value.

This means that if the lead is created with a Warm rating value, the system can autonomously choose the previous/above value (Hot) or the next/below value (Cold); this is valid for picklist fields only.

The **Re-evaluate Workflow Rules after Field Change** option allows another workflow rule evaluation (meaning any lead workflow and not only the current one) if this field update actually changes the source lead field (no workflow is further evaluated if the lead is created with the Hot rating, in this example)—this is needed if we have a special behavior related to the rating field (there may be other workflows on the rating field, after all).

If the target field is not a picklist (for example, a text field), you can select to put a blank value or use a formula field to calculate a value; in the following example, we'll be using the **Description** field to concatenate some critical fields in a readable format:

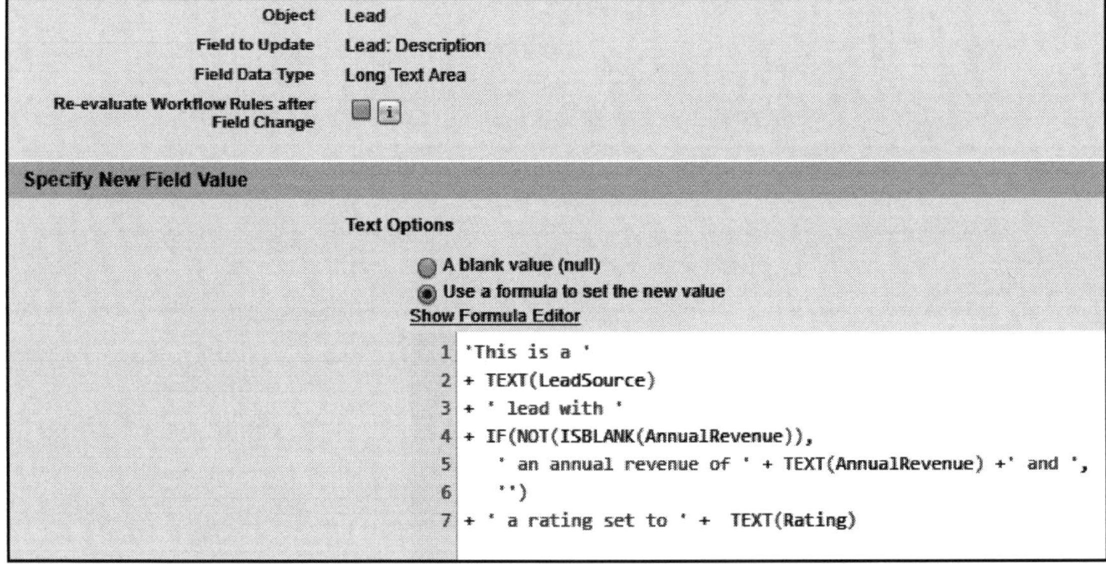

Field update with formula

In this example, we don't want the workflow to be re-evaluated (it's just a description field); the formula is used to create a description such as *"This is a lead with an annual revenue of 100,000 and a rating set to Warm."*

Once the following field updates have been created and associated with the workflow, activate it by using the **Activate** button:

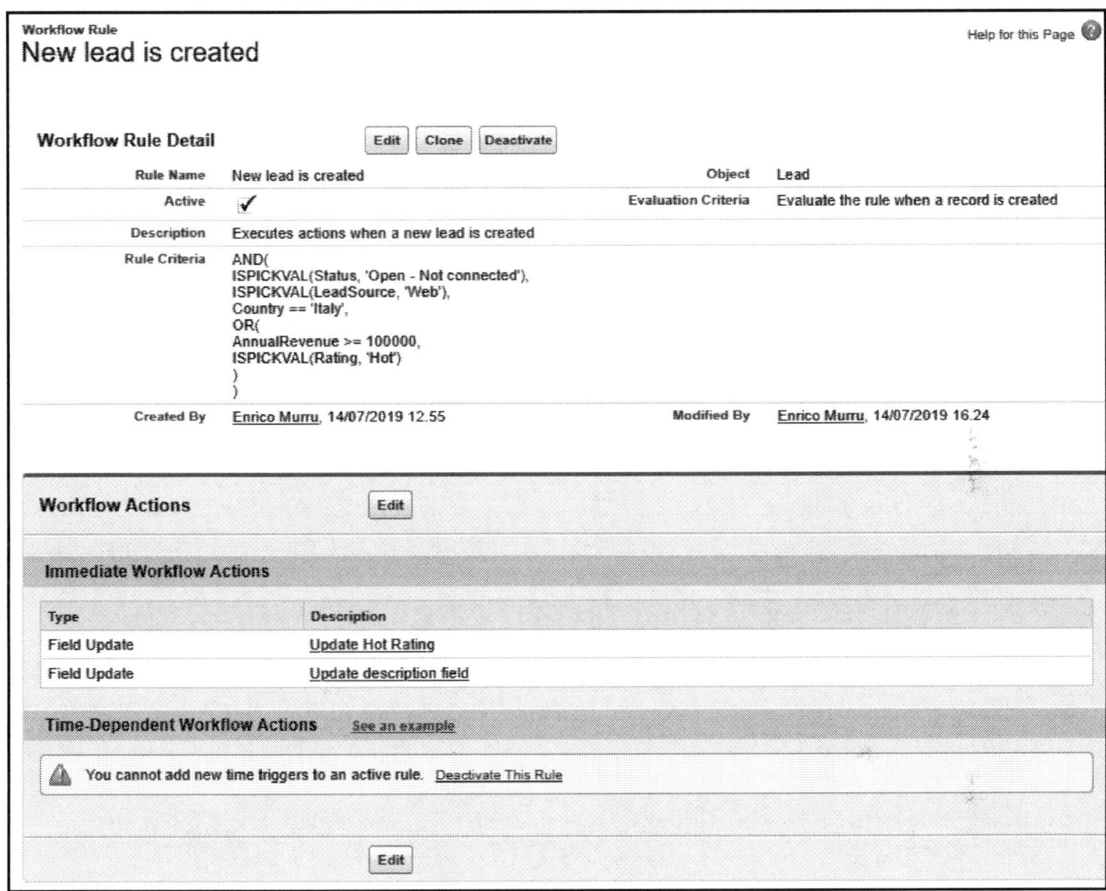

Activated workflow rule with two field update actions

Let's now create a new lead with the following values:

- **Lead Source**: **Web**
- **Annual Revenue**: **1,000,000**
- **Lead Status**: **Open - Not Contacted**

- **Rating**: **Hot**
- **Country**: **Italy**

The following picture shows the new lead:

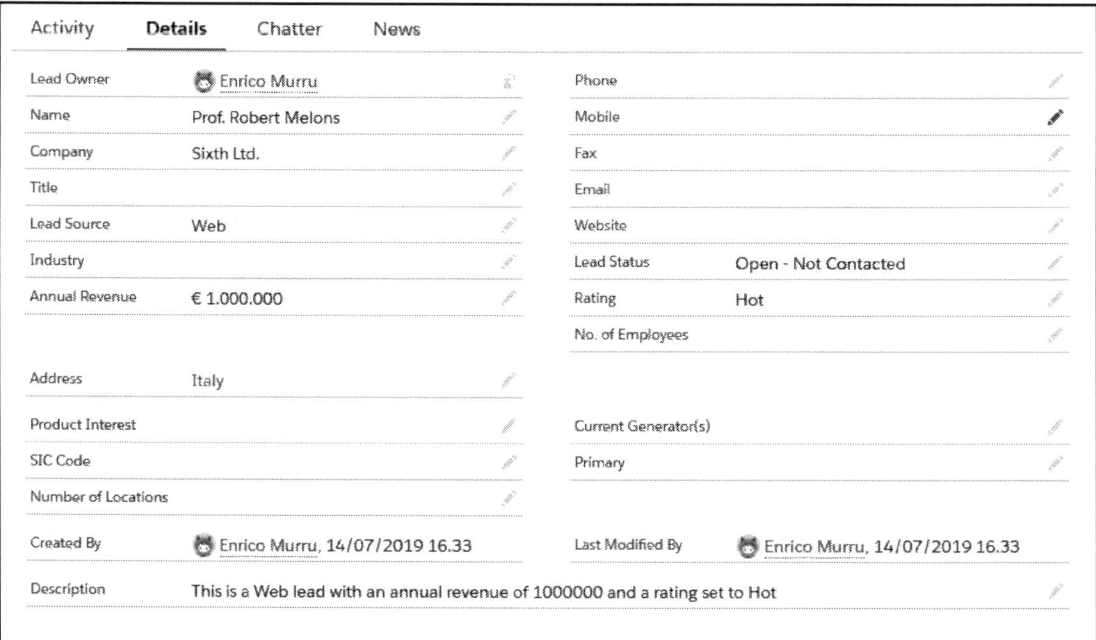

Workflow rule applied to a new lead

The rating field has been updated to **Hot**, and the description is filled in with a readable description with a concatenation of the most important key fields.

With field updates, it is also possible to select a new record owner by selecting the owner field, a user, or a queue (if a queue is available for the target object) and even notify the new owner (via email) of the new ownership, as shown in this screenshot:

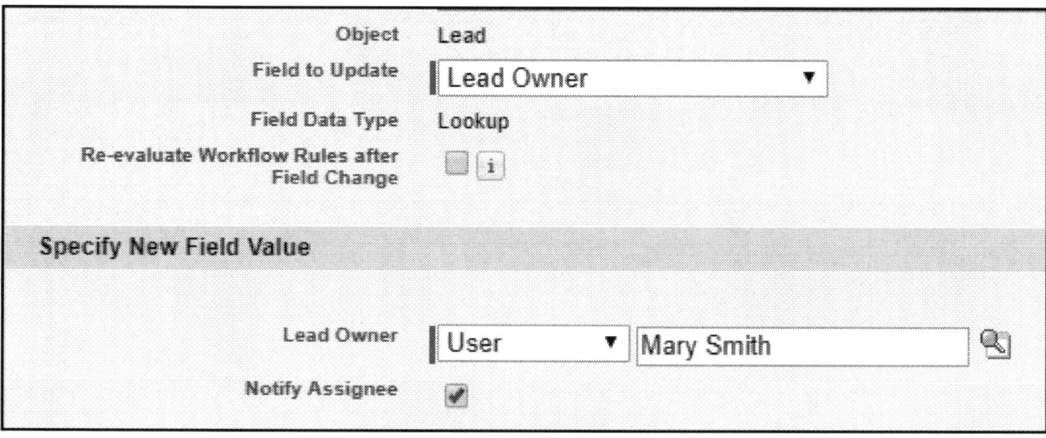

Owner field update

This can be an alternative way to assign records (remember that the lead object has its own assignment rules, along with the case object).

Remember the following peculiarities of field updates:

- Field updates are executed before email alerts, tasks, and outbound messages, but after case/lead assignment and auto-response rules.
- Field-level security is not enforced (they can update any field, even if current users don't have access).
- Field updates are shown on debug logs.
- If **field history tracking** is enabled and field update actions are executed on tracked fields, they'll be displayed on the history related list.
- Validation rules are executed before workflow execution, so it is possible to update a field, making its object inconsistent with its validation rules.
- A field that can be set to blank (null) by a field update cannot be set as required.

Cross-object field updates

When an object is a child of another object, it is possible to update a parent object field from a child object field update; this feature only works on custom-to-custom, custom-to-standard, and some standard-to-standard master-detail relationships.

Only the following parent standard objects are supported in custom-to-standard master details:

- Account
- Asset
- Campaign
- Case
- Contact
- Contract
- Contract line item
- Entitlement
- Opportunity
- Order
- Question
- Quote
- Service Contract
- Solution

For standard-to-standard master-details, these are the only supported field updates:

- Case comments updating a case
- Email updating a case
- Opportunity product updating an opportunity
- Opportunity updating an account

The special standard relation field updates cannot be used in approvals, though.

It is possible to update a parent record even if the user can't access it.

Task actions

This kind of automated action is quite straightforward; it is used to create a new task assigned to a specific user.

Here it is an example of a task action:

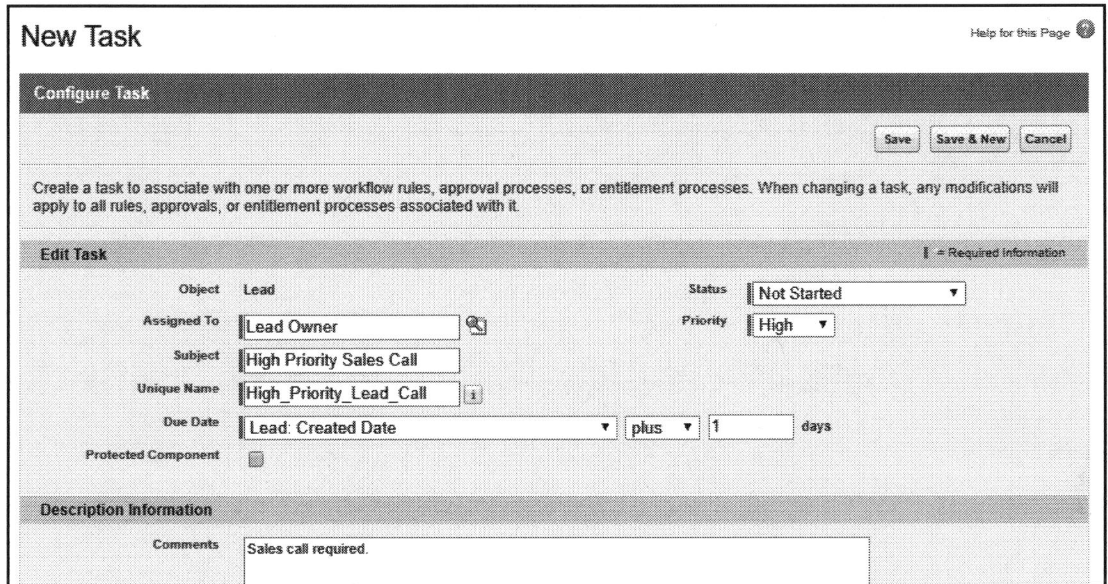

Example of task action

A new task is created with the following:

- **Task owner**: This can be an object owner, a specific user (internal or partner), or a role (internal or partner).
- **Task Subject**: free text to add a subject to the task
- **Due Date:** Select a specific date (trigger date, target/related object date fields, or user date fields) plus/minus a predefined amount of days.
- **Status:** Taken from the task status field.
- **Priority:** Same as the status.
- **Comments**: free text for task comments

After successful task action execution, this is what you see on the lead object:

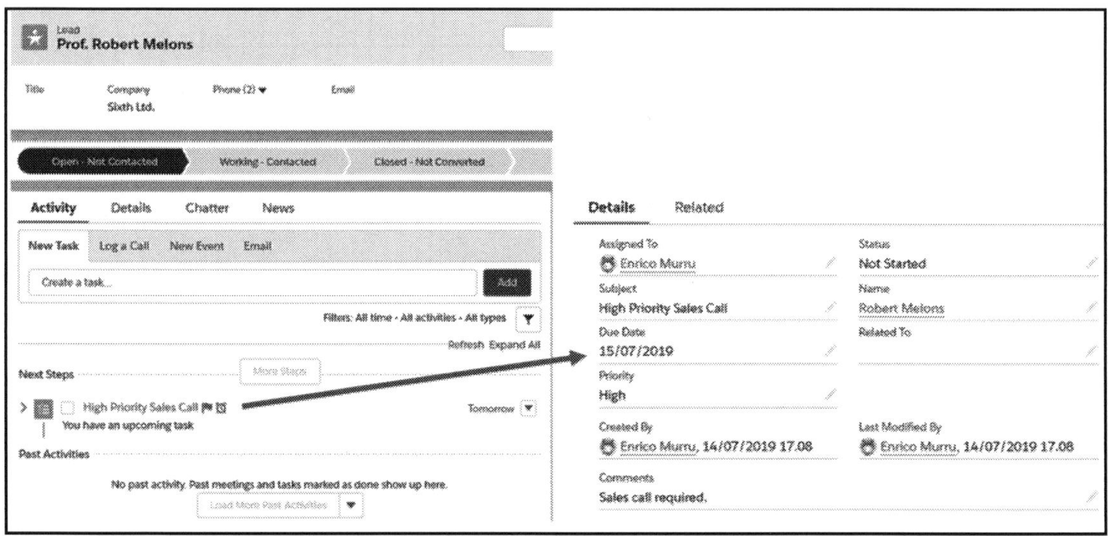

Task created from a task action on a lead record

Email alert actions

We have seen how to create an email alert in `Chapter 6`, *Service Cloud Applications*, when we dealt with entitlement processes—we created an email alert when case SLAs were hit.

We will create a new email alert to notify the user that the lead has not been contacted for two days (we'll be using time-dependent actions in the next sections), but for the moment we'll attach it as an immediate action on the same lead workflow.

First, create a new email template from **Setup** | **Email** | **Classic Email Templates**:

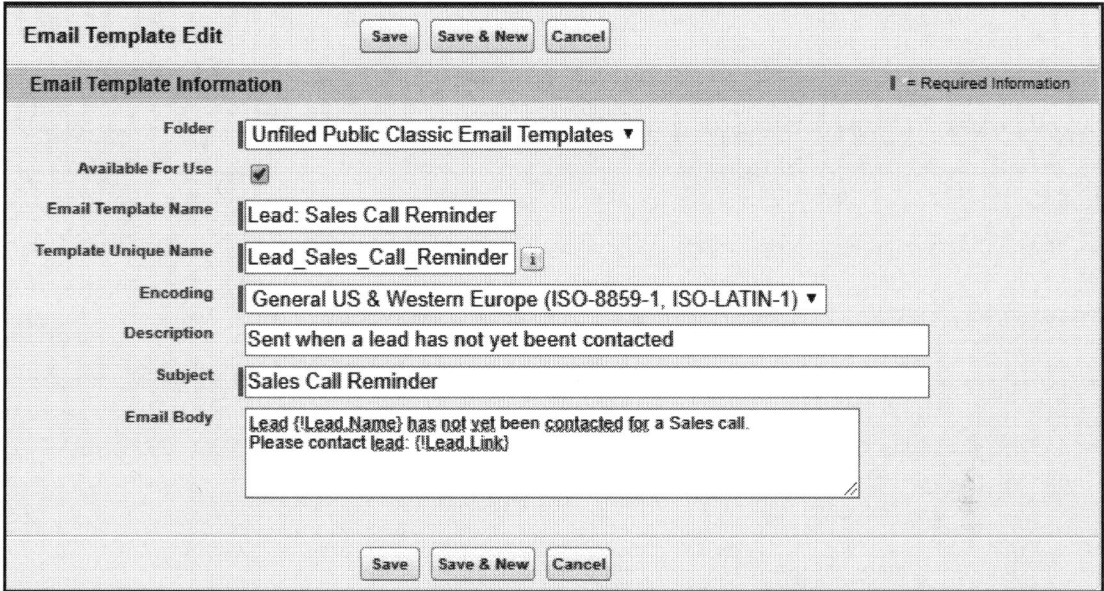

Email template example for an email alert action

Now let's create a new email alert action:

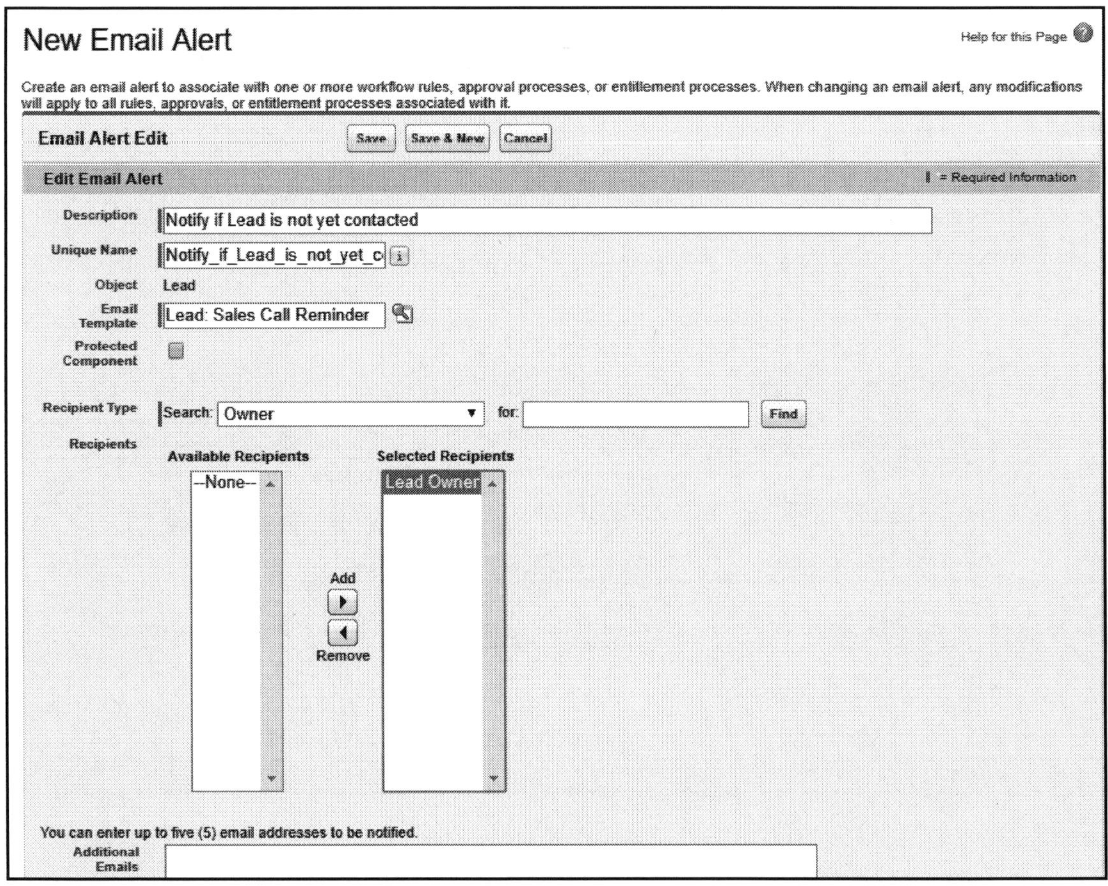

Email alert action example

We can select the following:

- Email template: The one created in the previous screenshot.
- Recipients: The lead owner is selected, but you can choose other options (for more info about recipients, refer to Salesforce Help at `https://help.salesforce.com/articleView?id=customize_wfalerts_recipienttypes.htm type=5#workflow_field_updates_reevalute_wf`).
- Additional email addresses that are not Salesforce users, leads, or contacts (up to five).

This is the result as the action is executed:

Example of email received after email alert action execution

There is an important limitation to consider when implementing email alerts: the daily allocation for emails sent with email alerts is 1,000 per the standard Salesforce license (except for the developer edition and trial organizations, where the limit is 15), up to 2 million.

Outbound message actions

Outbound messages are used to send some of the record data to an external system (it can be an ERP, an inventory system, a product management system, or whatever your CRM is integrated with).

Although outbound message actions can be configured in point and click mode, they require a bit of developer's knowledge to make everything work: the remote system needs to implement a specific set of APIs so that it can be able to get the message and reply correctly.

This can be a valid configuration for a lead-based outbound message:

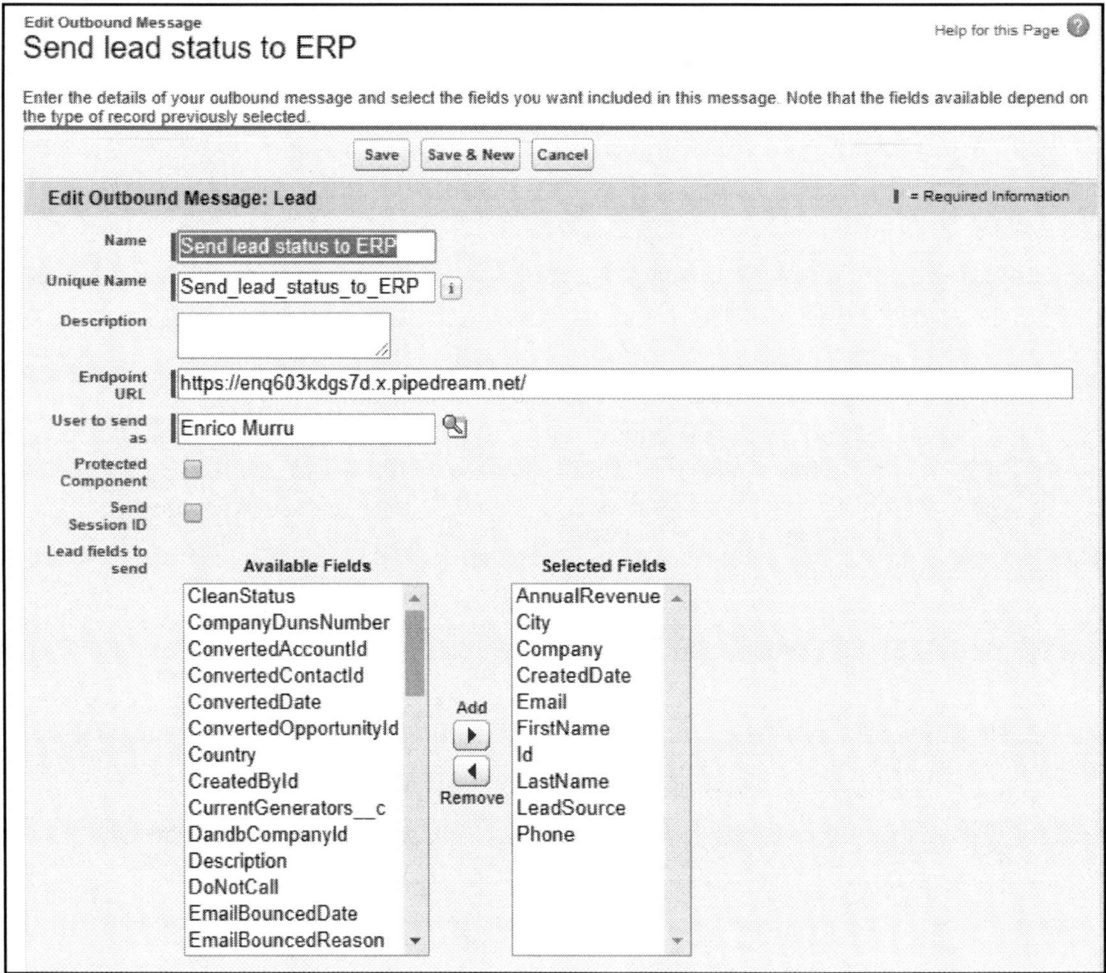

Outbound message configuration

This configuration states the following—when the automation triggers this action (it can be a workflow rule, an approval, or entitlement process) the external system identified by a remote endpoint URL is notified with a selection of the object fields (nothing can come from other related objects).

To test it out and see what message is actually sent between systems, open `https://requestbin.com/` and hit **Create a Request Bin** (deselect the **Private** checkbox); a request bin is an automated software that accepts any request that comes on its endpoint (there are several tools online that provide the same features for free).

Once the bin is created, you are provided with a dedicated endpoint that you can use to test outbound messages:

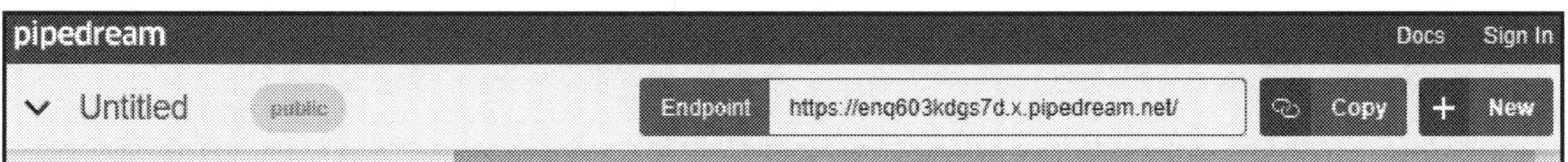

Request bin dedicated endpoint

From now on, the service stays idle and waits for any incoming request (called HTTP requests).

Create a new lead to trigger the workflow rule, and in a few seconds you'll see an upcoming request on **Request Bin**:

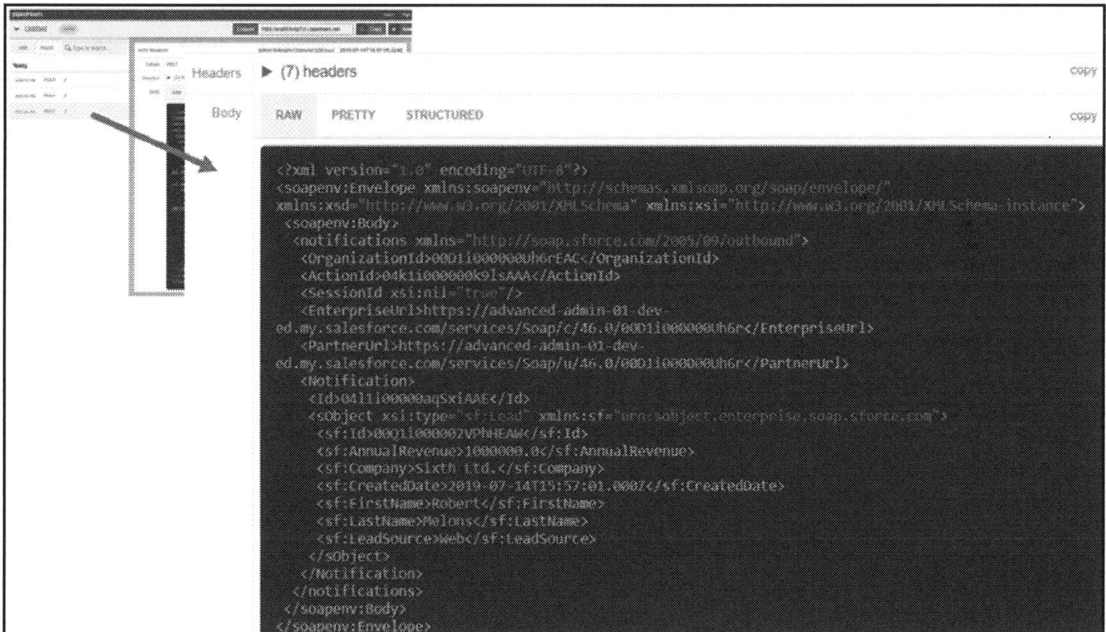

Example of outbound message received on the remote system

This is an XML formatted message; in the middle part, the **Notification** tag conveys the lead fields we selected on the outbound message.

If you keep waiting, you'll see other requests coming—this is a result of the missed implementation on the Request Bin side. It accepts any incoming requests, but it is not able to respond as Salesforce expects, but that is another story.

For further details on implementation using **Outbound Messages**, refer to Salesforce Help at `https://developer.salesforce.com/docs/atlas.en-us.api.meta/api/sforce_api_om_outboundmessaging.htm`.

You can monitor outbound message delivery status from **Setup** | **Environments** | **Monitoring** | **Outbound Messages**:

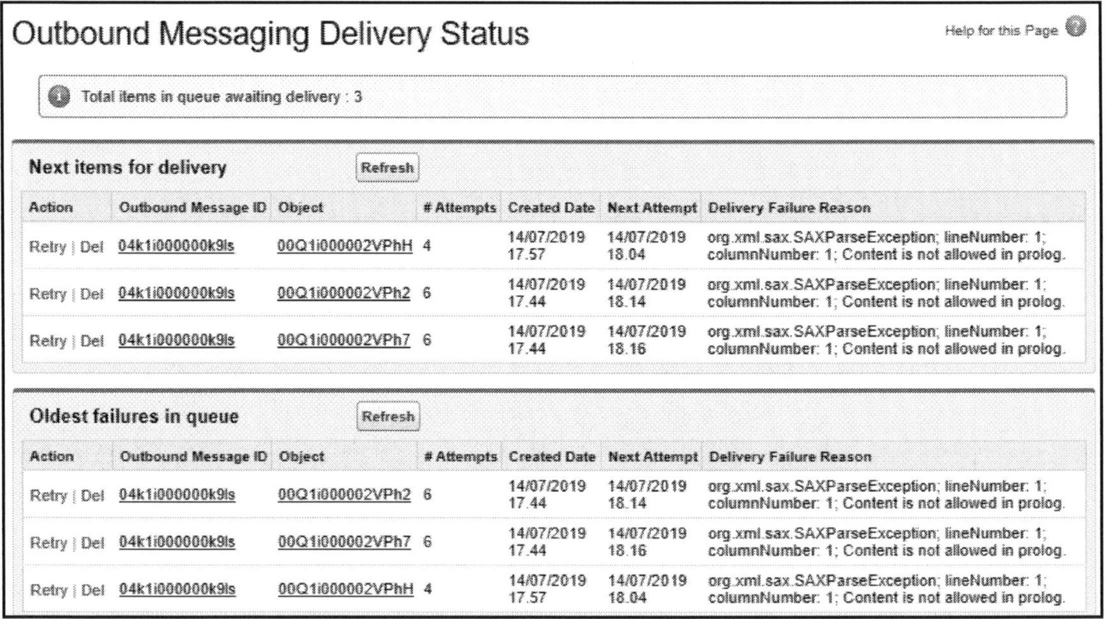

Outbound Messaging Delivery Status

Help for this Page

Total items in queue awaiting delivery : 3

Next items for delivery — Refresh

Action	Outbound Message ID	Object	# Attempts	Created Date	Next Attempt	Delivery Failure Reason
Retry | Del	04k1i000000k9ls	00Q1i000002VPhH	4	14/07/2019 17.57	14/07/2019 18.04	org.xml.sax.SAXParseException; lineNumber: 1; columnNumber: 1; Content is not allowed in prolog.
Retry | Del	04k1i000000k9ls	00Q1i000002VPh2	6	14/07/2019 17.44	14/07/2019 18.14	org.xml.sax.SAXParseException; lineNumber: 1; columnNumber: 1; Content is not allowed in prolog.
Retry | Del	04k1i000000k9ls	00Q1i000002VPh7	6	14/07/2019 17.44	14/07/2019 18.16	org.xml.sax.SAXParseException; lineNumber: 1; columnNumber: 1; Content is not allowed in prolog.

Oldest failures in queue — Refresh

Action	Outbound Message ID	Object	# Attempts	Created Date	Next Attempt	Delivery Failure Reason
Retry | Del	04k1i000000k9ls	00Q1i000002VPh2	6	14/07/2019 17.44	14/07/2019 18.14	org.xml.sax.SAXParseException; lineNumber: 1; columnNumber: 1; Content is not allowed in prolog.
Retry | Del	04k1i000000k9ls	00Q1i000002VPh7	6	14/07/2019 17.44	14/07/2019 18.16	org.xml.sax.SAXParseException; lineNumber: 1; columnNumber: 1; Content is not allowed in prolog.
Retry | Del	04k1i000000k9ls	00Q1i000002VPhH	4	14/07/2019 17.57	14/07/2019 18.04	org.xml.sax.SAXParseException; lineNumber: 1; columnNumber: 1; Content is not allowed in prolog.

Outbound message delivery logs

This is the list of messages that, from the Salesforce point of view, have not been correctly delivered to the external system. If the error was caused by a temporary system flaw, by hitting retry you can send again the given notification, although the system will continue its retries for 24 hours with an exponential interval between retries of up to two hours.

Time-dependent actions

Actions can be executed hours or days after a given date.

To add time-dependent actions, the workflow must be inactive and the evaluation criteria must not be set to **Evaluate the rule when a record is created**, and any time it's edited to subsequently meet the criteria.

Remove the **Notify if Lead is not yet contacted** email alert from the immediate actions, as shown in the following screenshot:

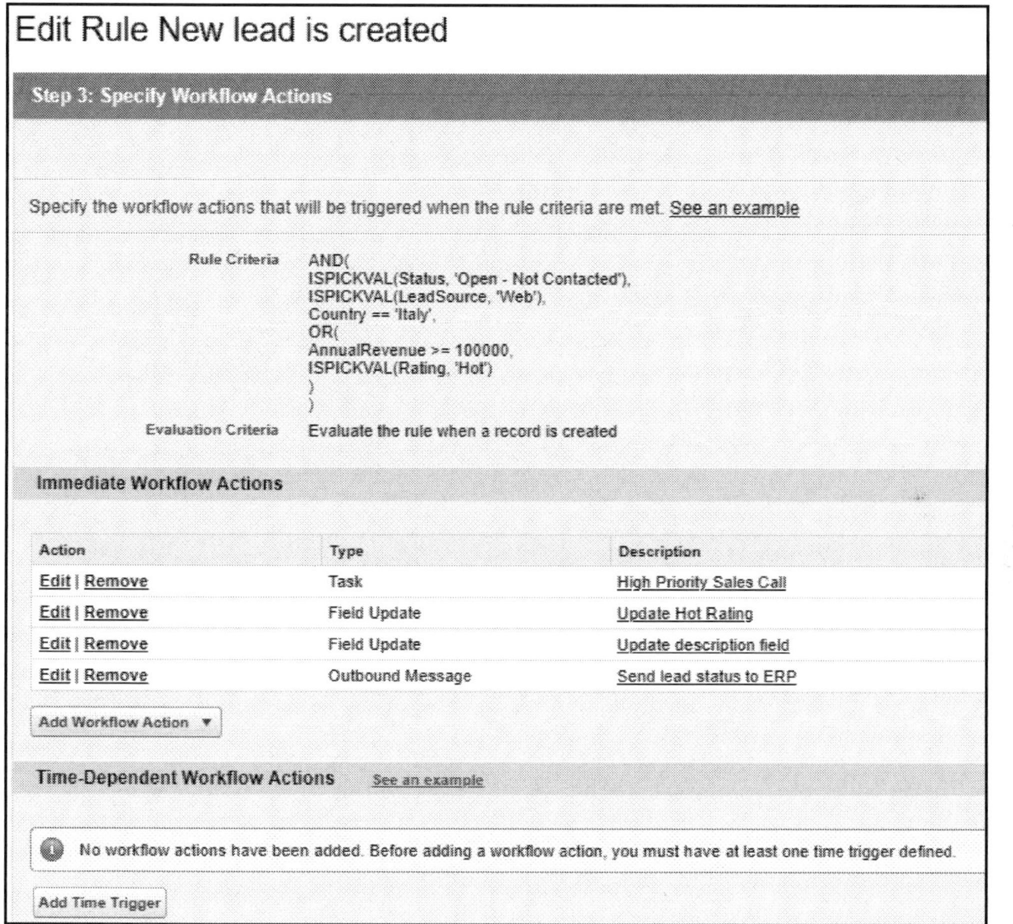

Workflow rule ready to be linked with a time-dependent action

Now click the **Add Time Trigger** button and select the appropriate time definition:

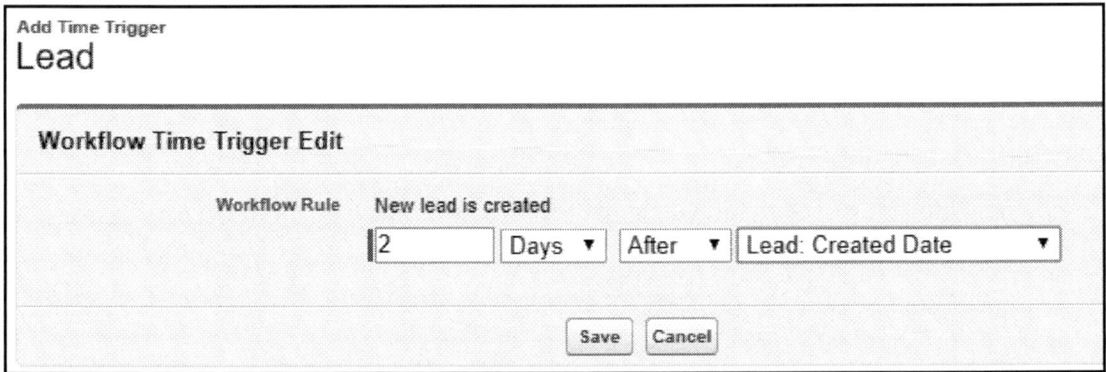

Time-dependent trigger editing

This is what you see on the workflow editing form:

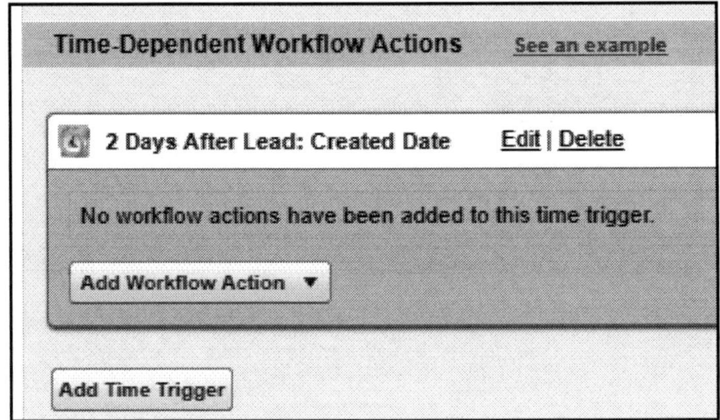

Time-dependent trigger enabled on workflow

Now you can add the existing email alert:

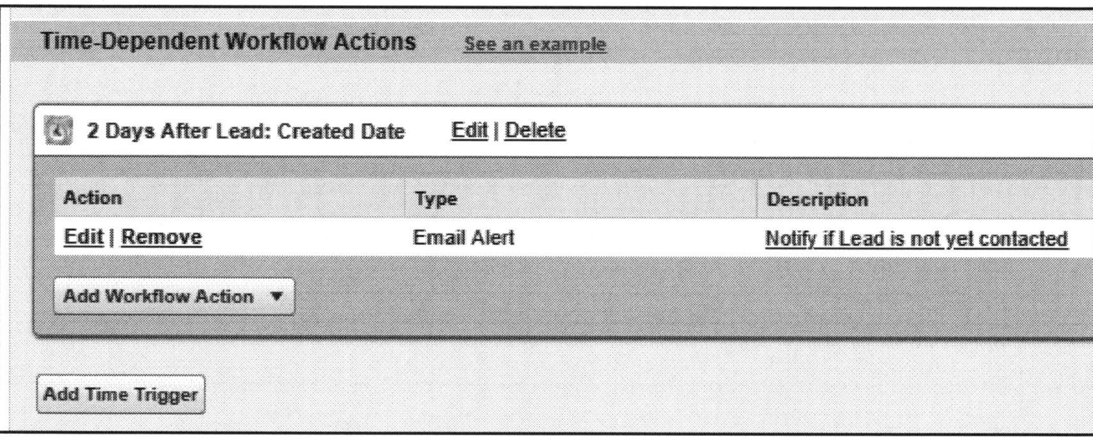

Action added to the time-dependent trigger

After the lead is created, the action executes after two days, and only if the rule criteria is still valid; this means that if the lead changes its status, the email is not sent (this prevents unwanted email alerts being sent if the record changes).

You can add multiple actions to the same time trigger and add more than one time-trigger per workflow.

The most notable limitation when using time-dependent actions is that Salesforce limits the number of executions to 1,000 per hour; any extra workflows are executed during the next hour.

Another requirement when using time-based workflows is that we need to define a default user in case the user that fired the workflow is no longer active when the action executes; this can be done from **Setup** | **Process Automation** | **Process Automation Settings** on the **Default Workflow User** field.

It is possible to monitor pending time-based executions from **Setup** | **Environments** | **Monitoring** | **Time-Based Workflows**:

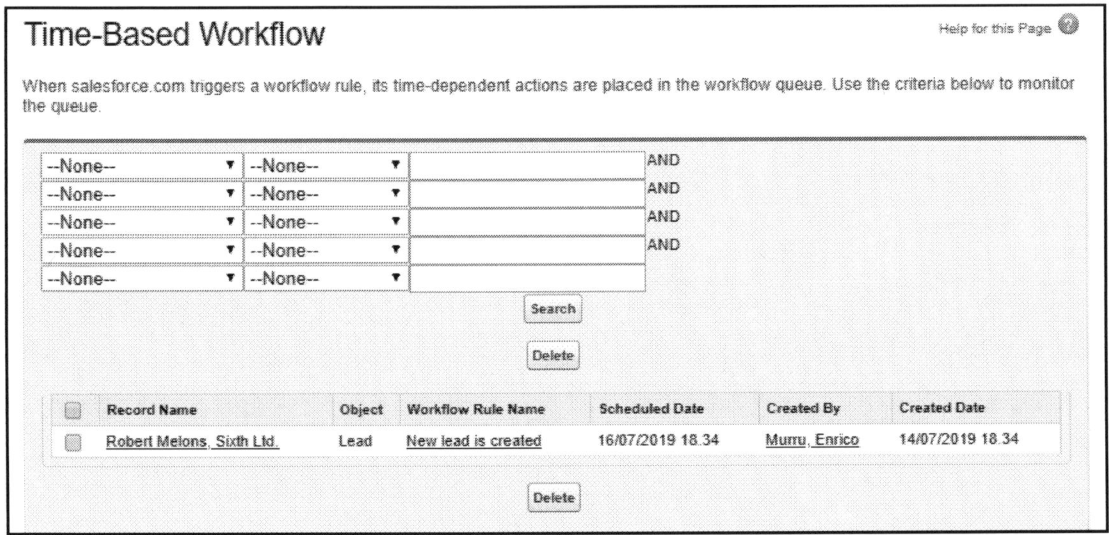

Time-based workflow monitoring panel

For further considerations on time-based workflows, refer to Salesforce Help at `https://help.salesforce.com/articleView?id=workflow_time_action_considerations.htmtype=5#workflow_field_updates_reevalute_wf`.

Further considerations on workflows

Workflows has a few limitations that should be considered when choosing this technology; here are some of the most relevant (as of winter 2020):

- Total inactive and active rules across objects (including workflows, assignment rules, auto-response and escalation rules): 2,000
- Total inactive and active rules per object: 500
- Active rules per object: 50
- Immediate actions per workflow: 40 (up to 10 for each action type)
- Time-based trigger per workflow: 10 (up to 10 for each action type)
- Time-based workflow execution per hour: 1,000
- Email alerts allocation per day: 1,000 alerts per standard license, up to 2 million

For more details on workflow limits refer to Salesforce Help at `https://help.salesforce.com/articleView?id=workflow_limits.htmtype=5`.

Before closing the chapter, let's list some considerations about adopting workflows on your business automations:

- When a custom object is deleted, workflow rules on that custom object are deleted as well.
- It is possible to run cross object field updates on accounts/opportunities when a lead is converted (use the **Require Validation for Converted Leads** on the **Setup | Features Settings | Marketing | Lead Settings** page).
- The order of the automated actions is not guaranteed, although field updates are always executed first.
- If you replace one or more workflow rules to replace an Apex trigger (or vice versa) remember to disable the trigger before activating the workflow rules; otherwise, both will be executed and you get unexpected automated behavior.
- Workflow rules are executed when a child standard or custom object with a master-detail field is re-parented.
- If the organization uses multiple languages, create a workflow using your own language (up to 25 filter criteria of 255 characters each), but remember that if you are using picklist filtering, the system uses the default value in the criteria, so you should use the values of the original language the workflow rule was created with when editing the rule (change the company default language accordingly).
- When using filter on record type labels, always use the master label and not the translated label; otherwise, the workflow won't trigger at all.
- A workflow rule doesn't fire if a condition has a reference to a field that doesn't have a value. For example, if a criteria is defined on the contact object where `Account.Active__c == true`, but the `Contact.AccountId` field is blank, the criteria is not matched and the workflow won't fire at all. In this situation use formula criteria to check whether the field is filled in or not.
- There are some actions on the Salesforce setup that don't trigger rules:
    - Replacing picklist values
    - Changing territory assignments on accounts and opportunities
    - Converting leads to person accounts
    - Deactivating self-service portal, customer portal, or partner portal users

For more information about using workflows, see Salesforce Help at `https://help.salesforce.com/articleView?id=workflow_rules_considerations.htmtype=5`.

This section helped us understand further the work considerations of workflows.

Summary

We have seen what process automation is and the declarative tools that the platform supports. We dug into workflows and how they can be configured with different kinds of actions with field updates, task actions, email alerts, and outbound messages to help us understand how they work and how to use them.

In the next chapter, we'll analyze approvals, another useful automation feature, which delivers approval processes for our records.

Questions

1. Which tools are used to deliver process automation?
    a. Page layouts
    b. Field-level security
    c. Workflows, approvals, and entitlement process
    d. Process Builder and Flow
2. A workflow is composed by:
    a. One rule and many actions
    b. Many rules and many actions
    c. One rule and one action
    d. Many rules and one action
3. Which evaluation criteria is executed every time a record is created or updated (even without changing any field)?
    a. Created and any time it's edited to subsequently meet criteria
    b. Created and every time it's edited
    c. Created

4. Which evaluation criteria are executed when the record is created?
    a. Created and any time it's edited to subsequently meet criteria
    b. Created and every time it's edited
    c. Created
5. What are immediate actions?
    a. Time-based actions triggered after one minute
    b. Actions executed when the record is created/updated and the workflow criteria matches the record
    c. Actions executed when the record is created but the workflow criteria doesn't match the record
6. Which automated action can be used within Flow and the Lightning Process Builder?
    a. Field update
    b. Task creation
    c. Email alert
    d. Outbound message
7. How can a field update action trigger a new workflow rule execution?
    a. Flagging the **Re-evaluate Workflow Rules after Field Change** option on the process automation settings
    b. Flagging the **Re-evaluate Workflow Rules after Field Change** option on the workflow rule configuration
    c. Flagging the **Re-evaluate Workflow Rules after Field Change** option on the field update
8. Which is the correct order of execution?
    a. Email alerts, field updates, tasks, outbound messages
    b. Field updates, email alerts, tasks, outbound messages
    c. Outbound messages, tasks, email alerts, field updates
    d. Field updates, outbound messages, email alerts, tasks
9. Can a field update action on the opportunity object update the related account object?
    a. Yes, it is one of the few standard-to-standard cross-object field updates available
    b. Yes, it is one of the few standard-to-custom cross-object field updates available
    c. No, only the target record can be updated with a field update action
    d. No, only the custom parent record can be updated with a cross-object field update action

10. Can email alerts be sent without any limitation?
    a. They are a standard automation feature; it is possible to send all the email alerts needed
    b. They are limited to 1,000 alerts per day
    c. They are limited to 1,000 x the number of standard licenses and up to 2 million daily
    d. They are limited to 2 million daily
11. What are time-based workflows?
    a. Workflows that have date fields on the rule definition
    b. Workflows that have email alert and task actions
    c. Workflows that can execute actions with a time-dependent trigger after a given number of days/hours to a defined date field
12. Which of the following applies to outbound messages?
    a. Must be monitored with a dedicated delivery monitoring page
    b. Must be attached to a time-dependent trigger
    c. Requires an external endpoint to deliver the message
    d. Can contain fields from related objects

12
Automating Record Approval with Approval Processes

After workflow rules, another important member of the process automation family is approval processes. They are a way to define criteria to decide whether Salesforce users can submit a record for approval to managers and automatically apply the required actions depending on whether the record is approved or rejected. Think of a sales VP who needs to explicitly approve discounts applied to opportunities if they exceed 10%, or an HR manager who needs to approve employees' expense logs. This can all be done through approval processes.

In this chapter, we'll learn about the following:

- Setting up approvals
- Using approvals
- Limits and considerations when using approvals

Understanding approvals

Approvals are the standard way to allow record approval in our company hierarchy. If a record meets some specific criteria, the current user's manager must evaluate it so that the business process can keep going according to business rules.

Let's look at an example.

Opportunity creation has a two-tier approval process, based on the opportunity's amount:

- **Lower than $ 100,000**: The opportunity is automatically approved.
- **Between $ 100,000 and $ 1,000,000**: The opportunity must be approved by the record owner's manager.
- **Higher than $ 1,000,000**: The opportunity must be approved by the manager and CEO.

After the approval process is completed, the opportunity custom field **Approval Status** must be set to **Approved** or **Rejected**, depending on the outcome. In the meantime, the record must be kept locked so that no one can edit it until the approval evaluation is completed by the managers.

Before you start to build a new approval process, go through the following checklist (an example response for our previous use case). I have answered each question for your reference (the text in italics is the answers).

- Who should be allowed to submit the approval?
    - **Any user related to the record (the creator, owner, or whoever makes sense).**
- How many approval steps do we need and who are the required actors?
    - **There are two steps, and the required actors are the manager and CEO.**

- What are the conditions on the target record and related records that should trigger approval?
    - **The opportunity amount; the opportunity amount must be filled in and greater than $0.**
- What should happen when a record is submitted, approved, or rejected?
    - **The approval status field needs to be updated and the record should be locked until it is approved or rejected.**
- Which email templates are needed to notify managers of upcoming approval requests? Do you need Chatter posts to start approvals?
    - **Use an email template and Chatter posts to notify managers about approval requests and to notify approval requesters whether their opportunity has been approved/rejected.**
- Can the approving user edit the locked record before the record is approved/rejected?
    - **The approving user cannot edit the record: the requesting user will be able to update the record based on their manager suggestions, which will be added along with the rejection (if it occurs).**

After answering these questions, you should be able to start creating a new approval process.

Creating an approval process

To begin creating a new approval process, go to **Setup** | **Process Automation** | **Approval Processes**, select the object type (**Opportunity**), click the **Create New Approval Process** button, and select **User Standard Setup Wizard**: the **Jump Start Wizard** will take care of some default options for you.

For more information about how the Jump Start Wizard handles default options, refer to Salesforce Help at `https://help.salesforce.com/articleView?id=approvals_jump_start_defaults.htmtype=5`.

For the sake of learning only what we need to know, we'll skip the Jump Start Wizard and go straight to the Standard Setup Wizard, a more complex wizard that will give you more control over approval configuration:

1. The first step of the wizard asks for the usual general information for the current approval, something we haven't seen for other configurations:

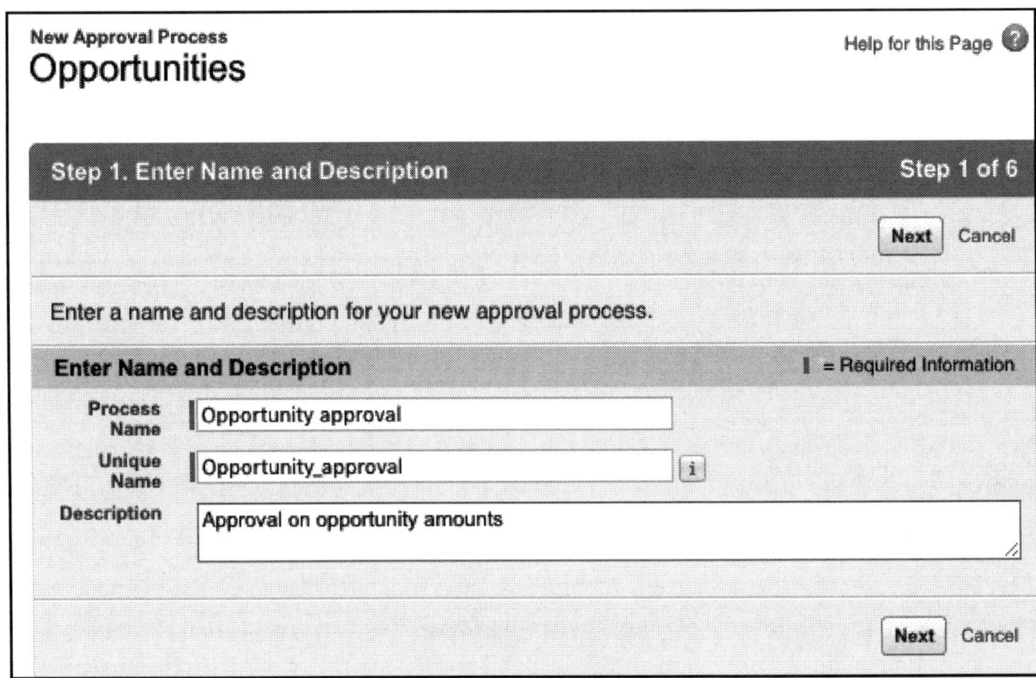

New approval wizard, step 1 – defining the approval name

2. Click **Next** to jump to the following step, which is used to filter down approval records based on criteria or a formula. Our criterion should be that the **Opportunity: Amount** is **greater than** 0:

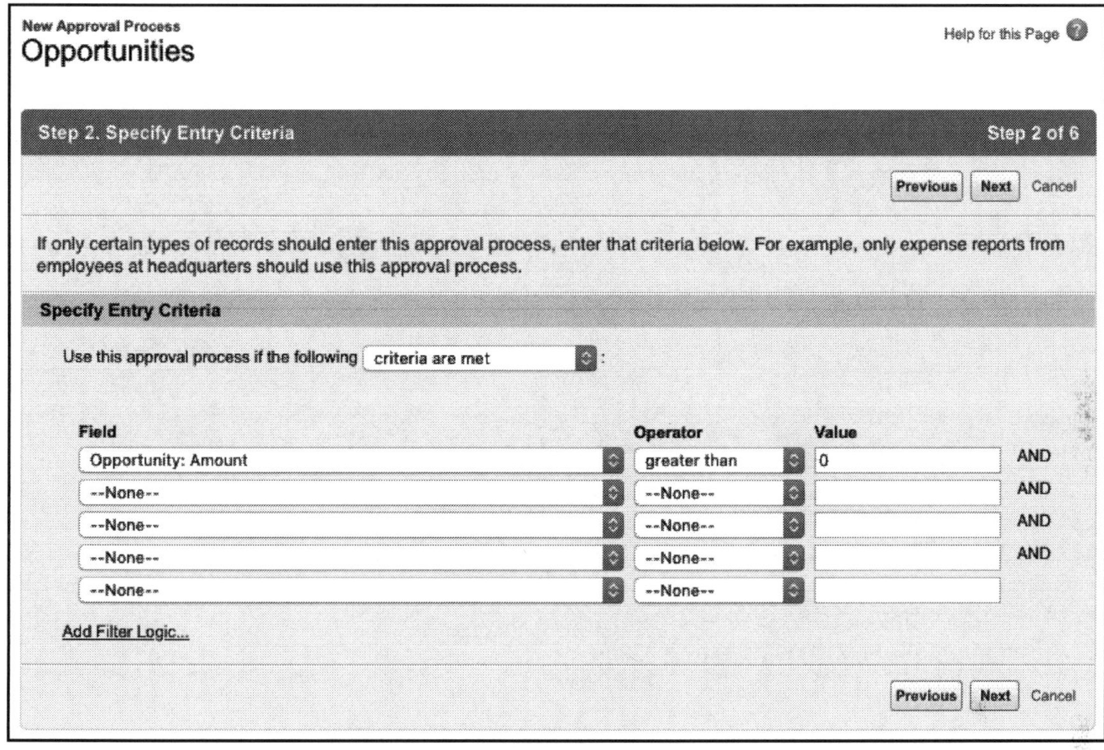

New approval wizard, step 2 – defining the approval criteria

If you want to use formulas instead of a plain criterion, select the **formula evaluates to true** value on the criteria selection picklist and enter a valid formula criterion as shown in the following screenshot:

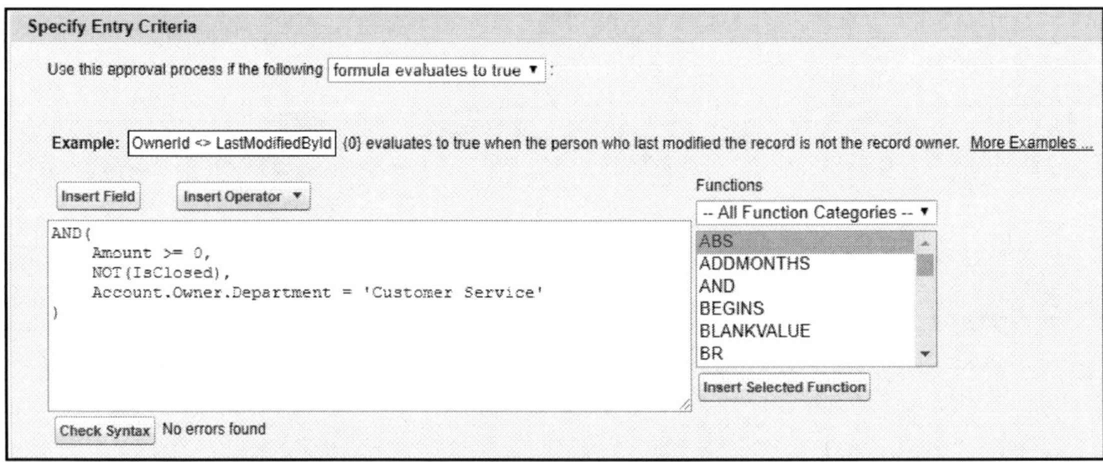

Defining an approval criterion using a formula

Formulas are especially useful when your entry criteria cannot be defined with a plain list of conditions, such as in the previous example where we defined a condition based on the opportunity account's owner, which is not listed in the fields in the **criteria are met** selection.

3. Go on with the plain criterion definition and click **Next** to jump to the third step:

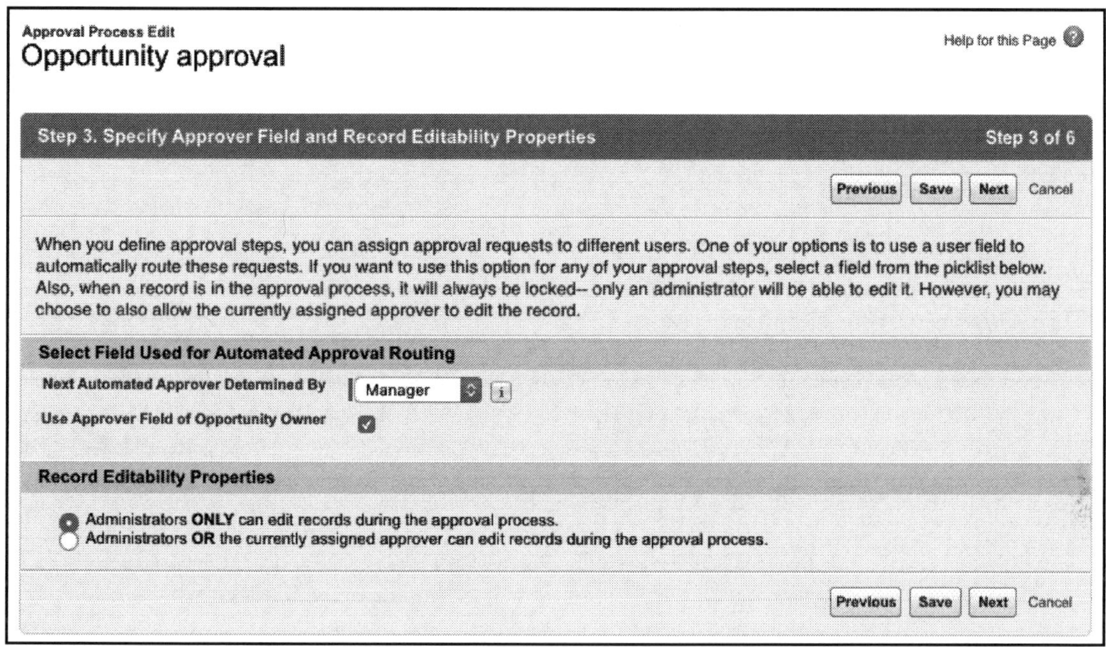

New approval wizard, Step 3 - configuring the manager and record editability

This step is used to select the approving user based on the user's hierarchy: do you remember the hierarchical relationship fields on the `user` object that we saw earlier in this book? The `user` object contains the **Manager** field (which is a standard hierarchical relationship), but you can create more hierarchical relationships from user to user (for example, **Area Manager** or **Country Manager**).

This step allows us to select the user that will be required to handle the approval using the **Next Automated Approver Determined By** picklist. The **Use Approver Field of *Opportunity* Owner** checkbox (the label will change depending on the object you are creating an approval for) takes the kind of approver selected in the previous picklist, selects the approver directly from the current record's owner (in this example, the opportunity object) if flagged, or from the current user who is submitting the approval if it is not flagged: this means that if you are submitting an opportunity record for approval and this flag is not checked on the approval, the automation will select your direct manager as the approver (your user's record's **Manager** field), whereas if the flag is checked, the manager will be selected from the user record of the opportunity owner.

Another important feature of approvals is the ability to lock a record while it is being approved: this prevents users from updating the records while the approver decision is being taken (we'll see how to apply this action in the next sections).

The **Record Editability Properties** section states the following:

- Only administrators can edit the locked record (they must have the **Modify All** object-level permission or **Modify All Data** permission)
- Administrators and approvers can edit the locked record.

There is no one-size-fits-all solution, so it is up to how you want approvals to work for your org. You should be very careful when using the record lock permission, as when a record is locked, no workflow, process builder, or trigger can modify that record until and unless we unlock the record itself.

For our scenario shown in the previous screenshot, let's select the **Manager** field on the **Next Automated Approver Determined By** picklist and select the **Use Approver Field of *Opportunity* Owner** checkbox.

4. Click **Next** to jump to the next section:

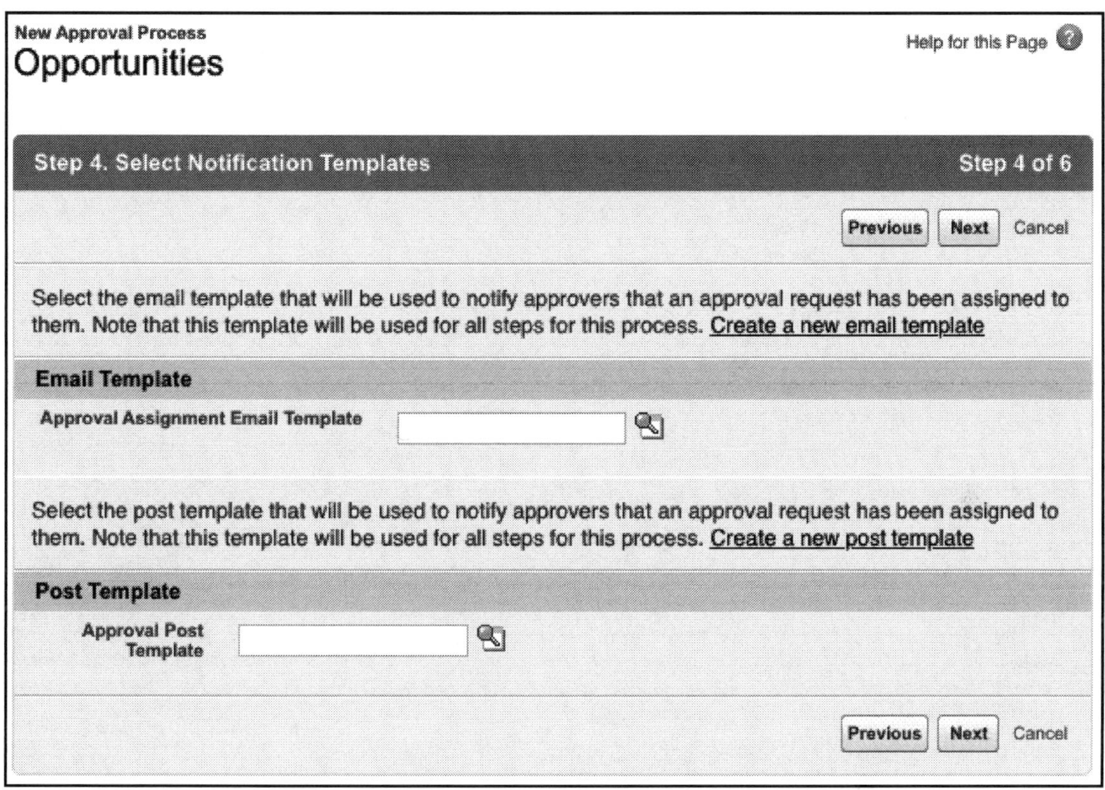

New approval wizard, Step 4 - defining the notification templates

This step is used to set up email and Chatter post templates for the approval request notification. Leave a blank field if you want to use the standard email and Chatter post templates. Let's now have a quick reminder about Chatter notifications:

- To enable approvals on Chatter, go to **Setup** | **Features Settings** | **Chatter** | **Chatter Settings**, look for the **Approval Posts** section, and flag **Allow Approvals**.

- To create a new **Post Template**, go to **Setup** | **Process Automation** | **Post Templates**, as shown in the following example:

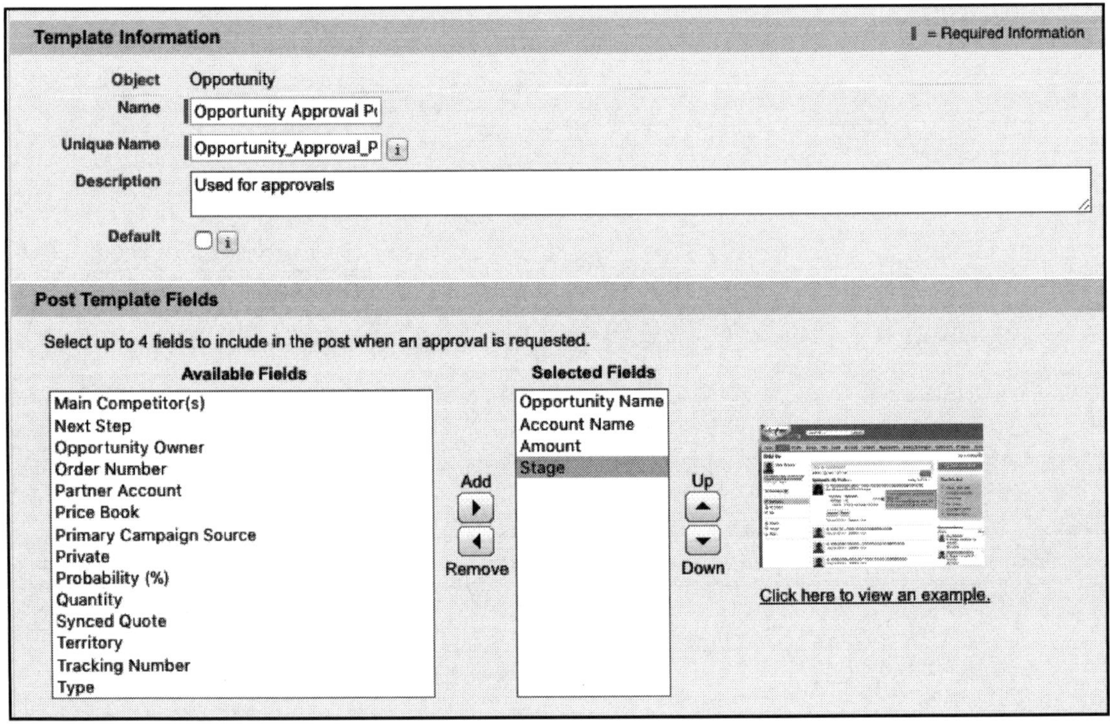

Post template creation

The post is basically used to define the fields to be displayed when the approval is notified (click on the example image to have a look at how the post looks in Classic).

In Step 4, leave the **Email Template** and **Post Template** fields blank and click **Next**.

5. You will see the following screen. This step configures the approval page, which is the page where the approver responds to an approval request, as shown in the following screenshot:

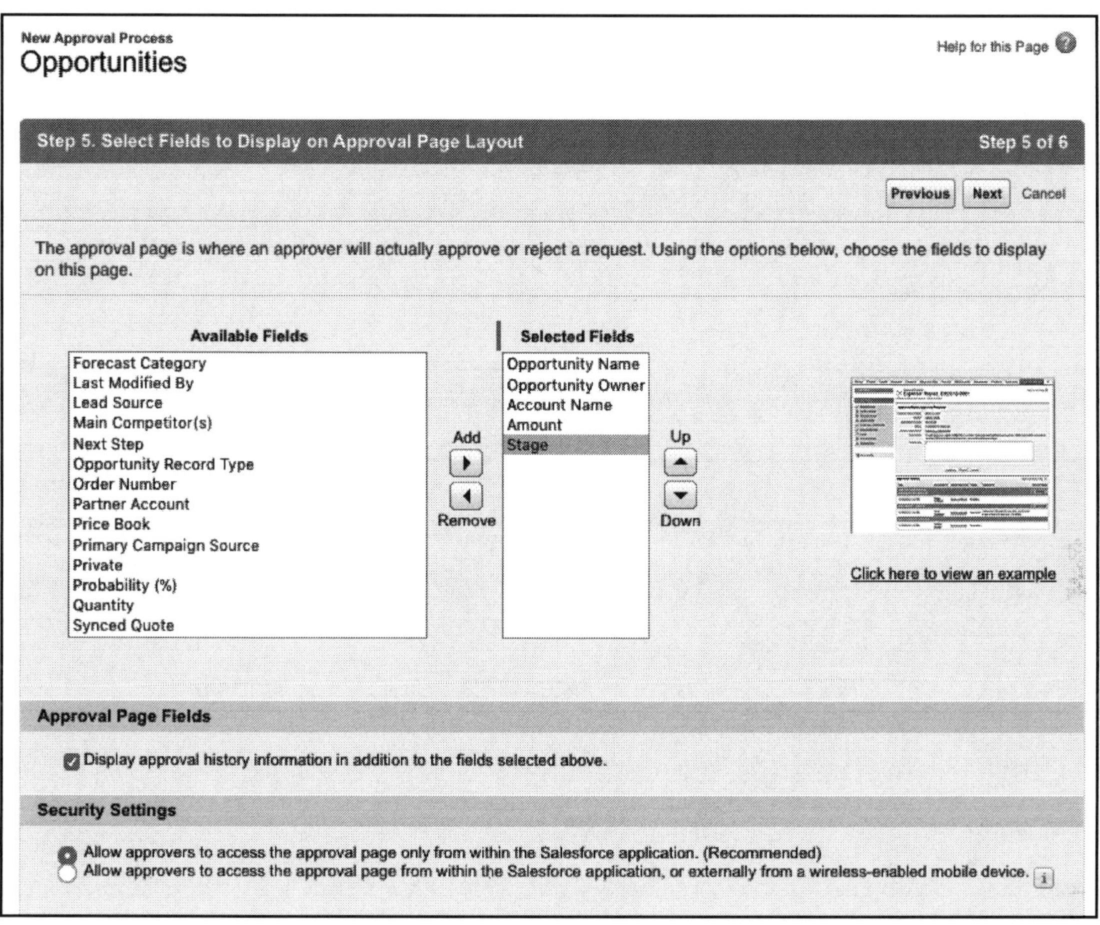

New approval wizard. Step 5

The first thing to select is the list of fields to be displayed to the approver. You should select only the most important fields as this page can be viewed using a mobile device, so too many fields can make the approval page uncomfortable for the approver.

In the **Approval Page Fields** section, check the **Display approval history information in addition to the fields selected above** option only if you want to display all of the approval history in a dedicated section of the approval page (the example screenshot gives you a hint of what the page may look like in Classic style).

Last but not least, you can decide to show the approval page only to authenticated users (this is, of course, the recommended option) or by using a mobile device, but without authentication (this way is less secure but, for sure, easier to use for approvers that are usually on the move).

6. Click **Next** for the last step:

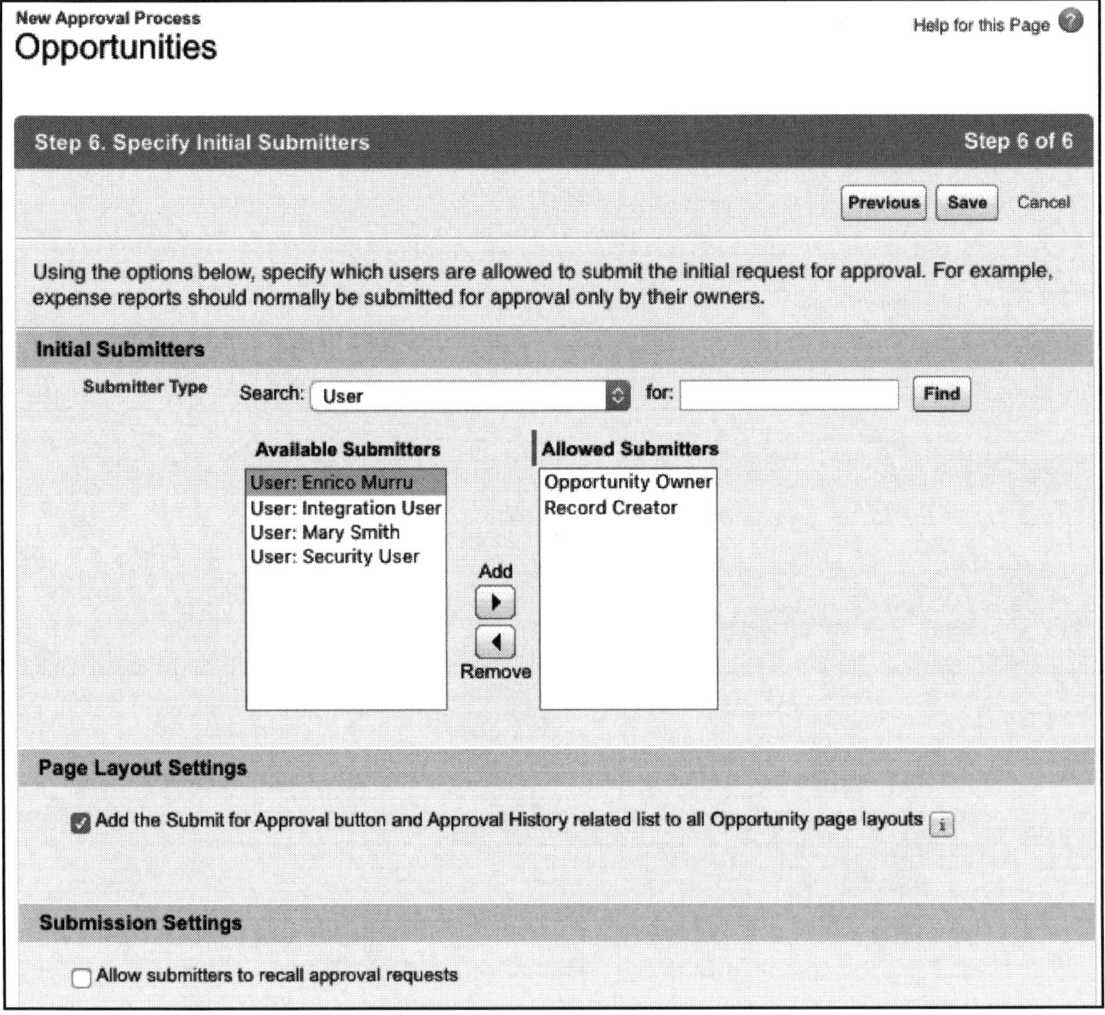

New approval wizard. Step 6

The first section allows us to select which users should be able to submit a record for approval. It gives us the following options:

- Record-related users (such as the creator or owner)
- Specific users
- Specific roles and subordinates

If the user who is watching the record does not belong to the categories selected in this list, they won't be able to submit a record for approval.

The **Page Layout Settings** are used to automatically add the **Submit for Approval** button and the **Approval History** related list to the object layouts.

The last option allows the submitter to recall an approval request; this may be useful when the conditions on the submitter side change over time.

7. Now click **Save**. A quick popup will appear to help you decide what you want to do next:

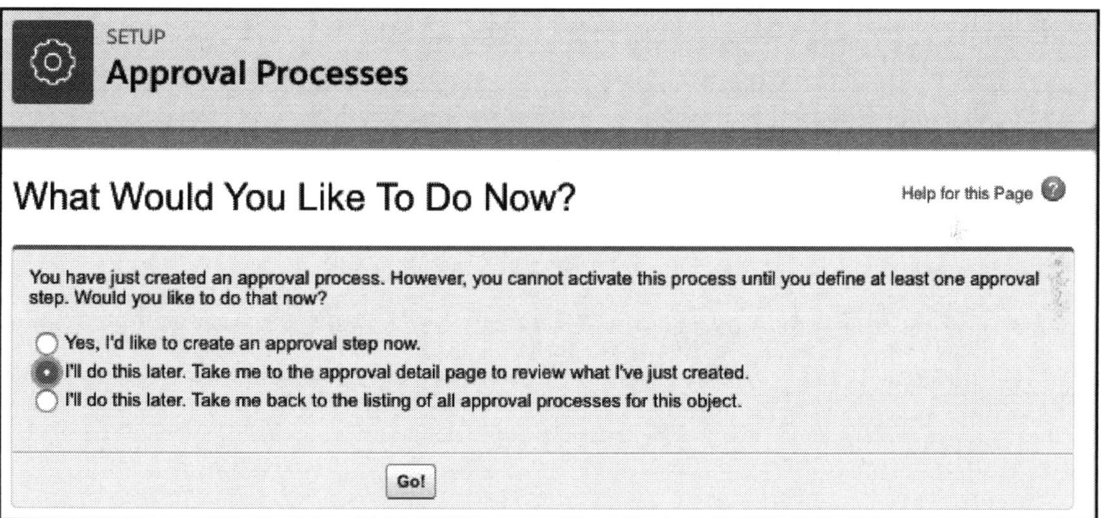

Last step of the approval wizard

Select the second option to jump to the approval just created. The approval detail page is divided into two main parts:

- A details section that shows the main configurations on the current approval:

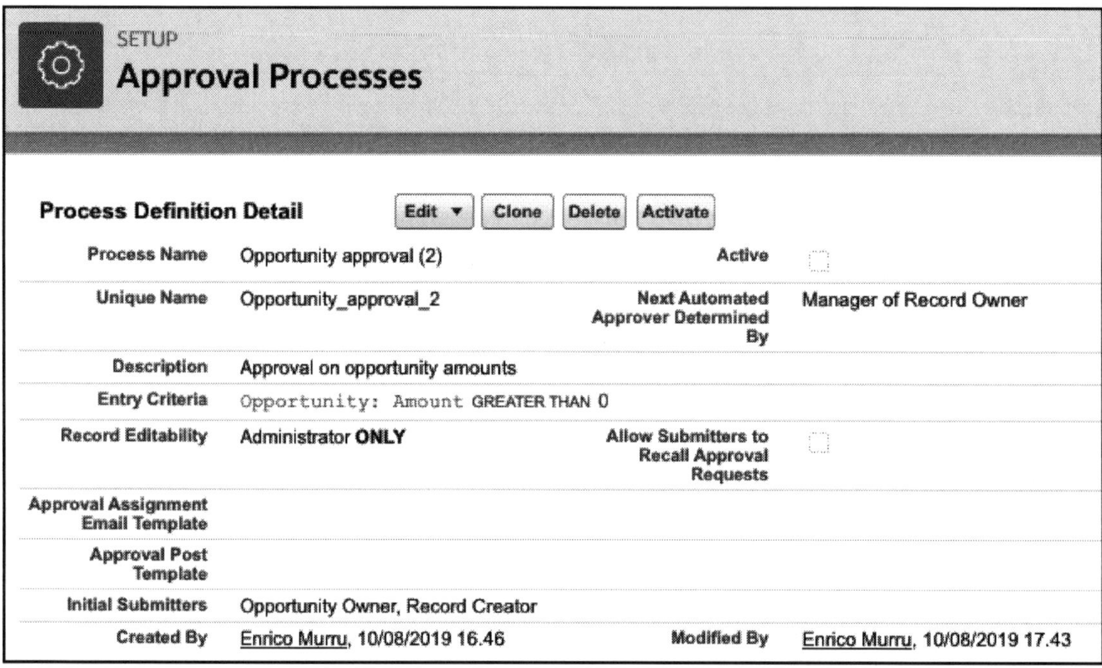

Approval details page

- The sections for the steps and actions related lists, which show everything about the approval steps and all other kinds of actions:

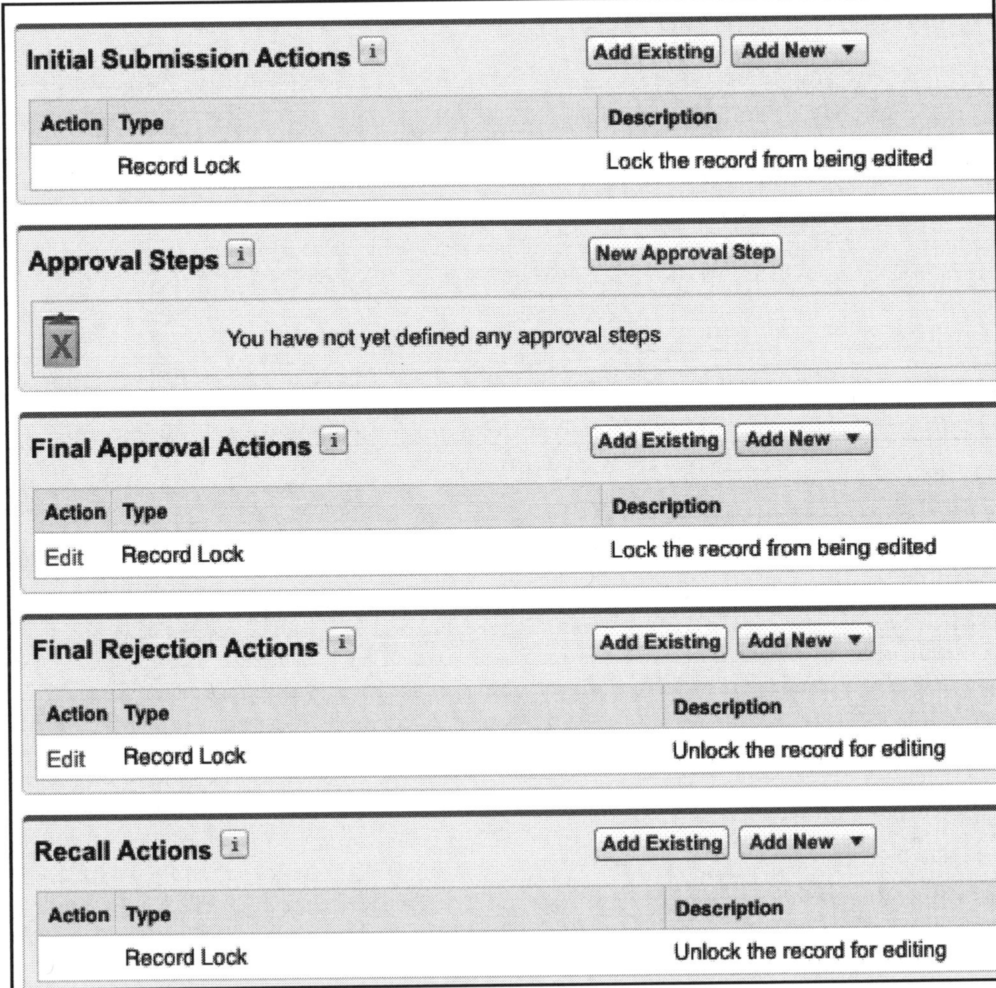

Approval actions and steps sections

Now that we have a brand new approval, we need to configure the steps that make up the approval process and the related actions that are automatically executed when a record is approved or rejected. Let's dive into this in the next sections.

Creating approval steps

Approval steps define the number of levels of approval and the users who should handle the approval. To sum our example up again, we have two tiers of approval (one for the direct manager and one for the CEO) with two users needed to handle the request (the current user's manager and the company CEO), and every step is determined by the opportunity's amount (again, if the amount is between $100,000 and $1,000,000, then only the manager is needed to handle the approval, while if the amount is higher than $1,000,000, the opportunity must be approved by both the manager and the CEO).

Let's see how we can create the steps required for our example:

1. To create a new step, click on the **New Approval Step** button in the header of the **Approval Steps** section of the approval details page (as shown in the previous screenshot). The **New Approval Step** wizard will appear:

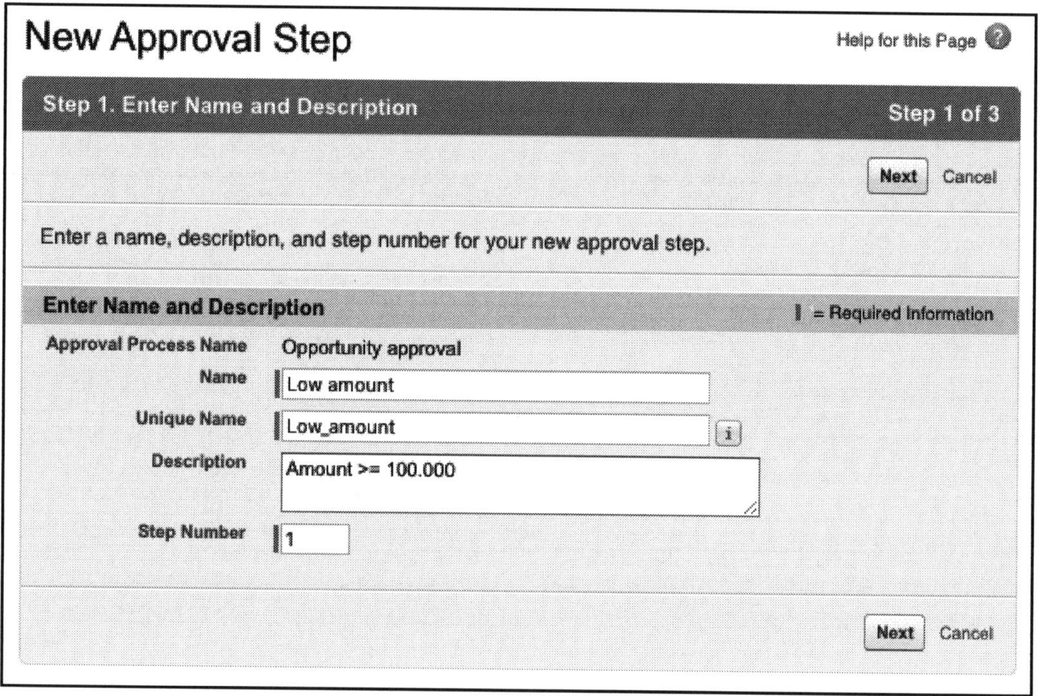

Approval step creation wizard. Step 1 - defining the step name

Select the usual identification fields and the **Step Number** that identifies the step order of evaluation.

2. Click **Next** to define the step's criteria:

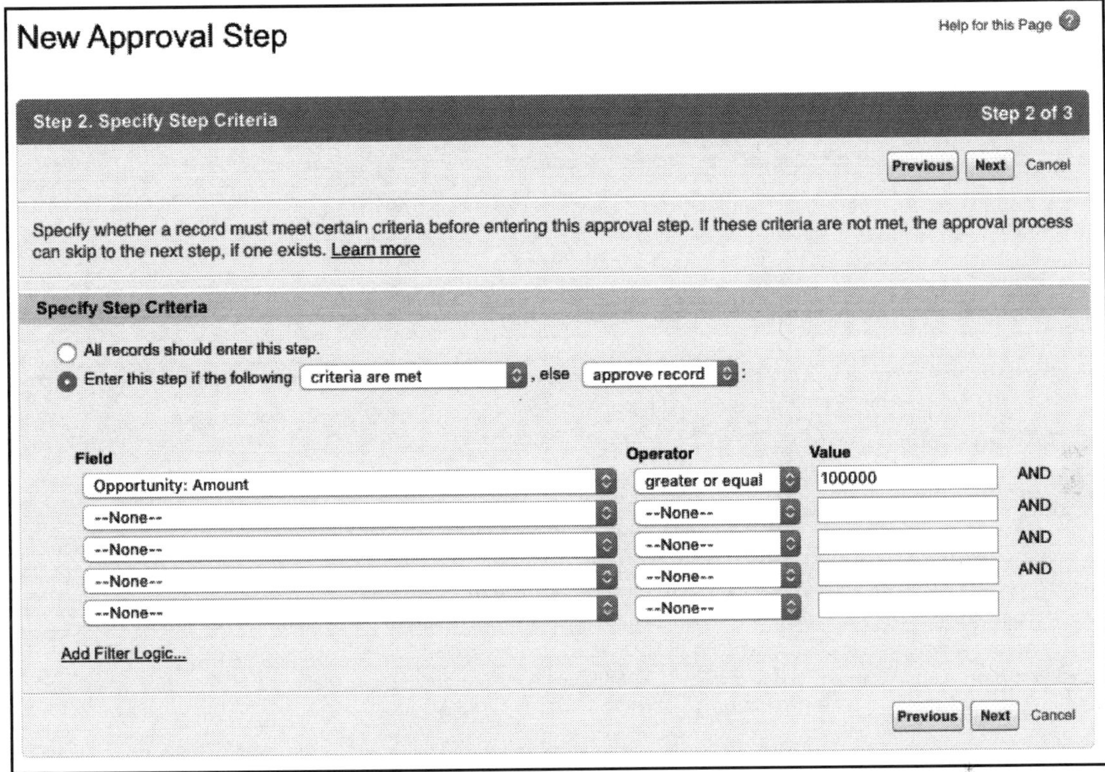

Approval step creation wizard, Step 2 - defining the step criteria

We can choose whether this step should be entered by all records regardless of any condition (for example, in our example, if any opportunity, disregarding its amount, needs a specific approval, we should mark **All record, should enter this step** and configure this step as the first one).

If we choose to select a condition, we can even select the **else** condition picklist with certain values (this is set to **approve record** in the previous screenshot):

- **approve record**: If conditions are not met, the record is automatically approved (this is our automatic approval step).
- **reject record**: If conditions are not met, the record is automatically rejected (this is our automatic rejection step).
- **go to next step**: This is available only if there are later steps. If none of the conditions of the later step match, the record is rejected.

Being the first step, this is the first condition to be checked against, and this will be the first approval the record will be submitted to; if the record has an amount lower than $100,000, then the record will be approved without any need for human intervention.

3. Click **Next** to bring up the next screen to select the approver:

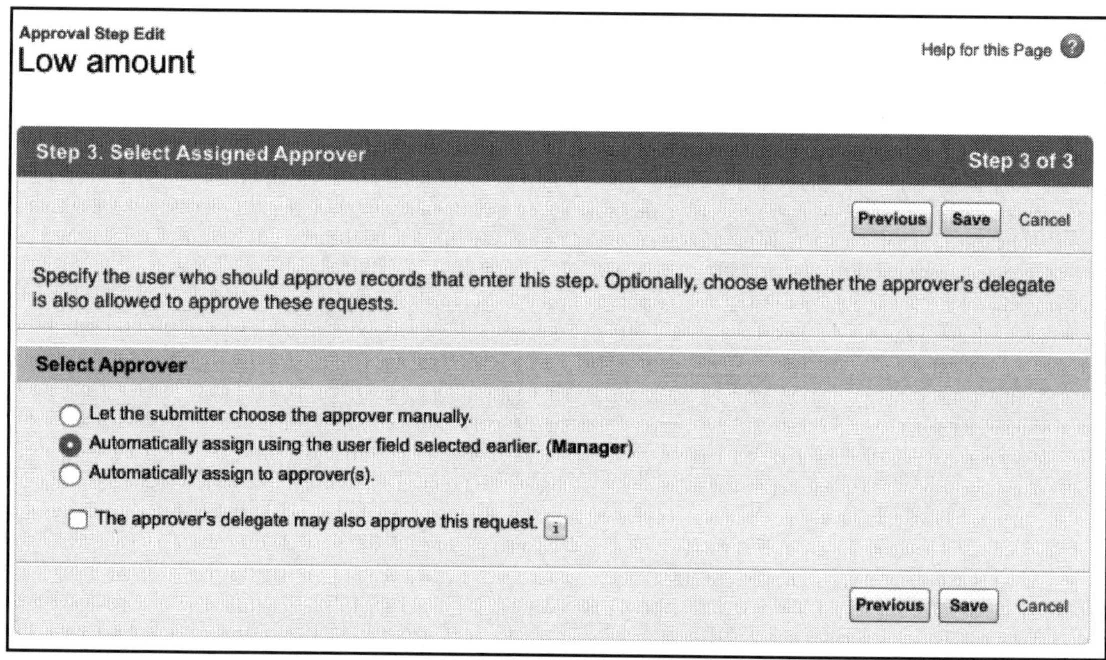

Approval step creation wizard, Step 3 - defining the approvers

This step selects the user who will be accepting the approval request, and can be set to the following:

- **Let the submitter choose the approver manually**: The user is selected manually by the submitter.
- **Automatically assign using the user field selected earlier: (Manager)**: The user referenced through the hierarchical relationship based on the approving record's owner user (which is our choice for the current step: the **Manager** field). This option is only available if the approval process has been configured to support this behavior (as seen earlier).

- **Automatically assign to queue**: The users from a specific queue, only if the approval object supports a queue (such as the case object (bear in mind, however, that this option is not shown in the previous screenshot as the opportunity object doesn't support queues)).
- **Automatically assign to approver(s)**: The statically selected users (this will be our choice for the next step, where the CEO will be required to approve deals over $1M). This configuration can contain up to 25 users.

When you select **Automatically assign to approver(s)**, the form will show newly available configurations:

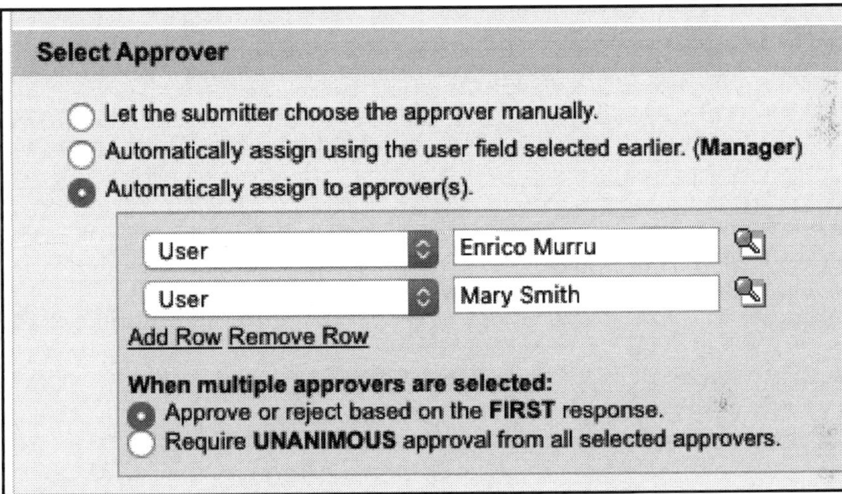

Select approvers on the approval step wizard

By selecting more than one approver, you can even decide whether the decision should be unanimous or whether the first approval/rejection considered will be the final response.

Another option is **The approver's delegate may also approve this request** checkbox, which is used to allow approvers to delegate an approval to their delegated user. In our scenario, the CEO may not be available to inspect the deal and provide an approval, so they can delegate their **Delegated Approver**, a standard user lookup found on the user layout, which is not a hierarchical relationship field:

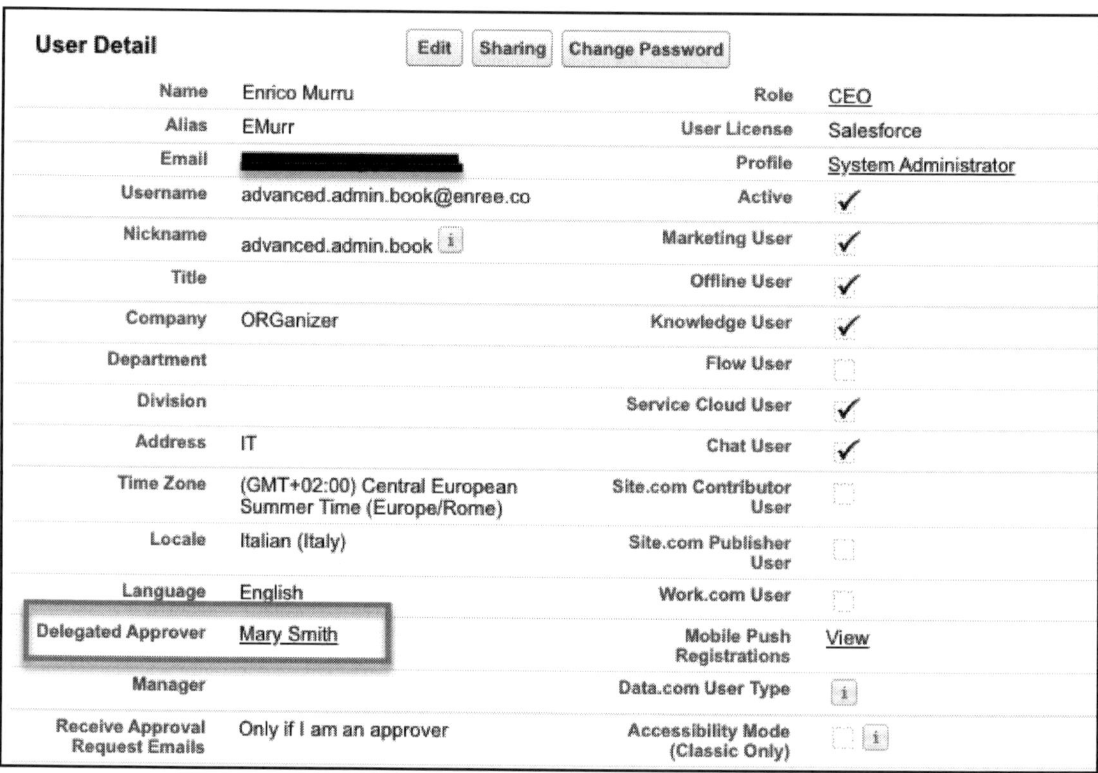

Delegated approver field on the user object

In our scenario, we'll have the following users:

- Laura Gnite, sales rep
- Mary Smith, sales SVP and manager of Laura Gnite
- Enrico Murru, CEO and manager of Mary Smith

Click **Save** to complete the step:

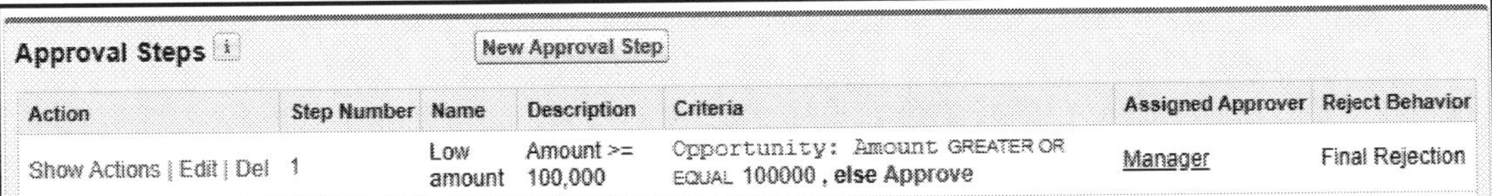

Action	Step Number	Name	Description	Criteria	Assigned Approver	Reject Behavior
Show Actions | Edit | Del	1	Low amount	Amount >= 100,000	Opportunity: Amount GREATER OR EQUAL 100000 , else Approve	Manager	Final Rejection

First step configured

4. Hit the **New Approval Step** button once again (as we did in *step 1*) to create our last step. Here are the configurations needed to complete our approval:
    - **Name**: **Big deals**
    - **Step Number**: **2**
    - **Step Criteria**: **Opportunity: Amount greater than or equal to 1,000,000**
    - **Reject Behavior**: Perform all rejection actions for this step *and* all final rejection actions. (**Final Rejection**)

The last configuration is only visible from any step that has a previous step (so it won't be visible from the first one):

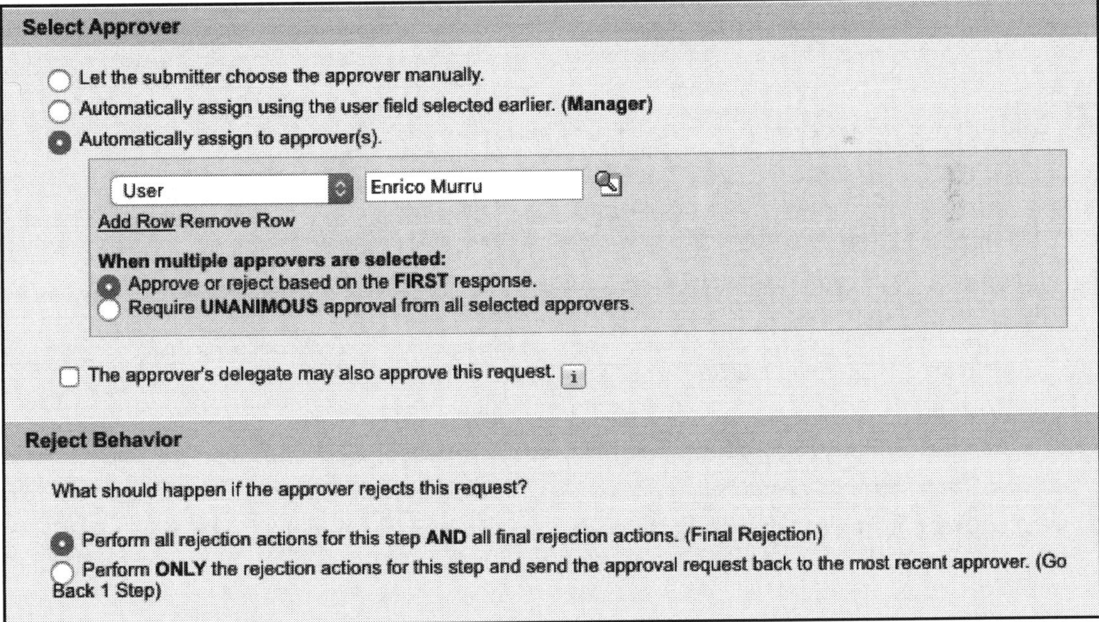

Reject behavior selection on Step 4 of approval step configuration

We haven't seen actions yet, but from this rejection configuration, it is possible to either consider the rejection as final (and so all final rejection actions should be executed) or as just a step rejection, which means that only the current step's rejection actions should be executed and the approval will go back to the previous step for further modification (for example).

5. Now click the **Save** button for the last time and get back to the process details page:

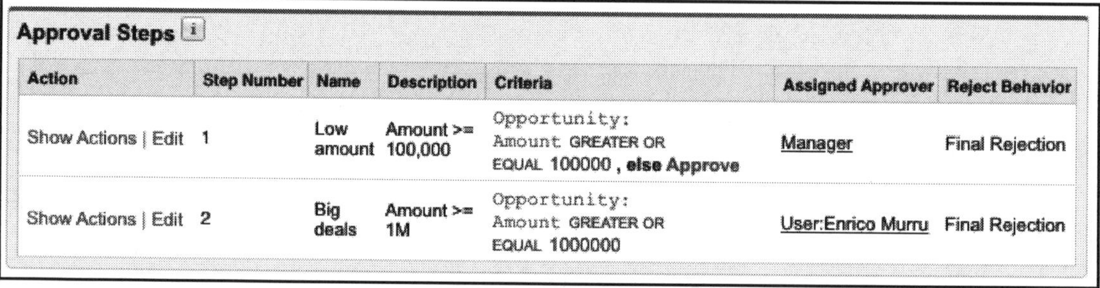

Approval Steps

Action	Step Number	Name	Description	Criteria	Assigned Approver	Reject Behavior
Show Actions | Edit	1	Low amount	Amount >= 100,000	Opportunity: Amount GREATER OR EQUAL 100000 , **else Approve**	Manager	Final Rejection
Show Actions | Edit	2	Big deals	Amount >= 1M	Opportunity: Amount GREATER OR EQUAL 1000000	User:Enrico Murru	Final Rejection

Approval steps related list on the approval process details page

We will now close the configuration, but we still need something to complete the approval, namely, the actions to be performed to allow the process to be completed.

Adding actions to approvals

The approval process flow can be seen from the **Approval History** related list, but it would be cool to have a way to make modifications to the record when approval stages are passed.

In our scenario, we want to update a custom opportunity field named **Approval Status**, a simple picklist defined as follows:

- **Name**: **Approval Status**
- **Type**: **Picklist**
- **Values**: **Pending** (default), **Submitted**, **Approved**, **Rejected**
- **Restricted values**: Yes
- **Field-Level Security**: All profiles except System Administrator have read-only access

This picklist could be used to avoid closing deals that haven't been approved yet (for example, by creating a validation rule on the opportunity object that uses the **Approval Status** and the **Closed** fields) or even to enable a new approval run if the amount field is updated (using a workflow rule or a process builder): we can even add more conditions to the approval entry criteria to avoid submitting a record if it has already been approved or rejected.

As we saw in the previous chapter, there are several automated actions available. Approval processes can use the following actions:

- **Task**: Assigns a task to the approver to set a schedule for the approval or a task to the submitter after a rejection to discuss the reasons behind the rejection with their manager.
- **Email Alert**: Sends an email when a response is done.
- **Field Update**: Updates a field on the opportunity.
- **Outbound message**: Notifies an external system of an approved billing request.
- **Record lock**: An approval-specific action used to lock/unlock the record during the approval flow. If the record is locked, it cannot be updated by anyone. An exception in this regard is made for the system administrator or any user with the **Modify All Data** permission or **Modify All** object-level permission.

We won't discuss how automation actions work in this chapter; refer to the previous chapter for more details.

Where can actions be added on the approval? As we have already seen in the previous section, the approval process detail page shows a diverse related list:

- **Initial Submission Actions**: Actions are executed when the user submits the approval. A default lock action is preconfigured when the approval is created.
- **Final Approval Actions**: Actions are executed when the record is successfully approved. A default lock action is already there (from the submitter's point of view, the record is approved and should not be changed).
- **Final Rejection**: Actions are executed when the record is rejected. A default unlock action is already preconfigured when the approval is created.

- **Recall**: A submitter could recall the approval request. Actions are executed in this eventuality (for example, to restore the approval status to the **not-yet-submitted** value).
- **Approval Step Approval/Rejection**: Actions can be added on a specific step's approval/rejection events. Default lock/unlock actions are already configured. To show step-specific actions, click on the **Show Actions** link next to a step definition, as shown in the following screenshot:

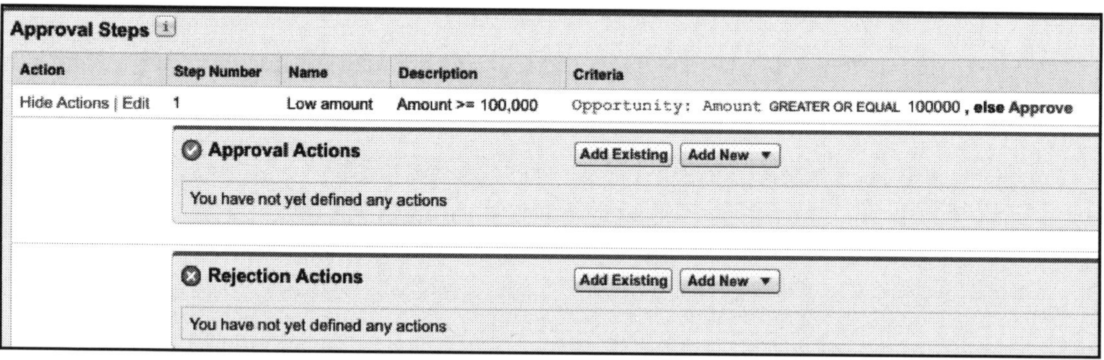

Approval step actions configuration

We won't add any step-related actions but only **Initial Submission**, **Final Approval**, and **Final Rejection** actions, according to our scenario.

Let's configure three different **Field Update** actions on the **Approval Status** picklist that set the following values:

- **Action: Set Submitted Approval**
    - **Position: Initial Submission Actions**
    - **Approval Status value: Submitted**
- **Action: Set Approved**
    - **Position: Final Approval Actions**
    - **Approval Status Value: Approved**
- **Action: Set Rejected**
    - **Position: Final Rejection Actions**
    - **Approval Status Value: Rejected**

That brings us to the following configuration:

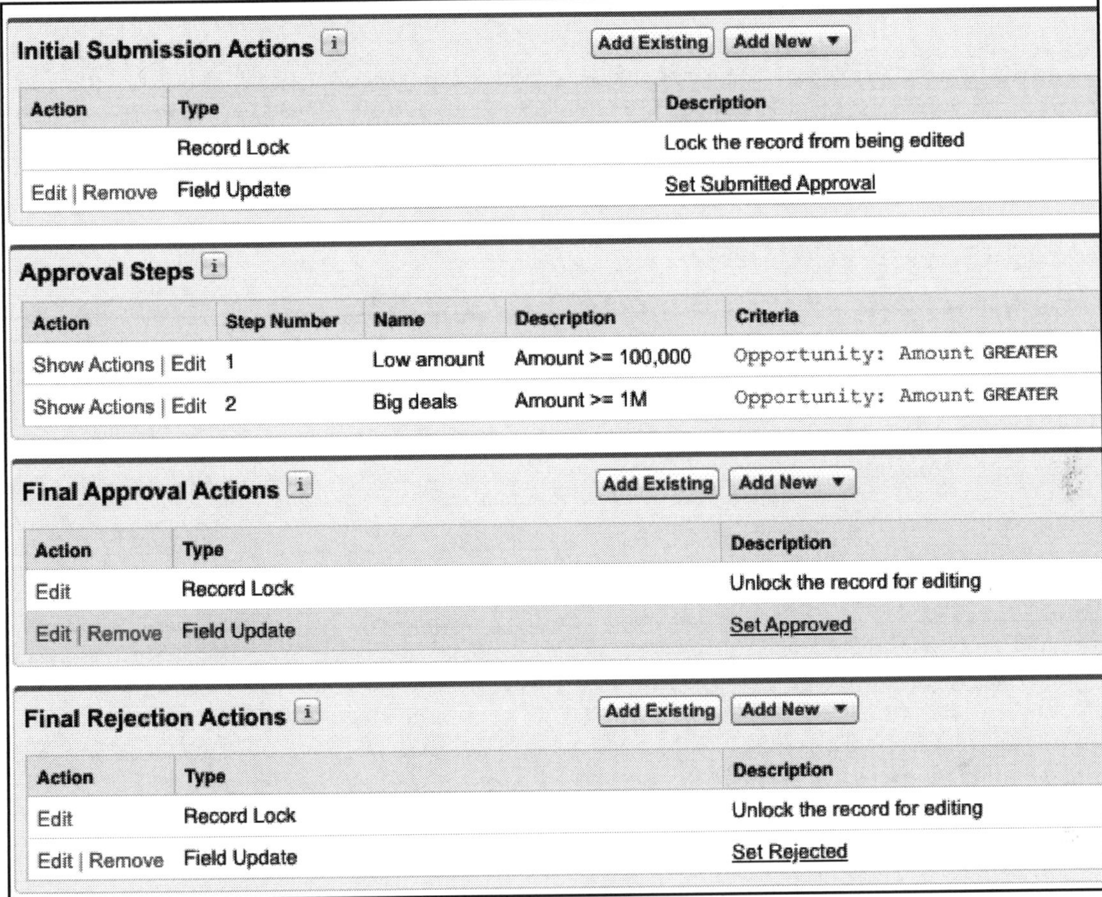

Approval actions configured

Note that the **Record Lock** action in the **Final Approval Actions** section has been changed to **Unlock the record for editing**, as we want the submitter to be able to update the record if they want.

The approval process is ready. We can activate the approval process by clicking the **Activate** button on the details page header.

Once an approval process has been activated, no more steps can be added or removed. Deactivate it and clone it to create a new version with more or fewer steps. Bear in mind that some attributes cannot be modified, such as step order.

Using approvals

Let's test our new approval. But before this, let's create a workflow rule on the **Opportunity** object that resets the **Approval Status** field if the amount field is updated, as shown in the following screenshot:

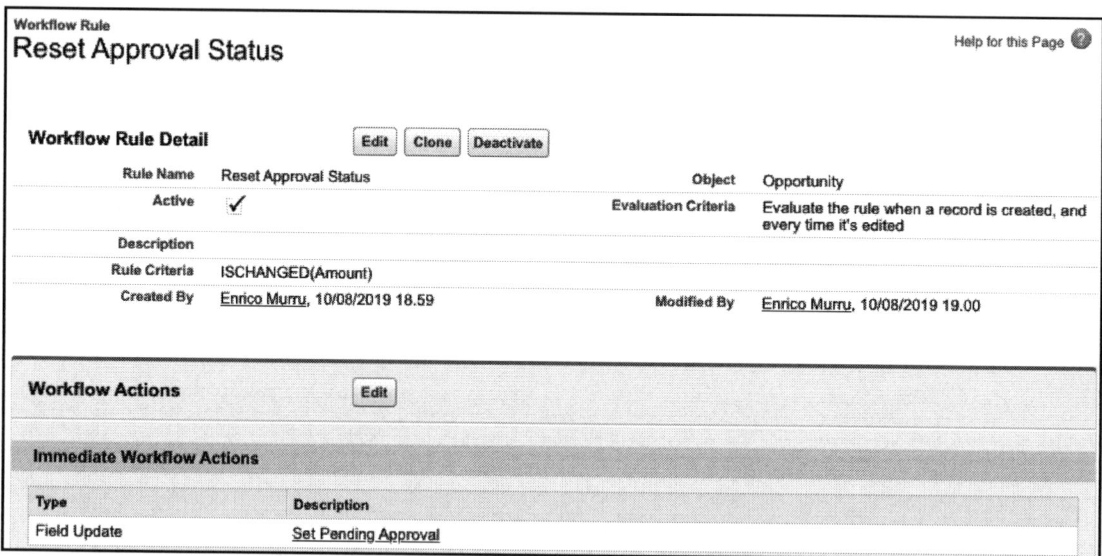

Workflow rule to reset the approval status on the opportunity record

Note that the rule criteria is **ISCHANGED(Amount)**, which states that the rule fires any time the **Amount** field is updated.

We are now ready to test. Let's proceed with the following steps:

1. Using a **lower hierarchy** user (which should have a **Manager** defined), create a new opportunity by setting the following values:
    - **Name:** Whatever you like
    - **Stage:** Any
    - **Close Date:** Any
    - **Amount: $15.000,00**
    - **Approval Status:** Pending (defaulted)
2. Now click on the **Submit for Approval** button (it should be next to the **Clone** button, depending on your layout configuration) and add a note on the modal (this should be used by the approver to take a decision). Nothing will appear to happen, but a green message will pop up stating that all went okay, and if you look at the **Approval History** related list, you can see two new items:

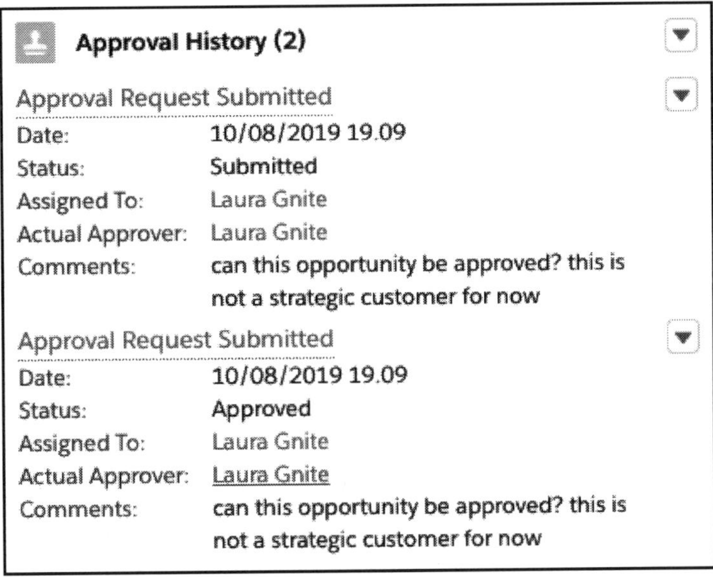

Approval history example

What has just happened?

As the opportunity amount was lower than $100,000, the approval process automatically approved the record. Approved actions were automatically executed, as we can see in the following screenshot:

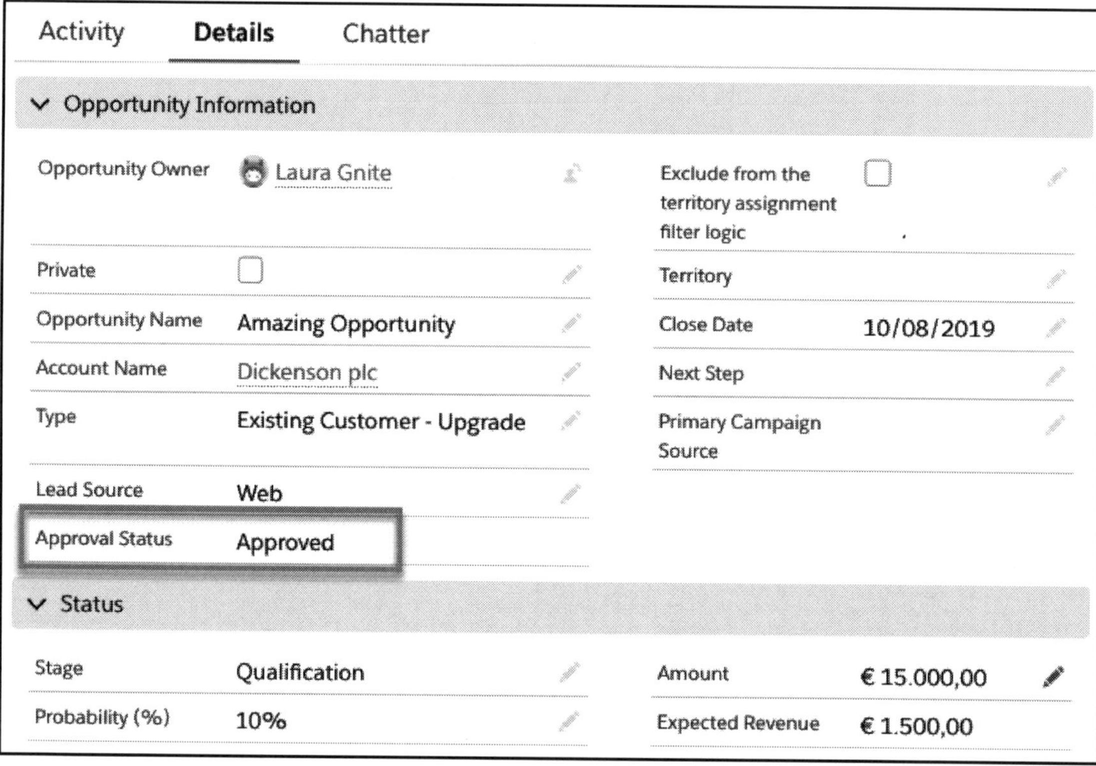

Approval actions executed on the Opportunity record

The **Approval Status** automatically changed to **Approved** and the record is also unlocked. Try to edit any record: nothing will prevent you from updating the opportunity.

Let's change the **Amount** field to a value greater than $100,000; we expect the **Approval Status** to be changed back to **Pending** by the workflow rule created earlier.

3. Now let's submit it for approval again. The record **Approval Status** will change to **Submitted**. Now click the **Submit for Approval** button again and try to edit the record:

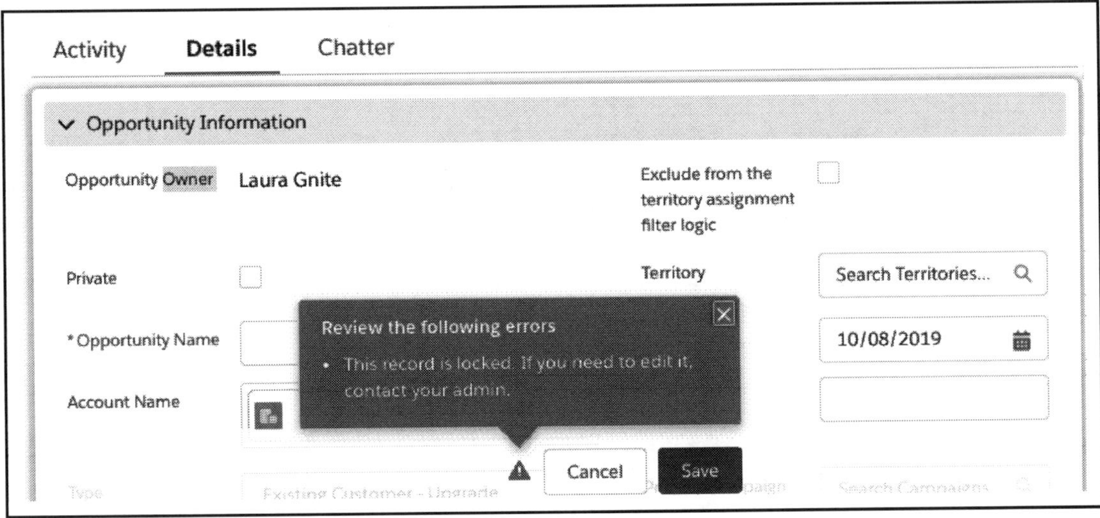

Record lock error

Now the record has been submitted for approval, but as the amount is greater than $100,000; the record needs explicit approval by the user's **Manager** (which in this example is **Mary Smith**) and has been locked:

Pending approval on the approval history

We have configured the approval to notify the approver with a standard email template and a Chatter post. This is what she gets via email:

Email notification for approval request

This is the standard Chatter post:

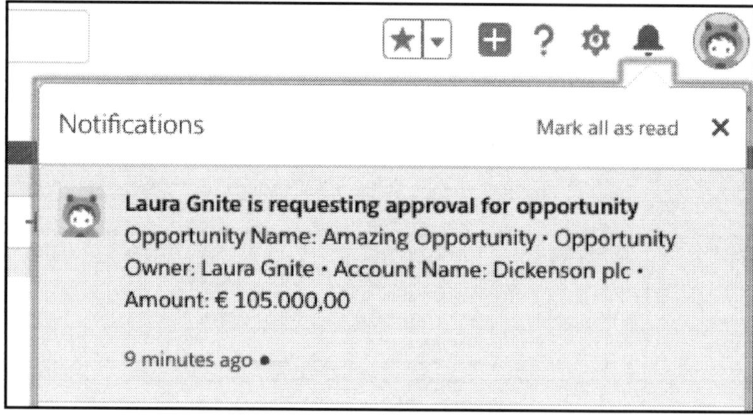

Chatter notification for approval

Click on the notification to jump to the approval page:

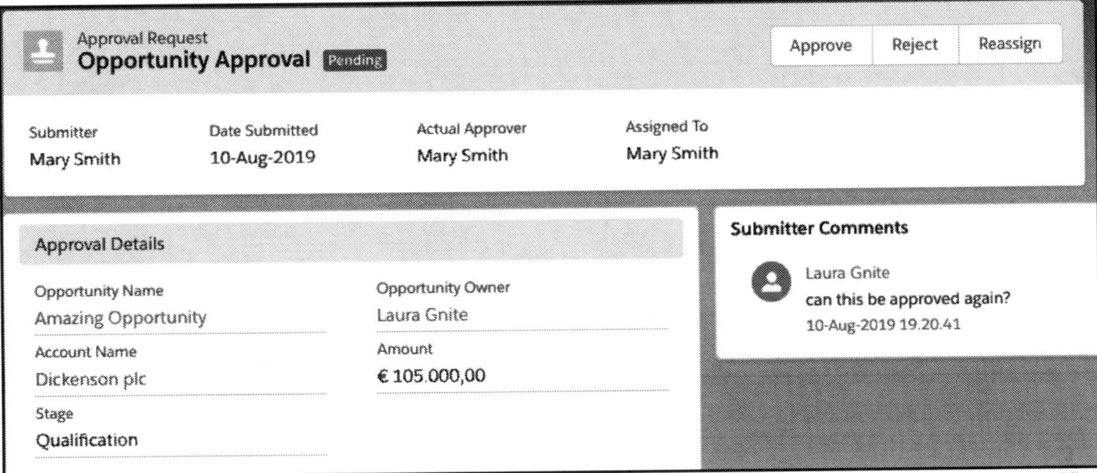

Approval page

By approving or rejecting the request, the approver can add a comment to justify their choice.

4. Approve the request. The **Approval History** related list will now show the last entry with the **approved** status:

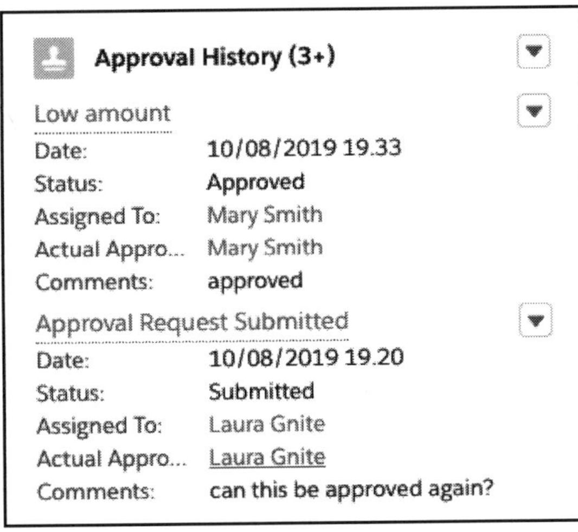

Approval history with the last step approved

What happens if we change the **Amount** field to be greater than $1,000,000?

The approval must be approved by Mary Smith (the Sales SVP) and then by Enrico Murru (the CEO), in subsequent steps: this means that if Mary rejects the record, Enrico won't have any actions to perform.

This is the approval history when both requests have been approved by the manager and the CEO:

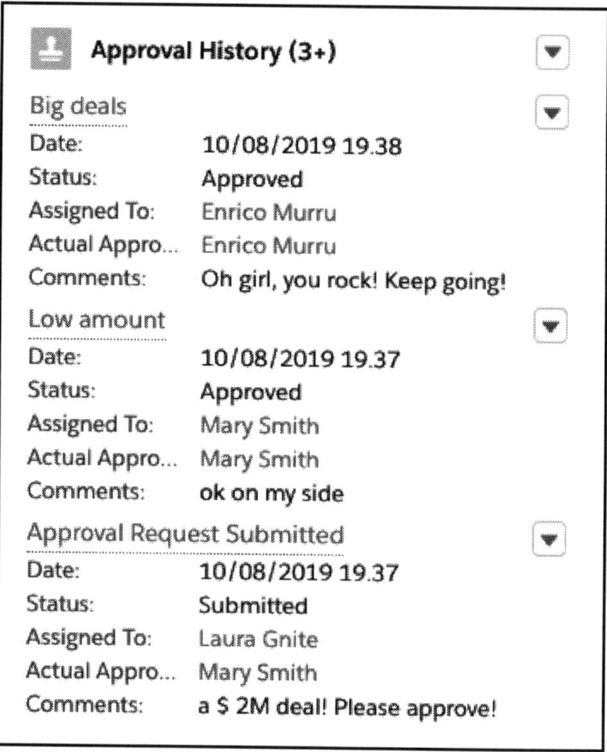

Approval history with two steps

The following configurations and components are available on the platform to speed up approval on the user's side:

- **An Items to Approve Lightning** component only for the home page in Lightning Experience (use the **Lightning App Builder** to set up home pages)

- **An Approval Requests** navigation item only for Lightning apps in Lightning Experience (go to **Setup** | **App Manager** to edit an app)
- Add the **Approval Items** to the Salesforce app navigation menu for the Salesforce Mobile App
- Add the **Items to Approve** related list to the required home page layouts in Salesforce Classic

Approvals can be handled by approvers simply by replying to the notification email response, a feature that can be enabled from **Setup** | **Process Automation** | **Process Automation Settings** by checking the **Enable email approval response** checkbox.

The approver can then respond to the notification email with an **APPROVE** or **REJECT** on the first line and a comment on the second line, without even accessing Salesforce, which will lead to the same result on the **Approval History** related list.

For more information about this cool feature, refer to Salesforce Help at `https://help.salesforce.com/articleView?id=approvals_email_parent.htmtype=5`.

Limits and considerations

Like any other platform feature, approval processes come with limitations (with great powers come great responsibilities, after all!). The following limits refer to the winter 2020 platform release:

- **Total active approval processes per org:** 1,000
- **Total approval processes per org:** 2,000
- **Total approval processes per object:** 300
- **Steps per process:** 30
- **Actions per section (initial submission, final approval, final rejection, recall):** 40
- **Maximum number of approvers per step:** 25
- **Maximum number of characters in approval request comments:** 4,000 (for Chinese, Japanese, and Korean the limit is 1,333 characters)

Approval submission is a manual operation. The user must click the **Submit for Approval** button to start the approval, but with a process builder (or Apex code) you can automatically start an approval process when specific conditions apply (for example, if the opportunity has not yet been submitted and we are approaching the **Closed Won** stage). We'll look at this in the next chapter.

To close this chapter, one last suggestion: if you need a more dynamic way to link approval requests to approvers (and the approval step definition wizard or the hierarchical relationships on the `user` object are not enough), refer to this great post by Automation Champion about dynamic approval routing at `https://automationchampion.com/tag/dynamic-approval-process-in-salesforce/`.

For more details about approver limitations, refer to Salesforce Help at `https://help.salesforce.com/articleView?id=approvals_considerations_approver.htmtype=5`.

Summary

In this chapter, we learned about a key process automation feature: approval processes. Using these, we can let our *low-level* users create business-critical records and make them mandatorily submit each record for approval if some conditions on the record are met. This ensures that their managers can review record data and decide whether the record should be approved (and continue the business flow) or rejected (by requiring some changes before the flow can continue). Throughout this chapter, we learned how to master approval process creation by using the creation wizard. Then, we learned how to add approval steps and configure their criteria and approvers, and then how to configure actions to be automatically executed on the approval or rejection of the approving record. We finally learned how the whole approval flow is executed on the Salesforce user side.

In the next chapter, we'll be dealing with workflow rules 2.0, or Lightning Process Builder, to increase the automation power of your data flow.

Questions

1. Approval processes can be defined across objects (for example, the same approval can be active for opportunity and case objects).
    a. False; approvals are related to a single object type.
    b. True; you can define up to five object types.
    c. True; only if objects are related with hierarchical relationships.
2. Approval entry criteria define:
    a. The steps needed in the approval.
    b. The conditions that a record must match to enter any approval step.
    c. The conditions that a record must match to enter the approval process.
    d. The actions to be applied to specific approval stages.
3. To deliver automated approval routing, what should you do?
    a. Create a custom object that defines a dynamic routing matrix and add a process builder to select the approver once the record is submitted for approval.
    b. Select a hierarchical relationship field from the `user` object.
    c. Select a hierarchical relationship field from the `opportunity` object.
    d. Automated approval routing is only supported on orgs created before summer 2019.
4. A submitted record whose approval is pending can be edited by whom?
    a. By the record owner's manager.
    b. By no one, if the record is locked.
    c. By admins and approvers, only if the approval has been configured to allows this.
    d. By any user whose profile has the **Modify All Data** user permission or **Modify All** object-level permission.
5. To notify an approver of an incoming submission, what should you do?
    a. Set a custom email template on the approval configuration.
    b. Set a custom Chatter post template on the approval configuration.
    c. Leave the custom email template and post template blank; standard email/post templates will be used instead.
    d. Set up a live chat with Omni-Channel to deliver the approval to the approver via the Service Console.

6. The approval page:
    a. Defines the record's fields that the approver will be presented with when deciding approval/rejection.
    b. Can be configured to show the approval history list with comments.
    c. Can be accessed by unauthenticated users.
    d. Is configured within the approval creation wizard.
7. If a user tries to submit a record for approval, they will get an error if:
    a. They don't own the record.
    b. They are the record owner, but the approval is configured so that only the record creator is allowed to submit the record.
    c. They are not enabled to submit the record.
8. Any approval step is composed of:
    a. An entry criteria, the designated approver, and zero or more approval/rejection actions.
    b. An entry criteria and the designated approver.
    c. An entry criteria, the designated approver, and one or more actions.
9. Which of the following actions can the approval process use?
    a. Process builder and flows.
    b. Task, email alert, field update, outbound messages, and record lock.
    c. Workflow rules.
10. Action can be added as:
    a. Initial submission actions.
    b. Step approval/rejection actions.
    c. Final approval/rejection actions.
    d. Recall actions.

13
Lightning Process Builder

We can bring workflow rules to a new level with the Lightning Process Builder, a point and click tool that was made to easily automate business processes using a modern and intuitive graphical designer.

Each Process Builder is made up of certain criteria based on a specific Salesforce object and is used to trigger groups of actions (just like workflow rules), both immediate and scheduled (just like workflows, you can update a field when a specific time condition is met). We'll also learn how to troubleshoot a process in order to understand why errors crop up, as well as how to speed up debugging and deliver a slick automated experience for your organization.

In this chapter, we'll learn about the following topics:

- Setting up a Lightning Process Builder
- Defining action groups
- Managing the Process Builder
- Final considerations for building with a Process Builder

Setting up a Lightning Process Builder

The Lightning Process Builder is a modern way to develop **state machines** within a graphical representation. This is because a picture is worth a thousand words.

This modern tool is basically an **If This Then That** (**ITTT**) tool and like workflow rules and other automation processes (such as approvals or entitlements), it holds a conditional statement (IF), along with the corresponding actions to perform (THEN).

Do you remember what workflow rules can do? They can do the following:

- Update one of the fields of a source object or of a parent record (with a master-child relationship)
- Create a task
- Send an email
- Send an outbound action

What can a Process Builder do instead?

- Create a record (not only tasks)
- Update related records or the source record itself
- Launch a quick action
- Post to Chatter (A Salesforce collaborative tool. For more information about Chatter, please refer to Salesforce Help at `https://help.salesforce.com/articleView?id=collab_overview.htmtype=5`).
- Launch a flow
- Submit a record for approval
- Invoke another Process Builder
- Launch an automated flow
- Send an email
- Send a custom notification
- Call Apex code

Besides the differences in the number of available actions, the Process Builder also allows us to apply actions in a specific order. This is something that is lacking in workflows. In workflows, we don't have a way to predict which action was performed first. Moreover, the Process Builder works with platform events, while workflow rules don't.

For more details about platform events, please refer to Salesforce Help at `https://developer.salesforce.com/docs/atlas.en-us.platform_events.meta/platform_events/platform_events_intro.htm`.

The ability to aggregate conditions and actions on the same instance of the Process Builder, along with having a clear graphical representation of the state machine, provides administrators with a powerful tool they can use to automate their processes.

Note that Salesforce is no longer enhancing workflows. This doesn't mean that workflows will be discontinued – they just won't receive any new features in the future since the Process Builder will become the next preferred automation tool (source: `https://trailhead.salesforce.com/en/content/learn/modules/workflow_migration/workflow_migration_intro`).

Also, it's not good to mix workflow rules and Process Builders: evaluate a migration to Process Builder from older workflow rules, as pictured in the Trailhead module referenced in the previous information box. That way, you'll have a more consistent automated process implementation and a better way to predict the automation behavior of any record.

The ability to have different versions of a given Process Builder also gives you the power to try new versions of an automation process, along with the chance to roll back if things go wrong.

While dealing with Process Builders, you'll find the same concepts as the ones that are found in workflow rules, but with some enhancements and cool features.

Now that we know what a Process Builder is, let's look at how we can build one.

Shaping a Process Builder

To create a new Process Builder, perform the following steps:

1. Click on **Setup** | **Process Automation** | **Process Builder** and then click the **New** button:

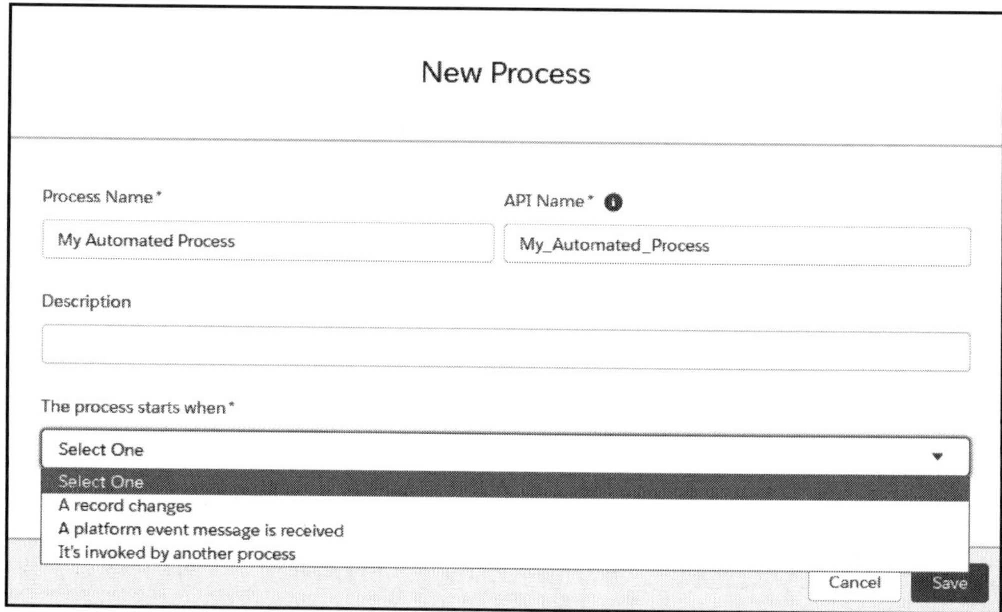

Creating a new Process Builder

Apart from the **Process Name** and **API Name** (which cannot be updated after creation), the process trigger event (which event the process should start on, that is, **The process starts when*** picklist in the preceding screenshot) will help you define what you want to do. Here, you can use one of the following trigger criteria:

- **A record changes**: The process is triggered by a Salesforce record that has been created/updated.
- **A platform event message is received**: The process is triggered by a platform event message that is received from Salesforce (more information about platform events can be found on Salesforce Help at `https://help.salesforce.com/articleView?id=platform_events.htmtype=0`).

- **It's invoked by another process**: The Process Builder you are creating is invoked by another process (it is not triggered by any record modification; it is triggered by a *parent* Process Builder). With this option, you can create recurrent Process Builders, thus avoiding repetition. This is often called an **invocable Process Builder**.

2. Click **Save.** You will see the graphical tool. If you click the **Edit Properties** button, you can change the name and description of the process, and a new **Template** checkbox will appear. With this checkbox, we can define the current process as a template process that can act as the *base automation* for a specific kind of business process. This way, it can be cloned, which can help create slightly different modifications that can be adapted to specific/local circumstances (for example, an opportunity-related process can differ from country to country, but its main structure applies globally).

The following diagram shows the base structure of a Process Builder:

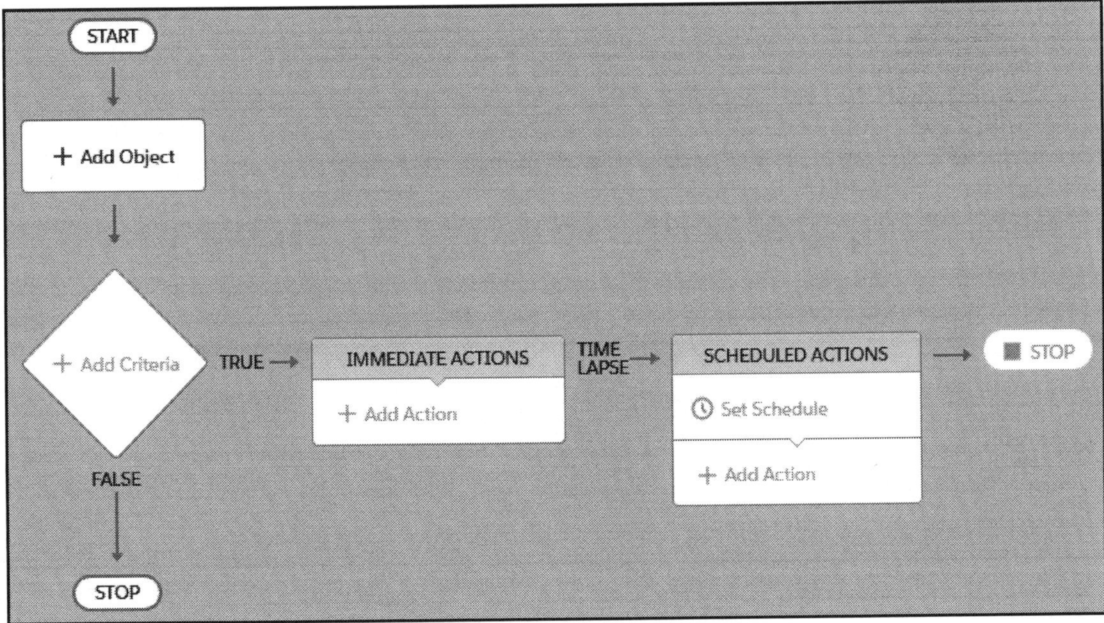

The base structure of a Process Builder

The preceding diagram will help us understand the following building blocks of a Process Builder:

- **Trigger**: What object/event the process should start from (the **+ Add Object** button).
- **Criteria(s)**: These are matching conditions that state whether a process should execute certain actions (the **+ Add Criteria** element).
- **Immediate Actions**: These are actions that are executed immediately if the criteria match.
- **Scheduled Actions**: These are actions that have been scheduled to run if the criteria match and are executed with a time-based schedule (depending on what's been specified in a date/time field or at the time the process is executed).

Now that we've set up our Process Builder, it's time to trigger it. Let's look at how we can do this.

Trigger selection

In the previous section, we looked at the Process Builder designer and all the blocks that we need to create a new instance of a Process Builder. The first step is creating a triggering condition. To do so, we need to use the **+ Add Object** button to open up the triggering conditions modal. The following screenshot shows the Process Builder's trigger selection for the record changes Process Builder:

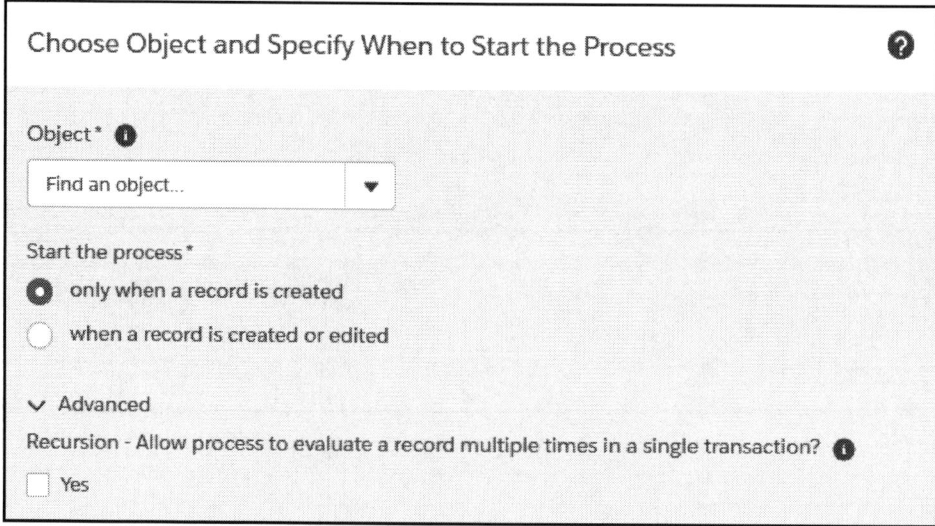

The **Start the process*** radio buttons look like the same options we had on the Workflow rule definition page, where we could define the triggering conditions, whereby a record may trigger the given workflow (if you don't remember this, please refer to `Chapter 11`, *Automation with Workflows*) exception that was made for the **created, and any time it's edited to subsequently meet criteria** option that's available later on in the configuration process.

To set everything up, perform the following steps:

1. Select the object type.
2. Set the **Start the process** option (this triggers the process when the record is created and/or updated).
3. Flag the **Recursion - Allow process to evaluate a record multiple times in a single transaction?** checkbox if you want the same Process Builder to be evaluated more then once in a single save transaction (up to five times per transaction). By flagging this checkbox, any record change that is executed after this Process Builder has completed its actions (there is no reason for this Process Builder to update the record so that another Process Builder can be triggered) can trigger the same Process Builder repeatedly until the recursion level has been reached (the five-times limit). Simply put, a Process Builder can trigger itself up to five times if this checkbox is flagged.

Every time the Process Builder is executed, it will handle a *new version* of the record by taking the modifications of the automations that preceded it into account.

When dealing with platform events and selecting the **A platform event message is received** option on the **New Process** modal, the subsequent form changes slightly:

Creating a new Process Builder to handle platform events

You can check how the form has changed by clicking on the **+ Add Trigger** button (which replaces the **+ Add Object** button), which displays the following options:

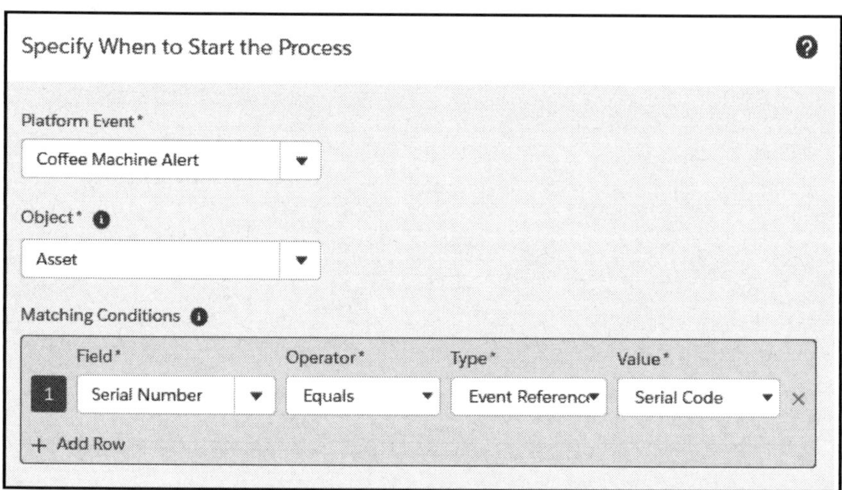

Process Builder Trigger selection for platform events

In this example, a **Coffee Machine Alert** platform event (which may tell Salesforce that we have run out of water) must be matched with a contextual Salesforce object, which, in our scenario, is an **Asset** object. The match is made using the **Serial Code** field on the platform event and the **Serial Number** on the **Asset** object.

In this case, we don't have a **Start the process** radio button since the platform event cannot be updated. For the same reason, it isn't possible to loop on the same Process Builder more than once.

If the matching conditions that should match a Salesforce object to give the platform event a context on the CRM find none or more than one related Salesforce objects, the Process Builder fails (it is not possible to relate none or multiple objects to a given platform event).

If we were building an invocable Process Builder, the trigger form would have been even simpler:

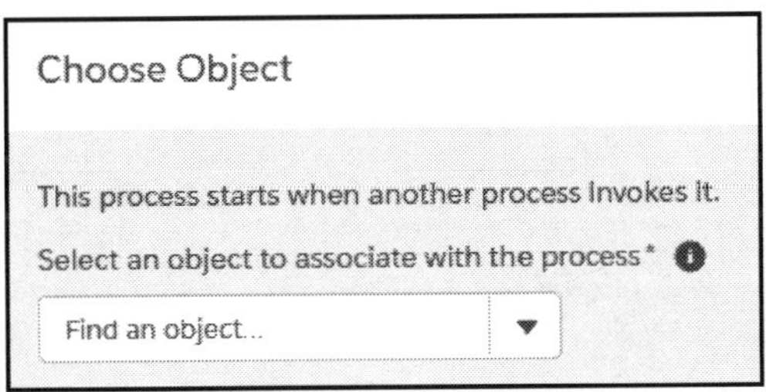

Process Builder Trigger selection for the invocable type

When the process is invoked by another process, it only carries out the object type it is referring to.

Now, we need to sort out the criteria definition.

Criteria definition

This is the process of matching criteria to make the Process Builder execute the actions group that has been defined for that criteria. Let's see how we can do this.

To add the criteria, click on **+ Add Criteria**:

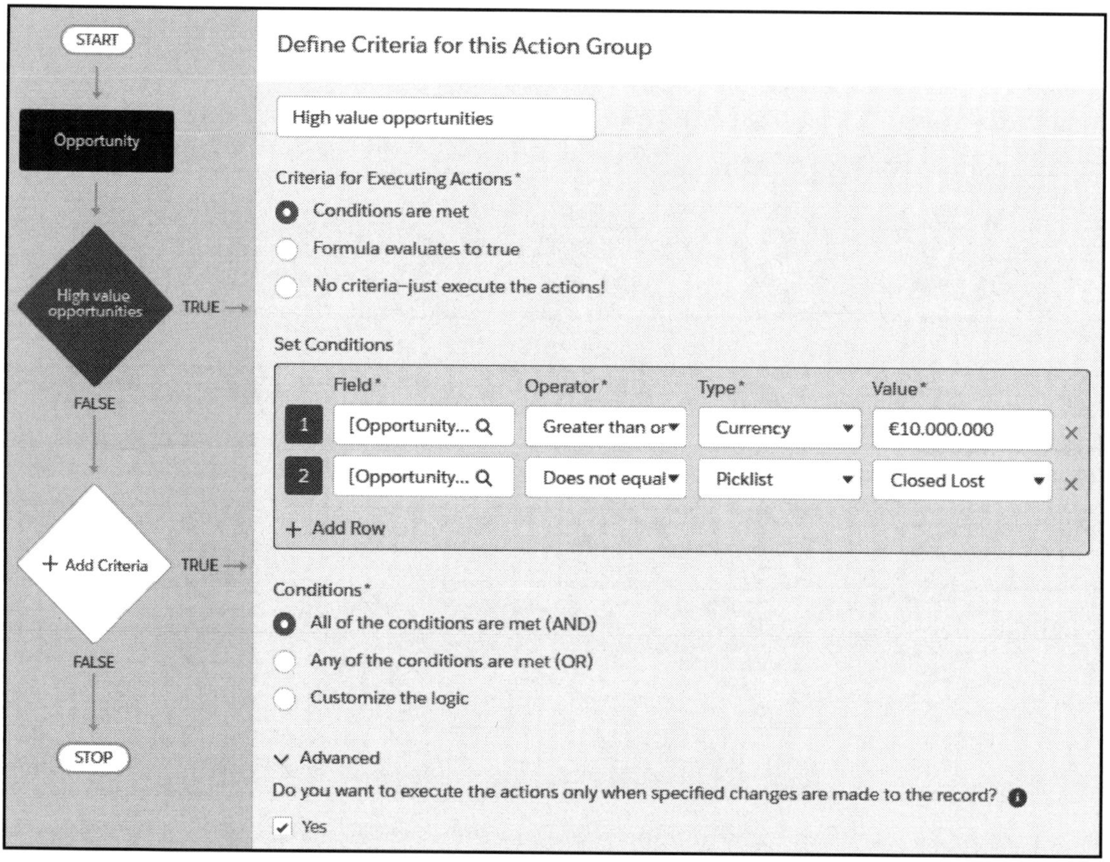

Criteria definition

Criteria are defined by the following three things, as shown in the preceding screenshot:

- By a list of conditions
- A formula
- No criteria

Note that the criteria always evaluates to true.

Of these three, the formula selection can be a little different from what we are used to; the following screenshot shows how previous conditions can be written using a Process Builder formula:

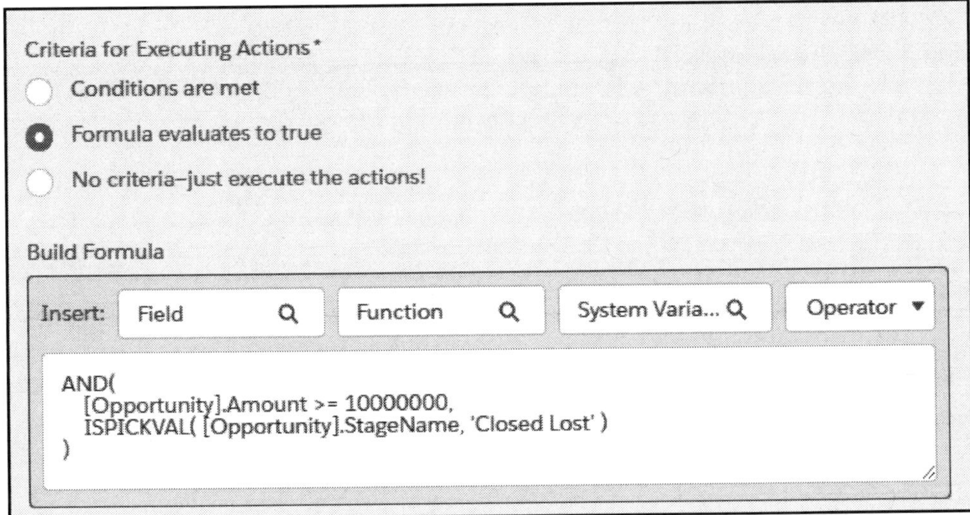

Process Builder formula

Remember the following when using formulae:

- They must return true/false.
- They can contain up to 3,000 characters.
- They must reference the process trigger object (with the right capitalization).
- The `ISCHANGED` function cannot be used if it's related to a parent object. For instance, `ISCHANGED([Opportunity].Account.Name` fails, while `ISCHANGED([Opportunity].AccountId)` is correct.

If we use conditions instead of formulas, the **Conditions** section grants the selection of AND/OR/custom conditions logic.

The **Advanced** tab is only shown if the trigger event is set to **when a record is created or edited** and the criteria node has conditions (the **No criteria—just execute the actions!** options is not selected) or formulas (but it has to contain a reference to the record that started the process) where the **Do you want to execute the actions only when specified changes are made to the record?** flag is used to prevent the Process Builder from executing the related actions if no significant change has been made to the record (that is, no field in the criteria condition/formula has changed). This is extremely useful when we don't want to generate multiple actions on subsequent updates of a record, such as an email notification.

As an example, let's configure the second criteria for medium-valued opportunities:

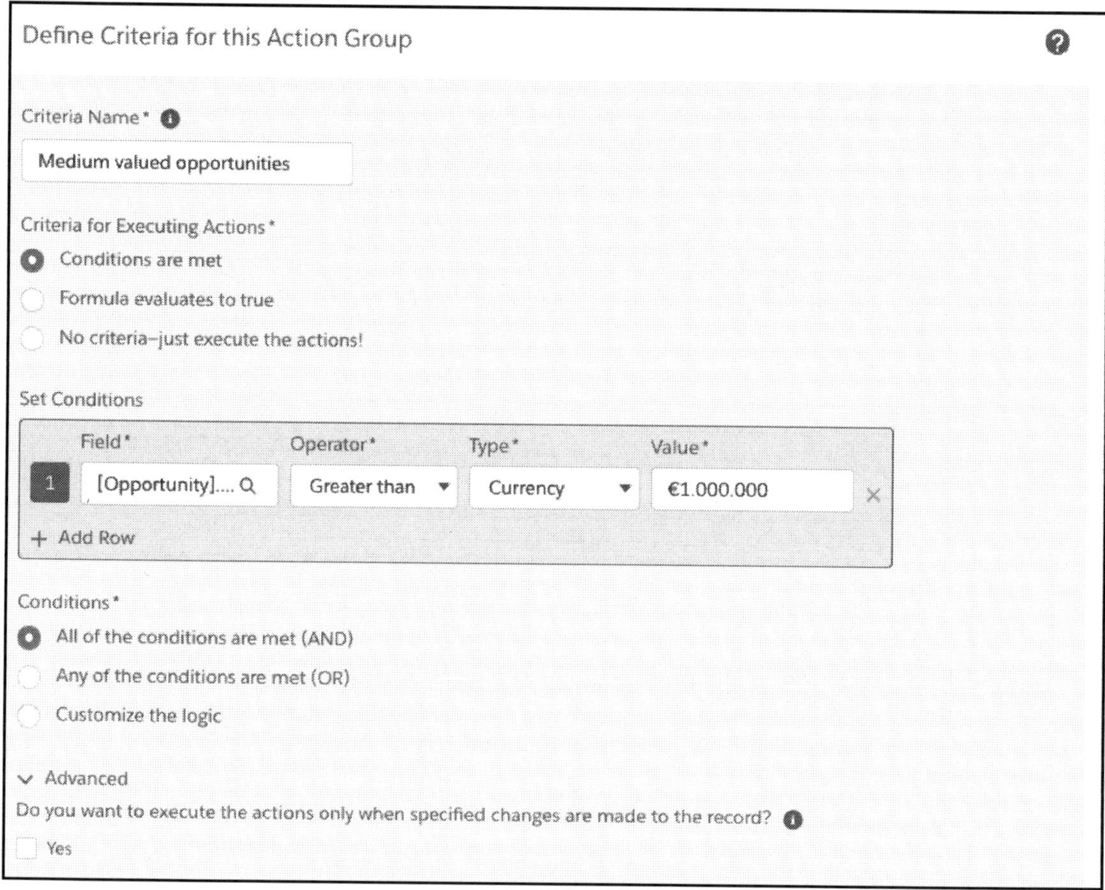

Definition of the second criteria

Another interesting feature is the option to stop the process when actions have been executed or continue to the next node (if the conditions match):

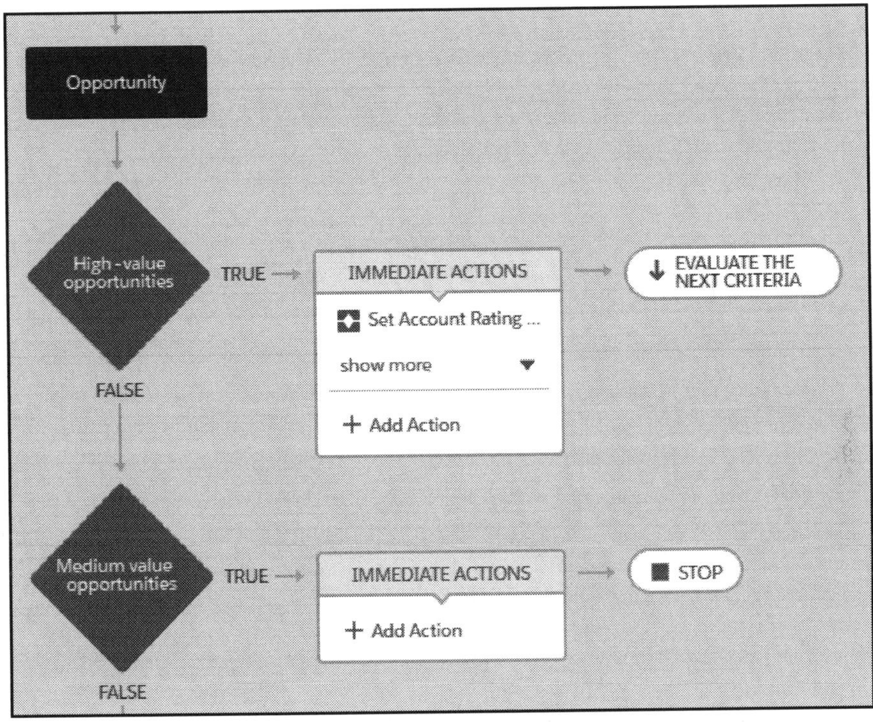

Actions for multiple criteria

In this example, if a high-value opportunity executes its actions (as we'll see shortly), the next node is evaluated (this is defined by the **EVALUATE THE NEXT CRITERIA** button, but it can be set to **STOP** to avoid Process Builder continuation, as you can see in the criteria branch that follows). So, if an opportunity record with an amount of $500 M triggers the Process Builder's automation, since the first criteria requires that the opportunity's amount is greater than $100 M and the second criteria requires an opportunity with an amount of at least $1 M, both actions' groups will be executed.

In the next section, we'll deal with actions and action groups.

Defining action groups

So far, we've seen how we can configure a Process Builder so that it's triggered by conditions on the fields of its triggering record. This is the **IF** part of the tool. Now, we want to talk about the **THEN** part, that is, the actions that the automation should execute in response to thc **IF** criteria.

Actions are defined in action groups, which can be of two different types:

- Immediate actions
- Scheduled actions

The first group is executed immediately when the criteria conditions match.

Scheduled actions are executed after a time frame has been defined and they are only available if the **Start the Process** setting is set to the following:

- *Only when a record is created*
- *When a record is created or edited* and the advanced option, **Do you want to execute the actions only when specified changes are made to the record?** is checked

The time frame can be defined using the **Set Schedule** action on the **Scheduled Actions** panel:

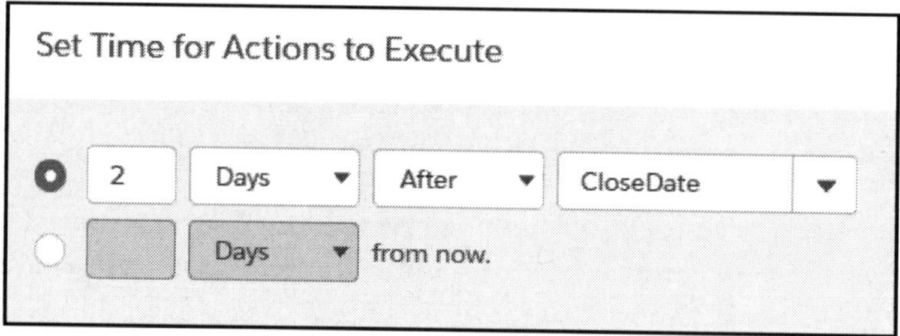

Scheduled Actions time frame selection

It is possible to select a time schedule based on a record date/time field or the Process Builder's execution time. We can select a number of days or hours after the selected date/time value and (only for record-related fields) before a given amount of time.

When the execution time is reached and the conditions have been met, the scheduled actions are executed.

You cannot go back in time, so if the scheduled time is less than **now**, actions are executed **as soon as possible**.

There are some limitations regarding scheduled actions (as of the Winter '20 platform release):

- You can have up to 20,000 process schedules based on a given field.
- Field-based schedules can't refer to a formula that includes related object fields.
- An organization can execute up to 1,000 groups of scheduled actions per hour. If the limit is hit, the remaining groups are executed in the next hour.
- An organization can have up to 50,000 pending schedules at a given time.
- The current time schedules are executed based on the time zone of the user that triggered the process.
- If the field at the base of a schedule has a null value, the schedule is ignored.
- If a record is deleted and has scheduled actions, these schedules are deleted as well.
- For processes that start when the record is created, scheduled actions are executed even if the initial conditions were changed at the time the schedule was executed.
- Processes based on the `SignupRequest` object don't support scheduled actions.
- If a scheduled criterion is configured as **0 Days Before** a date, the Process Builder engine automatically changes it to **0 Days After** the date when you reopen it, but the condition is still valid.

We can define more than one scheduled action, thereby providing different time schedules. This is shown in the following screenshot:

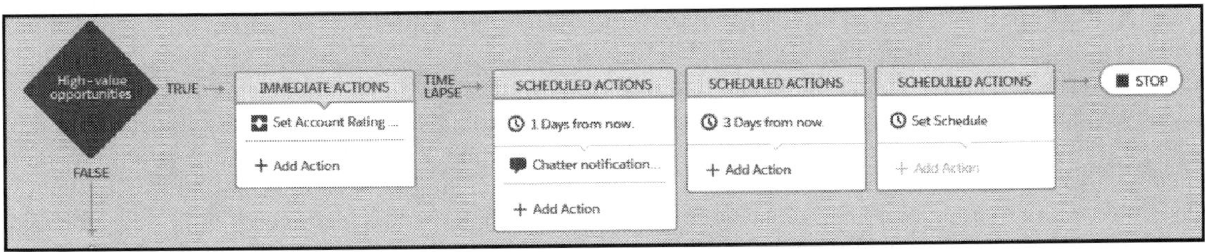

Defining multiple scheduled actions

Here, we've listed all the actions that are available for the Process Builder. In the upcoming sections, we'll quickly explain how they work.

Creating records

Select an object type and manually define the mapping for its fields:

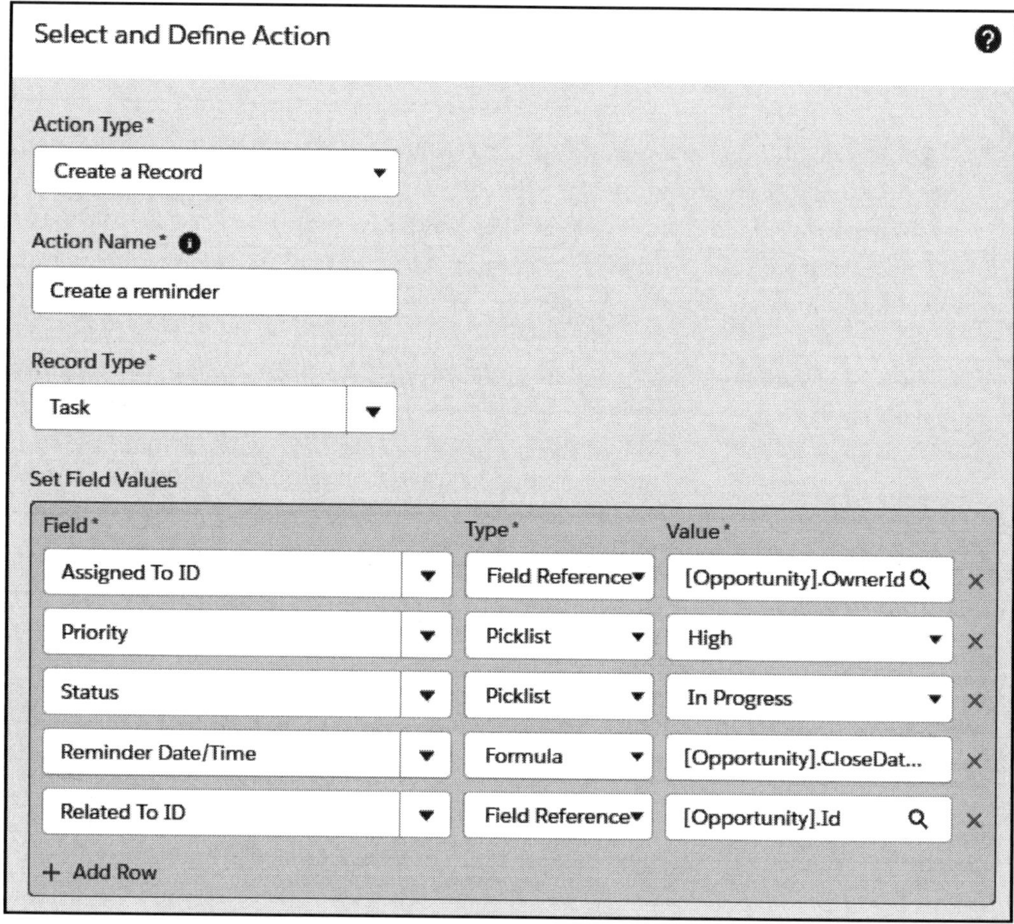

Record creation action

Mandatory fields appear automatically on the form.

You can use the current record's related object to set field values.

Updating records

In workflows, we used to create field update actions to update record fields and the parent's fields if a master-child relationship was in place. With the **Update records** action, we can update the following:

- The current record
- Any parent record (whether it is related to a master-child relationship or not)
- Any child record of the current record or any parent object (for example, in our scenario, the Opportunity Products or all the Cases related to the current opportunity's account). The following screenshot shows these:

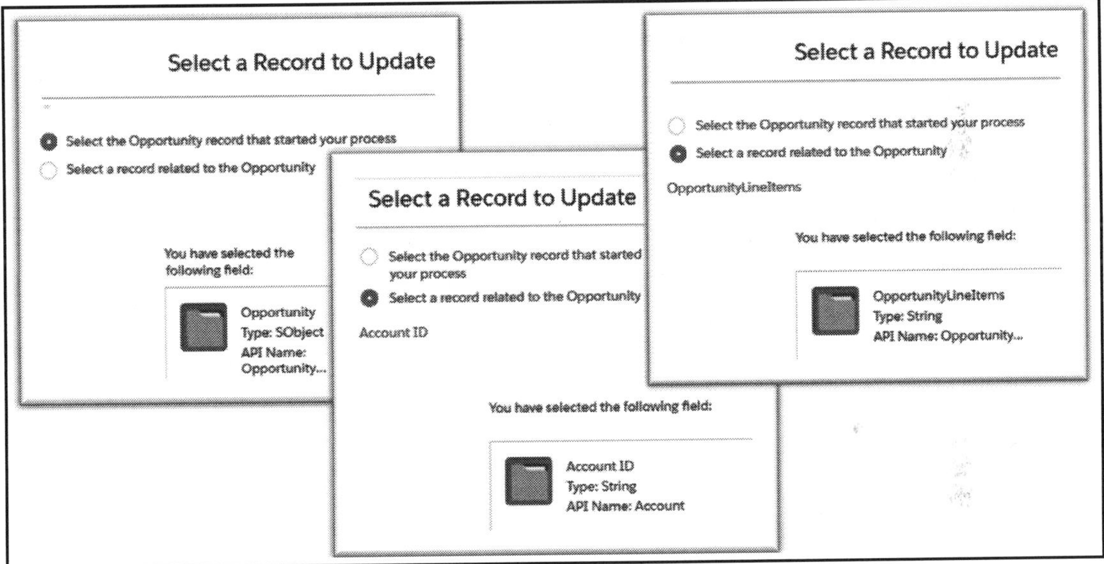

Record selection on the Update Records action

When selecting to update related child records, we can even select the conditions those records have to match and which need to be updated:

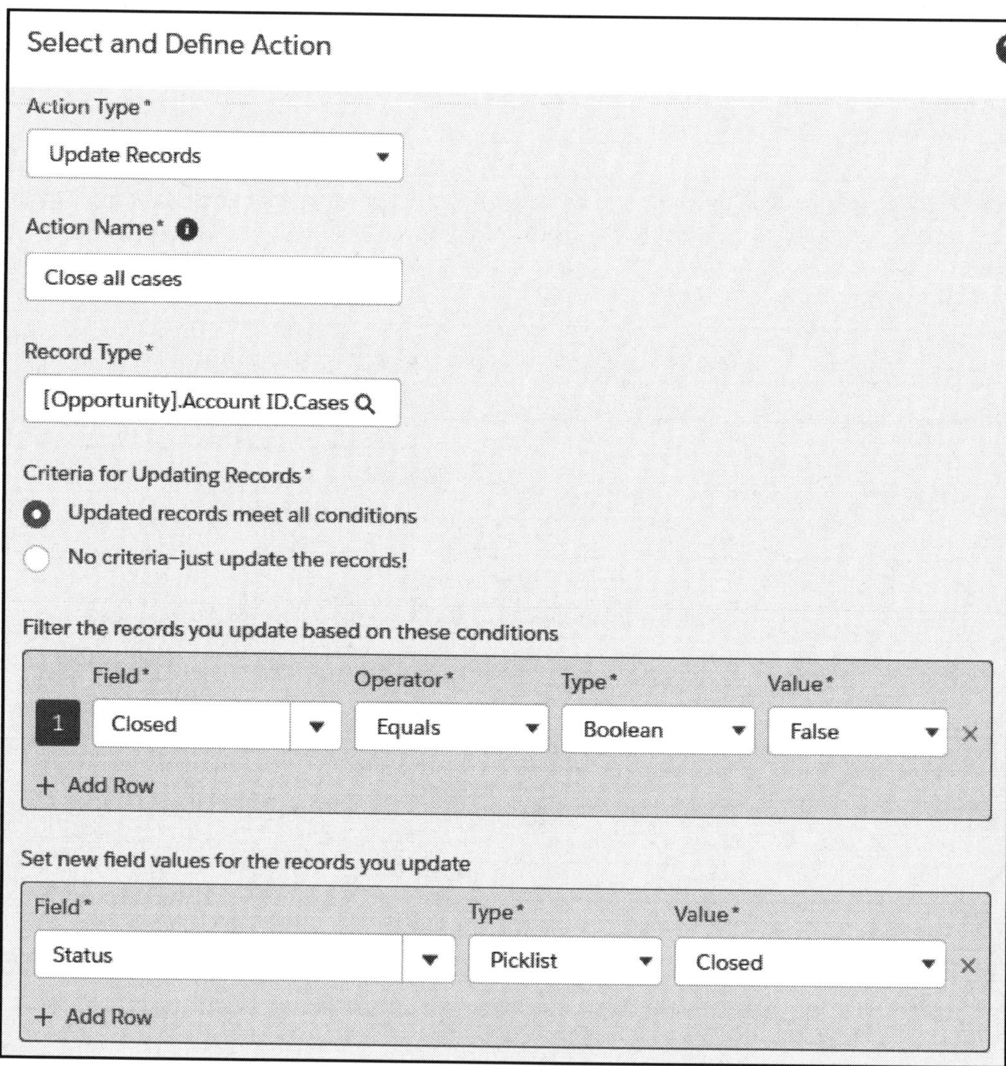

Record update configuration with child objects

In this example, we want to close all the open cases related to the opportunity's account by selecting the condition cases that must match (cases must not be closed) and then the field updates that will be applied to every record (status set to **Closed**). For this, in the **Criteria for Updating Records** section, set the value to **No criteria–just update the records!** in order to update all the records that come from the related children list.

Processes

It is possible to invoke another invocable process. This is extremely useful as it can save you time when dealing with repetitive actions.

In our scenario, we have created a simple invocable process that sets the account rating to hot:

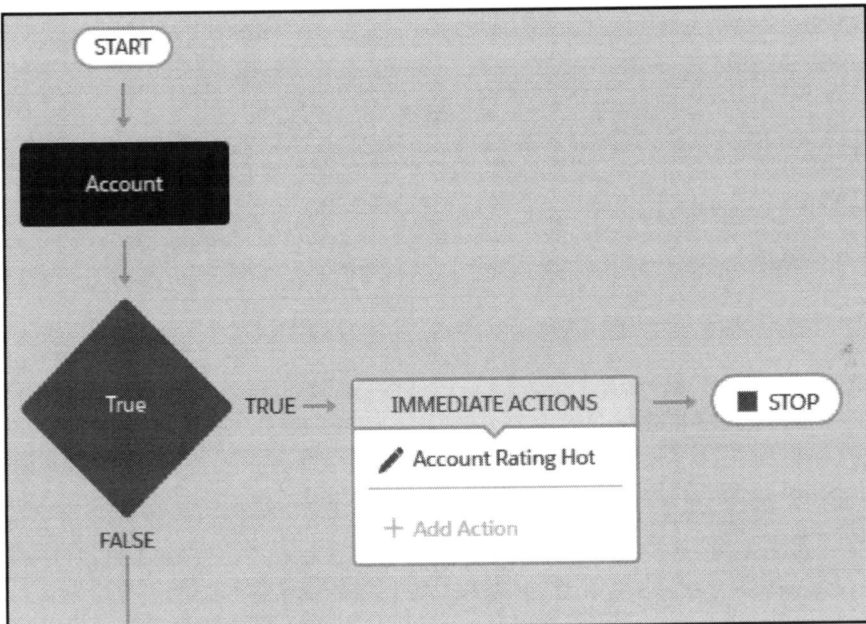

Invokable Process Builder example

The main Process Builder can select this process in order to execute all its actions:

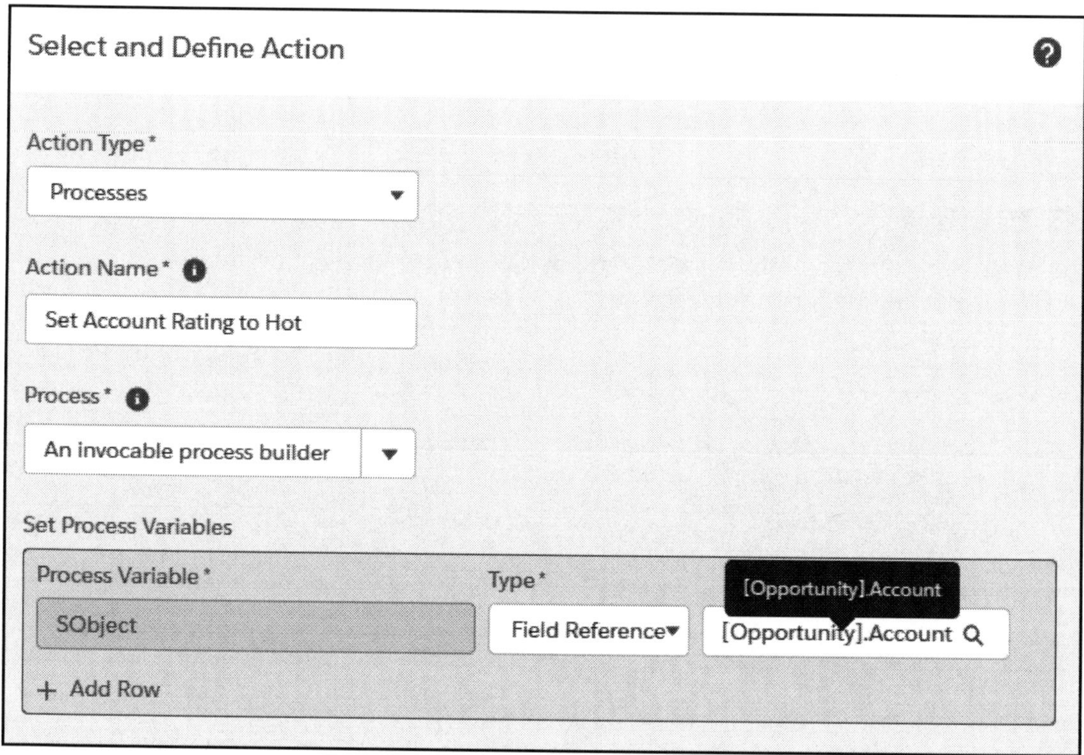

Processes action definition

Select an *active* process whose trigger object has at least one unique ID field in common with the current object. For us, the **Opportunity** object shares the **AccountId** field with the **Account** object of the invokable process that was selected.

The child process on an immediate action group will receive the record as it was when the process started, while on a scheduled action group, it will receive the last version of the record.

Posting to Chatter

As you already know, Chatter is a Salesforce collaboration tool that can be built into any record of your organization. This is automatically enabled on any organization created after June 10, 2010.

To find out more about Chatter and how it can leverage Salesforce collaboration, please refer to Salesforce Help at `https://help.salesforce.com/articleView?id=collab_overview.htmtype=5`.

Posting to Chatter is easy with the Process Builder:

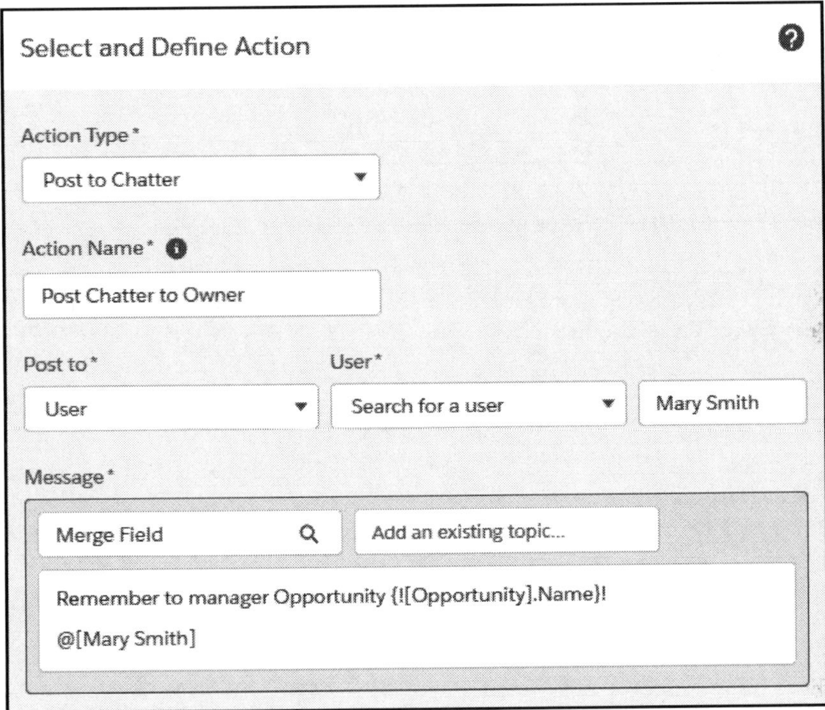

Post to Chatter action configuration

We can select to post to a **User** (by selecting a specific user or referencing an object field, such as `OwnerId` or `CreatedById`), to a chatter group, or to the current record Chatter feed.

The message can contain up to 10,000 characters with text, merge fields, already existing topics, and mentions (up to 25 per message).

To *dynamically* mention a user based on a record's field value, use `@[{!fieldReference}]` as the syntax; for example, `@[{![Opportunity].OwnerId}]`.

Remember that if you use Microsoft Internet Explorer 11 (which will be officially deprecated at the end of 2020; see `https://help.salesforce.com/articleView?id=getstart_browsers_sfx.htmtype=5` for more details), you won't be able to copy and paste text into a message, so be careful.

Finally, remember not to start the message with a field reference (for example, `{![Opportunity].Name}`) because that action won't be saved at all. This is a known issue – just add a blank space at the beginning of the message as a workaround.

Email alerts

Like workflows, with approvals and entitlements, you can send emails using **Email Alerts** actions. This is shown in the following screenshot:

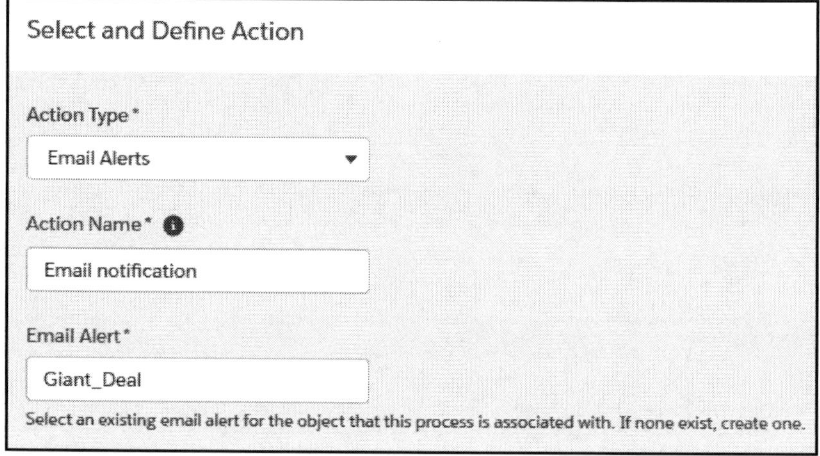

Email alert action

Simply select an email alert that's already on the system (remember that your organization can send 1,000 email alerts per standard Salesforce license (up to 2,000,000 in total)).

Submitting for approval

Do you remember `Chapter 12`, *Automating Record Approval with Approval Processes*, when we talked about automatic approval?

You can enter a record into an approval process by using a Process Builder action that's configured like so:

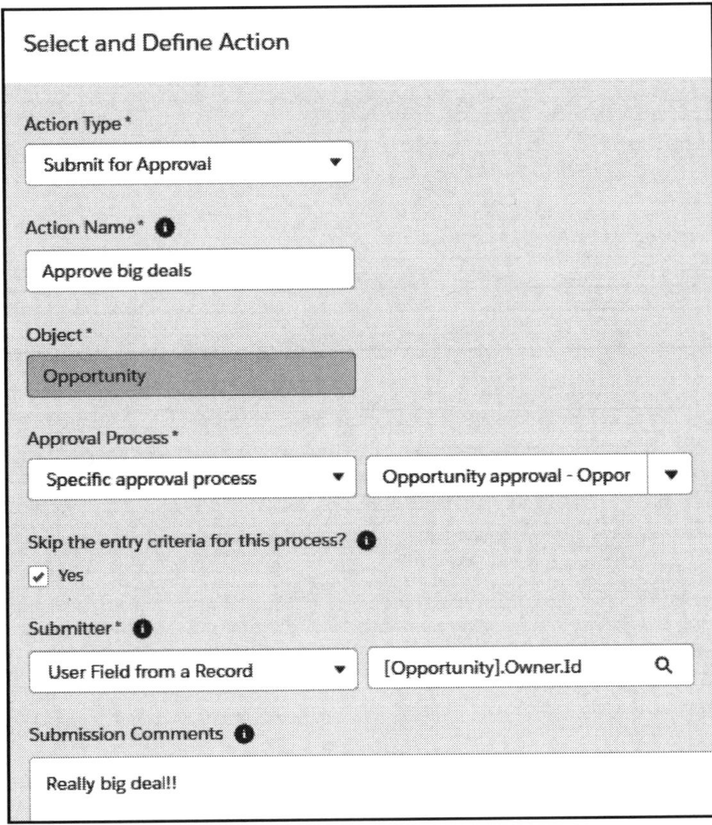

Submitting for approval action

When selecting the approval process, remember that the Process Builder will fail if you select a default approval process in the **Approval Process** section and no active approval has been set up or if you select a **Specific approval process** and the entry criteria do not match. In the latter case, flag **Skip the entry criteria for this process?** if you want to force the current record to enter the approval process while disregarding the entry criteria.

Then, select the submitter, who can be the current user running the process, a user who got it from the record (as shown in our example, this is the **Opportunity** owner), or any other user in the organization. If the selected user isn't listed in the initial submitter list, the Process Builder will fail.

Finally, insert an optional submission comment.

Flows

A flow can be launched from a Process Builder to make complex automations. The only limitation is that the flow must be an *autolaunched* flow. Flows will be covered in depth in the next chapter, that is, `Chapter 14`, *Lightning Flows*.

To configure a flow action, select an autolaunched flow and set up any relevant flow variables by picking from the current and related records:

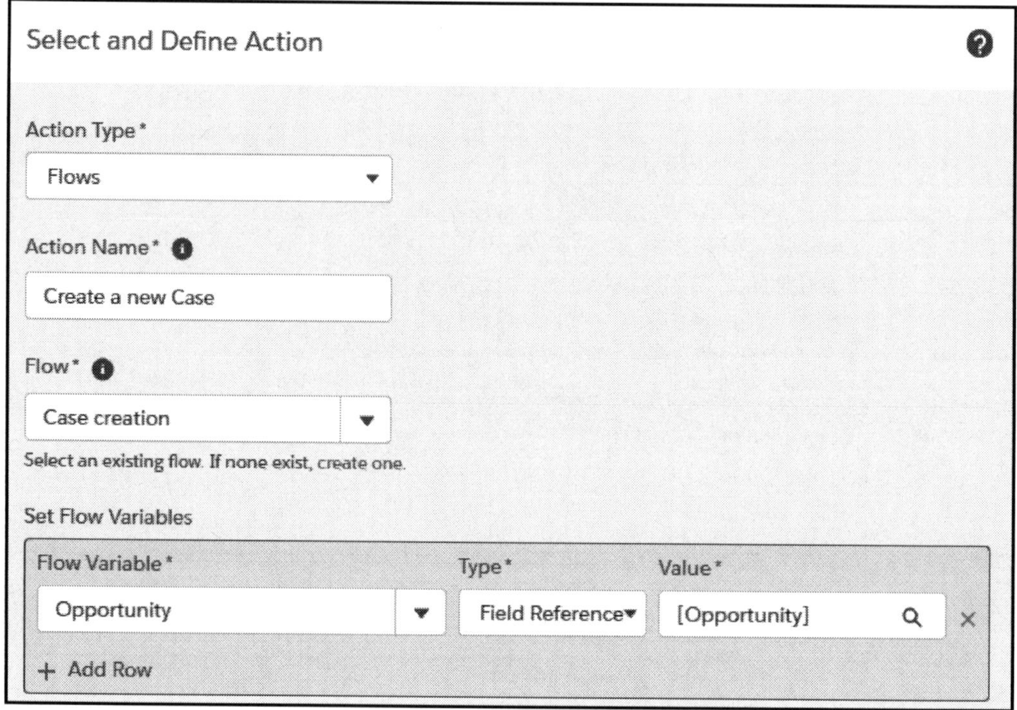

Flow action

Remember, only active flows can be selected for this configuration.

Quick Actions

A Process Builder action can execute a quick action (global or object-specific), but is limited by the fact that you can only select Quick Actions that can create or update a record or log a call (Quick Actions can also be used to launch a Lightning component on a record page, which is not something that the Process Builder is capable of doing):

Quick Actions are not covered in this book. Please refer to Trailhead at `https://trailhead.salesforce.com/en/content/learn/modules/lex_customization/lex_customization_actions` for a quickstart guide and Salesforce Help at `https://help.salesforce.com/articleView?id=actions_overview.htmtype=5` for more information.

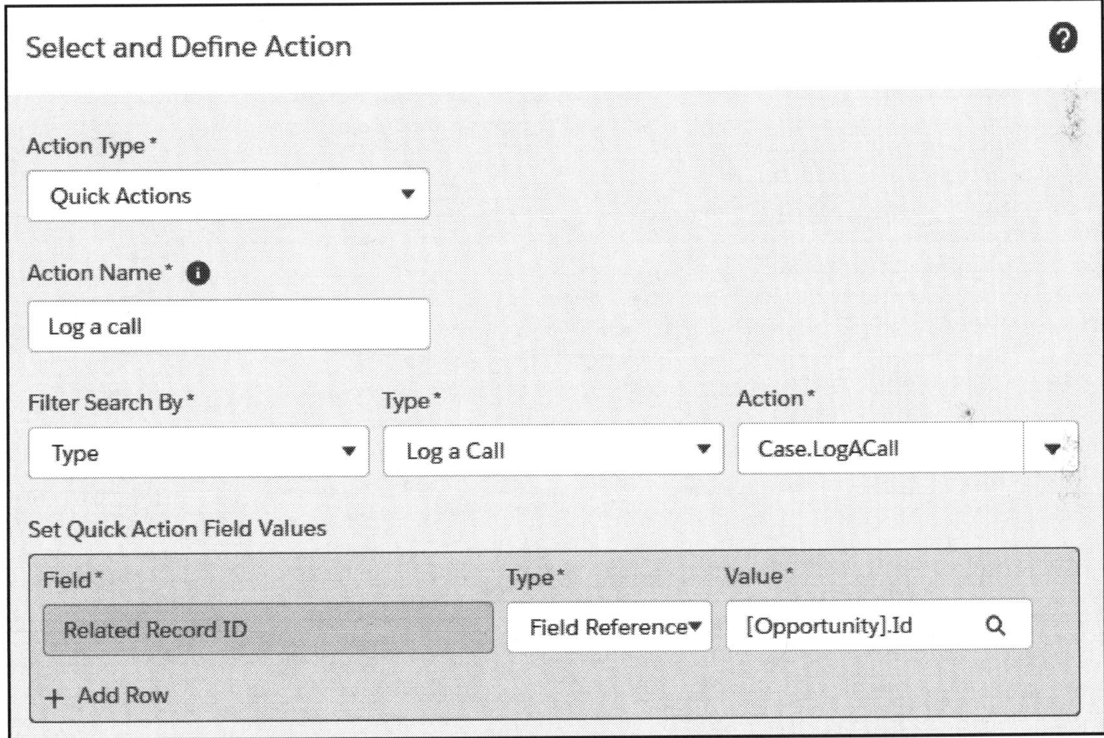

Quick Actions

The required fields are automatically added to the **Quick Actions Field Values**. You can add any other field that is available on the Quick Action definition and select static values (for example, a string or picklist) or reference a related field. In this example, we can create a renewal opportunity by copying the relevant fields from the current opportunity and putting this action into a scheduled action group so that the renewal is created after a given amount of days (let's say, 1 year or 365 days).

Custom notifications

Custom notifications are a great introduction to the summer 2019 release of Salesforce. Here, you can define custom notifications that can be sent to users via mobile or desktop.

To define a custom notification, go to **Setup** | **Notification Builder** | **Notification Types** and click the **New** button, as shown in the following screenshot:

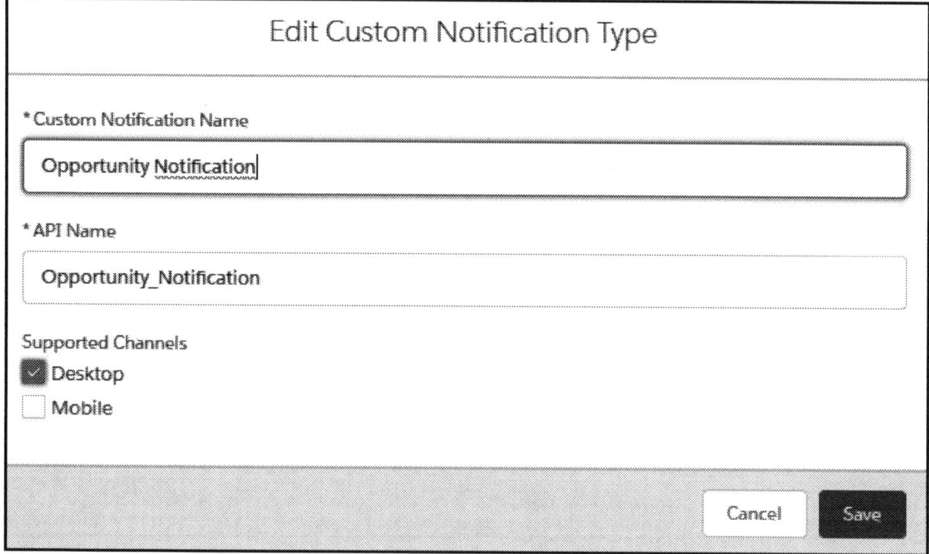

Custom notification type creation

From here, you can customize a new action on the Process Builder in order to send custom notifications, as shown in the following screenshot:

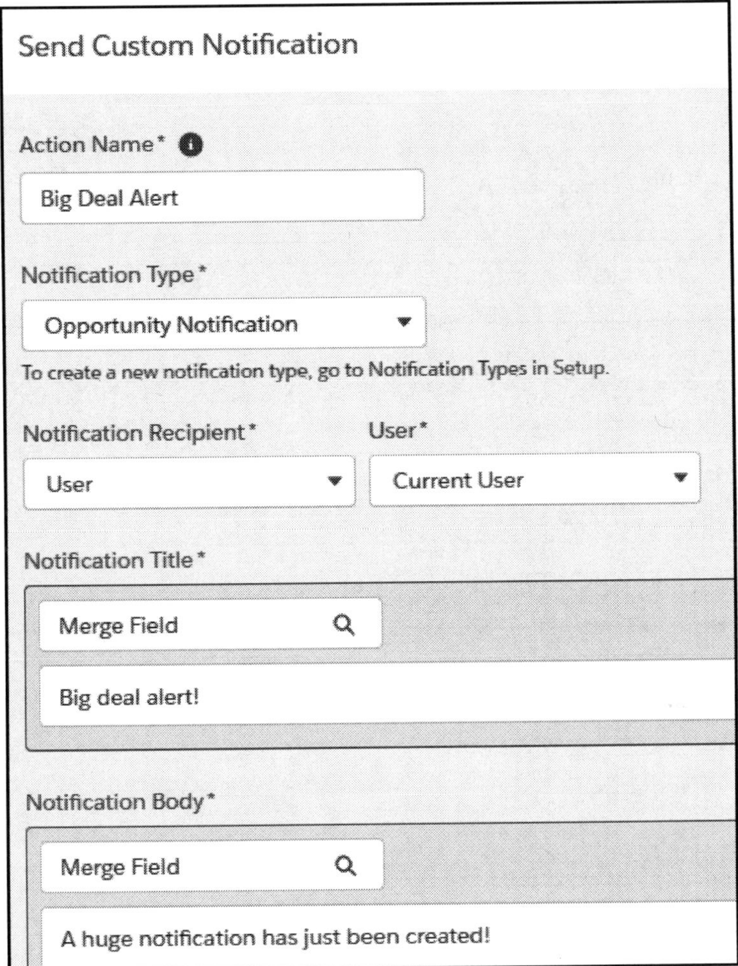

Custom notification action

When the action is executed, a new notification appears for the selected user or group of users:

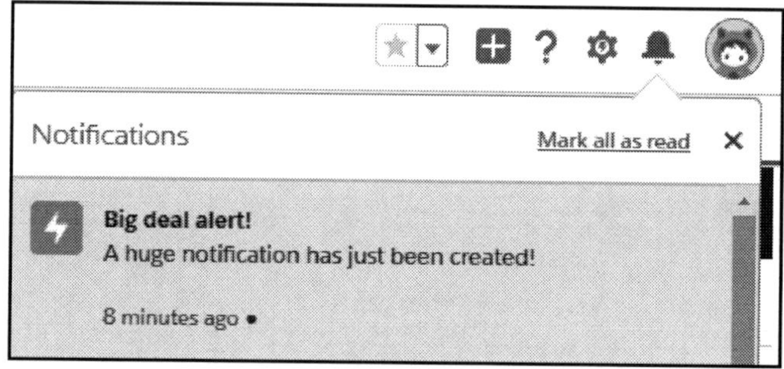

Custom notification on the user side

If you click on the notification, you will be redirected to the opportunity.

Apex

If the previous actions are not enough to define your process, you can use an Apex class to execute custom code and implement the necessary algorithm:

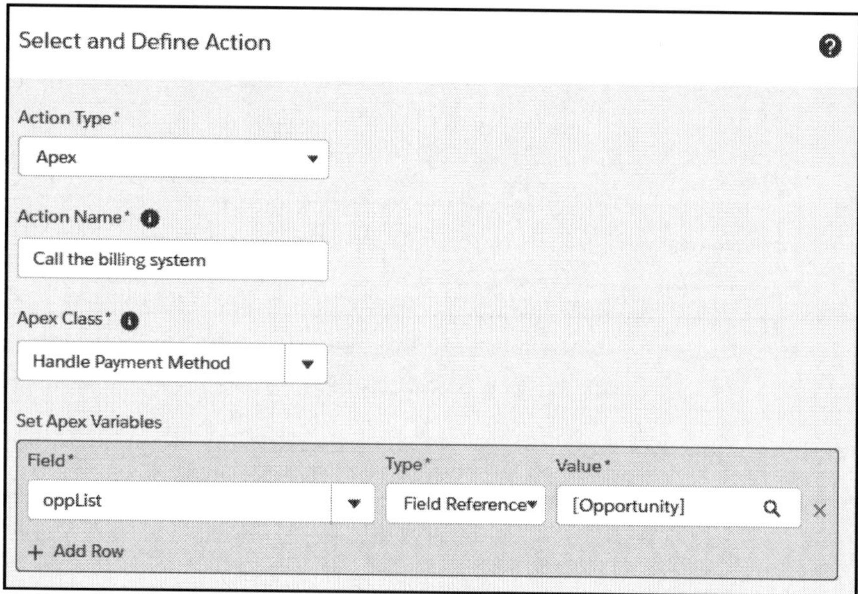

Apex action definition

In this example, we are calling a custom Apex class to communicate with the external billing system in order to set up a payment method (this operation can't be done without using custom Apex integration).

The Apex class must contain the `@InvocableMethod` annotation and must be shaped in a specific way so that it can be called by the Process Builder. Tell your developers to refer to Salesforce Help at `https://developer.salesforce.com/docs/atlas.en-us.apexcode.meta/apexcode/apex_classes_annotation_InvocableMethod.htm` for more information.

Managing the Process Builder

A process can be set with two different statuses:

- Inactive
- Active, that is, the process cannot be changed, only cloned

When cloning a process, you can clone the current process as a new version (so that it can be activated when your job is done) or as a brand-new Process Builder (this is particularly useful when you're using templates).

We can have up to 50 versions of a given process but only one can be active at a time.

To activate a process (by using the **Activate** button on the builder), we need to have at least one criteria node and one immediate or scheduled action group; once activated, all the other versions will become inactive.

To monitor pending scheduled actions, click on **Setup** | **Process Automation** | **Flows** and refer to the **Paused and Waiting Interviews** page. In fact, when a process schedules an action, Salesforce creates a flow interview record and pauses it until the scheduled time occurs. This is why we have to go to the **Flows** page to get the list of awaiting actions.

To troubleshoot errors on the Builder, we can use the **Apex Debug Logs** (which we looked at the beginning of this book); they work more or less like they did when we looked at the workflow rule example.

For more details about debugging a Process Builder, please refer to Salesforce Help at `https://help.salesforce.com/articleView?id=process_troubleshoot_debuglogs.htmtype=5`.

Final considerations for building with a Process Builder

Before closing this chapter, let's look at the things we need to take into consideration when building automation using a Process Builder.

The first suggestion is to use one automation tool for each object because it becomes very difficult to predict when actions will take place if you have a Process Builder, Apex triggers, and workflow rules active at the same time.

When replacing a workflow rule or an Apex trigger with a Process Builder, remember to deactivate them before activating the Process Builder, otherwise you may get unexpected results, such as the record being overwritten several times or multiple email notifications being sent (we don't want to spam our precious users).

Moreover, use only one record-change triggered process per object. That way, you will have an idea of what's happening behind the scenes, be able to predict the order of execution, and avoid hitting the platform's **governor limits**.

Transaction governor limits are an important part of the developer life cycle because they state how many operations Apex code can perform when a database transaction is done (that is, a record is created/updated/deleted). Since each Salesforce organization lies with other Salesforce organizations in the cloud, Salesforce has to ensure that no organization consumes too many resources so that the other organizations suffer (an organization can become unstable or slow). By limiting the resources each transaction can consume, Salesforce attains better performance and reduces the chance of system failures.

Governor limits are more than this, but by referring to our scope, we can define the following limits (as of Winter '20 release):

- Total number of SOQL queries: **100**
- Total number of records retrieved by SOQL queries: **50,000**
- Total number of DML statements (that is, CRUD database operations): **150**
- Total number of records processed as a result of DML statements: **10,000**

In a Process Builder, a SOQL query is executed on Update Record actions (which can return one record if the update is done on the trigger object or several records if we are getting, for example, all the cases for a given account) and a DML is executed on Quick Actions, Record Creations, or Update Records actions (for the latter, if you update all the cases for a given account, we will have 1 DML, but several records processed on that DML).

This means that it is good practice to combine actions when possible: don't create different Record Updates to update the same object; instead, create one Record Update action that updates all the required fields for the same record.

For a complete list of execution governor limits, please refer to Salesforce Help at `https://developer.salesforce.com/docs/atlas.en-us.apexcode.meta/apexcode/apex_gov_limits.htm`.

Pay attention and avoid infinite loops; for example, Process A triggers Process B, which creates a new record that triggers Process A, and so on. This is a possible cause of a governor limit outbreak.

Before moving on to the next chapter, take a look at the Automation Champion's Process Builder blog at `https://automationchampion.com/learning-process-builder/`. From there, you will have access to tens of examples and countless hints that can empower your Process Builder knowledge and expertise.

Process Builder is a powerful tool that can leverage process automation in your organizations and create exceptions in certain situations. This tool should cover all your needs. There's no doubt that Salesforce will push this technology further in its next releases to allow administrators to write complex automation, thus reducing the need for custom development (we'll talk about this in more detail in `Chapter 15`, *The Coding Approach*).

Summary

In this chapter, we've dealt with the Process Builder, a reliable, efficient, and featureful process automation tool that is meant to provide the same features that workflow rules provide, but with enhanced abilities.

Here, we've seen how we can create a new process related to object and trigger events and define criteria to execute immediate and scheduled actions that span from simple record updates to custom notifications or Apex classes.

We also looked at how we can manage Process Builder instances by cloning them and creating new versions. Finally, we looked at some best practices for aligning an action's execution with Salesforce governor limits.

In the next chapter, we'll inspect Flows, which provide even more automation so that we can collect, create, and update Salesforce data using automated actions or user interface forms.

Questions

1. What is a Process Builder?
    a. A set of actions that can be applied to workflow rules
    b. Another way to call workflow rules
    c. The natural evolution of workflows
    d. A mixture of workflow rules and approval processes
2. What is the process trigger event?
    a. An Apex trigger that's used to start a Process Builder
    b. The specific event a Process Builder should start on
    c. A workflow rule to start the Process Builder
3. When defining the Trigger object for a record change Process Builder, what do you need to do?
    a. Select a Salesforce object
    b. Select whether the process starts on its creation and/or when it's updated
    c. Select a Salesforce platform event
4. When using a platform event trigger, what should you do?
    a. Select a matching Salesforce object (and the matching conditions)
    b. Select the **Start the process** radio button, but **only when the record is created**
    c. There is no need to select the **Start the process** radio button since platform events cannot be updated; they can only be created
5. What is true when defining criteria?
    a. You cannot use a formula
    b. You can use only a list of conditions
    c. You can use a formula and a list of conditions, or no conditions at all

6. Immediate actions:
    a. These are executed in the same context as the Process Builder, that is, whether or not the criteria match
    b. These are executed in the same context as the Process Builder, but only when the criteria match
    c. These are executed after a time frame has been defined
7. Scheduled actions:
    a. These are executed in the same context as the Process Builder, that is, whether or not the criteria match
    b. These are executed in the same context as the Process Builder, but only when the criteria match
    c. These are executed after a time frame has been defined and the criteria still match at the time of execution
    d. These are available on record creation and are updated if the **Do you want to execute the actions only when specified changes are made to the record?** box is checked
8. Can we define more than one scheduled action group?
    a. Yes
    b. No
    c. Yes, but only with immediate actions
9. What can you do with the **Update Records** action?
    a. Update the current record that triggered the Process Builder
    b. Update any parent record (only with a master-detail relationship)
    c. Update any child record (and provide conditions in order to select specific children)
10. What can you do with the Chatter Post action?
    a. Mention up to 25 users
    b. Use merge fields
    c. Post to a user, group, or record Chatter feed
11. A Process Builder:
    a. Can have one of two statuses: **Inactive** or **Active**
    b. Can have one of two statuses: **Inactive** or **Cloned**
    c. Can be versioned but only one version can be active at a time

14
Lightning Flows

Lightning flows collect data and perform actions in your Salesforce organization or external system. Their configuration requires point-and click -interactions; no code is required. In this chapter, we will look at screen flows, which collect data from agents or customers (for example, tutorials or wizards), and autolaunched flows, which automatically execute data logic after a record change event (triggered by Process Builder or Apex).

In this chapter, we will cover the following topics:

- How to build a screen flow
- How to build autolaunched flows
- How to manage a flow
- How to debug a flow
- Limits and considerations

Flow concepts

Lightning Flow is one of the most powerful automation frameworks on the Lightning Platform and requires no code. It has countless features and more are added every year. This means that covering every aspect of flows in this chapter is nearly impossible.

That's why, in this chapter, we'll cover the basic concepts of flows and their main building blocks: to make you aware of a flow's power and flexibility. To master flows, you'll need to practice with them. Dedicated resources regarding flows can be found online and in book shops.

As we've already mentioned, with great power comes great responsibility, and flows are no different: if you keep using flows without carefully architecting and designing your processes, you will end up with monster flows, which are hard to maintain and troubleshoot (believe me, this comes from experience).

That's why, when developers are not skilled at working with flows, I suggest that they build Lightning components and Apex Triggers to the same level of complexity they wanted to reach with Flows. This isn't because developers cannot learn about flows and master the subject, but because, sometimes, customers don't even know what they want, and developers quickly find themselves frustrated as they try to adapt a badly architected flow, thus creating a big monster with tens of blocks.

I don't want to scare you, but before you start building a flow, take your time when designing it and ensure that your business process requirements are completely fulfilled (and documented in every step).

The following diagram is an example of a flow (taken from Salesforce Labs at `https://appexchange.salesforce.com/appxListingDetail?listingId=a0N3A00000FAB4hUAH`):

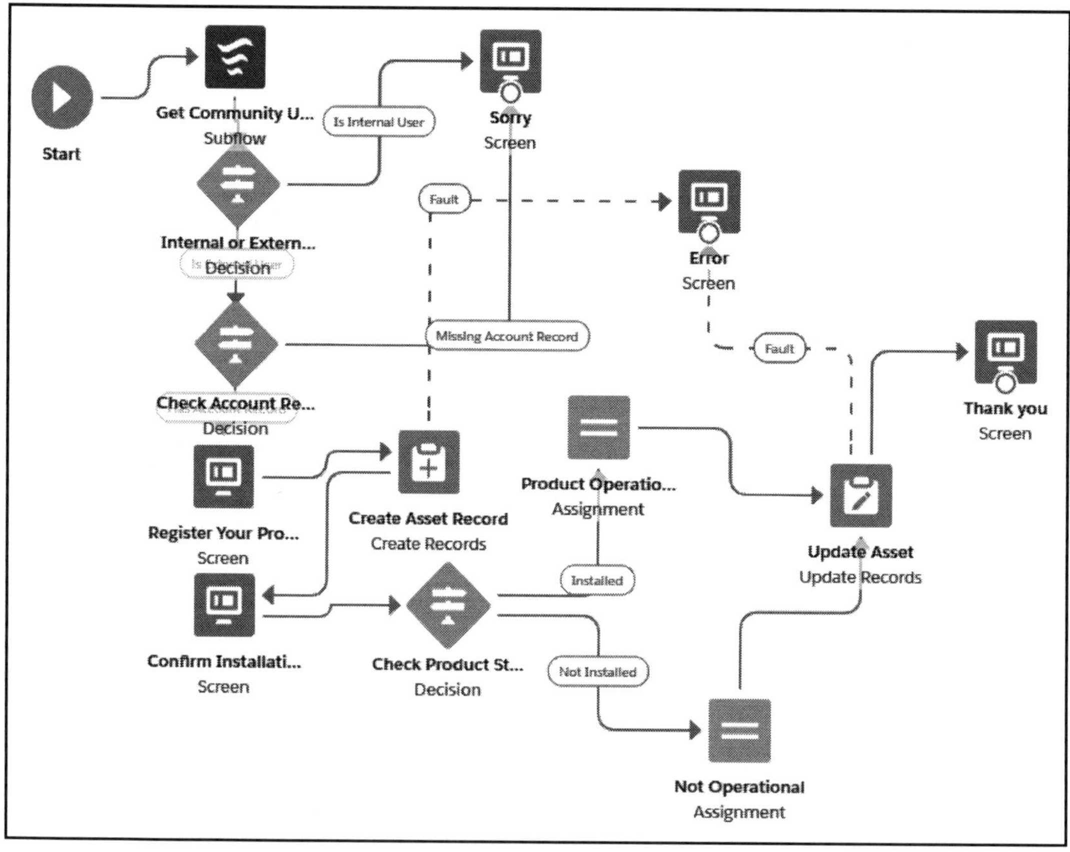

Flow example

A flow is composed of the following components:

- **Elements**: These are the functional actions that a flow can execute, such as exchanging data with a Salesforce database, displaying/gathering information from users, or manipulating data.
- **Connectors**: These connect elements and thus define the path that the flow will be following.
- **Resource**: These represent any data references that the flow uses throughout its execution.

To start creating flows, go to **Setup** | **Process Automation** | **Flows** and click on the **New Flow** button. You will see the following screen:

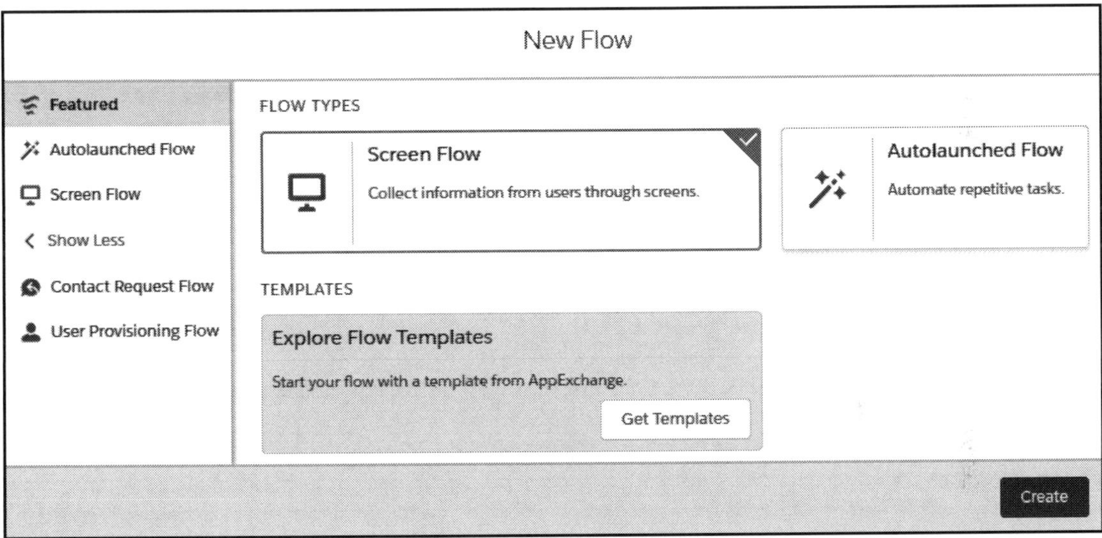

The first step of the Flow creation wizard

The first thing we need to select is the kind of flow we are going to build, which will filter out the different kinds of elements and resources that are supported by it:

- **Screen flow**: This requires user interaction as it's mainly used to grab data from users (it's like designing custom wizards using no code)
- **Autolaunched flow**: This doesn't require user interaction as it's mainly used to execute complex process logic (this can be triggered via Process Builder, Apex, or REST APIs)

While there are other kinds of flow types, we'll be concentrating on the screen flow and autolaunched flow types here as they will cover 90% of your needs. However, if you want to find out more, please refer to Salesforce Help at `https://help.salesforce.com/articleView?id=flow_concepts_type.htmtype=5`.

Building a flow

Let's build a simple screen flow so that we can gather contact and account data from the user's interactions by using the **Cloud Flow Designer** (this is the new version of the old **Flow Builder** app and was introduced in Spring 2019). This is shown in the following screenshot:

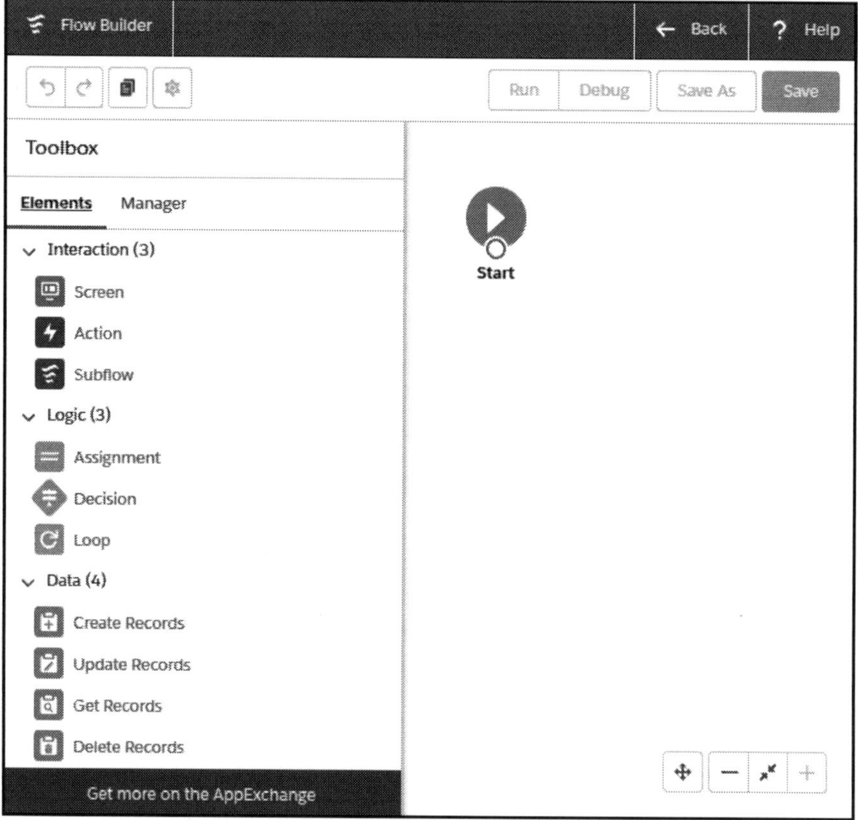

Cloud Flow Designer

Grab the **Screen** element and drop it onto the flow canvas. The specific element's modal will appear, as shown in the following screenshot:

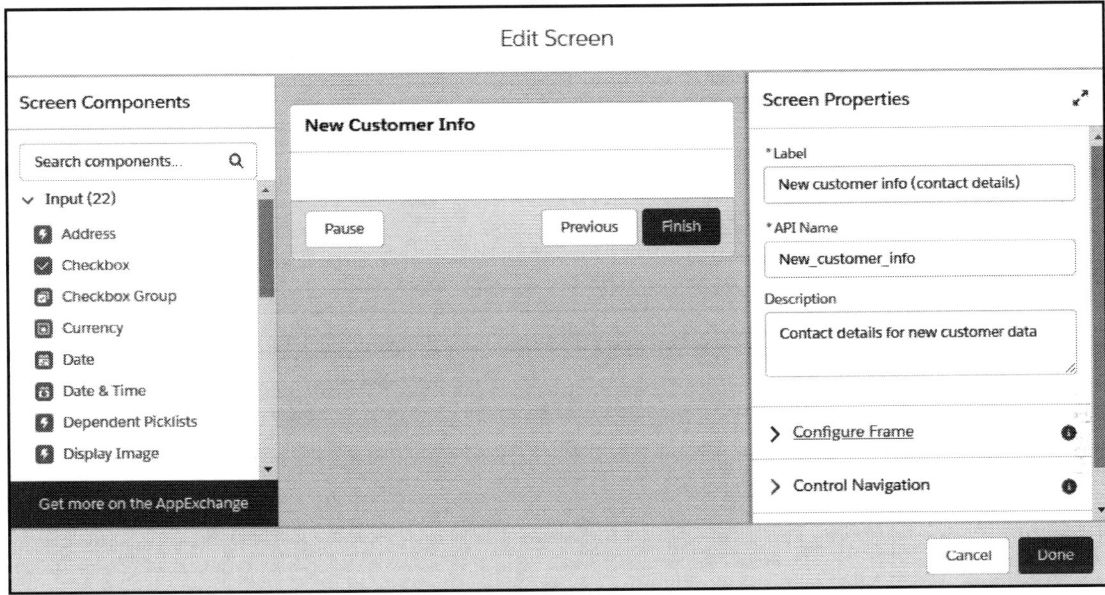

Screen element modal

Add a label and a unique API name for the modal (this is automatically filled in for you when you leave the focus of the label input).

We'll be creating a form here, so let's start by adding the **Name**, **Email**, **Phone**, and **Address** input components, as shown in the following screenshot:

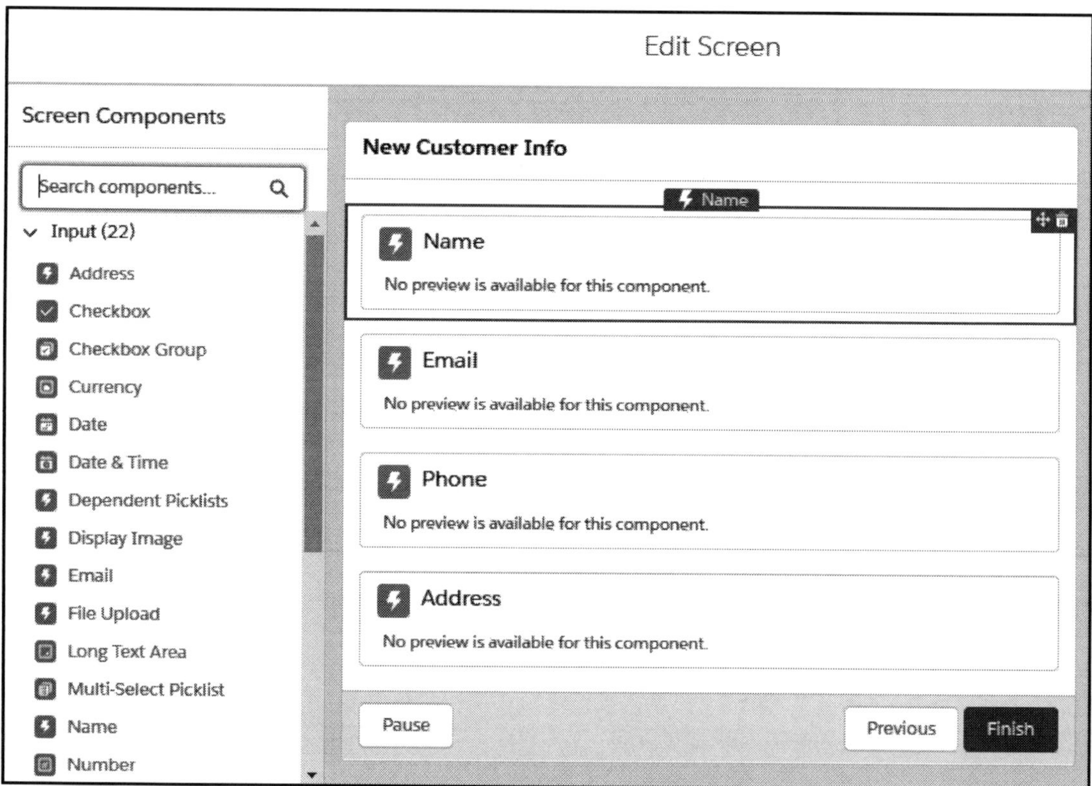

Screen element with form components

For each component, provide a valid API name. In this example, we have used the `contact_component_type` format; for example, `contact_name` or `contact_phone`. In flows, all the input components are considered variables or resources. For example, you can use the `contact_component_type` variable to fill in another component.

Click the **Done** button to return to the canvas.

Next, we need to define that we are going to put our values into a Contact object, so we need a resource that will host the values that are grabbed from the screen element.

On the Flow Designer's **Toolbox**, click on the **Manager** tab to show the list of resources and elements that have already been defined on the current flow (you will see the components that we just added):

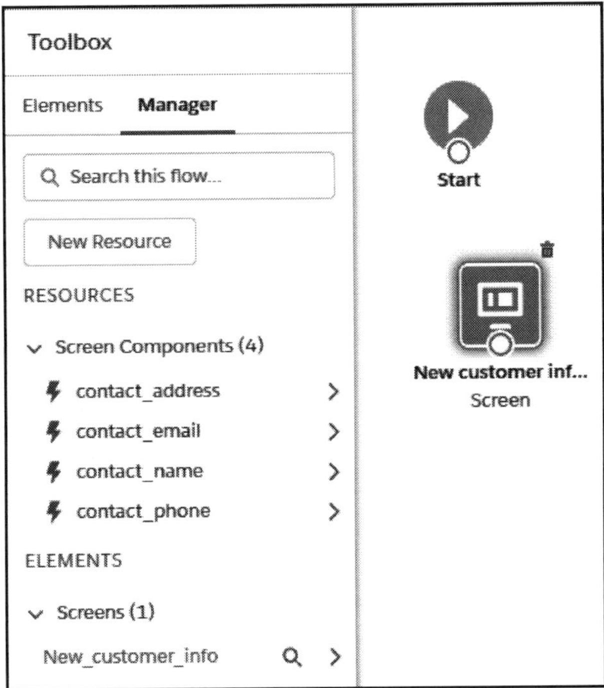

Manager tab of the Cloud Flow Builder toolbox

Now, click on the **New Resource** button; the **New Resource** modal will appear:

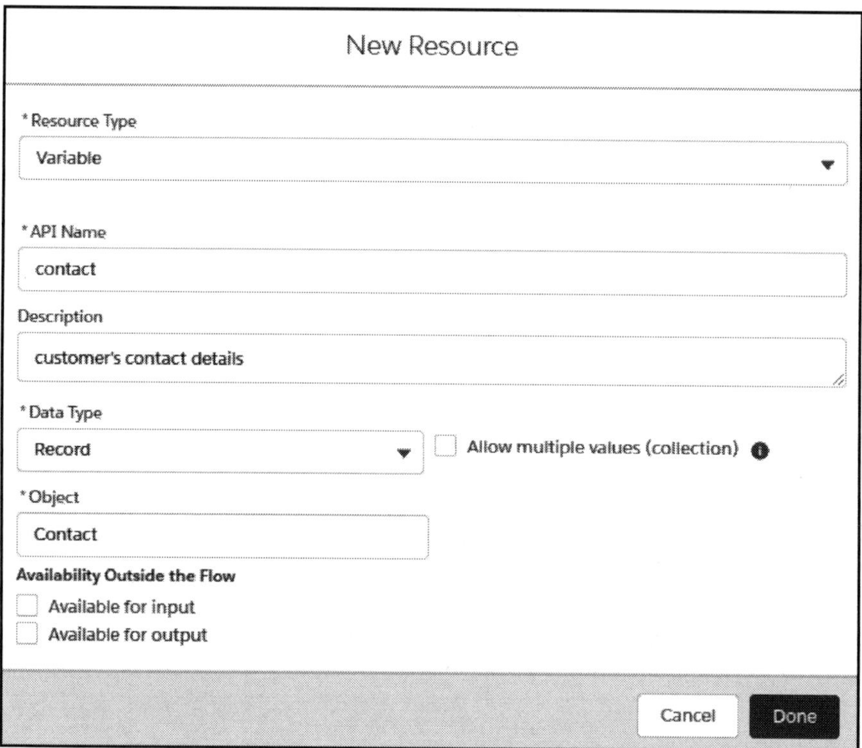

New Resource configuration modal

On this modal, select the following values to configure a new flow variable of the **Contact** type:

- **Resource Type:** Variable
- **API Name:** Contact
- **Description:** Customer's contact details
- **Data Type:** Record
- **Object**: Contact

Spoiler alert: Now we have a brand-new contact record that will be used to create a Salesforce contact at the end of the flow.

To link form components to the contact variable, double-click on the screen element. Then, for each component, click on the corresponding attribute to tell the screen element where each value should be grabbed from:

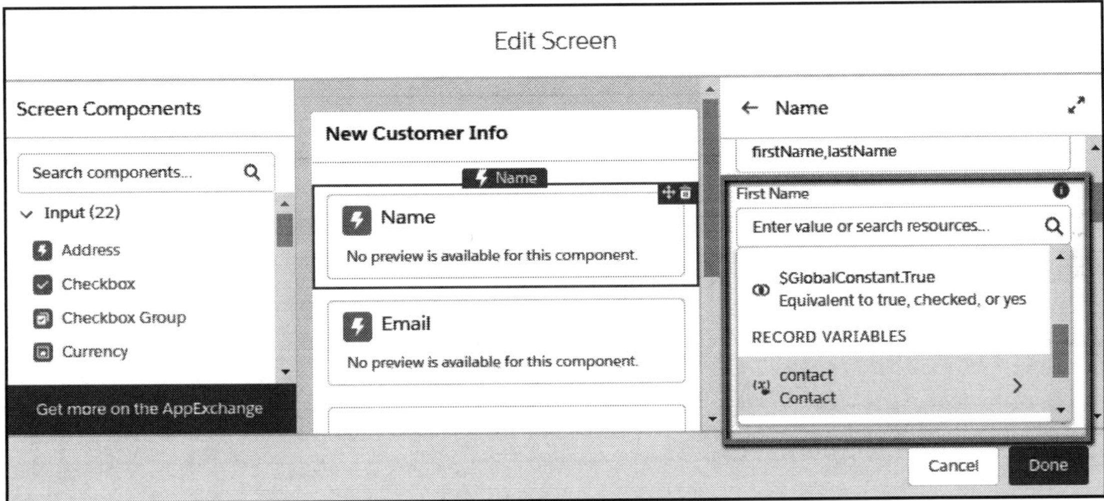

Linking screen components with variables

For this example, we'll be configuring the following attributes:

- **Name component:**
    - **First Name**: `{!contact.FirstName}`
    - **Last Name**: `{!contact.LastName}`
- **Email component**:
    - **Value**: `{!contact.Email}`
    - **Required**: `{!$GlobalConstant.True}`
- **Phone component:**
    - **Value:** `{!contact.Phone}`

- **Address component**:
  - **City Value**: `{!contact.MailingCity}`
  - **Country Value**: `{!contact.MailingCountry}`
  - **Postal Code Value**: `{!contact.MailingPostalCode}`
  - **State/Province Value**: `{!contact.MailingState}`
  - **Street Value**: `{!contact.MailingStreet}`

Repeat this configuration for the **Store Output Values** attributes section of each component's value to tell the flow engine where the data should be stored:

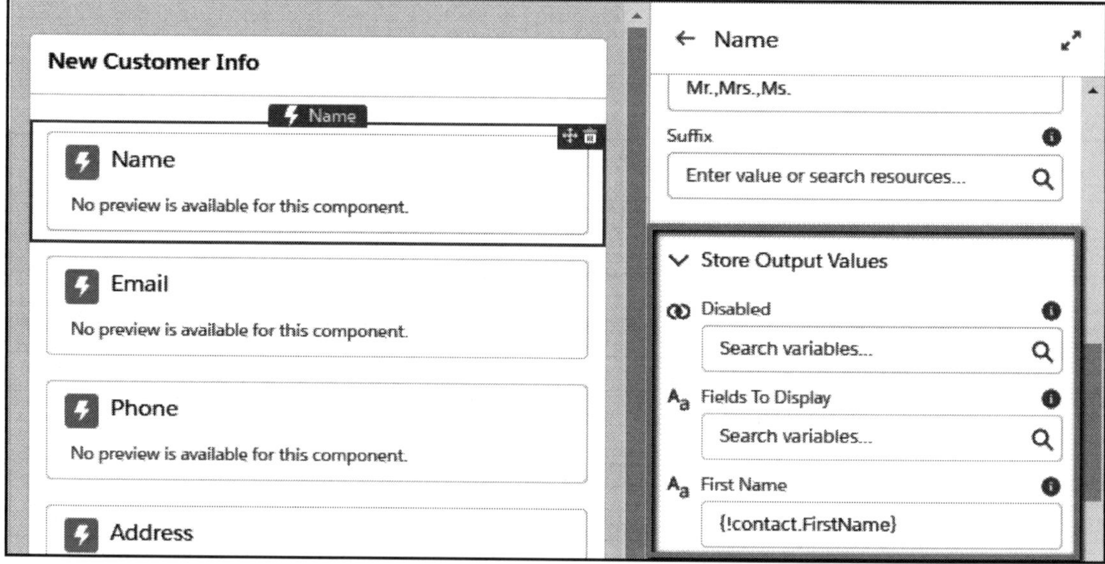

Setting output attributes

Why do we have this double configuration?

The first configuration is used to get the component's data from an already defined variable, while the second configuration sets up where the component's data should be stored. In our example, the two configurations match.

But why do you need to do this? You may want to get the component's initial values from the previous elements, which may have stored another kind of data. In our scenario, we are doing this so that we can go from the input screen to the verification screen and back without losing the data that we've inserted (using the **Previous** button on the flow screens). In other words, we'll go back and forth without losing any form fields.

In our scenario, we'll be using the email field as the unique field for contacts (for the email component's **Required** attribute, we selected the `true` global value):

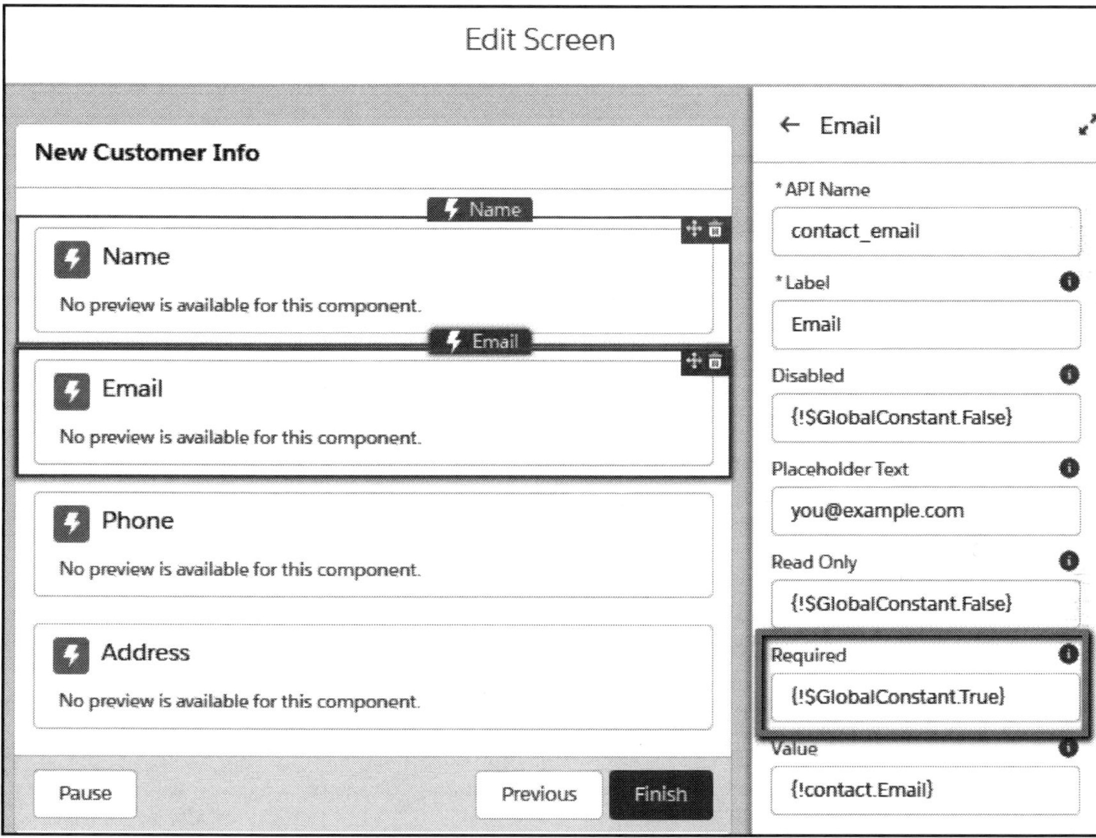

Attribute definition using global values

Close the modal and link the **Start** element to the **New Customer Info** screen element by dragging the white circle of the `Start` element to the white circle of the next block, called **New Customer Info**, as shown in the following screenshot:

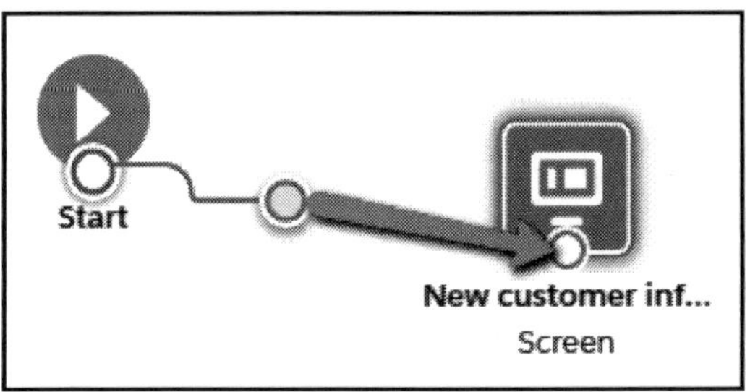

Linking flow elements

Now, we need to create a new screen element. This is where we'll be reviewing the data we've just filled in:

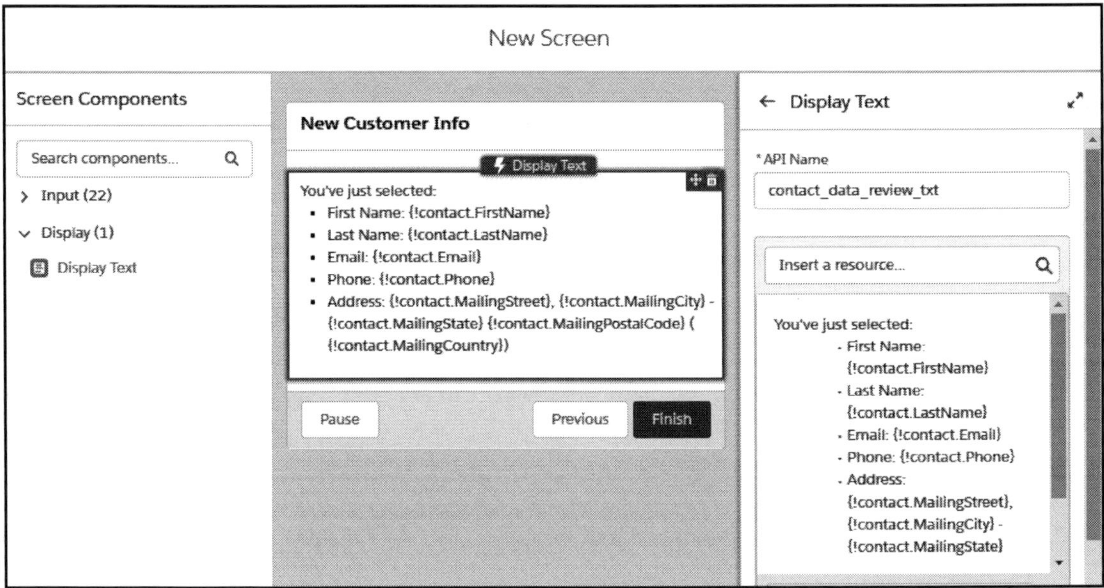

Review screen element

This element contains a **Display Text** component, which is used to display the data stored in the `contact` variable.

Next, link this element to the previous one:

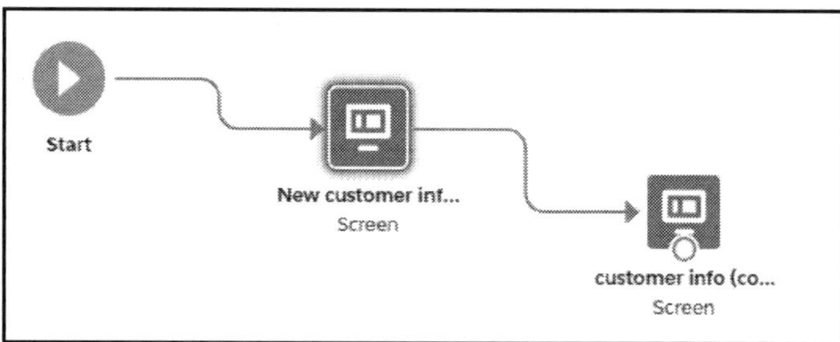

Simple flow example completed

At the moment, we don't have any database interaction, but we can test it anyway by clicking the **Run** button at the top of the Cloud Flow Designer (remember to save the flow first). To do this, compile the form with some values:

Example flow – input form screen

Click **Next** to go to the review screen:

Example flow – review screen

If you repeatedly click the **Previous** and **Next** buttons, you'll see the form keeping its data, thanks to the previous configuration of the *value* and output `value` attributes of the screen components.

Did you try to leave a non-required field blank? If so, you should have received an error message (and an email message with a log) stating that *"The flow failed to access the value for contact.field because it hasn't been set or assigned."* This is just Salesforce telling you that the variables associated with that input box were not initialized.

Flow variables need to be initialized before we can use them.

To initialize a variable, we'll be using the **Assignment** element and appending it between the **Start** element and the **New customer info** element. Let's see how we can do this:

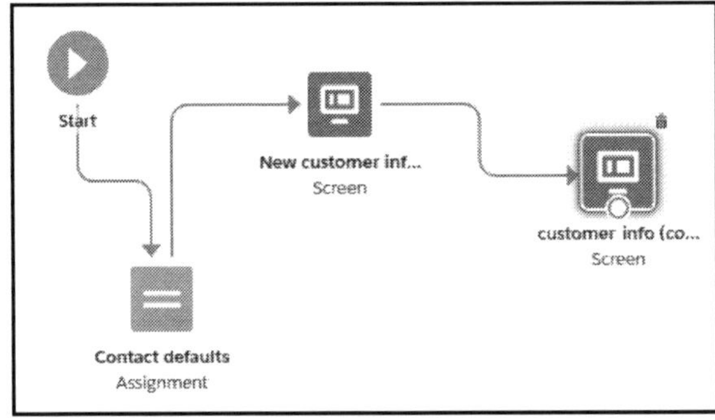

New assignment element used to initialize the contact variable

In our example, the element is being configured so that it assigns all the required fields to the *empty string* global variable, which a safe way to initialize a value to the empty value (use this global variable instead of a *blank text input* value):

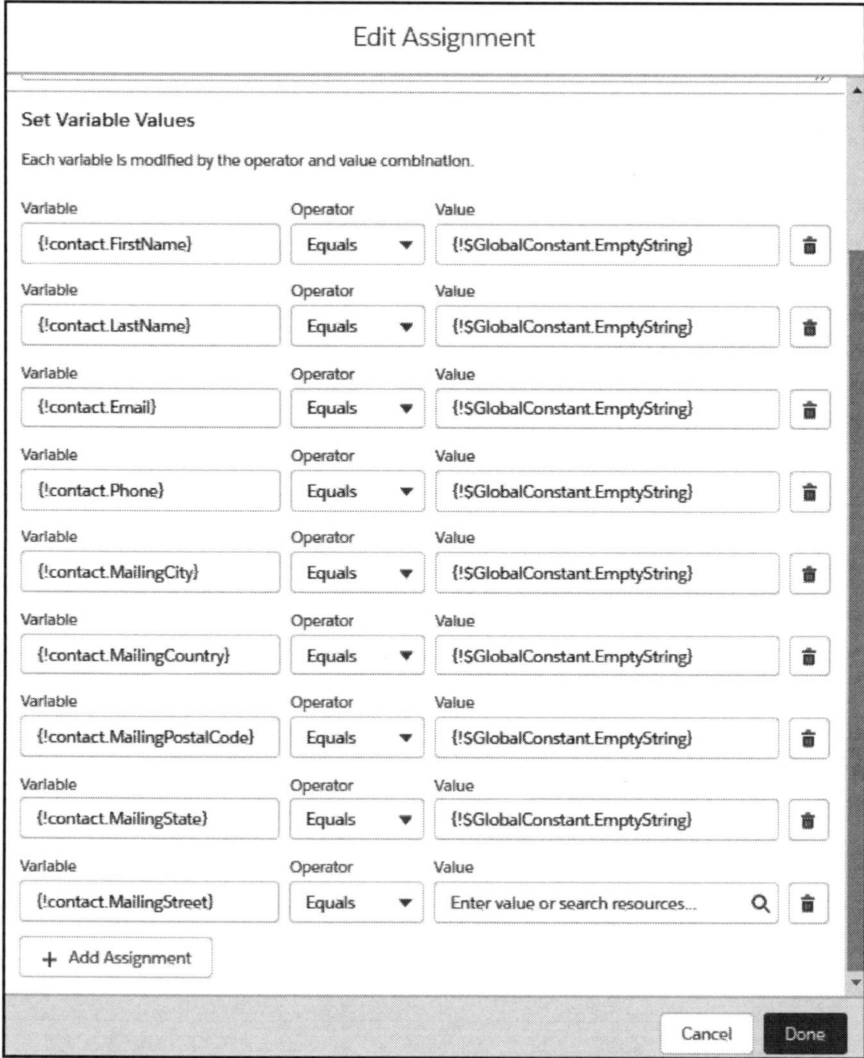

Contact variable initialization

The next step is adding the account's data.

Create a new screen element called **account details** with the following components:

- **Text component:**
    - **Name**: **Account name**
    - **API name**: `account_name`
    - **Required**: `True`
    - **Default value:** `{!account.Name}`
- **Text component:**
    - **Name**: **Duns Number**
    - **API name**: `account_duns`
    - **Required**: `True`
    - **Default value:** `{!account.DunsNumber}`
- **Currency component:**
    - **Name**: **Annual Revenue**
    - **API name**: `annual_revenue`
    - **Required**: `False`
    - **Default value:** `{!account.AnnualRevenue}`
    - **Decimal places**: 2

The following screenshot shows the screen element's account details:

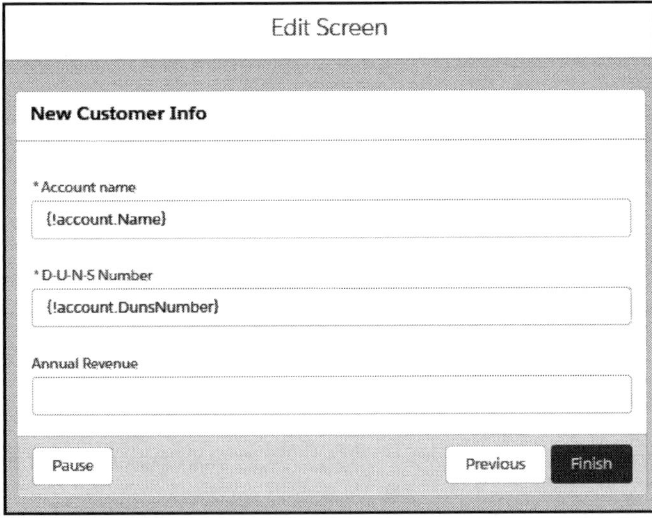

Account details for the screen element

Have you noticed that none of the components have the **Set Output Values** attribute section? This is because these are simple components that do not convey complex logic.

Does this mean that we cannot set text or currency components for variables like we've done for the contact details screen?

The answer is that we can; however, we need to use the assignment element again to map the form components to the proper variable fields. Let's look at how we can do this:

Create a new resource variable of the **Account** type by going to **Toolbox** | **Manager** | **New Resource**:

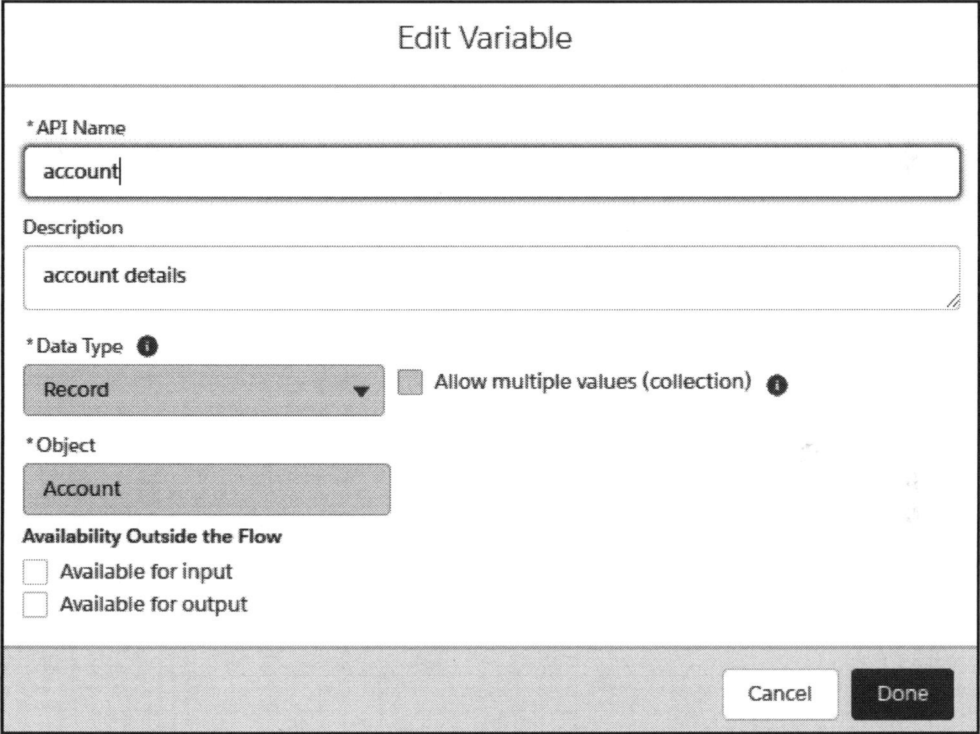

New account resource definition

Next, create a new **Assignment** element so that you can store the screen components, values in the account resource:

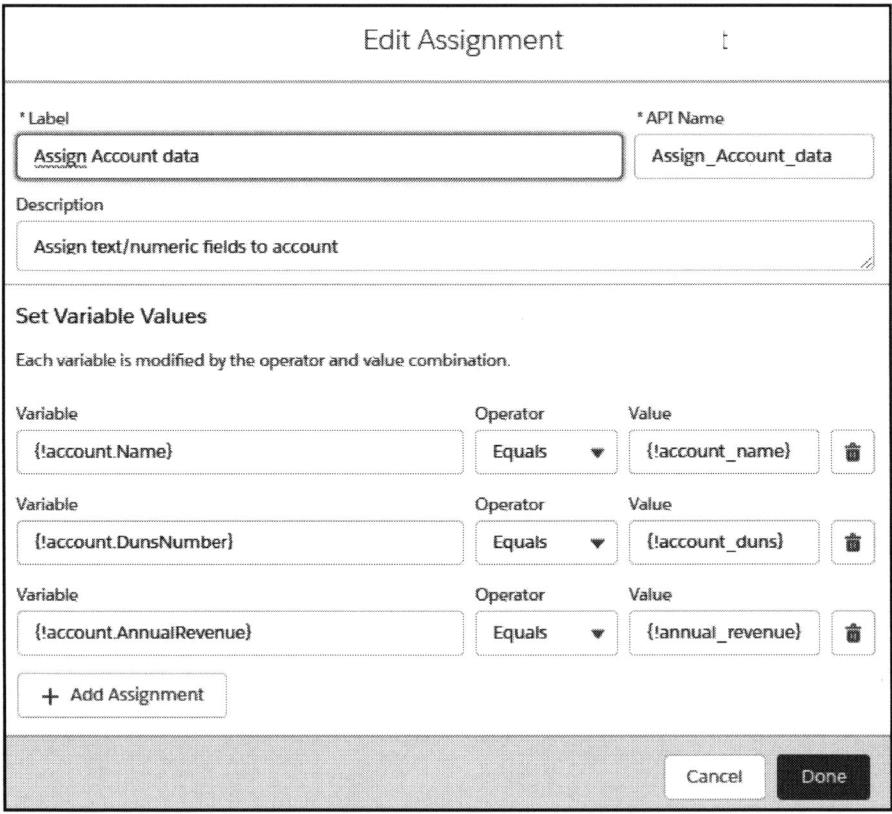

Components being assigned to variables

Remember to update the **Contact Defaults** element in order to initialize the account fields as well:

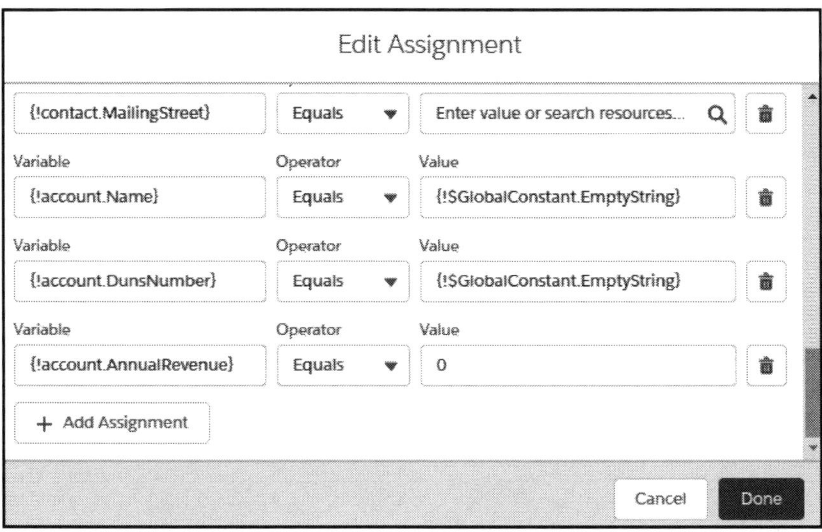

Contact Defaults element screen with new defaulted values for the account resource

Now, let's modify the customer info verification screen so that it displays the account data:

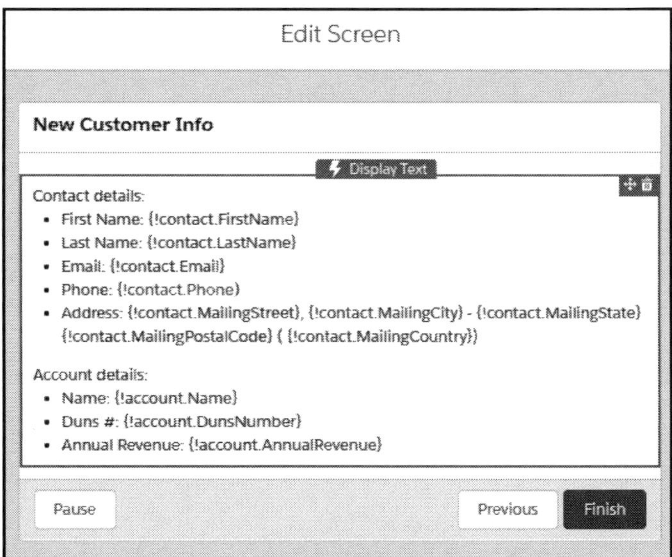

Data verification screen

Finally, detach the **Customer info** review and link everything together, as follows:

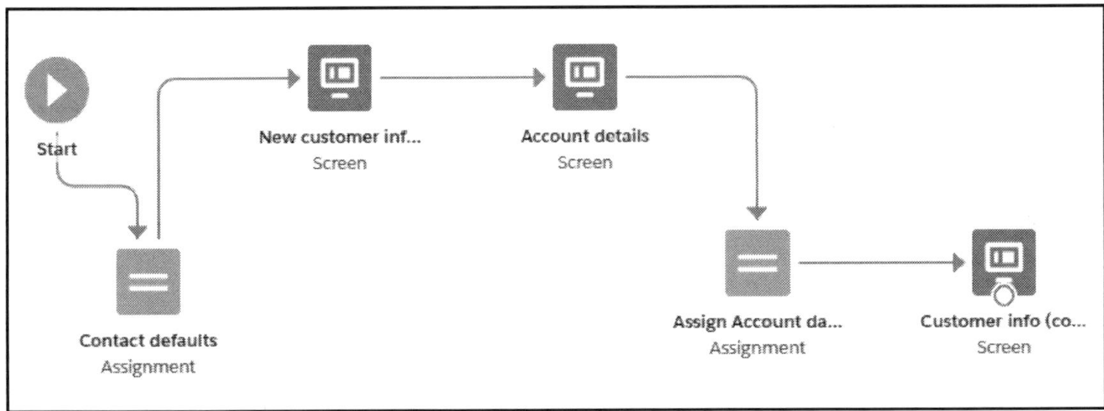

New flow configuration with account data

The whole flow can now be summarized in the following steps:

1. Initialize the contact and account data
2. Get contact details
3. Get account details
4. Finalize variable assignment
5. Review the data

For the last few steps, we'll be creating some logic to handle contact/account creation.

First, we need to know whether the contact and account are already in our database.

We'll be using the **Email** field on the contact and the **Duns Number** on the account. Initially, they were unique fields.

For this, we need a **Get Records** element that can query a given object type based on specific conditions.

We'll be creating a **Find Contact by email** element with the following configuration (this is shown in the following screenshot):

- **Label**: Find Contact by email
- **Get Records of This Object:**
    - **Object**: Contact (name of the object that the element will query)
- **Filter Contact Records:**
    - **Condition Requirements:** Conditions are Met
    - **Field:** Email
    - **Operator:** Equals
    - **Value:** `{!contact.Email}`
- **Set Contact Records:**
    - **Sort Order**: Not sorted (we don't need sorting)
    - **How Many Records to Store:** Only the first record (this is based on the fact that we consider the email field to be unique across all the contacts)
    - **Where to Store Field Values**: In separate variables (we want to get the contact ID field only; the rest of the contact data will be received from our flow)
    - **When no records are returned, set specified variables to null**: Set this to true so that if no contact is found, no value is set on the variables we'll define in the next section
- **Select Variables to Store Contact Fields:**
    - **Field:** ID field of the contact object
    - **Variable:** `{!FoundContactID}` (this text variable has been created inline and will contain the matched contact, if there is one)

The following screenshot summarizes this configuration:

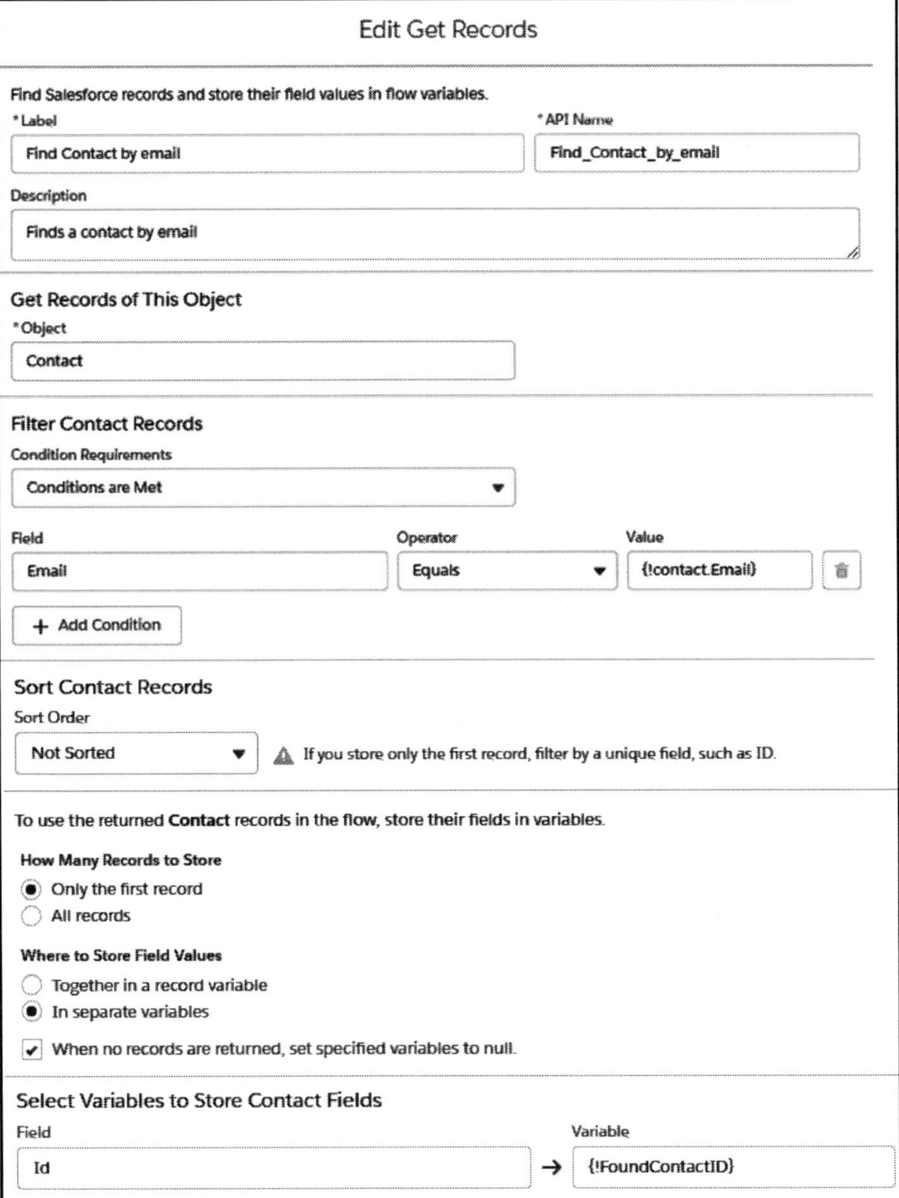

Get Records screen configuration for contacts

Create another **Get Records** element for the **Account** object with the same configuration that's shown in the preceding screenshot; the only things we need to change are the object type (which should be set to **Account**), the matching condition based on the **Duns Number** field (instead of the **Contact.Email** field) and the new **FoundAccountID** text variable, which we will use to store the matching Account ID (instead of the **FoundContactID** variable).

Now, based on the fact that the account has not been found, we can create or update a new record.

Connect the **Customer Info Review** screen to the **Find Contact By Email** element and the **Find Contact by Email** element to the **Find Account by Duns Number** element.

Let's create a new **Decision** element that will decide on whether the account is created or updated:

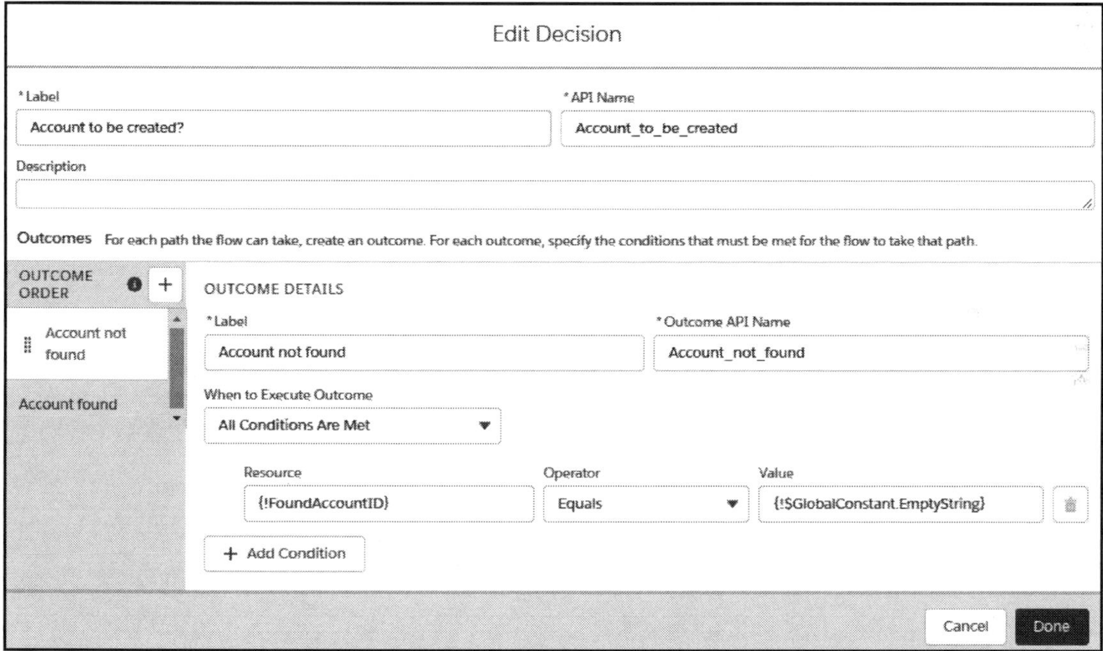

Decision element on the Account not found condition

Here, we have two outcomes (we can have more, but in our scenario, we only have a two-way decision): that is, either the account has been found or it hasn't, depending on the **FoundAccountID** variable value (the **Account found** outcome has no conditions as it is the **else** path of the **Account not found** outcome). Use the **EmptyString** global value whenever you need to check null/empty values.

Connect the **Find Account by Duns Number** element to the **Account to be created?** decision element.

Let's create a **Create Records** element so that we can create the account and an **Update Records** element so that we can update the account (they are quite similar):

Create Records screen configuration for the account record

Connect the **Account to be created?** element to the **Create Account** element and select the **Account not found** outcome.

Before connecting the **Update account** element, we need to set the ID of our account record with the `FoundAccountID` value (we are going to be doing an `upsert`).

Then, we need to create a new **Assignment** element to set this value:

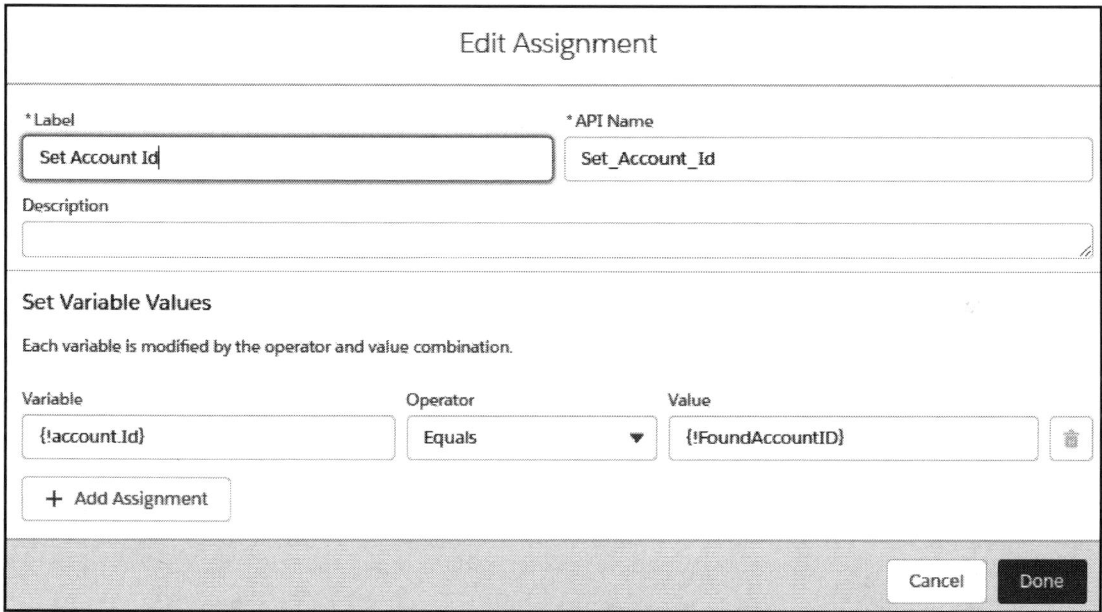

Setting the account's ID

Now, connect the **Account to be created?** element to the **Set Account Id** assignment screen and select the **Account found** outcome. Then, connect it to the **Update Account** element.

At this stage, we have created/updated the account record. We need to do exactly the same for the contact record, but with a few modifications. For this, we need to do the following:

1. Create a new **Assignment** element to set the contact's account ID with an assignment set to `{!contact.AccountId} Equals {!account.Id}`. This has to be connected to the account's Create/Update elements of the previous flow branch.
2. Create a new **Decision** element (contact to be created?) based on the `FoundContactID` variable with two outcomes: **Contact not found** and **Contact found**. This new element will follow the previous **Assignment** element.
3. Create a new **Assignment** element to put **FoundContactID** into our contact variable.
4. Create a **Create Records** element to create a brand-new contact.
5. Create an **Update Records** screen to update our contact with its **old** ID.
6. Create a final screen to tell the user that customer acquisition has been completed.
7. Create an error handling screen to tell the customer whether any of the database operations (the **Get Records** or **Create/Update records** elements) went wrong.

In order to show flow error messages, we need to use the `$Flow.FaultMessage` global variable, as shown in the following configuration for the **Error Message** screen:

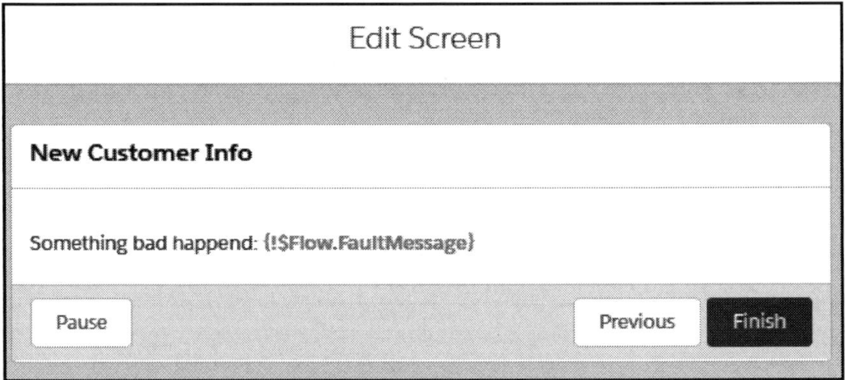

Screen to show flow error messages

If you followed previous instructions correctly, this is what you will have:

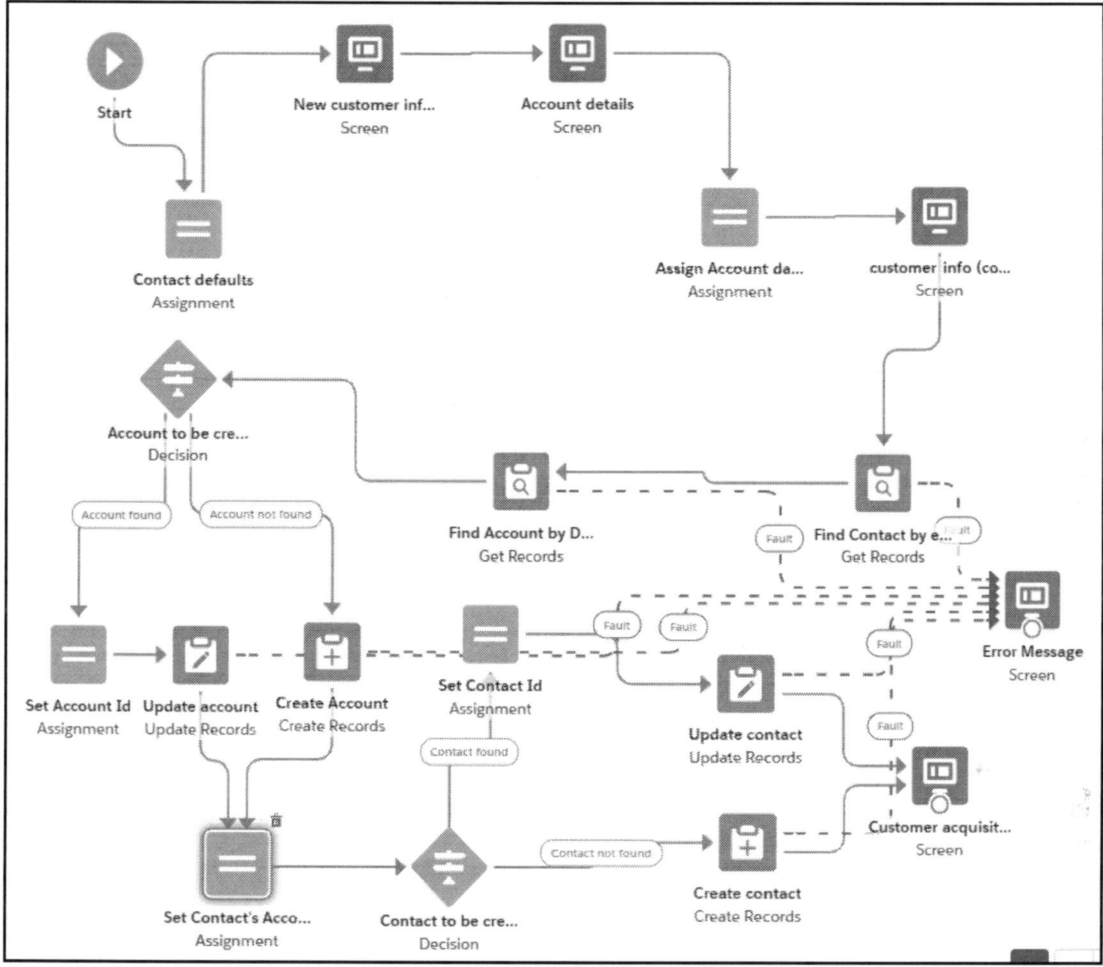

Final flow example

Mission accomplished – easy, eh?

So far, we have created a few actions, but the flow has already become a bit messy. The secret is designing simple flows that can be linked with one another using the **subflow** element, which can call subflows.

Connecting flows and subflows

We can connect data between flows using input/output resources. When you set up a new resource, you can specify whether that resource can be seen from outside its flow, as shown in the following screenshot:

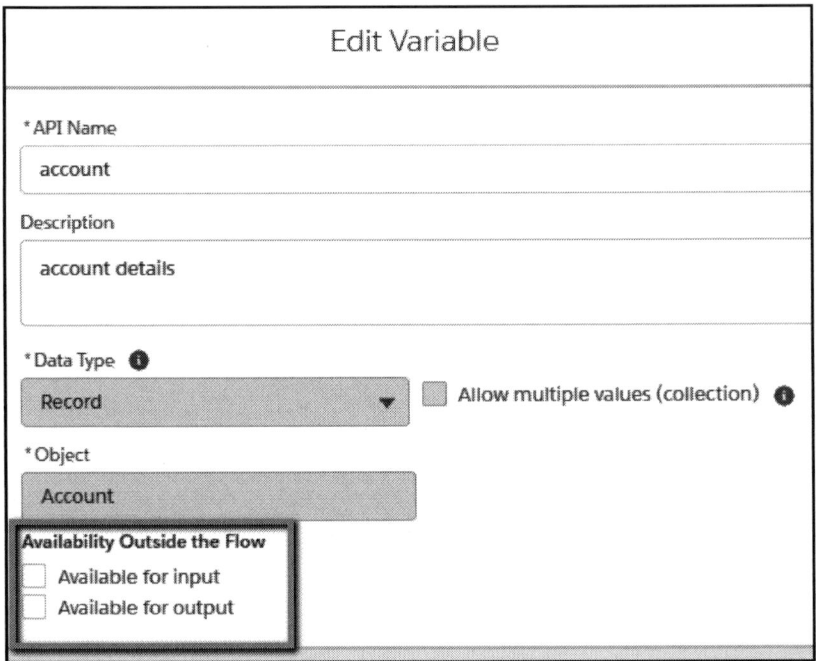

Setting our resource's availability

Let's say we want to create a flow to help sales reps create opportunities. The first step would be to get customer data and then use that data to compile the opportunity object. Our previous **New Customer Info** flow can be configured to have the contact and account resources set as input and output variables that can be accessed outside of the flow itself (so that they're accessible from the other flows that are connected to it).

In the new **New Opportunity** flow, we start by gathering account details that are not used to identify the account (for example, the company's website, or any other field that is not set to **empty** in the first assignment screen of the **New Customer Info** subflow) and that we actually want to store in the account record. To do this, we simply created a new screen element and a new **tempAccount** resource to store those fields.

By adding a new subflow, we are selecting the whole customer identification form without creating every element again, as shown in the following screenshot:

Subflow configuration

After selecting the **New Customer Info** flow, we can set up the input variables (in our scenario, this is only the account resource), along with two new resources for the output account and contact resources coming from the subflow:

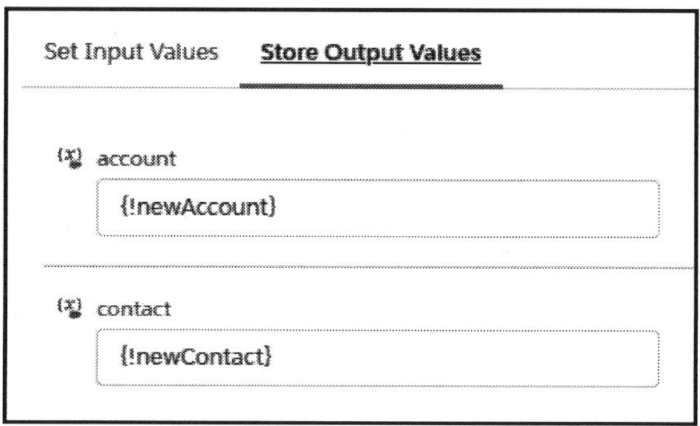

Output Values definition for a subflow

This way, when the **New Customer Info** flow ends, we are able to take account and contact data and use it in our opportunity flow. We can even create a new flow for service management, which creates a case, and still use the **New Customer Info** flow to identify the customer.

Cool, huh? This may seem complicated at first sight, but hopefully, this section has proved otherwise.

Autolaunched flows

What if you don't need a user interface but want to implement complex automated logic for your records?

This is where the autolaunched flow type comes into play. Here, we can define a Process Builder with a flow action to trigger the flow logic when a specific event occurs on an object type (for example, an opportunity is created).

The toolbox changes slightly for autolaunched flows:

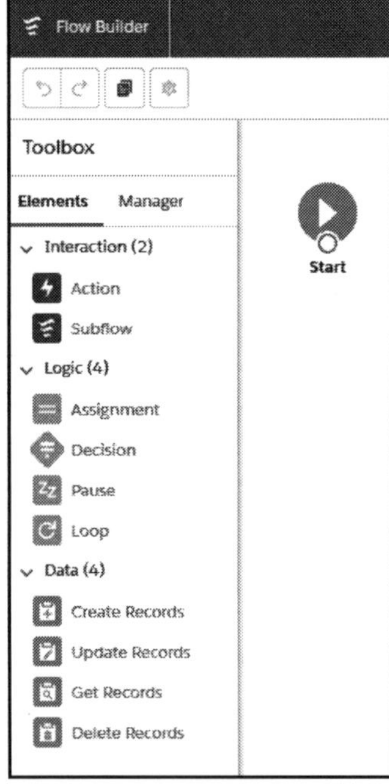

Autolaunched flow toolbox

The **Screen** element disappears, while the **Pause** element is added to the **Logic** elements section.

This particular element, which can only be run on autolaunched flows, is used to put the logic in a waiting state until specific conditions are met.

It is composed of the following:

- **One or more pause configurations**: These define (pretty much like we've seen in the **Decision** element) different **paused paths** that can be resumed with specific configurations:

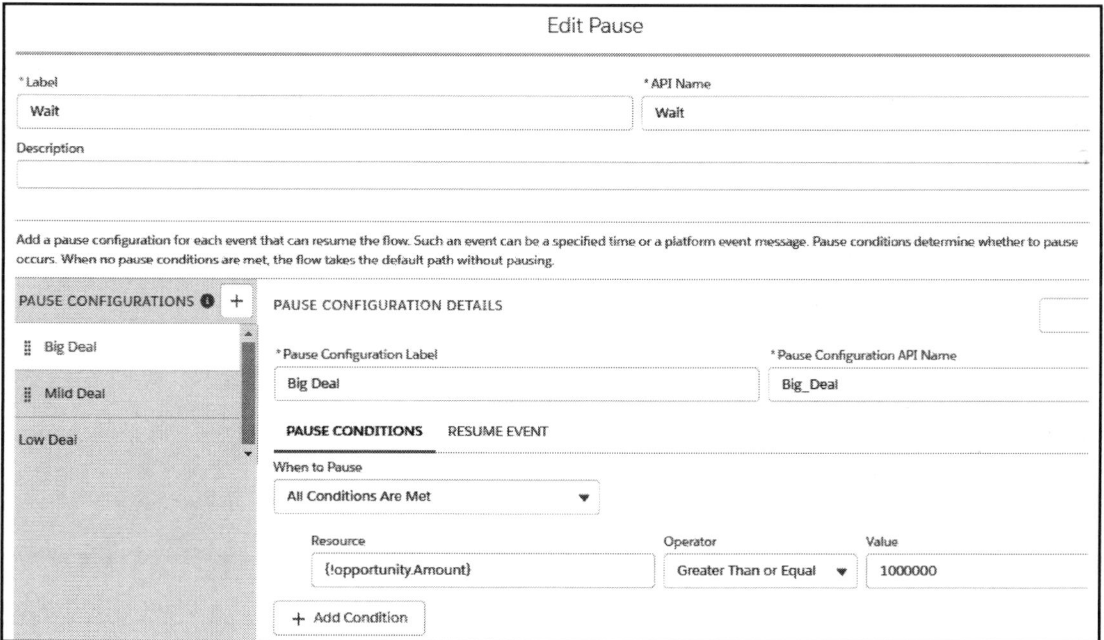

Pause configuration and conditions in the Pause element

- **One or more resume events**: These define the events that resume the flow for a given path; they can be based on a simple date/time value (fixed or resource-based) or on a platform event:

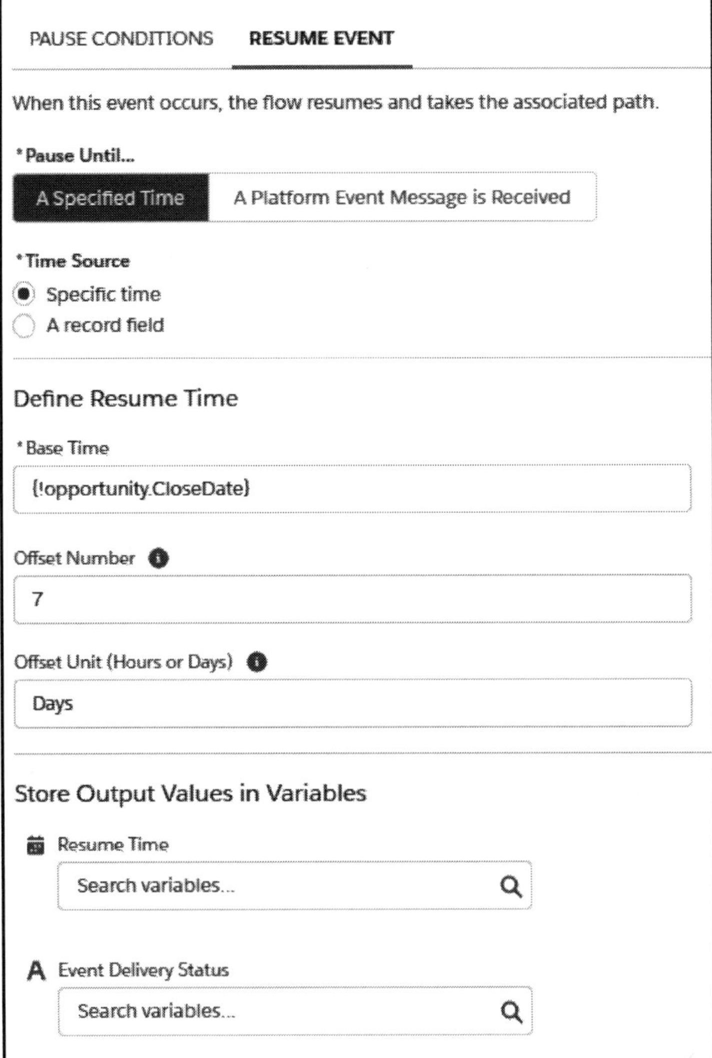

Resume event for a given pause configuration

Here is a quick example:

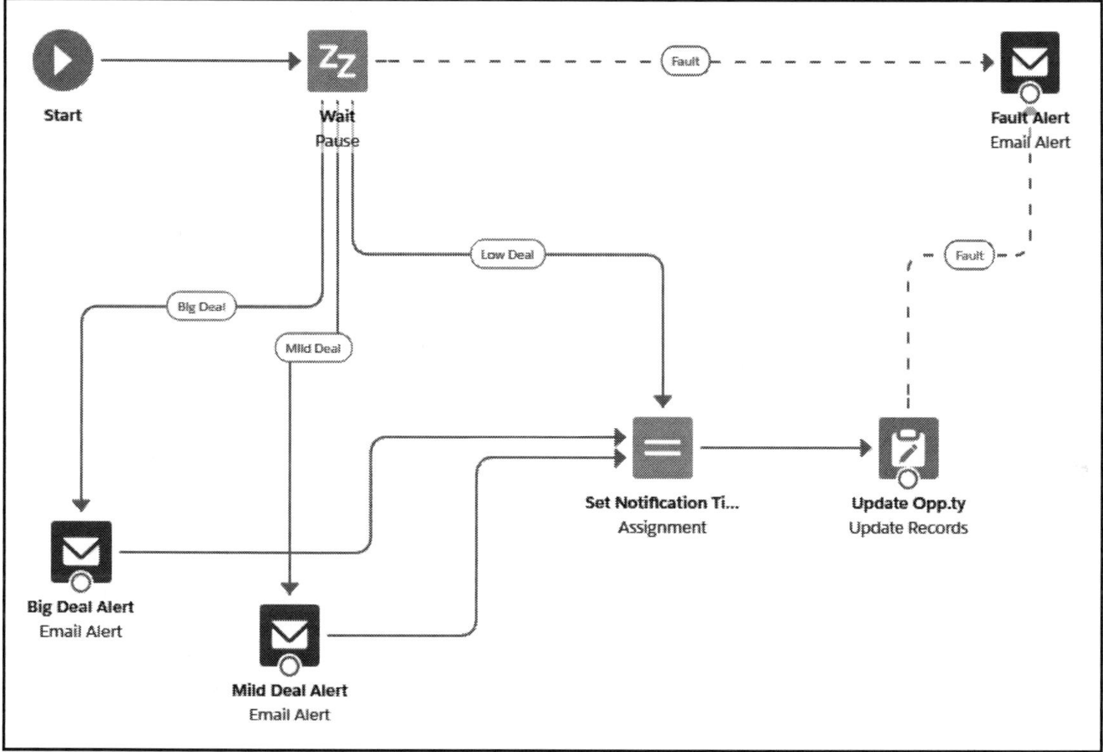

Example of an autolaunched flow with a Pause element

This flow, coupled with a Process Builder on the opportunity object, sends an email alert (using an Email Alert action):

- 7 days after the Close Date for opportunities with an amount greater than $1M
- 14 days after the Close Date for opportunities with an amount greater than $100k and less than $1M
- No notification if the opportunity is less than $100k
- Updates the opportunity's **Notification Date** (a date/time custom field) when the flow has completed

The flow is configured like so:

- The opportunity resource, which is of the variable and record type (of the Opportunity type), is available as an input resource (it can be passed in from the calling Process Builder).
- A Pause element, which specifies three configurations:
    - One for an amount greater than $1M with a 7-day resume event (Big Deal).
    - One for an amount greater than $100k with a 14-day resume event (Mild Deal).
    - A default one with no resume event

  This is the configuration of **Mild Deal** pause conditions:

Pause Configuration for mild deal path

This is the configuration of the **Resume** event for the **Mild Deal** path:

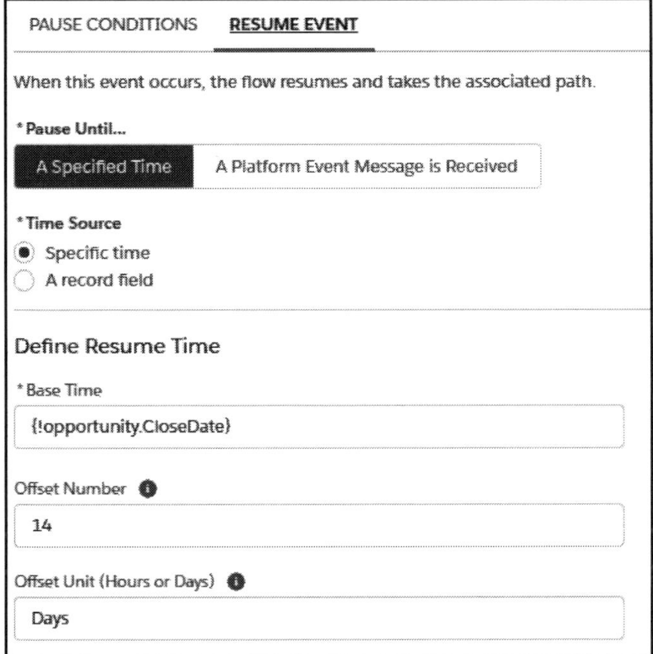

Resume configuration for mild deal path

- Three Action elements for opportunity notification and one for Pause element failure (even the Pause element can fail). To do this, select the Action element, filter the actions by **Type**, select **Email Alert**, look for an already defined Email Alert action (we saw these when we talked about Workflows, Approvals, Entitlements, and Process Builder), and then set up the record ID, which should be the base for the email alert:

Edit "Giant Deal!" email alert
Use values from earlier in the flow to set the inputs for the "Giant Deal!" email alert. To use its outputs later in the flow, store them in variables.
*Label: Big Deal Alert
*API Name: Big_Deal_Alert
Description
Set Input Values | Store Output Values
*Record ID: {!opportunity.Id}

Email Alert action element configuration

- One assignment element to assign the current flow date/time to the Notification Date custom field:

Edit Assignment
*Label: Set Notification Time
*API Name: Set_Notification_Time
Variable Values
variable is modified by the operator and value combination.
{!opportunity.Notification_Date__c} | Operator: Equals | Value: {!$Flow.CurrentDateTime}

Assignment element configuration

- One Update Records element to update the opportunity with the new assignment.

If the opportunity has an amount greater than $100k, an email alert is sent 7 or 14 days after the close date (depending on the actual amount); if the amount is lower, no email is sent. Regardless of whether or not the email is sent, the opportunity's **Notification Date** custom field is set up with the current flow's execution date/time, which will be set:

- to the current date/time of flow execution for **low deals**
- to the opportunity's Close Date field, plus 14 days (as for the resume event), for **mild deals**
- to the opportunity's Close Date field, plus 7 days, for **big deals** (again, as for the resume event)

This means that the final Update Records element is executed in different contexts, depending on the path that the flow has passed through.

When the flow is paused, it is listed in the **Paused and Waiting Interviews** section of the **Setup | Process Automation | Flows** page:

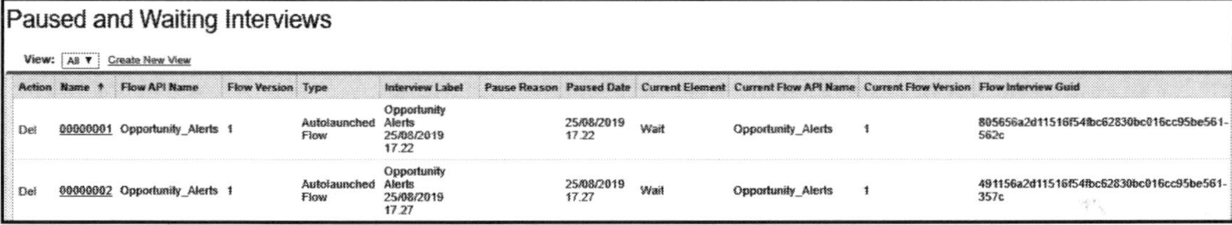

Paused and Waiting Interviews

View: All ▼ Create New View

Action	Name ↑	Flow API Name	Flow Version	Type	Interview Label	Pause Reason	Paused Date	Current Element	Current Flow API Name	Current Flow Version	Flow Interview Guid
Del	00000001	Opportunity_Alerts	1	Autolaunched Flow	Opportunity Alerts 25/08/2019 17.22		25/08/2019 17.22	Wait	Opportunity_Alerts	1	805656a2d11516f54fbc62830bc016cc95be561-562c
Del	00000002	Opportunity_Alerts	1	Autolaunched Flow	Opportunity Alerts 25/08/2019 17.27		25/08/2019 17.27	Wait	Opportunity_Alerts	1	491156a2d11516f54fbc62830bc016cc95be561-357c

Paused flows list

Now, you should have all the key elements so that you can start building your flows.

Unfortunately, it wasn't possible to cover all the properties and configurations that are available for flows. To deepen your knowledge of these additional elements, resources, and operators, please refer to Salesforce Help at `https://help.salesforce.com/articleView?id=flow_ref.htmtype=5`.

Managing a flow

Like any other automation process, a flow can be activated and deactivated. It supports versioning (and so cloning is a good choice if you wish to experiment with different versions) and, as in Process Builder, only one version of a flow can be active at a given time.

A flow can be distributed in the following ways:

- A Lightning page using the standard flow component from the Lightning App Builder
- A record quick action using the Flow action type
- In the Lightning Console
- In the utility bar so that the flow is available from any page of the given Lightning app
- By URL (for more details, please refer to `https://help.salesforce.com/articleView?id=flow_distribute_internal_url.htmtype=5`)
- Using a custom Aura component (ask your developer about how you can do this)
- Using a custom Visualforce page (ask your developer about how you can do this)
- Using Process Builder, a workflow with a flow trigger (beta feature), and Apex and REST APIs for autolaunched flows

When a flow fails, Salesforce sends a detailed email to the admin who last modified the flow or to the Apex exception mail recipients (this can be set up from **Setup** | **Email** | **Apex Exception Email**). You can choose which recipients to use from **Setup** | **Process Automation** | **Process Automation Settings**:

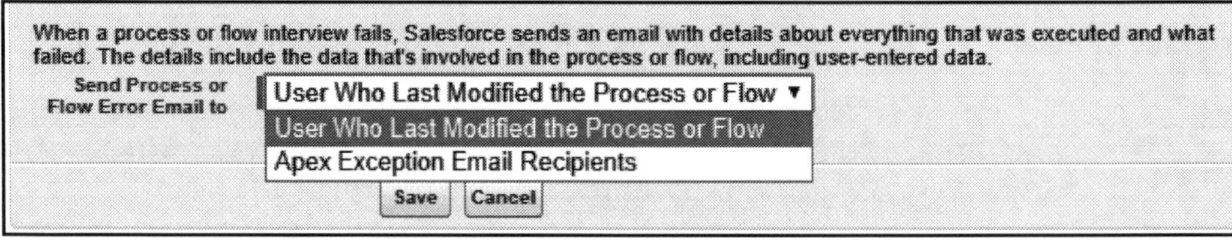

Flow error email recipients definition

I suggest that you select **Apex Exception Email Recipients** to prevent common users from receiving error log mail messages.

Testing a flow

As with any other feature, before releasing a flow into production, remember to test any available path so that you don't run into any unexpected surprises.

Debugging a flow is quite straightforward; select a flow and click on the **Debug** button. A new window will open:

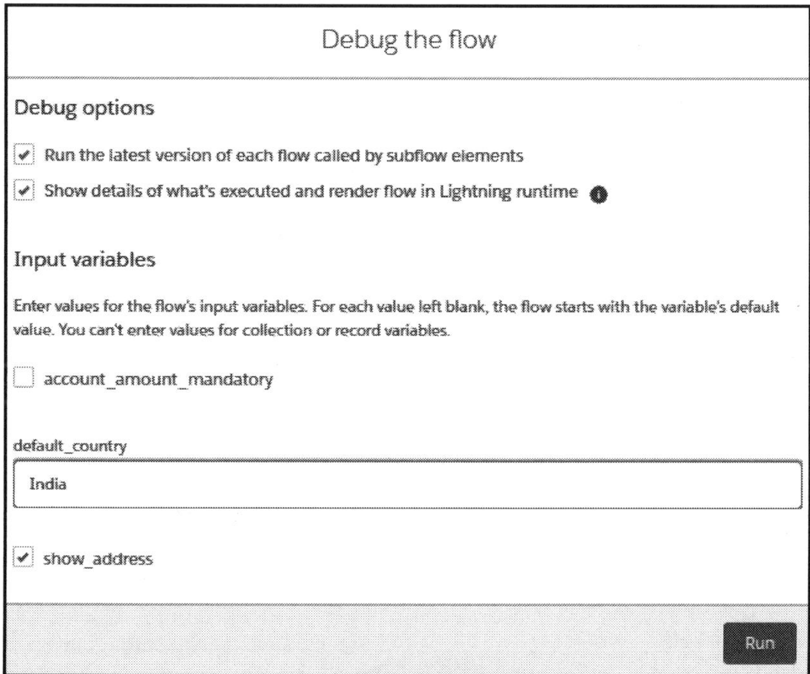

Flow debugging options

If the flow has inputs that are not collections or record variable resources, you can set them up on this initial box (like in the picture above).

When you click **Run**, the flow is executed. On the right-hand side of this window, you can take a look at the whole context:

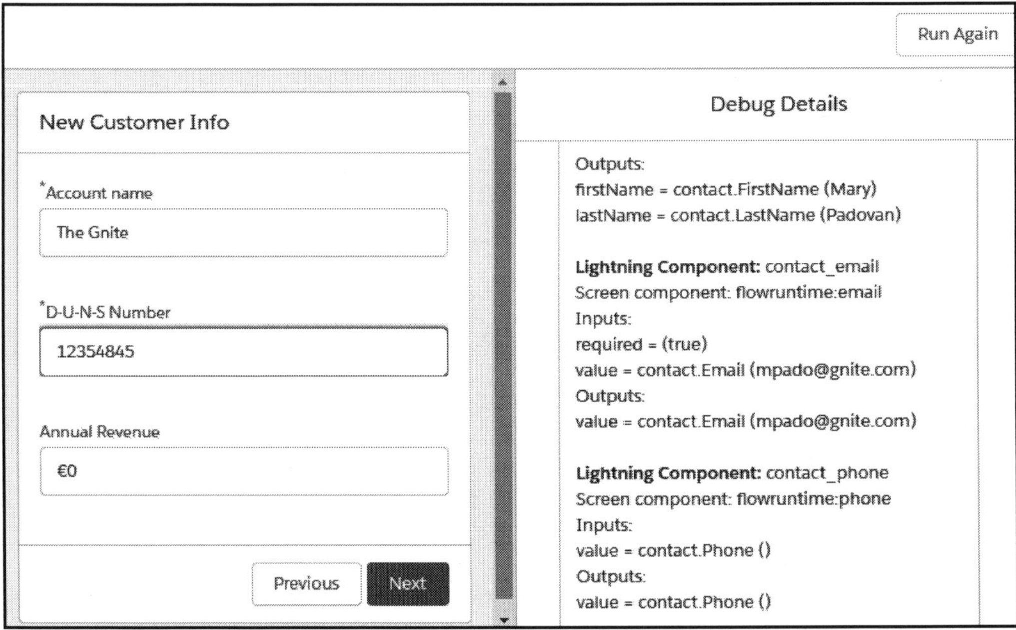

Debugging a flow

After each **Next** click, you'll see the right-hand side being updated with new data for each element that composed the flow.

Remember that, even in debug mode, transactions are committed to the database, so be careful when debugging in production.

Transactions and governor limits

Do you remember what we said about governor limits for Process Builder?

The same considerations apply for flows as well.

DMLs (or update/create/delete actions) are done when we use Create/Update/Delete Records elements or Actions (such as quick actions to create a Chatter post), while SOQL queries are done when using, for example, the Get Records element.

One of the best coding practices is to *bulkify* coding, that is, avoiding repetitive SOQL queries or database operations one after the other and preferring to use a single database operation to commit more than one record at a time.

The cool thing about flows is that their engines are automatically bulkified, so if you make a Create Records element that executes after a massive record operation on the system (for example, massive data loading that triggers for each record of Process Builder that calls a flow action), then chances are, the system will bulkify the flow interviews, thereby keeping your transactions under governor limits as much as possible.

For more details about flow bulkification, please refer to Salesforce Help at `https://help.salesforce.com/articleView?id=flow_concepts_bulkification.htmtype=5`.

Limits and considerations

Before closing this chapter, please take note of some of the limits that flows have (as of the Winter 2020 release – some depend on your Salesforce edition):

- **Max number of paused/waiting flows**: 30,000-50,000.
- **Max UI flows per monthly executions**: 2,000-20,000,000.
- **Max non-UI flows per monthly executions**: 10,000,000-10,000,000,000.
- **Versions per flow**: 50.
- **Total flows**: 5-4,000 per flow type.
- When a flow is added to a Lightning page, don't add an action (such as a record edit) before the first screen element; this will help you avoid unwanted actions being performed without the user actually being aware of them.
- When using change sets or the metadata API, a flow is deployed in an inactive state (and users can't run it), so remember to activate flows if a Lightning page contains a flow after its deployment.
- When a flow is used within a Lightning page, the following variable types are not supported: collection, record, and record collection. Each component only supports the input variables that are manually entered. The text input accepts a maximum of 4,000 characters.

Take a look at Salesforce Help at `https://help.salesforce.com/articleView?id=flow_considerations.htmtype=5` to find out more about the limits of flows, as well as what to take into consideration.

Summary

In this chapter, we have learned how to build complex business logic using a declarative approach (that is, the point-and-click approach) and used flows with and without a user interface. We also learned about the key elements and resources that compose flow automation and the considerations we should take into account regarding how to manage a flow, how to test it, and its limits. Everything that we've learned about in this chapter will help us collect data in a certain flow.

In the next chapter, we'll complete the *Process Automation* section of this book by introducing automation from a coding approach.

Questions

1. What is a flow?
    a. An automation tool so that we can use Apex code more easily
    b. Something we can use to build complex automations with or without a user interface
    c. A point-and-click process automation tool
    d. An evolution of workflows
2. What is a flow composed of?
    a. Resources
    b. Trigger objects
    c. Connectors
    d. Elements
3. What can we use to define a variable in a flow?
    a. A connector
    b. A trigger
    c. An element
    d. A resource
4. A flow that has no user interface is called a what?
    a. A user provisioning flow
    b. An autolaunched flow
    c. A screen flow
    d. A contact request flow

5. What is a screen element used for?
    a. To present an input form
    b. To present a decision branch
    c. To pause an autolaunched flow
6. How can a Salesforce Object record (for example, an opportunity) be stored?
    a. In a resource of the **variable** type
    b. In a resource of the **constant** type
    c. In a resource of the **record data** type
7. How can we set variable values?
    a. Using a Create Variables element
    b. By configuring the component's output value attributes on a screen component (if this is supported)
    c. Using an Assignment element
    d. Using a Decision element
8. How can we assign a variable a blank value?
    a. Use `{!$GlobalConstant.Null}`
    b. Use `{!$GlobalConstant.False}`
    c. Use `{!$GlobalConstant.EmptyString}`
    d. Leave the text input blank
9. If we wish to query records, which element should we use?
    a. Records Search
    b. Search for Records
    c. Query Records
    d. Get Records
10. How can we split flow paths?
    a. Use a Decision element
    b. Use a Split element
    c. Use a Pause element
11. How can we upsert a record?
    a. Use a Decision element
    b. Use the Update Records element
    c. Use the Create Records element
    d. Use the Upsert Records element

12. Which of these statements is true about autolaunched flows?
    a. They are used to automatically execute business logic without the use of a user interface.
    b. They can be triggered by Process Builder or an Apex trigger.
    c. They can use Screen elements.
    d. They can use Pause elements.

15
The Coding Approach

When deeper customization is needed, the coding approach is a win-win situation. In this chapter, you will learn how Apex triggers can provide complex automation for your processes when a point & click approach is not enough. Also, we will see how to evaluate Visualforce and Lightning Components customizations (which you won't be required to develop unless you want to learn to be a developer) when user interface constraints require coding magic.

So, in this chapter, we'll cover the following topics:

- What Apex triggers are and how they are shaped
- The order of execution of automation on the Lightning Platform
- The frameworks that can be used to implement custom user interfaces

Exploring Apex triggers

All the automation we have seen so far is related to rules that are defined to interact with record change events (called **DML** events, or **Data Manipulation Language** events). To sum up, these are the topics we've already covered in the previous chapters:

- **Workflow rules**: They execute actions on the originating record (or on its master record) when certain criteria on the originating record applies.
- **Approval processes:** They define entry criteria that are used to determine whether a record should be further evaluated by approvers (we configure criteria and actions as well).

- **Process Builders:** Like workflow rules, they are based on record events such as insert and update (but also on platform event creation), but they can execute actions on a wider variety of records (the record itself, its parents, or its children). Also, the kinds of actions available vary from updating a record to launching another Process Builder or an autolaunched Lightning flow.
- **Lightning flows**: They are used to create complex algorithms without any lines of code and can be launched from a Process Builder, which becomes its *triggering criteria,* and so the flow is called an **autolaunched flow**) or can be launched from another Lightning flow. Flows can also be used to create wizards composed of multiple steps to grant user input (but in this case, we can't talk about process automation but rather in user experience customization).

But what if you need to execute an algorithm involving a complex logic that cannot be executed from the aforementioned tools?

You have two choices:

- Unleash Apex actions from Process Builder or Lightning Flow (which is where Salesforce is going to be in the near future).
- Unleash a complete Apex customization with Apex triggers.

The first approach is limited by how Process Builder/Lightning flow is executed, while Apex triggers deliver more fine-grained control of what's happening on the database.

Before explaining the pros and cons of Apex triggers (and a quick tour of how to build one, which we'll hack together), we'll need to understand a basic concept of automation, the order of execution of automation within the Lightning Platform.

Order of execution

We can basically do five different operations on Salesforce records:

- Insert
- Update
- Upsert (which is just an insert or update operation, depending on the fact that the record may already be in the database, given a unique field such as its ID)
- Delete
- Undelete

While the delete and undelete operations have never been mentioned when we talked about automation (and this is one of the reasons Apex triggers are most suitable for certain scenarios), insert and update operations (and upsert) follow a determined order of events (which should become your mantra when designing automation) as follows:

1. The original record is loaded from the database (or a new record is initialized in case of insert).
2. The new field values coming from the DML request (whether it comes from the **Save** button on a page layout, from a Process Builder or workflow rule, or from Apex code or a SOAP/REST API call) overwrite old values:
    - If the record is updated/inserted from the user interface (for example, page layout), the Salesforce engine executes some system validations to check the record before submitting it:
        - Checking required fields defined at the layout level or the field level
        - Field format validation (for example, the email field)
        - Field length
    - If the record comes from Apex code or a REST/SOAP API call, Salesforce only validates foreign keys and checks whether they refer to the object itself (for example, it checks whether the `Case.ParentCase` field refers to the object itself. They are usually called **circular references** and are not allowed.).
3. Any Apex trigger is executed with the *before* event: without going into further detail, Apex triggers respond to events that occur around a record's database commit. The *before* event happens right before the record is saved into the database but not actually committed.
4. All validation rules are run, both system (required fields at the field level) and user-defined ones. In this step, layout-specific rules are not enforced again.
5. Duplication rules (refer to `Chapter 7`, *Improving Data Quality with Duplicate Management*) are evaluated, and if the *block* action is in place and a duplicate is found, the record is not saved at all and this flow breaks.
6. The record is saved to the database (but not yet committed).
7. Any Apex trigger is executed with the *after* event.
8. Any assignment rules are executed. We haven't talked about assignment rules. They are just used to assign cases and leads to the proper users/queues. Refer to Salesforce Help at `https://help.salesforce.com/articleView?id=creating_assignment_rules.htmtype=5` for more details.

9. Any auto-response rules are executed. They are used to send quick email responses to customers when a lead or case is created. Refer to Salesforce Help at `https://help.salesforce.com/articleView?id=creating_auto-response_rules.htmtype=5`.
10. Workflow rules are executed: no order of execution on workflow rules is enforced, as we already said we cannot determine which workflow rule is run first.
11. If workflow rules execute field update actions, the record is updated a second time, leading to the following automation chain:
    - *Before* and *after* trigger code is executed one more time (and only one).
    - Standard validation rules (such as on required field) are reevaluated (custom validation rules and duplicate rules are excluded from this round).

    This means that you can create records with invalid field values according to validation rules: take this into account when troubleshooting issues.

12. Process Builder is launched along with autolaunched flows: if a process or flow executes an update or insert, the affected record walks through this path one more time.
13. Escalation rules are executed. This is used for allowing a case to be escalated if certain conditions are met. Refer to Salesforce Help at `https://help.salesforce.com/articleView?id=rules_escalation_create.htmtype=5`.
14. Entitlement rules are executed (refer to `Chapter 6`, *Service Cloud Applications*).
15. If a parent record's roll-up fields need to be updated or is part of a cross-object workflow, the parent is then updated and walks through this same order of execution path.
16. If a grandparent record needs to be updated (because of a roll-up field or another cross-object workflow on the parent), it is updated and walks through this same save path.
17. Criteria-based sharing rules are evaluated (refer to `Chapter 1`, *Secure Data Access*).
18. The record is committed to the database (meaning that nothing can go wrong from now on, and the record is finally available to anyone in the organization with its new values).
19. Any post-commit logic event is executed, such as sending emails.

With a recursive save (that is, the same record that started this path is updated in one of these steps), *step 8* to *step 16* are skipped and only executed for the first iteration.

Trigger features and rules

In the previous section, we saw that the order of execution of Salesforce automation has to deal with all of the available automation tools within the Salesforce platform and that Apex triggers are called twice, *before* and *after* the record is saved to the database.

This is one of the pros of using Apex triggers:

- *Before save* events are not available on Process Builder actions. That is, on Process Builder, any action or logic is done only after the record has already been saved to the database; with *before* triggers, we can implement complex logic that deals with unrelated objects and that can be used to validate records in a better way. The example I usually use is validating Italian fiscal code: the code is composed of characters that come from the first name, last name, date of birth, a code that refers to the town of birth (called the Belfiore Code), and a check character (more details at `https://en.wikipedia.org/wiki/Italian_fiscal_code_card`). The algorithm is quite complex, so it is not suitable to be developed using validation rules (I bet there is an awesome administrator out there someone who can do it, but believe me, it would be easier using Apex code): that's why the *before* trigger is the best place to validate whether your Italian customer has a valid fiscal code. If you try to make a SOQL query asking for the current record from within the *before* trigger, you won't find anything, as the record has not been saved yet. The *before* trigger is also used to fill in current record fields without the need for further DML operations, just like setting a default value or a formula value in a custom way: if you change a value or a field in a *before* trigger, the system considers it as a new value that comes from the original save request.
- *After* save events happen only after the record has already been saved to the database (but not yet committed).

Another important feature of triggers is the possibility of accessing new and previous values of a given record: that is, if you update the `Account.Name` field, you are able to get the old and new values at once (we'll see it shortly), and this allows a more complex scenario of record validation.

When a trigger is executed (whether it is in a *before* or *update* event), all records for the given save action are passed through: this can be easily tested using some Apex code (running anonymously from the Developer Console, as we have seen in `Chapter 2`, *Auditing and Monitoring*) or using Data Loader by creating/updating more than one record at once. While in tools like Process Builder we have an *all or none* approach, that is, if something goes wrong everything is *rolled back*, while using Apex triggers you can selectively make a record pass the save process (while the rest of records won't), so partial success is possible and easily achievable.

Finally, delete and undelete operations are only available through Apex triggers: you can develop a complex cascading delete action (for example, by deleting the parent record or even *physically* unrelated records), or simply restore a record with an undelete operation and simultaneously alter the record itself to keep track of the undeletion (for example, undeleting an opportunity may need the close date to be postponed to a future date).

One last thing that's useful for developers is that, using triggers, you can get a full and precise debug log that allows a developer to uncover a bug easily, while using Process Builder and Lightning Flow error messages are more generic and usually more difficult to address (and even worse if automation logic simultaneously involves multiple automation tools).

One of the main rules when using Apex triggers is to have only one trigger per object: if you have more than one, you won't know which trigger is executed first. For example, let's say you have two triggers on an opportunity object, both related to the *after* save event:

- The first trigger gets all the opportunities related to an account and updates a field on that account, setting it to the overall sum of opportunities (without considering their stage or closure status) created in the last month.
- The second trigger is used to delete a set of opportunities related to the same account that in the last month has been lost.

As there is no way to determine which trigger is run first, you can have trigger 1 executing *before* trigger 2 or vice versa, delivering a significantly different result.

In fact, if trigger 1 is executed first, it will sum all the opportunities of the last month, including the lost ones, which are then deleted by trigger 2.

If trigger 2 is executed first, the lost opportunities are deleted *before* trigger 1 sums the amounts, delivering a potentially lower sum.

The solution is to merge the code into one trigger, delivering a more stable and predictable code.

Apex trigger anatomy

So far, we know that a trigger is defined by the following:

- An object type
- One or more events (before, after)
- A DML action (insert, update, delete, and undelete; upsert is just a short way to say *do an insert or an update if the record already exists*)

This is more or less the code involved in a trigger's definition:

```
trigger OpportunityTrigger on Opportunity (before insert, before update,
before delete, after insert, after update,
after delete, after undelete) {
    //code goes here...
}
```

All possible event combinations are referenced:

- *Before* events support insert, update, and delete operations.
- *After* events support insert, update, delete, and undelete operations.

If you want to refer to the specific event or operation, you would go with the `Trigger` keyword like this:

```
trigger OpportunityTrigger on Opportunity (before insert, before
update, before delete, after insert, after update, after delete,
after undelete) {
    if(Trigger.isBefore){

        if(Trigger.isInsert || Trigger.isUpdate){
            //before logic goes here...
        }

        if(Trigger.isUpdate){
            //before logic goes here...
        }
    }else if(Trigger.isAfter){
        if(Trigger.isUpdate || Trigger.isInsert){
            //after logic goes here...
        }
    }
}
```

As an experienced admin, I bet you get what it's all about: it's just a simple algorithm with a bunch of `if` statements that checks whether we are in a *before* or *after* event and, within each event, checks for a specific DML operation (the double slash indicates a comment, code that is never executed but is used to clarify what's happening, and is a language feature that's available in formulas and validation rules as well). When the trigger is fired (as we've seen in the order of execution list of automated actions), all the trigger's code is executed, and it is important to define which lines of code may make sense for the *before insert* event but not for the *after update* event, and vice versa.

The before event

Where is the record that is being saved?

The `Trigger` keyword comes in handy as well and gives us access to current record values (and even to old ones):

```
trigger OpportunityTrigger on Opportunity (before insert, before
update, before delete, after insert, after update,
after delete, after undelete) {

    //current record (supposing only one opportunity can be saved at once)
    Opportunity currentOpp = Trigger.new[0];

    //treating before and after events separately
    if(Trigger.isBefore){

        //following logic 0runs in before insert and update
        if(Trigger.isInsert || Trigger.isUpdate){

            //error if opportunity has a negative amount
            if(currentOpp.Amount <= 0){
                //the addError() method is used to break the save process
                //and is shown to the current user on the page layout
                currentOpp.addError('Invalid negative amount on opportunity.');
            }
        }

        //folowing login runs only for before update
        if(Trigger.isUpdate){

            //gets the old values for an opportunity
            Opportunity oldOpp = Trigger.old[0];
```

```
27.
28.             //error if opportunity amount is discounted of more than 50%
29.             Double newAmount = currentOpp.Amount;
30.             Double oldAmount = oldOpp.Amount;
31.
32.             if(newAmount > 0 && oldAmount > 0
33.                 && newAmount < (oldAmount * 0.5) ){
34.                 currentOpp.addError('Discount policies forbit discounts '
35.                 + 'higher than 50%. Please review the deal. '
36.                 + newAmount + ' vs '+oldAmount);
37.             }
38.         }
39.     }else if(Trigger.isAfter){
40.         if(Trigger.isUpdate || Trigger.isInsert){
41.             //after logic goes here...
42.         }
43.     }
44. }
```

We have covered only the *before* event.

What's happening?

Line 1 creates a new *variable*. A variable is just a temporary place where you can store a piece of data in Apex. It can store complex types such as Salesforce objects or simple types such as a string, an integer, or a date, for example.

Our first variable has the opportunity type, and it will contain the current opportunity record (supposing only one record is in the context of current trigger execution) that is taken from the `Trigger.new` property.

This property is a list of records of the opportunity type that contains all records that are part of the current trigger execution (and that have the most recent field values). A list is just a complex Apex type that is used to store a set of items of the same type. These elements can be taken using the `[n]` operator, where `n` is the element's index, which spans from 0 (the first element) to the maximum number of elements minus 1 (the last element).

Basically, on *line 1* we are storing the first element of the saved opportunities in a single variable of the opportunity type called `currentOpp`.

On *line 8*, the *before* event section starts, and on *line 11* we are executing a piece of code for insert and update operations. Basically, if the current opportunity amount is less than 0, we add an error to the opportunity stating that the value is not correct. This check could be done using validation rules as well.

The `addError()` method (a method is another way of calling a function, as you saw with formulas and validation rules, but methods are related to a specific Apex object) is used to attach an error to the record (that is displayed on the page layout, as we'll see shortly), flagging it as *not committable* to the database, thus interrupting the *order of execution*. We saw this in the previous section.

From line 23, we are concentrating on the *before* update condition (that is, if we create a record, this piece of code won't be executed). We can see a new variable that stores the old valued opportunity (`Trigger.old` is a list just like `Trigger.new`, but it contains the opportunities with the old values) and two new double variables that contain the new and old values.

The `Trigger` Apex class supports many static variables that can be used to understand the executing context: the most common ones are `Trigger.newMap` and `Trigger.oldMap`, which convey the same records as `Trigger.new` and `Trigger.old` but using a special Apex class called `Map`, which organizes records based on their Salesforce ID field (which in some algorithms is really useful). For more information, refer to Salesforce Help at `https://developer.salesforce.com/docs/atlas.en-us.apexcode.meta/apexcode/apex_class_System_Trigger.htm`.

Why has the `oldOpportunity` variable been defined inside the `Trigger.isUpdate if` statement and not just after the `currentOpp` definition? This is because insert operations do not convey an old value (there is nothing on the database so far), thus accessing the `Trigger.old` list in an insert operation leads to a critical error on Apex execution, which interrupts trigger execution and prevents the whole save operation from closing.

The two `newAmount` and `oldAmount` variables are then compared, and if the new amount is less than 50% of the previous amount, an error is attached to the record (this match could have been implemented using a validation rule as well).

Let's test it out:

1. Open the **Developer Console** (click the **Settings** icon and then select the **Developer Console** item). When the console loads, click on **File** | **New** | **Apex Trigger**, select the **Opportunity sObject**, and call it `OpportunityTrigger`:

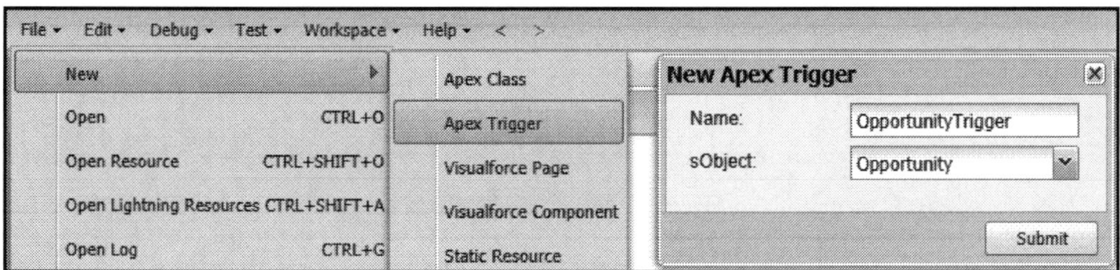

Trigger creation

2. Now copy the whole code in the previous example (or cut and paste it from the book's GitHub repository) and click **File** | **Save** or just *Ctrl* + *S* on your keyboard. If you have made some errors while writing your code, you'll see where the error lies on the **Problems** tab:

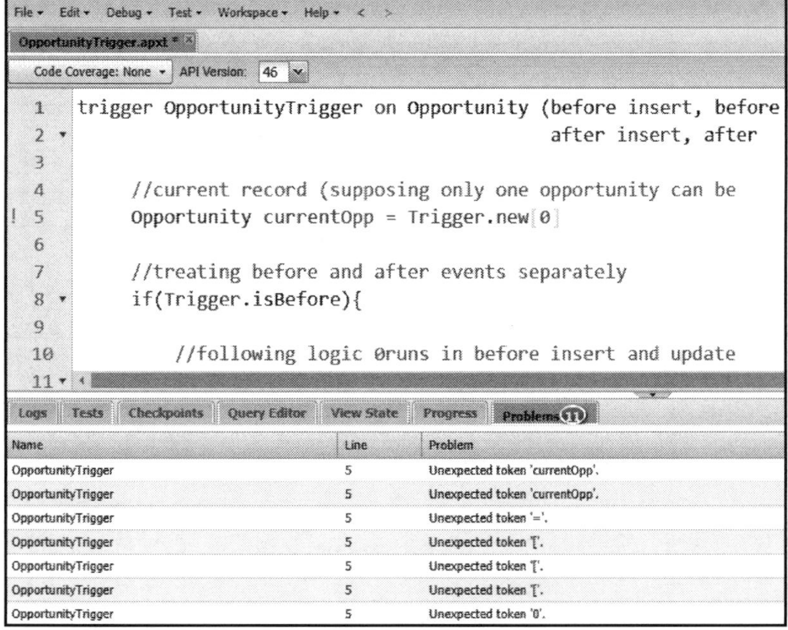

List of problems generated by miswritten code

Line 5 simply didn't terminate with a semicolon (required by Apex syntax), and this leads to a chain of errors on the subsequent lines: if we add the semicolon, all the compile errors disappear.

Do you remember debug logs from `Chapter 2`, *Auditing and Monitoring*? When we open the Developer Console, a new debug log is opened on the fly (have a look at the **Logs** tab):

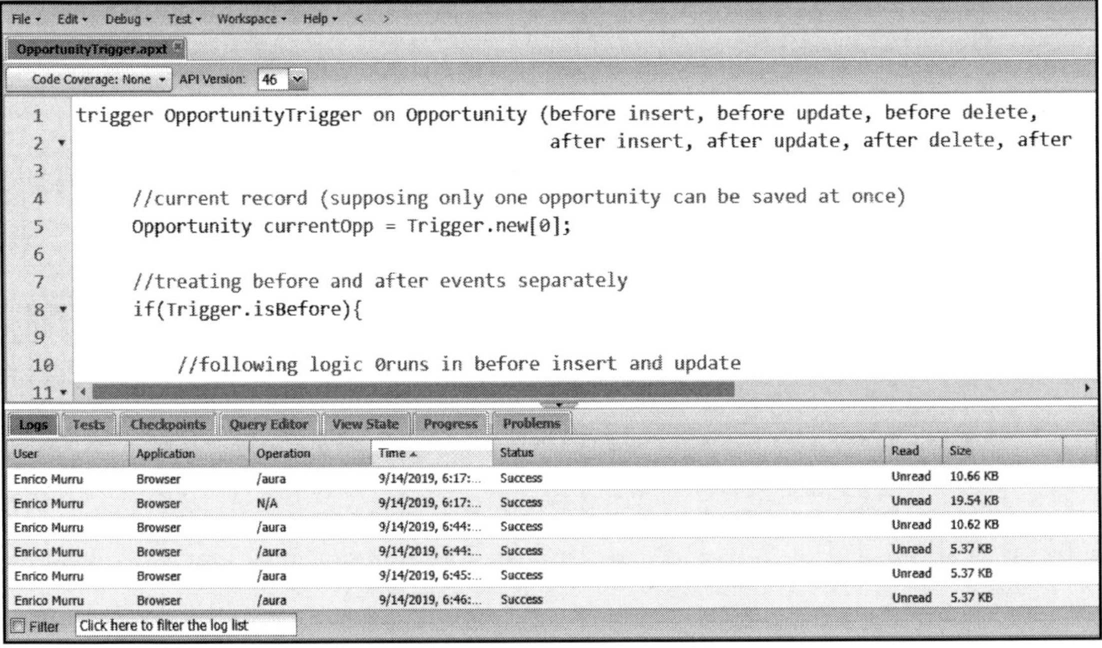

Debug logs on the Developer Console

3. Now that the trigger is in place, don't close the **Developer Console** window. Instead, jump to the CRM and create a new opportunity (or update an existing one) with a negative amount:

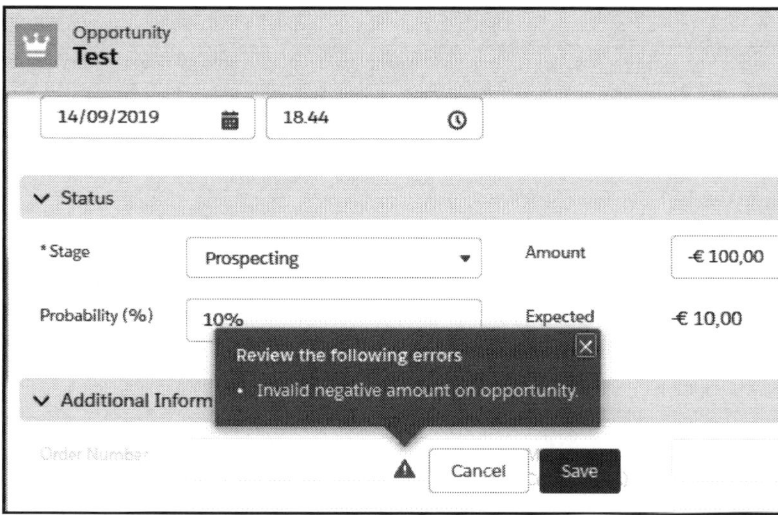

Trigger error for negative amount value

4. Now save the opportunity with a positive value (let's say $1,000) and then try to update the amount with $400 (which is lower than 50% of the original value):

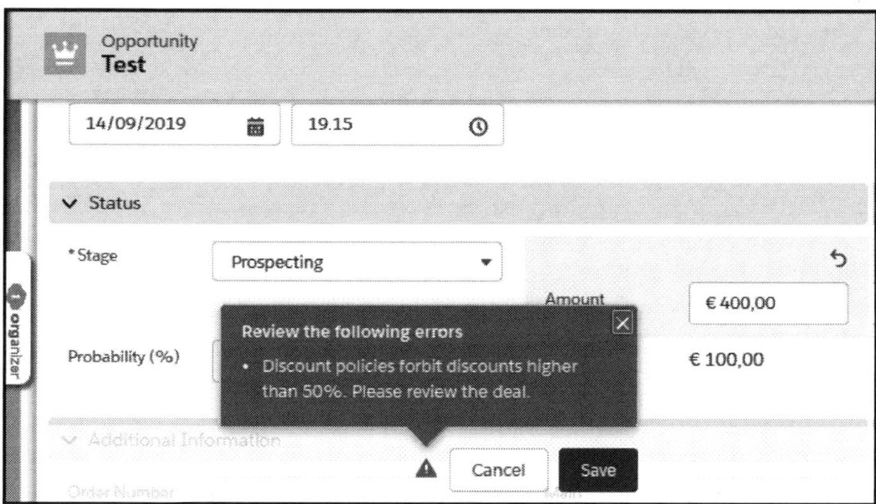

Trigger error for business rule on the amount field

The trigger logic worked as we expected! What if we try to delete the record?

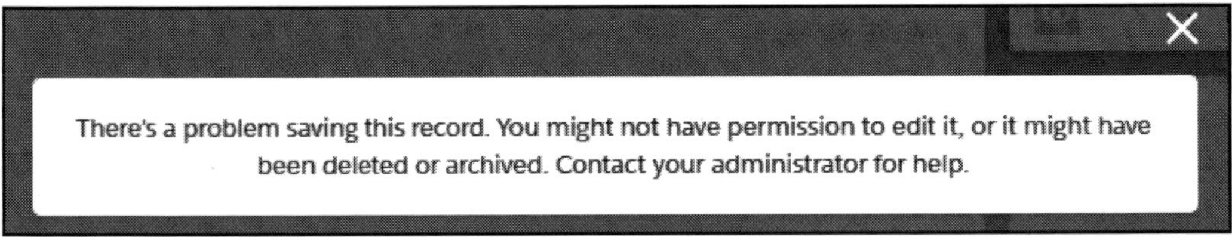

Unexpected error when deleting the opportunity

How's that?

This is related to how the trigger is written. Let's jump back to the Developer Console and the **Logs** panel:

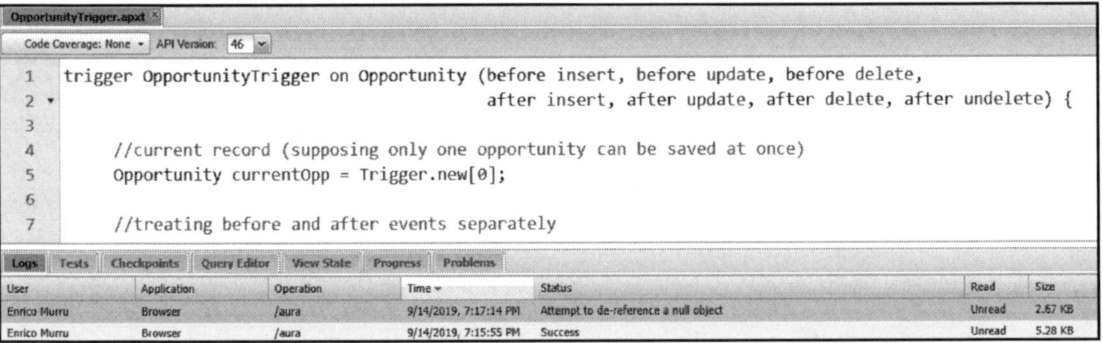

Debugging log after an unexpected record on a save operation

5. Double-click on the row whose **Status** shows **Attempt to de-reference a null object** (one of the ugliest errors a developer can face, not because it is not recoverable but because it means that they haven't designed their code in the best way). Scroll down on the **Execution Log** or use the **Filter** input box and write `FATAL_ERROR`:

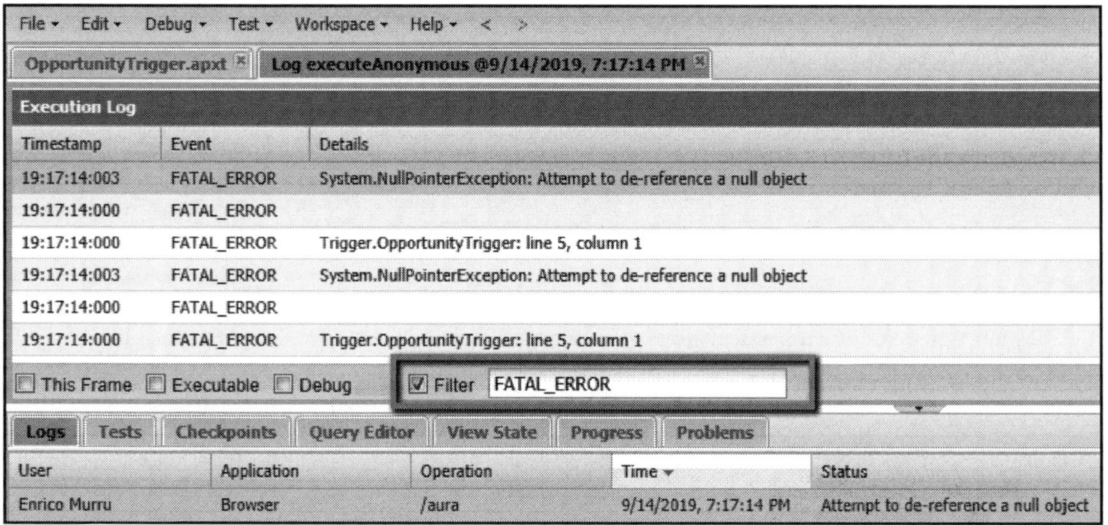

Filtering a debug log

This is called an unexpected exception: exceptions are a way that Apex uses to tell the developer that something went wrong, and the code failed to execute as expected.

The problem is related to `OpportunityTrigger` on *line 5*, where the `currentOpp` variable is being set. So, what's the problem?

We are doing a delete operation and the trigger is set up to support it (its definition supports the *before delete* and *after delete* events), but the delete operation does not contain any new value, so if we actually had to handle a delete operation we should have used the `Trigger.old` property instead (like we did for the old values on the `if` statement of `Trigger.isUpdate` in the `Trigger.isBefore` section).

We have two options:

- Move the `currentOpp` variable assignment inside a statement that explicitly refers to insert and update operations.
- Simply edit the trigger not to support delete (and undelete) operations.

We'll go with the second way, as we are not actually supporting delete/undelete operations. If for some reason in the future we want to support these events, we'll go through trigger refactoring to support the new DML operations.

The trigger declaration becomes simpler:

```
trigger OpportunityTrigger on Opportunity (before insert,
    before update, after insert, after update) {
. . .
```

From now on, no other exception will be thrown.

We said that in *before* triggers we can even change the record fields without executing a new save operation (a new DML), such as filling in default values using Apex code.

Let's create a new custom field on the opportunity object, a checkbox that is used to tell whether the opportunity is the first opportunity ever created for its account in the current month:

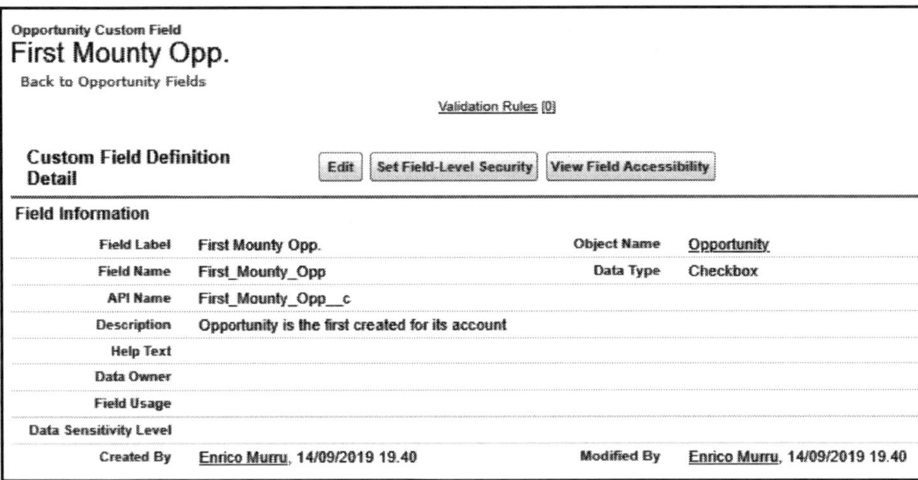

New custom field on the Opportunity object

Let's add some logic for the *before insert* event after the amount validations:

```
trigger OpportunityTrigger on Opportunity (before insert, before
update, after insert, after update) {

    //current record (supposing only one opportunity can be saved at once)
    Opportunity currentOpp = Trigger.new[0];

    //treating before and after events separately
    if(Trigger.isBefore){

        //following logic 0runs in before insert and update
```

```
        if(Trigger.isInsert || Trigger.isUpdate){
            // . . .
        }

        //folowing login runs only for before update
        if(Trigger.isUpdate){
            //. . .
        }

        //following logic runs in before insert only
        if(Trigger.isInsert){

            //checks if current opportunity is the first opp.
            //for the current month for its account
            if(currentOpp.AccountId != null){
                Integer monthOppties = [Select count()
                                       From Opportunity
                                       Where AccountId =
                                       :currentOpp.AccountId
                                       and CloseDate = THIS_MONTH];
                currentOpp.First_Mounty_Opp__c = monthOppties == 0;
            }

        }
    }else if(Trigger.isAfter){
        if(Trigger.isUpdate || Trigger.isInsert){
            //after logic goes here...
        }
    }
}
```

This piece of code must run on the *before* event and only for insert operations (that's why there's the new `if` statement of `Trigger.isInsert`); then we check whether the `AccountId` field is filled in (otherwise, the opportunity is not related to any account and our business requirement makes no sense).

`monthOppties` is an integer variable that contains the result of the SOQL query used to get the number (the `count()` SOQL function) of opportunities that are related to the same account as the current opportunity, whose created date is in this month (`THIS_MONTH` is a SOQL constant that can be used when referring to date/time filters).

The new `Opportunity.First_Month_Opp__c` field is then flagged only if the total number of opportunities is 0.

As you can see, after this field assignment no insert/update statement is executed (we've seen how to insert a new record in `Chapter 4`, *Extending Custom Objects*, using the `update` Apex keyword). This is because it is not needed, as we are in the *before* event, and so any modifications to the fields are propagated in the save operation.

If you try to create a new opportunity with a new account that hasn't got any other opportunities for the current month, the new checkbox is flagged and if you try to create a new one, it doesn't.

Try setting other fields yourself and see what happens after the record is saved.

To finish this complex example, let's complete the *after* event logic.

The requirement is to set a new field on the Account object that stores the total number of deals that are closing in the current month.

The first thing we do is create a new field on the account object:

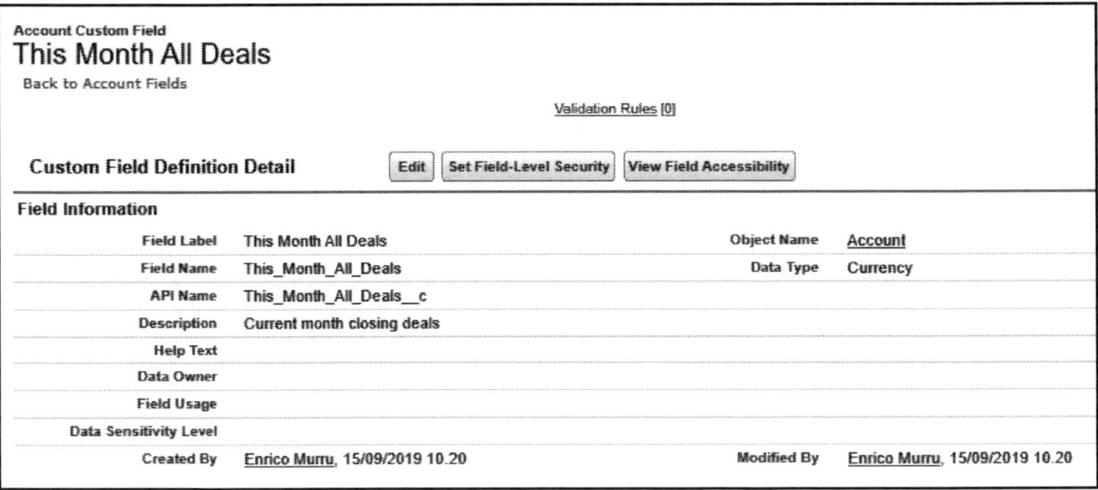

New field on the Account object to store all closing deals

The after event

Then, we can update the *after update* part on the trigger (some parts of the code have been hidden for simplicity; refer to this book's GitHub repository for the full code):

```
trigger OpportunityTrigger on Opportunity (before insert, before
update, after insert, after update) {

    //current record (supposing only one opportunity can be saved at once)
    Opportunity currentOpp = Trigger.new[0];

    //treating before and after events separately
    if(Trigger.isBefore){
        //. . . hidden for brevity
    }else if(Trigger.isAfter){
        if(Trigger.isUpdate || Trigger.isInsert){

            if(currentOpp.AccountId != null) {
                //query current account
                Account acc = [Select Id From Account
                               Where Id = :currentOpp.AccountId];
                //gets the sum of the amounts of all opportunities
                //that will be probably colosing this month
                Double totalAmount = 0;
                List<Opportunity> oppList = [Select Id, Amount From Opportunity
                                      Where AccountId = :currentOpp.AccountId
                                      and CloseDate = THIS_MONTH
                                      and StageName != 'Closed Lost'];
                //iterates trhough the opportunity list
                for(Opportunity opp : oppList){
                    totalAmount += opp.Amount;
                }

                //sets the value on the Account object and update it
                acc.This_Month_All_Deals__c = totalAmount;
                update acc;
            }
        }
    }
}
```

Whether it is an insert or update operation, we execute a SOQL query on the `Account` object getting the one that is related to the current opportunity.

Then, we get all opportunities related to the same account that are closing in the current month (we used `THIS_MONTH` again) and that are not lost. Like the `Trigger.new` property, the query returns a list of the opportunity type (the triangular brackets state that the list will be of the opportunity type).

With this list, we can iterate through all the elements using a `for` loop. Element after element, we are summing all the amount fields from the preceding query, thus getting the total amount for all closing deals (this part could have been easily done using the SOQL `sum()` function).

This cumulative amount is then assigned to the `Account. This_Month_All_Deals__c` field, and then the account is updated.

This could have been implemented using point and click with the following:

- A formula field on the opportunity object that returns the amount if we are in the current month, or 0 if not.
- A roll-up field on the account object that sums all the formulas of the previous step, getting the total number of closing deals.

Point and click mode may seem easier, but you may have other roll-up fields and formulas on your objects, and you may be close to object limits, so you may be required to write (or make your developers write) a trigger to implement the requirement.

To test it out, try to create some new opportunities. This is the current list of opportunities:

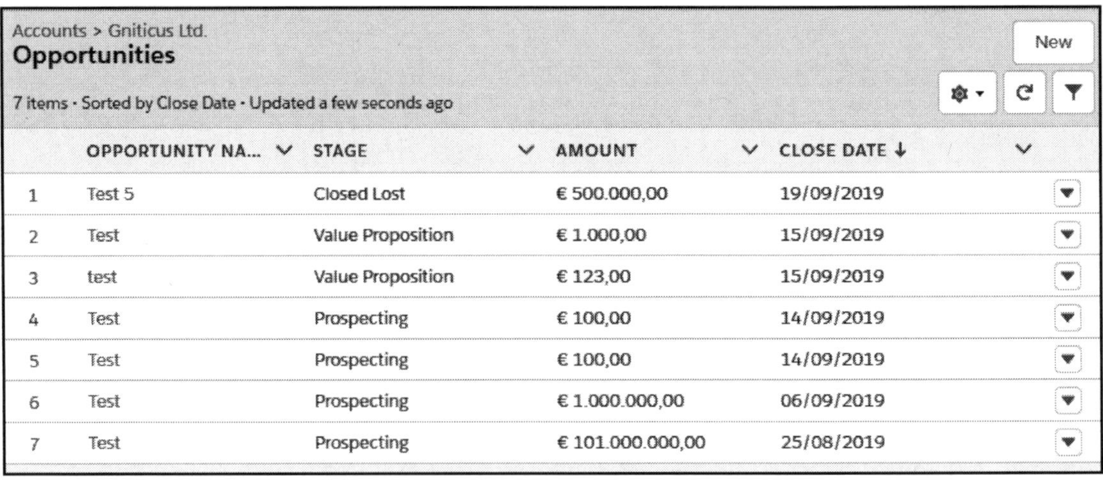

Accounts > Gniticus Ltd.
Opportunities
7 items • Sorted by Close Date • Updated a few seconds ago
New

	OPPORTUNITY NA...	STAGE	AMOUNT	CLOSE DATE
1	Test 5	Closed Lost	€ 500.000,00	19/09/2019
2	Test	Value Proposition	€ 1.000,00	15/09/2019
3	test	Value Proposition	€ 123,00	15/09/2019
4	Test	Prospecting	€ 100,00	14/09/2019
5	Test	Prospecting	€ 100,00	14/09/2019
6	Test	Prospecting	€ 1.000.000,00	06/09/2019
7	Test	Prospecting	€ 101.000.000,00	25/08/2019

Account's opportunities list

The current month is September 2019, so this is the total amount on the **Account** object that is calculated on the trigger any time a new opportunity is updated/created:

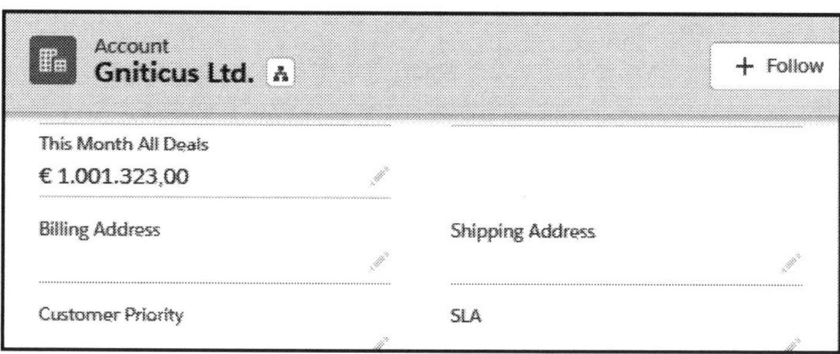

Total amount of current month opportunities

Without considering opportunities closed and lost in other months, the total is exactly what the requirement wanted us to implement.

There are some other concepts that a developer should understand and master to write triggers following best practices, such as the concept of bulkification (which is covered extensively in this great Salesforce Developers blog, `https://developer.salesforce.com/page/Apex_Code_Best_Practices`) to deliver a more robust code, or the better ways to organize the code within a trigger using one of the frameworks out there (have a look at this great video by our trailblazer MVP rockstar Adam Olshansky on the Apex Hours series: `https://www.youtube.com/watch?v=U5ZOA9EY3Kg`).

The purpose of this section was not to make you the best Apex developer in the world. It is impossible to share all the necessary knowledge without a solid programming background in just one chapter, but I hope you've just got a clearer idea of the possibilities that Apex triggers can deliver to your organization.

What else can you do with a trigger that you cannot do with any other automation tool?

- Integrate with an external system (using Apex callouts)
- Manage Apex sharing with complex criteria that cannot be defined using sharing rules
- Handle the update of unrelated objects
- Delete records

If all of this talking about Apex triggers tickled your imagination and you thought *why not start on the developer trail?*, I suggest you go out your comfort zone of awesome admin and start learning some nerdy Apex stuff from one of the best blogs out there that talks directly to administrators who want to change their careers. SFDC99.com (`https://www.sfdc99.com/beginner-tutorials/`), built by our MVP David Liu, has a special Apex Tutorial section that's meant for administrators who want to learn Apex coding, but I also suggest starting with a Trailhead from the following Trailmix, with selected topics dedicated to admins and beginner developers, at `https://trailhead.salesforce.com/en/users/enreeco/trailmixes/apex-for-admins`.

The code presented here is a simplified version of how a trigger can be implemented, so it may not respect all Apex best practices and coding principles, but it allows a more readable and understandable code. If you plan to start the developer trail and want to master triggers, I challenge you: take the code provided in this example and try to apply the bulkification principle to make it the most performant code ever!

User interface development

Way back in 2009, when I took my first steps into the Salesforce world, the first thing my boss asked me to develop was a four-step wizard in Visualforce for our most valuable customer, to be used to grab customer data to activate a new contract in the utilities industry. I had about 2 months of Salesforce training, and I was not sure I was able to develop it...but I did!

This is the power of the Lightning Platform. The learning curve is not very steep, and after an initial moment of difficulty you start coding like crazy by putting together everything you have learned. This skill comes with experience, of course, but it's not as hard as you might expect.

10 years ago, all I had was a huge PDF file with loads of Apex and Visualforce information and no Trailhead at all, but luckily Knowledge is now so accessible that you can get everything you need to become a pro. Experience is still the key, but you won't find any issue to get all the necessary resources to blaze your trail as a developer.

Visualforce is the first supported way to code custom user interfaces. These pages are kind of HTML pages (yes, the ones that your browser can read to output your favorite sites) with special tags (the instructions used to represent components in the page, from input text to buttons to labels) used to output server-side data (for example, table of **Account** records) or to interact with the client (that is, the user's browser) by displaying forms to get specific input data (which then can be processed using Apex code classes, called Visualforce controllers).

Visualforce pages can easily be represented by the following diagram:

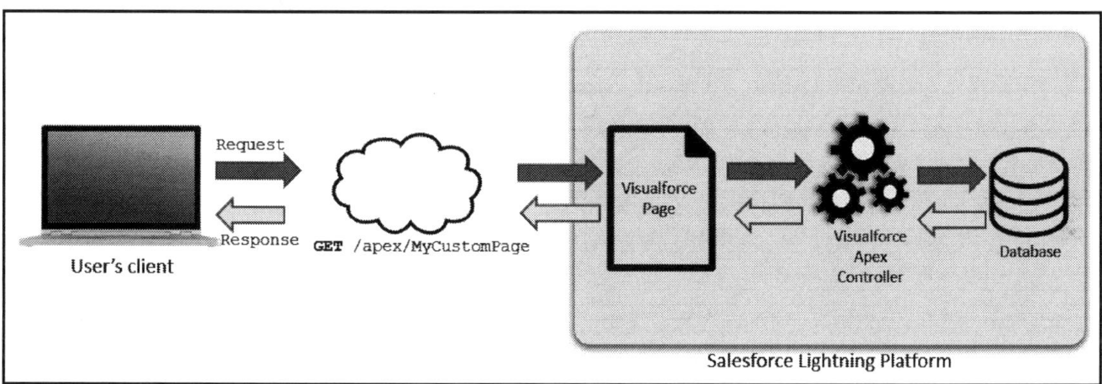

Visualforce page request flow

The following list explains the preceding page request flow diagram:

1. The user requests a specific page (Visualforce pages usually have the `/apex/` path in their URL).
2. The Salesforce platform gets the request and loads the corresponding Visualforce page.
3. If needed, the page returns control to its Apex controller, which handles any server-side logic.
4. If needed, the controller talks with the underlining database (making a SOQL query or doing a DML statement).
5. The database returns the requested result (a query result or an update operation).
6. The Apex controller gets the results and elaborates them and returns control to the Visualforce page.
7. The page, using standard and static HTML tags, images, JavaScript resources, and proprietary Visualforce tags, compose the final HTML page that is sent back as a response to the user's client.
8. The user's browser outputs the resulting HTML page.

Any time a user interacts with the same page, this request/response process restarts, and a new HTML page is generated with the updated data.

With the Visualforce framework, developers can generate any kind of form with any logic inside (they can use any JavaScript library to enhance the user experience), interact with the database, or even interact with external systems (for example, to get a list of all the bills for a given customer from the billing system, integrated using custom Apex callouts).

Where can we access a Visualforce page?

- From the LEX App Launcher
- From the LEX navigation bar
- From a standard page layout (Visualforce pages can be added within a layout section)
- From a Lightning page made with the Lightning App Builder
- From a quick action
- From an overridden object action (for example, override the edit action for the account record by showing a Visualforce page to users)
- From custom links or buttons
- From manually jumping to `/apex/MyPageName` in your browser

If you want to start building your first Visualforce page, I suggest you have a look at the Trailhead at `https://trailhead.salesforce.com/en/content/learn/modules/lex_dev_lc_basics/lex_dev_lc_basics_intro`.

Visualforce is a technology that is becoming outdated in favor of the Aura Framework and the brand-new **Lightning Web Components** (**LWC**) framework. As many customers still use Visualforce pages (I guess there are millions and millions of pages out there live in production), there are no current plans to retire it, but it is highly recommended to implement any new user interface customization using the Aura or LWC framework.

Why a new framework?

In Salesforce Classic, with each click you did on the user interface, you could see the browser loading a new page, waiting for the results to be composed by the server (basically what happens on a Visualforce page).

When Lightning Experience rolled out, the user experience became quite different, calling the **one-page app** paradigm: the client (that is, the browser) initially loads all the required client-side code (that is, JavaScript files), which contains most of the logic (things such as *when you hit the* **New** *button on the* **Account Lightning** *page, show a modal window containing a form with all input fields*), except for the server-side calls to the database (which, of course, cannot be **pre-loaded** on the client). With this technology in place, although the first load of the web app may take a while, the code is cached by the browser and any other subsequent access becomes quick as a flash (or *lightning*).

Moreover, developers don't have to build big monolithic pages but, with componentization, they now develop small pieces of the app that can be put together to build a bigger app and convey reusable developments (for example, an account selection form with custom filters can be applied to an order creation app or when creating a new opportunity).

In 2015, Salesforce released the Aura Framework (and the concept of Lightning Components), which was meant to follow the componentization and one-page app concepts, a modern way to develop web apps, but also the *responsive* concept, which is the ability to adapt to different form factors (smartphone, tablet, or desktop). In late 2018, Salesforce announced the definitive framework, the Lightning Web Components framework, that should bypass the Aura Framework (which hasn't actually been retired, although Salesforce suggests going with LWC for new developments); the announcement was made at the following developer blog post: `https://developer.salesforce.com/blogs/2019/05/introducing-lightning-web-components-open-source.html`.

The main difference between Aura and LWC is that LWC uses web standards (which contain built-in security for the code that is being run by clients) that are now common on most browsers, while Aura delivers the same features but with a lot of underlining JavaScript code (because at the time Aura was introduced, some of the features of the framework were not fully supported by major browsers). Using LWC is better in terms of performance because most of the code is already built into the browsers (this is a simple explanation, but it explains why LWC is preferable to Aura components).

As LWC is still a new framework, some of Aura's features are not yet fully functional, but the Salesforce engineering team is working hard to get this done. So, don't worry if your development team will use Aura instead of LWC in certain conditions.

Where can we access Aura or LWC components (some limitations may still apply to LWC)?

- From the LEX App Launcher
- From the LEX navigation bar
- From a Lightning page made with the Lightning App Builder or the Community Builder

- From a quick action
- From an overridden object action (for example, override the edit action for the account record by showing a custom Lightning component to users)
- As a standalone app using Lightning applications (a special kind of Lightning Components), which permits the use of a Lightning component outside of the LEX framework
- Inside Visualforce pages (this is a trick that is used when your organization still relies on the Classic interface but you want to start using the new Lightning framework)
- From external sites/portals using the Lightning Out technology (it's like loading a part of the LEX framework outside Salesforce to make Lightning Components available on external sites)
- From a flow screen to enhance the flow's user experience

If you want to learn more about Lightning Components, have a look at Trailhead modules for Aura Components at `https://trailhead.salesforce.com/en/content/learn/modules/lex_dev_lc_basics/lex_dev_lc_basics_intro` and LWC components at `https://trailhead.salesforce.com/en/content/learn/modules/lightning-web-components-basics/discover-lightning-web-components`.

Summary

Although this was an introductory chapter on Apex triggers and user interface customization, it should have given you the tools to understand how customization works with the coding approach. Summing up, we can build Apex triggers to deliver highly customized automation and provide granular control over what happens when a record is inserted, updated, deleted, or even undeleted. We have also learned how the process automation engine handles the order of execution among all the automation tools when a record is being saved in the database.

After a bit of theory, we created a complex trigger to handle some opportunity-related automation and also learned how to debug any unwanted exceptions that may be thrown.

In the last section, we saw how to create user interface customizations using the Visualforce, Aura, and Lightning Web Component frameworks, and we discussed the key differences between these customization frameworks.

In the next chapter, we'll go through some suggestions on how to successfully pass your Advanced Administrator certification, which will be an amazing ending to your study trail.

Questions

1. How can Apex code be executed when responding to a DML event/operation?
    a. Implementing an Apex trigger
    b. Calling Apex actions from Process Builder or Lightning Flow
    c. Executing Apex code from within the Developer Console
    d. Configuring a workflow rule with an Apex action
2. Which DML operation is not supported by Process Builder?
    a. Insert
    b. Update
    c. Delete
    d. Undelete
3. What is the order of execution?
    a. The order in which Process Builder executes all its actions related to a record save operation
    b. The order in which the Salesforce Lightning Platform executes all automation related to record save operations
    c. The order of precedence if an object has more than one trigger defined
4. Following the order of execution for automation, is a trigger's code executed before validation rules?
    a. Yes, validation rules are checked before a trigger's code execution.
    b. No, validation rules are checked right after loading the original record from the database.
    c. A trigger's code is run before and after validation rules are checked.
5. After the *before* event is completed, the record is committed to the database:
    a. True, and then the after trigger event is called.
    b. False, the record is saved to the database and not yet committed.
    c. False, the record is committed only at the end of the save path defined in the order of execution.
6. What happens when a trigger is run during the before event?
    a. The record is not yet on the database.
    b. Any value set on the fields of the triggering record is not automatically saved to the database but requires a recursive save instruction.
    c. Any value set on the fields of the triggering record is automatically saved to the database.

7. What happens when a trigger is run during the before event?
    a. Variables
    b. Object type
    c. A combination of events (before/after) and DML actions (insert, update, delete, and undelete)
    d. Lists
    e. A name
8. Visualforce can deal with the database:
    a. No, only Visualforce tags can access the database.
    b. Yes, using an Apex controller.
    c. Only if Visualforce has been enabled with Lightning Experience.

    a. Quick actions
    b. Lightning Out
    c. Standard page layout
    d. Overridden object actions
    e. Flow screen
10. Where can Lightning components be accessed from?
    a. Quick actions
    b. Lightning Out
    c. Standard page layout
    d. Overridden object actions
    e. Flow screen

7
Section 7: Taking Your Certification Exam

In this section, you will learn how to plan your studies, how to register for an exam, and how to schedule your exam. You will also learn about the best tips and tricks you can use to complete the exam, how to get an optimal score, how to utilize this book to its fullest potential, and what to consider while solving questions.

This section includes the following chapters:

- `Chapter 16`, *Tips and Tricks for Passing Your Exam*
- `Chapter 17`, *Mock Tests A and B*

16
Tips and Tricks for Passing Your Exam

This whole book is meant to be a structured trail to give you all the content you need to increase your chances of passing the Salesforce Advanced Administrator test (and to improve your skills, of course).

Throughout the chapters so far, I've tried to give you hints and pointers, as well as links to online official documentation and useful blogs for further reading and digging into the topics. If you plan to pass the Advanced Administrator certification test, then this means that you have already passed the Administrator certification test, so the exam day should not be a surprise for you, but I'm sure you'll find the tips and tricks covered in this chapter useful in helping you to be confident on exam day.

In this chapter, we'll learn the following:

- How to deepen your knowledge and find the right resources
- How to calculate question scores
- How to face your exam and optimize your final score
- What to expect on the exam day

Keep studying

We have covered all the required topics, providing diverse examples and use cases to increase the chances of this book helping you achieve the ultimate purpose of scoring well in the certification. However, it is important to keep studying these subjects to ensure we stay on top of things.

Topics and scores

The topics that the chapters and sections have covered haven't been randomly chosen, as the Salesforce Advanced Administrator certification guide clearly states what is covered in the exam and what percentage of questions will cover that topic (as of Winter '20):

- Security and Access: **20%**
- Extending Custom Objects and Applications: **8%**
- Auditing and Monitoring: **6%**
- Sales Cloud Applications: **10%**
- Service Cloud Applications: **10%**
- Data Management: **10%**
- Content Management: **3%**
- Change Management: **10%**
- Analytics, Reports, and Dashboards: **10%**
- Process Automation: **13%**

We have probably covered more than what's strictly necessary for the exam, but more is better when dealing with knowledge.

Given that each exam session contains 60 questions (optional 5 more questions may be added by Salesforce to the exam for internal checks, but they are not scored; unfortunately, you don't know which questions those are), you get the following average number of questions per topic:

- Security and Access: **12**
- Extending Custom Objects and Applications: **4-5**
- Auditing and Monitoring: **3-4**
- Sales Cloud Applications: **6**
- Service Cloud Applications: **6**
- Data Management: **6**
- Content Management: **1-2**
- Change Management: **6**
- Analytics, Reports, and Dashboards: **6**
- Process Automation: **7-8**

The pass score is **65%**. Doing the math, you can tell that you need to answer at least 39 questions correctly.

This doesn't seem too much, but each question generally has a multiple-choice format, which means that each question can have more than one right answer, increasing the difficulty level.

Need more resources?

This book covers all the topics, but some more examples and point of views on the same subjects can give you even more confidence.

I suggest you to jump to **Trailhead** and complete the Advanced Administrator Trailmix at `https://trailhead.salesforce.com/en/users/strailhead/trailmixes/prepare-for-your-salesforce-advanced-administrator-credential`, which covers a bunch of the topics as well. This is not a comprehensive guide (at least as of Winter '20), so you need to search online for further guides and training (chances are you chose this book to deep dive into certification topics).

I suggest reviewing the Administrator certification topics as well to refresh your knowledge of administration stuff (a dedicated Trailmix is at `https://trailhead.salesforce.com/en/users/strailhead/trailmixes/prepare-for-your-salesforce-administrator-credential`, a certification that is a prerequisite for the Advanced Administrator certification).

Besides the Trailmixes, a good way to test your skills is to go through the Trailhead Superbadges (located at `https://trailhead.salesforce.com/superbadges`), which are intended for administrative staff, such as the following:

- Lightning Experience Specialists
- Lightning Experience Rollout Specialists
- Process Automation Specialists
- App Customization Specialists
- Security Specialists
- Business Administration Specialists
- Lightning Experience Reports and Dashboards Specialists
- Service Cloud Specialists

This list may vary month after month when the Trailhead team releases new content; follow Trailhead on Twitter at `@trailhead` to hear about the new content.

Throughout this book, we have given you plenty of references, which I politely suggest that you look at to get a comprehensive view of all the main topics.

Remember that Google is your friend: search for **Salesforce Advanced Administrator Certification** and you'll find plenty of blogs and online courses to read and use to progress.

The Trailhead Academy provides the following classes (virtual and on site). You can find them at `https://trailhead.salesforce.com/en/academy`:

- Administration Essentials for Experienced Admins (ADM 211) (`https://trailhead.salesforce.com/en/academy/classes/adm211-administration-essentials-for-experienced-admins`)
- Certification Preparation for Advanced Administrator (CRT 211) (`https://trailhead.salesforce.com/en/academy/classes/crt211-certification-preparation-for-advanced-administrator`)

Another amazing place to increase your skills to the maximum levels is the Trailblazer Community (`https://success.salesforce.com`), where you have a few options:

- **Local community groups** (`https://trailblazercommunitygroups.com`): Find local meetups and join (or even organize) training sessions with your local pals.
- **Advanced Certification Study groups** (`https://success.salesforce.com/_ui/core/chatter/groups/GroupProfilePage?g=0F93A00000020CqSAI`): Virtually join other trailblazers and exchange knowledge with them.
- **Training groups** (`https://success.salesforce.com/featuredGroups?filter=a0L3000000Rq7K5EAJ`): Official Salesforce training groups.

Finally, you can even join Salesforce's Certification Days at `https://pub.s7.exacttarget.com/ryqkengawga`. These webinars are free for all, and will help you get an insight into the key topics for various certifications, and you can even get a discount for your next exam.

Facing the exam with the right attitude

I'm not lying when I say that it took me seven years to get my first certification, the Platform Builder I.

I cleared it with my eyes closed. I'm not kidding: some of the answers were wrong for sure (I'm not infallible). I was super excited after I saw the **Result: PASS** message, and I felt so dumb that it had taken me so long to get the first certification.

After this first certification, I got one after the other, following the Administrator, Consultant and Architect paths, reaching an outstanding 20 total certifications (at the time of writing):

A list of all the certifications I got from 2016 to 2019

Two things helped me to achieve this result:

- Hard work and, of course, daily experience as a Salesforce technical and solutions architect (in WebResults, Engineering Group)
- No fear of failure (perhaps even a drop of recklessness)

Failure is an option

First, don't be afraid to fail. Failure is the perfect way to learn.

Would you believe me when I say that I passed all these tests without a **Result: FAILED** message?

Let's take the Advanced Administrator certification as an example. It took me two attempts to clear the exam: in the first attempt, I was sure I could get through it without any issue, but I discovered that I hadn't studied the right way and I was actually bad at some key topics that I had no experience in.

After the completion of the exam, you will receive an email from Salesforce with your percentage score for each topic (you don't know which questions you failed, but you get a clear view of your deficiencies). I can show you my first attempt scores (with the weights for each topic as shown earlier):

- Security and Access: **50%** (weight 20%)
- Extending Custom Objects and Applications: **80%** (weight 8%)
- Auditing and Monitoring: **66%** (weight 6%)
- Sales Cloud Applications: **50%** (weight 10%)
- Service Cloud Applications: **33%** (weight 10%)
- Data Management: **66%** (weight 10%)
- Content Management: **50%** (weight 3%)
- Change Management: **100%** (weight 10%)
- Analytics, Reports, and Dashboards: **33%** (weight 10%)
- Process Automation: **75%** (weight 13%)

Multiplying each score by its weight, I got almost a 60% overall score.

Given that the **passing score is 65%**, it was close indeed!

What lessons did I learn? Never underestimate your exam, study all the topics, and test the features out. Learning through doing is way better; you'll remember how something works just by remembering how you configured it on the org.

Never skip a topic just because it is boring or because you already know it: there could always be a feature that you don't know or that is crucial for success in the exam.

I know you are wondering about the scores of the second attempt (the first score mentioned for each topic is the second attempt's score):

- Security and Access: **58%** versus **50%** (weight 20%)
- Extending Custom Objects and Applications: **80%** versus **80%** (weight 8%)
- Auditing and Monitoring: **33%** versus **66%** (weight 6%)
- Sales Cloud Applications: **83%** versus **50%** (weight 10%)

- Service Cloud Applications: **83%** versus **33%** (weight 10%)
- Data Management: **83%** versus **66%** (weight 10%)
- Content Management: **50%** versus **50%** (weight 3%)
- Change Management: **83%** versus **100%** (weight 10%)
- Analytics, Reports, and Dashboards: **33%** versus **33%** (weight 10%)
- Process Automation: **75%** versus **75%** (weight 13%)

If you do the math, it's about **76%**: the worst parts were the Analytics, Reports, and Dashboards (where I supposedly missed 2 out of 3 questions), Auditing and Monitoring (2 out of 3 wrong), and Security Access (where I probably missed 7 out of 12 questions) sections.

An exception should be made for the Analytics, Reports, and Dashboards section, where I admittedly skipped some study because I didn't like the topic at that time. I probably answered the other topics without understanding the question, or some of the topics I studied were not as clear in my mind as I expected (for the Security and Access section, I had another blast a few months after I cleared this exam as I had to design the whole sharing configuration for one of my company's biggest customers!).

All of this is to let you know that we can all make mistakes and fail a certification, but you can get a lot of experience just by preparing and appearing for a single exam.

Schedule it right now!

In the previous section, I demonstrated that even after hours of study, you can make mistakes and get the wrong answer.

This shouldn't mean that you should procrastinate and forestall signing up to your exam forever: believe me, you can study as much as you can, but there will always be a question that you won't fully understand (it may happen if English isn't your mother tongue) or simply that won't find a fit with your knowledge base.

If you schedule the exam, you'll find yourself committed to that date and efficiently use the remaining time to study and prepare for a successful result.

Preparing for the exam

Whether you'll be doing the exam online or onsite, no books, notes, smartphones, smart watches are allowed: it's you and the screen (and the people behind the webcam or the exam room who are checking that you are not cheating).

I've never attended an exam at a proctored site for the following reasons:

- None of the cities on the beautiful island where I live have a certified exam site.
- To do the online proctored exam, you just need a laptop, a webcam, a reliable internet connection, and a quiet place.

If you plan an online exam, remember the following:

- Don't wear watches.
- Put your smartphone in silent or plane mode.
- Don't use multiple screens.
- Don't drink/eat during the exam.
- Don't wear sunglasses, and if you (like me) have to wear normal glasses, they'll ask you to show the glasses to the webcam (to prove they are not *smart glasses*).
- Don't talk or read the questions out loud or point out to the screen with your fingers (I did once and was asked to stop).

Have a read at the following Trailhead article to get more info about both types of exams at `https://trailhead.salesforce.com/help?article=Scheduling-an-Exam`.

Question format

If you have already passed any other certification, the question formats should already be clear: a single or multiple-choice format.

Whether there are 1, 2, or 3 right answers (I have never seen more than 3 right answers), there is always a completely wrong answer (if not more than one), and the other ones are quite similar. I'm not saying you have to roll the dice to get the right one, but choosing between a narrow set of questions is definitely a plus.

And if you are not that sure about your answers, flag the **Mark this item for later review** checkbox so you can skip to the next question later at the end of the exam: later on you, can even find a related question that can help you answer (or simply remember) a previous question, so don't be rushed: take a breath and use all the allotted time you have. The Advanced Administrator certification test must be completed in 105 minutes (as of Winter '20); that is a little less than 2 minutes per question (enough time, if you have studied).

The final step

Are you ready to ace this? Schedule your exam, take a deep breath, and start your Advanced Administrator certification exam: you have studied a lot, you have deepened your knowledge, and can face another certification with enough confidence.

In the next and final chapter, you'll have a chance to prove your skills with two mock exams: start your stopwatch and prove you are an advanced, awesome admin!

Good luck!

Summary

In this chapter, we traced the path to the exam day by linking further resources to improve your knowledge (outside of this book) and looking at how scores are calculated.

Finally, we described how failing an exam could be a great source of learning (although I bet you won't fail!) and that you should schedule the exam as soon as you have completed study all of the topics because procrastination leads to **no exam at all**!

Before closing this long journey, you'll be presented with two mock exams to test your skills for the last time!

17
Mock Test A and B

This chapter contains two mock exams with 60 questions that cover the entirety of the Salesforce Advanced Administrator topics and are designed to test out your knowledge. In `Appendix A`, *Assessments*, you'll find the solutions, as well as the topic each question is related to, so that you can easily compute the final score on your own (as shown in `Chapter 16`, *Tips and Tricks for Passing Your Exam*).

Unlike the final assessments following each chapter in this book, each question in this chapter suggests the total number of correct answers (whether the question has a single- or multi-choice format), similar to what you'll see in the exam.

Start the stopwatch and prove you are an awesome Salesforce advanced administrator!

Mock Test A

1. What can you debug on the debug log? [three answers]
    a. Delegated administration tasks.
    b. Workflow rules.
    c. Apex triggers.
    d. Custom layouts.
    e. Validation rules.
2. A business wants to make sure that all **Invoice** (custom object) records have at least one invoice line item (which is a custom objec, with master-child relation to **Invoice**) record marked as **Discounted**, and a custom invoice line item field. How can you report on this? [one answer]
    a. Use a standard report type of **Invoice** with invoice line items, use a cross filter to get all invoices without line items, and then filter by `Discounted equals True`.

b. Create a custom report type of **Invoice** with invoice line items, use a cross filter to get all invoices without line items, and then filter by `Discounted equals False`.
c. Create a custom report type of **Invoice** with invoice line items, use a cross filter to get all invoices with line items, and then filter by `Discounted equals False`.
d. Create a custom report type of **Invoice** with invoice line items, use a cross filter to get all invoices without line items, and then filter by `Discounted equals True`.

3. Gianna is a service manager user who wants to access a contact record, but she is receiving an **Insufficient privileges** error. The contact-sharing configuration has the **Grant Access Using Hierarchies** option flagged, and the contact's owner has a role that is junior to that of Gianna. How is this possible? [two answers]
    a. The Contact **Organization Wide Defaults (OWD)** is **Controlled by Parent**, but the account's owner, referenced by the contact record, is not below Gianna's role in the hierarchy.
    b. The Account OWD is **Controlled by Parent**, but the account's owner, referenced by the contact record, is not below Gianna's role in the hierarchy.
    c. The **Grant Access Using Hierarchies** flag on the Contact OWD must be unchecked.
    d. The Contact OWD is private and no account is related to the contact record.
4. The Opportunity OWD is set to **Private** for internal users. A criteria-sharing rule grants read/write access to closed opportunities owned by any internal user to all service manager role users. Michael is a user with that role and his profile has read access only on the opportunity record. That said, Michael: [two answers]
    a. Can only view closed opportunities assigned to him.
    b. Can edit any closed opportunity.
    c. Can neither create opportunities nor edit them.
    d. Can edit any opportunity that he owns.
5. Team selling is enabled on opportunities; a sales VP does not have edit access on the opportunity object, but wants to have edit access to opportunities owned by his sales team. How can he be granted this kind of access? [one answer]
    a. By disabling team selling.
    b. By enabling **Edit** permission on the opportunity object from his profile or creating a new permission set.

   b. By setting the Opportunity OWD to Public Write only.
   c. By configuring team selling by adding the sales VP to each opportunity's team with read/write permission.

6. As an administrator, you need to create some new text fields on the **Survey** custom object and a brand new picklist on the **Invoice** custom object. You have also been asked to manually change 20 user profiles from **Read Only** to **Sales Rep custom profile**. You want to let Jennifer, a capable agent within your call center, prove her Salesforce administration skills. What are the steps required to enable Jennifer to complete the tasks on your behalf? [three answers]
   a. Create a new delegated group.
   b. Add Jennifer to the delegated administrators list and the 20 users to the **User Administration** list.
   c. Add **Invoice** and survey objects to the **Custom Object Administration** list.
   d. Add the **Delegated Administrator** standard Permission Set to Jennifer's user.
7. What happens if the current Salesforce administrator changes the role of a given user? [one answer]
   a. All sharing rules are recalculated.
   b. Only criteria-based sharing rules are recalculated.
   c. Only ownership-based sharing rules are recalculated.
   d. Sharing rules are recalculated only if the new role is higher in the hierarchy.
8. What are the possible reasons as to why a user doesn't see the **Sharing** button on a given **Invoice** (custom object) record? [two answers]
   a. OWD on the **Invoice** object is private.
   b. The **Enable Manual Sharing** settings option is not checked.
   c. OWD on the **Invoice** object is Public Read/Write.
   d. The button has not been added to the **Invoice** page layout assigned to the user's profile.
9. OWD on the **Container** custom object is set to **Private**, and no sharing rule is activated in relation to the object. You want service agent (role) users to have access to all container records with the record type **Transoceanic**. What can you do to fulfill this requirement? [one answer]
   a. Create a permission set with **View All Data** permission.
   b. Modify the service agent profile.

   b. Create a sharing rule.
   c. Create a permission set with **View All** permission on the container object.

10. A junction object has been created to link **Invoice** and bundle custom objects. Only bundles with the **Available** field set to **true** can be linked to invoices. How can you achieve this? [one answer]
    a. Create a validation rule on the bundle object based on the **Available** field.
    b. Use Process Builder to block junction object creation if the **Available** field is not checked.
    c. Add a third master-detail field to the bundle object that points to the **Invoice** object.
    d. Create a lookup filter on the master-detail field of the junction object that points to the bundle object.
11. A master-detail field on a custom object must be converted to a lookup field. You should remember that: [one answer]
    a. You need to delete any roll-up field on the master object based on that master-detail relation.
    b. For the conversion to be executed successfully, all records must have the master-detail field populated.
    c. All records' master-detail fields must be set to a blank value prior to conversion.
    d. Fields must be deleted first.
12. There is a small subset of users from diverse profiles and roles who need to have **Modify All Data** permission. How can you enable this? [one answer]
    a. Create a permission set with **Modify All Data** permission and assign it to the required users.
    b. Create a permission set with **Modify All Data** permission and assign it to the required roles and permissions.
    c. Assign the **Modify All Data** permission to the required profiles.
    d. Assign the **Modify All Data** permission to the required roles.
13. The **Controlled by Parent** OWD configuration can be applied to: [two answers]
    a. Contact, order, and campaign member objects.
    b. Custom objects that have a master-detail field.
    c. Custom objects that have at least one lookup field.
    d. All standard objects with a master-detail field.

14. For any account, you need to get the sum of all related opportunities' amount fields. How would you do this? [one answer]
    a. Create a roll-up field on the opportunity object.
    b. Create a roll-up field on the account object.
    c. Use Process Builder to total all the opportunities.
    d. Create an Apex trigger to total all the opportunities.
15. When a customer contacts the call center, the agent should be able to append one or more contract details (that each involve at least five different fields) to the case record that is being created. What is a good implementation approach here? [one answer]
    a. Create a lookup field on the case object that points to the contract object and vice versa.
    b. Add a master-detail field to the contract object that points to the case object.
    c. Create a contract detail junction object that links cases and contracts.
    d. Use Process Builder to create contract detail objects at the time of case creation.
16. You want to be sure that all changes to your org configuration can be tracked. What can you do? [one answer]
    a. Add all users to a **Delegated Administrator** group.
    b. Setup Audit Trail automatically keeps track of all setup changes.
    c. Give all users the system administrator profile.
    d. Create a report on the setup audit standard object.
17. What is a content delivery? [one answer]
    a. A feature that allows content to be shared in a web-optimized version for online viewing.
    b. A feature that allows content creation in libraries within Lightning Experience.
    c. A feature that segments content files using record types.
    d. A feature that allows content files to be entered within an approval process.

18. The **Active** custom checkbox on the account record must be set to **true** anytime an opportunity reaches the **Closed Won** stage. What tools are available to deliver this automation? [three answers]
    a. Process Builder.
    b. Approval process.
    c. Workflow rules.
    d. Entitlements.
    e. Apex trigger.
19. The **Invoice** object needs a lookup field that points to the account object. What is true about this lookup? [two answers]
    a. You can define lookup filters.
    b. If the account is deleted, then the **Invoice** is deleted as well.
    c. The account lookup must always be filled in.
    d. Unless the field is not declared as required, **Invoice** records can exist independently from account records.
20. Recently, a validation rule is not working as expected and you suspect that one of your junior administrators may have added a bug. Where can you take a look to establish what changes have been made? [one answer]
    a. Debug log.
    b. Setup Audit Trail.
    c. Email log.
    d. Validation log.
21. Which of these statements about Territory Management is true? [one answer]
    a. It cannot be used if Collaborative Forecasts are in use.
    b. A user can be assigned to a single territory.
    c. It cannot be used if Customizable Forecasting is in use.
    d. Accounts, opportunities, cases, and contacts that belong to a territory can be given a **Controlled by Parent** access level to users.
22. IT operations want to get a full extraction of all cases on a weekly basis. What measures can you put in place? [two answers]
    a. A **Data Export** wizard.
    b. A **Data Export** app available for iOS and Android.
    c. A **Data Import** wizard.
    d. Configure **Data Loader** with some scheduling using the command-line utility.

23. When an opportunity record is closed in the **Closed Won** stage, a workflow action creates a task related to the owner of the opportunity and an email is sent to the user who most recently modified the record. Where can you check what's going on? [one answer]
    a. The debug log only.
    b. The email log only.
    c. Setup Audit Trail.
    d. Both debug and email logs.
    e. The Org Monitor Setup page.
24. What is quote syncing used for? [one answer]
    a. To sync up products from opportunity to quote.
    b. To sync up products from quote to opportunity.
    c. Quote fields are mapped into **Opportunity** fields.
    d. Quote custom fields are mapped into custom Opportunity fields.
25. Which of these statements are true regarding content libraries? [two answers]
    a. Library permissions cannot be customized.
    b. A library does not contain any tagging rule.
    c. You can add users and groups to content libraries.
    d. You can add a specific content access level to each member in the library.
26. Your company has both business and retail customers, and so has different prices for the products sold, depending on the customer type. How can you configure this kind of pricing? [one answer]
    a. Create two standard price books.
    b. Create one custom price book with two record types.
    c. Create two custom price books.
    d. Create one custom price book and a new price book custom field named **Customer Type**.
27. Forecast adjustments allow [one answer]:
    a. Price books to be assigned to users on a massive scale.
    b. Managers and sales reps to adjust the expected revenue/quantity regarding their forecast roll-ups.
    c. Sales reps to significantly change opportunity amounts.

28. What can you activate in order to set up monthly or quarterly goals assigned to sales teams? [one answer]
    a. Forecast quotas.
    b. Opportunity splits.
    c. Opportunity teams.
    d. Forecast managers.
29. How are article types defined in Lightning Knowledge? [one answer]
    a. Each article type is defined by a different knowledge object type.
    b. Each article type is defined by a knowledge object record type.
    c. Each article type is defined by a data category.
    d. Each article type is a standard picklist on the article standard object.
30. By enabling Chat (live agent) on your org, you can deliver the following features: [two answers]
    a. Skill routing becomes unavailable.
    b. Supervisors can whisper to their agents.
    c. Real-time chat can be delivered to customers in Salesforce communities and external websites using Snap-ins.
    d. Agents can whisper to their supervisors.
31. Agents want to quickly establish if calling customers have phone service support enabled. How can they be enabled to do this? [two answers]
    a. Deliver the entitlements-related list on the **Account** page layout.
    b. Deliver the entitlements-related list on the **Product** page layout.
    c. Deliver the entitlements-related list on the **Contact** page layout.
    d. Enable the entitlements-related list from the **Entitlement Settings** page.
32. When the status (custom field) of an **Invoice** record (custom object) is set to **Paid**, and the **Recurring** custom checkbox field is set to **true**, a new **Invoice** record has to be created with the same data of the current invoice and the **Previous Invoice** lookup field needs to be filled in. Which tool would be the best choice for this? [one answer]
    a. The workflow rule with a cross-object field update action.
    b. Autolaunched flow triggered by Process Builder.
    c. Apex trigger on the **Invoice** record.
    d. Add the **Clone** button to the **Invoice** page layout.
    e. Process Builder with a **Create a Record** action.

33. Which automation tools support the sending of emails? [three answers]
    a. Workflow rules.
    b. Entitlements.
    c. Process Builder.
    d. Validation rules.
    e. Formula fields.
34. You don't want users to be able to re-open cases closed with the cancelled status. What can you do? [one answer]
    a. Configure a workflow rule with the following criteria: `AND ( IsClosed = FALSE, ISCHANGED(IsClosed), ISPICKVAL( PRIORVALUE(Status), 'Cancelled' ) ).`
    b. Configure a validation rule with the following error condition: `AND ( IsClosed = FALSE, ISCHANGED(IsClosed), ISPICKVAL( PRIORVALUE(Status), 'Cancelled' ) ).`
    c. Configure a validation rule with the following error condition: `AND ( ISCHANGED(IsClosed), PRIORVALUE(Status) = 'Cancelled' ).`
    d. Configure a workflow rule with the following error action: `AND ( IsClosed = FALSE, ISCHANGED(IsClosed), ISPICKVAL( PRIORVALUE(Status), 'Cancelled' ) ).`
35. When defining a duplicate rule on the account object, what are the valid actions in terms of finding a duplicate? [two answers]
    a. Block the record delete operation.
    b. Delete a record prior to saving.
    c. Block the creation and update.
    d. Allow the creation and update (and optionally alert and report).
36. When are duplicate rules unable to run? [two answers]
    a. When records are undeleted.
    b. When leads are converted to accounts or contacts and the **User Apex Lead Convert** flag is enabled.
    c. During Salesforce update time.
    d. When records are merged.
37. In order to add a new product to a custom price book: [two answers]
    a. The product must already be added to the standard price book.
    b. The product must already be added to another custom price book.
    c. The user needs to have access to the product record.
    d. The product needs to have the **Family** field filled in.

38. The business has requested that the **Invoice** custom object's sharing configuration must be set up as follows:
    - Service managers must have read access on all invoices.
    - Every **Invoice** must be viewable and editable by the owner and their managers.

    All profiles have the correct permissions required to read/write the **Invoice** object.
    How can you achieve this configuration? [two answers]
    a. Set the **Invoice** OWD as **Private** and flag **Grant Access Using Hierarchies**.
    b. Set the **Modify All** flag on the **Service Manager** profile for the **Invoice** object.
    c. Set the **View All Data** flag on the **Service Manager** role.
    d. Set the **View All** flag on the **Service Manager** profile for the **Invoice** object.

39. You want to report on accounts that have at least one contact record and that show the contact owner's name, role, and profile. Which technology should you use? [one answer]
    a. Standard report types (accounts with contacts, select the fields from the contact owner's lookup).
    b. A joined report.
    c. Custom report types (accounts with contacts, select the fields from the contact owner's lookup).
    d. A matrix report.

40. A case exits an entitlement process when: [two answers]
    a. It is created.
    b. A combination of conditions in relation to its fields are met.
    c. It is closed.
    d. It depends on a custom date/time field.

41. In which type of sandbox must Apex tests always run when an inbound change set is deployed? [one answer]
    a. No tests should be run on sandboxes.
    b. A full sandbox.
    c. A partial sandbox.
    d. A Developer Pro sandbox.
    e. A Developer sandbox.

42. When using Visual Studio Code to execute a deployment, what do you have to provide the tool with? [three answers]
    a. The type of destination org (sandbox, production, or custom domain).
    b. The username, password, and (optionally) a security token.
    c. Access to the debug log.
    d. The name of the inbound change set.
    e. Metadata elements to be deployed
43. What is required in order to deploy from sandbox A to sandbox B using change sets? [one answer]
    a. A deployment connection enabled on sandbox A (flagging **Allow outbound changes**).
    b. A deployment connection enabled on sandbox B (flagging **Allow inbound changes**).
    c. A deployment connection enabled on sandbox B (flagging **Allow outbound changes**).
    d. None of the above
44. What is it not possible to achieve using change sets? [two answers]
    a. Deploy from a sandbox to production.
    b. Delete a custom field from a custom object.
    c. Delete a custom field from a standard object
    d. Deploy from production to a sandbox
45. Paarth is a service agent profiled with read and edit access on the case object. The Case OWD is set to Public Read Only. Paarth's boss wants to have edit access to his subordinates users' cases. What do you have to do in order to enable the boss to have case edit access? [one answer]
    a. Set the Case OWD to **Public Read/Write/Transfer**.
    b. Add the **Modify All** permission for the case object on Paarth's boss's profile.
    c. Add the **Transfer All** permission for the case object on Paarth's profile.
    d. Nothing; using **Grant Access Using Hierarchies** allows Paarth's boss to have edit access to his subordinates' owned cases.

46. Which of these statements is true regarding Lightning Knowledge? [two answers]
    a. Once you turn it on, it cannot be disabled.
    b. It requires collaborative forecasting to be enabled.
    c. Articles are grouped by data category groups and data categories.
    d. It requires Enterprise Territory Management to be enabled.
    e. It requires Classic Knowledge to be enabled.
47. What happens if the deploy of an inbound change set fails? [one answer]
    a. The org is locked until such time as the problems are solved.
    b. You need to remove any new component using metadata APIs (for example, the Ant Migration tool)
    c. Nothing; the entire deployment is rolled back.
    d. Once a change set is uploaded, it can no longer fail.
48. You want to track all historical trends of opportunities month by month and report on opportunities that are closed at the end of every month. Which feature is perfect for this scenario? [one answer]
    a. Reporting snapshots.
    b. Historical reporting.
    c. Joined reports.
    d. Scheduled report runs.
49. You want to enable conditional highlighting on a given report, but somehow this is not possible. What are the possible causes? [two answers]
    a. The features expect at least one custom summary formula or a summary field.
    b. You must be in Salesforce Classic mode.
    c. The report must have a joined or tabular type.
    d. The report must have a summary or matrix type.
50. A user is not able to edit the list price for the **EU Price book** custom price book. How is that possible? [two answers]
    a. The price book is not shared.
    b. The price book is private.
    c. The price book entry is using the standard price.
    d. The user's profile is missing the requisite **Field-Level security** (**FLS**) permissions on the price book object.

51. You want to be sure that there are no accounts without contacts. What feature should you use? [one answer]
    a. Cross filter on contact to accounts.
    b. Joined reports.
    c. Cross filter on account to contacts.
    d. Summary reports.
52. Your company sells only one product, which is an online service, so support cases fall into just two categories: billing issues and service issues. Which kind of routing would you choose? [one answer]
    a. Queue-based routing with **Billing Issues** and **Service Issues** queues.
    b. Skill-based routing with billing and service skills.
    c. External routing.
    d. Einstein Analytics routing.
53. When an opportunity is won, the following actions need to be executed:
    1. Email the manager of the record owner with the details of the deal
    2. Post on the Sales Success Chatter group
    3. Update the account's **Last Won Deal** custom date field

    Which is the best tool to accomplish this? [one answer]
    a. Process Builder.
    b. Process Builder + Lightning Flow.
    c. A workflow rule.
    d. Approval Process + Automated Actions.
    e. Lightning Flow.

54. A user is trying to submit an **Invoice** record for approval to his manager (an approval process is configured to use the **Manager** field on the submitter user), but he's getting an error stating that the submission could not be processed. What are the possible reasons? [three answers]
    a. The user does not have read access to the **Invoice** record.
    b. The submitter user record does not have the **Manager** field filled in.
    c. The submitter's manager is an inactive user.
    d. No approval process is defined for the **Invoice** object.
    e. The **Submit for Approval** button is not on the **Invoice** page layout.

55. Contact has an OWD set to **Private**, and a standard duplicate rule on the contact object is active. A user tries to insert a potentially duplicated contact. What happens? [two answers]
    a. If record-level security is set to **Enforce Sharing rules**, any duplicate contact the user doesn't have access to is not detected.
    b. If record-level security is set to **Bypass Sharing rules**, any duplicate contact is detected.
    c. If record-level security is set to **Enforce Sharing rules**, any duplicate contact is detected.
    d. If record-level security is set to **Bypass Sharing rules**, no duplicate contact is detected.
56. A validation rule is defined by: [three answers]
    a. A name, an optional description, and the active status
    b. An error condition
    c. An error message and a place to put the message
    d. A list of actions
    e. A success condition
57. The Service VP has asked you to build a two-step wizard to allow service agents to insert customer info, query for any customer on the database to look for a match, and then complete a second step with case details that should create a new case. You want to use Lightning Flow. Which elements will you be using? [one answer]
    a. One autolaunched flow, one Record Update action, and one Record List action.
    b. It is not feasible using flows.
    c. Two screen components, one **Get Records** element and one Create Records element, and one Apex trigger on the case object.
    d. Two screen components, one **Get Records** element, and one Create Records element.
58. When an opportunity is created with an **Amount** field greater than $100,000,000, it should be automatically submitted for approval to the CEO of the company. What do you have to configure? [one answer]
    a. An approval process and an Apex trigger with the `submitForApproval()` Apex function
    b. An approval process and Process Builder with a **Submit for approval** action

c. An approval process and a workflow rule with a **Submit for approval** automated action
d. An entitlement to define the SLA and Process Builder with a **Submit for approval** action

59. What tool would you use to deploy from a developer edition org to one of your org's sandboxes? [three answers]
    a. A package
    b. Inbound change sets
    c. Data Loader
    d. Visual Studio Code
    e. The Force Migration Tool
60. When a new **Invoice** record (custom object) is created, its name should include the current date as well as the account's name and country, in the following format: **dd/mm/yyyy - AccountName [Country]**. Which tool can be used? [two answers]
    a. A workflow rule with multiple Field Update actions
    b. An autolaunched flow triggered by an approval process
    c. Process Builder with a single Record Update action
    d. An approval process with a single Field Update action
    e. A workflow rule with a single Field Update action

Mock Test B

1. Which of these is a feature of delegated administration? [two answers]
    a. It manages standard objects.
    b. It adds users to certain groups.
    c. It unlocks users.
    d. It configures standard objects picklists.

2. You want sales reps (with different roles) to access the **Overall Sales Performances** dashboard. At the same time, they should not be able to access the **Service Status** dashboard. The service agents (all grouped in a service group) need to be granted access to **Service Status**, but not to **Overall Sales Performances**. And finally, the CEO should be able to see any dashboard. What can you do? [three answers]
    a. Create two different folders for the sales and service dashboards.
    b. Share the sales folder with the sales reps group and with the CEO with view access.
    c. Share the sales folder with the sales reps roles and with the CEO with view access.
    d. Share the service folder with the service agents roles and with the CEO with view access.
    e. Share the service folder with the service agents group and with the CEO with view access.

3. The **Invoice** custom object has nearly 200 custom fields that should be visible to any user in the org, and only one user (editor) needs to have edit access to about 20 of them. How can you achieve this configuration? [one answer]
    a. Modify the editor user profile by setting the FLS for the invoice's 20 fields to **Edit Access**.
    b. Clone the editor user profile and give **Edit All** object-level access to the **Invoice** object.
    c. Set all the requisite profiles with field-level security for all fields set to **Read Access**, create a new permission set with FLS for the given 20 fields set to **Edit Access**, and assign it to the required user.
    d. Set all profiles with field-level security for all fields set to **Edit Access**, create a new permission set with FLS for the given 20 fields set to **Read Access**, and assign it to all users except the editor.

4. Which statement is correct regarding default user access to accounts and (related) opportunities in a given territory? [one answer]
    a. The default access level of accounts and related opportunities can be set up at the territory-type level.
    b. The default access level of accounts and related opportunities can be set up at the territory level.
    c. When a user is assigned to a territory, they automatically receive view and edit access to cases, but not opportunities.
    d. When a user is assigned to a territory, they automatically receive view and edit access to cases, accounts, and opportunities, but not contacts.
5. Marketing users need to be able to manage the campaign member object (such as adding fields or setting up layouts). How can you achieve this? [one answer]
    a. Use **Delegated Administration** on the campaign object.
    b. Change the marketing users' profiles to have **Modify All** object-level permission for the campaign member object.
    c. This is not possible.
    d. Use **delegated administration** on the campaign member object.
6. Which of these statements are true regarding content libraries? [two answers]
    a. You can restrict the record type content.
    b. Content on a library that has been added before a record type restriction has been added is automatically removed from the library.
    c. You can restrict the file type of the content in a library.
    d. You can define open, guided, or restricted tagging.
7. Quotes and opportunities are related objects, but which of these statements are true as regards their relationship? [two answers]
    a. If an opportunity product is deleted from an opportunity, the same product is deleted from all related quotes.
    b. An opportunity can have multiple child quotes.
    c. Synced quotes sync all their products with opportunity products.
    d. A quote can be related to multiple opportunities.

8. The sales rep user has **Edit** object-level permission on the **Inventory** custom object and **Read Access** on the type custom picklist field. This field is required on the inventory layout. What will the sales rep user see? [one answer]
    a. The field will become editable.
    b. The record won't be available with a **Missing FLS on Type field. Please update profile** error.
    c. The field will remain read-only on the layout.
    d. The field will be hidden.
9. The **Invoice** custom object cannot be accessed by any sales user with a standard profile. 15 users need to have read access on the object (and on its fields), and only 6 of them require edit access on the object (and on 5 fields). Which of the following options are valid solutions? [two answers]
    a. Create 7 permission sets, 2 for the Read and Edit object-level permissions, and 5 for the Edit FLS on custom fields, and assign them to the 21 users.
    b. Edit the standard profile with the required permissions.
    c. Create 2 new custom profiles with read and edit access on the **Invoice** object, and assign them to the 21 users (15 on the first **View** profile and 6 on the **Edit** profile).
    d. Create 2 permission sets with read and edit access on the **Invoice** object and assign them to the 21 users (15 on the first View profile and 6 on the Edit profile).
10. Gaurav is assigned to a **Delegated Administrator** group. What can he do now? [two answers]
    a. Manage standard objects (if defined in the **Delegated Administrator** group)
    b. Log in as another user (if granted administrator access)
    c. Log in as any other user
    d. Manage custom objects (if defined in the **Delegated Administrator** group)
11. A record has been manually shared with a specific user who couldn't access that record previously due to the sharing configuration. The record's owner is changed. Then what happens? [one answer]
    a. Manual sharing is deleted.
    b. Manual sharing is kept.
    c. Criteria-based sharing rules are not recalculated.
    d. Owner-based sharing rules are not recalculated.

12. Process Builder and workflow rules can execute actions on a time-based schedule by using scheduled actions and time-dependent actions. Where can we monitor pending actions? [one answer]
    a. Process Builder's time-dependent actions: The **Paused and Waiting Interviews** section on the flow setup page
    Workflow rules' scheduled actions: The **Time-Based Workflows** setup page
    b. Process Builder's scheduled actions: The **Time-Based Workflows** setup page
    Workflow rules' time-dependent actions: The **Paused and Waiting Interviews** section on the flow setup page
    c. Both from the **Scheduled Actions** setup page.
    d. Process Builder's scheduled actions: The **Paused and Waiting Interviews** section on the flow setup page
    Workflow rules' time-dependent actions: The **Time-Based Workflows** setup page

13. The case object needs to be related to five different types of junction objects, leading to five different many-to-many relations. Will you be able to complete this configuration: [one answer]
    a. Yes, without any restrictions.
    b. No, there can only be two master-details fields per object,
    c. Yes, but you have to be sure you can still create five custom objects.
    d. No, standard objects cannot be the master side of a master-detail relation.

14. Validating a change set: [one answer]
    a. Is a mandatory step to be executed prior to deployment.
    b. Can be optionally executed prior to deployment.
    c. By default, executes all Apex tests when run in a sandbox.
    d. Is done on the source org.

15. The project object, which already contains 200 records, needs to be related to the department object with a master-detail relation. What do you have to do? [three answers]
    a. Create a lookup field on Project that points to Department.
    b. Fill in all lookups in any Project record.
    c. Convert a lookup field into a master-detail field.
    d. Create the master-detail field.
    e. Use Process Builder to automatically populate the lookup field.

16. When a record is deleted and is referenced in a lookup field from another record: [two answers]
    a. Deletion will always be executed.
    b. The lookup field is blanked if otherwise configured.
    c. The related object where the lookup lies is deleted as well.
    d. Deletion can be blocked if the lookup has been configured in this way.
17. Which kind of relation ensures that a child record gets its parent record sharing settings? [one answer]
    a. Master-detail relation.
    b. Lookup relation.
    c. Hierarchy lookup.
    d. Parent-child relation.
18. You have just imported 1 million invoices into the new **Invoice** custom object and you want to see the weight of these new records in terms of the total data storage usage. Where can you check this? [one answer]
    a. The **Storage Usage** page
    b. The **Data Usage** page
    c. The **File Usage** page
    d. Issue a SOQL query on the **Invoice** object using the `PERCENT` SOQL function
19. Where can you monitor the importing of thousands of records using the Import Wizard? [one answer]
    a. From the Bulk Data Load Jobs page.
    b. From the Import Wizard Jobs page.
    c. The Debug Log.
    d. Only Data Loader jobs can be monitored.

20. When an opportunity is created, it should be submitted for approval only if the total amount is greater than $150,000, otherwise it is automatically approved. If the amount is greater than $1,000,000, it should be approved by the user's manager and, if it is greater than $10,000,000, it should also be approved by the Sales VP and the CEO. Which steps do you need to configure in this approval process? [one answer]
    a. One for the automatic approval, one if the amount is greater than $100k, and one if it's greater than $10M.
    b. One if the amount is greater than $100k, and one if it's greater than $10M.
    c. One if the amount is greater than $100k, one if it's greater than $10M for the Sales VP, and one for the CEO.
    d. One for the automatic approval, one if the amount is greater than $100k, one if it's greater than $10M for the Sales VP, and one for the CEO.
21. Following a sandbox refresh, users are not getting any email from Process Builder configured on Opportunity creation: what can you do? [three answers]
    a. Check the email deliverability settings.
    b. Have a look at workflow logs.
    c. Check Setup Audit Trail.
    d. Take a look at the email logs.
    e. Check whether users' email addresses are valid.
22. When adding a product to an opportunity, which price can a sales rep fill in? [one answer]
    a. The list price.
    b. The standard price.
    c. The opportunity price.
    d. The sales price.
23. Which is the correct order when setting up Enterprise Territory Management? [one answer]
    a. Territories, Territory Types, and Territory Model.
    b. Territory Types, Territories, and Territory Model.
    c. Territory Type, Territory Model, and Territories.
    d. Territory Model, Territory Type, and Territories.

24. To customize the metadata provided with each content file, what can you do? [two answers]
    a. Define content version record types.
    b. Define data categories and article types.
    c. Add new values to the content version's typc standard picklist.
    d. Create custom fields on the content version object and assign them to custom layouts assigned to different record types.
25. The service agent users (with a standard service agent profile assigned) need to have Read, Edit, Create, and Delete permissions on the **Container** custom object. How can you provide this feature? [one answer]
    a. Create a new custom profile (cloning the service agent profile), add all required container object-level permissions, and then apply the profile to the service agent users.
    b. Edit the standard service agent profile by modifying the container object-level permission.
    c. Create a permission set with the container object-level permissions and assign it to all users.
    d. Create a new custom profile (cloning the service agent profile), add a container object-level **View All** permission, and then apply the profile to the service agent users.
26. A survey object needs to be related to the campaign object so that a survey can be related to many campaigns and vice versa. Which feature will you choose? [one answer]
    a. Lookup fields.
    b. Junction object.
    c. The master-detail field from survey to campaign.
    d. Cross-object validation rules.
27. Which of these statements are correct regarding profiles and roles? [three answers]
    a. Profiles are mandatory on users, while roles are not.
    b. Profiles are used to set object-level and record-level access.
    c. Profiles control access to records through hierarchies.
    d. Roles are used to set object-level and record-level access.
    e. Roles define access to records through hierarchies.

28. Which of these statements are true regarding collaborative forecasting? [three answers]
    a. Multiple currency is not supported.
    b. It cannot be enabled if Customizable Forecasting is enabled.
    c. It is possible to enable up to four forecast types.
    d. You can enable users to forecast from the Forecast Hierarchy page.
    e. Forecast Adjustments is only supported by Customizable Forecasting.
29. What do you need in order to enable Lightning Knowledge? [three answers]
    a. Use the **Knowledge Setup** flow on the **Service Setup** page.
    b. An article record type must be created first.
    c. Data categories must be defined.
    d. Assign **Knowledge User** to selected users.
    e. Be careful to have enough knowledge user **Feature Licenses** on the company information page.
30. The audit department needs to be sure who modifies sensitive fields on the **Invoice** record, such as the **Amount** field (of currency type) and the **Account** lookup. How can you configure this requirement? [two answers]
    a. Enable Field History Tracking on the **Invoice** object and select the two fields to be tracked.
    b. Monitor Setup Audit Trail.
    c. Add the **History** related list to the **Invoice** page layout.
    d. Monitor Record Audit Trail.
31. You need to enable omni-channel routing to enable agents to be assigned to cases depending on attributes such as **Chinese speaking** and **Fault parts**. Which kind of routing would you choose? [one answer]
    a. Skill-based routing.
    b. Queue-based routing.
    c. External routing.
    d. Einstein Analytics routing.
32. A case can enter an entitlement process when: [two answers]
    a. The milestone hits the warning action.
    b. It is created (created date).
    c. Business hours are met.
    d. Depending on a custom date/time field.

33. What do knowledge components allow? [two answers]
    a. They can be used in Salesforce Classic.
    b. They suggest articles based on a case's details.
    c. They attach/remove articles from the current case.
    d. They attach knowledge entitlements to the current case.
34. Agents from Indian and Italian call centers are using invalid knowledge articles to resolve shipping-related issues because they visibly don't take into account the countries those articles are related to. How can you provide any assistance to this inferior service support? [one answer]
    a. Enable data categories (country-related) and assign role visibility to data categories.
    b. Create different article record types based on countries and assign their visibility to agents' profiles.
    c. Deliver the MyTrailhead feature to skill up agents.
    d. Suggest using Trailhead to better understand how Knowledge works.
35. In Lightning Knowledge, an article can be: [two answers]
    a. Created and edited.
    b. Published and deleted.
    c. Attached to a workflow rule.
    d. Sent via SMS with Live Chat.
36. Which objects are supported by duplicate rules? [one answer]
    a. Accounts, leads, contacts, and custom objects.
    b. All standard and custom objects.
    c. Accounts, leads, opportunities, contracts, contacts, and custom objects.
    d. Contacts, leads, and accounts.
37. To increase data quality, which entities can you reference in a lookup filter? [two answers]
    a. Validation rule criteria.
    b. Custom metadata settings.
    c. The current and related objects.
    d. User records, a user's profile, and roles.

38. The **Invoice** and **Payment** custom objects both have the **Origin** picklist, and the business wants them both to have the same values. How can you achieve this? [one answer]
    a. Use a global picklist value set.
    b. Use dependent picklists.
    c. Use a lookup field on the **Invoice** object to the payment object and apply a custom filter.
    d. Create a workflow rule to automatically copy the **Invoice** origin value to the **Payment Origin** field.
39. On the case object, you have defined an **Issue Reason** picklist with over 200 values. it is therefore no surprise that agents often use the wrong reasons when opening an issue case. What can you do to help agents? [one answer]
    a. Create a validation rule with the `VLOOKUP` function to look up the **Issue Reason** custom object.
    b. Use dependent picklists: Create an **Issue Category** picklist to organize issues, and make it the controlling field of the **Issue Reason** picklist.
    c. Create an Apex trigger to perform the validation logic and block record creation/update.
    d. Create an **Issue Reason** custom object and add a master-detail field to the case object.
40. The **Product Code** field of the product object needs to be strictly defined by a specific format (something along the lines of **XXXX-XXX-XX**). How can you achieve this requirement? [one answer]
    a. Create an Apex trigger on the product object to check the field format.
    b. Create a validation rule with a `REGEX` function.
    c. Create a workflow rule to block record creation if criteria are not met.
    d. Create a Lightning flow to send an error to the **Product Information Management** (**PIM**) system.
41. A sales rep is configuring product pricing within a custom price book. Which price are they going to fill in? [one answer]
    a. Sales price.
    b. List price.
    c. Standard price.
    d. Opportunity price.

42. A sales rep wants to make sure that the newly created quote is synced up with its opportunity, given that an old quote is already synced. What can they do? [one answer]
    a. Use the **Start Sync** button on the quote record after disabling any previous quote with the **Stop Sync** button.
    b. Use the **Start Sync** button on the quote record; any other quote sync instantly stops.
    c. Any new quote is automatically synced and overrides the previous quote.
    d. Update the **Sync Status** picklist to **Enabled** on the new quote.
43. Which of these statements are true regarding forecast categories? [three answers]
    a. Forecast categories' labels cannot be aligned with the company's sales process.
    b. It is not possible to change opportunity stage values to forecast category mapping.
    c. Forecast categories are mapped to opportunity stage field values.
    d. More than one opportunity stage value can belong to a single forecast category.
    e. It is not possible to forecast on the **Omitted** forecast category.
44. Once an inbound change set is deployed: [one answer]
    a. It can automatically be rolled back using the **Rollback** button on the outbound change set page.
    b. It can be rolled back with Data Loader.
    c. It cannot be automatically rolled back.
    d. It can be rolled back with Data Export.
45. When two or more contacts are identified as duplicates, what can you do with the merge tool? [two answers]
    a. For each field, select which record is the master of the info (the value is copied into the master record).
    b. The master record is automatically selected as the first record ever created.
    c. For each field, select which record is the master of the info ONLY if it is not blank (the value is copied into the master record).
    d. Select the master record.

46. What tools would you use to incorporate changes from production to the UAT Full sandbox? [two answers]
    a. It is not possible to deploy metadata from production back to a sandbox.
    b. Visual Studio Code or the Force Migration Tool.
    c. Only Developer or Developer Pro sandbox types can receive an inbound change set from production (Full Sandboxes are a full copy of production, so they cannot be changed).
    d. A change set.
47. A change set contains custom fields emanating from different objects (standard and custom). How can you deploy field-level security configurations along with the change set? [two answers]
    a. Add permission sets to the change set components.
    b. Flag **Push Field Level Security Permissions** on the change set details.
    c. Field-level security permissions must be configured by hand on the target org once deployment is complete.
    d. Add profiles to the change set with the **Add Profile** button.
48. What can you transfer from a sandbox to production using change sets? [three answers]
    a. Apex classes.
    b. Owned contacts and leads.
    c. Workflow rules.
    d. Validation rules.
    e. Opportunity teams.
49. Maria has a profile with read access on the account object with the **Prospect** record type. A criteria-based sharing rule grants Maria's role read/write access to accounts with the **Prospect** record type. Will Maria be able to access the **Prospect** accounts? [one answer]
    a. No; an owner-based sharing rule is needed.
    b. Yes; the sharing rule opens up the access level.
    c. No; her profile prevents her from editing the object despite the sharing rule.
    d. Yes; Maria's profile is automatically updated to follow the record's level of access defined by the criteria sharing rule.

50. The Case OWD is set to **Private**, and sharing rules are used to open up access to case records. A report has been scheduled and sent by email to service managers on a daily basis to receive all open cases at the end of the day. Service managers (who have the **View All** object-level permission on the case object) are reporting that the emailed report is missing some of the cases. What could be the cause? [one answer]
    a. Scheduled reports require the **View All Data** permission.
    b. Service managers may not have **View** permission on the case object.
    c. The report's running user does not have read access to all case records.
    d. Records have been deleted once the report has run.
51. Account object has the industry standard picklist field with about 200 values that can be divided into 5 categories that you want to report against Accounts. What reporting feature can you use to get the total number of accounts per category? [one answer]
    a. Cross filter
    b. Simple filter
    c. Custom summary formula
    d. Bucket column on the industry picklist
52. The sales VP wishes to see the trends of opportunities' amounts week after week (up to three weeks in the same report). How can you configure it? [one answer]
    a. Use reporting snapshots with a custom opportunity history object.
    b. Use field history tracking in the **Amount** field.
    c. Use historical trend reporting (by tracking the Amount field).
    d. None of the above.
53. You need to build a dashboard for all of your company's sales VPs (no pressure!), with each leading a specific continent division (Americas, Africa, Europe, Asia, and Oceania). They need a comprehensive dashboard with all the company's KPIs to be emailed weekly on a Friday night. What is the best way to configure this? [one answer]
    a. Create five dashboards (with a different running user each), and then schedule them.
    b. Create one dashboard with different filters per continent, and then schedule it.
    c. Create one dashboard with five components, one for each continent, and then schedule it.
    d. Create five dashboards with a running user with the **View All Data** permission and a filter to the continent, and then schedule them.

54. A user wants to submit an opportunity for approval, but they cannot see the **Submit for Approval** button. What can you do to solve this issue? [one answer]
    a. Add the **Submit for Approval** button to the custom buttons box of the opportunity standard layout.
    b. Configure a new approval for the current user's role.
    c. Add the **Submit for Approval** button to the standard buttons section of the opportunity layout associated with the user's profile.
    d. Activate the approval process.
55. When a master support case is closed, all related cases (child cases with the `ParentId` field set up to the master support case) must also be closed. Which is the best solution? [one answer]
    a. Deliver an autolaunched Lightning flow triggered by Process Builder.
    b. Deliver a workflow rule on the case object with one field update action for each child case.
    c. Ask your developers to build a Case Apex trigger to code this logic.
    d. Deliver Process Builder with an Update Records action on the case object.
56. When a new case is opened, the `ContactId` field should be automatically filled in: this contact should be looked up from any contact that matches the case's **Web Email** field, taking into account a custom unique field on the contact object called **Unique Email**. How can you achieve this? [one answer]
    a. Use Workflow Builder to trigger Process Builder.
    b. Use Process Builder to trigger an autolaunched Lightning flow.
    c. Use Process Builder to trigger a Lightning flow with at least one screen element.
    d. Instruct your support agents to search for contacts using Global Search.
57. When an **Invoice** record (custom object) holds the **Waiting for payment** status value (custom picklist field) for more then 60 days, an email should be automatically sent to the billing VP role users, and then the status should be set to **VP Notified**. Which tools are available to this end? [two answers]
    a. A workflow rule with one immediate action and one time-dependent action.
    b. A workflow rule with two immediate actions.
    c. A workflow rule with two time-dependent actions.
    d. Process Builder with two scheduled actions.
    e. Entitlements with two milestones.

58. After the platform checks validation rules before an account is committed to the database, a complex logic on the Security Number field is required. This involves a query on a security region code object and a complex check digit algorithm (that could not be configured using regular expressions) to validate the value in the field. If validation fails, the record operation should fail as well. Which tool would you unleash? [one answer]
    a. An Apex trigger on the account record, using the **after** event.
    b. Process Builder and a **Get Records** action.
    c. A validation rule with VLOOKUP and REGEX functions.
    d. An Apex trigger on the account record, using the **before** event.
    e. A Lightning flow with screen elements.
59. You can move change sets (provided a valid connection exists): [two answers]
    a. Between any developer org and a production org.
    b. Between production orgs.
    c. Between sandboxes that rely on the same production org.
    d. Between production orgs and any sandbox under it.
60. When an **Invoice** record (custom object) is marked as paid (custom Status field set to **Paid**) and the custom numeric field, **Number of Payments**, is set to N (where N is any number greater than 0), an automation should automatically create **N** invoice line item records (custom object with a master-detail with invoice). Now, each invoice line item should have the **Amount** custom currency field set to the invoice's Total Amount custom fields divided by the number of invoice line items (**N**). Which tools would you prefer? [one answer]
    a. Process Builder to trigger an autolaunched flow that handles the creation of all invoice line item records.
    b. Process Builder with a screen flow that displays a wizard to create the invoice line item records.
    c. An Apex trigger on the invoice line item object that handles the creation of all invoice line item records.
    d. Process Builder and one workflow rule per invoice line item record.

Assessments

Chapter 1

1. a
2. c
3. a
4. b
5. b
6. b
7. b
8. b, c, and g
9. b
10. a
11. b
12. a
13. b and c
14. c
15. b
16. a
17. a, c, and e
18. c
19. b

Chapter 2

1. c
2. d
3. a
4. d
5. a, b, and d
6. d

7. c
8. a, d, and e
9. d
10. a
11. a and c
12. a
13. b
14. b and d
15. c and d
16. c and d

Chapter 3

1. b
2. a
3. a, b, and c
4. c, d, and e
5. d
6. b, c, and e
7. c
8. a
9. b, c, and d
10. a, b, c, and d
11. b
12. a
13. a, b, d, and e
14. e
15. a and b
16. a, b, and c
17. c

Chapter 4

1. b and c
2. c
3. a
4. a
5. b
6. c
7. d
8. c
9. c
10. b
11. d
12. a
13. b
14. a
15. b
16. b
17. c
18. a

Chapter 5

1. b and c
2. a
3. a
4. c
5. c and d
6. b
7. a
8. b
9. a and d
10. c and d

11. b
12. a, b, and d
13. b
14. a
15. c

Chapter 6

1. c
2. a
3. c
4. c
5. b
6. c
7. a and b
8. a
9. c
10. c

Chapter 7

1. b
2. c
3. b
4. a
5. a
6. b
7. b
8. c
9. b and c
10. c and e

Chapter 8

1. b
2. a
3. a, c, and d
4. b, c, and d
5. c
6. b
7. a
8. a and c
9. a
10. b, c, and d

Chapter 9

1. a and c
2. a
3. d
4. b
5. a, c, and d
6. a, b, and d
7. b, c, and d
8. b and d
9. b and c
10. b and c
11. b and c

Chapter 10

1. d
2. c
3. c and d
4. a
5. a

6. d
7. a and b
8. a
9. a
10. a
11. b, c, and d

Chapter 11

1. c and d
2. a
3. b
4. a, b, and c
5. b
6. c
7. c
8. b
9. a
10. c
11. c
12. a and c

Chapter 12

1. a
2. c
3. b
4. c and d
5. a, b, and c
6. a, b, c, and d
7. b and c
8. a
9. c
10. a, b, c, and d

Chapter 13

1. c
2. b
3. a and b
4. a and c
5. c
6. b
7. c and d
8. a
9. a and c
10. a, b, and c
11. a and c

Chapter 14

1. b and c
2. a, c, and d
3. d
4. b
5. a
6. a and c
7. b and c
8. c
9. d
10. a
11. a, b, and c
12. a, b, and d

Chapter 15

1. a and b
2. c and d
3. b

4. c
5. b and c
6. a and c
7. b, c, and e
8. b
9. a, c, and d
10. a, b, d and e

Chapter 17

Mock Test A

1. b, c, and e (Auditing and monitoring)
2. d (Analytics, reports, and dashboards)
3. a and d (Security and access)
4. a and c (Security and access)
5. b (Security and access)
6. a, b, and c (Security and access)
7. a (Security and access)
8. c and d (Security and access)
9. c (Security and access)
10. d (Extending custom object and applications)
11. a (Extending custom object and applications)
12. a (Security and access)
13. a and b (Security and access)
14. b (Extending custom object and applications)
15. c (Extending custom object and applications)
16. b (Auditing and monitoring)
17. a (Content management)
18. a, c, and e (Process automation)
19. a and d (Extending custom object and applications)
20. b (Auditing and monitoring)
21. c (Security and access)
22. a and d (Data management)

23. d (Auditing and monitoring)
24. b (Sales cloud applications)
25. c and d (Content management)
26. c (Sales cloud applications)
27. b (Sales cloud applications)
28. a (Sales cloud applications)
29. b (Service cloud applications)
30. b and c (Service cloud applications)
31. a and c (Service cloud applications)
32. e (Process automation)
33. a, b, and c (Process automation)
34. b (Data management)
35. c and d (Data management)
36. a and d (Data management)
37. a and c (Sales cloud applications)
38. a and d (Security and access)
39. c (Analytics, reports, and dashboards)
40. b and c (Service cloud applications)
41. a (Change management)
42. a, b, and e (Change management)
43. b (Change management)
44. b and c (Change management)
45. d (Security and access)
46. a and c (Service cloud applications)
47. c (Change management)
48. a (Analytics, reports, and dashboards)
49. a and d (Analytics, reports, and dashboards)
50. c and d (Sales cloud applications)
51. c (Analytics, reports, and dashboards)
52. a (Service cloud applications)
53. a (Process automation)
54. b, c, and d (Process automation)
55. a and b (Data management)
56. a, b, and c (Data management)
57. d (Process automation)

58. b (Process automation)
59. a, d, and e (Change management)
60. c and e (Process automation)

Mock Test B

1. b and c (Security and access)
2. a, c, and e (Analytics, reports, and dashboards)
3. c (Security and access)
4. b (Security and access)
5. c (Security and access)
6. a and d (Content management)
7. b and c (Sales cloud applications)
8. c (Security and access)
9. c and d (Security and access)
10. b and d (Security and access)
11. a (Security and access)
12. d (Process automation)
13. c (Extending custom object and applications)
14. b (Change management)
15. a, b, and c (Extending custom object and applications)
16. b and d (Extending custom object and applications)
17. a (Extending custom object and applications)
18. a (Auditing and monitoring)
19. a (Auditing and monitoring)
20. b (Process automation)
21. a, d, and e (Auditing and monitoring)
22. d (Sales cloud applications)
23. c (Security and access)
24. a and d (Content management)
25. a (Security and access)
26. b (Extending custom object and applications)
27. a, b, and e (Security and access)
28. b, c, and d (Sales cloud applications)
29. a, d, and e (Service cloud applications)

30. a and c (Auditing and monitoring)
31. a (Service cloud applications)
32. b and d (Service cloud application)
33. b and c (Service cloud application)
34. a (Service cloud application)
35. a and b (Service cloud application)
36. a (Data management)
37. c and d (Data management)
38. a (Data management)
39. b (Data management)
40. b (Data management)
41. b (Sales cloud applications)
42. b (Sales cloud applications)
43. c, d, and e (Sales cloud applications)
44. c (Change management)
45. a and d (Data management)
46. b and d (Change management)
47. a and d (Change management)
48. a, c, and d (Change management)
49. c (Security and access)
50. c (Analytics, reports, and dashboards)
51. d (Analytics, reports, and dashboards)
52. c (Analytics, reports, and dashboards)
53. a (Analytics, reports, and dashboards)
54. c (Process automation)
55. d (Process automation)
56. b (Process automation)
57. c and d (Process automation)
58. d (Process automation)
59. c and d (Change management)
60. a (Process automation)

Other Books You May Enjoy

If you enjoyed this book, you may be interested in these other books by Packt:

Salesforce Platform Developer I Certification Guide
Jan Vandevelde, Gunther Roskams

ISBN: 978-1-78980-207-8

- Solve sample questions and mock tests and work with exam patterns
- Gain an understanding of declarative Salesforce tools such as Process Builder, flows, and many more
- Code in Salesforce using the Developer Console and IDEs
- Grasp the basics of object-oriented programming
- Write Apex classes, Visualforce pages, and Apex test classes with easy-to-follow steps
- Explore the different deployment tools that you can use to push metadata to different environments
- Build custom declarative apps and programs on Force.com platforms

Salesforce Lightning Platform Enterprise Architecture - Third Edition
Andrew Fawcett

ISBN: 978-8-17899-567-5

- Create and deploy AppExchange packages and manage upgrades
- Understand Enterprise Application Architecture patterns
- Customize mobile and desktop user experience with Lightning Web Components
- Manage large data volumes with asynchronous processing and big data strategies
- Implement Source Control and Continuous Integration
- Add AI to your application with Einstein
- Use Lightning External Services to integrate external code and data with your Lightning Application

Leave a review - let other readers know what you think

Please share your thoughts on this book with others by leaving a review on the site that you bought it from. If you purchased the book from Amazon, please leave us an honest review on this book's Amazon page. This is vital so that other potential readers can see and use your unbiased opinion to make purchasing decisions, we can understand what our customers think about our products, and our authors can see your feedback on the title that they have worked with Packt to create. It will only take a few minutes of your time, but is valuable to other potential customers, our authors, and Packt. Thank you!

Index

A

Accept Outbound Changes 125
account details 536
action groups
  Apex class, using 514, 515
  custom notifications 512, 513, 514
  defining 500, 501
  email alerts 508
  flow 510
  posting, to Chatter 506, 507
  processes 505, 506
  Quick Actions 511, 512
  records, creating 502
  records, updating 503, 504, 505
  submitting, for approval 508, 509
advanced highlighting
  for report data 360, 361
ANT Force.com Migration Tool
  about 137
  reference link 137
ANT Migration Tool
  reference link 120
Apex Code, best practices
  reference link 585
Apex managed sharing 42
Apex sharing 18
Apex triggers
  after event 583, 584, 586
  anatomy 571, 572
  before event 572, 573, 574, 575, 576, 577, 578, 579, 581, 582
  exploring 565, 566
  features 569, 570
  order of execution 566, 568, 569
  rules 569, 570
AppExchange
  URL 144
approval process
  considerations 483, 484
  creating 453, 454, 455, 456, 457, 458, 459, 460, 461, 462, 463, 464
  limitations 483, 484
approval steps
  creating 466, 467, 468, 469, 470, 471, 472
approval
  about 452, 453
  actions, adding to 472, 473, 474, 475, 476
  using 476, 477, 478, 480, 481, 482, 483
approver limitations
  reference link 484
Authenticated Website 61
autolaunched flows
  about 550, 551, 554, 556, 557
  components 551, 552
automated actions
  about 428
  cross-object field updates 433, 434
  email alert actions 436, 437, 438
  field updates 428, 429, 430, 431, 432, 433
  outbound message actions 439, 440, 442
  task actions 434, 435, 436
Automation Champion
  reference link 517
automation, implementing in CRM
  approvals 420
  custom code 420
  entitlement process 420
  flow 420
  lightning process builder 420
  workflows 420

B

background job monitoring 89
big objects
  reference link 78
blocks 355
bucket column 361
bucket fields
  about 361, 362, 363
  limitations 363
built-in report types
  reference link 345

C

cascading delete 172
case teams 45
certification exam
  facing 603
  failure scenarios 599, 600, 601
  preparing for 602
  question format 602, 603
  scheduling 601
change sets, components
  reference link 127
change sets
  deploying, with packages 133, 134, 135
  deploying, with tools 135, 136, 137, 138
  used, for deploying metadata changes 120, 121, 122, 123, 124, 125, 126, 127, 128, 129, 130, 131, 132, 133
charting option
  selecting 399, 400, 401, 402, 404, 405
charts
  adding, to reports 358, 359, 360
Chatter
  posting to 506, 508
  reference link 488, 506
child implicit sharing 19
Chrome extensions
  reference link 144
circular reference 172, 567
Classic and Lightning Experience, differences
  reference link 414
Classic Knowledge
  reference link 239
Clone quick action 206
collaborative forecasting, versus customizable forecasting
  reference link 222
collaborative forecasting
  about 222
  setting up 223, 224, 225, 226, 227, 228, 229, 230, 231, 232
content delivery 334, 335, 336, 337
content libraries
  handling 320, 321, 322, 323, 324, 325, 326, 327, 328
content packs 333, 334
content search 337, 338
cross-object formulas 174
cumulative forecast roll-ups 229
custom baseline file requirements
  reference link 100
Customer Community 61
customer relationship management (CRM) 13
customizable forecasting
  about 222
  reference link 222
customizing rules
  exploring 306

D

dashboard viewer 397
dashboard
  building 390
  filtering 406, 407, 408, 409, 410, 412, 413
  limitations 414
  report and dashboard folders 390, 391, 392
  setting up 393, 394, 396, 397, 398, 399
  subscribing to 413, 414
dashboards
  building 389
data changes
  handling 138, 139
Data Export feature 144
data field grouping options
  in Classic 353
  in Lightning 355
Data Import Wizard
  about 139, 140

data, importing with 139, 140, 141, 142, 143
Data Loader
about 139
data, importing with 143, 144
reference link 144
Data Manipulation Language events 565
data skew 47
data
exporting 144, 145, 146, 147
importing, with Data Import Wizard 139, 140, 141, 142, 143
importing, with Data Loader 143, 144
debug level 92
debug log
monitoring 90, 93, 94, 95
delegated administration 70, 71, 72, 73
dependent picklists 189, 190, 191, 192
Developer (Dev) 118
Developer Pro sandbox 115, 118
Developer sandbox 115
developer-admin (dev-min) 91
duplicate management
about 289, 290
considerations 313, 314
duplicate rules
customizing 306, 307, 308, 309
dynamic approval routing
reference link 484
dynamic report 397

E

Einstein Bots 268, 269
email deliverability 96
Email Deliverability 119
email log
about 95
monitoring 95, 97
reference link 97
enhanced folder sharing
about 390
Editor permission 390
Manager permission 390
Viewer permission 390
enterprise territory management 47, 48, 49, 50, 51, 52, 53, 54, 55, 56
event log files
about 101
reference link 101
event monitoring 100, 101, 103, 104, 105, 106, 108
Event Monitoring Analytics app
about 107
reference link 108
EventLogFile object
reference link 105
execution governor limits
reference link 517
Expected Revenue field 399
external data sources
reference link 176
external lookups 176
external relationships 175
external routing 257
external users
types 32

F

Field Audit Trail
reference link 89
field history tracking
about 86, 87, 88
limitations 87
Field-Level Security (FLS) 17, 28, 29, 30, 130, 161
file and data storage allocations
reference link 80
files
adding, to libraries 328, 329, 330, 331
Filters button 413
flow bulkification
reference link 561
flow
connecting 548, 549, 550
distributing 558
managing 558
testing 559, 560
Force.com IDE
reference link 136
forecast adjustments 229
Forecast Category 220, 223

Forecast Type 224
forecast type, properties
  Fields, displaying on list 224
  Forecast Date Type 224
  Forecast Measurement 224
  Forecast Type 224
forecast types, in collaborative forecasts
  reference link 225
forecasts
  deals, predicting with 220, 221
formula fields 158, 175
formulas
  in reports 364, 367, 368, 371
Full sandbox 117, 118, 119
functions, in formulas
  reference link 180

G

Gauge chart 399
global duplicate management 299, 300, 301, 302, 303, 304, 305
global picklist value set 188
Google Docs
  enabling 331, 332
governor limits 516, 560, 561

H

health check monitor 98, 99, 100
hierarchical relationships 173, 174
High Volume Customer Portal 61
high-volume community users 61, 62
Historical Tracking Reports 376, 377, 378
Historical Trend Reports
  reference link 378
history
  tracking, on reports 376

I

identity verification history
  monitoring 83
If This Then That (ITTT) tool 488
Illuminated Cloud
  URL 138
Image Field 218, 219
implicit sharing 19
indirect lookups 176
Integration 118
Integration sandbox 118
Invoice Reason 189
Invoice Type 189
ISV partner program
  reference link 133
Italian fiscal code
  reference link 569

J

joined reports 353, 373, 374, 375, 376
Jump Start Wizard
  reference link 453

L

libraries
  files, adding to 328, 329, 330, 331
licensing, groups
  about 15
  chatter-free license 16
  full sharing model usage users/licenses 15
  high volume customer portal licenses 16
licensing
  about 14, 15
  reference link 16
Lightning App Builder 405
Lightning Components
  reference link 590
Lightning Experience Dashboard Components
  reference link 402
Lightning Flow
  about 521, 522
  autolaunched flows 523
  building 524, 525, 526, 527, 528, 529, 530, 531, 532, 533, 534, 535, 536, 537, 538, 539, 540, 541, 542, 543, 544, 545, 546, 547
  components 523
  connectors 523
  considerations 561
  elements 523
  limits 561
  limits, reference link 561
  reference link 522
  resource 523

screen flow 523
Lightning Knowledge Migration Tool
about 239
reference link 239
Lightning Knowledge
concepts 239
Lightning Process Builder
considerations, for building automation 516, 517
criteria definition 495, 496, 497, 498, 499
debugging, reference link 515
managing 515
reference link 515
setting up 488, 489
shaping 490, 491, 492
trigger selection 492, 493, 494, 495
Lightning Report Builder 345, 355
lightning table 402
Lightning Web Components (LWC) 588
List Field 218
Live Agent chat
about 258
Setup flow 261, 262, 263, 264, 265, 266, 267, 268
local duplicate management 290, 291, 292, 293, 294, 295, 296, 297, 298, 299
login history
monitoring 81, 82
lookup relationships 171, 172
LWC components
reference link 590

M

managed packages 133
manual sharing 18, 39, 40, 41, 42
many-to-many relationships 170, 171
master–detail relationship 158, 160, 161, 163, 164, 165, 167
matching rules
customizing 309, 310, 311, 312, 313
matrix report 352
MAX roll-up type 168
Metadata APIs 135
metadata changes
deploying, with change sets 120, 121, 122, 123, 124, 125, 126, 127, 128, 129, 130, 131, 132, 133
Metadata SOAP APIs
reference link 120
metadata types
reference link 135
Metric chart 400
Milestones 273
Modify All Data permissions 28
multi-currency 207

N

Negotiation 213

O

object relationships
advanced aspects 155, 156, 157, 158
external relationships 175
formula fields 174, 175
formula relations 174
hierarchical relationships 173, 174
lookup relationships 171, 172
many-to-many relationships 170, 171
master–detail relationship 158, 160, 161, 163, 164, 165, 167
roll-up field 167, 168, 169
roll-up fields 170
object security 19, 20, 21, 22, 23, 24
Object-Level Security (OLS) 17, 27, 28
object-specific limits
monitoring 77, 78
Omni-Channel Supervisor app 257, 258
Omni-Channel
configuring 251, 252, 253, 254, 255
external routing 257
skill-based routing 255, 256
one-page app paradigm 589
Online Sales Process 202
Opportunities with Historical Trending 377
opportunity synchronization
versus quotes 219, 220
opportunity teams 44
Opportunity Territory Assignment 50
Organization-Wide Default sharing
about 30, 31, 32
values 31, 32

Organization-Wide Defaults (OWD) 17
ownership skew 47

P

package management
  reference link 135
packages
  used, for deploying change sets 133, 134, 135
parent implicit sharing 19
Partial Copy 118
Partial Copy sandbox 115, 116, 119
permission sets 17, 19, 20, 21, 22, 23, 24, 25, 26, 27
picklist management
  about 183, 184, 185, 186, 187, 188, 189
  dependent picklists 189, 190, 191, 192
platform events
  reference link 489, 490
pre-chat form 266
pre-loaded 589
pricebooks
  list price 207
  managing 200, 201, 202, 204, 205, 206, 207
  sales price 207
  standard price 207
PRIORVALUE function 182, 183
Probability fields 220
process automation tools
  classification categories 420
process automation
  about 419
  tools, selecting 420, 421
Product Information Management (PIMs) 205
product schedules
  about 207, 208, 209, 210, 211, 212
  default schedule 208
  managing 200, 201, 202, 204, 205, 206, 207
  quantity and revenue schedule 208
  quantity schedule 208
  revenue schedule 208
products
  managing 200, 201, 202, 204, 205, 206, 207
profile editor page
  section 21, 22
profiles 19, 20, 21, 22, 23, 24

Q

quotas
  about 232
  reference link 232
Quote PDF-related list 217
quote templates
  creating 217, 218
  managing 213, 214, 215, 216, 217
Quotes-related list 213
quotes
  managing 213, 214, 215, 216, 217
  versus opportunity synchronization 219, 220

R

Re-evaluate Workflow Rules after Field Change option 430
Record Editability Properties 458
Record Owner 141
record-level access 30
REGEX function 181, 182
regular expressions
  about 181
  reference link 181
report and dashboard folders, access levels
  reference link 390
report and dashboard folders, user permissions
  reference link 390
report and dashboard folders
  about 390, 391, 392
  features 390
report data
  advanced highlighting 360, 361
report formats
  about 350
  joined 353
  matrix 352
  summary 351
  tabular 350
Report type event
  reference link 106
report types
  about 345
  creating 345, 346, 347, 348, 349
  reference link 350

reporting 343
Reporting Snapshots
about 378, 380, 381, 382, 383
reference link 384
reports, with formulas
about 364
column summaries 364, 365, 366
row-level formulas 369, 370, 371
summary formulas 367
reports
building 344
chart, adding to 358
charts, adding to 358, 359, 360
filtering 356, 357
history, tracking on 376
subscribing to 384, 385, 386
Request Bin
URL 441
Required attribute 531
Review 213
role hierarchies 33, 34
role hierarchy 18
roll-up field 158, 167, 168, 169
roll-up field, limitations
reference link 170
row-level formulas
reference link 372
rules
customizing 306

S

Sales Amazing Dashboard 406
Salesforce baseline standard
reference link 100
Salesforce Classic Dashboard
reference link 393
Salesforce communities
about 258
setup 259, 260
sharing within 56, 57, 58, 59, 60, 61
Salesforce CRM Content
options 319
setting up 317, 318, 319
Salesforce Data Loader
reference link 144
Salesforce DX development 138
Salesforce DX
reference link 120
Salesforce Event Log File Browser
reference link 107
Salesforce Extension Pack for Microsoft Visual Studio Code 138
Salesforce Help
reference link 422, 438, 442
references 567
Salesforce IDs
reference link 184
Salesforce Knowledge 237, 238, 239
Salesforce Lightning Knowledge
articles, handling 242, 243, 244, 245
data categories, managing 246, 247, 248, 249
external knowledge, importing 249, 250
setting up 240, 241
Salesforce organization
data visible, creating 13, 14
Salesforce product pricing
reference link 15
Salesforce sharing model
about 30
OWD sharing 30, 31, 32
role hierarchies 33, 34
sharing rules 35
Salesforce Shield platform
reference link 107
Salesforce, forecasting types
collaborative forecasting 222
customizable forecasting 222
Salesforce, licenses
reference link 16
Salesforce, storage
data storage 78
file storage 78
Salesforce
URL 114
sandbox types
reference link 119
sandbox, setup consideration
reference link 120
sandboxes
Developer Pro sandbox 115

Developer sandbox 115
flow architectures 117, 118, 119, 120
Full sandbox 117
Partial Copy Sandbox 116
Partial Copy sandbox 115
reference link 117
used, for testing 114, 115
using, for testing 113
Schema Builder 155
scores 596, 597
self relationship 172
Session-based permission sets
reference link 26
SetupAuditTrail
reference link 85
SFDC99
URL 586
sharing groups 18
sharing model 16, 17, 19
sharing rules
about 18, 35
Apex managed sharing 42
case teams 45
considerations 46, 47
criteria-based 37
manual sharing 39, 40, 41, 42
opportunity teams 44
owner-based 37
personal groups 35
public group 35
team sharing 42
working with 36, 37, 38, 39
sharing sets 18
skill-based routing 255, 256
SLA management
entitlements 269, 270, 271, 272, 273, 274, 275, 276, 277, 278, 279, 280, 281, 282
Standard price book 205
state machines 488
storage
monitoring 78, 80
subflows
connecting 548, 549, 550
subordinates 35
summary report 351
System Overview page
API usage limits 75
background job monitoring 89
business logic limits 75
debug log, monitoring 90, 93, 94, 95
email log, monitoring 96, 97
field history tracking 86, 87, 88
health check monitor 98, 99, 100
identity verification history, monitoring 83
login history, monitoring 81, 82
monitoring 74, 75, 76
object-specific limits, monitoring 77, 78
portal roles limits 76
schema limits 75
storage, monitoring 78, 80
user interface limits 75
user licenses limits 76
View Setup Audit Trail, changes monitoring 83, 84, 85

T

tabular report 350
team sharing
about 18, 42
account team 42, 43, 44
territory hierarchies 18
territory management (TM) 47
territory model state 49
territory object 48
territory type 47
Text Field 218, 219
time-based workflows
considerations, reference link 446
time-dependent actions 443, 444
about 445
tools
used, for deploying change sets 135, 136, 137, 138
topics 596, 597
trace flag 92
Trailblazer Community
advanced Certification Study groups, reference link 598
local community groups, reference link 598
reference link 598

training groups, reference link 598
Trailhead Academy, classes
reference link 598
Trailhead Superbadge
reference link 597
Trailhead
reference link 597
Training organization 119
transactions limits 560, 561
Trigger Apex class
reference link 574

U

UAT 119
user interface development 586, 587, 588, 589, 590
user object
private 32
public read-only 32
user permissions and access
reference link 20

V

validation rule
about 176, 178, 179, 180
defining 176
example 177
PRIORVALUE function 182, 183
REGEX function 181, 182
VLOOKUP function 180, 181
View All Data permissions 28
View Setup Audit Trail
changes, monitoring 83, 84, 85
Visual Studio Code
reference link 121
Visualforce 588
Visualforce page
reference link 588
VLOOKUP function 180, 181

W

Welkin Suite
URL 138
Workbench
reference link 101
workflow actions
423
workflow rules
about 423
building 422, 423, 424, 426, 427
evaluation criteria, values 424
workflows
considerations 446, 447
limits, reference link 446, 447
reference link 447

Made in the USA
Coppell, TX
16 November 2020